SOCIAL PSYCHOLOGY
OF EDUCATION

Theory and Research

Daniel Bar-Tal
SCHOOL OF EDUCATION
TEL-AVIV UNIVERSITY

Leonard Saxe
DEPARTMENT OF PSYCHOLOGY
BOSTON UNIVERSITY

HEMISPHERE PUBLISHING CORPORATION

Washington   London

A HALSTED PRESS BOOK

JOHN WILEY & SONS

New York   London   Sydney   Toronto

Hemisphere Publishing Corporation
1025 Vermont Ave., N.W., Washington, D.C. 20005

Distributed solely by Halsted Press, a Division of John Wiley & Sons, Inc., New York.

1 2 3 4 5 6 7 8 9 0   D O D O   7 8 3 2 1 0 9 8

Library of Congress Cataloging in Publication Data

Main entry under title:

Social psychology of education.

    Includes bibliographies and indexes.
    1. Educational sociology—Addresses, essays, lectures. 2. Social psychology—Addresses, essays, lectures. I. Bar-Tal, Daniel. II. Saxe, Leonard.
LC189.S669   370.19   77-28746
ISBN 0-470-26306-7

Printed in the United States of America

Contents

iii

Contributors

Elliot Aronson is professor of psychology at the University of California at Santa Cruz. He received his PhD in social psychology from Stanford University in 1959.

Daniel Bar-Tal is lecturer at the School of Education, Tel-Aviv University. He obtained his doctoral degree in social psychology from the University of Pittsburgh in 1974.

Diane L. Bridgeman is an instructor of psychology at the University of California at Santa Cruz. She did her graduate work in social psychology at the University of California at Santa Cruz, where she received her PhD in 1977.

Jere E. Brophy is professor of teacher education and educational psychology and is senior researcher at the Institute for Research and Teaching at Michigan State University. He received his PhD from the Department of Human Development at the University of Chicago in 1967.

Robert Geffner is currently completing his doctoral studies in social and educational psychology at the University of California at Santa Cruz.

John C. Glidewell is professor of education and social psychology at the University of Chicago. He received his PhD in psychology from the University of Chicago in 1953.

David W. Johnson is professor of educational psychology at the University of Minnesota. He did his graduate work in social psychology at Columbia University, where he received his EdD in 1966.

David F. Lancy is principal research officer at the Department of Education in Konedobu, Papua New Guinea. He received his doctoral degree from the International and Development Education Program at the University of Pittsburgh in 1974.

Gaea Leinhardt is a research associate at the Learning Research and Development Center at the University of Pittsburgh and is Research Assistant Professor in the Department of Psychology at the University of Pittsburgh. She did her graduate work in educational research at the University of Pittsburgh, where she received her doctoral degree in 1972.

Frederick F. Lighthall is associate professor of education and behavioral sciences at the University of Chicago. He obtained his PhD in educational psychology in 1957 from Yale University.

Henry Clay Lindgren is professor of psychology at San Francisco State University. He received his PhD in education from Stanford University in 1942.

Martin L. Maehr is professor of educational psychology and associate director of the Institute for Child Behavior and Development at the University of Illinois at Urbana-Champaign. He received his PhD in educational psychology from the University of Nebraska at Lincoln in 1960.

Philip J. Runkel is professor of psychology and codirector of the program on strategies of organizational change at the Center for Educational Policy and Management at the University of Oregon at Eugene. He obtained his PhD in social psychology in 1956 from the University of Michigan at Ann Arbor.

Leonard Saxe is assistant professor of psychology at Boston University and is a faculty member of Boston University's Center for Applied Social Science. He did his graduate work in social psychology at the University of Pittsburgh, where he obtained his doctoral degree in 1975.

Richard A. Schmuck is professor of educational psychology and codirector of the Program on Strategies of Organizational Change at the Center for Educational Policy and Management at the University of Oregon at Eugene. He obtained his PhD in social psychology from the University of Michigan at Ann Arbor in 1962.

Janet Ward Schofield is assistant professor of psychology at the University of Pittsburgh. She received her PhD in social psychology from Harvard University in 1972.

Dean Tjosvold is assistant professor in the Division of Counseling and Educational Psychology at Pennsylvania State University. He did his graduate work in the social psychology of education at the University of Minnesota, where he received his doctoral degree in 1972.

Preface

This book is designed to provide both educators and social psychologists with a view of the burgeoning field of the social psychology of education. As editors, we have tried to bring together a set of original articles that integrate the best current thinking about social processes in education with current research on these problems. Our hope is that this volume will stimulate increasing interest in social-psychological issues in education and that the book will lead to the further development of a social psychology of education subdiscipline.

We were both trained in experimental social psychology, and we have worked together closely, initially as fellow graduate students, later as faculty colleagues. In a sense, we were both part of the "crisis generation" of social psychologists, for we were trained during the period of the early 1970s when critiques of laboratory-oriented social psychology were a principal focus of our graduate seminars. Since graduate school, each of us has devoted the major portion of our time to applications of social psychology. Although we do not expect that our involvement in educational problems will, necessarily, lead to a solution of the crisis in social psychology, it seems to us to be a useful outlet for our energies. We hope that, in our work and through this book, we can advance the way in which social psychology is involved in important educational problems to benefit both social psychology and educational practice.

In developing this book, we were both tremendously influenced by our contact with the Learning Research and Development Center at the University of Pittsburgh. During 1974 and 1975, we participated in a seminar led by the late Paul Lazarsfeld and by Lauren Resnick. The seminar brought together an interdisciplinary group of scholars from basic disciplines such as sociology and psychology and from various areas of education. It was during this seminar that we began to think that it was possible to apply social psychology to educational problems in a truly problem-focused and useful way. Professor Lazarsfeld encouraged us to contribute to the development of social psychology of education by editing this volume, and he had intended to write a chapter, which, unfortunately, was not completed because of his untimely death in 1976.

Our initial contact with the contributors in this volume came as a result of a symposium we organized at the 1975 American Psychological Association Convention in Chicago. The symposium, "The Contributors of Social Psychology to Education," was cosponsored by the APA Division of Educational Psychology and Personality and Social Psychology, and it included presentations by Jere Brophy, Dale Lake, Frederick Lighthall, and Richard Schmuck and had, as discussants, Herbert Thelen and John Glidewell. The symposium group provided the core group of contributors for our volume; later, a number of other social psychologists of education were invited to join the project.

We assume responsibility for any problems that may be a part of the book, but as is probably the case with most edited books, any acclaim that is due should be directed to the contributors. They represent the very best current social psychologists of education. We thank each of them, not only for providing excellent chapters that should advance the field and stimulate thought about social processes in education, but also for their patience and understanding throughout the editorial process. During the time the book was being edited, we traded compliments, "suggested revisions," and even demands on a regular basis between Israel and a dozen or so universities throughout the United States. We hope that, in the end, this sometimes-lengthy correspondence will have been worth the effort in terms of the quality of the book. It is, of course, left to you, the reader, to make that determination.

Although the contributors are the principal individuals we want to thank, we would also like to express our appreciation to a number of others who provided support in various forms during the preparation of this volume. First, we want to thank the staff at Hemisphere Publishing Corporation, most particularly, Evelyn Pettit and Christine Flint. We also thank William Begell, President of Hemisphere, who encouraged us from the very beginning to bring this project to completion. Second, we thank Martin Greenberg and John Levine, our graduate school mentors, who stimulated us to think about the applications of social psychology and who taught us the skills to transmit these ideas. Although, in some cases, our mentors provided a model of psychology against which we could conveniently rebel, we are indebted to them in innumerable ways. Third, we thank our spouses, Yaffa Bar-Tal and Marion Saxe, who created the kind of environment in which we could be productive and who put up with our working vacations.

We also thank Susan Keator, at Boston University, who typed much of the correspondence between the editors and contributors. Other staff, at both Tel-Aviv University and Boston University, also assisted in various ways, and although the list is too long to individually identify them, we appreciate their help.

Daniel Bar-Tal

Leonard Saxe

Introduction

Daniel Bar-Tal and Leonard Saxe

It is obvious that schools are complex social environments, where, in addition to learning per se, social interaction takes place. It is not surprising, then, that social-psychological research has been carried out in educational settings and that social-psychological theories have been used to understand and explain educational phenomena (e.g., Fleming, 1944; Glidewell, Kantor, Smith, & Stringer, 1966; Henry, 1960; Withall & Lewis, 1963). Despite the fact that psychological thinking about social processes has been applied to educational problems, however, compared with other applications of psychology to education, this effort has been relatively minimal.

This volume is directed at improving this state of affairs. The book brings together a set of social-psychological analyses of educational problems intended to represent the best of currently available theory and research. We hope that, not only will the individual chapters contribute to better understandings of specific educational problems, but, in addition, that the volume as a whole will serve to stimulate systematic thinking about the entire range of social-process problems in education. In essence, our goal is to identify the social psychology of education as a specialized subdiscipline.

In this introduction, it seems appropriate to briefly indicate our view of the state of this subdiscipline and how this volume contributes to the development of the field. Because Chapter 1, by Henry Lindgren, reviews, in detail, current trends in educational social-psychology research, our analysis of the current state of knowledge need be only a general discussion of the utility of various frameworks offered to describe problems in social psychology of education. Then we turn to a discussion of the relationship between social psychology and education and of the symbiotic needs of social psychologists and educators. We close with a description of the chapters of volume in terms of their contribution to the social psychology of education.

STATE OF THE ART OF THE SOCIAL PSYCHOLOGY OF EDUCATION

Although, in recent years, a great deal of work has been published about social-psychological problems in education, only a small amount of this work can be considered to be a true contribution to the social psychology of education—at least as we define the field. Much of the past work is probably better classified as "social psychology *for* education." Understanding the difference between social psychology *for* education and social psychology *of* education is important in order to understand our view of the relationship between social psychology and education and our view of how this volume contributes to the understanding of educational problems.

Social psychology for education, as we refer to it, merely uses social-psychological principles to explain educational problems. The basic assumption of this approach is that social behavior that occurs in the classroom can be explained by a set of "basic" social-psychological principles that do not depend on the context in which the behavior occurs; that is, wherever human beings are, they perceive; have attitudes, motivations, and beliefs or values; and associate in groups. This perspective of social psychology is simply imposed on education. The research and conceptual work that represents the social psychology for education approach does not present social-psychological issues in an interrelated manner in terms of educational processes, but as separate topics. Such writings have been organized in terms of such topics as conformity, leadership, motivation, role, social perception, social climate, interpersonal interaction, group structure, personality, attitudes, group performance, organizations, socialization, and social learning. These topics have typically been explained in relation to the social-psychological literature and only followed by short discussions of their educational implications.

Moreover, the reported research in social psychology for education has often been carried out in laboratory settings (i.e., noneducational settings) where college students have served as subjects. Getzels (1969), who evaluated the contributions of social psychology to education in *The Handbook of Social Psychology,* has noted that "the lack of any theoretical restruction may have the consequence of making the social psychology of education only a grab bag of social-psychological notions and data perhaps relevant to education but unrelated in any systematic way to each other" (p. 461). The practice of applying social-psychological theories and findings to educational problems without an examination of their validity in educational settings has certainly been a useful first step. It has acquainted educators with social-psychological thinking. Without a problem focus on educational issues, however, it contributes little to the development of the theory and practice of educational social psychology.

In contrast, the social psychology of education defines its scope according to a problem focus on educational issues. The topics in social psychology of education are those social-psychological issues that concern the social functioning of individuals and groups in educational systems. Implicit in this definition of the social psychology of education is that social psychology is not automatically relevant to education. The social psychology of education focuses on education only to the extent that the educational system dictates specific sociopsychological problems not necessarily found in other systems. Thus, the problem is always located in education, although the conceptual and methodological tools to analyze it are distinctly sociopsychological. A result is that the topics of the social psychology of education do not necessarily correspond to the standard topics of social psychology.

RELATIONSHIPS BETWEEN SOCIAL PSYCHOLOGY AND EDUCATION

While the development of the social psychology of education should provide important benefits to education, the synergistic relationship between this subdiscipline and the generic field of social psychology should also be recognized. Thus, at one level, educational problems represent an important kind of problem that should stimulate social psychology to develop new methods and theories. Educational problems, occurring as they do in real-world settings where change is one of the most important features, require that social psychologists design new ways of thinking and studying behavior. At another level, it is clear that the development of a social psychology of education is tied to the methodological and theoretical development of social psychology per se. The degree of success of social psychologists of education must, in large part, depend on the sophistication of the conceptual and methodological tools of social psychology.

During the past several years, there has been a great deal of discussion within social psychology about its ability to be useful and about the degree to which a Kuhnian (Kuhn, 1970) paradigmatic crisis exists in the field. A number of social psychologists (e.g., Gergen, 1973; Harré & Secord, 1973) have argued, in essence, that the basic premises of the field are ill-founded and will not lead to understandings of social behavior, at least as understanding has been traditionally defined (i.e., lawful relationships). Critics, such as Gergen (1973), have argued that our understandings of social behavior have only temporal value; others, such as Harré and Secord (1973), have argued that our unit of analysis is faulty. Although a number of social psychologists have recently noted the futility of critiquing the field (see Elms, 1975), it is clear that the field is still faced by a series of difficult problems.

These problems of social psychology are not exclusively metatheoretical problems, as described above. For example, as Helmreich (1975) has noted, even though we currently have the tools to do large-scale multivariate research in field settings, not much of this kind of research has successfully been done by social psychologists. Within the field, there seems to be a continuing bias toward highly controlled laboratory-oriented research (cf. Higbee & Wells, 1972). The promise of Kurt Lewin's (1948) theorizing about social psychology—that it would be an interplay of theory and practice—has not yet been achieved.

This state of social psychology does not portend well for its use as a tool in understanding educational problems, but it does suggest how a synergistic relationship between social psychology and education could be achieved. In essence, educational problems provide sophisticated and complex issues to challenge social psychologists to utilize the best available theory and methods and to challenge the field to develop new approaches. In a parallel way, the social-psychological perspective is important for educators and may significantly improve educational practice.

Until recently, educators have, relatively, neglected social-psychological problems, but this seems to be changing with learning and cognitive skills. In recent years, educators have realized that, if they are to understand the impact of the social environments within which they operate, that they need the conceptual assistance of behavioral scientists, such as social psychologists. On a pragmatic level, educators have been faced with a series of social problems, such as prejudice, pupils' dislike of school, and conflicts among staff members, that can be solved only with the help of social scientists. In addition, the growing recognition that a school should be responsible, not only for the instruction in the three Rs, but also for the socialization of the child poses new problems for educators, such as formulation of social objectives for education, incorporation of social objectives into curricula, or design of classroom social processes as a means for achieving social goals. It would seem that social psychologists of education can be of great help in solving a range of social problems that preoccupy educators.

THIS BOOK

We hope that this book contributes significantly to both social psychology and education. Its chapters explore relationships between social psychology and education, emphasizing the contributions that each field can make to the other. Of course, the authors of these chapters do not share a unified view of problems in the social psychology of education. In addition to conceptual differences, some authors are very critical of current practices, while other authors see current developments as very exciting. What ties the chapters together is that they analyze social aspects of the educational process and they do so from a social-psychological perspective.

Each of the 12 original chapters in this volume discusses a selected topic in the social-psychological education. Although the topics are not inclusive of all of the areas of the social psychology of education, the scope of the field is represented, and the chapters cover the range of "levels of analysis" (see discussion below) of social processes in education. All authors attempt to provide a synthesis of theory and research in terms of a specific substantive problem or metatheoretical issue in the social psychology of education. An important feature of these syntheses is that their focus is distinctly educational.

The volume is organized in seven parts. The first three parts discuss general metatheoretical issues of the social psychology of education. The last four parts present theoretical and methodological analyses of specific topics. The first part consists of a single chapter by Henry Lindgren, which provides an overview of the historical roots of social psychology of education. The next part includes a chapter by Frederick Lighthall, which discusses the role of social psychologists of education. The third part consists of three chapters, written by Philip Runkel, Gaea Leinhardt, and David Lancy, which discuss methodological problems of conducting research in the social psychology of education. Runkel discusses the problems of an investigator working in a school setting; Leinhardt analyzes the stages of field research in education; and, Lancy proposes the use of ethnomethodology as a research strategy.

The remaining parts of the book are organized in terms of four levels of analysis. Each level of analysis refers to a particular perspective taken by social psychologists of education. The first unit of analysis is the individual. This perspective has, as its major point of reference, structures and processes that characterize the functioning of individuals. Work from the individual level of analysis has mainly been directed toward understanding behavior, in social situations, in terms of individual attitudes, motivations, perceptions, beliefs, and values. Because a teacher's behavior is directed toward individual students, rather than toward an entire class of students, the basic assumption of this level of analysis is that individual students should be the focus of social-psychological investigation. Four chapters that adopt this level of analysis have been included in Part IV. They are by Jere Brophy, Daniel Bar-Tal, John Glidewell, and Martin Maehr. Brophy discusses interactions between students' individual differences and instructors. Bar-Tal discusses the social outcomes of the education process. Glidewell analyzes the antecedents, symptoms, ways of management, and prevention of distress among school pupils. Maehr reviews the concept of achievement motivation and develops a new conceptual model that takes situational factors into account.

The second level of analysis is the group. From this perspective, the classroom is viewed as a group, and principles of group dynamics are applied to explain classroom situations. The basic assumption of this approach is that classrooms are separated and isolated and that each class functions autonomously. Research contributions in this area have focused on such variables as a teacher's leadership, patterns of interaction in the classroom, cohesiveness of the class, or social climate in the classroom. Two chapters are included here based on this group perspective, one by Richard Schmuck and one by Elliot Aronson, Diane Bridgeman, and Robert Geffner. Schmuck discusses the dynamics of learning groups in the classroom, whereas Aronson and his colleagues discuss the advantages of learning in small cooperative groups.

The third level of analysis is the school. From this perspective, one takes an organizational approach to viewing the school as a system with a concomitant social structure (which includes goals, norms, and roles). A basic assumption of this perspective is that a systemic view of the school organization is necessary to understand individuals' behavior in schools. Taking the organizational perspective, Dean Tjosvold discusses the effect of control on organizational life of schools, and David Johnson analyzes different types of conflict in the school organization.

The fourth level of analysis is the community. Educational settings are not closed systems. They are greatly affected by the community, just as community life is affected by the schools. Thus, the fourth perspective considers the interrelationship between community and school. One chapter, by Janet Schofield, represents this perspective. Schofield discusses the important problems of desegregation and how social-psychological knowledge can be applied to understanding its effects on intergroup relations.

REFERENCES

Elms, A. C. The crisis of confidence in social psychology. *American Psychologist,* 1975, *30,* 967–976.

Fleming, C. N. *The social psychology of education.* London: Routledge & Kegan Paul, 1944.

Gergen, K. J. Social psychology as history. *Journal of Personality and Social Psychology,* 1973, *26,* 309–320.

Getzels, J. W. A social psychology of education. In G. Lindzey & E. Aronson (Eds.), *The handbook of social psychology* (2nd ed., Vol. 5). Reading, Mass.: Addison-Wesley, 1969.

Glidewell, J. C., Kantor, N. B., Smith, L. M., & Stringer, L. A. Socialization and social structure in the classroom. In M. L. Hoffman & L. N. Hoffman (Eds.), *Review of research in child development* (Vol. 2). New York: Russell Sage, 1966.

Harré, R., & Secord, P. F. *The explanation of social behavior.* Totowa, N.J.: Rowman & Littlefield, 1972.

Helmreich, R. Applied social psychology: The unfulfilled promise. *Personality and Social Psychology Bulletin,* 1975, *1,* 548–560.

Henry, N. B. (Ed.). The dynamics of instructional groups: Sociopsychological aspects of teaching and learning. *The 59th yearbook of the National Society for the Study of Education* (Pt. II). Chicago: University of Chicago Press, 1960.

Kuhn, T. S. *The structure of scientific revolutions,* (2nd ed.). Chicago: University of Chicago Press, 1970.

Lewin, K. *Resolving social conflicts.* New York: Harper, 1948.

Withall, J., & Lewis, W. W. Social interaction in the classroom. In N. L. Gage, (Ed.), *Handbook of research on teaching.* Chicago: Rand McNally, 1963.

HISTORICAL
PERSPECTIVES
ON SOCIAL
PSYCHOLOGY
OF EDUCATION

Trends in Social Psychology Research in Education

Henry Clay Lindgren
Department of Psychology
San Francisco State University

DEFINITIONS

Education, in this discussion, refers to school-related behavior and related variables. *Social psychology* is more difficult to define because it is a field that is still developing an identity. Its practitioners may be psychologists or sociologists; its research may be theoretical or applied; its theories are often particularistic and trendy; and its findings for the most part have not undergone rigorous cross-validation in other cultures. There is, nevertheless, some agreement among social psychologists that their discipline is, as Gordon W. Allport (1969) described it, *"an attempt to understand and explain how the thought, feeling, and behavior of individuals are influenced by the actual, imagined, or implied presence of others"* (p. 3, italics in the original). Allport further defined "implied presence of others" to refer to the activities carried out by the individual as a result of his or her position or role "in a complex social structure and because of his membership in a cultural group" (p. 3).

Allport's definition of social psychology is a good starting point for a discussion of the extent to which social psychology appears in educational research, but a survey of the kind I am undertaking here requires something more descriptive. How does one recognize a social psychological variable when one encounters it in studies of education? What is needed here is a definition of social psychology that is more specific and detailed than the general statement made by Allport.

It can be argued that any field of endeavor is what its practicioners say it is, so one can turn to social psychology textbooks in the hope of finding some consensus on the content and dimensions of the area. Although authors are not in agreement on the structure of the field, there are a number of topics that appear with sufficient frequency to give the reader a general idea of what it is that commands the interest and attention of social psychologists. These topics are listed below as a way of providing a working definition of what is meant by the term *social psychology* in this chapter. Probably other social psychologists would use somewhat different terminology and would organize the topics differently, but I am confident that the majority of the following topics would appear on any list:

3

Social motives
    affiliation and association
    interpersonal attraction
    aggression and violence
    prosocial motives, including altruism
    identification
    deindividuation
    beliefs
    values
    moral development

Personality
    self-concept and self-structure
    needs for achievement, affiliation, and power
    independence and dependence
    anxiety
    alienation
    balance theory

Social learning (imitation, modeling)
    social attitudes
    liking and disliking
    prejudice and stereotyping
    authoritarianism and egalitarianism
    attitude change

Social perception
    person perception
    empathy
    attribution theory
    dissonance theory
    comparison level

Social (and group) structure
    status
    position
    role and role strain
    social norms

Social (and group) processes
    cohesiveness
    morale
    group task performance
    social exchange
    negotiation and bargaining
    communication and language

Social influence
    conformity to norms
    compliance
    leadership
    social power
    propaganda

Cross-cultural, ethnic, and socioeconomic differences
   desegregation and integration of public facilities
   sharing of resources
Organizational psychology
Social ecology

A review of the above topics indicates that social psychologists consider that their field is concerned with how people interact with their social environment, as well as with the structural and behavioral characteristics of that environment.

ROLES OF SOCIAL AND EDUCATIONAL PSYCHOLOGISTS

There are two areas that could legitimately be examined in order to gather data on the amount and kind of social-psychological research that has been conducted. One of these consists of the research conducted by social psychologists on educational problems and issues. This area poses a major problem, however.

Research conducted by social psychologists is sometimes focused on specific questions related to pressing issues—drug addiction, for one example—but social psychology usually deals with general issues. It is, as Allport (1969) described it, a branch of general psychology. Even when social psychologists conduct research on areas with a high degree of topical interest—alternatives to marriage, for instance—they usually are concerned with identifying basic trends in human behavior. For the investigator interested in fundamental research, education is interesting for three major reasons: (1) Exposure to educational processes has a demonstrable effect on the behavior and attitudes of people and can be measured fairly precisely in terms of the number of years of education; (2) certain education techniques, such as discussions and examinations, can be used to test hypotheses about social behavior; and (3) schools are a good source of relatively homogeneous samples of subjects.

Because social psychology, as a science, is more fundamental than applied, research published under this heading is only occasionally or incidentally concerned with educational topics. A survey I undertook of social psychology textbooks published within the last decade indicated that about half of them mention educational *effects* (but not processes) as contributing factors in socioeconomic variation. Social psychology textbooks published 20-30 years ago did concern themselves with racial prejudice and the ways in which schools might combat it, just as textbooks of the pre-World War II era proposed ways in which schools might prepare students to deal with propaganda. But, with a couple of exceptions, neither of these topics was of major concern to authors of social psychology textbooks.

In his review, "A Social Psychology of Education," which appeared in the second edition of *The Handbook of Social Psychology*, Getzels (1969) complained that social psychologists have tended to ignore educational issues. He pointed out that the earlier edition of the handbook, which appeared in 1954, contained chapters on the social psychology of industry and politics, but none on education. Getzels's own chapter is evidence that social psychologists are becoming aware of education, however belatedly, but there is little indication that their interest is more than tangential and incidental. For instance, less than 10% of the papers appearing in the *Journal of Personality and Social Psychology* for 1976 dealt with topics directly relevant to education, although a number of them were concerned with variables potentially interesting to educators. By way of an example, one of the studies appearing in the journal was an investigation by McClintock and Moskowitz (1976) of children's preferences for individualistic, competitive, and cooperative outcomes. This investigation produced findings that could be interesting to individuals involved in kindergarten and elementary school education, but the findings could be equally interesting to developmental psychologists, recreation directors, parents, or anyone concerned with early stages of altruistic or self-centered behavior.

Because few of the studies undertaken by social psychologists were focused specifically on educational problems and issues, I decided to take the alternative course of action open to me—namely that of determining the extent to which research of educational specialists has been concerned with social-psychological concepts and variables.

Surveying the research literature in education for the last 50 years or so in search of examples of social-psychological research could be a mind-boggling undertaking, but fortunately it is not necessary to cast so wide a net. Most of the literature in education is not primarily concerned with research, and such research as is done is conducted mostly by educational psychologists (Travers, 1969). Hence one can get a fairly accurate idea of the degree to which educational research involves problems of a social-psychological nature by examining the publications of educational psychologists.

Educational psychologists have the whole field of psychology to call upon. Standing on middle ground between psychology and education, they can draw on any subfield of psychology they believe is relevant to educational problems. If a concept or technique holds the promise of providing insight into an educational problem, the educational psychologist appropriates it, irrespective of whether its source is physiological psychology, the psychophysics laboratory, the psychology of aesthetics, or psychoanalytic theory. The educational psychologist's only standard is—or ought to be—a pragmatic one. Pragmatism, however, is not the only consideration employed by educational psychologists, for there are other concerns that guide their choices, as we shall see.

CONTENT ANALYSES OF RESEARCH IN EDUCATIONAL PSYCHOLOGY

I have analyzed two sources of data to identify trends in educational research: the *Journal of Educational Psychology* (JEP) and the educational psychology section of *Psychological Abstracts* (PA). My analyses were for the years 1920, 1930, 1940, 1950, 1960, 1966, 1970, and 1976 (PA was not published until 1927, hence 1920 is represented by JEP only). Since its inception, PA has provided a section for publications in educational psychology, and the listings included in this section might be expected to provide one measure of the extent to which educational psychologists have carried on research employing social-psychological variables. A comparison of the contents of both JEP and the educational psychology section of PA would thus yield information as to the reliability and validity of the method being used. In analyzing the contents of the JEP, I classified every article in a given year. In PA, I randomly sampled articles by taking the topmost complete listing in each column. Each article in JEP and each publication sampled from PA, I classified according to content and tallied under one of nine categories (see Table

1-1), which in turn were based largely on the educational psychology subdivisions employed in recent years by the editors of PA.

In classifying the content of a listed publication, I gave priority to material of a social psychology nature. In other words, if the author of a publication included a social variable in his or her research plan, I classified the work under the appropriate social psychology category (1, 2, or 3 in Table 1-1) even though its main focus would otherwise suggest another category. For instance, an article dealing with instructional techniques to be employed with socially disadvantaged children would be tallied under Category 1, rather than 7, because of the author's implied use of social status or cultural identity as a variable.

The rationale for setting the classification scale to "overrespond" to the use of social variables is as follows. Social psychology is a field that appeared fairly late in the history of psychology and received relatively little attention from most psychologists, especially in the earlier years of its development. There were, furthermore, only a few investigations, like Wickman's (1928) survey of teachers' attitudes toward children's problem behavior and Hartshorne and May's (1928–1930) study of students' cheating, that studied social variables in an educational setting. In most educational research, when social variables were included at all, they played a secondary role to variables that researchers considered to be more significant. Hence, in order to respond to any indication of interest in social-psychological data, it was necessary that the classification process be programmed to pick up weak signals. As a consequence, the data in Tables 1-1 and 1-2 should be interpreted in terms of the proportion of scholars using social-psychological variables in their research, and they only indirectly reflect the emphasis researchers placed on data and concepts drawn from social psychology.

In interpreting the data presented in Tables 1-1 and 1-2, it is important to keep in mind that the figures for each year reflect the activity of researchers for up to 5 years preceding that year. The figures for 1930, in other words, reflect research that was probably conceived as early as 1925, planned in 1926, carried out in 1927, published in 1928, and abstracted in 1929 in order to appear in the 1930 PA.

The correlations between the classifications for JEP and PA for each year suggest a fair degree of relationship between the proportions of publications falling in each category, especially in the years from 1940 onward. Indeed, the only major difference between JEP and PA in recent years has been the increased specialization of articles appearing in JEP, which now publishes proportionately fewer studies that include variables associated with either mental health or guidance and counseling.

As one reviews the data for the years sequentially, one finds few great surprises, but the data do indicate how the interests of educational researchers have shifted over the two generations represented by the span of years. Educational psychologists in the post-World War I era, as indicated by the data for 1920 and 1930, were concerned largely with instructional methods, evaluation, and testing. Much of their research involved the teaching of reading and arithmetic. Only one-fifth or less of their research included any social-psychological variables.

About one-eighth of the 1930 articles were concerned with guidance and counseling, largely of a vocational nature. Table 1-1 shows the percentage of publications in this category declining over the years, but this showing is largely an artifact of the method of classification used. In later years, researchers in guidance and counseling gave greater attention to personality, attitudes, and social behavior. When they did so, the entries were classified under one of the social-psychological

TABLE 1-1 Percentages of Articles in the *Journal of Educational Psychology* (JEP) and Randomly Sampled Publications Listed in the Educational Psychology Section of *Psychological Abstracts* (PA) Categorized according to Content

Categories	1920 JEP (43)[a]	1930 JEP (74)	1930 PA (125)	1940 JEP (67)	1940 PA (99)	1950 JEP (41)	1950 PA (108)	1960 JEP (59)	1960 PA (85)	1966 JEP (51)	1966 PA (114)	1970 JEP (72)	1970 PA (234)	1976[b] JEP (54)	1976[b] PA (344)
1. Social structure and social processes	2	3	10	1	7	10	20	20	9	20	12	14	18	24	33
2. Social motives (attitudes, beliefs, values, percepts)	12	5	2	6	10	12	1	14	23	6	12	14	12	11	9
3. Personality	7	9	5	7	6	12	3	14	11	10	12	7	10	11	10
4. Mental health (psychopathology, diagnosis, treatment)	0	1	3	0	3	5	10	5	4	0	4	0	8	0	4
5. Guidance and counseling	0	0	12	0	9	5	3	2	5	0	4	0	2	0	1
6. Special education	5	4	7	1	11	2	8	5	4	2	11	1	5	2	8
7. Instruction, curriculum, programs	21	15	42	28	31	20	29	22	21	47	28	57	27	41	24
8. Tests, measurements, evaluation, selection	51	58	18	54	20	32	26	19	23	14	14	4	15	9	8
9. Philosophy, miscellaneous	2	3	2	1	2	2	0	0	0	2	4	3	3	2	3
r between JEP and PA		.37		.73		.73		.80		.93		.86		.84	

[a]Figures in parentheses refer to the number of articles in JEP or to the number of listings sampled in PA.
[b]Only 6 months of 1976 were included in the survey; in previous years, the entire year was surveyed for JEP and January through September for PA.

TABLE 1-2 Summary of Table 1-1 Categories Collapsed

Categories	1920 JEP	1930 JEP	1930 PA	1940 JEP	1940 PA	1950 JEP	1950 PA	1960 JEP	1960 PA	1966 JEP	1966 PA	1970 JEP	1970 PA	1976 JEP	1976 PA
Social-personality (1, 2, 3)	21	17	16	14	23	34	24	48	43	36	36	35	40	46	52
Individual-centered (4, 5, 6)	5	5	22	1	23	12	21	12	13	2	19	1	15	2	15
Methodology, programs, tests (7, 8, 9)	74	76	62	83	53	54	55	41	44	63	46	64	45	52	35

categories, as I noted in my description of the classification method. In the 1970s, for example, many of the guidance publications were concerned with group counseling and were as a consequence tallied under Category 1. PA has for some years included vocational guidance under applied (or industrial) psychology, rather than under educational psychology.

In the late 1930s, as reflected by the data for 1940, educational psychologists began to become interested in student interests and attitudes. This trend is reflected in the sharp percentage of increase in Category 2 in Table 1-1, but the overall use of social-psychological concepts and variables, as indicated in Table 1-2, increased only moderately.

The late 1940s, as reflected in the 1950 figures, saw the first major increase in studies dealing with social structure and processes. Most people in education and psychology viewed World War II at least to some degree as a struggle between fascist and democratic ideologies. There was a strong belief that one of the best ways to support democratic ideals was to teach them in school, and the best way to teach such ideals presumably was to maintain a democratic atmosphere in the classroom. The Lewin, Lippitt, and White (1939) study of autocratic, democratic, and laissez-faire social climates had attracted widespread attention, and the movement to train experts in group dynamics (which developed into sensitivity training in the 1960s) was well under way. Sociometry was a popular way of studying classroom dynamics in that era. Teachers were also experimenting with loosely structured discussion techniques, stimulated partly by the group dynamics movement and partly by Rogers's (1942) nondirective methods, which seemed suitable for working with groups as well as with individuals. Research dealing with cooperation and competition also appeared.

The data for 1960 indicate that the interest in social-personality variables continued to grow. This was an era when educators became interested in Maslow's (1954) needs, Snygg and Combs's (1949) phenomenology, authoritarian attitudes (Adorno, Frenkel-Brunswik, Levinson, & Sanford, 1950), and the effects of anxiety on learning (Taylor, 1953).

During the mid 1960s, as indicated by the figures for 1966, the relative interest in social-personality variables began to lag somewhat, as Table 1-2 shows. The drop was especially noticeable in Category 2. A separate analysis for 1964 (not included in the tables) indicates that this trend had actually got under way during the early 1960s.

The figures for 1970 and 1976 suggest that the tendency for researchers to be more interested in social structure and process than in social motives and attitudes continued. The 1970 data reflect the publication of research funded by War on Poverty grants. Studies of student unrest and activism also appeared during this period. Social learning (Bandura & Walters, 1963) and moral development (Kohlberg, 1958) were two additional areas that attracted the attention of researchers.

Going back to 1966, one sees the beginning of a trend away from problems specifically concerned with evaluation and testing, coupled with an increase in the proportion of studies of methodology and curriculum, reflecting interest in programmed instruction, behavior modification, and Bloom's (1956) taxonomy of educational objectives.

It is in the early 1970s, as reflected by the figures for 1976, that one finds social-psychological themes in about half the publications appearing in the two sources. The greatest gains are in variables related to social structure and process.

Studies generated by federally funded research related to the mid-1960s War on Poverty continued to appear during this period. The controversy over the relative importance of environment and heredity for variations in IQ led to the publication of theoretical comment, as well as original research. Rosenthal and Jacobson's (1968) field experiment on teacher-expectancy effects stimulated both debate and research, as did books and articles on attitudes toward women.

The declining percentages during the early 1970s of studies dealing with tests and evaluation may have reflected a growing hostility on the part of the public toward measurement of all types. On the face of it, it seems that the percentage gains of social psychology, as reported in Table 1-2, have occurred at the expense of testing and evaluation. One should not overestimate this trend, however. Note that the PA sample sizes for 1970 (January–September) and for 1976 (January–June) are much larger than those for previous years, reflecting a major increase in the total number of studies of an educational psychology nature. This means that the absolute number of studies devoted to some aspect of testing and evaluation has actually increased during the 1970s, even though the proportion has decreased relative to the total. One should also keep in mind that most of the studies included in the other categories make use of tests of some description.

The general conclusion to be drawn from the data reported in Tables 1-1 and 1-2 is that the typical educational psychology study today deals with a broader spectrum of variables, especially with those of a social-psychological nature, whereas in earlier years the typical study was more narrowly concerned with specific aspects of instruction or evaluation.

A REVIEW OF HISTORICAL TRENDS

In his brief history of educational psychology, Robert I. Watson (1971) placed the initial stages of educational psychology in the 1880s, when Galton conducted experiments with association and administered the first psychological tests, and when Ebbinghaus published his work on retention. The next few years saw considerable research activity both in learning research and in the development of testing techniques. These two areas were for many years the chief research areas for educational psychologists.

In the early twentieth century, the major figure in the psychology of learning was Edward L. Thorndike, "the first man to deserve to be called an educational psychologist in the modern sense of the term" (p. 17), according to Watson. Thorndike's (1898) early experiments were with animals. Within a few years, he had shifted his focus to human learning, and in 1905 he published his laws of learning: exercise, effect, and readiness. Thorndike also played a large part in the development of standardized tests for school subjects.

Thorndike's associationist concept of learning had no place for social psychology. For example, he reported that he could find no empirical evidence for imitation and he dismissed it completely. The fact that he included *readiness* in his learning theory might suggest an interest in social motivation, but his reasoning makes it clear that he thought of "readiness" in a largely neurological sense. For Thorndike, wants, interests, and motives were the products of instinctive satisfiers or likes and, hence, were not researchable.

It is perhaps going too far to say that, by excluding social factors from learning research, Thorndike set the pattern for the generation of educational psychologists who followed him. What is more likely is that his approach merely reflected the climate of opinion that prevailed among the experimentalists of his day. They preferred to conduct tightly controlled, empirically satisfying studies of learning behavior, and they did not want to be encumbered by any variables that seemed extraneous and which in any event were poorly understood. Thorndike's contemporary, Charles H. Judd, who did extensive work in the psychology of school subjects, especially reading, also displayed little interest in social or personality factors that might affect academic success or failure.

It seems fair to say that Thorndike and Judd represent an approach to learning that not only was characteristic of the educational psychologists of their day, but that also prevailed for a good many years. Learning, to these psychologists, was a process that occurred when the individual encountered certain environmental variables. This encounter could occur by chance or it could occur by design, as in a laboratory or a classroom. In the laboratory, the experimenter manipulated the variables that led to learning; in the classroom, it was the teacher who did the manipulation. Their learning theories took no account of the presence of other learners in the classroom nor of the learner's social environment outside the classroom.

Except for contributions to educational practice (but not to theory) in the form of programmed learning and behavior modification, laboratory research in learning has, over the years, largely followed the line laid down by Thorndike. This determination to hew to the line and produce scientifically elegant research with little direct relationship to the needs of the practitioner has baffled, frustrated, and even irritated psychologists with a humanistic orientation. Stone and Church (1973) voiced the views of many when they wrote:

> Learning theory is weak because it fails to come to serious grips with so many areas of learning. It is hardly concerned at all, or at most programmatically, with knowledge, the broad interconnected system of facts and ideas and meaning and values that school learning is supposed to deal with. It has very little patience with the learning of concepts and relations and principles, with . . . the cumulative consequences of learning . . . how learning can serve to make a person less egocentric or ethnocentric. (p. 189)

Although Stone and Church wrote as developmental psychologists, the complaints they utter could just as well come from either social psychologists or educators.

In defense of Thorndike, Judd, and their contemporaries, one should recognize that the social psychology of the day had little to offer the educator. McDougall's social psychology textbook, published in 1908, sold over 100,000 copies during the following quarter century (Murphy & Kovach, 1972), but it seems unscientific by today's standards. Whereas Thorndike used instinct as a kind of a wastebasket for troublesome variables like social motives, McDougall (1908) made instinct the keystone to his Darwinian theories of social behavior and expressed the hope that a relevant and systematic psychology would eventually disclose "the innate tendencies of thought and action that constitute the native basis of the mind" (p. 16). The year 1908 also saw the publication of another textbook on social psychology, by Ross, a sociologist who was interested in the ways in which the social interaction among human beings influences their behavior.

Everyday observation, armchair speculation, and logical analysis were the bases of the psychologies developed by McDougall and Ross, and it is surprising to note that the era of scientific experimentation in social psychology had already started 10 years before their books were published. The first experiment demonstrating the influence of the group on the individual was conducted by Triplett (1898), who found that children winding up reels of string to which flags had been attached worked faster in the presence of others than when alone. During the first two decades of this century, Moede (1920), a German psychologist, also conducted a series of experiments demonstrating a "group effect" on tasks involving a variety of cognitive skills. Münsterberg (1914) at Harvard was aware of Moede's studies and had carried out experiments that showed that individuals in a group influence one another in reporting such objective phenomena as the number of dots appearing on a screen.

None of these experiments had much impact on the psychological profession, however, and it was not until 1924, when Floyd H. Allport published his *Social Psychology*, that psychologists became aware that scientific experimentation could legitimately be undertaken in social behavior. The appearance of Allport's book marks the beginning of the modern era in social psychology, for it was the first social treatise to be based on the results of scientific experimentation, rather than on armchair logic. Allport rejected the instinctual theories of McDougall and viewed social behavior as resulting from what he termed "prepotent influences," which could be modified by conditioning. This line of reasoning established his work as compatible with Watsonian behaviorism, the prevailing ideology among psychologists of that day.

Research in social psychology was now on its way to becoming scientifically respectable, but this did not mean that it had much appeal to educational psychologists. Researchers in education were slow to be aware of the social dimensions of the behavior they were studying, while social psychologists, for their part, were concerned with basic, rather than applied, research. They were also preoccupied with developing methodologies with which to conduct social research—survey techniques, attitude scaling, and sampling methods, for example.

It is interesting that many of the major contributions to social psychology during the years before World War II were not made by social psychologists. One of these contributions was the well-known *Hawthorne effect*, reported in a series of studies conducted by industrial psychologists at a Western Electric plant during the late 1920s and early 1930s (Roethlisberger & Dickson, 1939.) Margaret Mead's (1928, 1930) anthropological research in the South Pacific raised questions about cultural relativism in the interpretations of behavior made by psychologists and laymen alike. The sociologists Warner and Lunt (1941) reported that, not only was social class alive and flourishing in the world's greatest democracy, but it could even be used as a way of predicting the attitudes, beliefs, and general behavior patterns of individual Americans.

But social psychologists did make some contributions of their own. The best known of their pre-World War II studies are the social-norm experiments of Sherif (1936) and the social-climate investigations of Lewin, Lippitt, and White (1939). Educational researchers were inclined to give more attention to the social-climate study, perhaps because its findings were supportive of democratic methods and placed traditional autocratic ideologies in a bad light. The research method employed by Lewin and his co-workers also showed how an independent variable (teacher behavior) could be manipulated or otherwise controlled in classroom experiments and other studies with small groups.

A review of textbooks in the 1930s indicates that some educational psychologists were becoming interested in social factors. By way of contrast, Thorndike's 1914 edition of his textbook contained a chapter entitled "The Social Instincts" and briefly made mention of Dewey's (1910) concepts of student needs and problem-solving attitudes, but they were not central to his arguments and he cited no supportive data. Some 20 years later, however, Pressey's (1933) text included a chapter on the social psychology of childhood and adolescence, in which he discussed such topics as the influence of the home environment, the influence of teachers, the social atmosphere of the schoolroom, the school as a center of student social life, community morale, the influence of adult amusements on children, and the integration of home, school, child, and adult societies. Other chapters in the text contained discussions of measurement of attitudes, character traits, and social adjustment; the effects of social incentives; and the relationship between socio-economic status and intelligence.

The contents of other textbooks of that period suggest that the social-personality emphasis found in Pressey's book was somewhat unusual. A more typical book was that of Eurich and Carroll (1935), who discussed the measurement of personality traits, attitudes, and interests but did not indicate how such variables are related to problems of learning and instruction. Otherwise the book contained little about social factors.

The tide was beginning to turn, however. In 1941, Trow complained that most educational psychologists were limiting their investigations to the psychology of the individual, neglecting the social aspects of the individual's behavior (Watson, 1971). Findings from longitudinal studies of child development, such as the Berkeley Growth Study, were making the point that the cognitive development of children— a major concern of educators—was closely tied up with their social and emotional development. Indeed, all aspects of children's behavior, both in and out of the classroom, were shown to be affected by such social factors as parental attitudes and child-rearing practices. To be sure, such studies were correlational in nature, and hard-nosed learning experimentalists expressed little tolerance for any data that were not based on properly controlled experiments in the classical design. Yet the consistent results reported in a steady progression of longitudinal studies were not easily dismissed. Even though the more experimentally minded educational psychologists rejected or ignored findings of such investigations, they found an eager market among professional educators and developmental psychologists. Evidence for this acceptance may be found in addresses, technical papers, and panel reports contained in the *Proceedings of the Midcentury White House Conference on Children and Youth* (Richards, 1951), almost all of which deal with variables in the realm of social psychology and personality, and which tacitly accept the validity of longitudinal and other correlational studies.

The midcentury years, in retrospect, marked a turning point in the orientation of educational psychology. Cronbach (1950) signaled the new trend in his essay on educational psychology, which appeared in the initial issue of the *Annual Review of Psychology*. In this paper, he discussed at some length such topics as the effect of social class on learning readiness, emotional factors in learning, and learning as a group process. About one-fourth of Cronbach's article dealt directly with social and personality factors in education, and an additional one-fourth was indirectly concerned with related topics. Authors of educational psychology chapters in the next few issues of the *Annual Review* tended to follow Cronbach's lead.[1]

Sherif's work on competition and cooperation in groups of preadolescent boys attracted some attention from educational researchers (Sherif & Sherif, 1953; Sherif, White, & Harvey, 1955). His earlier research demonstrating the effect of group norms on individual judgment seems largely to have been ignored, however, as were later studies by Asch (1956) and Crutchfield (1955), which confirmed Sherif's earlier work and provided further evidence of the way in which social norms can take priority even over the evidence of the senses.

It was the Lewin, Lippitt, and White (1939) study that commanded the most attention among educators, however, and the work on social norms was largely overlooked. This holds true even today. A review of the author indexes of 15 leading educational psychology texts that appeared in the 1970s shows that only 3 of them list the Asch study, and 4 mention Sherif's competition-cooperation research, but not his social-norm experiments. By way of contrast, 11 of the books—almost three-fourths—list Lewin.

The increasing interest in social-personality variables during the 1950s is indicated by the emphases in the more widely used educational psychology textbooks. Travers (1969), in his review of educational psychology in the fourth edition of the *Encyclopedia of Educational Research*, reported that texts by Cronbach (1954) and Lindgren (1956) were the predominant ones in the middle and late 1960s. He attributed their popularity to the fact that each of the authors attempted to present a consistent theoretical position—a model of learning in the case of Cronbach and a phenomenological approach in the case of Lindgren. They were not, however, the only texts of that era to be characterized by theoretical consistency. The book by Woodruff (1951) was also closely reasoned, theoretically consistent, and phenomenologically oriented. Although successful, it was not as widely used as the books by Cronbach and Lindgren. In retrospect, it seems likely that the popularity of the Cronbach and Lindgren books was to a large degree based on the fact that they included extensive discussions of the social aspects of classroom learning and also appeared at a time when educational psychologists were becoming very interested in social-personality variables.

The social-personality orientation of the Cronbach and Lindgren textbooks is clearly apparent from their subject headings. Cronbach wrote of education as a part of socialization, the development and satisfaction of social and personal needs, differences in home and community background, the teacher as a classroom leader, and personality structure and character development. When he discussed readiness, he described it in personal and motivational terms and said that teachers could understand it through classroom observation, peer judgments, and the student's self-concept. Lindgren dealt with self-perceptions, the influence of the family's emotional climate, social class, levels of aspiration, and unconscious biases in judging children's behavior. Chapter headings included "The Learner and His

---

[1] Educational psychology no longer appears as a chapter in the *Annual Review of Psychology* and has been replaced by chapters on instructional psychology, which appear every 3 years. Authors of these chapters have, in recent years, been inclined to ignore studies involving social and personality factors. The last review under the heading of educational psychology appeared in 1964. About 4% of its content dealt with social-personality variables. Percentages of space devoted to social-personality variables in instructional psychology reviews are as follows: 1969, 0%; 1972, 4%; and 1974, 12%.

Group," "Discipline and the Learning Situation," and "Learning through Group Methods." Both books also made extensive use of anecdotal material based on classroom experiences of teachers and students, which added a touch of reality that had been absent from other textbooks in the field.

This social-reality approach was taken up by other authors in the following years. Some of the more successful texts are those by Biehler (1971), Fransden (1957), and Perkins (1969). Educational psychologists' awakening social interests during the 1950s were appropriately reflected at the end of the decade by the publication of "The Dynamics of Instructional Groups: The Sociopsychological Aspects of Teaching and Learning," Part II of *The 59th Yearbook of the National Society for the Study of Education* (Henry, 1960). Although the society had been publishing a pair of yearbooks every year since 1902, this was the first one that was concerned with the social aspects of classroom learning.

Education in the late 1950s and early 1960s experienced a renewed burst of interest in laboratory studies of learning. This turning away from the "softer" social-personality psychology studies may have been due in part to the great increase in concern about science education and traditional curricula touched off when the Russians launched the first Sputnik in October 1957. The following year, B. F. Skinner (1958), who had become the major spokesman for laboratory psychologists, published his *Science* article on teaching machines. The teaching machine had actually been introduced by Pressey (1926) many years earlier, but Skinner's model had the advantage of appearing at a time when educators were ready to try a technologically novel approach. The method used in Skinner's machine was also an expression of the operant-conditioning model of learning, which he had done so much to popularize. In addition, the instructional formats developed for the new teaching machines were compatible for computer programs.

A new era of technological development was now under way in educational psychology. It was reflected in the emphases of a spate of new textbooks (Gagné, 1965; Klausmeier, 1961; McDonald, 1959; Travers, 1963). The renewed emphasis on research was also reflected in the second editions of texts by Cronbach (1962) and Lindgren (1962), who strengthened their coverage of empirical research, although they still maintained most of the social and personality orientation that characterized their first editions.

The attempt of learning psychologists to find new ways of applying their approaches to classroom instruction was only partially successful. Programmed instruction failed to revolutionize teaching and learning, as had been hoped, and its appeal to researchers eventually faded, but behavior modification continued to be a popular research area well into the 1970s. Its major use today appears to be in special education.

Another phenomenon of the 1960s was the appearance of theoretical formulations and research on social learning, variously labeled as "learning through imitation," "observational learning," and "modeling." Thorndike, as I noted, had excluded imitation from his theoretical formulations of learning. As far as laboratory learning research was concerned, observational learning virtually disappeared from view until Bandura (1962) revived it. Bandura and McDonald (1963) conducted an experiment demonstrating that moral development in children is responsive to social modeling and is little influenced by reinforcement. The study attracted a great deal of attention among developmental psychologists but was virtually ignored by learning theorists.

The reasons why learning theory remained oblivious to imitation or social learning are not difficult to discern. Hilgard and Bower (1966) noted that behaviorists were uninterested in observational learning because it could not be demonstrated clearly in animal experiments. They continued: "The notion of sensory-sensory conditioning boggled the biases of the S-R behaviorist, and the animal orientation of S-R learning theory was clearly what triumphed during the 1930s and 1940s" (p. 537).

This reaction tells one something about the isolation of laboratory psychology from educational problems. Actually, learning theorists were not really interested in educational problems, as Atkinson (1968) has pointed out. Gagné and Rohwer (1969) also observed that studies of human learning are unlikely to be of much value to teachers because the conditions under which the experiments were performed are unlike the situations in which most human learning occurs. Furthermore, the tasks set for subjects in learning experiments, such as the memorization of nonsense syllables, are inappropriate in that they "appear to cover a range from the merely peculiar to the downright esoteric" (p. 381).

EDUCATIONAL SOCIAL PSYCHOLOGY
COMES OF AGE

A review of the data reported in Table 1-2 indicates that educational researchers' use of social-personality variables peaked in the late 1950s and then declined for an extended period, whereupon it awakened in the 1970s with a renewed burst of activity. In retrospect, it seems likely that this revived interest in social-personality research was associated with the massive increases in federally funded studies concerned with the development and evaluation of programs undertaken as part of President Lyndon Johnson's War on Poverty, which had been initiated by the Economic Opportunity Act of 1964. The prevailing view among educators was that poverty is associated with, and probably caused in large part by, individual deficiencies in education. These deficiencies, in turn, were seen as partly due to shortcomings in the schools themselves and partly due to deficiencies in the preschool environment of children, which kept them from benefiting from their school experiences. According to this line of reasoning, the school performance of the children from impoverished homes would improve if their environment could somehow be enriched.

Federal grants made to researchers who were willing to investigate ways in which social-environmental variables could be effectively manipulated attracted a great many educational psychologists, who presumably would otherwise have devoted themselves to the kind of tightly designed experiments in learning and cognition that had been traditional in the field.

The researchers' involvement in problems that included social-personality variables was itensified by an event related to the War on Poverty: Jensen's (1969) paper on the heritability of IQ, a statement that challenged the very basis of Head Start and similar attempts to enrich the environment of disadvantaged children and thus facilitate cognitive development. The Rosenthal and Jacobson (1968) book, mentioned earlier, also had important implications for those interested in the education of the disadvantaged, for it not only posed doubts about the validity of all educational research; it also suggested that certain teacher attitudes, which are probably unconscious and may be uncontrollable, may have a profound effect on students' self-regarding attitudes and their subsequent performance. Both the

Jensen and the Rosenthal-Jacobson studies have come under severe criticism on methodological grounds (Cronbach, 1975), but they did attract a great deal of attention in and out of the education and psychology professions and raise questions that are still being researched.

Both the controversies and the intensified research activity of the 1960s led to the writing of textbooks designed to capitalize on the interest educators were beginning to show in social psychology. Three of these texts, authored by Backman and Secord (1968), Guskin and Guskin (1970), and Johnson (1970), appeared within a 2-year period.

Getzels's (1969) chapter, "A Social Psychology of Education," which appeared in the second edition of *The Handbook of Social Psychology*, was a significant milepost that marked how far educational specialists had gone in their use of the data and concepts of social psychology. Among the topics examined by Getzels were social class, socialization, social effects on mental ability, racial segregation, compensatory education, the school and the classroom as social systems, and the effect of both teacher characteristics and learner characteristics on learning.

Getzels's review was especially valuable because of its penetrating and objective treatment of such controversial issues as incongruities—between cultural values and institutional expectations, between personality dispositions and role expectations, and between roles—and as conflicts—arising from personality disorder, from personality differences, from incongruent interpersonal percepts, and from idiosyncratic definitions of expectations. He also raised important questions: "Can a program of compensatory education, even at its best, be salutary in any ultimate way without altering the racism and the disadvantaged environment giving rise to the disadvantaged child? Will the child's conception of life and of himself disappear if Appalachia, Harlem, and Watts are permitted to remain?" (p. 493). He asked, further, "Assuming, as seems justified, that certain cultural values provide inappropriate criteria for satisfactory socialization and personality formation, are the expectations of the school system as it is presently constituted likely to provide more satisfactory criteria for socialization and personality formation. . . ?" (p. 494). It is significant that these questions remain unanswered some 10 years after Getzels posed them.

THE CONTRIBUTIONS OF BEHAVIORISM, HUMANISM, AND SOCIAL PSYCHOLOGY TO EDUCATION

No one could have predicted during the late 1950s and early 1960s, when the shapers of educational policy were imbued with the spirit of scientism and were technologically pursuing excellence, that, by the mid 1970s, "soft psychology" would once again be in the ascendency. The most visible harbinger of this change was the spate of college student uprisings that broke out like fever blisters during the late 1960s. Perhaps the students were reacting to the toughness in teachers' demands and institutional requirements during the post-Sputnik era, but other factors were undoubtedly involved. Whatever the cause, many young people enthusiastically and noisily rejected middle-class adults and their carefully nurtured educational establishment. Those who attacked the values of educators and criticized instructional practices became instant heroes to these disgruntled youths, but they were especially attractive to dissidents who espoused values that were avowedly humanistic. In this, the young people were encouraged and applauded by the members of the education and psychology professions who strongly supported humanistic values.

The writings of Carl Rogers (1942, 1951, 1961, 1969) were a major source of ideas and inspiration to the humanists. In 1956, he and B. F. Skinner had conducted a celebrated debate on the question of the control of human behavior, in which the two had sharply delineated the differences between the humanistic and the behavioristic approaches to psychology.

The differences were shown to be fundamental and irreconcilable. Essentially, the Skinnerian behaviorist believes that if learning sequences are designed appropriately and students are placed on the proper schedules of reinforcement, the desired learning will occur. Rogerian humanists think of learning as a process in which individuals develop their own unique ways of dealing with their environment and thus of developing their best potential. Behaviorists see learning as a performance that is evoked from the students by their environment; Rogerian humanists perceive it as a process that does not have to be evoked, for it is inevitable and unique for each person.

Swain (1972), has analyzed the positions of Skinner and Rogers and has concluded that the basic difference between the two lies in their views of what humans are and what they ought to be. Skinner sees individuals in mechanical terms, as capable only of reacting to the stimuli in their environment. Rogers maintains that the individual is not dependent on environmental stimuli and is inherently capable, without outside help or direction, of making responsible decisions that lead to harmonious social behavior. Skinner is concerned about external control maintained by environmental manipulation, whereas Rogers looks for ways to eliminate external controls.

According to Swaim, Skinner's ideal educational environment is one that would provide precise control and predictable outcomes, whereas Rogers wants a school environment that would permit maximum personal choice for the learner, one that would permit each learner "to become." Skinner's approach would seem to be most useful in teaching basic skills; Rogers's concept appears to be more appropriate for students who are having problems of adjustment.

As applied psychologists, educational psychologists' chief role is that of helping educators perform more effectively. They can do this to a limited extent by developing and evaluating instructional techniques, but potentially, their major contribution is that of helping the educational profession gain a psychological understanding of the factors and forces that facilitate or interfere with school learning. The behavioral approach typified by Skinner and the humanistic approach of Rogers each has something to contribute to this understanding, but they share common shortcoming, for both tacitly assume a single learner who either responds to the environment the teacher has prepared for her or him or is freed to make choices reflecting her or his unique needs. Both viewpoints overlook the reality that the learner is never alone: One is always in the midst of a social situation that one is a part of and that is a part of one. Much of what one does or does not do is based on what family and peers have taught one to believe about oneself and the outside world, and much is in response to the expectations of others and to the norms imposed by one's social environment. Whether one deviates or conforms, it is always in respect to these norms and expectations.

What all this means is that Skinnerian teachers who attempt to manipulate the learner's environment do not have as much latitude as they believe. The reinforcement contingencies that they arrange may be negated or weakened by the demands made by the learner's social environment. The social environment can of course be manipulated, but such a task is vastly more complex than anything envisioned by the disciples of Skinner.

For their part, the Rogerians and other humanists who yearn to free learners to pursue their unique needs seem unaware that many of these needs were implanted, or at least shaped, by their social environment. An aggressive child who disrupts classroom activities may be expressing a sense of alienation and discouragement, but in most instances the child is also responding to peer-group norms and expectations and is also playing out a role defined by his or her position in the group. To be sure, every individual's needs may be viewed as unique, but it is also possible to make valid and useful generalizations about the ways in which groups perceive their environment and one another and in which group members are likely to respond to these precepts.

Rogerians and other humanists are inclined to view individuals' needs for group acceptance as something that interferes with their personal development, a position that is bound to create insurmountable problems for teachers. The failure of many well-intentioned humanistically oriented teachers to deal with reluctant learners and obstreperous students may be charged to this blind spot regarding the social realities of the classroom. The same criticism holds for Skinnerians as well, but in my experience, the teachers who are confirmed humanists far outnumber the confirmed behaviorists.

What psychologists who work with educators must do, in short, is to broaden their view of the learning process by helping them become aware of the social reality in which learning occurs. If we can address ourselves properly to this task, we will be moving with the major trends today in social psychology, which is shifting its focus from intraindividual to interpersonal processes and is becoming increasingly concerned about application (McClintock, 1976). It is to be hoped that the future development of social psychology in education will respond to these trends and will be typified by ventures such as that of Johnson and Johnson (1975), whose book, *Learning Together and Alone,* describes the classroom as a "social milieu in which there are a variety of possible forms of social interdependence that strongly affect its members both in terms of what is learned and how learning occurs" (p. 104), a viewpoint that "may come as a shock to many educators who are strongly influenced by current psychological theories of learning and performance, theories that assume that one can somehow abstract individual performance from the social matrix in which it occurs" (McClintock, 1976, p. 105).

As we enter this last quarter of the twentieth century, indications are clear that research conducted in education has taken on a distinct social-psychological flavor. There is still some preoccupation, however, with the social psychology of individual students—their attitudes and values, their locus of control, the influence of culture and social class on their thinking, the effect their teachers' expectations have on their performance, and the like. The educator who is aware of these factors has indeed made progress beyond the purely cognitive view of learning that has prevailed for so many years, but one dimension is still missing: an understanding of the way in which interpersonal relations in the classroom affect the learning behavior of students. Without this insight, the teacher will remain one step away from grasping the reality of the teaching-learning situation.

REFERENCES

Adorno, T. W., Frenkel-Brunswik, E., Levinson, D. J., & Sanford, R. N. *The authoritarian personality*. New York: Harper, 1950.

Allport, F. H. *Social psychology*. Cambridge, Mass.: Riverside, 1924.

Allport, G. W. The historical background of modern social psychology. In G. Lindzey and E. Aronson (Eds.), *The handbook of social psychology*, (2nd ed., Vol. 1). Reading, Mass.: Addison-Wesley, 1969.

Asch, S. E. Studies of independence and submission to group pressure: 1. A minority of one against a unanimous majority. *Psychological Monographs*, 1956, *70*, (Whole No. 416).

Atkinson, R. C. Computerized instruction and the learning process. *American Psychologist*, 1968, *23*, 225–239.

Backman, C. W., & Secord, P. F. *A social psychological view of education*. New York: Harcourt, 1968.

Bandura, A. Social learning through imitation. In M. Jones (Ed.), *Nebraska Symposium on Motivation*. Lincoln: University of Nebraska Press, 1962.

Bandura, A., & McDonald, F. J. Influence of social reinforcement and the behavior of models in shaping children's moral judgments. *Journal of Abnormal and Social Psychology*, 1963, *67*, 274–281.

Bandura, A., & Walters, R. H. *Social learning and personality development*. New York: Holt, 1963.

Biehler, R. F. *Psychology applied to teaching*. Boston: Houghton Mifflin, 1971.

Bloom, B. S. (Ed.). *Taxonomy of educational objectives*, Handbook 1, *Cognitive domain*. New York: McKay, 1956.

Cronbach, L. J. Educational psychology. *Annual Review of Psychology*, 1950, *1*, 235–254.

Cronbach, L. J. *Educational psychology*. New York: Harcourt, 1954.

Cronbach, L. J. *Educational psychology* (2nd ed). New York: Harcourt, 1962.

Cronbach, L. J. Five decades of public controversy over mental testing. *American Psychologist*, 1975, *30*, 1–14.

Crutchfield, R. S. Conformity and character. *American Psychologist*, 1955, *10*, 191–198.

Dewey, J. *How we think*. Lexington, Mass.: Heath, 1910.

Eurich, A. C., & Carroll, H. A. *Educational psychology*. Lexington, Mass.: Heath, 1935.

Fransden, A. N. *Educational psychology*. New York: McGraw-Hill, 1957.

Gagné, R. M. *Categories of learning*. New York: Holt, 1965.

Gagné, R. M., & Rohwer, W. D. Instructional psychology. *Annual Review of Psychology*, 1969, *20*, 381–418.

Getzels, J. W. A social psychology of education. In G. Lindzey and E. Aronson (Eds.), *The handbook of social psychology* (2nd ed., Vol. 5). Reading, Mass.: Addison-Wesley, 1969.

Guskin, A. E., & Guskin, S. L. *A social psychology of education*. Reading, Mass.: Addison-Wesley, 1970.

Hartshorne, H., & May, M. A. *Studies in the nature of character*. New York: Macmillan, 1928–1930.

Henry, N. B. (Ed.). The dynamics of instructional groups: The sociopsychological aspects of teaching and learning. *The 59th yearbook of the National Society for the Study of Education* (Pt. II). Chicago: University of Chicago Press, 1960.

Hilgard, E. R., & Bower, G. H. *Theories of learning* (3rd ed.). New York: Appleton, 1966.

Jensen, A. R. How much can we boost IQ and scholastic achievement? *Harvard Educational Review*, 1969, *39*, 1–123.

Johnson, D. W. *The social psychology of education*. New York: Holt 1970.

Johnson, D. W., & Johnson, R. T. *Learning together and alone: Cooperation, competition and individualization*. Englewood Cliffs, N.J.: Prentice-Hall, 1975.

Klausmeier, H. J. *Learning and human abilities: Educational psychology*. New York: Harper, 1961.

Kohlberg, L. *The development of modes of moral thinking and choice in the years ten to sixteen*. Unpublished doctoral dissertation, University of Chicago, 1958.

Lewin, K., Lippitt, R., & White, R. K. Patterns of aggressive behavior in experimentally created "social climates." *Journal of Social Psychology*, 1939, *10*, 271–299.

Lindgren, H. C. *Educational psychology in the classroom* New York: Wiley, 1956.

Lindgren, H. C. *Educational psychology in the classroom* (2nd ed.). New York: Wiley, 1962.

Maslow, A. H. *Motivation and personality*. New York: Harper, 1954.

McClintock, C. G. Social psychology in the classroom. *Contemporary Psychology*, 1976, *21*, 104–105.

McClintock, C. G., & Moskowitz, J. M. Children's preferences for individualistic, cooperative, and competitive outcomes. *Journal of Personality and Social Psychology*, 1976, *34*, 543–555.

McDonald, F. J. *Educational psychology*. Belmont, Calif.: Wadsworth, 1959.

McDougall, W. *An introduction to social psychology*. London: Methuen, 1908.

Mead, M. *Coming of age in Samoa*. New York: Morrow, 1928.

Mead, M. *Growing up in New Guinea*. New York: Morrow, 1930.

Moede, W. *Experimentelle Massenpsychologie*. Leipzig: Hirzel, 1920.

Münsterberg, H. *Grundzüge der Psychotechnik*. Leipzig: Barth, 1914.

Murphy, G., & Kovach, J. K. Historical introduction to modern psychology (3rd ed.). New York: Harcourt, 1972.

Perkins, H. V. *Human development and learning*. Belmont, Calif.: Wadsworth, 1969.

Pressey, S. L. A simple device for teaching, testing, and research in learning. *School & Society*, 1926, *23*, 373–376.

Pressey, S. L. *Psychology and the new education*. New York: Harper, 1933.

Richards, E. A. *Proceedings of the Midcentury White House Conference on Children and Youth*. Raleigh, N.C.: Health Publications Institute, 1951.

Roethlisberger, F. J., & Dickson, W. J. *Management and the worker*. Cambridge: Harvard University Press, 1939,

Rogers, C. R. *Counseling and psychotherapy*. Boston: Houghton Mifflin, 1942.

Rogers, C. R. *Client-centered therapy: Its current practice, implications, and theory*. Boston: Houghton Mifflin, 1951.

Rogers, C. R. *On becoming a person*. Boston: Houghton Mifflin, 1961.

Rogers, C. R. (Ed.). *Freedom to learn*. Columbus, Ohio: Merrill, 1969.

Rogers, C. R., & Skinner, B. F. Some issues concerning the control of human behavior: A symposium. *Science*, 1956. *124*, 1057–1066.

Rosenthal, R., & Jacobson, L. *Pygmalion in the classroom: Teacher expectation and pupils' intellectual development*. New York: Holt, 1968.

Ross, E. A. *Social psychology*. New York: Macmillan, 1908.

Sherif, M. *The psychology of social norms*. New York: Harper, 1936.

Sherif, M., & Sherif, C. W. *Groups in harmony and tension*. New York: Harper, 1953.

Sherif, M., White, B. J., & Harvey, O. J. Status in experimentally produced groups. *American Journal of Sociology*, 1955, *60*, 370–379.

Skinner, B. F. Teaching machines. *Science*, 1958, *128*, 969–977.

Snygg, D., & Combs, A. W. *Individual behavior.*. New York: Harper, 1949.

Stone, L. J., & Church, J. *Childhood and adolescence* (3rd ed.). New York: Random House, 1973.

Swain, E. E., *B. F. Skinner and Carl R. Rogers on behavior and education*. Unpublished doctoral dissertation, University of Oregon, 1972.

Taylor, J. A. A personality scale of manifest anxiety. *Journal of Abnormal and Social Psychology*, 1953, *48*, 285–290.

Thorndike, E. L. Animal intelligence: An experimental study of the associative processes in animals. *Psychological Review, Monograph Supplements*, 1898, *2* (No. 8).

Thorndike, E. L. *Educational psychology: Briefer course*. New York: Teachers College, Columbia University, 1914.

Travers, R. M. W. *Essentials of learning*. New York: Macmillan, 1963.

Travers, R. M. W. Educational psychology. In R. L. Ebel, Noll, V. H. & Bauer, R. M., (Eds.), *Encyclopedia of education* (4th ed.). New York: Macmillan, 1969.

Triplett, N. The dynamogenic factors in pacemaking and competition. *American Journal of Psychology*, 1898, *9*, 507–533.

Warner, W. L., & Lunt, P. S. *Social life of a modern community*. New Haven: Yale University Press, 1941.

Watson, R. I. A brief history of educational psychology. In H. C. Lindgren and F. Lindgren (Eds.), *Current readings in educational psychology* (2nd ed.). New York: Wiley, 1971.

Wickman, E. K. *Children's behavior and teachers' attitudes*. New York: Commonwealth Fund (Harvard University Press), 1928.

Woodruff, A. D. *The psychology of teaching* (3rd ed.). New York: Longman's, 1951.

II

THE ROLE OF THE SOCIAL PSYCHOLOGIST OF EDUCATION

2

Equity, Consequentiality, and the Structure of Exchange between Social Psychologists and Educators

Frederick F. Lighthall
University of Chicago

In this chapter, I shall present thoughts about bringing psychological research and researchers closer to educational practice and practitioners. These thoughts began developing more than a decade ago (Lighthall, 1963; Lighthall & Diedrich, 1965) and led to several years of effort, with my colleague Jack Glidewell, toward meshing the realities of schooling and social-psychological research (Lighthall, 1969, 1973; Lighthall & Braun, 1976). I am dealing with three thoughts here: first, contributions by psychology to education are illusory unless they occur as a part of a mutual, equitable, and valued exchange relation between psychologists and educators; second, some encompassing distinctions among kinds of social behavior and experience are necessary in order to bring the activities of educators and psychologists into a common framework of thinking; and third, the development within educational systems of data-gathering and data-rendering mechanisms, through new roles or group functions, is essential if exchange relations between educators and psychologists are to be more than trivial and fleeting.

THE CONTRIBUTIONS OF SOCIAL PSYCHOLOGY TO EDUCATION

Social psychology has, in principle, a unique contribution to make to both educational theory and the practice of educating. Its unique possibilities lie in the fact that it is the only branch of psychology whose concepts, theory, and data encompass interpersonal phenomena and processes. Education—fundamentally an interpersonal process, carried out through the interdependent cooperation of two roles, educator and learner—requires for its elucidation precisely the kinds of analytical tools and data provided by a social psychology. Educational psychology must be, fundamentally, not a cognitive or a developmental or a personality psychology, but a social psychology. Given this view, the immediate occasion for preparing the initial draft of this chapter—a symposium on contributions of social psychology to education—was of more than passing interest. Yet I had qualms about the contributions of social psychology to education.

For one thing, it seemed clear that, in any such contributing relation, the question of whether a potential contribution from A to B would become an actual contribution, used by B in B's ongoing being, was a question wholly dependent on B, not A, for an answer. It is the beneficiary, not the benefactor, who allows an intended benefit to become actual (Lighthall, 1975). Thus the question of whether social psychology could contribute to education was not one social psychologists were in a position to answer, as we were ostensibly doing in that original symposium. The symposium, thus, seemed to me then, and seems even more so now, to represent a certain degree of smugness, like the snobbism of the missionary out to civilize a primitive people. There are two domains of contribution one can imagine, the first one easier and less smugly claimed for social psychology than the second.

The first domain of contribution is what social psychologists can give to educational theorists, primarily educational psychologists, curriculum theorists, and philosophers. Social psychologists write theoretical and empirical articles for social psychological journals. Educational psychologists and others actively thinking about education read them. It is a kind of passive contributory process; the educational theorist eavesdrops, as it were, on a conversation among social psychologists. The social psychologist may not even be aware, in this journalistic conversation, that she or he is contributing to an educational theorist's thinking. I think this is the kind of contributing process many of my colleagues have in mind when they speak of psychological contributions to education.

This process goes on among academics. Even on those rare occasions when social psychologists address themselves directly to an educational question in a publication read primarily by educational scholars (e.g., Getzels & Thelen, 1960; Strodtbeck, 1965), it remains essentially a conversation among academics via media and language familiar to academics. It seems to me that all such contributions are fundamentally weakened without a second kind of contribution. This second kind of contribution is at once much more difficult, and claimed as possible only with much more smugness, than the first, given the current methodological commitments and repertoires of social psychologists. This kind of contribution is now also much more needed than further academic collections like this volume, if both education and social psychology are to overcome their respective weaknesses.

The second kind of contribution of which I speak is the kind social psychologists might make to the practice of educating. It is sometimes suggested, even claimed outright, that the writings among academics become, sooner or later, contributions to the practice of educating. Such claims are at least debatable. Even the more modest of such claims (e.g., Getzels, 1974), suggesting only that a certain critical mass of psychological research was *necessary* (not sufficient) for changes in educational practice to take place, are unconvincing for at least three reasons.

First, educational changes that appear after the flowering of a certain domain of research (e.g., changes to the group-centered or discussion-centered classroom after the flowering of group dynamics research) do so selectively, ignoring other earlier or simultaneous flowerings (e.g., individual learning as a function of carefully managed contingencies among drive, cue, response, and reward). Second, educational changes cannot be considered contributions to effective educational practices just because the changes are visible. Educational systems are notoriously vulnerable to fads, many of which are justified by reference to research, but which go as easily as they come, with nothing changed except the presence of so many television sets (used, then dropped, in the teaching of foreign languages), revamped textbook series (used, then dropped, in the teaching of mathematics or biology), or movable desks (moved, then lined up again in rows). Third, the process of educational decision making regarding changes does not include examination of the details of research conditions or the limits on extrapolation set by subject samples or kinds of treatments actually employed. Educational changes are a complex function of community sentiment, Zeitgeist, the economy, and uses of global reference to selected research conclusions as justifications of advocates' viewpoints. It is more likely that pervasive social and economic conditions (e.g., wars and arms races, depressions, inflations, witch-hunts, and social movements for racial and sexual equality) generate both research flowerings and educational changes, than it is that the academy has any systematic or appreciable influence on educational practice.

By considering social psychologists as educators, one gains some perspective on the influence of social psychology, as academic knowledge, on the practice of educating. The overwhelming majority of social-psychological researchers are also university educators. One may wonder whether their broad and intimate knowledge of their own discipline's methods, theories, and findings exerts an influence on their own educating. If social psychology, as knowledge about phenomena in general (it is claimed), has a special contribution to make to the practice of educating, it surely ought to show up in the ways social psychologists prepare curriculum materials; interact with students in seminars, in lecture courses, and in tutorials; invent assignments and examinations for students; and organize themselves in faculties as working units.

I know of no studies or data that bear on social psychologists' educational practices or effectiveness. Informal observation of myself and my colleagues, however, strongly suggests that social psychologists are no more effective in working together as colleagues, are no more creative or effective in preparing and conducting courses and seminars, and in general are no different in their educating from musicologists, scholars of literature, or anyone else who knows nothing of the methods, theories, or findings of social psychology. It is ironic, by the way, that one of the least effective courses taught by the social psychology faculty at the University of Chicago in recent years—a judgment in which both faculty and students concur—has been the common-core overview course for incoming graduate students in social psychology, taught jointly by several senior members of the faculty. One faculty member now teaches that course. Social psychologists, like just about everybody else, teach better alone than they do as a social unit. If I am correct in my assessment that social-psychological knowledge exerts no influence even when the knowledge operates in the head of the practitioner, how likely is it that knowledge among social psychologists will exert some influence on the ways other educators educate?

There are objections, then, to the claim that social psychology can exert either a remote influence or an immediate influence on educational practice; but a crescendo of voices is leveling an even more trenchant criticism against any claim for social psychology's contribution to educational practice. Internal weaknesses of social-psychological method are increasingly being pointed out that render questionable even contributions to general social-psychological knowledge.

Koch (1965) argues authoritatively that experimental psychology generally settled prematurely on its methods before sufficient exploration of its subject matter and, as a result, produces "ameaningful" knowledge. Social psychologists themselves, from a wide range of vantage points, are extending and particularizing Koch's criticisms (Argyris, 1975; Bass, 1974; Fried, Gumpper, & Allen, 1973; Gergen, 1973; Israel & Tajfel, 1972; McDavid, 1965; McGuire, 1973; Menges, 1973; Orne, 1962, 1973; Proshansky, 1976; Resnick & Schwartz, 1973; Rosenberg, 1965; and Rosenthal & Rosnow, 1969). The thrust of much of this criticism is that the social-psychological experiment in particular yields precious, arcane, or artifactual knowledge rather than knowledge usefully generalized. McGuire (1973) points out shortcomings of even the field experiment as a way of avoiding artifacts.

To those familiar with the "action research" of Lewin and his students, my review of criticisms of social-psychological research may seem one-sided. Has not the work of Rice (1958), of Marrow and his associates (1967), and of Sanford (1976) demonstrated at least a potential for social psychology's contribution to educational practice? Surely such research has contributed in the realm of business and industry. There are two answers to such objections.

First, analysis of the relations between the researchers and the research "subjects" in these action-research projects shows that (a) the relations are very different from the relations obtaining between the overwhelming majority of social psychologists and educators, and (b) where an impact endured, the relation between researcher and subject developed many of the characteristics of exchange relations I am at pains to describe below.

The second answer to those who might object to my ignoring action research as the means social psychologists might contribute to education is simply that social psychologists avoid action research—like the proverbial plague. Whatever happened to action research? Sanford (1976) has the following answer: "Contrary to my impression in the late 1940's, I would say now that it never really got off the ground, or was widely influential in psychology or social science (p. 21). Action research is not and never was in the mainstream of social psychology.

There are, in summary, at least three grounds for skepticism regarding the contributions of social psychology to educational practice. First, the weaknesses just referred to: Social-psychological knowledge is vulnerable to criticisms, from Argyris and Bass at the intervention end of the spectrum, and from McGuire, Orne, and Rosenberg at the polar opposite of laboratory experimentation. Note also: To the extent that social-psychological knowledge is vulnerable to these scholars' criticisms, even the claim that social psychology can contribute to educational theory within the academy is vitiated. Second, even if a number of social-psychological research methods can withstand such criticism, the impact that knowledge resulting from those methods can remotely exert on educational practice is reduced to the vanishing point by the vicissitudes of a long decision chain outside the academy. Third, even if social psychologists can produce sound knowledge that does traverse the distance from the scholar at the academy to the practitioner in the school system, the transduction of academic knowledge about the general to practical action on the particular remains an impediment to any potential contribution. It seems apparent that social psychologists have been unable to make such transductions even within their own heads; their educating in their roles as professors seems relatively untouched by their knowledge of social psychology.

To understand contributions of knowledge to practice, one must, in the final analysis, watch how knowledge brings practitioners into greater awareness of, and control over, their own actions—their own behaviors, yes, but also their own thoughts, values, and feelings leading to and away from their behaviors. The Skinnerian hope of modifying behavior via external control over the environment without attending to events inside the skin is an illusion supported only by very special social-psychological conditions. Subjective contingencies running counter or parallel to objective ones are usually far more powerful and precise predictors of behavior than are objective contingencies (see, for example, Alegre & Murray, 1974; Dulany, 1968; Levine, 1971; Page & Kahle, 1976). To know how knowledge from A can become contributions to action by B, one has to know how B's ongoing subjective minding interacts with A's knowledge in such a way as to render A's knowledge about the world in general both compatible and relevant *in B's mind* to B's knowledge about the particular of B's own actions.

The foregoing discussion of the contributions of social psychology to education lays the foundation for a problem that can now be formulated. I have claimed that social psychology, that branch of psychology that gathers data and develops theories about interpersonal relations, has unique contributions to make to educational practice by virtue of the fundamentally interpersonal nature of educational phenomena and processes. I have also taken some pains to show not only that the methodological bases of much of social-psychological knowledge were being authoritatively questioned on a number of grounds by social psychologists themselves, not only that the impact of even unimpeachable knowledge on educational practice was completely dependent on the vicissitudes of societal conditions and on superficially informed decision processes outside of the academy, but also that, even within the academy and within the social psychologist's person, it was doubtful whether even intimate and accurate knowledge of that social psychology had any detectable influence on the social psychologist's own educating. Not only is the message that social psychology might send to education of questioned validity, but the channels for transmission also seem to be jammed. What hope is left for any contribution to educational practice from social psychology?

The problem that needs to be addressed, then, is the incompatibility between the claim that social psychology is in principle uniquely suited to contribute to educational practice and the conclusion that dubious messages and jammed channels reduce to insignificance social psychology's contribution to educational practice. The problem is an incompatibility between a possibility and an actuality. Solutions to such problems always take one of three forms: (1) verification that the possibility is nonexistent and that the actual already approximates the desirable, (2) modification of the actual so that it realizes the possible, and (3) joint modification: diminishing conceptions of the possible and augmenting actual achievements. In this context, I advocate the second kind of solution.

Modifications of both the methodological underpinnings of social psychology and the channels by which social-psychological knowledge has an impact on educational practice are required before any claim for contributions from the one side to the other can legitimately be regarded as more than missionary smugness. Both of these weaknesses can be addressed by shifts in the exchange relations (Blau, 1964; Gouldner, 1960; Homans, 1958) between educators and social psychologists.

FOUR KINDS OF ACTION: ON-LINE, NO-LINE, SIDELINE, AND OFF-LINE

Distinctions are needed between kinds of action engaged in by educators and social psychologists to provide a suitable framework for thinking about an exchange relation between them. Let me distinguish two broad classes of behavior and experience (I use the term *action* to refer jointly to behavior and experience) and, within one of these kinds of action, two special subclasses. The first, broader, distinction is between what I call "on-line action" and "no-line action." The distinction is based on the fact that in social action much depends on the distribution of discretionary power influencing (a) whose purposes are served and (b) whose schedules or timing preferences are followed.

On-line and no-line behavior are distinguished by degrees of discretion over purposes and schedules. One is fully on line when one is pursuing one's own goals in one's own time.[1] (The goals and schedules may, of course, be interdependent with others' goals and schedules: Being on line does not necessarily mean being independent or alone in one's action.) One is totally caught in no-line action when one has discretion over neither the direction nor the timing of one's actions. At the on-line extreme, outcomes of action are important and sought after; at the no-line extreme, they are either inconsequential or avoided.

The adolescent, slumped on the couch and disengaged from on-line action ("engaged" in no-line action), expresses the no-line experience by saying, "There's nothing to do. No one's around." Nothing from the external world stands out from anything else; all of it is equally uninteresting. Nothing from the internal world is more salient than anything else, either; all contents of minding are equally bland. All conceivable goals are equally low in priority. Attention to consequences of any action is absent. Such experience and behavior do not usually last long. Under most circumstances, humans are inveterate generators of unattained goals, doers in their own time, and sensitive to consequences.

Often people suspend these three tendencies voluntarily, that is, they follow a larger goal of giving a certain—sometimes devastating—control over their behavior to someone else's purposes for a time. That is what one means by *compliance*. Sometimes compliance is precipitated by force, sometimes not; but wherever compliance is, so too is no-line behavior. To clarify: The act of complying for a purpose and for a time is itself on-line action; but within the duration of compliance, the directions and timings of behavior are under someone else's minding and are of consequence to the compliant person so long as they do not violate that person's purpose for suspending her or his own control over purpose and timing in the first place. When the demands of others violate compliant people's purposes for complying, they no longer comply. They suspend their suspension of control. They move on line.

For the most part, no-line behavior and experience are short-lived; yet one is

---

[1] The on-line experience—pursuing one's own goals in one's own time—is parallel in some respects to the experience of *flow* formulated and investigated by Csikszentmihalyi (1975). My emphasis in the on-line–no-line distinction is on the balance between external and autonomous control over the aim and timing of action. Csikszentmihalyi explores the balance of resources *demanded* by a task and resources *commanded* by the actor engaged in the task. The experience of flow assumes what I am calling "on-line experience" as a precondition, necessary but not sufficient.

reminded, by the literature on the effects of minority repression and the effects of imprisonment, that universal tendencies toward maintenance of discretion over direction and sequence of behavior can be blunted to the point of deadened quiescence. The behavior and experience of people assigned to prisons, hospitals, and, alas, some schools is frequently characterized by pervasive compliance to encompassing regimes of treatment—compliance to others' comforts and conveniences; others' values, norms, rules, and schedules; others' desires and whims. A salient feature of no-line experience is a sense of the arbitrariness of the actions of the powerful others. Both mild forms (see, for example, Cusick, 1973, pp. 88, 128; Jackson, 1968, pp. 1–37, 83–111) and extreme forms (see Bettelheim, 1960, pp. 107–235) stand in stark contrast to action under goal direction and discretionary control over the sequencing of actions. Calling such behavior and experience "no line" keeps salient the fact that such action leads nowhere of choice or favored consequence in the life of the person so controlled. No-line action is either meaningless or utterly fearful to those caught up in it; for them, it does not fit into their life. They are "doing time," doing someone else's bidding, complying, waiting for their own suspended life to start up again. The most important contrasting characteristics of on-line and no-line action can be described by the terms in Table 2-1.

It is important to distinguish on-line from no-line action because the value and endurance of any intended contribution between psychologists and educators will depend on the contribution's actual usefulness to the beneficiaries in their on-line action. Intended contributions to people or groups under no-line conditions necessarily partake of no-line qualities: They are not owned, are seen as inconsequential and arbitrary, are merely complied with, lead to minimal investment of energy, and are dropped as soon as the reasons for polite or grudging compliance disappear. Enduring and consequential contributions to the actions of educators (and, reciprocally, to the actions of psychologists) are inescapably contributions on line.

Within on-line action, there are two kinds that are important to distinguish in order to rethink the possibilities for a contributing relation between social psychol-

TABLE 2-1   Contrasting Characteristics of On-line and No-line Action

Dimension of action	On-line characteristics	No-line characteristics
Demands of others	Understandable, predictable	Unclear, arbitrary
Purposes being served	Own—valued	Others'—devalued
Consequences of of action	Important	Unimportant
Sense of efficacy	Potent, proactive	Impotent, reactive, passive
Energy	Invested	Protected or withheld
Relation of action to other actions and purposes	Relevantly connected	Disconnected, irrelevant
Attention	Focused, concentrated	Diffused, distractable
Interaction with participating superordinates	Communicative, overtly cooperative, or overtly rejecting	Uncommunicative, compliant, docile

ogists and educators. These two subclasses of action are reflexive: They involve the examination of behavior and experience. *Off-line action* examines one's own behavior and experience; *sideline action* examines others' behavior and experience.[2]

I draw special attention to these two kinds of action because they appear to me to be the means sine qua non by which people performing tasks at intermediate levels of effectiveness become aware of and eliminate the performance habits that keep them at merely intermediate levels. Sidelining action on behalf of people seeking higher levels of performance usually takes the form of performance observations by experts that lead the performers to make off-line comparisons of the observations with their own behavior. Sidelining action by a supervisor or coach or tutor is useful, too, but only if it includes communication between the sideliner and the performers about the sideliner's observations. Such communications are the sion for broadened awareness—on the performers' parts—of the dysfunctional moves, postures, and positions they are unwittingly engaging in; on the sideliner's part, of the performers' thoughts and experiences that lie behind performance patterns.

Clearly, sidelining action is useless in improving performance unless it leads to off-line action on the part of the performers: Thinking about and visualizing actual and desired behaviors, analyzing other changes that are required to support the new behaviors, planning for future occasions of the performance, and the like. Equally clear, off-line action by the performers without sideline support is difficult and short-lived at best. It is in the joint operation of sideline and off-line action that the possibilities for effecting improved levels of on-line performance are maximized.

Watch practicing educators upon whose success in educating depends their own jobs or the safety of their students' clients. One finds such educators usually in the role of supervisor or coach, bent on improving the performance of, for example, aircraft pilots, scuba-diving instructors, and competitive athletes. Such educators are found in greatest numbers in the world of competitive sports, particularly professional sports. The stakes in all of these situations are high: On-line action is richly (or bitterly) consequential. To engage in such consequential on-line action without supportive sideline and off-line action would be unthinkable. In such situations, one of the educator's crucial contributions, along with proddings and programs of physical conditioning, is that of an intervening sideliner, providing objective information about performers' blunders and advances in skill.

If enhancing the effectiveness of people in the performance of tasks or roles requires sideline and off-line action, then one stumbles immediately upon a resource that is almost totally unavailable to public (and most private) school educators. Whereas professional athletes work constantly in the presence of opportunities (and requirements) for examining their on-line behavior with the assistance

---

[2] Strictly speaking, both off-line and sideline action could be subclassifications of no-line action as well as of on-line action. That is, one could comply with commands or suggestions to examine one's own behavior, or someone else's, with little investment, no sense of its connection to other purposes, and so on. Granting this, it seems useful here to consider only sideline and off-line actions that have on-line qualities. To clear up another terminological matter, I speak of on-line action, separate from sideline or off-line action, even though the latter are subclasses of the former. I could introduce a new term (mainline?) to denote all on-line action that is neither off line nor sideline, but that seems unnecessary. In general, "on-line action" refers to people's everyday work and leisure action that is neither sideline nor off line and that is characterized by serving their own or valued purposes according to schedules they perceive as fitting to those purposes.

of staffs of sidelining observers, educators typically have no such opportunity. Indeed, educators are relentlessly on line. They are constantly obliged, at the classroom level, to make unassisted choices among fluidly changing alternatives and, at the staff and administrative level, to work their way through an almost unending stream of interruptions toward a succession of immediate goals. Educators' time for planning is severely limited, but regular time and mechanisms for retrospective assessment of their own individual or collective actions are simply nonexistent.

Teachers, administrators, and staff specialists are similar to professional athletes in two respects: (1) They are advanced performers, not still acquiring the skills necessary to perform; and (2) while performing, they are unable to be aware of their own postures, moves, and thought processes, attending as they must to the immediate world facing them and the next moves they must make to complete a task or simply to avoid disaster. But educators, particularly public educators, are at opposite poles from professional athletes with respect to opportunities to improve their respective levels of performance. Educators who seriously intend to become more effective in their action, therefore, must address the virtual absence of mechanisms and opportunities for sidelining assistance and off-line analysis if they are to fulfill their intentions. Before I turn to a consideration of the off-line actions of educators who were serious about improving their performance, let me return to the problem formulated earlier.

There are, recall, two kinds of impediments standing in the way of social psychologists' contributions to educators' educating. The first are methodological weaknesses, increasingly acknowledged by social psychologists, weaknesses that render the data, findings, and conceptions of much of social psychology of questionable validity. These weaknesses also impede contributions of social psychology to educational theory. The second kind of impediment to social psychologists' contribution to education is the jammed channel of communication—jammed by the long decision chain between psychologists and educators and by other, unknown impediments preventing social psychologists from using their own knowledge of social psychology in the improvement of their own educating. How does the fourfold distinction among kinds of action help illuminate these impediments and suggest ways around them?

As it happens, by using the distinctions to examine methodological weaknesses of social-psychological studies and by considering remedies that would increase their validity and ultimate generalizability, one also examines the exchange relation between social psychologists and their subjects. An altered relation between social psychologists and the people they study turns out to be central, not only to the problem of validity, but also to the problem of jammed channels of communication between social psychologists and educators. How do the distinctions between on-line and no-line action and between sideline and off-line action clarify and suggest remedies for these two kinds of impediment?

The core of an answer I am suggesting is that social-psychological studies are vulnerable to the kind of criticisms being leveled at them only to the extent that the behavior studied is no-line behavior. Argyris (1975) points out that the values and strategies of interpersonal control implicit in social psychologists' methodologies bear a striking resemblance to their substantive findings. Social psychologists' data, findings, theory, and inferences reflect governing values and research strategies whose common fulcrum is the control of other people. Such a criticism is validly leveled at any method that recruits and treats subjects according to purposes and schedules set unilaterally by investigators and followed by subjects without regard for (i.e., data gathering about) subjects' priorities and in which variations in behavior do not covary with consequences to the behaver. Such is no-line behavior. Argyris's criticism could not be validly leveled at any study of on-line behavior in which the investigator had to negotiate with subjects as equals and in which, in exchange for intimate data about on-line action, the investigator had to provide the subjects with, for example, easily interpretable arrays of data reflecting their actions.

Orne (1962, 1973) and others criticize experiments and other data-gathering procedures for allowing artifacts to creep into data by virtue of subjects' responses to the special demand characteristics of the data-gathering procedures, but such criticisms are validly leveled at any data-gathering procedure to the extent that it induces no-line action. When people volunteer or are recruited to do someone else's bidding, they do so, of course, out of their own purposes; they are to that degree on line. Within the period of doing the other's bidding, they may either succumb to the no-line inducements or transform the situation into on-line action. If they succumb—giving over control to the other—they are, whatever else they may be doing, engaging in that special kind of docile, "irresponsible," dependent behavior called mere compliance; they have become self to some master. In some experiments the "demand characteristics" are sufficiently clear that the compliant subject merely carries out the demands. When this happens, that is, when subjects merely carry out experimenters' (unwitting but discernible) demands, results become trivial.

If, on the other hand, people volunteering or recruited to do experimenters' bidding do not simply give over direction to the experimenter, they engage in active, but covert, construing and evaluation of the experiment's hypotheses, which become powerful determinants of their behavior. (See, for example, Alegre & Murray, 1974; Bem, 1965; Dulany, 1968; Farber, 1963; Levine, 1971; Page & Kahle, 1976.) If subjects agree with the experiment's purposes and hypotheses as they construe them, they engage in behavior that would confirm their constructed purposes and hypotheses. If they oppose the experimenter's purposes and hypotheses as they construe them, they engage in behavior intended to disconfirm them. Either way, their private construings and evaluations introduce "artifacts."

Thus, two kinds of artifacts occur in research in which subjects are induced to serve others' research purposes. The first is simple compliance with clear demand characteristics. The second is the subjective construing and evaluation that subjects introduce covertly and that become guides to their own cooperative or antagonistic behavior. Either kind or both kinds characterize the action of subjects whenever they are induced to respond to others' purposes and schedules, in other words, whenever they are constrained toward no-line action. Orne's criticisms could not validly be leveled at studies of on-line action in which data-gathering purposes and procedures were openly negotiated as part of an exchange in which the purposes of both negotiating parties influenced and were being served by the data collection.

Finally, McGuire (1973) criticizes both laboratory and field experiments on the grounds that "simple a-affects-b hypotheses fail to catch the complexities of parallel processing, bidirectional causality and reverberating feedback that characterize both cognitive and social organization" (p. 448), but such a criticism is validly leveled at any study in which the subject's behavior must be constrained by what the superordinate investigator wishes (unilaterally) to study and by schedules of action and forms of response established by the investigator. The complexities of which McGuire speaks have been controlled right out of the data-gathering procedure (though never out of the subject's cognitive or social processes). Studies of no-line action, which predominate in social psychology, are bound to be vulnerable to the criticism of causal simplicity because the central criterion of success is whether subjects' behavior comes under the control of the experimenter's manipulations. The identification during the last 15 years of the wide variety of artifacts that operate in studies is testimony to the validity of McGuire's conceptions of subjects as capable of parallel processing and reverberating feedback and of their behavior as bidirectionally caused.

Although McGuire is undoubtedly correct that a shift to field experiments will not, of itself, eliminate the deficiencies he and others point out in social-psychological research, studies of on-line action—with a variety of methodologies used in the context of equitable and consequential exchanges between researchers and educators—would mitigate much of the narrow, "a-affects-b" thinking. Once psychologists negotiated with educators to study their consequential, on-line action, educators would demand more than a written report in exchange. Meetings with educators to discuss patterns, interpretations, causes, and consequences of action studied would be a part of the equity.

It is in the exchange, not in the study of on-line action by itself, that social-psychological data, interpretations, and theories would become more valid. There, observers and observed would trade views about patterns in the data, interpretations of their meanings, assessments of their causes, and speculations about their consequences and modifications. Explanations of causality of the "a-affects-b" kind, the unilateral control of behavior, deception, and what McGuire (1973) calls "demonstrations" of "the obvious correctness of our hypotheses" would be minimized in such exchanges. It is in the exchange, not in the mere availability of sideline data, that educational practice would feel the effects of social psychologists' contributions. In the trading of views about patterns, meanings, causes, consequences, and modifications, educators would become aware of their blunders, yes, but aware also of their resources and their opportunities for improvement.

My argument can now be more fully stated. Most nontechnical educational systems have developed no mechanisms for improving performance through sideline and off-line action: No observational, recording, data-displaying, or data-interpreting capabilities that would focus on actual performance of educators have been developed or stabilized in educational organizations.[3] Substantial improvement will not be possible without substantial increases in sideline and off-line action. A large number (though not a large proportion) of educational systems are under pressure to improve substantially.

In a complementary fashion, most social psychologists have avoided studies of phenomena and processes in natural settings. Substantial improvement in the capacity of social psychology to deal validly with the complexities of cognitive and social life will not be possible without substantial increases in the study of consequential on-line action. An increasing number (though not proportion) of social

---

[3] A noteworthy exception to this valid generalization is the daily general staff meeting of the Orthogenic School of the University of Chicago (see Bettelheim, 1974). Although the content is indelibly stamped with Bettelheim's outlooks and personality, the form and much of its process are generalizable as a mechanism for off-line action.

psychologists want substantial improvements in the validity of social-psychological research. A complementarity of needs and resources is developing that points toward the development of an exchange between educators and social psychologists who want to improve their respective practices and outcomes.

Consider an example of social psychologists working with educators in an exchange oriented toward both an impact on practice and a contribution to social-psychological knowledge. Although the achievements of both goals were modest, the episode, and the data about on-line action gathered and discussed in the course of the episode, illustrate the kind of exchange of which I have been speaking abstractly.

AN EXCHANGE BETWEEN SOCIAL PSYCHOLOGISTS
AND EDUCATORS

Almost a decade ago, John Glidewell and I began a program of training to prepare social-psychological specialists for work as internal organizational consultants in schools. At that time, the idea that social psychologists might contribute directly and practically to schooling was new (Lighthall, 1969), although the role of sociopsychological clinician in schools had been hinted at earlier (Lighthall & Diedrich, 1965) and, of course, similar roles had operated for some time in commercial and industrial organizations. After 3 years of experience with the training program, a field test was undertaken of a number of game plans for using data to increase educators' awareness of their own individual and collective action. The field test kept Susan Allan and me in a private religious high school about 1½ days a week for a school year. We carried out what it now seems most accurate to call a "research consultation" involving the intensive study of, and interventions into, two organizational groups: a student-faculty council and a three-person administrative team (the executive council).

In the course of that year, one of the teachers at the school, Sister Janet Acker, who was a member of the student-faculty council, became interested in our data and procedures and in the new role of social-psychological specialist. She pursued the possibility that she might develop the role within her school on a part-time basis. The ethos of the religious order that owned and managed the school, the goals of the most influential administrator, the sentiments of many of the students' parents, and economic pressures that closed many religious schools constituted a strong force for program improvement and self-scrutiny. The executives responded favorably to Sister Janet Acker's request to begin training at the University of Chicago to continue the kinds of observation, recording, and discussions of data that Susan Allan and I had started. She would work toward a role in the school that would be one- or two-fifths-time teaching (social sciences) and three- or four-fifths-time studying problems of communication, coordination, and problem solving among various sectors of the school's organization.

The intended role of the social-psychological practitioner as we conceived it has been described in detail elsewhere (Lighthall, 1969, 1970, 1973; Lighthall & Braun, 1976). Briefly, the role was to be nested within a steering committee composed of staff members from different roles and levels of authority in the school. The steering committee's functions were twofold: (1) to set priorities among the organizational problems or focuses to which the specialist would attend, and (2) to help the specialist in her entry into various parts of the school, in planning and foreseeing the consequences of actions, and with interpretation of data. The problems to be selected for consideration would concern organizational processes, in other words, the ways in which individuals and groups communicated, exerted influence, dealt with conflict, cooperated, and solved problems. The specialist's expertise was to be in the gathering and analysis of data; in assisting others in clarifying and following priorities; in noting and directing attention to contradictions and conflicts; and in helping others to manage tensions, communicate more clearly, and confront problems more forthrightly—all within the substantive priorities set by the steering committee.

In actuality, the first year of Sister Janet's work as an internal social-psychological consultant was divided between courses and supervision at the university and her initial involvement in school problems. She also taught one senior seminar in problem solving. In the second semester, she introduced her students to a practical problem that the administrators were trying to deal with and that her steering committee had thought to be a useful initial focus for her work: the increasing amounts of debris and garbage being left by students after their lunch periods.

Now this surely was a "safe" and organizationally peripheral problem for a budding consultant to take on, but it was viewed as a problem and it did involve social behavior. Data were gathered on degrees of littering (reliably rated) over a 2-week period, cross-tabulated by lunch period (first through fourth) and class of student (freshmen through seniors, inasmuch as students sitting at the same table tended overwhelmingly to be from the same year in high school). Data analyses, showing differences in lunch periods and year of student, were presented on bulletin boards, and a closed-circuit television program was carried out highlighting various aspects of the problem. It came to light from interview data that part of the problem was crowding. Many seniors who had almost enough credits to graduate, and consequently had time on their hands during the day, spent two or three periods in the lunchroom, crowding out the underclassmen. The problem of litter and garbage and of underclass resentment was lessened to some extent by the creation of a dining annex.

Thus, an initial problem was perceived; data were gathered; analyses revealed a hidden problem; widespread discussion of the data led to tangible changes, lessening tension, and to some extent, mitigation of the undesirable crowd behavior that had initiated the inquiry. Not bad for a novice consultant, but this contribution was not very central to the organization. It did serve to display to students, teachers, and administrators, however, the usefulness of systematic observations and analyses of data in solving organizational problems; and some senior students had, moreover, become active sideliners!

Before describing other aspects of the new role as it developed, a brief summary of some background information is useful. The year before Sister Janet began her internship as a social-psychological specialist in the school was a year of considerable change in the administrative and governing structures of the school. During that previous year, the year in which Susan Allan and I carried out our research consultation and in which Sister Janet became interested in a new role for herself in the school, two kinds of change took place.

First, the large all-school faculty and student council was reorganized into separate councils: student councils for each class year, each chaired by a member of the administrative team (executive council); a faculty council; and a parent council. A new kind of all-school council was established, which was to be made up of representatives from each of the other smaller councils from the various roles and sectors of the school and chaired by the school's director, who also chaired the executive council. Second, the executive council was enlarged from three to six members, a change that reflected also an innovation in roles. A new role, that of counselor-administrator (separate from the regular guidance and counseling role in the school) was added, one administrator-counselor for each of the 4 class years. These four counselor-administrators, who came to be called "class consultants," were to sit as executive-council members along with the school's director and associate director. The purpose behind the role of class consultant was to strengthen the frequency and quality of contact between administrators and students, especially with respect to student disciplining. The role of class consultant was, thus, a regular, on-line administrative role, not to be confused with the sideline role of social psychological specialist.

These organizational changes, of course, brought about not only needed solutions but also new problems and confusions, which were the subject of discussions at executive-council meetings the subsequent year, the year Sister Janet began assuming the functions of an internal organizational consultant.

One of these problems had been sensed the year before, in discussions among the director and associate director of the school, Susan Allan, and me. This problem took Sister Janet much closer to the mainsprings of the school organization. The executives met once a week to coordinate events and efforts in solving emergent problems. They had come to realize that once solutions or decisions had been reached in these executive meetings, the necessary follow-up was too often long delayed, weak, or nonexistent. The course of problem solving on one problem was preempted by the emergence of another problem. In short, they had become vaguely aware of a metaproblem: a problem of losing track of problems.

A problem accounting system was therefore attempted. It involved the development of what we called the role of "problem accountant." A member of each group into which the problem accounting system was to be introduced would fill out a problem accounting sheet, which simply called for notes to be taken on any problem or difficulty that emerged in the group, its source, the date it surfaced, a brief description of the resolution or referral, the date of resolution, and other descriptive data. Accounting procedures were introduced at two levels: the junior and senior class councils and the executive council.

The senior and junior class councils, however, engaged in such noncommunicative discussions (parallel talk) that the problem accountant could not even keep track of the subject under discussion, let alone the course of problem solving. Problem accounting was therefore abandoned in these councils. (This failure, however, by virtue of its even rudimentary planning and organization, focused attention on an even more central problem, the nature of communication in these class councils. I am omitting discussion of that attention here.)

The problem accounting system introduced into the executive council was more successful. Training of the class consultant who volunteered to take on the role of problem accountant in executive meetings was pushed much farther than was possible with the students who had assumed the new role in the junior and senior councils. Revisions of accounting sheets and procedures were also accomplished through experience with the executive council.

A number of problems were followed completely, from their first appearance in executive meeting discussions through follow-up interviews by Sister Janet with the person most directly responsible for referring the problem to the executive committee in the first place. These follow-up interviews obtained testimony and ratings regarding the extent to which the executives' actions on the problem were felt to be satisfactory to those most directly affected by the problematic conditions and the executives' actions. Still, the accounting task did require continuous refinement, absorbing a considerable amount of time on the parts of Sister Janet and of the class consultant who had assumed the new role to monitor the executives' problem solving.

Flaws and ambiguities in the problem accounting procedures among the executives were still being worked out when Sister Janet's attention and energies were preempted by other priorities. Sister Janet was asked to help the executives assess strengths and weaknesses of their performance during the first semester. They were planning for the following year and wanted input from teachers and from each of themselves individually regarding their functioning as an executive group and in their separate roles as directors and class consultants. Discussions with her advisor and steering-committee members (at that point, the executive council) led Sister Janet to give most of her energies to the evaluation task. Thus, the problem accounting system was discontinued, prey to the very forces it was designed to reveal in detail. The accounting system had worked sufficiently long and well, however, for data to be gathered that were useful in Sister Janet's assessment of some of the qualities of the executive group's functioning.

Evaluation activities of two kinds were undertaken: (1) assessment of the effectiveness of the executives' functioning in their weekly meetings and (2) assessment of the strengths and weaknesses of the ways in which each of the four class consultants carried out her role. Space limits require me to confine the discussion to the first kind of data only, that bearing on the executives' use of meeting time. I describe first some data the executives did consider together and then further data and analyses they were prevented from discussing (by delay in their analysis and by a shift in personnel) but that would otherwise have been on the executives' agenda. These data illustrate the kind of focus and exchange possible when a sideliner who is trusted, as Sister Janet was, helps administrators step off line to examine their own administrative behavior. They also illustrate how data gathered for off-line purposes can also contribute more broadly to social-psychological knowledge of on-line phenomena and processes.

Sister Janet examined the administrators' responses to 11 agenda items of executive meetings. The problems to which the items referred had been followed intensively through the problem accounting procedures during the first semester of the school year. These 11 items were not randomly sampled, but they seemed to us and to the executives to represent the range of complexity and importance of items they regularly dealt with in their weekly meetings held September–December. Analysis was later extended to 10 additional items from meetings held January–April.[4]

Six kinds of data were examined, only the first three of which are of concern here: (1) the duration of discussion of each of the 11 (and later, 10 more) agenda

---

[4] All of the meetings of the executive group were openly recorded during Sister Janet's internship year. The recordings were part of a separate study I was conducting of the executives' communication and problem solving. The recordings became routine early on: The director would open the meeting by going to the tape recorder, turning it on, and testing for proper recording volume. The only people at these meetings were on-line participants.

items; (2) ratings of each of the 11 (and then 10 more) items for their importance for discussion at an executive-committee meeting; (3) samples from three meetings across the year of duration and frequency of participation of each executive during a dozen 2-minute periods (four per meeting); (4) the problem accountant's and Sister Janet's judgment of the form in which each agenda item was presented to the executives (as a question to be answered, as a vague problem to be formulated and acted on, as a formulated problem to be acted on, or as a proposal or solution to be adopted, modified, or rejected); (5) the degree of satisfaction of the beneficiaries of the executives' action on items they had acted on, as rated by Sister Janet from interviews she held with the person most responsible for routing the problem to the executives; and (6) excerpted interview comments from the executives about their reactions to arrays and discussion of data described in 1, 2, 4, and 5, above. I should emphasize that this last kind of data was second-order, reflexive data: verbatim expressions of responses to arrays of other data.

The first meeting between Sister Janet and the executives in which data were portrayed dealt with all but the third and sixth of these kinds of data. In that meeting, little more was accomplished than assimilation of the information, arrayed in six tables, and a brief discussion of each kind of data. Successive meetings and interviews moved toward an increasingly sharp focus on the relation between the executives' priorities regarding the problems they actually discussed in their weekly meetings and the amount of time they actually devoted to discussing each one. My examination of data can move to a much sharper focus than Sister Janet and the executives were able to achieve, given the competing goals of an internship and the skill of an intern.

The first array of data that was presented by Sister Janet to the executives and that is of interest in this discussion appears in Table 2-2 (actual names, not these pseudonyms, were used in the original displays). Although the fourth column, showing rough indexes of consensus about priorities, was the primary focus of discussion of that table in the initial meeting, subsequent comments by the executives in interviews about their interpretations of the data in Table 2-2 provided greater focus on the relation between discussion time and priorities. Several of the executives commented on their collective tendency in meetings to "spend an awful lot of time on little things and very little time on essentials."

Sister Janet summarized the recorded comments made in these interviews and provided the executives in a second meeting with verbatim excerpts of their comments about the data arrays that had been discussed in the first meeting, of which Table 2-2 was one. Uneven participation by the executives had been noticed by Sister Janet in more than one meeting. Because participation in such meetings had a bearing on the question of how effectively they were working together, Sister Janet assembled the data reported in Table 2-3 for the executives' perusal and discussion in their second meeting.

The questions that the data of Table 2-3 raise are of both the obvious and the nonobvious kinds. Obvious: How functional is it for scarce coordination time of the executives to be allocated so unevenly among the six executives? Not so obvious: To what extent do the three underclass consultants give predominant attention to their consultant role, viewing their administrative responsibilities and role as increasingly peripheral? More particularly: What has happened to Sister Katherine's sense of her role in the executive council? If some of the regularities of participation across the three meetings can be taken seriously, still other questions might be

TABLE 2-2 Agenda-item Content, Discussion Time, and Rated Importance of Each of 11 Actual Items and 5 Hypothetical Items

Content	Time spent (min)	Sum of ratings[a]	Range[b]
1. Intraschool communication: establishing a daily bulletin to read during homeroom	90	21	2
2. Cafeteria student behavior needs to be regulated—crowd behavior . . . how to control?	65	18	2
3. How well the executive council is performing its functions	c	18	4
4. Cafeteria: lack of sufficient seating to accommodate students	60	4	2
5. School policies and procedures for school activities and trips	43	13	4
6. Determining the admission policy for accepting incoming freshman	40	19	3
7. How effectively the school councils are functioning	c	19	2
8. Functioning of homeroom advisors—Some are not performing all their duties . . . difficulties of getting cooperation	40	14	3
9. Stealing—among students, from library, homeroom decorations, etc.	c	17	4
10. Student uniform policy: Should the policy be relaxed?	32	8	1
11. Room allocations: What group should be given the use of a room that is no longer in use—as a meeting room, office, etc.?	20	4	2
12. Conflicts between faculty subgroups relative to school policies, departments, etc.	c	13	4
13. Evaluation of policies made by the executive council—What procedures, if any, should be used?	18	18	4
14. School parking policies: parking lot—which and how much space is given to students? to teachers?	c	2	2
15. Role definitions of executive council positions	15	21	1
16. School security—police in attendance at school dances, activities, etc.	16	10	2

[a] A high rating (4 on a 0–4 scale) indicated that the item was considered important enough to be discussed at an executive-council meeting. The highest possible sum of ratings was 24 for the six executives.

[b] The difference between the lowest and highest rating on a scale of 0–4.

[c] Hypothetical items were rated along with other items but never came up for discussion; these were introduced as one test of the extent to which time allocations to items were made on the basis of executives' estimates of importance.

generated. The question of regularity itself, of course, naturally arises when only four periods of three meetings are sampled. An important function of such data at the organizational level, however, is not only to settle questions but to raise them—to draw conscious attention to organizational behavior and thereby increase thought about, first, the relation between actuals and ideals and, second, alternative modes of behavior not before contemplated. Does Miss Carey want to be

TABLE 2-3 Samples of Frequency and Duration of Participations from Four 2-Minute Periods in Each of Three Executive Meetings

	September 22				December 7				April 2			
	Frequency		Time[a]		Frequency		Time		Frequency		Time	
	N	%	Sum	%	N	%	Sum	%	N	%	Sum	%
Sr. Claudia (dir.)	6	27	232	48	10	30	281	59	14	44	179	37
Sr. Patricia	5	23	64	13	7	21	52	11	6	19	149	31
Sr. Catherine (assoc. dir.)	4	18	27	6	9	27	43	9	3	9	53	11
Sr. Katherine	5	23	114	24	0	0	0	0	3	9	59	12
Sr. Mary Ann	2	9	43	9	2	6	15	3	2	6	3	1
Miss Carey	0	0	0	0	0	0	0	0	4	12	37	8
Other staff	[b]				5	15	89	19				

[a]In seconds.
[b]Two staff members were present at the December 7 meeting only. Zeros opposite other participants represent not absences but nonparticipation of members present.

as peripheral in executive discussions as these data show her to be? Do the directors and their fellow consultants want more complete participation from Sister Mary Ann and Miss Carey? Such questions, along with the other ones I have suggested, are virtually never considered by educators in their relentless on-line work unless a sideliner can present the looking-glass opportunity that only data can provide.

How the discussions about the data of Table 2-3 actually went, I cannot say. They were taken up, along with other matters, at a retreat away from the school, which went unrecorded and unobserved. The fact that, about this time in the school year, Sister Claudia decided to give up her innovative administration of the school and to accept a position of greater responsibility undoubtedly meant that discussion of the patterns and implications of Table 2-3 was truncated.

What do Sister Janet's activities described thus far illustrate? They illustrate first of all the activities of a rank neophyte: All of the activities described so far were undertaken in her first year of graduate training in social psychology. They illustrate the fact that simple arrangements of data, without inferential statistics, can be meaningful to on-line educators. They illustrate that simple data can be used to confront people with their own consequential, on-line, collective behavior. Sister Janet's activities also illustrate the use of a variety of kinds of data: recorded verbatim testimony, behavioral frequency counts, time measures, ratings of satisfaction and importance, frequency counts of discussion contents, and data about responses to data. They illustrate many small, specific things.

By and large, however, these activities illustrate the beginnings of a sidelining role of a social psychologist in interaction with educators who want to step off line, to plan for more effective functioning, and who are willing to take a retrospective look at their behavior. The ready context of a possible contribution from Sister Janet as a sideliner was, and had to be, provided by the educators: They wanted to learn because enough of them felt pressures from their own value systems, from economic conditions facing the school, and from the commitments of the director to accountability to feel that much depended on their learning about their own behavior. Without a sidelining role or mechanism, however, that commitment to learn would not have received the informational support that even a beginning social psychologist could provide: an attention to actual social processes through the systematic gathering and arranging of a variety of kinds of on-line data.

I can move to an even sharper focus on some on-line organizational processes with additional data gathered by Sister Janet after her initial presentations. Consider the following modest extension of the inquiry into the relationship between Sister Janet's executives' use of their meeting time and their subjective individual ratings of 21 problems that they had discussed in meetings over the year.

Just how strong is the relation, we asked, between the rated importance that a problem be discussed in executive meeting and the amount of time the executives actually devoted to it in executive meetings? Of course more than mere priorities would influence discussion time. Degree of consensus about a problem's importance, problem complexity, and the amount of prior discussion are variables that would probably influence the amount of discussion time taken in any one meeting. Without sufficient data about these other possible influences, we wondered how a simple assessment of the executives' priorities about discussing the items, after they had been discussed, would relate to the amount of meeting time devoted to them. Despite the grossness of the inquiry, we decided to compute simple rank order correlations between (a) summed ratings of the importance of problems discussed in executive meetings (i.e., how important the rater believed it was that each problem be discussed at an executive meeting) and (b) the amount of time taken in the meeting or meetings in which it was discussed. Overall, it did seem reasonable to expect that there should be some positive correlation between length of discussion time and the rated importance of discussing a problem.

Because there seemed to be a distinct difference in the average participation in these meetings between Sisters Claudia, Patricia, and Catherine, on the one hand, and Sister Katherine, Sister Mary Ann, and Miss Carey on the other, correlations were computed separately for these two groups and for first- and second-semester items. The coefficients of rank order correlation between discussion time and rated importance of the 11 first-semester items was −.07 for the three most frequent participants and +.16 for the three less frequently participating executives. For the 10 second-semester items, the coefficients were .41 and .53, respectively.

Frequency of participation seemed not at all important in affecting the relation between importance of considering an item and the amount of consideration time it received in a meeting. Time of year, however, did seem to have some effect on the size of the relation. In examining the content and other characteristics that might differentiate first-semester from second-semester agenda items, we could find only one that stood out with even moderate salience, namely, the origin of the agenda item. Of the 11 items introduced during the meetings of the first semester, 7 were introduced by Sister Claudia, the director. The next-nearest number of items introduced by anyone was 2. In contrast, during the second semester, the director introduced only 3 of the 10 items, whereas Sister Patricia, the next-most actively participating executive, introduced 5 items.

It was at least plausible that items introduced by a strong director, as Sister Claudia clearly was, might consistently receive more exploration in meetings irrespective of importance simply because of deference to the top administrator. Items introduced by anyone else, however, would more likely be explored only for what they were worth, uncontaminated by deference.

We reexamined the data, therefore, differentiating the items with respect to who had introduced them, dropping the first- and second-semester distinction. Now that power had reentered our thinking, we differentiated ratings, as well as source of item, according to our estimates of power, the frequency of participation summed across the rows of Table 2-3. Of the 21 items for which we had data across the year, 10 had been introduced by Sister Claudia and 7 by Sister Patricia, the second-most active member. The separate correlations suggested by these considerations appear in Table 2-4.

The rather clear and consistent pattern that resulted from these differentiations was made even clearer when items introduced by the least participating members were combined with those introduced by Sister Patricia. The resulting coefficients, reading down the right-hand column, were .60, .62, and .75. The pattern becomes still clearer if participation times are used instead of frequencies.

The pattern that comes through is simple in its gross outlines. If anyone but the director introduced an item, it tended to be discussed by the executives for a length of time commensurate with the executives' sense of the item's importance for discussion at an executive meeting; but when the director introduced an item, it tended to be discussed for a length of time inversely related to executives' (including the director's) sense of its importance for discussion by them in executive meeting.

TABLE 2-4 Correlations (Rho) between Rated Importance of Items Discussed in Executive Meetings and Time Taken in Discussion, Differentiated according to Frequency of Participation of People Introducing and Rating the Items

	Originators of agenda items in discussion	
Source of rating of importance	Sr. Claudia: director	Sr. Patricia: second-most frequent participant
Sr. Claudia	−.46	.55
Sr. Patricia and Sr. Catherine	−.41	.56
Three less powerful executives	−.12	.74

A discussion of the data of Table 2-4 among the executives would probably create tension as it explored how it was that some of the very items the director felt were most important to discuss at the executive meetings were considered most briefly, whereas some of the ones she regarded as trivial were given extended consideration. Why that was so for items introduced by her and not by others would more than likely, with a social-psychological consultant participating, prompt some discussion of the effects of positional power and deference on members' participation. It is hard to imagine, too, that consideration of who trusts whom with what responsibilities and information could long be kept out of a discussion of these data. As noted earlier, the executives did not receive the data of Table 2-4 because the director had been promoted by the time the analyses had been completed.

If such discussions had taken place, Sister Janet's competence in dealing productively with her own and with the executives' tensions would be every bit as important to the success of her contribution as would competence in the arts of data collection, analysis, and display. Off-line action prompted by such data, exploring influence, the control over events, trust, and deference, for example, frequently occasions strong emotions. Deciding to give up or to defend an action tendency of consequence that is one's own is usually not accomplished without considerable uncertainty and ambivalence. The implications for training social psychologists to develop exchange relations with educators (or others) for research about on-line phenomena and processes are obvious: Trained researchers will have to be competent in participating productively, not only in theoretical discussions of data, but also in the full range of interpersonal forces released in off-line action.

THE STRUCTURE OF EQUITABLE
AND CONSEQUENTIAL EXCHANGE

Something of the role that Sister Janet, her colleagues, and I fashioned in her school has been glimpsed, largely through the windows afforded by some of the data she collected. The data were also incomplete and too simple to capture the complexities latent in the phenomena with which she was dealing. Yet in their simplicity was also a strength: Subject matter was focused for educators' examination. The data were sufficient to serve, if modestly, two distinctly different purposes in two different kinds of collaboration.

One collaboration faced outward to the university. Being concerned with regularities in the processes of communication and influence, and more broadly with the processes by which collective behavior is or is not under the control of participants, the collaboration produced the data of Table 2-4. These data bring together the findings of Cohen (1958), Kelley (1951), and Read (1962), on "upward communication" on the one hand, and those of Strodtbeck (1954) and Strodtbeck, James, and Hawkins (1957) on interpersonal influence as a function of verbal dominance, on the other hand, with the added ingredient of subjective priorities.

The other collaboration faced inward to highly influential colleagues. Being concerned with improving the effectiveness of collective performance, the collaboration produced the data of Tables 2-2, 2-3, and 2-4, along with excerpts of verbatim comments about the data of Table 2-2. The data of Tables 2-2 and 2-3 focused attention, as the data of Table 2-4 might have, on the relation between colleagues' actual collective behavior, on the one hand, and their values and aspirations regarding their collective behavior, on the other.

It is important not to construe these two kinds of collaborations separately. They developed out of a single collaboration that combined their purposes and should be considered as two overlapping parts of a single three-party collaboration. Consider the structural diagrams of Figure 2-1, which provide some perspective on the collaboration illustrated above and which suggest some conditions necessary for an equitable exchange between social psychologists and educators.

The three columns of Figure 2-1 allow for sidelining roles both in the university and in the school, and they include the on-line roles of educators. The first row of Figure 2-1 depicts the structure of the typical research contact that social psychologists have with school personnel: serving researchers' (theoretical) purposes only and without any contact with a sidelining role or group in the school. The second and third rows depict the structure of interactions described earlier, while the fourth and fifth rows add information, not previously discussed, about the development and termination of the three-party collaboration.

The structure of interactions and activities depicted in rows 3, 4, and 5 developed out of the structure of row 2: a research consultation between a couple of us from the university and two groups of on-liners in a school. This research consultation (row 2) differed from the typical kind of contact (row 1), not only in combining theoretical with practical ends (studying ongoing social systems in the process of change and intervening in parts of that process), but also in the fact that the research consultation itself grew out of a training program preparing social-psychological practitioners for schools. Susan Allan and I were enacting the role that Jack Glidewell, our colleagues, and I were providing training and supervision for at the university. The training program itself had dual purposes built into it: There was a 2-year training program for practitioners at the MA level and a full PhD program to train social psychologists who could both conduct research and carry out interventions in school (and other) systems (see Lighthall & Braun, 1976).

A glance down the five rows at the incidence of t, tp, and p brings to the foreground shifts in relative emphases on theoretical and practical goals in the interactions between social psychologists and educators. With the introduction of the new role, through Sister Janet, my own goals shifted away from study and intervention toward study and supervision and finally toward study of processes predominantly. Despite that shift, however, the three-party collaboration continued to address practical issues because of the presence of a siderliner in the school who

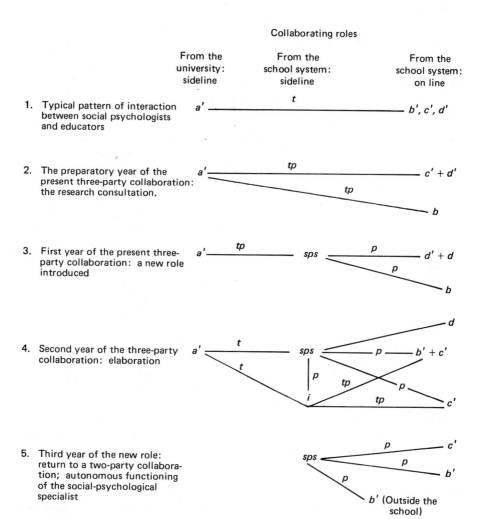

FIGURE 2-1 The structure of various contributing relations between social psychologists and educators: *a*, social psychologists at the university; *b*, school administrators; *c*, school faculty; *d*, students in school systems; *i*, interning student from the university; *a′, b′, c′, d′*, subgroups (or subsamples) of *a*, *b*, *c*, and *d*; *sps*, social-psychological specialist; *t*, collaborations pursuing theoretical goals; *p*, collaborations pursuing practical goals; *tp*, collaborations pursuing theoretical and practical goals.

could collaborate in two directions. The new role constituted a link between the university sideliners and the educational on-liners.[5]

The link provided more than a data-gathering extension of university purposes, too. During the second year, Sister Janet was sufficiently on top of things to work alongside an intern from the university. The intern not only gathered data that threw light on change processes in general but also increased the school's capacity for sideline support of off-line action.

Sister Janet worked with the university intern in supporting the off-line efforts of the class consultants and the school's department chairpersons in working out a conflict and worked with members of the guidance department in examining their corporate functioning and purposes. During this second year, Sister Janet continued to teach a course whose students (d' in Figure 2-1) again assisted in organizational problem solving that required collecting and rendering arrays of data. During this time, my collaboration with Sister Janet and the intern took the form of discussions of the theoretical bases for collecting data and for expecting this or that to happen, of planning adequate data collections, of critiquing the intern's written report, and in general, of relating what I knew of social psychology (being primarily an educational psychologist with social-psychological leanings) to the situations and data they were encountering.

The important lesson that is highlighted by the comparisons made possible in Figure 2-1, however, is what happens when either the university sideliner or the school sideliner operates alone. The first kind of unilateral action, shown in the first row, yields knowledge oriented wholly to the theoretical interests of the researcher. The result is a report published for other academics with interpretations unchallenged by, and usually irrelevant to, educators. The second kind of unilateral action (row 5) is just as deleterious to the development of valid knowledge of complex, on-line processes. Cut off from the collaborative influence of the knowledge-generating researcher, the practitioner must succumb to the relentless on-line pressures of the educational system, helping solve this or that problem, perhaps even with the continued use of data-supported sidelining action, but operating beyond the discipline of pulling together all of the data to examine larger implications or of writing out formulations of phenomena or processes. From such circumstances, without a theoretical sideliner to offer perspectives to the practicing sideliner in the school and to demand equity from the practicing sideliner, intervention practices easily develop that ignore broader accumulated knowledge and contravene more broadly tested principles. Indeed, the pressures on Sister Janet to help solve organizational problems induced her to begin consultations in the larger religious order even before the end of her second year, consultations that increased substantially in her third year.

This briefly described three-party collaboration is a single instance developed out of special circumstances. The collaboration lasted only 2 years but might well have

[5] For a description of a different kind of three-party collaboration, involving groups of educators as the mechanism for intervening and for (some) sidelining, see Schmuck, Murray, Smith, Schwartz, and Runkel (1975). That account shows degrees of intervention success as a function of the extent to which the purposes and schedules of the on-liners meshed with those of the intervening outsiders. The fit between the goals of the interveners and those of the system intervened in is an issue dramatically underscored in the events of 2 years described by Smith and Keith (1971), who observed the effects of insiders as they imposed a plan within an educational system, creating conditions for no-line action at many levels.

endured except for a shift in priorities outside academia. Sister Janet left the religious order that operated the school and, with inflationary pressures and a shift in the directorship, the school's administration decided not to continue the new role at the salary that Janet, now a layperson, would require; nor did the school's new administration find a new Sister Janet to assume the role.

CONCLUSION

Does this illustration add up, then, to just another shaggy dog story? Yes and no; the development of three-party collaborations of this kind can happen, but only when the priorities of both educators and social psychologists are complementary. Educators, after all, receive data that are useful from such an exchange only if they feel sufficient dissatisfaction with present performance that they can stand the tension of improvement involving descriptions of their own actual, not merely intended, behavior. Social psychologists, too, will find such exchanges equitable only if they want on-line data sufficiently to forego unilateral control over subjects and variables and to handle the tensions, in themselves and in educators, inevitably generated by data renderings that describe on-liners' behavior.

To explore the conditions that are necessary for educators and social psychologists to develop such complementary goals would lead to an examination by social-psychological researchers and educators of the resources, opportunities, rewards, and constraints of improved performance; but that is too long a story to begin here. Let me summarize this one. It is a story about contributions between educators and social psychologists. Its center is not educational practice or scientific research; it is the improvement of both through an exchange. At the center of exchange is *equity* and *consequentiality*. Equity alone is not enough; trivialities can be exchanged equitably. Consequentiality, too, is insufficient by itself; consequentiality for only one party in an exchange soon aborts the exchange relation. This story distinguished four kinds of behavior in order to bring both the weaknesses of education and social psychology and their complementarities into the same framework. The framework provided by the distinctions was based on the assumption that what goes on in any contributing relation depends fundamentally on the distribution among the parties of discretionary influence over the purposes and schedules of action. Too much of social psychology studies no-line action; too much of education is relentlessly on line. Both suffer: the one from invalidity; the other from unawareness of behavior and effects. Under favorable conditions, each can offer solutions to the other's ills. The illustration given here shows how a modest effort was made in that direction. Its analysis suggests a conclusion: If both educators and social psychologists who want to improve their respective practices can find each other, they will best be able to contribute to each other's on-line lives by forming and nourishing a three-party collaboration. The third party, an individual or group within the educational system, forges the link between scientific inquiry and practical inquiry by collecting data fitting the priorities of both the educator (revelant to improvement goals) and the social psychologist (relevant to theoretical problems) and by using the data in arrays appropriately differentiated for the edification of scientists and educators. The coinage of value in the exchange is data, not conclusions or explanations. The social-psychological, political, and economic conditions necessary to increase the number of social psychologists and educators who want to invest in improving their professional practices are not addressed in this story. The most fruitful starting point for such an inquiry would seem to be answering the question: Who has what to invest in such improvements with what promise of valuable net gain?

REFERENCES

Alegre, C., & Murray, E. J. Locus of control, behavioral intention, and verbal conditioning. *Journal of Personality*, 1974, *42*, 668–681.

Argyris, C. Dangers in applying results from experimental social psychology. *American Psychologist*, 1975, *30*, 469–485.

Bass, B. M. The substance and the shadow. *American Psychologist*, 1974, *29*, 871–886.

Bem, D. J. An experimental analysis of self-persuasion. *Journal of Experimental Social Psychology*, 1965, *1*, 199–218.

Bettelheim, B. *The informed heart*. New York: Free Press, 1960.

Bettelheim, B. *A home for the heart*. New York: Knopf, 1974.

Blau, P. M. *Exchange and power in social life*. New York: Wiley, 1964.

Cohen, A. R. Upward communication in experimentally created hierarchies. *Human Relations*, 1958, *11*, 41–53.

Csikszentmihalyi, M. *Beyond boredom and anxiety*. San Francisco: Jossey-Bass, 1975.

Cusick, P. A. *Inside high school*. New York: Holt, 1973.

Dulany, D. E. Awareness, rules, and propositional control: A confrontation with S R behavior theory. In T. R. Dixon & D. L. Horton (Eds.), *Verbal behavior and general behavior theory*. Englewood Cliffs, N.J.: Prentice-Hall, 1968.

Farber, I. E. The things people say to themselves. *American Psychologist*, 1963, *18*, 185–197.

Fried, S. B., Gumpper, D. C., & Allen, J. C. Ten years of social psychology: Is there a growing commitment to field research? *American Psychologist*, 1973, *28*, 155–156.

Gergen, K. J. Social psychology as history. *Journal of Personality and Social Psychology*, 1973, *26*, 309–320.

Getzels, J. W. Images of the classroom and visions of the learner. *School Review*, 1974, *82*, 527–540.

Getzels, J. W., & Thelen, H. A. The classroom as a unique social system. In N. B. Henry (Ed.), *The dynamics of instructional groups: The sociopsychological aspects of teaching and learning. The 59th Yearbook of the National Society for the Study of Education* (Pt. II). Chicago: University of Chicago Press, 1960.

Gouldner, A. W. The norm of reciprocity: A preliminary statement. *American Sociological Review*, 1960, *25*, 161–179.

Homans, G. C. Social behavior as exchange. *American Journal of Sociology*, 1958, *63*, 597–606.

Israel, J., Tajfel, H. (Eds.). *The context of social psychology: A critical assessment*. London: Academic, 1972.

Jackson, P. W. *Life in classrooms*. New York: Holt, 1968.

Kelley, H. H. Communication in experimentally created hierarchies. *Human Relations*, 1951, *4*, 39–56.

Koch, S. The allures of ameaning in modern psychology. In R. E. Farson (Ed.), *Science and human affairs*. Palo Alto, Calif.: Science & Behavior, 1965.

Levine, M. Hypothesis theory and nonlearning despite ideal S-R reinforcement contingencies. *Psychological Review*, 1971, *78*, 130–140.

Lighthall, F. F. School psychology: An alien guild. *Elementary School Journal*, 1963, *63*, 361–374.

Lighthall, F. F. A social psychologist for school systems. *Psychology in the Schools*, 1969, *6*, 3–12.

Lighthall, F. F. A dialogue and three principles. *School Review*, 1970, *78*, 403–413.

Lighthall, F. F. Social psychologists in schools: Some concepts and interventions. *School Psychology Digest*, 1973, *2*, 10–15.

Lighthall, F. F. Psychology and education: In a contributing relation, who controls whether the contribution will be actual or merely potential? In L. Saxe (Chair), *Contributions of social psychology to education*. Symposium presented at the meeting of the American Psychological Association, Chicago, 1975.

Lighthall, F. F., & Braun, J. W. *The twenty-second case* (National Institute of Mental Health Project 5-T21-MH11217, final rep.) Chicago: University of Chicago, 1976.

Lighthall, F. F., & Diedrich, R. C. The school psychologist, the teacher, and research:. Willing and reluctant cooperation. *Psychology in the Schools*, 1965, *2*, 106–110.

Marrow, A. J., Bowers, D. G., & Seashore, S. E. *Management by participation.* New York: Harper, 1967.

McDavid, J. W. Approval-seeking motivation and the volunteer subject. *Journal of Personality and Social Psychology*, 1965, *2*, 115–117.

McGuire, W. J. The yin and yang of progress in social psychology: Seven Koan. *Journal of Personality and Social Psychology*, 1973, *26*, 446–456.

Menges, R. J. Openness and honesty versus coercion and deception in psychological research. *American Psychologist*, 1973, *28*, 1030–1034.

Orne, M. T. Communication by the total experimental situation: Why it is important, how it is evaluated, and its significance for the ecological validity of findings. In P. Pliner, L. Krames, & T. Alloway (Eds.), *Communication and affect.* New York: Academic, 1973.

Orne, M. T. On the social psychology of the psychological experiment: With particular reference to demand characteristics and their implications. *American Psychologist*, 1962, *17* 776–783.

Page, M. M., & Kahle, L. R. Demand characteristics in the satiation-deprivation effect on attitude and conditioning. *Journal of Personality and Social Psychology*, 1976, *33*, 553–562.

Proshansky, H. M. Environmental psychology and the real world. *American Psychologist*, 1976, *31*, 303–310.

Read, W. H. Upward communication in industrial hierarchies. *Human Relations*, 1962, *15*, 3–16.

Resnick, J. H., & Schwartz, T. Ethical standards as an independent variable in psychological research. *American Psychologist*, 1973, *28*, 134–139.

Rice, A. K. *Productivity and social organization: The Ahmedabad experiment.* London: Tavistock, 1958.

Rosenberg, M. J. When dissonance fails: On eliminating evaluation apprehension from attitude measurement. *Journal of Personality and Social Psychology*, 1965, *1*, 28–42.

Rosenthal, R. & Rosnow, R. L. (Eds.). *Artifact in behavioral research.* New York: Academic, 1969.

Sanford, N. Whatever happened to action research? In A. W. Clark (Ed.), *Experimenting with organizational life—The action research approach.* New York: Plenum, 1976.

Schmuck, R. A., Murray, D., Smith, M. A., Schwartz, M., & Runkel, M. *Consultation for innovative schools.* Eugene: University of Oregon, 1975.

Smith, L. M., & Keith, P. M. *Anatomy of educational innovation.* New York: Wiley, 1971.

Strodtbeck, F. L. The family as a three-person group. *American Sociological Review*, 1954, *19*, 23–29.

Strodtbeck, F. L. The hidden curriculum in the middle-class home. In J. D. Krumboltz (Ed.), *Learning and the educative process.* Chicago: Rand McNally, 1965.

Strodtbeck, F. L., James, R. M., & Hawkins, C. Social status in jury deliberations. *American Sociological Review*, 1957, *22*, 713–719.

III

METHODOLOGICAL
ISSUES
OF SOCIAL PSYCHOLOGY
OF EDUCATION

3

A Consultant's View
of Research Methods

Philip J. Runkel
*Center for Educational Policy and Management
and Department of Psychology,
University of Oregon*

Most educational psychologists have always hoped that their ideas and empirical findings would have beneficial effects on the practice of education in the near future. The school itself has seemed to us the testing ground we could not and should not avoid. However, the methods of research and evaluation most of us learned to use in evaluating educational experiments are methods handed down to us from agriculture and animal psychology—methods well suited to the controlled agricultural plot and the controlled rat laboratory but not to the natural setting of the school and its embedding community. Only recently have some penetrating thinkers broken loose from the older mode and offered us some new logics—among others Argyris (1968), Barker (1963, 1965), Brandt (1972), Bronfenbrenner (1976), Bruyn (1966), Fairweather (1967), Friedlander (1968), Glaser and Strauss (1967), House (1976), Scriven (1967), Stake (1975), Stufflebeam and others (1971), and Willems and Rausch (1969). Some of those writers are consultants seeking evidence of organizational change. Some are evaluators who have come to believe that evaluation is most useful when it becomes a joint enterprise between peers (client and evaluator) in partnership. All urge a reassessment of the research strategies that in the past have acquired the greatest prestige and attracted the greatest confidence.

In the older mode, those of us studying education have found ourselves in curious contradictions. Despite our wish to have effects on practice, we have typically designed our research under the tenet that it should ideally have no effect on the clients at all. When we have interviewed clients, we have wanted them to give no further thought to the questions after the interview; we have not wanted them to "react" to the interview. We have sought "unobtrusive" methods of getting data. We have tried to prevent our "control groups" from learning anything from our "experimental groups."

When we have intervened in a school to produce an experimental group, we have typically tried to limit our effects to that group and to the variables we ourselves wanted to study. Making a distinction between the clients' problem and the research problem (our problem), we have typically postponed investigation of ways the clients might themselves alter the variables with which they were ready to deal; instead, we have investigated the ways *we* might alter the variables with which *we* were ready to deal. While carrying on our experimental studies, we have often refused to tell clients our hypotheses and findings until we had no further need of the clients. We have refused, sometimes, even when we were convinced that clients were pursuing unproductive or even harmful courses of action; and when we believed the experimental group was reaping clear benefits from a new course of action, we have typically refused to tell the control groups.

In experimental studies, we have usually examined carefully only those aspects of the clients' behavior we were trying to affect, paying little attention to side effects or long-term effects, despite the fact that those effects might often have been more costly or more beneficial to the clients than the effects we ourselves sought. Nor have we paid much attention to the ways that changes in school organizations change the conditions that help or hinder further changes, or to the effects of study and experimentation in schools upon the long-term relationships among researchers, consultants, clients, and publics. In short, despite our wish to have practical effects on the school, our research methods have persuaded us to postpone practical applications, to pass over opportunities to give practical help to a ready client, and to reject opportunities to learn about conditions and variables lying outside the convenience of our research designs.

We have pursued this paradoxical policy, of course, because of our yearning for "clean results." We have been committed to a logic of research design that would, we hoped, enable us to reach, with high confidence, a logical conclusion about the effect of Variable A on Variable B, while only entertaining with low confidence suppositions about the effects of other variables on B. We have wanted our conclusions from any one empirical study to withstand the threat of alternative explanations that might be proposed by critics. The yearning is understandable. The policy of "rigorous" research design, however, has failed to provide us with the means of offering practical help to school people.

More than that. The customary attitude of researcher toward "subject" has allowed us to stumble into an ethical quagmire, as the proliferating recent literature on ethics in social science testifies. But I shall not discuss ethics here: The topic of this chapter is a consultant's view of the difficulty of making research useful to practice in education.

The policy of rigorous research has failed our hopes in two ways. First, it has established a distrustful and unproductive role relationship between us and our clients.[1] Second, it has weakened, rather than strengthened, our confidence in generalizing from research to practice. After a few words about the first point, the bulk of the rest of the chapter is devoted to the second point.

THE AUTHORITARIAN RESEARCHER

When social science researchers ask "subjects" for information (or for behavior the researchers will observe), the researchers have usually been authorized to make the request either because of the organizational hierarchy, such as a school district,

---

[1] By *clients*, I mean throughout this chapter the school people, those whom our research or consultation is supposed to benefit, not the funders.

in which both they and the subjects work, or because the entry of the researchers into the organization from outside has been legitimized by someone of authority within the organization: "Dr. Scaramouche is here from the university to conduct a very important study, and we can be a key source of information. I want you to give him your full cooperation." No matter how gently the researcher talks, that mode of entry inevitably puts the researcher into a relationship of some authority over the subjects. The relationship is crystallized, indeed, when it becomes apparent that the researcher is the one who will unilaterally make all the decisions about what to investigate, about who will be studied, about the instructions that will be given to the subjects, about what will be done with the data, and so on.

Arygris (1968) has pointed out that researchers and "subjects" almost always come together through organizational channels. This is especially true of socio-psychological research in schools. Consequently, organizational norms are likely to govern the interaction. In his article entitled "Some Unintended Consequences of Rigorous Research," Argyris (1968) compares the relationship between experimenter and subject with that between superior and inferior in a workaday organization:

Like management principles, [the assumptions underlying rigorous research design] are expected to work if subjects cooperate. It is precisely at the point when people are brought into the picture that the difficulties arise. Why is this so? . . . to answer this question, let us examine the basic qualities of rigorous research. Most methodologists agree . . . that rigorous research tends to occur when:

1. The research is deliberately undertaken to satisfy the needs of the researcher and where the pace of the activity is controlled by the researcher to give him maximum possible control over the subjects' behavior.

2. The setting is designed by the researcher to achieve his objectives and to minimize [the role] of the subjects' desires [in] the experiment.

3. The researcher is responsible for making accurate observations, recording them, analyzing them, and eventually reporting them.

4. The researcher has the conditions so rigorously defined that he or others can replicate them.

5. The researcher can systematically vary the conditions and note the concomitant variation among the variables.

These conditions are remarkably similar to those top management defines when designing an organization . . . rigorous research criteria would create a world for the subject in which his behavior is defined, controlled, evaluated, manipulated, and reported to a degree that is comparable to the behavior of workers in the most mechanized assembly-line conditions.

If this similarity between conditions in organizations and those in research systems does exist, then the unintended consequences found in formal organizations should also be found, in varying degree, in the temporary systems created by research. These consequences . . . are:

1. Physical withdrawal . . . absenteeism and turnover.

2. Psychological withdrawal while remaining physically in the research situation. . . . To give a researcher what he wants in such a way that the researcher does not realize that the subject is doing this [is] a skill long ago learned by employes and students. . . .

4. Covert hostility . . . includes such behavior as knowingly giving incorrect answers, being a difficult subject, second-guessing the research design and trying to circumvent it . . . , producing the minimally accepted amount of behavior, coercing others to produce minimally, and disbelief and mistrust of the researcher.

5. Emphasis upon monetary rewards as the reason for participation.

6. Unionization of subjects. (pp. 185–186)

One result of the policy of rigorous research, in brief, has been that great chunks of our data come to us with certain defects of validity that would be much less likely to have occurred if the data had been produced from a more equal partnership of client and researcher.

So far as I know, no one has made a direct empirical comparison between the results of research conducted in the traditional, authoritarian way and research conducted in a partnership between "subjects" and researcher. In the meantime, the evidence from two domains of research seem to me worth taking very seriously. One is the large domain of research on organizational life cited by Argyris (1968)—research that includes some educational organizational organizations. The other is the smaller domain of studies of the effects of the relationship between experimenter and subject on the experimental outcomes—even though this body of work has not included, to my knowledge, a full negotiation between subject and researcher as an experimental condition. Some examples from the second domain are those of Blum (1952), Brock and Becker (1966), Edwards (1961), McGuigan (1963), Orne (1962), Piliavin, Rodin, and Piliavin (1969), Riegel (1975), Rosenthal (1967), and Sroufe (1970). A third domain of evidence is less well documented but is well known to consultants: the common experience of consultants that they get superficial and "safe" information from clients at first acquaintance and then deeper and more risky information after trust has increased. Even though indirect, the evidence from these three domains, taken together, seems convincing to me.

GENERALIZATION

Given that traditionally rigorous empirical studies must, more often than not, produce data of severely restricted generalizability, one should expect the findings from studies conducted with that kind of rigor to be replicable chiefly among humans who are engaged in a certain kind of activity—an activity originated by a supervisor or other person in authority, conducted for the supervisor's purposes, designed and paced by the supervisor, recorded and judged by the supervisor, and eventually reported by the supervisor. One should not, however, expect humans to show that same kind of behavior when they are engaged in self-initiated, self-guided activity for their own purposes, judging it by their own standards.

Beyond the features of traditional research pointed out by Argyris, there are others that impede the application of research to practice. One is the widespread supposition that some strategies of research are superior to others.

Complementarity of Research Strategies

Despite the disadvantages Argyris has pointed out in the strategy of rigor and other disadvantages that could be mentioned, I do not want to be understood to be saying that rigorous research designs are "bad" and should be scrapped. All research strategies have advantages and disadvantages, and all should be kept in the repertoires of the social scientist and the consultant. A few years ago, McGrath and I (Runkel & McGrath, 1972) sorted research strategies into eight types and diagrammed the relations among them as in Figure 3-1. I see no reason to change what we said at that time, namely,

> The purpose of the framework presented here is to show how various strategies are related to one another and, hence, the relative advantages and disadvantages of their use. It is true, of course, that all of these strategies are useful and should be employed in a programmatic fashion, since they tend to compensate for one another's weak points. But in any given study, the investigator almost always has to choose one strategy rather than the others. . . .

> The choice among the strategies should be made with an eye to their respective advantages and weaknesses and on the basis of (1) the nature of the

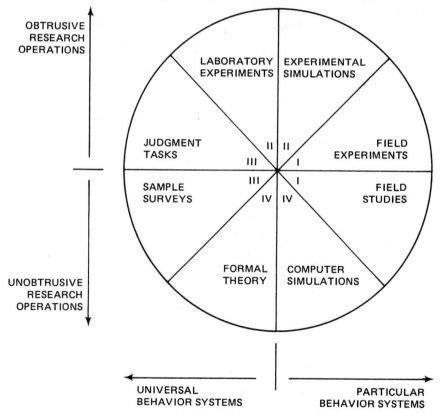

FIGURE 3-1 Research strategies. I, settings in natural systems; II, contrived and created settings; III, behavior not setting dependent; IV, No observation of behavior required. (Adapted from Runkel & McGrath, 1972. Reprinted by permission of Holt, Rinehart, and Winston.)

problem the investigator wants to study, (2) the state of prior knowledge about this problem, and (3) the amount and kinds of resources available to the investigator. We cannot emphasize too strongly our belief that none of these strategies has any natural or scientific claim to greater respect from researchers than any other. A researcher may find one strategy more comfortable than another for temperamental reasons, or he may find that his colleagues admire him for using one rather than another. From the point of view of the grand strategy of science, however, all of these methods are complementary; each serves the others. (pp. 88–89)

Figure 3-1 arranges research strategies according to two dimensions. Laboratory experiments and experimental simulations (the sectors marked "II") are typified by a great degree of intervention, manipulation, and intrusion on the part of the researcher. Formal theory and computer simulations (marked "IV") require, in contrast, no operations on the empirical world at all. On the other dimension, field experiments and studies (marked "I") take data from unique, concrete settings—from actual events in the natural world. In contrast, the strategies marked "III" typically assume that the real-world setting in which the data are collected has no significant effect on the phenomena being studied. The labels in the sectors are not meant to be definitive. The message the diagram is intended to convey is that there are many kinds of strategies for developing knowledge about behavior, and the strategies differ in their advantages and disadvantages. Two of the ways in which strategies differ are their obtrusiveness and their particularity. The diagram is discussed at length in Runkel and McGrath (1972, chap. 4).

The common belief that laboratorylike experiments are always superior to the other strategies in Figure 3-1 has led researchers to strive to establish laboratorylike controlled conditions in schools, and that has led, in turn, into the pitfalls Argyris has described. Laboratory research should continue, and we should use the results of laboratory research as hypotheses to be tested in field studies and field experiments. We should, however, spend more of our resources in field studies and field experiments than we have done in the past, and we should do so without the apologies we have been making. Controlled laboratory experiments are excellent strategies for developing confidence in hypotheses that can then be tested in actual schools; but, for the very reason that many important variables *are* controlled in laboratory experiments, the results of those experiments should never be expected to replay themselves in a particular school—or even in a majority of randomly selected schools. Because the variables controlled in the laboratory are not controlled in the school, trying a finding from the laboratory in the school becomes a new experiment. Later, I suggest some ways of strengthening the logic of field studies and field experiments.

When Will We Know Enough?

I sometimes encounter colleagues in the social sciences who look askance at the consulting I do with schools. "We do not know enough," they say, "to give practical advice to people." (I have never asked whether they mean I do not know enough or they do not know enough.) They go on to say, "We need to do a lot more research. When we learn how enough variables fit together, then we'll be able to make confident predictions in the natural setting."

Some of my colleagues hope that we can, as the years and decades (or centuries?) go by, gradually develop exhaustive lists of variables and their interrelations that encompass all that can be important to know about learning and living in schools. We can eventually, they seem to hope, find every variable that accounts for any appreciable amount of variation in students, teachers, administrators, parents, and their interaction; in social composition of class; in scheduling; in curriculum; in social structure of curriculum and learning task (cooperative or competitive, for example); in social structure of school; in style of school management; in socio-economic distribution of students, staff, administrators, parents, and community; in influences from interfacing community organizations and individuals (for example, social workers, PTA, police, courts, Boy Scouts); in amounts of local, state, and federal moneys available for schooling and their deployment; in home characteristics and their distribution in the student body; in amounts of education or training given outside the school by home, peers, church, businesses; and so on. If we find all the variables that have any ponderable importance, find ways of measuring them with very little error, and assess their relations to various kinds of learning on the part of students singly and in all their combinations, then (such is the hope) we shall find ourselves able to specify categories of students or schools so finely that the few students or schools in any one category will be very, very similar—so similar, indeed, that their uniqueness will not matter. We can then prescribe a "treatment" for those few highly similar students or schools that will fit them extremely well and cause important improvement in students' learning, or important reductions in staff turnover, or strong changes in whatever other outcomes we may have in mind.

But the argument that we ought to wait until we know enough before we try to be helpful to actual schools fails in five important ways: It fails to (1) take into account the nature of diagnosis; (2) note that relations among variables change as the years go by; (3) treat clients the way they want to be treated—as unique individuals or organizations, not as statistics; (4) recognize the uncertainties of inductive logic; and (5) face some of the practical difficulties of gathering data and testing outcomes in the natural setting.

Diagnosis and Consulting

Part of the argument for waiting until we "know enough" is the assertion that we can eventually specify all the really important conditions in the school necessary to produce a desired outcome. Then, if some of those conditions are not present, we can produce them and thereby produce the desired outcome. That reasoning implies that we can ascertain the state of conditions in the school; it implies that we must diagnose the present state of the school. But how is diagnosis done?

Diagnosis cannot be done sight unseen; it must be done by someone on the ground, by someone who has the time and knows how to do it. Whether the diagnostician is at other times a teacher in a school, a research specialist in the district's central office, a professional evaluator, or a college professor is of small moment, except for the probability that an otherwise full-time teacher or principal cannot usually muster the single-mindedness, the detachment, and the time that competent diagnosis requires. The duty cannot simply be added, like making announcements at assemblies, to the existing jobs of school personnel.

The point is that a role must be inserted between research and practice—the role of the consultant. Sometimes consultants also go on to help clients to act upon diagnoses.[2] Here, however, I am pointing to the fact that someone—let us agree to use the term consultant—must ascertain the conditions and readiness characterizing student or school and choose the relevant portions of theory to guide action. In conducting a diagnosis and choosing actions that will bring about desired outcomes, consultants must work with two facts: that errors are inevitable in diagnosis and that prediction is probabilistic.

Diagnosis is never free from error. All our theories of measurement include error terms, and no one has yet asserted that measurement can ever be made free from error. Even if theory is developed to the point that hypothetical students or schools can be categorized very finely and very precise predictions can be attached to each of the categories, the problem remains of ascertaining, in the natural setting, the category in which a student or school belongs. Ascertaining the category will never be error free. Some client will inevitably be put in the wrong category and will therefore be assigned the wrong treatment.

Predictions are never certain. The probability can never be 1.0 that a given treatment will produce a certain outcome, even when the diagnosis is correct. Some client will inevitably be disappointed when the treatment fails to bring the promised outcome.

Those two facts alone, even without the other difficulties set out below, are enough to tell us that we are bound to disappoint some of our clients if we prescribe a course of action for them and then sit back in the expectation that our predications will be borne out; and we shall disappoint them even when the experimental evidence is what we are wont to call overwhelming.

In working within the natural, uncontrived world of human affairs, one cannot generalize from past experience to future experience in the sense that one will know what to do in the new situation before it arrives. In the laboratory, the future can often be predicted very well. One can specify the conditions under which certain reinforcement schedules with 8-year-olds should have specified results, and one can be confident that one's instructions to the laboratory assistants will bring those results, at least a very large part of the time. In the natural world, however, the conditions are not easily replicable, and predictions bring many surprises.

Predictions, nevertheless, are worth making. Our knowledge of human behavior is good enough so that, through hypotheses made before an event arrives, we can be better prepared for the event than if we went into every event with undifferentiated expectations. For example, we know enough about risk taking, learning plateaus, creativity, anxiety, role taking, cooperation, competition, relaxation, stereotyping, and other features of human behavior so that we can make better bets if we make different predictions about the social norms we shall discover in a college mathematics class and a high school dance class, in a political convention and an industrial board meeting, and so on. Nonetheless, being able to make better bets means only that we can save ourselves chasing down a lot of blind alleys. It does not mean we can guarantee results to our clients.

Social science gives us *hypotheses* to carry with us to the brink of our next

---

[2] Here I am talking about diagnosing conditions necessary to the application of new knowledge from research—diagnosis not already routinely a part of the work of school or district. Certainly, teachers and counselors diagnose dispositions of their students and the conditions surrounding them; administrators diagnose pressures on school and district; and so on. I am talking here about diagnosing conditions that will help or hinder making changes—not merely routine adjustments—in the present way of doing things.

interaction with our fellow humans. We should be ready to look for likely outcomes while remaining alert for information that will confirm or disconfirm the hypotheses we brought with us. Indeed, we should usually take special pains to search out additional information in the local school so that we can more surely increase or decrease our confidence in the hypotheses we brought with us. We should never suppose that the next week, the next year, or the next innovation will go just as the last. We should make a careful diagnosis, select some possible courses of action, specify some likely reactions, and then walk into the next week, year, or innovation alert for every corroboration or contradiction and ready to push one hypothesis down and raise another into its place at a moment's notice. We should act when our confidence in our best guess about what is going to happen in the next hour or day sufficiently exceeds our confidence in our next-best guess.

I have just said that the consultant, to be maximally helpful to clients, must diagnose repeatedly and must be ready to change hypotheses and treatments as events unfold. That instruction is quite contrary to the instruction our methods books give for rigorous research. In controlled research, the paradigm calls for choosing one or more hypotheses, finding or producing the specified conditions and treatments, and then sitting back to see whether the hypotheses are borne out. Clients naturally feel betrayed when they are left to the harsh mercies of the rigorous experiment.

Meanwhile, Conditions Change

The ground shifts under our feet even while we are learning how to examine it, and social scientists now and then complain. Cronbach (1975) recently wrote:

> Our troubles do not arise because human events are in principle unlawful; man and his creations *are* part of the natural world. The trouble, as I see it, is that we cannot store up generalizations and constructs for ultimate assembly into a network. It is as if we needed a gross of dry cells to power an engine and could only make one a month. The energy would leak out of the first cells before we had half the battery completed. (p. 123)

Cronbach's forewarning concerning *knowledge* about the world applies equally to social and organizational pattern of *action* that humankind has developed through which to deal with the world. Wisdom both in thought and action is wisdom about past worlds, as Campbell (1975) has said: "Wisdom produced by any evolutionary system is always wisdom about past worlds, a fittedness to past selective systems. If those worlds have changed, the adaptations may no longer be useful, may in fact have become harmful" (p. 1106).

The relations among our variables change faster than we might think. Among studies with which I am acquainted, the one that best sets forth the experimenter's plight is that of Bronfenbrenner (1958). He examined all the available studies of the relation between social class and permissiveness in rearing children. When all studies were tallied, about as many showed the middle class to be more permissive as showed the lower class to be so. That tally did not mean, however, that the findings were in error, that no relation actually existed. Bronfenbrenner went on to show that, over the 25 years or so of the studies, parents in both classes had become more permissive, with the middle-class parents increasing their permissiveness at a faster rate than the lower-class parents. The result was that the middle-class parents overtook the lower-class parents in permissiveness. A relation existed all right, but it was a dynamic one, not a static one.

During the years when studies were accumulating that showed lower-class parents more permissive than middle-class ones, many social scientists pointed with pride to the accumulating evidence, and much theorizing was built on those findings. When studies showing the converse began to appear, the first thought was that they were somehow defective, and the next thought was the despairing one that another promising hypothesis had succumbed to siege by extended study and that we did not, after all, know as much as we had thought. As it turned out, we knew more than we had thought. In assessing what we know about categories of people, we can be wrong in the lesson we draw from a series of studies that seem to agree with one another, and we can be wrong in the lesson we draw from a series of studies that seem to contradict one another.

It is not difficult to think of social attitudes and readinesses that are probably changing while we study them. Many females perceive potentialities for themselves that few perceived 20 or 30 years ago. Although the majority of people in the United States probably still believe that competition is always an unmitigated good, the proportion is probably dropping. The economic expectations of the very poor are probably becoming even more hopelessly pessimistic. The proportions among types of crime, including those committed in schools, have changed during the last three decades or so. And so on. Knowledge is always knowledge of the past; it can give us hypotheses to test in the present and future, but it cannot ever enable a consultant to prescribe out of an encyclopedia.

The Client, the Researcher, and the Consultant

Clients always care about the accuracy or validity of information about themselves, but they rarely care much whether that information accurately describes schools elsewhere. The local superintendent wants valid information about whether *this* district is functioning well. Ordinarily, when the superintendent on this side of the river comes to a conclusion about the best next step to take on the basis of data collected in the district, this superintendent has little curiosity about whether that would be a good step to take in the district on the other side of the river.

Researchers[3] are always interested in whether they have learned something about people or schools they have not yet observed. Typically, they are interested in the veridicality of the information about the local school only to the extent that it bolsters generalization to other schools not directly observed. Ordinarily, the

---

[3] We should remember, when we talk about researchers, experimenters, or consultants, that we are not talking necessarily about separable people. We are talking about *roles*. When physicians receive patients, the physicians begin the relationships in the role of consultant. When physicians begin a course of treatment, they then move into the role of experimenter, checking the outcome of each part of the treatments and altering the prescriptions (experimental interventions) to suit the situations. When the physicians compile their experiences with groups of their patients and write up their conclusions for medical journals, they are then presuming to say something about patients they have never treated (generalizing from the groups), and they move into the role of the researcher. When I use the terms *consultant, experimenter*, and *researcher*, I am using them to refer to types of *relationships* (roles) one can take up with clients and audiences, not as descriptions of types of people.

researcher in the district on this side of the river is halfway across the river in spirit before the last questionnaire from this side has been filled out.[4]

Consultants must be as concerned with the validity of their evaluations for use in the local school as their clients are, and they will often be concerned with a certain kind generalizability as well. They will rarely be concerned, however, with the kind of generalization served by the logic of random sampling. That is, consultants will not often feel a need to make a statement such as, "I am 95% confident that if I repeated in 100 schools the training I just finished conducting in these 10, and if the 100 were selected from the same population as these 10, then the mean scores on the posttests in 98 of those schools would lie between 67 and 83." The kind of statement the consultant wants to make is different, more like: "When I go into a school that differs from these 10 in respect to _____ , _____ , and _____ , the best bets among variables to give me useful diagnostic information (after which I would take some trial steps and then gather more diagnostic information) would be _____ , _____ , and _____ ." In other words, the consultant does not expect to draw the next school from a listable population (certainly not randomly), does not wish to make a statement about what the next school is like or what might happen in it before collecting diagnostic information about it (not to speak of specifying a degree of confidence in such a statement), and is not interested in the proportion of schools out of 100 in which some preconceived statement might be correct.

Nevertheless, consultants, like researchers, want to learn from experience. Consultants want to go into the next school able to make diagnoses that are more valid, quicker, or less of a nuisance to the school people than in the last school. It is very important, therefore, that consultants keep careful, systematic records of their own experience, that they make counts and cite base rates where possible, that they periodically publish their experiences formally or informally, and that they urge other consultants to do the same. The resulting body of lore can help us choose likely hypotheses, and the experiences in it can someday be counted as instances or case studies.

In sum, if researchers are to "apply" their knowledge to students and schools in the natural setting, researchers must not ask students and schools to give up their ordinary business to make use of the researchers' knowledge. If researchers ask students and schools to behave as "subjects" would in a laboratory (doing whatever the experimenter tells them, refraining from asking what the experiment is all about, and so on), then the researchers are failing to apply their knowledge to the ordinary workaday world.[5]

---

[4]   The distinction between getting information for local people to use in guiding their action and selecting a locality or series of localities to represent a population is the same distinction made by Cronbach and Suppes (1969) when they talk of decision-oriented and conclusion-oriented research. The distinction Campbell and Stanley (1963) make between internal and external validity is similar, though perhaps not identical. Some recent writings on evaluation have delved deeply into the special problems of generating information useful to practice (see, for example, House, 1976, and Stake, 1975.

[5] There is an exception to this statement. If schools were to adopt an experimental stance themselves, including the adoption of appropriate experimental controls, then researchers could fit their experiments into the experimental paradigms being used by the schools. The experimental setting would become the natural setting. There are parallels in other fields of human activity. The study of the various substances in petroleum has led not so much to predicting the

Researchers can greatly increase the likelihood of their findings being applied to schools if they include the role of the consultant in their field experiments—if they include in their designs someone to be at hand at every step while the clients are trying to use new knowledge to learn a new way of doing things, someone who will adapt, step by step, to the needs of the clients.

Inductive Logic

All scientific induction rests on the postulate that the more instances we find of what we predict, the more confident we can be that we shall encounter more confirming instances in the future; but that postulate is not as reasonable as it sounds at first. The classic example is that of the black ravens. Let us hypothesize that all ravens are black. That hypothesis is equivalent, logically, to saying that no raven is included among not-black things—that is, that all not-black things are not-ravens. Consequently, every instance we find of a not-black thing that is not a raven should increase our confidence that all ravens are black in the same way as finding more black ravens. So suppose that we find a yellow daffodil. Logically, that event should increase our confidence that all ravens are black; but somehow, most of us are not convinced that finding a yellow daffodil, a purple grape, or a white heron should make us more confident that all ravens are black.

In brief, the very logic that underlies empirical research is suspect. I cannot take space to do justice to the topic (see especially Carnap, 1962; for a brief overview, see Gardner, 1976). Suffice it to say that we should not be overconfident that the symbolic combinations and permutations that go on in the heads of researchers (or in the circuits of computers) will lead to accurate descriptions of future events, either in the laboratory or in the natural settings of schools. We cannot yet measure the extent that our inductive logic mirrors reality. That is one more reason the consultant should stay close by the client, ready to substitute new hypotheses for old whenever a prediction seems to be going wrong.

The logic of statistical inference rests on the inductive postulate, too, for it counts proportions of confirming instances. A more transparent reason that the logic of statistical inference does not serve consultants well is that clients are interested in whether a prescription will work *for them, today*. They are not interested in whether a prescription will work for some proportion out of 100 instances. The results of experimentation with a sample, even a thoroughly random sample, do not tell consultants anything reliable about their next particular client. Random sampling guarantees only that the conclusion from that sample will be unbiased. That is not the same thing as accurate. One does not know that one's next sample will show a result like that of the last. The experimentation with the sample does, it is true, enable one to estimate what the result of so many out of 100 such experiments will show; but the consultant does not work with so many out of 100. The consultant works with one particular client after another. Each client hopes the

---

behavior of oil shales as to the erection of huge laboratorylike devices called refineries. The result of the scientific study of the growth of chickens has not been the greater predictability of the growth of chickens running a free range; rather, it has been the construction of highly controlled environments for raising chickens. Refineries and the new chicken "ranches" are essentially greatly enlarged laboratories. Schools could be designed similarly, but I am not advocating it. In the meantime, researchers can help schools directly only by giving up the controls customary in the laboratory.

experiment will be successful, and the consultant wants to be successful with all.

Even for the researcher, our usual methods of statistical inference offer little help in building knowledge about the natural setting. The probabilistic conclusions from results with a sample are reliable only when a random sample has been taken from a population. A sample can be taken randomly when the population is listable, but that is often impossible. For example, suppose one is a consultant in school administration and has developed a training program for establishing new patterns of interpersonal collaboration within school staffs. Suppose, also, that the training program has been designed for use with school staffs that knowingly and voluntarily invite consultants to come and work with them for that purpose. Then the appropriate population within which the new training technique should undergo experimental testing is the set of schools with staffs that knowingly and voluntarily invite consultants to come and work with them. But how will one find and list that population? The only way would be to carry out negotiations with every school in turn until one had reached a firm agreement, or had clearly failed to reach an agreement, to carry out training with each school, for it would be very inaccurate merely to ask, "Would you be willing if . . . ?" For practical reasons, one would then have to break one's promises with all but a very few. Not only would that be highly unethical, it would certainly make one unwelcome the next time around. It would be extremely expensive, too. Furthermore, the readiness of many schools to seek help from consultants would change after that kind of treatment, and one's list of the population would immediately be inaccurate. For those reasons and more, listing such a population is impossible, and therefore random sampling from it is impossible. So far as I know, interventions in schools, classrooms, and similar bodies have never been done randomly, and the statistical inferences from such experiments to "the population" are therefore without foundation.

The difficulty of sampling randomly to study sociopsychological processes in schools is, compared to studying individuals, especially formidable. Because social psychology is the study of interaction, a sociopsychological study must sample interactions or settings for interaction (such as classrooms, schools, or triads from a specifiable population of triads), not individual humans. I do not know of any sociopsychological study that has ever sampled settings for interaction randomly.

PRACTICAL DIFFICULTIES

So far, I have discussed some obstacles to the application of new knowledge to practice that are obstacles in principle. I now turn to a few obstacles of a practical nature that delay the accumulation of knowledge about the functioning of students and schools.

The Time It Takes

One of the difficulties of assessing any important outcome of consultation or experimentation in schools, especially effects of organizational and other sociopsychological changes, is the fact that it takes a long time to lift a school from the typical level to a high state of sociopsychological capability. (On the complications of choosing indicators of capabilities of schools, see Schmuck, Runkel, Arends, & Arends, 1977, chap. 11.) It is difficult to persuade school districts or governmental agencies to provide money over a period of 3, 4, or perhaps 10 years so that the effects of a training project, for example, can be charted.

From the point of view of natural history, change in social norms runs long indeed. D. T. Campbell (1975) says:

> I am convinced that in past human history, an adaptive social evolution of organizational principles, moral norms, and transcendent belief systems took place.... For a social evolution to have taken place, the selective system must have operated consistently over extended periods of time, for hundreds and hundreds of years. (p. 4)

Among the many examples from earlier technologies is Delort's (1973) remark that windmills were in use in Castille as early as the tenth century but were hardly known in the rest of Europe before the twelfth.

Those of us offering consultation in organizational structure and process are hoping that consultation and training can speed the natural pace of change in schools and districts. Even so, serious changes in sociopsychological functioning of schools and districts must be granted years to reach completion, not months. An example from the National Institute of Education is instructive. In 1974, the NIE announced that it wanted to encourage schools to develop a sustained capacity for solving their local problems. The institute made it plain that they were not thinking of something like sending bunches of people off to a series of lectures on problem solving. On the contrary, they visualized an organizational capacity for dealing with unique local problems—a capacity that had to be homegrown; the organizational processes for making organizational adaptations to local environmental and organizational problems had to be built within the local organization. With this conception in mind, the NIE advertised for schools or clusters of schools that had already set in motion an institutionalized, organizational mode of meeting and coping with local problems. The NIE wanted to select nine schools, or clusters of schools, to be awarded funds to speed the development of local modes of organizational problem solving. In answer to NIE's call, hundreds of schools and districts submitted proposals from which nine were chosen to receive funds.[6] The NIE chose schools or clusters that seemed to have the firmest foothold in their communities, the best support from interfacing agencies, the most stable personnel, and so on. It turned out that none of those most promising projects was new in 1974; all had histories ranging from 2 to 7 years. Nevertheless, the NIE judged all of the funded groups to be in need of further help; none seemed already to have become a model for local problem solving. Still more years would be necessary to ascertain whether those promising schools would be successful in their efforts.

Obviously, school people want to have an estimate of the time a change will require before they commit themselves to the effort. It is also obvious that the laboratory cannot deliver those estimates. Finally, it is obvious that few schools or districts will want to invest 2 to 7 years of strenuous work toward serious sociopsychological change merely to provide a researcher with an estimate of the time required; the schools or districts will want the probability to be high that they will reap some benefit for themselves. That benefit is the price more and more schools are demanding of researchers. Because it ordinarily takes 2 or more years to be even fairly sure one is giving dependable sociopsychological help to a school, not to speak of systematically assessing the results and documenting them, only long-term

---

[6] The Grants for Development of Organizational Strategies for Sustained Improvement of Urban Schools: grant numbers NIE-G-74-0079 through -0085, -0087, and -0088.

projects have a good chance of testing the applicability of sociopsychological hypotheses.

The Routine Year

Field experiments require not only the time it takes to teach and practice the new way of doing things but also the time it takes to ascertain whether the new way has become stable. To ascertain whether the outcome of a field experiment will last, the new functioning of the school or district must be evaluated after the clients are on their own. To speak more exactly, the outcome should be evaluated amid the same conditions under which the clients will be routinely carrying on their work in the new way.

Some activities in schools occur in short cycles. Examples are getting the attention of students at the beginning of a class period, learning how to use the card catalog in the library, and planning a basketball game. Other activities have yearly rhythms. Organizational processes usually manifest themselves in the yearly cycle. If a school undertakes a project to improve its problem-solving capacity as a school, its new skill will be tested throughout the turning of the academic year. A single trial of the new skill must be a year in length. The first adequate trial of that skill comes in the *routine year*. When researchers or consultants want to evaluate the outcome of an intervention into processes that operate on the yearly cycle, they have the following choices:

First Year after the Departure of the Consultants. This is the first year the clients are operating without the direct help of the consultants, but this is not a routine year, a routine year being one in which things are operating the way they have done in the past.

Second Year. In this year, the clients are operating with a year's experience behind them, but that previous year not having been a normal year, this one is not fully so.

Third Year. This is the first routine year; it is the first year that was preceded by a year that was not that of the clients' first trial on their own. This year offers the first fair test of whether the clients *can* make the innovation a routine.

Fourth Year. This is the first year after which a researcher or evaluator has a fair chance to estimate the *stability or change* that the new way of doing things is showing—by comparing performance at the end of this second routine year with that at the end of the first routine year.

Fifth Year. This is the first year after which the researcher or evaluator has a fair chance to estimate the trend of the new way of doing things, inasmuch as three points can provide a first approximation to the acceleration or deceleration of a curve.

If conditions affecting the innovation change, then 1 or more years of the 5-year sequence must be recycled if the innovation is to be fairly assessed. Few projects undertaken to alter sociopsychological processes in schools have been assessed for 5 years after the end of the intervention, or even for 3 years. When evaluations are made over any shorter time, however, prognostications about stability, not to speak of trend, must be very shaky. Shaky assessments of outcome, in turn, produce shaky "knowledge" to be offered to school people.

The "Good" School

Sometimes, when a school undertakes a complex, difficult organizational change and succeeds, some onlooker is heard to say, "Well, sure. That school was a good school when they started. They didn't have far to go." The implication seems to be that the school was already in motion toward "good" or "better" and that therefore the observed change owed little to the consultants. Such a view is a little right and a lot wrong. I agree that some schools are more ready for successful change than others, but even "good" schools show considerable oscillation in their performance from year to year. There are several subtleties in the abilities and readiness of schools (see, for example, Schmuck, Runkel, Arends, & Arends, 1977, chaps. 1 and 2), but I am limiting myself here to oscillation.

It is commonplace to find a school that is superior in some one respect. Every year, in any school district, one school stands at the top of the list in percentage of last year's graduates enrolled in the next higher level of education; another stands at the top of the list in percentage of staff contributing to the community chest; another at the top of the list in length of time a curricular innovation has been maintained; and so on. It is inevitable that some school will stand at the top of a given list, even if no school is particularly trying to stand there, and it is inevitable that some school must stand at the bottom. The typical school oscillates within any given list. The unusual school stays in the same place over several years. The very unusual school stays at the top (or the bottom) of some list year after year. The remarkably unusual school stays at the top (or the bottom) of more than one list.

Runkel, Wyant, and Bell (1975, chap. 8), for example, studied the kinds of innovations reported by elementary schools in two districts near Seattle over 4 years and four administrations of questionnaires. They divided the innovations teachers reported to be going on in their schools into five classes: structural, collaborative, curricular, cloistered, and nothing. Omitting reports of "nothing" and tallying the classes of actual innovation reported by the greatest percentage of teachers in each of 22 elementary schools that gave data at least 2 years, Runkel, Wyant, and Bell found that

6 schools reported the same type of innovation over 3 consecutive years
5 schools reported the same type of innovation over 2 consecutive years
11 schools changed every year

Those statistics argue that an outcome evaluator must expect to watch at least two elementary schools to find one that sticks with one type of problem even for 3 years, and of course, sticking with it does not necessarily mean solving it well. This oscillation is one more phenomenon that lengthens the time it takes to assess outcomes of complex interventions in schools and districts.

Trust

Arygris (1968) has pointed out some debilities of rigorous research strategy, but there are also disadvantages to the collaborative research strategy in which consultant and client build an investigation jointly, as peers. I have to content myself with discussing just one. When consultants stand beside clients and confer with them about each new difficulty encountered, sometimes offering alternative paths of action, the relationship between clients and consultants typically becomes more intimate, trusting, and committed as the weeks go by. The attitude of clients toward consultants becomes radically more favorable when the clients feel they have received a clear benefit from the consultants. If the consultants are also the collectors of evaluative data, the answers they get from the same question asked at different times differ, not only because the objective reality may have changed, but because respondents will be willing to tell the consultants things at a later time, when they feel more trusting, that they were not willing to tell them earlier.

The growing intimacy will have that effect even though the consultants give over the collection of evaluative data to evaluators who have no other interaction with the clients. The clients come to associate the evaluators with the consultants; they come to feel they are the same bunch. Their trust of the consultants rubs off on the evaluators.

Consider the example of job satisfaction. When the consultants first collect data (assuming they are collecting their own) before they have carried out any important amount of consultation, respondents will salt their answers to questions about satisfaction with a large proportion of protectiveness. Respondents will give answers like, "Sure, I like it here OK—I have no complaints." If they are given multiple choices to check, a majority will check something on the favorable side of the list, even if they do not check the most favorable response offered. At first acquaintance with the consultant, school staff have no way of knowing whether their answers will be passed on to their superiors—department head, principal, or superintendent. Parents, especially poor parents, have no way of knowing whether their answers will be passed on to school authorities, social-service agencies, police, or whomever. Students have no way of knowing whether their answers will be passed on to all of the above. But as time goes by without the consultants bringing any hurt upon the clients from superiors or publics, the clients become willing to trust the consultants with information the consultants could possibly use against them.

Some of the information clients at first hold back is information about happy feelings, but most of it is information about unhappy feelings. As trust grows, the clients begin to tell the consultants the kinds of unhappiness they have with their school, their jobs, their working conditions, and the people they work with. The result is that clients will frequently answer questions about satisfaction more unfavorably 2 or 3 months after consultation begins than they did before it started, even though they may actually be feeling more hopeful than they did before.

In short, a collaborative relationship between clients and consultants can often yield estimates of relationships within school and district that actually change in meaning from one assessment time to another, especially during the early phase of a project, even though the questions asked remain the same. That kind of invalidity can only be untangled by using a good deal of judiciously chosen supplementary data.

WHAT TO DO

Some of the difficulties I have mentioned can be circumvented. Others must be met head on. None requires despair.

Complementarity of Research Strategies

Sociopsychological hypotheses about schools, students, and their communities should continue to be tested by all the eight strategies I mentioned earlier. Each strategy has its own strengths and weaknesses. Laboratory experiments, for example, with their strong control, are excellent for ruling out precise alternative hypotheses—for making sure that variables uninteresting to the experimenter are not causing the effect sought—but they are weak in generality over situations. The controlled laboratory becomes a very special behavior setting in itself, as Argyris (1968), Edwards (1961), McGuigan (1963), Orne (1962), Rosenthal (1967), Webb, Campbell, Schwartz, and Sechrest, (1966), and others have so persuasively argued. Results of controlled laboratory experiments are general in the sense that they hold constant, randomize, or ignore many variables that are active in natural situations; that is, they greatly simplify reality. That is an advantage in making sure of the relations among a few variables under the conditions of the experiment. The results, however, cannot be generalized in the sense that one can be sure they will replicate throughout a large range of natural settings. Furthermore, simply because too many variables are controlled, a laboratory experiment cannot even tell one very clearly the kinds of natural settings that will be the best bests for application.

Field experiments are excellent for testing the practicality of a "treatment"—testing whether it will work in at least one natural setting. A series of field experiments, furthermore, can develop a catalog of conditions that affect the outcome of the treatment. Field experiments suffer, however, from confounding of variables. In a natural setting, it is rarely possible to separate even a few of the important variables into different treatments; often, some cannot even be assessed. The variables necessary and sufficient to produce the outcome of a field experiment can never be ascertained with confidence from a single experiment, or even from several. The variables acting are too many.

All eight strategies have both advantages and disadvantages. Knowledge from research will be more easily applicable if researchers and consultants make use of all eight strategies in their work, testing their hypotheses by more than one strategy whenever possible.

Building a Body of Knowledge

We are more likely to build a practically useful body of sociopsychological knowledge about schools and students from weak studies than from strong studies. First, because every research strategy has weaknesses as well as strengths, there really is no such thing as a sociopsychological study that is strong overall, especially if one of the prime criteria is the applicability of the conclusions to practice. All studies are weak in some respects. We can make best use of experimentation if we treat the outcome as a possibly useful hypothesis for our next job of consultation, using the strengths of the study of strengthen our own imagination and the weaknesses to guide diagnosis.

I have often heard colleagues say of a study, "I am not going to pay attention to the results of that study, because the study had several weaknesses in its design." That is like saying, "I'm not going to accept a ride in that automobile, because they may bring out a better model next year." The way to make good use of a study is to ask oneself, first, whether the study increases or decreases one's confidence in its conclusion, even ever so little, compared to what one's confidence would have been without the study.

We must resist the temptation to reject the contribution of a study that has faults. We must not ask, "Is the investigator's conclusion unassailable?" for there is no such study. We must ask, instead, "Is the investigator's hypothesis even a little better bet than the competing hypotheses not adequately controlled in this study?" No matter how weak the investigator's data and analysis may be, if they are stronger than other possible explanations for his or her results, then we should add that much strength to our confidence in the hypothesis. One does not test a coin for balance by taking excruciating care with each toss. The confidence any one toss gives one is very small; one decides by accumulating tosses. Similarly, we should accumulate studies, but we should not forget to include the whole range of strategies in the studies we accumulate.

If a study can add an increment to one's confidence, one should next ask oneself, "Suppose I were to act in my next consultation (or experiment) as if the conclusions from this study were true? What might I do, then, that would be productive?" and, "Suppose I were to act in my next consultation (or experiment) as if the faults in this study affected its conclusion appreciably? What, then, would I look out for?" Both these questions can bring a profit to the consultant or researcher. If consultants or researchers treat a large number of studies in this way, they will find some fitting together theoretically and operationally in the next consultation or experiment and some not. That is the strategy of construct validity, and that is the surest way to winnow studies for their usefulness. Because most studies, as I have said, are weak in some respects, the strategy of construct validity leads one to make use, along with the hypothetical attitude, of a large body of weak studies instead of waiting for a few "strong" studies.

In brief, when a collection of weak studies fit together and help a consultant or researcher to make a correct prediction in the next consultation or experiment, the studies have made an important contribution to knowledge. As a body, they are stronger than any single one of them, and often stronger than any single "strong" study could be. Such a chain is stronger than its weakest link.

A large number of studies, even if they are weak studies, can inspire us with many more hypotheses than a single study. Furthermore, there are always many weak studies available, but we may have to wait some time before a strong study relevant to our next consultation or experiment appears. We can get to work sooner, therefore, if we build hypotheses from the available weak studies instead of waiting for the definitive one to appear. For all these reasons, I think we shall make better headway if we build our body of sociopsychological knowledge about schools upon weak studies (and upon any strong studies, too, that may happen along) instead of insisting upon using only the (supposedly) strong studies.

Diagnosis and Consulting

We are more likely to build a practically useful body of sociopsychological knowledge about schools if we use consultants to help clients try new ideas. I have given the chief arguments for that statement earlier. The kernel of the argument is that the natural condition of schools does not allow an experimenter to specify conditions at the outset and then to insist that they be maintained until the experimental period has come to an end. Schools must meet problems as they arise, and the experimenter's needs will properly be low in priority. The consultant must be there to alter hypotheses, treatments, measures, and schedules as conditions change. The project will contribute most to the body of scientific knowledge about schools, of course, if the consultant keeps meticulous records of everything relevant to the experiment.

Time

Earlier, I gave several reasons that the more productive field experiments in the social psychology of education require much longer time periods than are now typical. There is no way to get around that requirement. Hypotheses about limited sets of variables can be tested in short studies outside the natural setting, but there is no way to test whether the resulting findings are practical without putting them through the natural cycles in the natural setting. It may be difficult to persuade funding agencies to fund projects running 7 years instead of 1 or 2, but a reliable body of knowledge, easily applicable to practice, will be postponed until they do.

Causal Sequences in Practice

One of the nastiest problems in experimentation is that of causality. It seems to me that a field experiment of some length, carefully monitored by consultants or evaluators or both, can give us confidence in causality in a way that has rarely been used by social scientists. The sequence of causation from the beginning of a socio-psychological intervention of any scope to its end is very complicated, and the evaluator who has made assessments only at beginning and end has a hard time answering the question of what caused what. Critics sometimes put it something like this: "Yes, this school seems to be better off now than it was, but how to you know it was what you taught them that did it? Maybe they worked out some problems just because you broke loose some time for them to do it and gave them a chance to get reacquainted. How do you know a beer bust wouldn't have worked as well?"

The evaluator who wants to be able to present data to justify the claim that the outcome of a project took form through a series of planned and understandable steps, each one making the later ones possible, will assess the state and functioning of the system receiving consultation after every important step. The evaluator's calendar will be marked, so to speak, with the dates on which important interventions were made, with the dates before and after those interventions when assessments were made, with the designations of the subsystems from which data were taken, and with the abilities, qualities, or conditions assessed. With careful documentation of each important step, the evaluator can show the causal chains that existed—the way one step made possible the next.

Consider a confrontation designed around *imaging*—a procedure often used as a first step in resolving conflicts between groups in an organization. The procedure requires each group to describe behavior it thinks is characteristic of itself and behavior it thinks is characteristic of the other group. Each group is required to state, in its own words, the statements made about it by the other group, to assure that correct meaning has been conveyed. Finally, each group is required to cite examples of behavior or evidence to back up its assertions about the other group and the other group's assertions about it. Through this procedure, verifiable observations of behavior are brought to everyone's attention, and vague impressions, along with suppositions about motives, are discarded. The two groups, then, are usually in an improved position from which to state the problems they are making for each other and to generate solutions.

The evaluator might not be able to make an airtight case that the imaging, by itself, enabled the opposing groups to agree on some subproblems that were obstructing the solution of larger problems and to agree on things that both groups were doing that were maintaining the subproblems obstructing their solution. The evaluator might, however, have data showing the rates with which the two groups usually brought out unpleasant facts about themselves, tried to reach an understanding of each other's opinions, asked each other's views on disagreements, and agreed upon some common problems the solution of which could admittedly work to the benefit of both groups. Moreover, the usual rates of doing those things might be very low or even zero. "Well, you have a pretty good case there," a critic could say, "but you had them together for 10 hours of talking and game playing before you did the imaging, and maybe they were just ready to make progress, and the imaging itself was irrelevant," and the evaluator, always reasonable, would have to admit, "Yes, that's possible."

But suppose the evaluator has been tracking and documenting the consultation over the weeks, and can tell how, in each group, the problems came to be reconceived as the groups worked on them; how, in each group, people gradually faced up to the fact that the other group was intimately involved in their problems and vice versa; how they first said it was hopeless to try to talk with the other group but after some weeks began seriously to consider doing so and at last did; how they conducted themselves during the imaging; the remarks made by each group that drew comment from the other; how they took joint and coordinated steps to solve problems as joint problems after the imaging; how they kept mentioning, during those sequential events, agreements they had made in earlier events about intended later events; how they kept mentioning information or skills that came out of the consultation; and how they kept comparing the steps of action they were taking with the planning they had done along the way. In such a case, inasmuch as problems came to be conceived that had never been so conceived before; joint steps were taken by groups that had never taken joint steps before; the two groups joined in discussion and work that many of them had said was impossible at the start; the groups appealed to information and skills presented during the consultation; and the people evidently coordinated their actions by referring to planning they had done during the series of events and by comparing their actions with that planning— because of the concatenation of the events and the clients' use of the products of events for coordinating later events, any reasonable person would admit to little doubt that the chain of events must have had a strong causal effect on the outcome. It remains true, of course, that one's confidence in the causal importance of the imaging (or in any other single episode) must remain less than one's confidence in the whole chain as a container of causes. Documenting the links in the causal chain does not do away with the basic weakness of the field experiment—that is, the difficulty of pinpointing the effects of separate variables. The documentation does, however, drastically weaken the competing hypothesis that the cause of the outcome lay chiefly with events extraneous to the intervention.

In brief, when the connections between the links in a chain of events are clearly documented, one will almost always find oneself placing more confidence in the causal effect of the chain as a whole than in the causal effect of any one of its links. The chain, in other words, is stronger than its weakest link. Such a chain can provide one with strong confidence that it contained causal effects, even though one cannot ascertain the relative contributions of the separate links.

Direct Behavioral Evidence

Finally, we can strengthen confidence in a field study simply by documenting the direct behavioral evidence to be found in the natural life of the school. We can get interesting information, of course, from interviews and questionnaires, but the most obvious and direct thing to do is to look to see whether the clients are *doing* the things we hoped they would be doing. If one hoped one's clients would be talking or writing of problems in terms of situation, target, and plan; if one hoped they would be using the systematic problem-solving method in choosing solutions and trying them out; if one hoped they would be probing their resources and playfully exercising abilities their jobs do not usually demand; if one hoped they would be more often trying out courses of action and less often defensively explaining problems away; if one hoped they would be regularly assessing the progress of their courses of action, and deliberately and periodically reassessing their goals— then one can get the most direct information about outcomes by looking to see whether they are doing those things.

I suppose there are two reasons, among others, that most social scientists shy away from offering descriptions of gross behavior as evidence of outcomes. First, it often happens that effects are too weak to show up in gross observable behavior and can only be detected by the subtleties of questionnaires or other indirect methods. In that case, the method of direct behavioral evidence is of no use. Second, actions of clients in their daily work cannot usually be counted easily. To take some examples, how easy is it to tell when a school faculty is probing its own resources to keep them ready at hand? Should one give equal weight to an action by an individual and a joint commitment among staff? How easy is it to tell when an instance would have been routine without the intervention and when it is clearly an instance shaped by the intervention? Questions like those are not easy to answer.

Because it is difficult to get unambiguous counts of gross behavioral instances,[7] it is to the same degree difficult to throw instances into an analysis for statistical inference; but that is a small loss, as I explained earlier. The more important point is simply that we must take the risk of using judgment in every instance and sometimes very shakily. The solution, however, is to exercise judgment resolutely, describe the instances adequately, and leave it to our audiences to agree or disagree with us. Judgment is always required in analyzing empirical information. Statistical analysis does not remove it, because one's audience can disagree with one about one's alpha level, about the statistical test one chose, about one's number of cases, about the importance of the strength of one's result quite aside from its statistical significance, and about other matters. The more persuasive count of gross behavior is one that displays easily distinguishable instances, that displays strong effects, and that makes clear comparisons with base rates.

It is is still necessary to judge whether our clients are showing the desired behavior in greater degree (more often, more judiciously, more successfully, or

[7] Hiring judges and checking their reliability only begs the question.

whatever we choose) than they were doing before consultation, or in greater degree than schools do without consultation. In other words, the necessity of comparing our results with base rates remains. There are other judgments we will want to make, too, such as whether the change over time of the difference from other schools was worth the cost of mounting the project.

Sometimes our judgment of outcomes will differ from our clients' judgment or from the judgment of other audiences. In the group with whom I work, we have found that our judgment about the worth of outcomes has rarely differed to a surprising degree from the judgment of our clients. Audiences such as central-office administrators or parents, however, when they were not participants in the project, have now and then judged our projects in ways that surprised us.

To be more specific, let me describe a couple of actual cases of comparing gross behavioral outcomes with judgments of base rates. The first illustration comes from a project in which our group at The Center for Educational and Policy Management established a cadre of organizational specialists in a school district. Runkel, Wyant, and Bell (1975, chap. 12) explain how the cadre deepened their personal and team resources by accepting consulting engagements outside the district. After listing a couple of pages of gross behavioral episodes as evidence, those authors appeal to base rates in the following manner:

> The question arises whether these excursions of the cadre should be considered remarkable. Don't teachers teach outside their jobs—Sunday school, for example? Don't administrators give talks at the Rotary Club and at conventions? Certainly they do; but we think the Kent cadre displayed some distinctive features. To match the record of the Kent cadre, we think one would have to find a group of a couple of dozen people in a school or district whose outside ventures showed the following features.
>
> 1. They generally made their excursions not as individuals but as teams. When the cadre received a request for consultation, it was not enough for one member to be available. Two or more persons had to be broken loose from their regular schedules, and they had to be persons suited to the task and to one another. It is more difficult to put together a team to respond to a request for consultation than to find an individual.
>
> 2. A request for services was always passed along to the cadre's coordinator and the Decision-Making Task Force. A field team was then built to meet the needs of the client, of the individuals on the team, and of the cadre as a whole. In a clear sense, the cadre as a whole delegated its consulting work to sub-teams of itself. These sub-teams were strongly conscious that they had to answer demands from two sources: the client and the cadre.
>
> 3. They nearly always went out for at least half a day at a time—more often two or three days at a time—not just an hour (and of course they did not merely give talks). Teams went outside the district on six different occasions in 1970–71, four in 1971–72, and four in 1972–73. This was done in addition to all the work within the Kent schools and district.
>
> 4. They went into organizations and tasks considerably different from those back home: poverty-stricken adults, a Model Cities Council, a Community Committee on Child Care, the administrators of a strife-torn urban school district, and the like.

It is true that individuals exist in many school districts—especially in larger ones—whose activities range as far as the most active cadre member and farther. We claim, however, that it is not easy to find an identifiable group of 24-or-so showing a record as active as this, with the consulting performed in teams, done as part of the work that was the smallest part of their regular jobs, done in consultations that stretched their abilities, and maintained over five years. (chap. 12, pp. 6–7)

The second example comes from a report by Duffin, Falusi, and Lawrence (1972). Although part of their data is a count of books (and even that was difficult), they focus on the organizational processes of inventorying and decision making. They appeal to the knowledge they presume the reader has about those processes in other school districts.

The discovery that certain textbook titles were being ordered in one school while another school was taking the book out of service . . . led to the question of whether a more economical use of these resources could be made.

Before September 1971, approximately 46,000 books that were usable, or usable if rebound, were picked up and delivered. This operation generated data to indicate that there were 85,000 such usable texts which were excess to the system's current needs.

In 1972, we have 29,011 usable books to be distributed and 24,358 to be rebound. This cycle has generated data to show that there is another known surplus of 25,770 usable books and 24,334 usable if rebound. From the 1971 surplus we have retrieved for use approximately 7,000 usable and 6,000 rebound books.

Think about these figures. Initially we might feel that York County is the most inept school system in the world. How could anybody have so many unknown surplus books? And yet we know that York County's general efficiency has never been in question. We can logically assume that the same general situation obtains in all the other school systems of comparable size and complexity everywhere. However, *try to find out!* It could be predicted with some degree of confidence that such data could not be obtained unless the trust level in the organization was quite high. It is also obvious that if such data were used punitively, we could expect to get honest answers exactly once. The data has not been used punitively but as an opportunity to learn to be more effective in the future.

It is important to understand that we are not talking about stupid management of resources or inefficiency. Our principals and superintendents were about as efficient as anyone else. . . .

[When] we do not know what we have, we cannot know we need. . . . Many principals plan for a personal reserve for emergencies. Multiply these "reserves" by the number of schools in the system and you are talking about a lot of resources.

Marshaling evidence by reporting direct observations of gross behavior in the manner illustrated above requires large, obvious, relevant actions as outcomes and common, confident knowledge on the parts of the reporter and audience alike of base rates against which to compare the outcomes. (Sometimes, of course, the reporter can supply base rates in the form of data.) The researcher or consultant should report the outcomes in enough detail so that the reader can get a fair picture of the kinds of instances the researcher or consultant chose as outcomes and so that the reader has a fair picture of the base rates being used for comparison. The reporter can then only hope for agreement from the reader, as I am doing here. Finally, I repeat that evidence becomes more reliable as it accumulates from several strategies of research.

CONCLUSION

For too long, now, the relationship between researchers and the researched has focused upon the benefit to the researcher and has treated the needs of the people in the schools—the clients—more or less as a nuisance. There remain few places in the United States where school people will allow that relationship to continue much longer. Quite aside from the morality of that older relationship, it has crippled our efforts to make research useful to clients.

The methods of rigorous research have led clients into a deep distrust of researchers and consultants. Nevertheless, we have been reluctant to admit the weaknesses of the rigorous strategy and the strengths of other strategies. We have come to think we could learn all about the natural world in the laboratory if only we kept at it long enough, and we have not put our attention on the steps necessary to enable school people to make use of new knowledge. These assertions are especially true when we are trying to reach a new understanding of the organizational and sociopsychological nature of school life.

Schools need consultants when they contemplate change, especially organizational change. The duties of the consultants are to help clients adapt to the stresses that change inevitably brings and to help them make new plans when the original hypotheses show faults. The relationship between consultants and clients, to be most helpful, must be one of peers; and that new relationship must honor the day-to-day needs of both partners. If we do not learn to work with clients as peers, we shall find our clients becoming fewer and fewer, because they will be refusing to be "subjects."

The new peer relationship cannot permit the strong control over experimentation that researchers are now accustomed to demanding. We need to develop skills and attitudes that permit us to use a variety of research strategies, capitalizing on the strengths of each and admitting their weaknesses. We need to learn how to extract confident knowledge from collections of "weak" experiments.

We also need to face squarely the practical difficulties. The natural setting of schooling is very complex, and the complexity is different in different places. We shall not develop knowledge suitable for very many places from a single experiment. Sociopsychological conditions in schools oscillate, too, from year to year. We should not expect to ascertain the trend of those conditions by taking one or two measurements after the consultants have gone home. When an experiment is promising, we shall get much better information from it if we follow up its effects for 5 years or more.

Studying effects for longer periods and drawing together the results of many experiments, even "weak" ones, into plans for consultation can enable the new peer relationship, if it takes in hypotheses from more controlled experimentation and gives hypotheses back to it, to produce much more useful information than we have done in the past.

REFERENCES

Argyris, C. Some unintended consequences of rigorous research. *Psychological Bulletin*, 1968, *70*, 185-197.

Barker, R. G. On the nature of the environment. *Journal of Social Issues*, 1963, *19*(4), 17-38.

Barker, R. G. Explorations in ecological psychology. *American Psychologist*, 1965, *20* 1-14.

Blum, F. H. Getting individuals to give information to the outsider. *Journal of Social Issues*, 1952, *8*, 35-42.

Brandt, R. M. *Studying behavior in natural settings*. New York: Holt, 1972.

Brock, T. C., & Becker, L. A. "Debriefing" and susceptibility to subsequent experimental manipulations. *Journal of Experimental Social Psychology*, 1966, *2*, 314-323.

Bronfenbrenner, U. Socialization and social class through time and space. In E. E. Maccoby, T. M. Newcomb, & E. L. Hartley (Eds.), *Reading in social psychology* (3rd ed.). New York: Holt, 1958.

Bronfenbrenner, U. The experimental ecology of education. *Educational Researcher*, 1976, *5*(9), 5-15.

Bruyn, S. T. *The human perspective in sociology: The methodology of participant observation*. Englewood Cliffs, N. J.: Prentice-Hall, 1966.

Campbell, D. T. On the conflicts between biological and social evolution and between psychology and moral tradition. *American Psychologist*, 1975, *30*, 1103-1126.

Campbell, D. T. & Stanley, J. G. Experimental and quasi-experimental designs for research on teaching. In N. L. Gage (Ed.), *Handbook of research on teaching*. Chicago. Rand McNally, 1963.

Carnap, R. *Logical foundations of probability* (2nd ed.). Chicago: University of Chicago Press, 1962.

Cronbach, L. J. Beyond the two disciplines of scientific psychology. *American Psychologist*, 1975, *30*, 116-127.

Cronbach, L. J., & Suppes, P. *Research for tomorrow's schools*. Don Mills, Ont.: Collier Macmillan Canada, 1969.

Delort, R. [*Life in the middle ages*] (R. Allen, Trans.). New York: Universe, 1973.

Duffin, R., Falusi, A., & Lawrence, P. Organization development, P. II: Problems can only be solved from the inside. *School Progress*, 1972, *41*(10), 62-64.

Edwards, W. Costs and payoffs are instructions. *Psychological Review*, 1961, *68*, 275-284.

Fairweather, G. W. *Methods for experimental social innovation*. New York: Wiley, 1967.

Friedlander, F. Behavioral research as a transactional process. *Human Organization*, 1968, *27*, 369-379.

Gardner, M. Mathematical games: On the fabric of inductive logic, and some probability paradoxes. *Scientific American*, 1976, *224*(3), 119-124.

Glaser, B. G., & Strauss, A. *The discovery of grounded theory: Strategies for qualitiative research*. Chicago: Aldine, 1967.

House, E. R. Justice in evaluation. In G. V. Glass (Ed.), *Evaluation Studies Review Annual* (Vol. 1). Beverly Hills, Calif.: Sage, 1976.

McGuigan, F. J. The experimenter: A neglected stimulus object. *Psychological Bulletin*, 1963, *60*, 421-428.

Orne, M. T. On the social psychology of the psychological experiment: With particular reference to demand characteristics and their implications. *American Psychologist*, 1962, *17*, 776-783.

Piliavin, I. M., Rodin, J., Piliavin, J. A. Good samaritanism: An underground phenomenon? *Journal of Personality and Social Psychology*, 1969, *13*, 289-299.

Riegel, K. F. Subject-object alienation in psychological experiments and testing. *Human Development*, 1975, *18*, 181-193.

Rosenthal, R. *Experimenter effects in behavioral research*. New York: Appleton, 1967.

Runkel, P. J., & McGrath, J. E. *Research on human behavior: A systematic guide to method*. New York: Holt, 1972.

Runkel, P. J., Wyant, S. H., & Bell, W. E. *Organizational specialists in a school district: Four years of innovation*. Tech. Rep. of the Center for Educational Policy and Management, University of Oregon, 1975. (Eric Document Reproduction Service No. ED 111 107)

Schmuck, R. A., Runkel, P. J., Arends, J. H., & Arends, R. I. *Second handbook of organization development in schools*. Palo Alto, Calif.: Mayfield, 1977.

Scriven, M. The methodology of evaluation. In R. W. Tyler, R. M. Gagné, & M. Scriven (Eds.), *Perspectives of curriculum evaluation*. Chicago: Rand McNally, 1967.

Sroufe, L. A. A methodological and philosophical critique of intervention-oriented research. *Developmental Psychology*, 1970, *2*, 140–145.

Stake, R. E. *Program evaluation, particularly responsive evaluation.* Paper presented at a conference on New Trends in Evaluation at Göteborg, Sweden, October 1973. Center for Research and Curriculum Evaluation, University of Illinois at Urbana-Champaign, November 1975. (Available from Evaluation Center, College of Education, Western Michigan University, Kalamazoo, Michigan 49008)

Stufflebeam, D. L., Foley, W. J., Gephart, W. J., Guba, E. G., Hammond, R. L., Merriman, H. O., Provus, M. *Educational evaluation and decision making.* Itasca, Ill.: Peacock, 1971.

Webb, E. J., Campbell, D. T., Schwartz, R.D., and Sechrest, L. *Unobtrusive measures: Nonreactive research in the social sciences.* Chicago: Rand McNally, 1966.

Willems, E. P., & Rausch, H. L. (Eds.). *Naturalistic viewpoints in psychological research.* New York: Holt, 1969.

4

Coming out of the Laboratory Closet

Gaea Leinhardt
Learning Research and Development Center,
University of Pittsburgh

The purpose of any research is to add to knowledge about a particular phenomenon. In some cases, there exist clear-cut paradigms and focused, isolable phenomena for study (Kuhn, 1968). In other cases a phenomenon exists in a web of other unknowns, and it is inappropriate to isolate it because the boundaries of "it" cannot be well defined. The majority of the research questions in education fall in between these extremes: Some information can be gained by studies of isolated phenomena under manipulated and controlled conditions, whereas some must be studied within the contexts of their own ecological niches (Bronfenbrenner, 1976). In some cases, both approaches are useful. For example, teacher expectancies (Rosenthal & Jacobson, 1968; Seaver, 1973) and parent-child interactions (Lamb, 1975) have been studied with success in both laboratory and field settings. In both cases, the information obtained in the field helped to provide a convincing level of generalizability beyond that generated by laboratory research.

Field-based research[1] can complement laboratory work in the acquisition of knowledge by the kinds of questions that it can answer. Field settings are often the most appropriate context in which to investigate certain questions, especially in education. My purpose in this chapter is not to argue against laboratory work, which is frequently both a parsimonious and an elegant way to contribute to the

The research reported herein was supported by the Learning Research and Development Center, which is supported in part as a research and development center by funds from the National Institute of Education (NIE), U.S. Department of Health, Education, and Welfare. The opinions expressed do not necessarily reflect the position or policy of NIE, and no official endorsement should be inferred. The author wishes to acknowledge the assistance of Daniel Bar-Tal, William Bickel, Audrey Champagne, Kathy Engel, Mary Engel, Connie Faddis, Janet McGrail, and Len Saxe.

[1] The term *field research* refers to the conduct of studies in settings in which the phenomena of interest naturally occur. The researcher in such a situation attempts to be minimally disruptive to the natural flow of events (Webb, Campbell, Schwartz, & Sechrest, 1968). The term *field research* is not meant to prescribe or proscribe a particular approach to information gathering such as experimental, quasi-experimental, or ethnomethodological techniques (Aronson & Carlsmith, 1968; Cook & Campbell, 1976). The techniques described in this chapter can be utilized both for traditional research and for action or applied research (Lazarsfeld & Reitz, 1975; Lewin, 1946; Sanford, 1970). The term *applied research* refers to the utilization of findings and problem selection; the term *field research* refers to the context in which research is conducted, whether applied or not.

knowledge pool, as many have noted (Aronson & Carlsmith, 1968; Cook & Campbell, 1976; Kaplan, 1964); rather, it is to show how and why field research is conducted. The information obtained from a field-research paradigm—whether descriptive, quasi-experimental, applied, or field experimental—has some unique properties, especially with respect to how generalizable the findings are.

Field-based research has several characteristics that both separate it from the more controlled situation of the laboratory and constitute its advantages. One characteristic is that the phenomenon of interest in field-based work has a raison d'être other than being the object of research; it exists, for example, to educate children, to reform alcoholics, to punish criminals, to train soldiers. The treatments, or independent variables, *may* once have been the brainchild of a researcher, but in the field, they are out of the researcher's control and, thus, exist in a web of interrelated circumstances. Field-based research takes place in settings with minimal researcher interference and with maximal external interference, and it requires some skillful and thoughtful work if the research is to contribute to knowledge.

The characteristic of a phenomenon existing independently of the results of the research situation contributes to field-based research. For instance, one has the opportunity to observe the phenomenon of interest in situ. The researcher need not look at an event that is isolated from other elements but can witness its interaction with all other elements. Two things usually emerge from such an experience: (1) a healthy respect for alternative explanations of events normally studied in the laboratory and (2) a sense of proportion—how important or how extensive the phenomenon of interest really is. In controlled situations, in which all "other" influences are held constant, a hypothesis may be confirmed; but in natural settings, there may exist other forces that are competitive with the one under study and that may exert a more powerful influence.

An example may help to make the point more clearly. Behavioral psychology has established a strong link between human actions and their consequences (Holland & Skinner, 1961). Behavior of a certain type is more or less likely to increase in frequency dependent upon its consequences. In controlled settings, certain consequences (such as receiving M & M's or getting tokens) may act as quite powerful reinforcers for a desired behavior, but in other settings, they may fail to act in this way. This is not because reinforcement does not work but because some other "natural" reinforcer (or perhaps social punishment) is acting more powerfully on a competing behavior.

Bouchard (1976), in his excellent review of field methods, lists several other advantages of the field situation that are usually unavailable or not manipulatable in laboratory work: (a) the ability to examine boundary conditions of the phenomenon with respect to the intensity, range, frequency, and duration of its occurrence; (b) the existence in the field of natural life-spans of phenomena and natural units for investigation; (c) the ability to examine the setting effect, or as Bronfenbrenner (1976) refers to it, the "ecological structure" in which the phenomenon occurs; and (d) the opportunity for hypothesis generation, reformulation, and extension. One also has the opportunity to study a variety of phenomena that converge to establish factors or accrue knowledge. Thus, the field challenges researchers to move beyond the narrow, clean conception of a problem into the broader, messier, and often more relevant way of looking at problem sets. The presence of these features in the natural setting is what contributes to a dramatic increase in capacity to generalize results on the one hand, and on the other hand makes such research produce mental indigestion in the well-trained laboratory psychologist.

To be sure, field research has some difficulties that are more pronounced than other types of research paradigms. Four major ones are: systematic, as opposed to random, error; difficulty with causality; increased cost; and messy analyses. In field research, error or unexplained sources of variance often cannot be controlled by random assignment of subjects to treatments. Therefore, much greater effort must be made to document probable or possible sources of "natural" influence *other* than the treatment, on both the independent and dependent variables of interest. Thus, factors influencing the degree of implementation of a treatment and conditions under which measurement itself takes place must be described (Fullan & Pomfret, 1975). In field-based research, one does not make assumptions about "the treatment"; one studies it. This in turn often makes the use of statistical methods like analysis of covariance (ANCOVA) inappropriate.[2]

Clearly related to the problem of nonrandom error is the problem of establishing causality in field-based research. Much of modern science uses a particular form of logic in order to maximize the likelihood of establishing a causal chain. The logic is that, all other things being equal, a change was observed in Y following the introduction of X (or several Xs) and that such a change was not observed without X; further, such an association between X and Y had a probability of occurring by chance in only very rare circumstances (Blalock, 1964; Kaplan, 1964; Kuhn, 1968). In order to play this particular game, not only must treatment be assigned to randomly chosen units, but treatment itself must be easily definable and a contrast group must be available. All of this can be summarized as the ability to manipulate the treatment conditions, a situation usually unavailable in the field. Not only is it rare for a field researcher to manipulate treatment, but even less often can appropriate contrast groups be found. This makes it very difficult to say either that all other things were equal or that the change would not have occurred without the treatment.

The tools that are both available and convincing for supporting causal arguments in field research are: (a) replication over time or over diverse settings, (b) logical argument or causal models, and (c) replication of the production of the results through simulation. The establishment of convincing inferential chains of causality through theory, models, or both (Blalock, 1964) is necessary as the data from fieldwork accumulates. Field research is generally (but not always) conducted when descriptive information about the phenomenon is still useful and prior to the need for, or availability of, conditions for more restrictive research approaches. It benefits greatly from the presence of models of the phenomena for both problem specification and analysis.

An additional disadvantage to field research is its high cost. In contrast to laboratory work, it is costly in time, money, and effort. Much time and energy goes into laying the groundwork, and large amounts of effort are expended without "anything happening." The results of field research, however, have the possibility of being highly significant—and the data accumulated can frequently be of great value to other researchers. Ways of minimizing wasted time and money are discussed later in the chapter.

The most taxing problem for field research is analysis and synthesis. Masses of data accrue and very few approaches to attacking it emerge. The nature of the data is such that the majority of the statistical tools are not usable—this fact alone makes

---

[2] For a related discussion on evaluative research and the need to study the treatment range itself, see Edwards, Guttentag, and Snapper (1975).

many otherwise interested researchers very wary of approaching the area. The task of cataloging the information, pulling it apart, and recombining it in a variety of ways is indeed tremendous, but also feasible.

Considering all of the pitfalls, such as nonrandom error, elusive causality, high cost, and primitive tools for analysis, one might well question why such research should be undertaken. As a minimum, field research provides the chance of exploring the applicability of theory developed in the laboratory. As a maximum, field research attacks and occasionally answers highly significant social problems. Thus, the field provides both a final testing ground for existing theory and a primordial soup for question specification and question asking.

The major points of this argument can be summarized as follows: In all research, it is critical that the investigatory paradigm chosen follow (not precede) the problem being addressed; for certain classes of researchable problems, field-research approaches are the most useful paradigms; there is always a trade off between method and question.

In this chapter, topics covered are relevant to the conduct of field research. The specific areas covered are: problem formulation, review of the literature, instrument construction, working in the field, time and cost, implementation, data reduction, analysis of results, and finally, an example of a field-research effort. Two points should be borne in mind when considering these topics. First, although the topics are discussed in a sequence, real research conditions often alter this sequence with no damage to the study. Second, specific types of research may not require attention to some of the topics covered, whereas other types may require additional elements not discussed in this chapter. Thus, this is not a model or map for how field research should be conducted. Rather, it might be considered one of many possible annotated strategies.

PROBLEM FORMULATION

Usually there is more to be learnt from a study of disarray
than is gained by intentionally disregarding it.
(Scriven, 1961, p. 93)

Problem formulation is the process of assessing what is currently known about a phenomenon and what needs to be known and of deciding as well on the best way of gaining that knowledge. It is sometimes the case that the objective of a line of inquiry is to decide precisely what the relevant problem is. Psychology as a whole, and social psychology in particular, normally define problems out of an existing literature base. Often, a pair of experimental results are slightly incongruous with one another, or the answer to one question leads to the generation of another. This results in an orderly, if often esoteric, approach to the gaining of knowledge (Cronbach, 1975). (A harsher statement of the sterility of this approach is reported, in separate discussions of applied versus laboratory research, by Gross, 1976; Helmreich, 1975; Higbee & Wells, 1972; Lowe, 1976; Sanford, 1970; and Weissberg, 1976.) In general, the procedure is to formulate the problem, select the most appropriate paradigm for its investigation, generate the most plausible sets of hypotheses, and proceed to carry out a study (Aronson & Carlsmith, 1968; Cartwright, 1973; Kaplan, 1964; Kuhn, 1968). The work is often of three kinds: (1) replication of previous research on a different population, (2) resolution of two or more conflicting opinions, or (3) an extension of old questions into new areas through a challenge to the paradigm or the posing of new questions.

Formulating problems in the field is a less direct task and may require much travel between the field setting and the home work base before the problem emerges and before the study can begin. Although problem formulation can occur at any phase of research (Schatzman & Strauss, 1973), the assumption here is that some degree of formulation will take place near the beginning of the effort. A major difficulty in problem formulation arises from the lack of control of "intervening variables" on the one hand, and the multiplicity of significant factors on the other. For the most part, one does not wish to control these disruptions but to study them (Bronfenbrenner, 1976). Clearly, if the disruptions are both unpredictable and important, the problem cannot be exhaustively stated a priori. Does this mean that one should just go out and soak up the object of study with no sense of direction? Certainly not, but it does require a more flexible position for interpretation of observations than do the controlled situations. Mitroff and Turoff (1974) and Mitroff and Blackenship (1973) describe the difficulties of problem formulation in some detail, especially the probability of selecting the "wrong" object of study. Cronbach (1975) suggests that scientists often study the easier or more familiar phenomenon rather than the more significant or appropriate one. It is the opportunity to study a highly significant problem that is so available and tempting in field research.

Problem formulation goes through two basic phases, *area selection* and *problem specification*. The first, area selection, can be tackled in several ways. One possible way is to follow somewhat traditional research steps, for example, determining if laboratory findings replicate in the field and resolving consistently conflicting findings (the conflict often is between intuition and science rather than between two scientific positions). After a general area has been identified, the setting can be visited to begin the task of problem formulation. Careful attention needs to be paid to what information to collect in order to carry out the study and what additional information to examine to explain potential findings. Frequently at this stage, a more interesting or relevant problem presents itself. If that happens, it is often appropriate to follow up on it. In any case, the next step is to have a period of observation in order to narrow the range of possible questions to be asked.

To display the process of problem specification more precisely, some of the major steps are charted in Figure 4-1. The first step, opportunity knocks, represents an event or question that can be fruitfully explored in a field setting. Its occurrence is sometimes controllable, but frequently it is a happy partnership between curiosity and availability.[3] The first three activities after seizing the opportunity (boxes 1, 2, and 3) represent the parallel behaviors of reading, observing, and discussing both the situation or setting of interest and the general domain, for example, learning in the classroom. The next two activities (boxes 5 and 6) represent possible attacks on the task of problem formulation: (a) listing questions as they emerge, or forming them from observed differences or discontinuities

---

[3] It should be noted that Schatzman and Strauss (1973) do *not* feel that the mere presence of an interesting site should determine substantive interests. It really is a matter of degree. It would be absurd to do research as if one were chasing butterflies in a field (with apologies to Nabokov); however, it is appropriate to be aware of interesting and unusual opportunities. The distinction is both arbitrary and subtle.

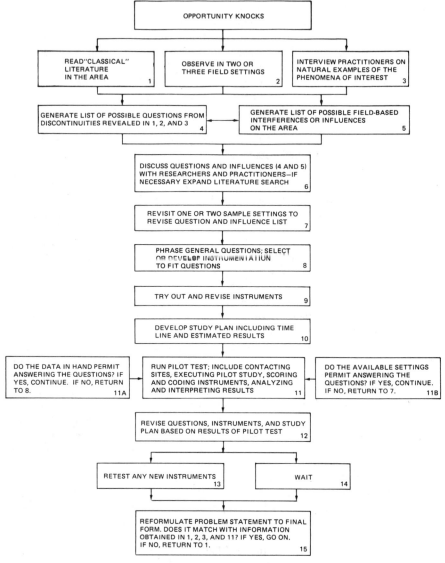

FIGURE 4-1 Problem formulation.

discovered while carrying out the first three steps and (b) listing the kinds of interferences the natural setting might provide that would result in outcomes that are discordant with theory or laboratory findings, or both (a) and (b).

The next three steps (boxes 6, 7, and 8) involve using colleagues and other sources of information to generate a tentative list of questions to be examined in the study. This is the first attempt to narrow the range. As soon as tentative questions are developed, instruments need to be found or developed to help guide the generation of data that will, in turn, be the basis for answering the questions (box 9). It should be noted that the initiation of field-based research frequently comes about because a researcher has access to an available data base to which questions can be posed; in fact, the existing data can sometimes be the foundation for an elegant quasi experiment, such as that conducted by Seaver (1973) on teacher expectations. This chapter, however, deals primarily with field-research activities that generate their own data.

To return to Figure 4-1, after instruments are revised, a study plan is drawn up and a pilot test is conducted. Boxes 11a and 11b of Figure 4-1 are control checks on the entire process. They represent attempts to assess the fit among questions, data, and settings. Three of the next four steps in Figure 4-1 represent processes of revision (boxes 12, 13, and 15).

The fourth step (box 14) is to wait and think. This is perhaps the most difficult step. The incubation or mulling process is crucial, however. It is at this time that one develops the courage to consider major revisions to the study plan, takes a broader view of the entire effort, and seriously considers whether the study is focusing on the important questions at hand rather than on the ones that are easy to answer. Much of the rest of the work in conducting this kind of study can be reduced if this stage is carefully done.

A final caveat is required. The steps outlined above are only one approach; they are not the only approach. The main points are that problem formulation must be conducted seriously and systematically and that it is a messy and time-consuming affair. As Kuhn (1968) puts it, "Early fact-gathering is a far more random activity than the one that subsequent scientific development makes familiar" (p. 15).

One specific kind of problem formulation is the kind that results from specific attempts to apply existing theory to field situations. This is really a kind of reformulation. An example of how problems can be reformulated as they move from the laboratory to the field comes from the behavioral psychologists. Their work started with laboratory studies with animals, with whom treatment and subjects could be easily manipulated; moved to laboratory work with humans; and finally, came to examining humans in situations of more or less limited control such as prisons, hospitals, schools, and bars. Consider some of the problems facing these researchers as they made these transitions: redefining reinforcers (clearly, one cannot semistarve school children to insure that food acts as a reinforcer); total alteration in the speed with which reinforcement could be given, from microseconds to hours or days; and finally, the presence of competing reinforcers or punishments in the situation (it might just be more fun to goof off than to work 10 minutes at the computer or do a puzzle).

The first attempts at applying the new techniques were often little more than attempts to make natural settings into field laboratories, that is, to conduct field experiments controlling all intervening situations in a most artificial way. As Sommer (1977) put it, they seemed to think of field research "as laboratory studies done outdoors" (p. 1).

Two problems emerged from these attempts: (1) Results were temporary and not particularly generalizable and (2) controlling everything was an absurdly dysfunctional activity for the researchers and the subjects. As the behaviorists moved into more natural, less controlled situations, new questions and problems emerged to replace the previous set. For example, where reinforcement in the form of food had been studied previously, the effects of secondary reinforcers (such as tokens) were of interest, as well as more abstract ones (such as control of time and task) (Klein & Thompson, 1976; Wang & Stiles, 1975). Where the reinforcer had been taken for granted and where increases in desired behavior had been the focus of study, new research examining long-term consequences or possible *overjustification phenomena* began to be studied (Greene, Sternberg, & Lepper, 1976) as well as more negative social abuses (Holland, 1975a).

Another illustration of new problems for research is available in a paper that criticizes some of the attempts to apply behavioral theory (Holland, 1975b).

> Advocates of aversion therapy base confidence in their techniques on their understanding of laboratory findings. However, the facts of discrimination learning are neglected. The home, the bar, or streets in which the problem drinking normally takes place are easily discriminated from the contrived conditions of the clinic or even the simulated bars used to promote transfer of training. Differences between these contrived settings and the real-life situations are still far greater than those found in laboratory discrimination learning studies where responding regularly comes under stimulus control. Behavior is adaptable. It adjusts to the contingencies of reinforcement or punishment. (p. 5)

> If the very theory on which behavior therapy is based is correct, then the solution to a behavioral problem cannot rest in the specially arranged contingencies in the special environment of the clinic. The contingencies of the natural environment must be modified if the problem is to be corrected. The abject misery and loneliness of Gallant's skid-row alcoholics could provide a solid operant basis for drinking as a means of escape into unconsciousness. That the long-term effect adds to the poverty and loneliness simply makes moderation more difficult by deepening the problems and establishing a vicious cycle. (p. 10)

The point of this example is to illustrate both the need to revise the problem under consideration when moving from the laboratory to the field and the advantages of doing so. Classical studies of aversion, for example, had not taken into account the relative magnitudes of competing situations, such as the need for social interaction and companionship. In reexamining the situation and expanding the scope of the problem, new approaches to studying it and finding solutions were generated.

Problem formulation in the field is a more complex, interactive, and critical task than in most laboratory work. Extreme care must be taken to fit the data collection and analyses to the questions that are eventually defined, whether those questions emerge from the processes described or from the more conventional use of causal models. In addition to formulating the problem, a careful review of the literature should be carried out. This research process can go on simultaneously with the later stages of problem formulation, or during instrument construction.

REVIEWING THE LITERATURE AND THE FIELD

> *It includes an active desire to listen to more sides than one; to give heed to facts from whatever source they come; to give full attention to alternative possibilities; to recognize the possibility of error even in the beliefs that are dearest to us.*
> (Dewey, 1974, p. 224)

The Literature

In order to prepare oneself appropriately for conducting any study, laboratory or field, one must return to the library and review literature that is salient to the issues at hand. This is done both to renew and expand one's understanding of the area and to avoid reinventing the wheel. In laboratory research, a review is made of the most current indexes in the field of interest, for example, *Psychological Abstracts, Educational Index, Current Index to Journals in Education,* and *Resources in Education* (ERIC). One can also employ computerized searches of the literature. In field research, careful reviews should be made of all of the sources, including articles and books in the fields of anthropology, policy research, and survey research. It is also important to seek out the narrative descriptions of field experiences regardless of the time in which they were generated. Excellent samples of descriptions of working in schools can be found in Froebel's (1906) description of setting up his kindergarten; Mayhew and Edwards' (1936) description of the first 7 years of the University of Chicago Laboratory School set up by Dewey; Ashton-Warner's (1963) description, in novel form, of teaching in New Zealand; Kohl's (1967) description of teaching in inner-city American classrooms; and Cazden's (1976) description of an academic taking a sabbatical in an elementary school teaching setting.

Perhaps the most complex literature to review, at least in the United States, is government documents. A large body of educational research is conducted under the auspices of federal, state, or local governments. This research is almost always reported in lengthy documents. Although such reports are often labeled "dull" by their readers, they represent gold mines of information. Frequently, the federal government convenes a special panel and requests position papers on a topic. These papers often serve as the basis for requests for proposals, which in turn generate final reports. Such reports usually include original instruments, coding schemes, and other data not often found in journals. A classic example is *Equality of Educational Opportunity* (Coleman, Campbell, Hobson, McPartland, Mood, Weinfeld, & York, 1966). This report became the basis for several books, articles, and theses, among them *Inequality* (Jencks, Smith, Acland, Bane, Cohen, Gintis, Heyns, & Michelson, 1972). Much of the work done after the original study consisted of reanalysis of data presented in the initial report.

The Field

In addition to reviews of written literature, there is another kind of review crucial to the success of field-based research. It is a review of the situation in which the research is to be conducted. For school work, one must learn about the particular school organization, the custodial and secretarial personnel, the number of classes per grade, the makeup of the student population, the kind and strengths of local parent groups and relevant unions, and so on. This should be done as systematically as possible, always remembering that, although only a few individuals have the power and authority to grant permission to do a study, an extremely large number of individuals possess the ability to stop a study on almost any grounds. Researchers often approach this problem by avoiding (or going around) local power groups. A far better policy is to secure as much support for the study as possible before starting. One way to secure the support is to involve various groups in the stage of problem formulation.

Reviewing information from the theoretical perspective is no more or less important than finding out about the setting as a whole. Researchers should learn how they are likely to be perceived, what the history of research is in the setting, and what the relevance of the particular research is to the situation under examination (Coleman et al., 1966; Schatzman & Strauss, 1973). If this is accomplished in a thorough fashion, it will greatly facilitate working in the field. To work successfully in the field, however, several other things need to be taken into consideration; these are discussed in a later section.

INSTRUMENT CONSTRUCTION

Observation is less likely to involve special instruments than special circumstances.

(Kaplan, 1964, p. 126)

A variety of recording devices or instruments constitutes the tools of most social science research These tools are important. Social psychology, whether laboratory based or field based, uses tests, questionnaires, interviews, and observational instruments to monitor the attitudes or reported behaviors of subjects. The majority of these instruments are either modifications of previously used instruments or instruments specially developed for the situation. In this section, some guidelines for the construction and modification of instruments for use in field-based research are reviewed. All the finer details of measurement theory are not, however, covered. For more information on measurement theory, see Cattell (1973), Buros (1938-1972), Lord & Novick (1968).

The purpose of any instrument is to permit the researcher to gain information *relevant* to solving the research problem of interest. The investigator should be able to answer why any bit of information was gathered. This information, whether quantitative or qualitative, becomes the data base for all further analysis and hypothesis testing. Information should therefore be gathered in a form that permits easy and logical summation across incidents. This should be obvious, but it is frequently overlooked in research, especially field-based research.

Form of Instrument

The form of the instrument to be used depends on what information is desired and on the availability of resources, principally time and money. It does not depend on whether one is doing research in schools, hospitals, prisons, or noninstitutional settings or on whether the instrument is being used to assess independent or dependent variables. There are at least four categories of instruments in field-based research: observational schedules, interviews, questionnaires, and tests. A comprehensive review of the first three kinds of instruments and methods of using them is presented by Bouchard (1976). It is also possible to record—as opposed to measure—almost all behaviors by audio or video mechanisms. One might use these devices, but one would then want to condense the information from them.

Direct observation yields very detailed information about behaviors, from which attitudes and perceptions can sometimes be inferred. Records of observations include: anecdotal field notes with minimal structure; systematic field notes in which categories of information are maintained but which permit one to add additional points of information that one feels are necessary; and finally, categorical frequency counts or ratings. The differences between the kinds of instruments are in degree rather than type, although anecdotal field notes are usually considered more subjective than frequency counts. This is true only from the perspective that the subjectivity is more blatant, and hence more suspect, than in frequency counts. Surely the decision of *what* to count is a subjective one. Inclusion and exclusion events, however, are public rather than private, as in the case of anecdotal notes. Systematic forms of observation are best generated from more informal anecdotal observation. Observation, in general, is often the first step in constructing other kinds of instruments, and it is one of the best ways of producing information about the total environment as opposed to just the objects in it.

Interviews are another technique for gathering information. They require an interviewer and a respondent. Interviews differ in the degree to which the questions and answers are structured or open. They may have a fixed set of questions or have some general guidelines for questions. They may be open-ended (any answer is taken) or fixed-choice (the possible answers are predetermined) (Bouchard, 1976). Interviews yield information on the respondents' reported behavior, on the respondents' attitudes and perceptions, or on both. Given that most behaviors can be directly observed, relying on reported behaviors is a less precise way of obtaining the necessary information than observing it. Interviews take much less time and money than observations, however, and for certain things they are more appropriate. For example, to obtain information about class scheduling, the number of girls and boys in a classroom, or the textbook series being used, it is clearly sufficient to ask a teacher, even though the answers may deviate somewhat from the observed situation.

Questionnaires are very similar to interviews. They do not require an interviewer, however, and are therefore less costly to administer. Questionnaires can vary in the same way as interviews; in other words, they may call for open-ended or fixed-choice responses; it is impossible, however, to have an unstructured set of questions for a questionnaire. The information obtained from questionnaires is of similar reliability to interviews, with possible misinterpretation of questions by the respondent being traded off against possible increases in truthfulness obtained because a respondent can answer privately in written form. This same privacy, however, may result in a lower response rate for questionnaires than for interviews.

Tests are the most common data-gathering technique. They are heavily used in educational research, especially as measures of dependent variables. They are also the most frequently misused form of instrumentation. This misuse often stems from a mismatch between the questions of research and the instrument or between the subject population and the instrument. Tests may require one-to-one administration or they may be group administered. Tests generally have the characteristic of having one correct answer to an item or, at a minimum, having a directionality to the answers; in other words, answer X is better than answer Y. Tests may represent direct samples of behaviors (such as a math test), may be reports of behaviors (attitude tests), or may be direct samples of behaviors that are then interpreted in some way (projective tests). Tests yield information that is usually not costly, can be easily summarized, and can be quite complete within the domain of interest.

How to Select or Construct an Instrument

The various steps in constructing an instrument are shown in some detail in Figure 4-2. The first step is to decide on the kind of information desired. The desired information is identified from a combination of observational work and problem formulation. Another step is to select the most probable mode and to observe in the setting. A third step is to search for existing instruments that can be modified or refined in order to meet the specific requirements of the study.

Excellent sources for the listings and descriptions of instruments are: Buros (1938-1972); Center for the Study of Evaluation (1966-1976); Educational Testing Service (1973-1977); Lake, Miles, and Earle (1973); Robinson and Shaver (1969); Shaw and Wright (1965); and Simon and Boyer (1967-1970). These books

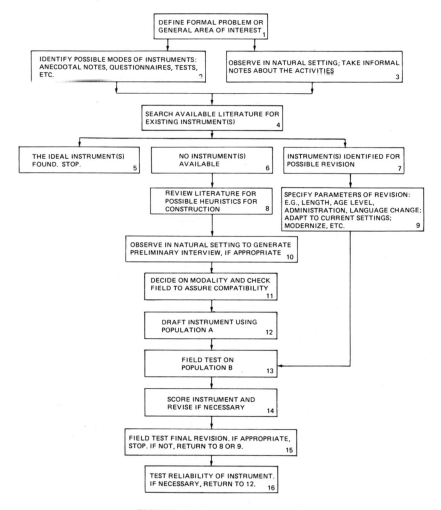

FIGURE 4-2 Instrument construction.

reflect a heavy psychological and educational bent; they are, however, complete and excellent sources of information for social psychologists working in educational settings.

Another way of obtaining information about available instruments is to write directly to authors about unpublished instruments that they have used in reported studies. Most authors are willing to share instruments, revisions, and comments with a fellow explorer. The advantage to using existing instruments or revising them is that one can build on available validity research and, in some cases, reliability information. Revisions usually require several trials on different populations, but the process is still far easier than generating instruments from scratch.

Sometimes, totally new instruments must be developed. The procedures recommended are borrowed heavily from anthropological and participant observation work. The first stage in development is to review the literature for possible heuristics in order to guide development and to observe the phenomenon of interest. One observes for a long period of time, looking for cases in which relevant events occur, and noting each case. This is not systematic observation; it is a more open, flexible observation. The process is time consuming and sometimes quite tedious, but it serves to focus the work so that a lot of data on nonevents will not be collected. After a feel for the setting has been obtained, information interviews can be started. These interviews are most often open-ended and should form the basis for content analysis. The content analysis of the informal interviews can then serve as the basis for returning for more formal observations, for more focused interviews, or for the construction of trial instruments.

Regardless of the eventual form of the instrument, objectives should be specified; mechanisms for obtaining information on the objectives should be devised; and instruments should be field tested. Newly created instruments should, in general, be developed on one group, tried out on another, and revised on a third. For most observational schedules and interviews, several trials and revisions are necessary. The major difficulty in this work is that instrument development becomes an end in itself rather than a means for gathering information. Techniques and rules for measurement begin to replace concern for the problem. Of course, the more precise the instrument, the better the information—but it is far better to have a "noisy" instrument focused on the right question than a clean one focused on the wrong one. "Measurement, in short, is not an end in itself" (Kaplan, 1964, p. 171).

An area of concern in instrument construction, especially in fieldwork, is stability. Observational data, especially the informal kind, is seductive. Researchers may be quite sure, after observing in a classroom for 5 minutes (and much more so after a month), that they know the "truth" about the situation; being the human creatures that we are, we generate hypothetical explanations for every phenomenon we see. We say that something occurred because the teacher did not do this; something else occurred because the subject did not do that; and so on. The most sobering way of assessing the validity of these assumptions is to attempt to estimate the stability or repeatability of any observed characteristic. This has a psychometric base in test-retest reliability. The question asked is, how consistent is the particular behavior? That is, how likely is it that the behavior or a similar behavior occurs regularly (if infrequently)? In general, variation occurs, not only in the measuring technique, but also in the exhibition of the behavior itself. Behaviors that tend to be highly unstable in their occurrence tend not to be useful predictors or explainers of other events.

There are many kinds of instruments available for research. Instruments should be selected or developed because they aid in answering the questions of interest, not because they are convenient or already exist. If instruments need to be revised, care should be taken in selecting both the mode and the content and in field testing the final instrument. Finally, instrument construction should not become an end in itself.[4]

WORKING IN THE FIELD

> *If field research is not the same as doing laboratory studies*
> *out of doors, what is it?*
>
> (Sommer, 1977, p. 1)

There are substantial differences between appropriate laboratory behavior and field behavior. In laboratory research that causes no physical or mental pain, compensation (in terms of money, grades, or something else) permits researchers to deceive their subjects, to require appearances at fixed times and places convenient to the researchers, and to engage in minimal levels of social interaction with the subjects. These norms do not hold in the field. The discussion of appropriate field behavior covers five areas: recognizing self-interest, respecting different knowledge bases, explaining the study, being truthful to subjects, and respecting the hierarchies.

One thing to acknowledge is that there are very few altruistic research programs. Researchers may select an area of work out of moral commitment or political belief, but usually the product of such research has payoff to the researchers in terms of theses, published papers, or general visibility. This is not inappropriate. It does require that the researchers try to offer something in exchange for the benefits received—not favors, but a fair trade.

As important as acknowledging the self-interest of researchers is acknowledging the expertise of the practitioners in the field. Researchers may disagree with policies, may be frustrated by bureaucratic decision making, and may become infuriated by an apparent lack of understanding of the value of the research being carried out. Practitioners are in the field daily, though, and have a massive wealth of clinical information that should not be ignored. It is vital that researchers explain clearly the purpose and hypotheses of the study, listen to and answer questions, and solicit and, if possible, incorporate practitioners' explanations or counter-hypotheses into the study.

Explaining the purpose and methods of the study is perhaps the hardest thing for researchers to do. In general, there is a belief that some things can only be understood by a trained scientist. If researchers cannot adequately explain the purpose of a study, the methodology to be employed, and the conclusions to be drawn, then it could be argued that the researchers, and not the practitioners, are most probably confused as to the basic issues at hand.

---

[4] Two areas not covered by this section are the role of the observer in research situations and the conception of "angles of observation" (Schatzman & Strauss, 1973). The role of the observer is almost totally dependent on the kind of research being done, whereas the angle of observation is similar to the idea of using multiple techniques to get convergent information (Leinhardt, 1975).

A second widely held view is that, if one tells subjects the truth about a study, they will falsify or alter their behavior. Although the ethics committees of many professional organizations (education, psychology, and sociology) and universities strongly discourage the use of the "harmless" lie, the practice continues, and papers whose authors have deceived subjects continue to appear in the official journals of these organizations. It is never desirable to lie to subjects, but in the field it is both unnecessary and totally inappropriate. Researchers should explain as much of the study as possible and then define what portions of the study cannot be discussed and why, promising to explain everything after the conclusion of the study. For example, one can tell teachers that the research involves studying teacher-student interaction in a reading class and that an observation scheme will be used. One can go on to explain that people tend to become self-conscious if they know others are looking for something specific. Therefore, the particular observation schedule cannot be examined until after the study is over. The main point is to be explicit about what cannot be discussed rather than substituting a deception. The likelihood is that the study participants who receive limited knowledge will react in at least as desirable, if not more desirable, ways than those who have been deceived or assume that they have been. It is also a good practice to distribute the final reports of the research to the participants.

The final point to be made regarding collecting data in the field involves respecting the organizational hierarchies. Information is always a source of power, and information about a new event, such as a study, is no exception. It is important, therefore, to make information available to all participants. For example, the principal should know everything the teachers are told and the teachers should know what the children are told. This procedure tends to reduce the degree to which individuals feel threatened by a research study.

The main point here is to encourage researchers to interact with field personnel in a manner that reflects the researchers' limitations and the practitioners' skills. Inevitably, researchers will need the help of practitioners at some critical and unforeseen point in the study. If the practitioners have been treated with respect, such help is usually received. In addition, there will be a greater chance that the setting can be used in the future for additional research.

TIME AND COST

A well-organized research laboratory with several researchers sharing the same facility can be a very efficient operation (Cronbach, 1975). In a matter of months, studies can be designed by the principal researcher, carried out by research assistants and graduate students, and analyzed by all three. Studies can be run back to back and simultaneously. There is very little down time for the principal researcher or for the staff. Unexpected results can and should lead swiftly into additional work, or modifications and reruns of the original study (Aronson & Carlsmith, 1968).

By contrast, field-based research goes on in agonizing slow motion. The principal researcher must stay active, and the study cannot easily be turned around after planning is completed. Rarely can more than one researcher share a facility such as a classroom unless the studies being conducted are very unobtrusive. The entire staff spends days and weeks waiting for decisions, meetings, and clearance from the field. For the average situation, a well-organized and carefully planned study will yield 1 hour of data collection for every 4 or 5 hours of effort. The effort includes contacting officials, meeting with supervisors of participants, obtaining permission from all relevant groups, and planning and scheduling. In general, one or two studies per year can be accomplished in a classroom. Of course, the results may lead to several products, but one basic intervention is probably all that can be done.

In order to operate successfully in the field, the time frames of the object of study must be learned (Schatzman & Strauss, 1973). The researcher's schedule must be adjusted to fit that of the cooperating participants. For example, interviews with teachers cannot be conducted all morning, only at the scheduled class breaks. Unfortunately, these breaks occur at roughly the same time for most teachers rather than in a staggered fashion. The major point is that time must be well planned in conducting the study. Additional time is also required for data coding and multiple analysis. This increase in time, naturally, leads to increase in costs.

The cost of doing field-based research is usually quite high because of the time required (Bouchard, 1976; Bronfenbrenner, 1976; Cronbach, 1975). Naturalistic research *can* be done on a shoestring; but if several people are doing observations, if reasonable forms are used, if a test or instrument is built, and if field trials are carried out, then the chances are that the cost will be high (Schwitzgebel, 1970).

After formulating the problem, constructing the instruments, reviewing the literature, and preparing the groundwork, one is ready to conduct the first step in implementing the study: pilot testing.

IMPLEMENTATION

> *Civilized man . . . sets up in advance of any particular ship-wreck warning buoys, and builds lighthouses where he sees signs that such an event may occur.*
>
> (Dewey, 1974, p. 214)

In this section, some of the major activities associated with most middle-to-large–sized field-research studies are dealt with; pilot testing, staffing and training, scheduling, and meetings are covered. The assumption is that several people are involved, but even if only one or two people are conducting the study, the major activities are still relevant.

Pilot Test

A pilot test is a practice run of the entire study, from the planning stages up to and including the data analysis (Borg & Gall, 1974). The need for and purposes of pilot testing are the same for both laboratory- and field-based research. Because of complexities of problem formulation, data analysis, and time expenditure, however, pilot tests are even more necessary in field research than in controlled settings.

The ideal pilot study is a complete run-through. Frequently, the difficulties associated with field research preclude such a trial. If a complete pilot test is not feasible, portions of the total study can be tried out separately in different settings. The advantage of this approach is that the small pieces are more manageable and more easily tested. The disadvantage is that there is no test of how the pieces fit together.

The results of the pilot study aid tremendously in the refinement of the problem, the overall study plan, and the specification of hypotheses. The results of the analyses of preliminary data constitute a good check on the kind of results likely to be obtained and the precision with which the techniques permit questions to be answered. Finally, the pilot study is a last check for instruments that have not been previously used.

Staffing and Training

Most field-research efforts require the help and expertise of several individuals in addition to the principal investigators. The discussion that follows assumes a staff of 2-18 people. Recruiting and selecting these individuals is a major undertaking and is not dealt with in detail. The members of a research team should be interested in the topic of study, get along well, and be willing and eager to learn new skills (Schatzman & Strauss, 1973). The roles to be filled become obvious in the rest of the section; of course, one person may fill many roles. Highly technical personnel, such as computer programmers, need to be well informed about the study and well integrated into it as soon as possible because they are valuable in spotting conceptual and technical errors. Members of the team for a specific project should know each other and their various roles.

Clear lines of communication from the field to home base and within the project itself should be established, maintained, and tested. Any participant in the study—parent, teacher, principal—must know whom to call for a problem. Any research team member should know whom to contact about a problem and to whom to refer a participant. During the actual data collection, master schedules should be posted publicly and, if possible, distributed so everyone knows where everyone else is at any time.

All necessary members of the team and their backups should be trained thoroughly in the performance of any given task, such as interviewing, prior to performing the task (this means prior to piloting). Training should be updated, and changes in procedure should be discussed regularly during the implementation of the study, rather than when crises occur. Training involves learning how to perform certain tasks and certain roles. Often in the course of performing a single task, the researcher will wear many different hats and must have thought about how best to don each one.

Scheduling

Each segment of the study needs to be scheduled carefully, starting with the field time clock, not the researcher's time clock. Considerations in scheduling should include sufficient personnel for backup, the temporal and spacial proximity of another activity, and levels of fatigue of both researchers and participants.

One of the most frustrating realities of fieldwork is that something almost always goes wrong in the field that upsets the plan. The degree of disruption can be minimized *if* the disruptions are concentrated in the field and not in the research team. Careful scheduling and staffing selection can help assure this by avoiding the planning of difficult tasks on top of one another and by avoiding the overtaxing of any one researcher. Another tactic that helps limit the frequency and intensity of crises is having frequent meetings.

Meetings

Brief daily meetings of all members of the research team should be held during the main data-collection phases of the study, and weekly meetings should be held at all other times during the study. The main purpose of the meetings is to keep all members informed of current developments, changes, and procedures, as well as to try to head off any difficulties—interpersonal or technical—before they become serious. These meetings are analogous to the participant observers' review and write-up of daily field notes. Meetings conducted early in the study help the group to draw maps of the field—spacial, temporal, and social (Schatzman & Strauss, 1973). Meetings conducted later on help to maintain a sense of where team members are in the total picture and to remind members of approaching deadlines.

Each meeting should provide all team members the opportunity, but not the requirement, to report on their activities, the chance to relieve tension, or both. Each meeting should have a report concerning snags in the field, last minute changes, and the need to pick up missing data from the individual who is acting as troubleshooter. Obviously, if the fieldwork is being conducted over a wide geographic area, face-to-face meetings are not possible on a daily basis. The function of the meetings should still be filled through some system of reporting.

The role of the principal investigators, the necessity of meetings, and the degree of precision of scheduling that is required are all dependent on the size and duration of the study. The larger the study, the more defined all roles must be, and the more precise the planning. The successful implementation of a study is dependent on overplanning of details while simultaneously maintaining a high degree of flexibility toward those plans. Once the study is underway, the next task is to manage the incoming information effectively.

REDUCING THE DATA

> *Water, water everywhere/Nor any drop to drink.*
> (Coleridge, *Rime of the Ancient Mariner*)

In laboratory studies, researchers define a problem, carry out a study, analyze the results, and write them up. Theoretically, they do the same thing in field-based research, but somehow, at the end, there is always much more material than can be organized and described in a useful fashion. If care has been taken in problem formulation, reformulation, instrument construction, and pilot testing, the problem can be kept to a minimum. In the discussion that follows, *some* behaviors that lead to data swamp, and some solutions, are indicated.

Sources of the Problem

There are two powerful temptations in field-based research. First, after investing the time and energy to get into the field, there is the "While we're at it, why not ask it;" syndrome. Symptoms of this first syndrome are an inability on the part of the researcher to state why a particular question is being asked and how the answer will be used. A less common but similar symptom is a defense of data collection that relies on historical precedent (e.g., "we've always collected data on *X*"). Second, there is the desire to depart from agreed-on instrumentation to further document the independent (or occasionally the dependent) variables. Symptoms of this second syndrome are high levels of anxiety in the researcher that important data will be missed or that some extenuating circumstance will be overlooked. A general symptom of disorder is the presence of boxes of unanalyzed data (or, for the more sophisticated, mountains of untouched computer output), which start to appear midway into the study.

Ongoing Data Processing

One way of guaranteeing immunity from these plagues is to completely analyze and write up pilot results before starting the study; but, like not drinking the water in a foreign land, one often forgets about the ice cubes or the reconstituted orange juice. Some protection can be provided, however, if all data from a study are reviewed, coded, and made machine ready or filed daily. This permits organization and cleanup of field notes and rapid recognition of wasteful data-collection efforts, as well as the discovery of what is not being collected. Ongoing data processing also allows researchers to decide whether to stop collecting a specific kind of data midway in the study. The disadvantage of ongoing data collection is the real possibility of biasing the study's future data collection in an inappropriate way. Clearly, a balance must be struck through judgment on the potential value of information and the risk of data swamp.

Sorting Data

At or near the end of a study in which masses of data have been collected despite one's best efforts to keep the quantity at a minimum, procedures for sorting the data need to be set up. The first sorting involves pulling out easily quantifiable variables from the rest of the data, for example, test scores and coded questionnaires. The remaining data should be separated into four groups: (1) descriptive data that support either independent or dependent variables (e.g., descriptions of the general classroom setting or of the testing procedures); (2) descriptive data that can be quantified and used in the analysis (e.g., content analyses of interviews); (3) descriptive data that cannot be quantified but can support analyses; and (4) descriptive data that, though it may be fascinating, have no apparent relevance to questions in the study.

Estimating Central Tendency and Spread

Having grouped quantifiable variables by idea or concept, each variable should then be described in terms of its mean and standard deviation (or an equivalent estimate of the central point of the distribution) and of the spread of the values that the variable has taken. An excellent way of getting a feel for data is described by Tukey (1977). He recommends using stem-and-leaf displays and box plots to obtain a picture of data. Variables that have no variation in a particular sample may still be important in a different study. Data that have no variation, however, are of no further use statistically, although they may be descriptively significant. (That everyone was exactly 6 feet tall is informative, but the height cannot be used to explain other information in the study.) Estimating central tendency and spread also permits obvious errors in the data to be discovered and gives the researchers at least a feel for the data in hand. They may even discover that the same information has been collected twice, thus permitting the combination of the two or the elimination of one. A general scan of the quantifiable variables should permit the discarding of some variables and the combination of others, thus reducing some of the mass. In making the scan, one looks for low measures of spread and low means. Little spread indicates little variation; low means can indicate infrequent occurrence of an event. Every decision to delete variables should be carefully and thoroughly documented so decisions can be defended and, if necessary, revised.

Collapsing by Concept

Having sorted the data and deleted some measures, the researchers are ready to begin reducing the information in a way that will permit presentation and description of results. The first and most important idea is that one collapses by concept, not by instrument. Thus, if the researchers have collected data from tests, observations, and interviews, they should pull related variables from all three sources and group them. It is useless to present the data in the form collected. One cannot draw inferences based on instrument form (unless that is the point of the exercise). One has to draw conclusions along conceptual lines. The way the researchers should organize the data depends on the problem statement and on the underlying theoretical models if they are available. Variables should be grouped in a manner that is consistent with the original questions and the original variables. It is at this stage that incomplete data should be reviewed for possible deletion. If there are numerous blanks for any given variables the remaining data points are unlikely to be representative of the part that is missing.

There are many ways of actually combining measures that can help to reduce the numbers of variables and more clearly present the findings. One way is to use some kind of statistical grouping procedure, such as principal components (on the data that is already sorted), weighting each measure by its factor loadings, and then summing measures to create a factor score. This assumes that, for any given concept, all of the measures of that concept should group together. This is not always the case. For example, the opportunity to learn subject matter in school might include measures of numbers of days in the school year (Wiley & Harnischfeger, 1974) or the amount of time on task (Bloom, 1974) or the overlap between curriculum and test (Cooley & Leinhardt, 1975b). Although these measures are important estimates of opportunity to learn, there is no theoretical reason why they should be correlated. If they are uncorrelated in a given sample and one of the measures tends to relate consistently to other measures of opportunity in that sample, then the second measure will not be heavily weighted in the first factor, or even in the first few factors, of an analysis.

There are statistical ways around this problem, but there is also a different approach to grouping the data. Measures can be transformed to a common metric (such as z scores) and then added together to make a composite score of a variable within a concept. Such a score would then distinguish between classrooms with many days of school and high amounts of on-task behavior and classrooms with many days of school and low amounts of on-task behavior, but the composite permits compensation of dearth in one area by using plenty in another. Creating composites in this way is similar to creating composites of factor scores, except that the weights for the measures are equal rather than variable, and inclusion of a measure is logical and based on theory or knowledge, rather than empirical.

ANALYSIS OF RESULTS

The field researcher is a methodological pragmatist.
(Schatzman & Strauss, 1973, p. 7)

The purpose of this section is to describe the further analysis of information gathered in the field. The section includes a brief description of some of the available analytic techniques, both statistical and logical; however, the ways of applying them are not covered in detail.

Quantifiable field-based data can and should be analyzed in exploratory and confirmatory ways (Tukey, 1977; Tukey & Mosteller, 1977). Just as information has been gathered by several techniques, the data should be examined from several angles before trying to confirm or test hypotheses. The first point to be borne in mind is that any act that involves more than merely recording the data is an analysis. Thus, descriptions drawn from field notes are a legitimate form of analysis. Of course, descriptions may include some quantitative summaries to support them, such as multidimensional scaling or discriminant analysis.

A few of the more common statistical techniques are described in this paragraph. Questions about differences in means are usually answered by some form of analysis of variance (ANOVA), which contrasts means of different groups while adjusting for the spread within each group. Analysis of covariance (ANCOVA) contrasts means while adjusting for both the spread and some other variable or variables. Regression analysis is descriptive of variation in the means of the dependent variables, but it permits inclusion of information about variation in the independent variables as well, rather than assuming the treatment to be fixed. Other techniques incorporate prior information about the situation or focus more on differences between expected and observed situations. Each technique has multiple versions, some of which do not use ordinary least squares but rely on more robust estimations of the parameters of interest, for example, ridge regression. Still other variations use systematic ways of combining information to describe relationships, for example, path analysis and structural-equation models. The important points to remember are: No one technique should be considered absolutely correct or final; in most cases, several techniques can be tried and used in combination; and, the analysis should fit the question, *not* the other way around. As Kaplan (1964) said, "It comes as no particular surprise to discover that a scientist formulates problems in a way which requires for their solution just those techniques in which he himself is skilled" (p. 28). This tendency should be avoided.

Remaining descriptive data should fall into two groups, data relevant to the identified questions, and data irrelevant to the questions. Relevant descriptive data can be incorporated into discussions of background, collection efforts, or results, or they can be the focus of a more narrative description of the entire study. For example, some recent research on differences in teacher behavior toward girls and boys focused on female teachers (Seewald, Leinhardt, & Engel, 1977). All but 2 of over 50 teachers in this research were women, so the study described and analyzed their behaviors. The 2 male teachers behaved somewhat differently. Because of such a small sample, these differences could only be described and were not included in the main analysis. The observed differences in in-class behavior did permit speculation and the generation of hypotheses. Descriptive data that are not relevant for the questions addressed in a study either can be stored away or can serve as the basis for another study addressing different questions.

Nonquantifiable data can also be subjected to analysis based on "reflective thinking" (Dewey, 1974). That is, systematic and intelligent consideration of information can be carried out without the use of statistical tools. Individuals trained in the traditions of statistical analysis are often terrified by such an approach. One way of looking at a reasoned analysis, however, is that it is the reflective (pun intended) approach to statistical analysis. The following steps of criticism are used: (a) gathering the evidence, (b) evaluating the evidence, (c) understanding the meaning of the information, and (d) presenting the information (Kent, 1967, pp. 6-7). At each step, statistical information can also be merged to help move to the next step in a way analogous to the use of narrative information in a statistical presentation.

The two major points in this section bear emphasizing once more. First, before and during the entire field-based study, every effort should be made to limit the quantity of data and to keep the data clean while not losing information; in other words, data should be focused and complete. Second, all analyses that are carried out should help to clarify the phenomenon under consideration rather than being carried out for their own sake.

AN EXAMPLE OF FIELD BASED RESEARCH

An example of a long-term, field-based research program (1971-1975) comes from a study of the impact of classroom practices on student achievement. The research was conducted in some 60 classrooms (per year) throughout the United States. The classrooms were all second-grade rooms, were all using some version of the Learning Research and Development Center's (LRDC) individualized curricula, and were all part of the Follow Through compensatory education program. The research was iterative and changed over the 4-year period, but it retained a common theme of documenting the relationship between student learning and classroom processes. The reason for studying this problem in the field rather than the laboratory was twofold. On the one hand, we wished to study natural variation in classroom practices; on the other, we needed information on how an instructional program changes when it goes from controlled to field settings.

A number of problems occurred during the course of the study that made occasional changes in direction and other compromises necessary. These are mentioned wherever appropriate. The study, on the whole, was reasonably successful and fulfilled its own goals sufficiently to serve as an example here.

Problem Formulation

The "opportunity that knocked" (see Figure 4-1) for these particular studies consisted of access to the large number of classrooms using the LRDC curricula and of a willingness of the schools to cooperate in research combined with our desire to find out more about the relationship between processes of instruction and learning.

Prior to 1970, LRDC had kept very sketchy and informal notes on the educational program in the field. These notes were little more than an inventory of equipment. Toward the end of 1970, it became clear that it would be useful to document program implementation on an expanded basis. Two researchable questions were defined: To what degree is the program implemented in the Follow Through classrooms; To what extent does variation in the degree of implementation result in observable differences in students' academic growth? Over the next 3 years, the questions were modified as data from each study became a literature base for future problem formulations. The broadest restatement of the problem became: What is the nature of individualized instruction in the Follow Through classrooms? To what extent does the degree of individualization affect student academic growth (Cooley & Leinhardt, 1974, 1975a, 1975b; Leinhardt, 1972, 1976, 1977a, 1977b)? As Schatzman and Strauss (1973) suggest, the "problem" was continuously changed as information came in from the field situation. The steps outlined in Figure 4-1 were in fact the basic ones followed; however, the sequence was repeated many times and stretched out over several years.

Instrument Construction

During the 4 years of study of the Follow Through program, three basic instruments were used: standardized achievement tests, teacher interviews, and observational schedules. The specific forms of each changed slightly, depending on external policies of testing and the refocusing of questions. The major instrument construction, however, occurred in the first 2 years of the study and is therefore described in some detail.

A search for available instruments made use of Simon and Boyer's instrument survey, *Mirrors for Behavior* (1967-1970) and of existing studies of LRDC programs. It was clear that teachers' instructional behaviors should be documented in some manner and that overall teacher practices should also be monitored, but no existing instrument could meet those needs adequately. It was decided that new instruments would have to be constructed.

The classroom behaviors of the teacher seemed to be most easily captured by direct observation—and later, by coding videotape segments taken in the classrooms. The more general classroom practices seemed best gathered by an interview and questionnaire combination. Specific instruments were developed over several months of tryout and revision in six different classrooms. The general content of the instruments was decided after observing in several rooms, talking to curriculum developers, and reading relevant literature.

The specific content of the observational schedules was decided by using two converging techniques. Available schedules were reviewed, including unpublished and published instruments. Simultaneously, long sessions (3 hours a day for several weeks) were spent in classrooms tracing the behaviors of individual students. After a reasonably complete picture of an average student day was established, the process was repeated for teachers. The behaviors of teachers were analyzed into three groups: those behaviors that involved students in interaction; those behaviors that did not involve students but would directly affect their learning, such as lesson writing or correcting work; and those behaviors that did not involve students and were not expected to affect learning directly. The first group of behaviors were further defined and became the basis for observation. Obviously, this process itself also contributed to the reformulation of the problem under study. Each year of the study resulted in further refinement of the observational techniques. These refinements were based on new instruments as they came out, such as Stallings's Classroom Observation Procedure (Stallings, 1972), on data from the previous years' instruments, and on the redefinition of the problem.

The specific content of the interview and questionnaire combination came primarily from the teacher activities that were observed in the tracing period but that did not involve interaction with students. The content also came from an analysis of existing LRDC curricula, which focused on the key features of implementing and using the curricula. The interview and questionnaire format was developed in the second year as a way of permitting teachers to control the accuracy of the content of responses while insuring a high response rate (100%) and a relatively consistent interpretation of items.

Usability in the field was established by the extensive help of two colleagues, who administered questionnaires, made observations, noted times for each item, and noted needed revisions to improve clarity or precision of the items. Another group of colleagues was assigned the task of providing data with which to estimate the stability of the characteristics and the instruments under development. When the first stage of development was completed, care was taken to see that the resulting measures yielded information relevant to each domain specified in the problem formulation: classroom context, time allocation, space allocation, assignment procedures, management procedures, and student independence (Leinhardt, 1972). After 4 years of work, the instruments were altered to match new domains: motivators, opportunity, structure and placement, and quality of instruction (Cooley & Leinhardt, 1975a). These new domains reflected an expanded interest in a variety of educational approaches, not just those of LRDC.

Reviewing the Literature

For the study of Follow Through, four sources of background literature were relevant: evaluation literature, classroom observation literature, curriculum descriptions, and government documents on the Follow Through programs. These sources were reviewed prior to the study and continued to be consulted during the course of the study. A more difficult and significant task was that of becoming acquainted with all of the factors involved in the particular study.

The LRDC-based Follow Through staff consisted of a project director and between 5 and 11 staff members. During the first few years of program implementation, different individuals kept filling different roles, and roles were constantly being slightly altered to fit the needs of the project. Thus, the "literature" base was usually in flux. The field staff remained the most important link in learning about the significant situations in the field: local floods, flu epidemics, and new buildings. Information was almost always obtained orally and informally.

Working in the Field

In general, work in the field went relatively well. Good relations were established and maintained with the sites. Several individuals made suggestions for ways to improve the study, which were often followed. Usually, the suggestions centered around variables to be included or around the appropriate timing for an interview or observation. The sites were never deceived nor promised anything that was not delivered. The coding of tapes and questionnaires was made as open as possible, and many school supervisory personnel were taught how to code, how to construct new instruments to suit their own needs, or both. In four cases, these activities helped in the efforts of local supervisors to achieve higher academic degrees. At the end of each phase of data collection, letters were written to all site personnel acknowledging their help. Both oral and written reports on the outcomes of the studies were made at least once (and often twice) a year.

Data Organization and Interpretation

Fortunately, data in this study were always collected according to some scheme, and no unmanageable data flood ever developed. The most difficult problem over all 4 years was how to present the results in a way that exhibited some conceptual clarity while maintaining sufficient detail in the information.

Data were analyzed by reading them over, examining means and standard deviations, and calculating correlations and partial correlations. Data were reduced according to several conceptual models, starting with domains specified by developers and moving to those specified by evaluators (Cooley & Leinhardt, 1975a). The data were analyzed initially by describing the patterns of correlations among variables, and later by using commonality analysis (a modification of regression). This analysis permitted the examination of both unique and shared contributions of process constructs to student outcomes. The problem with this approach was a lack of usable detail in the final discussions.

Essentially, two points have emerged from these studies: (1) Classroom practices make a consistent, if small, difference in what students learn, and (2) some practices, especially some of those associated with individualizing instruction, have a positive impact on learning. There are five general findings that seem to have consistent replication: (1) The most powerful predictor of student achievement is initial student ability; (2) an increase in clarity and cognitive focus on the part of teachers is associated with higher student achievement; (3) an increase in managerial focus and negative affect is associated with lower achievement; (4) reasonably frequent *formal* assessment of student mastery is associated with student achievement, whereas lack of such assessment is associated with depressed achievement; and (5) some forms of student autonomy for which students have received instruction result in increased student growth (Leinhardt, 1976, 1977a, 1977b).

A final point about field research should be made. Although the product is painfully attained, data kept in a reasonably organized fashion can be reanalyzed. This reanalysis can be based on slightly redefined, but similar, questions or on totally new ones. The data can thus serve as a continuation of a line of research or as a point of departure for new research.

This review demonstrates how an actual series of field-based studies was carried out within the framework presented in this chapter. My experiences with the LRDC studies have confirmed, for me, the viability of the strategies for practical field research. Admittedly, field research is not always successful; this section could have been a narrative of crises encountered during the various stages of problem formulation, instrument development, and so on. The possibility of such crises can be minimized, however, by careful attention to the experience-based strategies described here.

CONCLUSION

> *It is less important to draw a fine line between what is "scientific" and what is not than to cherish every opportunity for scientific growth. There is no need for behavioral*

> *science to tighten its immigration laws against subversive aliens.*
>
> (Kaplan, 1964, p. 28)

After an opening discussion of the importance and advantages of field research, this chapter is focused on strategies for planning, implementing, and making use of such research. By observing and questioning educational phenomena in a natural environment, social scientists can expand tremendously their understanding of complex phenomena. Both the process and the product of problem formulation must change in response to the exigencies of the real world. Such changes can be fed back into continued laboratory work to challenge the questions and paradigms of previous research.

In the process of conducting field studies, researchers are required to deal with new problems and solutions in methodology. For instance, producing the necessary detailed documentation of treatments is a new skill for many researchers, who are more accustomed to directing their energies toward design of treatments than toward documenting them. The recording process itself may lead to new ideas for future design efforts, which will in turn result in subtle or gross modifications of treatment conditions. Each task, design, and documentation will tend to improve the quality of the other.

The relative significance of research findings should be considered. Because the problems tackled in field research are complex and reality based, it is likely that the successful solutions that are generated will have great impact. This is essentially the issue of generalizability. (Cronbach, 1975). Field research becomes generalizable as findings are replicated over time and situation. Most researchers are interested in ultimately generalizing to the real world. Field research, like a glacier, accomplishes its task slowly—but surely.

REFERENCES

Aronson, E., & Carlsmith, J. Experimentation in social psychology. In G. Lindzey & E. Aronson (Eds.), *The handbook of social psychology* (Vol. 2). Reading, Mass.: Addison-Wesley, 1968.

Ashton-Warner, S. *Teacher*. New York: Bantam, 1963.

Blalock, H. M. *Causal inferences in nonexperimental research*. Chapel Hill: University of North Carolina Press, 1964.

Bloom, B. S. Time and learning. *American Psychologist*, 1974, *29*, 682–688.

Borg, W., & Gall, M. *Educational research: An introduction*. New York: McKay, 1974.

Bouchard, T. J. Field research methods: Interviewing, questionnaires, participant observation, systematic observation, unobtrusive measure. In M. D. Dunnette (Ed.), *Handbook of industrial and organizational psychology*. Chicago: Rand McNally, 1976.

Bronfenbrenner, U. The experimental ecology of education. *Educational Researcher*, 1976, *5*(9), 5–15.

Buros, O. K. (Ed.). *Mental measurements yearbook* (7 vols.). Highland Park, N.J.: Gryphon, 1938–1972.

Cartwright, D. Determinants of scientific progress: The case of research on the risky shift. *American Psychologist*, 1973, *28*, 222–231.

Cattell, R. B. *Personality and mood by questionnaire*. San Francisco: Jossey-Bass, 1973.

Cazden, C. B. *How knowledge about language helps the classroom teacher—or does it: A personal account*. Mimeographed version presented as an invited address to the annual meeting of the American Educational Research Association, San Francisco, April 1976.

Center for the Study of Evaluation. *Technical Reports*. Los Angeles: University of California at Los Angeles, 1966–1976.

Coleman, J. S., Campbell, E. Q., Hobson, C. J., McPartland, J. M., Mood, A. M., Weinfeld, F. D., & York, R. L. *Equality of educational opportunity.* Washington: U.S. Government Printing Office, 1966.

Cook, T. D., & Campbell, D. T. The design and conduct of quasi-experiments and true experiments in field settings. In M. D. Dunnette (Ed.), *Handbook of industrial and organizational psychology,* Chicago: Rand McNally, 1976.

Cooley, W. W., & Leinhardt, G. Evaluating individualized education in the elementary school. In P. O. Davidson, F. W. Clark, & L. A. Hamerlynck (Eds.), *Evaluation of behavioral programs in community, residential, and school settings.* Champaign, Ill.: Research, 1974.

Cooley, W.W., & Leinhardt, G. *The application of a model for investigating classroom processes.* Pittsburgh: University of Pittsburgh, Learning Research and Development Center, 1975. (LRDC Publication, 1975/24) (a)

Cooley, W. W., & Leinhardt, G. *Design for the individualized instruction study: A study of the effectiveness of individualized instruction in the teaching of reading and mathematics in compensatory education programs.* Pittsburgh: University of Pittsburgh, Learning Research and Development Center, 1975. (b)

Cronbach, L. J. Beyond the two disciplines of scientific psychology. *American Psychologist,* 1975, *30,* 116–127.

Dewey, J. Why reflective thinking must be an educational aim. In R. D. Archambault (Ed.), *John Dewey on education.* Chicago: University of Chicago Press, 1974.

Educational Testing Service. *Test Collection Bulletins.* Princeton, N.J.: 1973–1977.

Edwards, W., Guttentag, M., & Snapper, K. A decision-theoretic approach to evaluation research. In E. Struening & M. Guttentag (Eds.), *Handbook of evaluative research* (Vol. 1). Beverly Hills, Calif.: Sage, 1975.

Froebel, F. W. A. *Letters on the kindergarten.* Syracuse: Bardeen, 1906.

Fullan, M., & Pomfret, A. *Review of research on curriculum implementation.* Toronto: Department of Sociology in Education, Ontario Institute for Studies in Education, 1975.

Greene, D., Sternberg, B., & Lepper, M. *Overjustification in a token economy.* Paper presented at the meeting of the American Educational Research Association, San Francisco, April 1976.

Gross, A. E. Applied social psychology—Problems and prospects. *Personality and Social Psychology Bulletin,* 1976, *2,* 114–115.

Helmreich, R. Applied social psychology: The unfulfilled promise. *Personality and Social Psychology Bulletin,* 1975, *1,* 548–560.

Higbee, K. L., & Wells, M. G. Some research trends in social psychology during the 1960s. *American Psychologist,* 1972, *27,* 963–966.

Holland, J. G. Behavior modification for prisoners, patients and other people as a prescription for the planned society. *Mexican Journal of Behavioral Analysis,* 1975, *1,* 81–95. (a)

Holland, J. G. *Behaviorism: Part of the problem or part of the solution?* Invited address presented to the convention of the American Psychological Association, Chicago, 1975. (b)

Holland, J. G., & Skinner, B. F. *The analysis of behavior.* New York: McGraw Hill, 1961.

Jencks, C., Smith, M., Acland, H., Bane, M. J., Cohen, D., Gintis, H., Heyns, B., & Michelson, S. *Inequality: A reassessment of the effect of family and schooling in America.* New York: Basic, 1972.

Kaplan, A. *The conduct of inquiry.* San Francisco: Chandler, 1964.

Kent, S. *Writing history.* New York: Appleton, 1967.

Klein, R. D., & Thompson, M. *The use of an individualized motivation system to modify accuracy and rate on a computer-based number facts program.* Paper presented at the meeting of the American Educational Research Association, San Francisco, April 1976.

Kohl, H. R. *Teaching the "unteachable."* New York: New York Review, 1967.

Kuhn, T. S. *The structure of scientific revolutions.* Chicago: University of Chicago Press, 1968.

Lake, D., Miles, M., & Earle, R. *Measuring human behavior.* New York: Teachers College Press, 1973.

Lamb, M. E. Fathers: Forgotten contributors to child development. *Human Development,* 1975, *18,* 245–266.

Lazarsfeld, P. F., & Reitz, J. G. *An introduction to applied sociology.* New York: Elsevier North-Holland, 1975.

Leinhardt, G. *The boojum of evaluation: Implementation, some measures.* Unpublished doctoral dissertation, University of Pittsburgh, 1972.

Leinhardt, G. *A strategy for program evaluation.* Pittsburgh: University of Pittsburgh, Learning Research and Development Center, 1975. (LRDC Publication, 1975/16)

Leinhardt, G. Observation as a tool for the evaluation of implementation. *Instructional Science,* 1976, *5,* 343–364.

Leinhardt, G. Evaluating an adaptive education program: Implementation to replication. *Instructional Science,* 1977, *6,* 223–257. (a)

Leinhardt, G. Program evaluation: An empirical study of individualized instruction. *American Educational Research Journal,* 1977, *14,* 277–293. (b)

Lewin, K. Action research and minority problems. *Journal of Social Issues,* 1946, *2,* 34–46.

Lord, F. M., & Novick, M. R., with Allen Birnbaum. *Statistical theories of mental test scores.* Reading, Mass.: Addison-Wesley, 1968.

Lowe, R. H. A survey of social psychological methods, techniques and designs: A response to Helmreich. *Personality and Social Psychology Bulletin,* 1976, *2,* 116–118.

Mayhew, K. C., & Edwards, A. C. *The Dewey School: The Laboratory School of the University of Chicago, 1896-1903.* New York: Appleton, 1936.

Mitroff, I. I., & Blackenship, V. On the methodology of the holistic experiment: An approach to the conceptualization of large-scale social experiments. *Technological Forecasting and Social Change,* 1973, *4,* 339–353.

Mitroff, I. I., & Turoff, M. On measuring the conceptual errors in large-scale experiments: The future as decision. *Technological Forecasting and Social Change,* 1974, *6,* 389–402.

Robinson, J. P., & Shaver, P. R. *Measures of social psychological attitudes.* Ann Arbor: Institute for Social Research, 1969.

Rosenthal, R., & Jacobson, L. *Pygmalion in the classroom. Teacher expectation and pupils' intellectual development.* New York: Holt, 1968.

Sanford, N. Whatever happened to action research? *Journal of Social Issues,* 1970, *26*(4), 3–23.

Schatzman, L., & Strauss, A. L. *Field research: Strategies for a natural science.* Englewood Cliffs, N.J.: Prentice-Hall, 1973.

Schwitzgebel, R. L. Behavior instrumentation and social technology. *American Psychologist,* 1970, *25,* 491–499.

Scriven, M. The key property of physical laws—inaccuracy. In H. Feigl & G. Maxwell (Eds.), *Current issues in the philosophy of science.* New York: Holt, 1961.

Seaver, W. B. Effects of naturally induced teacher expectancies. *Journal of Personality and Social Psychology,* 1973, *28,* 333–342.

Seewald, A. M., Leinhardt, G., & Engel, M. *Learning what's taught: Sex differences in instruction.* Paper presented at the annual meeting of the American Educational Research Association, New York City, April 1977.

Shaw, M. E., & Wright, J. M. *Scales for the measurement of attitudes.* New York: McGraw-Hill, 1965.

Simon, A., & Boyer, E. G. (Eds.). *Mirrors for behavior* (14 vols.). Philadelphia: Research for Better Schools, 1967–1970.

Sommer, R. Toward a psychology of natural behavior. *APA Monitor,* 1977, *8*(1), 1; 7.

Stallings, J. *Training manual for classroom observation.* Menlo Park, Calif.: Stanford Research Institute, 1972.

Tukey, J. W. *Exploratory data analysis.* Reading, Mass.: Addison-Wesley, 1977.

Tukey, J. W., & Mosteller, F. *A second course in data analysis and regression in statistics.* Reading, Mass.: Addison-Wesley, 1977.

Wang, M. C., & Stiles, B. *An investigation of children's concept of self-responsibility for their school learning.* Pittsburgh: University of Pittsburgh, Learning Research and Development Center, 1975. (LRDC Publication, 1975/11)

Webb, E. J., Campbell, D. T., Schwartz, R. D., & Sechrest, L. *Unobtrusive measures: Nonreactive research in the social sciences.* Chicago: Rand McNally, 1968.

Weissberg, N. C. Methodology or substance: A response to Helmreich. *Personality and Social Psychology Bulletin,* 1976, *2,* 119–121.

Wiley, D. E., & Harnischfeger, A. Explosion of a myth: Quantity of schooling and exposure to instruction, major educational vehicles. *Educational Researcher,* 1974, *3*(4), 7–13.

5

The Classroom as Phenomenon

David F. Lancy
Ministry of Education, Papua New Guinea

To Husserl . . . [the] attempt to cope with psychological problems by means of experiments [is] like trying to unravel lace with a pitchfork.

(Spearman 1930)

Most of the research that might fall into a category labeled "social psychology of education" is atomistic in that only certain features of the classroom are singled out for study at any one time. Occasionally, the atoms are combined into molecules of the size of teacher-student relationships, but one rarely gets a glimpse of the larger entity, the classroom. Call it a "society," a "culture," or a "collective," by whatever name, one must recognize that the classroom is larger than the sum of its parts. In order to study classrooms, one must try to build a theory and methods that do justice to the *classroom*, while not obscuring its constituent features such as roles, personalities, and organizational structure. By treating the classroom as a phenomenon in its own right and by drawing on the theory and methods of phenomenology for inspiration, one can at least make a start.

Phenomenology has been variously characterized as a method, a philosophy, and a theory. Its wellsprings are found in the earliest writings of Edmund Husserl (1859-1938) (see especially Husserl, 1962). As a method, phenomenology has been most fully elaborated by the ethnomethodology school in sociology; as a philosophy by the French existentialist school; and as a theory, by the gestalt school and by the symbolic interactionist school of social psychology.

Inasmuch as Husserl's writings offer little guidance to a program of research in classrooms and inasmuch as each of the aforementioned schools offers useful ideas for some areas of inquiry and not others, a synthesis is needed. I am drawing on phenomenology and its offspring to create a *perspective*, a way of looking at classrooms that is part philosophy, part theory, and part methodology.

The first and the central tenet of phenomenology is that reality is *subjective*. It can only be known through some combination of perceptual processes. There is no recording instrument known, least of all the human recorder, that can capture a piece of reality with perfect fidelity; there will always be some distortion. That is

I would like to thank the editors and Hugh Mehan for their detailed and helpful comments on earlier drafts of this chapter. I have tried to respond to their numerous concerns, without being entirely successful.

not to say that science is invalid. Science as a way of recording and knowing about the world is merely one way of perceiving, although it has become quite popular in the last 200 years. Phenomenology and science are not incompatible, but in employing the phenomenological perspective, certain cherished tools of the scientist are abandoned or at least handled with caution. Thus, a researcher taking a phenomenological approach, avoids, as much as possible, the use of *assumptions* about the phenomenon under study; avoids *reducing* complex reality to a few "variables"; and minimizes the use of instruments that are *reactive* and that greatly influence the reality she or he is trying to study. In effect, such a researcher tries to approach the classroom with an open mind, to carry out investigations in which the conclusions are post hoc rather than a priori. Operating like the natural historian, the researcher observes, records, classifies and concludes, seeking, wherever possible, to capture the reality of the subjects and not only her or his own reality.

The second tenet of phenomenology is that reality, any reality, is constantly changing. This change process may be described as "progress," as "evolution," as "entropy," or in any number of ways, but the researcher who employs the phenomenological perspective will be aware of it. Subjective realities are therefore often studied comparatively and historically to determine the kind and rate of change that affects them.

The third tenet of the phenomenological perspective is that there is a need for openness. The phenomenological researcher is open to alternative constructions of reality; open to many possible "explanations" for observed phenomena, few of which, in the absence of hypotheses or assumptions, can be ruled out in advance of the study; and open to a variety of data from many sources because no specified set of research techniques follows from the method. Finally, the openness is demonstrated in the open-ended time frame in which change becomes part of the study rather than invalidates it.

Hence, the phenomenological perspective is ideal for studying phenomena that are patently complex and about which little is known with certainty. Phenomenology probably has very little to contribute to advancing atomistic theories, for instance. For simple phenomena, phenomenology captures too much; it is wasteful (e.g., a phenomenological study of hiccupping). For phenomena about which a great deal is known, it would again be wasteful to throw away the known, to start from scratch as a phenomenological study would do (e.g., a phenomenological study of maze learning in the Norway rat in which nothing is assumed about the effects of handling, reward, or punishment). The phenomenological researcher is, above all, opportunistic. By being on the scene, the researcher observes and collects incidents, artifacts, and quotations that illuminate the phenomena. For this reason, phenomenology is best employed in situations that have relatively confined temporal and physical boundaries.

The contemporary classroom fits all these criteria neatly. Its activities begin and end at a set time each day and, in most cases, are confined to a space about 40 feet square. That we know very little about classrooms is in no way belied by the enormous volume of empirical and prescriptive works on the subject. It is the one public service with which almost no one is satisfied, and presumably, if we knew a lot about it, we could at least keep some people happy some of the time.

The complexity of the classroom has been consistently underestimated by education researchers, particularly by social psychologists. Attempts have been made, without notable success, to employ, in classroom study, theoretical perspectives that had been developed in a less complex situation (Bar-Tal, 1976). To make a point about the complexity of the classroom, I turn to a brief and, I hope, instructive digression.

TWO MODELS OF EDUCATION

Although the focus of this chapter is on classrooms, one must, of necessity, examine the larger world of which they are a part. Philosophies of education obviously play a role in the investigation, although the reality projected by a given philosophy of education and the reality one observes in the classroom may be far apart. Imagine the contrasting reality of classrooms guided by the following two statements of educational philosophy: "I hold that the aim of life is to find happiness which means to find interest. Education should be a preparation for life (Neill, 1960). "Education? It's just a weapon whose effect depends on who controls it and whom he wishes to strike with it" (Stalin, quoted in Michener, 1957).

Glaser (1976) has isolated key features of educational philosophy, which are bound to have an impact on the dynamics of classroom practices. He presents five models, of increasing complexity, that represent aspects of the education process in classrooms. Each of the models is presented as a flow diagram depicting a variety of instructional activities. The diagrams have boxes for decisions that are made on, for, or by the student. Model I, for instance, has 7 boxes; Model 5 has 17 (see Glaser, 1976, p. 41–48). I am taking Glaser's simplest and most complex models to their logical extremes to make a point about classroom realities.

The simplest model has two components, the teaching establishment and the pupil. The teaching establishment has three functions, a custodial function (it must house the education process and provide various amenities for physical comfort), a teaching function, and an assessment function. The pupil component has one function, to adapt to the functions of the teaching establishment. The pupil must adhere to the conventions imposed by housing, teaching, and testing. If the pupil fails to do this he or she is removed from the classroom and formal education for that person ceases. Assuming that the pupil manages to stay in step with the system for some fixed number of years, the pupil will "graduate"; his or her educational *career* is considered a success.

Several points can be made about this model classroom. First, it will be highly resistant to change, for it is a closed system. The only inputs to it that do change are the pupils, but they are treated as *tabulae rasae*, incapable of making any contribution to the education process. The reality of the classroom is as the teaching establishment defines it, typically an intransigent environment. Second, although it is recognized that no classroom actually looks like the model, some look more like it than others; classrooms of 100 years ago looked more like it than the classrooms of today. Third, despite the fact that the model is an inaccurate reflection of contemporary schools, many individuals doing educational research base their programs of research on this model.

Research in education has consistently assumed that the definition of reality as given by teachers is the reality of the classroom, and teachers have assumed that what children bring with them to the classroom (their culture, if you will) has little or no effect on what they do there. They have assumed that the main and only outcome of importance from the classroom experience is success or failure in academic tests, and they have assumed that this success or failure is largely a function of inherent and fixed characteristics of the pupil (i.e., sex, IQ, and race). Most of these assumptions, and others like them, are supportable only when a classroom faithfully duplicates this simple model. When it does not, and this is increasingly the case, then all such assumptions are premature.

As long as the teaching establishment could control access to the classroom via IQ tests and by language and class barriers, the static model I described here could be held intact. As long as the majority of pupils who could not or would not adapt to the functions of the teaching establishment were kept out of the system, it never had to face the challenge to its principles that this influx would eventually bring about. Universal, compulsory education was a watershed. It is impossible to estimate how many educational philosophies are ascendent in the United States today, and one must accept the fact that, inasmuch as no classroom faithfully copies the philosophy that spawned it, the number of possible classroom configurations must be approaching infinity. At the same time, one must be careful to recognize that the specter of this simple model haunts even the most "open" of classrooms. Hence, to paraphrase Cooley:

A classroom is like all other classrooms.
A classroom is like some other classrooms.
A classroom is like no other classroom.

Because of the importance of a historical perspective to their work, phenomenologists are in a position to evaluate whether what is claimed to be new and different in the classroom is just new wine in an old bottle. But let us look at the potential impact of a more complex model, drawing heavily on Glaser's (1976) conception.

The teaching establishment has now grown in size and become much more differentiated. It includes teachers, administrators, counselors, coaches, nurses, and curriculum specialists, many of whom add new functions. The pupil's physical and mental being is the focus of much greater attention and care. Teachers continue to teach, but they also tutor, diagnose, and remedy. There are still textbooks, but there are also cassette recorders, minicalculators, magazines, films, computers, posters, puppet theaters, and educational games. Pupils are no longer assumed to be empty vessels; they are now assumed to have initial competence, talents, aptitudes, and a cultural heritage. They make choices about what they will study, when, and through what media. They must still adapt to classroom conventions, but in "democratic" classrooms, they may participate in creating those conventions.

Children may still fail, but if they do, they are not necessarily forced out of the classroom. They may receive remedial instruction; they may retake tests after some further practice; and they may change majors. Most important, in the completely *individualized classroom,* each child operates autonomously from every other child. Instead of all pupils learning (or attempting to learn) the same material at the same rate at the same time, all these features are free to vary. Unlike the simple model, here the teaching establishment must change to meet the needs of pupils. Finally, an implicit feature of this model is that education is now open to scientific inquiry and manipulation. This inevitably means that classroom changes will be more frequent because the scientific perspective on reality, as contrasted with many other perspectives, sees change as necessary and desirable. Again, one cannot assume that any actual classroom looks exactly like this model, for some look more like it than others, but it describes contemporary classrooms better than those of 100 years ago.

I have deliberately chosen two extreme models in order to highlight the variation that exists from one classroom to another. We are not yet in a position to atomize the classroom into some set of constituent variables because we do not yet know enough about the reality of classrooms. One would not like to carry out research in a theoretical vacuum, nevertheless, particularly if one wants to discover some classroom universals, or characteristics that are found regardless of the model of education that motivates a particular classroom. One needs some organizing concepts, but these should be as free of assumptions and as open to modification on the basis of experience in the field as possible. Phenomenology and its intellectual descendants offer such concepts.

THE SOCIAL CONSTRUCTION OF CLASSROOM REALITY

Classrooms are complex and likely to become more so. In this section, I introduce some concepts that will begin to reduce this complexity. I start with some of the few knowns of the classroom—universal features of reality that all classrooms share.

If reality is subjective, it must be created by individual *actors* whose perceptions, in turn, are influenced by relatively permanent features of the environment called *rules* and *situations.* Actors are the human participants, the "subjects" of our study and, in the classroom, include, at a minimum, a teacher and some pupils. Rules may be glossed as "laws," "norms," "customs," or "standards." Rules are prescriptions for the behavior of actors (e.g., a pupil may not speak until called on). Situations consist of encounters between actors that are governed by rules. They are patterned in conspicuous ways and may even be named, such as the "conversation," the "math lesson," and the "pledge of allegiance." More than 25 years ago, Cottrell (1950) claimed that the study of situations was seriously neglected by social psychologists. It still is.

From the phenomenological perspective, some features of actors, rules, and situations are of greater concern than others. These features are important because they contribute to an understanding of the social construction of reality but also because they are so often neglected by researchers employing other perspectives. One feature of human actors as active agents is that they do not simply respond to stimuli; by their attention and their actions, they create the stimuli in their environment. Confronted with a situation, human actors first must define what that situation means to them. Then they check their definitions against the emerging definitions of other actors who are party to the same situation. This process of definition is seen in the continual interplay between the teacher and pupils over what can be got away with. In contrast to other kinds of researchers, the phenomenologist looks with scepticism on the idea that pupils are "socialized" in the school. It is not that pupils do not change as a result of their classroom experiences, but the socialization concept implies that children are moved passively toward some ultimate goal.

Each situation is not of course defined from the ground up. Individuals carry in their heads ready-made definitions collected together in what some have called a "cognitive map" (e.g., Kaplan, 1973). Via what Garfinkel (1967) has called "common understandings," these maps tend to become quite similar for any group of people who habitually confront the same situations. One cognitive map that is built out of common understandings is the domain of "subjects." Pupils possess a shared conception of the attributes of subjects, their temporal and spatial loci, their degree of difficulty, the pattern of classroom activities associated with each subject, and so on. What is important to point out here is that situations are never defined once and for all, nor are common understandings ever perfect. In any situation, no matter how commonplace, people make subtle adjustments to their perceptions and actions based on feedback from the situation, and vice versa, situations are subtly changed with each new encounter.

A second characteristic of actors that should be of concern is that they are *naive psychologists* (Heider, 1958). In interaction, it is not enough to know what the other person is doing; one would also like to know what motivates these actions. Human beings analyze the overt behavior and physical properties of others and make attributions about such things as mood, intelligence, and intentions. The actor as naive psychologist is nowhere more in evidence than in the classroom. Teachers constantly make attributions about their charges (e.g., that child's home-life is terrible), yet researchers usually dismiss these judgments as "biased." Instead, these attributions are central to the phenomenology of classrooms.

Third, actors have *careers.* In order to understand how actors perceive and are perceived, one needs to know something about their life histories. The teacher's statement that a child's homelife is terrible indicates that the pupil in question brings into the classroom some identifying characteristics that were achieved outside the classroom and at some earlier time point. Individuals' histories are important for understanding individuals' cognitive maps of the world as well as for understanding the judgments that others make about individuals. Another aspect of career and, perhaps, a more important one inasmuch as it is often neglected, is its quality of being "in the making." Actors all carry around their concepts of self, and although these do change, they also have a basic stability that gives rise to the idea of a career. One thinks of adults having business careers, but the term *career* encompasses much more than a job; it is possible to speak of pupils' careers as well. Pupils, too, are concerned about managing the impressions that others have of them and of changing their situations to better fit their careers. A big question that I take up later is how teachers, in the process of managing their own careers, also manage or shape the careers of pupils.

Many observers of the education scene have remarked on the number and apparent absurdity of classroom rules, and no account of life in the classroom is complete without a description of its explicit rule system. Two features of classroom rules warrant special attention. First, rule use is flexible; with each shift of actor, the rule is applied somewhat differently or may be suspended entirely. What action a teacher takes when a pupil is "late" will depend on who the pupil is, how late the pupil is, what the weather is like, etc. (cf. Stebbins, 1975). Second, rules arise from situations. Only a tiny fraction of the rules that govern an actor's behavior are ever written down; rather, they must be inferred from features of the situation (e.g., the placement of the teacher's desk vis-á-vis the pupils' desks).

Situations normally have physical features, or what Goffman (1959) has called "props." Classroom situations make use of desks, blackboards, books, etc. These objects are not simply neutral parts of the situation; through their patterned employment, they take on meaning and can be powerful agents in shaping situations. Consider, for instance, the importance of the wall clock to life in the classroom. The objects of the classroom and the behavior to which they are related together make up what Barker and Wright (1951) have called the "psychological habitat."

The goal of the phenomenological investigator, then, is to study some of the salient features of actors, rules, and situations in the classroom setting. Others, of course, have studied these before. What distinguishes the phenomenological perspective is that it separates actors, rules, and situations only for purposes of analysis. None of these three entities ever operates in isolation from the others, for "actors, rules and situations ceaselessly inform one another" (Mehan & Wood, 1975, p. 75).

From the phenomenological perspective, one should look at what lies behind social variables and at the nonmathematical relationships between variables. *Sex,* for example, is a characteristic of most actors, but unlike gender, it is not a fixed attribute but an *accomplishment* (Garfinkel, 1967). It is part of the actor's career, a part of the self that must be managed in front of others. Rather than treating sex as a category to be ticked off on a questionnaire or entered as a variable in a computer-run calculation, the phenomenologist is interested in determining such things as how sex as an attribute is displayed in classrooms, what part actors' self-concepts of sex plays in their careers, the extent to which the actor's sex plays a role in shaping classroom situations, and the extent to which rule application varies with the sex of actors.

The social construction of reality is possible because human beings *communicate.* They talk to each other; they gesture; they listen; they hear; they write; they draw pictures. Their bodies respond appropriately to the signals of chairs, doorways, windows, and bells. In the process of interaction, human beings imbue their entire environment with meanings. These meanings become shared or commonly understood. The objective of a phenomenological study, then, is to discover these meanings and describe the communication processes that create them. The data are human words and movements as responses to other words, movements, and things.

PARTICIPANT OBSERVATION IN THE CLASSROOM

This classroom research enterprise is most easily characterized as a *field study,* and an excellent introduction to this method, for the social psychologist, has been written by Katz (1953). Nevertheless I want to review here the methods and techniques that are most compatible with the phenomenological perspective. The research goal should at all times be "as naive and full a description of direct experience as possible" (Koffka, 1935 p. 73). No matter what language (e.g., prose, graphs, numbers, photographs) is used for description, it is important to strive for completeness and accuracy. Descriptions should be based largely on observations. The primary role of the researcher is *participant observation,* which Diesing (1971) has defined succinctly: "It is a process of waiting to be impressed by recurrent themes that reappear in various contexts" (p. 145) and at greater length:

> The participant observer method involves taking data as they come, and they usually come in scattered, disconnected fragments. Unlike the experimentalist, who can demand evidence on a specific question from his subject matter, the participant observer must adapt his thinking to what his subject happens to be doing. He has to observe each casual interchange as it happens, participate in the ceremony of the day since it may not occur again for two

years, talk to the informants who are available, and get involved in whatever problems and controversies are prominent at the moment. At the end of the day he comes home with a wealth of information on a variety of points, but nothing conclusive on any one point. Over the weeks and months his evidence on a given point gradually accumulates and the various points start to fit together into a tentative pattern. But there are always pieces of evidence missing, because the occasion for them did not occur. There are always themes whose meaning remains unclear or ambiguous and alternative interpretations and patterns that cannot be conclusively rejected. The researcher gradually becomes more active and tries to fill in the gaps, but he never quite finishes. (pp. 164–165)

Perhaps the hardest part of the enterprise comes at the beginning when researchers try to compromise between full access to the life of classrooms and influencing that phenomenon once they have gained access to it. Having resolved this difficulty (and each classroom will demand a different role for the participant observer so that no prescriptions are possible) researchers must begin to focus their observations. The first things to be observed and described are the things present in the room, such as the furniture, the decoration, the instructional materials. Here, participant observers function much like archaeologists, trying to make sense out of whatever material artifacts they can find. Next, behavior must be observed, and here the emphasis should be on recording what is said. Not only is verbal behavior easier to record than nonverbal behavior; it also is often easier to discover underlying meanings or implicit rules from talk than from actions. What pupils are not permitted to do may only be revealed in their talk.

At one extreme, participant observers are actively present in the classrooms, writing up descriptions only after leaving the room. At the other extreme, the observers may never enter the classrooms but instead use a remote-controlled video tape recorder to "observe" the classrooms. The former procedure is more likely to distort classroom reality; the latter is more likely to lead to the problem of *data flood* (see chap. 4 in this volume).

By the time the process of observing and recording is well underway, the researchers should have already begun to structure the data. The observers put names on things, ideally, names the actors themselves use. For example, the terms that actors use to describe various parts of the room reveal its psychological habitats, and "the short little girl with pigtails" in the researcher's notes becomes "Beth Ann." Naming is the first step in the process of classification. It can be presumed that all those things that have the same name *are* the same, so that, when there are two or more of them, researchers can henceforth describe the class by describing one. There are a variety of possibilities for reducing and structuring by developing typologies. Pupils may be classified as troublemakers, cool kids, brains, and so forth (cf. Davis, 1972). Time segments may be classified as classes, breaks, or study periods; situations, as playing with stuff, bugging someone, doing a lesson, getting your folder, and the like (cf. Lancy, 1976a).

Participant observation starts out in an unstructured, unfocused, and informal vein, but the researchers gradually narrow the field of inquiry and use more powerful techniques to gain information. The most straightforward means of systematizing observation is to count things. How many pupils are in the classroom? At what time of the day? The discovery that pupils spend an inordinate portion of their time in the classroom simply *waiting* (Jackson, 1968) comes as a shock and a revelation. One can combine a tally system with the emergent classification systems with informative results. How much time do "brains" spend at their desks as opposed to "troublemakers"?

The general aim is to describe the classroom setting so that the kinds of actors, rules, and situations are revealed. By recording and analyzing the communication patterns among individuals and things, one can begin to convey how reality gets constructed and how aspects of the classroom take on enduring meaning for the participants. As indicated earlier, however, particular features of actors, rules, and situations deserve attention.

SOME TECHNIQUES FOR CLASSROOM RESEARCH

I have said that the phenomenologist must be opportunistic and, following Diesing (1971), wait to be "impressed by recurrent themes." Investigators have a number of means at their disposal to eke out these themes or to follow up on suggestive leads. They must go beyond participant observation to probe more deeply into classroom reality, and to do so, they can employ some useful techniques for gaining an understanding of classroom actors and their careers, classroom situations, and the rules that operate in them.

With the objective of coming to understand the subjective reality of the classroom, one goal should be to discover how the actors themselves define what goes on, especially their own roles. Contrast the following definitions of the classroom situation by two teachers:

> If a teacher has a well-modulated voice and a pleasing disposition her children are more relaxed and quiet. Children are like kittens: if kittens have a full stomach and lie in the sun they purr. If the atmosphere is such that the children are more comfortable, they are quiet. (quoted in Henry, 1966, p. 311)

> You can't let them get the upper hand on you or you're through. So I start out tough. The first day I get a new class in, I let them know who's boss. (quoted in Becker, 1952, p. 459)

For both teachers, getting their children to act in a docile manner is a desirable end, but the apparent means to that end are strikingly different in the two cases. Both of these remarks were made in the course of open-ended interviews, but researchers can also discover teachers' definitions of classroom situations from their talk in the classroom and from their conversations with other teachers in the hallways and teachers' lounge of the school.

The cognitive maps of actors can also be uncovered in open-ended interviewing. Spradley and McCurdy (1972) have written an excellent guide to the interviewing strategies one can employ, in which they include several samples of cognitive maps drawn from their own work and that of their students. One of their students (Parott, 1972) interviewed second-grade pupils to discover their cognitive map of recess. Pupils named 31 activities that could take place during recess, and these were divided into three categories: games, goofing around, and tricks. Each of the categories was distinguished from the others on the basis of certain attributes, for example, whether the activity involved competition, had a goal, or required teams.

Two assumptions are built into this kind of inquiry: (1) that the actor's definition of the situation resembles a treelike or taxonomic structure and (2) that this structure will be shared by some homogeneous group of actors, like second-grade pupils. In fact, this may not always be the case. Lancy (1977) found that intermediate-grade pupils do not hold a shared cognitive map of the domain of pupils. In interviews, Lancy discovered that pupils had few names for types of pupils and, of these, there was little agreement on what the attributes of any given type were or on how a decision might be made to typecast any particular pupil.

When researchers can establish the cognitive maps that actors use to classify other actors, they will be a long way toward understanding the naive psychology operating in the classroom. A discussion of the attributes that pupils use to distinguish "brains" from "troublemakers" from "cool kids" should shed light on the way actors use inferred characteristics of others to form judgments. Even in the absence of anything so complete as a cognitive map, researchers can, via content analysis, learn about actors as naive psychologists from the transcripts of interviews and recorded conversations. The two teachers quoted earlier clearly differ in their assessment of the nature of pupils. One teacher probably sees pupils as essentially well behaved; they misbehave only when something perturbs the situation causing them to be uncomfortable. The second teacher sees pupils as essentially misbehaved; good behavior is the residue after all misbehavior has been suppressed.

The study of classroom actors' careers is of course quite difficult, requiring a relatively long period of contact with each single subject. The most complete career study to date has been done by Harry F. Wolcott (1974) on an elementary school principal. Several days a week, for a period of 2 years, Wolcott shadowed a single principal, in the school, at home, at meetings, wherever he went. He took notes on the behavior of the principal and his location; recorded what he said, who he talked to, and who did the talking; interviewed him about his philosophy and his opinions; collected all of the school's official notices and other written records; and conducted a time-and-motion study on the principal. In addition, he interviewed members of the principal's family and the school staff. Wolcott did all this because, after a review of the enormous literature on principals and school administrators, he came to the conclusion that most of it was useless for understanding any given principal as a real actor in a real school. It was useless because it consisted of (a) prescriptive works—recipes for what a principal *should* do, (b) reports that contained "factual data which tells us too little about too many" (Wolcott, 1977, p. 346) such as the average age or average number of years of teaching experience of principals, and (c) survey results that were totally uninterpretable because of the absence of prior fieldwork and description. These same criticisms can be leveled against the accumulated literature on teachers and pupils. Studies of the careers of classroom actors are long overdue.

If investigators have the good fortune to begin their studies on the first day of school, they will be treated to a full display of the formal rule system of the classroom. Discovering how these rules are applied, and the informal rules as well, will, however, take a bit more work. Mehan (1974), working with video tape records, carried out a thorough analysis of the teacher's application of rules in a typical lesson. Despite the fact that the teacher gave the pupils a set of instructions (i.e., rules) prior to the lesson and was able to give Mehan a coherent description (during pre- and postlesson interviews) of the rules she would apply, she did not adhere to these rules during the lesson and was apparently unaware of her deviation. One rule stated that, for a pupil's response to be judged correct by the teacher, it would have to be expressed in a complete sentence. As the teacher queried pupils, she indicated by word and action whether the response was acceptable. Mehan observed that she rejected logically correct responses that were not in complete sentences, but she also *accepted* responses that were logically correct but were not complete sentences. He concluded:

> Rule use in a social situation is an interpretive process. The "correctness" rule had to be interpreted against a constantly changing background of features of the setting which might include the child's behavior, the teacher's expectations, the question structure. Because the rule cannot anticipate those background features, the formal statement of the rule is incomplete. (pp. 124–125)

Lancy (1977) found a somewhat unusual source of classroom rules and, incidentally, evidence of differential deviation by sex: fifth graders' New Year's resolutions. The pupils were asked by the teacher each to write a resolution on a piece of construction paper, to print their names underneath, and to pin the resolutions to the bulletin board. Lancy retrieved the resolutions when they were taken down a month later. Here are the samples of the girls' New Year's resolutions:

I resolve to brush my teeth four times a day. (several of these)
I resolve to stop biting my nails. (several)
I resolve to do better in my math and reading.
I resolve to do better in my school work.
I resolve to stop fighting with my brother.

The boys' New Year's resolutions were different:

I resolve to stop talking. (several of these)
I resolve not to get any sentences. (as punishment)
I resolve to do my work and quit fooling around. (several)
I resolve not to play games before I am done with my work.
I resolve I shall not bug Thy [sic] teacher.

Another good opening for investigators is the arrival, in the middle of the school year, of a "new kid." Many conventions previously hidden from view will surface at this time. In general, however, studying classroom rules and their application requires researchers to collect data from many sources and constantly to compare what actors say with what they do.

Classroom situations are often anchored in objects or locations (e.g., the play corner), and part of the researchers' task is to locate these anchors. Lancy (1976c) found that a filing cabinet that contained cassette tapes for spelling drill and was located in a hallway served as such an anchor. Pupils could safely linger and chat or watch traffic in the hallway as long as they were "in the process" of finding or putting away a tape.

Researchers have a variety of means to describe the more permanent features of classroom situations. Diagrams of the room with furniture appropriately marked are useful. Counts can be made of the things one usually finds in the room. These data can be combined with other observations to give meaning to the classroom environment. Adams (1970) created a planar grid of the classroom and then took frequency counts of pupils' responses in each square of the grid. He showed by this method that responses came overwhelmingly from the grid squares just in front of the teacher's desk.

In describing and classifying the various features of classroom reality, researchers move, inexorably, toward a *model* of the classroom. Initially, of course, it is a model of *the* classroom, but by judicious comparison, a more general model may be achieved. One thing is important to point out here. Although the task appears difficult, given the many strictures the phenomenological perspective requires, teachers and pupils *do* accomplish it every day in millions of classrooms throughout the world. Teachers and pupils are thrown together some time around Labor Day every year and are told, in effect, to "make this room a classroom," and they do it with apparent ease. They create a model of the classroom.

TESTING THE MODEL

When social scientists use models, they sometimes contain variables that stand in some mathematical (or quantifiable) relationship to each other. These mathematical models are very useful for testing propositions contained in the model. From the phenomenological point of view, however, they are unsatisfactory. In describing classroom features mathematically, their meaning for classroom actors may be seriously distorted. Many investigators have taken up the study of a feature of pupils' careers called "success." Unfortunately, most such studies have assumed that success is reflected solely through test results and grades, both of which are easily quantified. Phenomenologists would argue that many aspects of success are not quantifiable and that many so-called objective measures of success are trivial.

There are, then, serious, but not insurmountable, problems in testing the model. The most basic kind of test to employ is to collect data on the same phenomena using a variety of different instruments. In Lancy's (1976a) study of intermediate-grade pupils, he found that an important aspect of school life for pupils was something they called "activities" (see Figure 5-1). He tape-recorded conversations among pupils, and these conversations revealed the salience of the activities domain and also yielded some names for activities. Open-ended interviews with a few pupils added some names and definitions for the named activities. A taxonomy showing the relationships among categories of activities was developed. To test whether this cognitive map was an accurate reflection of pupils' actual behavior, Lancy constructed a behavior observation scale with categories drawn from the taxonomy. He found that the taxonomy did indeed describe behavior. Pupils performed, at some time, all the activities listed in the taxonomy, and they never performed any activity not included in the taxonomy.

To test whether the cognitive map formed part of the common understanding of pupils, an instrument was constructed using 25 phrases containing activity terms. Each phrase was paired with every other phrase, and all 80 fourth- and fifth-grade pupils from the school were asked to judge (on a 5-point scale) the degree of similarity of each pair. These data were then analyzed with a clustering program that rearranges similarity distributions into a tree structure. This structure was compared to the taxonomy elicited from pupils in interviews and was found to be a

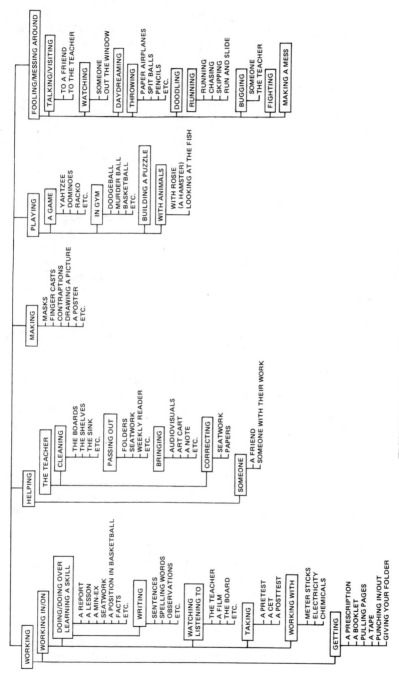

FIGURE 5-1 The elicited taxonomy of activities.

very close approximation. The data were also analyzed with a multidimensional scaling program to test whether there was more than one "solution" to the distribution of judgments. There was found to be only one solution, indicating that all pupils view the activities domain in much the same way, or that the cognitive map is shared by the group as a whole.

The model can also be tested by exposing it to the scrutiny of actors. The comments of teachers and pupils can be invaluable in correcting the model or in pointing out discrepancies between what actors do and what they think they do. Various kinds of comparisons are possible. Jackson (1968) was able to clarify some of his findings about life in classrooms by making comparisons with other settings: the church, the factory, and the home. These kinds of comparisons, as well as more conventional cross-classroom comparisons, allow one to distinguish features that are true for *the* classroom versus *a* classroom.

Finally, there are two tests to discuss that, in many ways, grow directly out of the phenomenological perspective. These are "passing" and "breaching" (Diesing, 1971; Mehan & Wood, 1975). In the literal sense, *passing* occurs when investigators have sufficient confidence in their understanding of the classroom setting to attempt to play actors' roles. Passing as a pupil would be difficult for the average researcher, although it might be attempted in a high school. Passing as a teacher should be easier and a very useful exercise for classroom researchers who have begun to construct a model. Investigators can, for example, volunteer to substitute when regular teachers are ill. The test of the model will be in how much perturbation in normal routines occurs during the substitution. If opportunities to play a full actor's role are not available, investigators can still be very conscious of how their behavior affects others and use these reactions to modify the model where appropriate.

Researchers can also consciously attempt to create a perturbation through *breaching*. Here, investigators deliberately violate what they think is a rule, or violate some common understanding, or call attention to some feature of an actor's appearance or behavior that is normally not employed in that particular situation. Harold Garfinkel (1967) must be credited with the invention of the breaching experiment, and I quote from two of the many he described:

> Students were instructed to engage an acquaintance or a friend in an ordinary conversation, and, without indicating that what the experimenter was asking was in any way unusual, to insist that the person clarify the sense of his commonplace remarks. . . .
> The victim cheerily waved his hand.
> (S) How are you?
> (E) How am I in regard to what? My health, my finances, my school work, my peace of mind, my . . . ?
> (S) (Red in the face and suddenly out of control) LOOK! I was just trying to be polite. Frankly I don't give a damn how you are. (pp. 42–44)

> In another procedure students were asked to spend from fifteen minutes to an hour in their homes imagining they were boarders and acting out this assumption. . . .
> In . . . four-fifths of the cases family members were stupefied. They vigorously sought to make the strange actions intelligible and to restore the

situation to normal appearances. . . . One student acutely embarrassed his mother in front of her friends by asking if she minded if he had a snack from the refrigerator. "Mind if you have a snack? You've been eating little snacks around here for years without asking me. What's getting into you?" (pp. 47–48)

Breaching reveals the common understandings that contribute to the maintenance of situations and also reveals the actor as naive psychologist. Many of the subjects in Garfinkel's experiments said or implied that they thought the experimenters were acting out of malice, were sick, or wanted something. For them, the abnormal behavior had to have a root cause.

In the final analysis, no created model can ever represent a perfect picture of classroom reality. It is bound to distort that reality because the model has been put together by a biased observer (every observer is biased) and because it is fixed in time, whereas classroom reality continues to change. All researchers can do is strive to improve the fit between the model and the reality.

THE PUPIL'S CAREER

Classroom studies that employ the phenomenological perspective are very scarce. Those investigators that have used this approach have tended to focus rather narrowly on one or another classroom phenomenon; hence, no single piece of literature offers a complete model of the classroom. In this section, therefore, I review a series of studies, all of which contribute something to the understanding of the pupil's career. Because the pupil is the raison d'être of the classroom, this review should contribute to a model of the classroom.

Although they do not have a complete monopoly on pupils' careers, teachers, by virtue of their vested authority, have considerable influence. Stebbins (1975) carried out a study in which he observed and recorded teacher-pupil interaction situations in 70 classrooms, then interviewed the teachers to elicit their definitions of them. He found that teachers shared a cognitive map of pupils delineated by the following dimensions: deportment (attentiveness and orderliness), academic performance, socioeconomic status, shyness, activeness, and tardiness.

By placing pupils on a scale in which each of these dimensions is employed, teachers can "understand" and "cope with" them. They actively work toward improving a pupils' behavior on all but the socioeconomic status dimension. The pupils improve by becoming more attentive and orderly, by getting better marks, by becoming less shy and more (or less) active, and by arriving on time more often. A teacher might decide that a pupil will not make any improvement on any one or all of these dimensions (and is still far from ideal), in which case the teacher could use tactics (principally ignoring the pupil) to isolate him or her so that he or she would not have an adverse effect on the others.

In channeling the pupils' careers teachers may base their actions on implicit predictions of each pupil's likelihood of improvement. These judgments are formed from observing pupils in a variety of classroom situations. One such situation that provides conspicuous milestones in pupils' careers is test taking. Tests are assumed to measure pupils' competence (either real or potential). The success of pupils' careers is built on the supposedly objective results from the tests they have taken. In a series of studies, Mehan (1973, 1974) and others have seriously undermined the assumption of objectivity in academic tests.

Mehan (1973) video-taped the administration of individualized language-development tests to a class of 23 first graders. After hearing a question read by the tester, a child was required to point to one among several pictures, only one of which demonstrates the correct answer. He found that testers "interpreted" a large number of answers, especially in situations in which children placed their fingers between two pictures, answered correctly before they had heard the entire question, or changed their responses. There was, furthermore, no evidence that these gray areas were governed by some hard and fast rule such as "score the first answer only." The many opportunities for a tester to interpret children's answers does serious damage to the claim of objectivity.

Well-known and respected self-administered tests fare no better. In a study of elementary schools carried out by Cicourel, Jennings, Jennings, Leiter, Mackay, Mehan, and Roth (1974), the investigators considered various aspects of the testing situation. For instance, after taking the California Reading Test, children were interviewed and asked to explain each of their answers. The format of the test is a series of items with a word or sentence printed on the left and three simple pictures to the right of the word or sentence. A child must cross off the picture that best represents the meaning of the word or sentence. In one case a child explained that he checked the picture of the elephant to the word *fly* (wrong answer) because the elephant was "Dumbo." In another case, a child who had done very poorly on another self-administered reading test (the Peabody) was questioned at length about the test items. He demonstrated the appropriate patterns of logical reasoning but, because words and pictures had different meanings for him than they did for the test constructor, he got many answers wrong. The testing situation, crucial to the careers of pupils, is controlled entirely by adults, whose world views are quite different from those of children. Cicourel et al. (1974) have demonstrated that objective tests, as presently constructed, cannot be seen as infallibly measuring the academic accomplishments of pupils.

Even if these tests did take into account the perceptions of pupils, pupils' careers would still be influenced by the well-meaning though subjective judgments of adult classroom actors. Shumsky and Mehan (1973) recorded an elementary school faculty meeting, called by the principal to determine which children should be promoted and which ones should be placed in a "special" classroom:

Principal:	And Mrs. Neal, do you have kids that you don't think should go on to second grade?
Mrs. Neal:	Well, Mike Brandon for one.
Mrs. Susan:	He's on my list.
Mrs. Neal:	Oh, he's on your list?
Mrs. Jones:	Did he take the reading test?
Mrs. Susan:	Yeah.
Mrs. Jones:	How'd did he do?
Mrs. Susan:	Wait a minute, I've got it here (pause). I think he did OK, yeah, oh he got a 1.7.
Mrs. Pollen:	That's good.
Mrs. Neal:	Yeah, but I was surprised by that. He can't read that good. He must have guessed a lot. I still have him in the Blue-birds (slow reading group).
Mrs. Jones:	I'm questioning Irene too.

Mrs. Neal: I don't think she's got it kid, I don't think she'll ever do any good.

Mrs. Sanction: I think three, not necessarily retained, but three that need mothers.
                (p. 5)

It is probably not an exaggeration to suggest that the careers of Mike, Irene, and other children placed in the special class will be profoundly affected. These discussions, however, are based on teachers' subjective impressions and are arrived at in a manner that could hardly be called logical or rigorous. Actually, most of the children were placed in the special class without any discussion at all. The principal and other teachers were perfectly willing to rely on the judgment of teachers who supplied lists of the children they thought should be put in special classes. How teachers form impressions of children's competence deserves a chapter by itself, but Mackay (1974) studied the teacher's assessment of children's competence in classroom lessons. He analyzed video tapes of teacher-child interactions and concluded:

> The teacher thus treats the child as empty of knowledge (i.e., correct answers) and moves him from this state of emptiness to a state of fullness (i.e. knowledge), a process she accomplishes by asking questions and reformulating them until the child gives the "correct" answer. In some instances the teacher not only asks the questions but also finally *gives* the "correct" answers. Instruction is the occasion for adults to exercise their preference for a certain meaning of the world for the child. (pp. 185–186)

In testing and in teaching situations, children's competence is measured by their success at choosing or producing answers deemed correct by adult actors. Pupils' rates of success can also be raised or lowered through the discretionary actions of these adults. Teachers can ignore correct answers or they can respond to incorrect answers by reformulating the questions until pupils respond correctly. Teaching and learning, far from being complementary activities, are often in direct conflict.

Hodgkinson (1967) observed a spelling baseball game that was supposed to improve pupils' spelling abilities. Afterwards he asked pupils to write down everything they had learned from the game. They gave a variety of answers, but *none* mentioned spelling, and in a test administered the following day, the pupils showed no improvement over their previous performance. "Clearly what the teacher thought she was teaching and what the students were actually learning were two different things" (p. 75). Teachers create academic rationales for teaching activities that may in fact contribute nothing to the stated goals of learning.

Carlson (1965) found that, when teaching machines were introduced in the school to individualize instruction, teachers gave slower learners extra materials and allowed them to do additional work at home. This had the effect of keeping all the children at the same place in the lesson. Teachers apparently judge their own effectiveness on the basis of how far along in the course the class is at a given time point. Under individualization, pupils are on different lessons at the same time, making it more difficult for teachers to compare their performances with those of their peers and with their own past efforts.

Even in situations in which pupils are encouraged to make original contributions, the timing and form of them is closely controlled. Bremme and Erickson (1977) carried out a video tape analysis of a teacher-pupil activity called "First Circle," in which 24 children and their teacher sit on the rug for about 15 minutes in the morning to discuss things and plan for the day. The authors found a subtle distinction between "teachers' time" and "students' time." There is no formal designation of these time periods, but pupils and teachers "know" which is which and act accordingly. Specifically, if pupils want to say something during teacher time, they have to chime in with it because, if they address the teacher or raise their hands, they will be ignored. Conversely, if they want to say something during students' time, they must raise their hands or address the teacher. There are also conventions on what may be said during the two times. These rules are entirely informal, and they are reinforced by the pupils as well as the teacher by attending or ignoring appropriate or inappropriate behaviors.

What these studies demonstrate is that there are at least three realities of the classroom. There is the teacher's view of reality, which predominates, because it is the teacher who defines situations (or redefines them, as in the individualization project). The pupil's view of reality is quite different from the teacher's view, and it is discussed at length later. A third reality is the reality that education is an objective, even scientific, enterprise that efficiently leads children to greater knowledge and skill. This is the official reality, but it is probably less important than the other two realities in governing pupils' careers.

I now turn to how it is that teachers' views come to dominate the classroom. Few studies have been done that document the teacher's career, but one common thread occurs. That is that teachers are subject to a great deal of peer pressure to conform very closely to group norms. Willower (1969) studied teachers in a large junior high school and found that the paramount topic of teachers' conversation was discipline. Teachers who appeared to be lax disciplinarians were severely ostracized by their peers. Even teachers who were not very "tough" in the classroom talked tough in the teachers' lounge and took special pains to keep their pupils in order during assemblies and other "public" gatherings where their classes were on display.

Teachers maintain a monopoly on the definition of classroom situations by virtue of the common understandings they share and by the assiduous management of impressions. Goffman (1959) developed a *dramaturgical model* for impression management, and his general description of its organization can apply very well to teachers:

> Within the walls of a social establishment we find a team of performers who co-operate to present to an audience a given definition of the situation. This will include the conception of own team and of audience and assumptions concerning the ethos that is to be maintained by rules of politeness and decorum. We often find a division into back region and a front region where the performance is presented. Access to these regions is controlled in order to prevent the audience from seeing backstage and to prevent outsiders from coming into a performance that is not addressed to them. Among members of the team we find that familiarity prevails, solidarity is likely to develop, and that secrets which could give the show away are shared and kept. A tacit agreement is maintained between performers and audience to act as if a given degree of opposition and of accord existed between them. Typically, but not always, agreement is stressed and opposition is underplayed. The resulting working consensus tends to be contradicted by the attitude towards the audience which the performers express in the absence of the audience and by carefully controlled communication out of character conveyed by the performers while the audience is present. (p. 238)

The "front region" is of course the classroom; the "back region," the teachers' lounge. The teacher's career is that of "performer"; the pupils', that of "audience." King (1973) provides further insights into the dramaturgical nature of classrooms.

There are occasions when pupils are permitted to play more than a passive role. Some classroom situations are left sufficiently ill-defined so that they are open to exploitation by the pupils. Lancy (1976b) studied intermediate-grade pupils' activities in an experimental science class. There were a variety of prepared activities in the course, such as lessons to be read and experiments to be carried out, but there was one activity that was left largely undefined. This was the student-initiated independent activity (SIIA). The object of the SIIA is to get pupils to voluntarily design and carry out experiments of the sort they have been doing in the planned activities. Because they must initiate the projects themselves, however, and because there are relatively few constraints on what they may do, they have redefined the SIIA so that it bears little resemblance to the curriculum developer's and teacher's model. A fourth-grade girl was interviewed about recent SIIAs she had done:

> Sally: Well, sometimes I make an experiment. Like my girlfriend and I once made an experiment. We put 1/3 dixie cup of lemon juice and sugar in it and we stirred it and then we put it in the freezer.
> D. L.: And what happened?
> Sally: Then in three days we came back and it was frozen.
> This is a description of a fairly typical "mixture" and mixtures are the most common experiments. Girls seem to prefer mixtures that "turn out nice". When there was snow on the ground, a frequent activity was collecting a beaker full of snow and then adding various food colour dyes until a pleasing effect had been achieved. Boys prefer making mixtures that either look or smell "awful". They delight in pouring unlikely materials (baking soda, honey, soap powder) together and then heating the whole thing until it boils. They also seem to relish in heating things, in general, because they get to wear asbestos aprons, gloves, and goggles. (p. 18)

Another area for student initiative is in the peer group. By junior high, students are very social. Their view of the classroom includes elaborate characterizations of their fellow pupils as "brains," "pets," "weirdos," and "hoods" (Everhart, 1975). The single, homogeneous cognitive map of the classroom held by elementary school pupils (Lancy 1976a) begins to break up as pupils form into socially distinct cliques, each with its own reality. These realities attain their maximum divergence in the high school, where one's group dominates over all other considerations. Cusick (1973), in a study of a midwestern high school, found that school life was organized almost entirely around several well-recognized student groups, including "athletes," the "power clique," and the "music-drama group." Every classroom situation was filtered through the particular group one belonged to and defined accordingly. For the "hood" group, to which Cusick attached himself, all classes were profoundly boring, and members put forth as little effort as possible. They tried to get away with as much as they could, and they constantly trod the border line of expulsion. The loyalty to one's group and its view of the school was unswerving: "I asked one of the athletes, Greg, about associating with those not in his group. The thought just did not make sense to him. 'You know, like if you came here and didn't hang around with us, I wouldn't even know you'" (p. 67).

Pupils' careers begin in the elementary school as series of successes or failures over which teachers exercise capricious control. By junior high, this pattern may have evolved to a point at which the children have acquired from their peers such labels as "brain." the label becomes a full-time role in high school and determines not only the academic side of individuals' careers but the social and athletic sides as well.

The picture of pupils' careers that emerges here is admittedly very sketchy, but take a second look at how some of these insights were achieved. First, note that most of the studies were not constrained by theory. Shumsky and Mehan (1973), for instance, set out to see how pupil placement is accomplished. They do not have a theory of how this happens, nor do they make predictions beforehand. Secondly, note that most of these investigators paid a great deal of attention to what class-room actors had to say, spontaneously or in response to general, open-ended questions. In doing so, they captured the subjective reality of these actors, as in Stebbin's (1975) study of teachers' characterizations of pupils. Third, these studies demonstrate that one can employ a wide variety of research techniques, ranging from clinical instruments (Willower, 1969) to "pure" participant observation (Cusick, 1973), and still retain the phenomenological perspective. Finally, a theme common to several of these studies is that they directly challenge accepted views of classroom reality, as in Hodgkinson's (1967) inquiries into whether an "instructional game" instructs. Whether the picture of pupils' careers and, by extension, the classroom as phenomenon, becomes less sketchy depends on whether a substantial amount of future research in classrooms includes these phenomenological features.

PHENOMENOLOGY AND THE ELIMINATION OF CLASSROOM AGONIES

Social research tends to gravitate to various contemporary social problems, and this is particularly true in social psychology. The various endeavors described in this book almost all have an orientation to particular classroom problems. These problems are indeed pressing, and I would like to speak briefly, in conclusion, about phenomenology's contribution to ameliorating these problems.

First of all, it is becoming increasingly clear that no single avenue, whether teacher training, curriculum development, classroom management, decentralization, or any other, leads directly to educational nirvana. Nevertheless, the fragmented perspective of most education researchers guarantees that the big picture of the classroom as system will remain unrevealed or presented in unintelligible formulas. Phenomenology is determinantly *holistic* and seeks to discover the overall patterns that give life to an institution. Lacking perhaps in precision and in capacity for generalizing results, a phenomenological study can nevertheless yield some measure of understanding, and understanding is the first step toward directed change.

Second, because phenomenologists eschew variables, their reports are usually readable by a lay audience, meaning teachers and perhaps even students. In an age when more information is stored than can be retrieved, it is refreshing to imagine some research findings that can be immediately fed back into the setting that generated them. This feedback might do a great deal toward bringing the three realities back into harmony. Teachers and pupils alike might be surprised to find how far apart their views are from each other and from the reality of education. This is not to say that all phenomenologists write in lucid, jargon-free English. On the contrary, many of the proponents of phenomenology cited in this chapter are read and understood only with the greatest stamina and persistence, but this need not be the case. As researchers attempt straightforward descriptions of classroom reality without trying to convince anyone they have rediscovered America, a valuable literature can emerge. The sad fact is that we know more about the customs of primitive people from obscure corners of the globe than about our own institutions because anthropologists have more often employed the phenomenological perspective than other social scientists.

Finally, because phenomenology is so transparent to the uninitiated, its employment can become a regular classroom activity. It might not be a bad idea for teachers to serve as participant observers in their own and others' classrooms and for pupils to be encouraged to conduct investigations into the routines of their classroom. The whole purpose of this work is to open up the classroom to continuous scrutiny and discussion. It is a mistake to assume that classroom actors relish the failure of their enterprise, and given the opportunity to explore it openly, unhindered by rules and "common understandings," some improvement, even in the most unhappy cases, might be achieved.

REFERENCES

Adams, R. S. The classroom context. In W. F. Campbell (Ed.), *Scholars in context.* Sydney: Wiley, 1970.

Bar-Tal, D. *Social outcomes of the schooling process.* Pittsburgh: University of Pittsburgh, Learning Research and Development Center, 1976. (LRDC Publication, 1976/1)

Barker, R. G., & Wright, H. S. *One boy's day: A specimen record of behavior.* New York: Harper, 1951.

Becker, H. S. Social class variations in the teacher-pupil relationship. *Journal of Educational Sociology,* 1952, **25,** 451–465.

Bremme, D. W., & Erickson, F. Behaving and making sense. *Theory into Practice,* 1977, **16**(3).

Carlson, R. *The adoption of innovations.* Eugene, Oreg.: Center for the Advanced Study of Educational Administration, 1965.

Cicourel, A. V., Jennings, K. H., Jennings, S. H. M., Leiter, K. C. W., MacKay, R. W., Mehan, H., & Roth, D. R. *Language use and school performance.* New York: Academic, 1974.

Cottrell, L. S., Jr. Some neglected problems in social psychology. *American Sociological Review,* 1950, **15,** 705–712.

Cusick, P. A. *Inside high school.* New York: Holt, 1973.

Davis, J. Teachers, kids and conflict: Ethnography of a jr. high school. In J. P. Spradley & D. W. McCurdy (Eds.), *The cultural experience: Ethnography in complex society.* Chicago: Scientific Research Associates, 1972.

Diesing, P. *Patterns of discovery in the social sciences.* Chicago: Aldine, 1971.

Everhart, R. B. *Cognitive mapping in the study of the social and formal organization of the school.* Paper presented to the meeting of the American Anthropological Association, San Francisco, December 1975.

Garfinkel, H. *Studies in ethnomethodology.* Englewood Cliffs, N.J.: Prentice-Hall, 1967.

Glaser, R. *Adaptive education: Individual diversity and learning.* New York: Holt, Dryden, 1976.

Goffman, E. *The presentation of self in everyday life.* Garden City, N.Y.: Doubleday, Anchor, 1959.

Heider, F. *The psychology of interpersonal relations.* New York: Wiley, 1958.

Henry, J. *Culture against man.* London: Social Science Paperbacks, 1966.

Hodgkinson, H. L. *Education interaction and social change.* Englewood Cliffs, N.J.: Prentice-Hall, 1967.

Husserl, E. *Ideas: General introduction to pure phenomenology.* New York: Macmillan, 1962.

Jackson, P. W. *Life in classrooms.* New York: Holt, 1968.

Kaplan, S. Cognitive maps in perception and thought. In R. M. Downs & D. Stea (Eds.), *Image and environment.* Chicago: Aldine, 1973.

Katz, D. Field studies. In L. Festinger & D. Katz (Eds.), *Research methods in the behavioral sciences.* New York: Holt, 1953.

King, E. W. The presentations of self in the classroom, an application of Erving Goffman's theories to primary education. *Educational Review,* 1973, **25,** 201–209.

Koffka, K. *The principles of gestalt psychology.* New York: Harcourt, 1935.

Lancy, D. F. *The beliefs and behaviors of pupils in an experimental school: Introduction and overview.* Pittsburgh: University of Pittsburgh, Learning Research and Development Center, 1976. (LRDC Publication, 1976/3) (a)

Lancy, D. F. *The beliefs and behaviors of pupils in an experimental school: The science laboratory.* Pittsburgh: University of Pittsburgh; Learning Research and Development Center, 1976. (LRDC Publications, 1976/6) (b)

Lancy, D. F. *The beliefs and behaviors of pupils in an experimental school: School settings.* Pittsburgh: University of Pittsburgh, Learning Research and Development Center, 1976. (LRDC Publications, 1976/21) (c)

Lancy, D. F. *The beliefs and behaviors of pupils in an experimental school: Interpupil variation.* Unpublished manuscript, University of Pittsburgh, 1977.

MacKay, R. W. Conceptions of children and models of socialization. In R. Turner (Ed.), *Ethnomethodology.* Harmondsworth, Middlesex: Penguin, 1974.

Mehan, H. Assessing children's language using abilities. In J. M. Armer & A. D. Grimshaw (Eds.), *Methodological issues in comparative sociological research.* New York: Wiley, 1973.

Mehan, H. *Ethnomethodology and education.* In D. O'Shea (Ed.), Sociology of school and schooling. *Proceedings of the Second Annual Conference of the Sociology of Education Association,* Washington, NIE, 1974.

Mehan, H., & Wood, H. *The reality of ethnomethodology.* New York, Wiley, 1975.

Michener, J. *The bridge at Andau,* New York: Random House, 1957.

Neill, A. S. *Summerhill: A radical approach to child rearing.* New York: Hart, 1960.

Parott, S. Games children play: Ethnography of a second-grade recess. In J. P. Spradley & D. W. McCurdy (Eds.), *The cultural experience: Ethnography in complex society.* Chicago: SRA, 1972.

Shumsky, M., & Mehan, H. *The structure of educational accounts.* Paper presented at the meeting of the American Anthropological Association, New Orleans, December 1973.

Spearman, C. E. Youth and military service. C. Murchison (Ed.), *History of psychology in autobiography* (Vol. 1). New York: Russell & Russell, 1930.

Spradley, J. P., & McCurdy, D. W. *The cultural experience: Ethnography in complex society.* Chicago: SRA, 1972.

Stebbins, R. A. *Teachers and meaning: Definitions of classroom situations.* Leiden: Brill, 1975.

Willower, D. J. Schools as organizations: Some illustrated strategies for educational research and practice. *Journal of Educational Administration,* 1969, 7(2), 110–126.

Wolcott, H. F. An ethnographic approach to the study of school administrators. In A. H. Yee (Ed.), *Social interaction in educational settings.* Englewood Cliffs, N.J.: Prentice-Hall, 1971.

Wolcott, H. F. *The man in the principal's office: An ethnography.* New York: Holt, 1974.

IV

INDIVIDUALS IN THE SCHOOL

6

Interactions between Learner Characteristics and Optimal Instruction

Jere E. Brophy
College of Education, Michigan State University

One of the ways that social psychology can contribute to the improvement of educational practice is by providing information about how learners might be instructed in ways that meet their individual needs more effectively than teaching everyone the same way does. This could be based either on status characteristics like sex or socioeconomic status or on acquired psychological characteristics such as needs, preferences, or personal traits. Differential treatment could be accomplished either by grouping for separate instruction those individuals who are homogeneous on a trait of interest or (more probably) by identifying ways to structure heterogeneous classrooms so that diverse needs are met effectively.

For example, it is possible to structure different learning experiences for boys versus girls, introverts versus extroverts, or students oriented toward competition versus students oriented toward cooperation, so that each group has educational experiences that will maximize group achievement, attitude, or both. Carried to its logical conclusion, this idea approximates true individualization whereby all students are taught with methods most likely to succeed specifically with them.

APTITUDE-TREATMENT INTERACTION

This idea is hardly new. It is implied in familiar terms such as *individualization, prescriptive teaching, diagnostic teaching,* and *teaching the whole child.* Cronbach (1957) introduced the concept of aptitude-by-treatment interaction, referring to the possibility of contrasting interactional relationships between different educational treatments and differences in learner aptitude. This term is too narrow for this discussion because it focuses on learner aptitude alone. As Cronbach (1975) himself noted in a later paper, numerous cultural, motivational, personal-preference, and personality characteristics are known or suspected to interact with instructional variables in determining educational outcomes. Consequently, the broader term *learner characteristics* is used in this chapter and includes any group difference or individual difference that might form the basis for differential educational practice.

The literature on aptitude-by-treatment interactions has been disappointing to date. Bracht (1970), after an extensive survey, found that the percentage of studies reporting a significant aptitude-by-treatment interaction was only about what would be expected by chance. A more recent and comprehensive review by Cronbach and Snow (1977) criticizes Bracht for being too narrow in his definition of a significant interaction. These authors take a more positive view of the earlier literature than Bracht did, and they review many studies done since that time that indicate probable interactions between learner characteristics and optimal instruction.

Statistically significant interactions between learner-aptitude variables and instructional variables are reported commonly, but the vast majority of them are ordinal interactions indicating that certain learners were able to profit more from a given form of instruction than were other learners. Typical findings are that high-aptitude learners succeed regardless of instructional approaches, although they prefer approaches that maximize their freedom to structure their own learning experiences. In contrast, learners with less aptitude seem to require (as well as to prefer) much more organization and structuring by the teacher (Cronbach & Snow, 1977).

Such ordinal relationships between learner characteristics and instruction are interesting, but they do not have the important implications for differential instruction that disordinal relationships would have. Ordinal relationships merely indicate that one group requires more help than another, whereas disordinal relationships imply that one group does better under one approach and the other group does better under a different approach. The discovery of disordinal relationships with practical implications for education seems unlikely with regard to learner-aptitude variables, but a variety of social and personality variables do seem promising. Before this can occur, however, a variety of methodological and conceptual issues need to be resolved.

Methodological Issues

Many of the studies that failed to find predicted interactions used very weak treatments that were unlikely to have effects of any kind. Many others used treatments such as individualized study of programmed materials, so that any results obtained would be unlikely to generalize to ordinary classroom instruction. Findings with practical significance are likely to appear only if investigators use settings and treatments with enough ecological validity to allow generalization to ordinary classroom teaching and use treatments powerful and extended enough to produce nontrivial differential effects.

Logical Issues

Aptitude-by-treatment interaction is often described as if different treatment approaches would take learners to the same ultimate goals, although by different paths. This idea is expressed explicitly by Cronbach and Snow (1977), and it seems to be an implicit assumption behind much of the research in the field. The theory is that if instruction is arranged to accommodate learner preferences and strengths and to avoid their dislikes or weaknesses, learning will be enjoyable and easy and, thus, will proceed efficiently. It may be true that learning will be easy and enjoyable this way, but it is not necessarily true that different learning experiences will lead different learners to the same ultimate goals. In fact, this outcome is probably the exception rather than the rule.

If preexisting differences are reinforced by treatments, these differences probably will increase. Thus, short-term learning might be maximized by presenting material visually to learners who are visually oriented and orally to learners who are verbally oriented. This does not mean, however, that either group necessarily will be better off in the long run if taught this way all of the time; in fact, both groups might be better off if given a more balanced learning experience.

A related point is that it is not always better to pitch to strengths and avoid weaknesses than to do the opposite. If weakness areas have societal importance, individuals may have to develop these weakness areas to at least minimal levels in order to cope successfully with societal demands, so that their long-run interests are best served by concentrating on their weakness areas even though they might find this less enjoyable and more difficult in the short run. These considerations have been recognized by several writers interested in the interaction between learner characteristics and instruction (Berliner & Cahen, 1973; Hunt, 1975; Salomon, 1972), but they have not yet begun to influence the design and conduct of research in this area.

Good and Power (1976) have developed a model that considers a variety of learner characteristics and suggests how teachers could take all of them into account simultaneously while optimizing instruction to heterogeneous groups. Student characteristics such as ability, achievement progress, expectations for success, value on success, attitudes toward school, sense of futility, sociability, dependence, and anxiety are taken into account in identifying general types of students and suggesting differential teacher treatment on variables such as task difficulty, level of abstractness of instruction and materials, availability of options and task variety, instructional-setting variables, and many others (for an elaboration of the original model, see Good & Brophy, 1977). Models like this will be essential for drawing upon knowledge of learner characteristics in planning instruction because it is not practical to form separate learning groups for each learner characteristic that can be identified. Instead, it will be necessary to capitalize upon and respond to a variety of learner characteristics simultaneously in the process of teaching heterogeneous groups.

In the meantime, let us consider some of the learner characteristics that might form the basis for designing systematically different approaches for different learners. The following list has been drawn from variables important in social and personality psychology. It is meant to be illustrative rather than inclusive. For each variable, the attempt is made, not only to show that groups of learners with contrasting characteristics can be identified, but also to speculate about how the contrasting types could be taught most appropriately.

INDIVIDUAL CHARACTERISTICS

Psychologists have identified a great many needs, preferences, traits, and other characteristics on which individuals differ. Some of these are known to interact with different educational approaches, so they have potential implications for school practice.

Introversion and Extroversion

Introverts usually do not volunteer information or call out answers during class discussion, and they are often shy or brusque in responding when called upon by teachers. They do not enjoy responding in public situations, and they usually will not do so on their own initiative. In contrast, extroverts usually are more than happy to "perform" in public. They often call out answers and have to be reminded to respect other students' turns, and they tend to give chatty and detailed responses when they do get a chance.

If teachers only call on students who volunteer, introverts will not respond very often. Conversely, if teachers want to equalize individual participation, they will have to ignore or even stifle extroverts and call upon introverts to participate involuntarily (Brophy & Good, 1974). This makes it difficult to draw implications for optimal instruction.

If teachers follow the students' preferences, introverts will rarely participate in public discussions. This strikes most observers as inappropriate, partly because it seems "unfair" to allow extroverts to dominate discussion, and partly because continued deference to the preferences of introverts will reinforce these preferences and perhaps ultimately harm both their achievement and their social adjustment. These arguments appear to have face validity, but the idea that teachers should try to equalize participation in classroom discussions has many problems connected with it. First, continually stifling extroverts will probably irritate them and perhaps diminish their motivation as well as cut short potentially creative and important contributions. Also, an experiment involving deliberately calling on students who did not volunteer indicated that this tactic backfired (Schultz & Dangel, 1972). Introverts did not become more willing to volunteer on their own, and their achievement suffered.

Neither extreme response to this student difference seems satisfactory. Teachers probably will get the best results by partially accommodating student preferences, allowing extroverts to participate more often and not trying to force introverts to participate when they clearly do not want to. At the same time, however, they could socialize extroverts to raise their hands and get recognition before speaking out, and more generally, to respect their classmates' rights to have the floor. They also could gradually condition introverts to respond more frequently by calling on them to do so in nonthreatening situations.

Achievement Motivation

Individuals high in achievement motivation, especially if they also are high in actual achievement, tend to respond better to criticism than to praise. Conversely, individuals low in achievement motivation, especially if they also are low in actual achievement, tend to respond better to praise than to criticism (Van de Riet, 1964). The educational implications of this difference seem straightforward, although they need heavy qualification.

First, criticism seems likely to be appropriate and to function as a motivator only when students have done poorly for lack of effort or because of some other failure to apply themselves. Criticism of students who have done their best obviously is self-defeating. Second, although there are no definitive data on the matter, it seems intuitively obvious that the relationship between criticism and performance is curvilinear rather than linearly positive and that criticism is likely to be counterproductive if used too much. Finally, to the extent that individuals high in achievement motivation can be described as functioning out of intrinsic motivation, neither praise nor criticism nor any other kind of extrinsic attempt to motivate is likely to improve performance (Deci, 1975). Incentives improve performance only when they are relevant to the motivational systems under which individuals are operating. Thus, praise or criticism can be useful for affecting the performance of individuals motivated at least in part by a desire to please the teacher, but they are unlikely to help and may in fact detract somewhat from the performance of individuals motivated by more intrinsic considerations (Eden, 1975).

In any case, knowledge of individual differences in motivational systems could help teachers optimize instruction by individualizing their use of praise versus criticism versus nonevaluative feedback. More generally, these three responses to students could be varied systematically along with other approaches (such as material reinforcement, opportunity to move ahead, or opportunity for self-chosen activity) in order to provide incentives that would be most relevant to each individual student's system.

Need for Structure

Individuals differing in conceptual level respond differently to structured versus unstructured educational experiences (Hunt, 1975). Those high in conceptual level prefer, and usually do better in, less structured classrooms that place a premium on individual initiative and independent learning through discovery and exploration. Those lower in conceptual level both prefer and do better in classrooms featuring tight structuring by the teacher, clear-cut assignments that maximize specific demands and minimize student choice, objective tests rather than essay tests, and the like.

Others working from different perspectives (e.g., those of the authoritarian personality, dogmatism, cognitive style, independence versus dependence, or anxiety) have noted similar differences between those who prefer structured situations in which authority figures spell out clear expectations versus those who prefer less structured situations in which they have more opportunity to choose and manage their own learning experiences (Domino, 1971; Dowaliby & Schumer, 1973).

Students who differ in locus of control also differ in need for structure (Arlin, 1975). Individuals with an internal locus of control believe that they can control what happens to them, and they tend to take action to try to do so and to assume personal responsibility for outcomes, good or bad. Given these qualities, it is not surprising that they also prefer more open situations in which they have freedom of choice about what to do and how to do it. Individuals with an external locus of control tend to feel powerless in the face of strong and unpredictable forces. Instead of taking control, they believe that their roles are limited to finding out what forces are operating and trying to respond to them. They feel less responsible for their own actions and their outcomes because they feel less in control of the situations they face. Consequently, they tend to prefer highly structured situations in which they know exactly what to expect. They are willing to give up the freedom associated with more open situations in exchange for the security that comes with structure.

It would be easy to pitch to strengths with respect to preference for structure by teaching those who prefer structure in a structured way and those who do not in a less structured way, thus maximizing the achievement and the attitudes of both groups. To a degree, this appears defensible and perhaps optimal. For those who are extreme in their performances on this dimension, however, reinforcing these preferences might create problems. For example, individuals who strongly prefer structure also tend to score in socially undesirable ways on several personality variables, and there is reason to believe that they would have difficulty in situations requiring independent thought and action. They may need at least a minimal amount of practice (preferably practice leading to success) at coping in unstructured situations independently.

Conversely, although independence is generally valued and valuable, some individuals will get into trouble with society if they become so independent that they ignore important environmental constraints or the rights and wishes of others. Also, certain situations inherently involve structure, and everyone must learn to cope with these effectively, regardless of preferences. Thus, although there may be some point in catering to differences in preference for structure, it cannot be carried too far, or else certain educational goals will be met at the expense of others.

The clearest potential applications of this individual-difference variable may be in occupational counseling and guidance. Unless there is evidence of a desire to change and some progress in doing so, individuals who prefer structure might be guided toward occupations that involve structure, and those who resent it might be guided toward occupations that place a premium on independence and creativity,

Reward Contingencies

Applied behavior-modification research has shown that some students prefer individual reward, and others prefer group reward. High achievers and "overachievers" tend to prefer individual rewards, whereas low achievers and "underachievers" tend to prefer group rewards (Hartup, 1970).

In this case, accommodating preferences will probably increase existing group differences and perhaps create elitist attitudes in individuals who prefer individual rewards and alienation in students who prefer group rewards. On the other hand, constant exposure to nonpreferred reward contingencies may irritate or discourage high achievers who feel (usually correctly) that they are pulling more than their weight. It may also cause the harder workers to blame or reject those who do not work as hard if the group does not get rewards it might have gotten for better performance. These considerations seem to indicate a combination approach in which each type of reward contingency is offered at different times (if contingent rewards are used at all).

Group reward contingencies could be made more attractive to certain students by adding bonuses for those who work the hardest and thus are most responsible for group success. This would retain some of the incentive for the harder workers to continue to work hard, but it also would provide incentive for them to help, rather than blame, their fellow group members. Meanwhile, those who do not work as hard probably would prefer this arrangement to individualized reward contingencies. They would get help from other students in the group, and the group performance usually would be higher than their own would be, so that they would get more rewards this way than if they worked alone. At the same time, there would be some group pressure on them to work harder and pull their own weight.

This arrangement involves going part way to satisfy both groups, but it retains elements of the nonpreferred incentive system in order to apply some pressure on both types to change in desirable directions. It should be noted that the assumption here is that rewards are scaled to ability levels and thus are contingent on effort, not on absolute performance level.

Orientation toward Cooperation Versus Competition

Some individuals are competitive and prefer competitive situations; others tend to cooperate and prefer cooperative situations (Johnson & Johnson, 1974). Large individual differences on this dimension can be seen in any culture. In addition, Kagan and Madsen (1972) and their associates have shown in a series of studies that Mexican and American students differ systematically on this dimension. Mexican students spontaneously form cooperative groups and work together in problem-solving situations, whereas American students (both black and white and both middle-class and lower-class) tend to compete as individuals. These tendencies are strikingly strong in both cultural groups, at least among boys, even to the point at which they become self-defeating. Mexicans sometimes are cooperative when it is in their best interest to be competitive, and Americans sometimes are competitive when it is in their best interest to be cooperative. Other researchers have noted cultural differences of a similar nature (Miller & Thomas, 1972), and there are related racial and rural-urban differences in American culture (Johnson & Johnson, 1974).

The educational implications are that some students will be motivated positively by opportunities to compete as individuals for some kind of prize or recognition and that they will respond neutrally or even negatively to attempts to get them to cooperate. Other students will cooperate eagerly and successfully but will resist attempts to get them to compete as individuals. Motivation could be maximized by catering to preferences, at least in the short run, but it should be noted that these differences can be so strong as to be inappropriate and self-defeating in certain situations. If schools are expected to socialize as well as to educate, it might be important to try to reduce, rather than reinforce, these preferences, or at least to orient students toward the nonpreferred coping style in situations in which the preferred style is self-defeating.

Learning in Individual versus Group Settings

A related individual and cultural difference is a preference for learning individually versus as part of a group. Mexican boys appear to prefer group settings; American boys, to prefer individual settings. Individuals within each culture differ even more on such preferences (Sutter, 1967). Here again, the implication for education seems to be that socialization toward an appreciation of (or at least an ability to exhibit when necessary) the nonpreferred mode of learning is needed.

DIFFERENCES BETWEEN EXISTING GROUPS

Some differences appear to be distributed more or less randomly across individuals, but others are more predictable and, in many ways, are better thought of as group differences than as individual differences. The differences between Mexican and American students discussed above border on this. Group differences with the potential for serving as the basis for differential education exist in every culture. To illustrate, consider some of the more obvious differences among students in the United States.

Language Differences

Few would argue with the point that students who do not speak English need to learn to express themselves adequately in English if they are to cope successfully with American society, but there is much disagreement about how schools should treat students who speak English but with racial or geographical dialects. Teaching to strengths has been advocated by those who argue that speakers of "black dialect" or other English dialects with specific names should be taught in their dialect, either throughout their schooling or at least for the first several years (Baratz & Baratz, 1970; Labov, 1972). Later arguments and data established that this approach would be a mistake, compounding, rather than easing, the problems of the people meant to benefit by it (Copple & Suci, 1974; Hall, Turner, & Russell, 1973).

Presently there is widespread agreement that teachers should not reject or punish students for spontaneously using the language spoken in their home, neighborhood, or cultural group, but there is also wide agreement that teachers should provide good language models for the students. There is no evidence to support the systematic use of dialects for instruction. For monolingual English speakers, at least, this whole topic is disappearing as an issue, as it becomes evident that everyone has a dialect, whether or not it is labeled.

The situation is different with individuals for whom English is a second language, most notably Spanish speakers originally from Latin America. Although it is agreed that these individuals need to learn English, it has been argued that they will progress most satisfactorily in school if taught initially in Spanish (if that is their dominant language) and then phased into English after basic concepts have been taught in the native tongue (Nedler, 1972). Presently, available data are sparse and inconclusive on this issue. If supported, this approach would represent a truly practical interaction between learner characteristics and instructional methods, and one of the few that would involve teaching to strengths, at least for a time.

Social-group Differences

Differences among racial, ethnic, cultural, or social-class groups provide a basis for developing educational experiences planned specifically for each group. So far, this is most evident in the special curricula and materials developed for use with black students. Based on findings that individuals tend to identify most easily with models similar to themselves (Bandura, 1969), efforts have been made to include black individuals in stories and pictures in school books, to include previously ignored blacks in history books, and at higher levels, to develop black studies programs.

Other attempts in this area have not fared as well. Rejection of the idea of teaching in black dialect has been mentioned already. A similar fate has met the notion that black students should be taught by black teachers. Most blacks now reject the notion of an entirely black faculty or student body as an ideal, although they do agree that it is important to introduce black teachers into schools serving black children if they are not already there.

The outcomes of efforts to build educational programs specifically targeted for blacks are representative of the outcomes of similar efforts aimed at other groups as well. After much trial and error, the ultimate resolution usually involves essentially negative prescriptions (e.g., do not punish culturally sanctioned behavior). Positive prescriptions usually are limited to the inclusion of appropriate models and historical figures in the curriculum and the accommodation of group preferences in food, sports, music, and other school activities outside of the basic curriculum.

Attempts to go beyond this by substituting culturally specific instruction for the "standard" curriculum are usually resisted, however.

An additional problem complicating attempts to change schools to accommodate the needs of minority groups is the tendency to confuse minority-group *behavior* with minority *culture*. Many individuals show certain behaviors habitually because they are accustomed to them or because they never have been exposed to anything else, but not because these behaviors are part of a "culture" that is positively valued or even consciously considered. This is especially true of many social-class differences. For example, lower-class parents use (on the average), more physical punishment in disciplining their children than middle-class parents do, but it would be incorrect to call this behavior "cultural" or to imply that it is done because the parents have considered the matter carefully and decided that this is the best way to raise children. On the contrary, research indicates that lower-class parents realize that physical punishment is futile in the long run but resort to it for lack of knowledge about what else to do (Hess, 1970). Furthermore, few such parents want the school to use physical punishment as the "standard" method for dealing with student problems.

Most lower-class individuals with limited education know what they want for their children (basically the same things that everyone else wants), although they often do not know how to get these things. They usually view the school as an instrument for upward mobility, so they want their children to get a good grounding in the basic tool skills. They want schools to teach the children what they need to know to succeed in society, not to reinforce what they know already (Hess, 1970).

There is some evidence that differential treatment of children from different social classes can be beneficial to all, but it is based on notions of matching instructional content and methods to student learning histories and levels of achievement, rather than on notions of matching school experiences to existing group preferences or strengths (Brophy & Evertson, 1976). In general, lower-class students tend to learn more if taught somewhat less but if taught more redundantly (in smaller chunks and with more individualized and frequent opportunities to get practice and feedback). They also tend to do better if taught with patience and friendly encouragement.

In contrast, children from higher social-class homes respond better when challenged with more difficult material and taught at a brisker pace. They can learn more in the same amount of time, and they respond positively to challenging and difficult (although interesting) assignments. Furthermore, they seem not to need patience, encouragement, and warmth to the degree that lower-class students do. Sometimes, in fact, they respond better to critical demandingness than to patient encouragement. Findings like these have rather obvious implications for differential treatment that would maximize the achievement of students from different social-class backgrounds, although it should be noted that they refer only to achievement and might need to be modified when other goals are taken into account (Brophy & Evertson, 1976). As far as they go, these data indicate that optimal teacher treatment of students from high social-class backgrounds is similar to the treatment they experience from the parents, but that optimal treatment of students from lower-social class backgrounds involves counteracting, rather than reinforcing, the motivational strategies to which most of them are accustomed. More generally, data on group differences indicate that such differences may be a starting point for making decisions about differential instruction of different groups, but these decisions probably will not involve providing each group with more experiences of the same kind they are already familiar with and that are important in producing the existing differences in the first place.

Victims of Discrimination

Related considerations apply to members of minority groups who are victims of discrimination by dominant majorities. St. John (1971) studied 36 teachers considered to be exceptionally successful in dealing with black children and concluded that, as with the lower-class children studied by Brophy & Evertson (1976), the teachers who were the most successful with these students were the ones who were the warmest and most patient and understanding. In general, liking the teacher and feeling that the teacher liked them was more important to the learning of these students than was the belief that the teacher was especially skilled, well organized, or otherwise effective in purely instructional matters. The reverse was true for white students.

Kleinfeld (1975) reported similar data in her studies of Alaskan schools. She found that Indian and Eskimo children experienced both culture shock and hostility and discrimination when they made the transition from their own schools to heterogeneous city schools. Anglo students who lived in the cities dominated these schools, and the Indian and Eskimo children who were bused into the schools suffered discrimination and related problems similar to those suffered by low-income blacks bused into predominantly middle-class Anglo schools.

Kleinfeld identified two types of teachers who were ineffective with the minority students and one type that was notably effective. Some of the ineffective teachers were prejudiced and discriminatory themselves, harboring negative attitudes and low expectations. Consequently, they accomplished little with the minority students. Other ineffectual teachers had more positive affective responses toward these students, but they felt sorry for them and tried to do what they could to make them feel comfortable and to help atone for the indignities they had suffered. These teachers, however, had low expectations concerning these students' learning potential. As a result, they tried to meet the students' affective needs (as they perceived them), but they did not try to teach them much. They were afraid to put these students on the spot or cause them to be embarrassed.

The teachers who were effective with the minority students harbored positive attitudes toward them and did what they could to personalize instruction and make them feel comfortable, but they also made every effort to teach them as much as they could and to hold them responsible for completing assignments. Like the effective teachers of lower-class children in the Brophy & Evertson (1976) study, these effective teachers combined high expectations and determination to teach with personalized instruction and a willingness to meet the students' affective needs. These data indicate that students who are alienated from school or learning experiences need a different kind of instruction than those who are highly motivated and generally successful. Even here, though, it is important to take a long-term developmental view. The long-range goal is to move learners along as far as they can progress, not merely as far as they can progress if treated as alienated learners who have special needs. Thus, to the extent that teachers are effective in meeting special needs, the learners should become more and more like majority-group students. As this occurs, their needs change, so that they will benefit more by being taught in ways similar to the ways that the dominant group has been taught all along.

Sex Differences

A long list of sex differences has been documented repeatedly, and it appears that almost all of those relevant to education are determined culturally rather than biologically (Brophy & Good, 1974). Yet, observers generally, and feminists in particular, usually concentrate on finding ways to reduce or eliminate these sex differences rather than upon separating the sexes or treating them differently. Thus, coeducational groupings are favored overwhelmingly, and few would suggest excluding girls from mathematics or science classes on the ground that girls tend to have more difficulty with these subjects than boys do.

It is difficult to give prescriptive guidelines about the implications of sex differences for education, because there is such disagreement among people of all walks of life concerning what are, or should be, idealized male and female sex roles. Consideration of simplistic extremes is helpful, however, in thinking about the implications of all kinds of individual and group differences for education.

Schools could build upon existing differences by segregating the sexes and having male students taught by male teachers and female students by female teachers. A few writers have advocated this, and not without supporting arguments and data. In particular, some feminists have argued that females are better off in all-female colleges, and comparisons of graduates of such colleges with graduates of coeducational colleges usually support the all-female colleges, at least to some extent. Thoroughness would, however, demand going beyond mere segregation of the sexes in order to systematically socialize boys to be more aggressive, competitive, independent, and spatially and mechanically skilled than they already are, and girls to be more affiliative, dependent, deferent, and verbally oriented than they already are. This strikes most observers as obviously counterproductive, but it is conceptually identical to the educational changes that are commonly proposed as ways to take into account other learner differences.

The opposite extreme would be a systematic attempt to obliterate all sex differences and produce androgenous people with identical sex roles (or, to be precise, with no sex roles). This strikes many as the ultimate solution. Even if it is accepted in theory, however, realism requires that it be approached slowly and carefully. Attempts to make dramatic and radical breaks with traditional practice could create havoc and almost certainly would backfire, even if overwhelming support for the idea could be gathered (and this is not likely in the foreseeable future). Furthermore, it should be remembered that any such program would be based on value judgments, essentially no different than those behind programs calculated to force students to stop using a foreign language or speaking English with a dialect.

CONCLUSION

These selected examples illustrate that existing individual and group differences *may* provide a basis for developing alternative educational treatment of different individuals or groups that would benefit all more than teaching everyone the same way would. The existence of differences does not, however, necessarily mean that differential educational treatment is needed; and if it is needed, it does not necessarily involve either the accommodation of differences in preference or strength or an attempt to eliminate these differences. This will depend upon the nature of, and the reasons for, the difference, and also upon the ages of the students in question.

Most theorizing about optimizing to match learner characteristics has come from writers concerned primarily with postsecondary education, and most of the successful implementations of these ideas have been in college and university settings. Reflection on the issues raised in this chapter suggests that this may not be accidental. It appears that the feasibility of individualizing instruction varies with the developmental levels of students involved. Most of the cautions expressed earlier about inappropriate responses to learner characteristics are based on the idea that long-run best interests might be served better by shoring up weaknesses or providing appropriate exposure to nonpreferred experiences while the individual is still in the formative years. It is usually argued, however, that students have attained status as adults who are responsible for themselves and free to decide what they want by the time they reach college, so that schools no longer have the socialization responsibilities that they did previously. Many observers would argue that schools do not have such responsibilities earlier, either. In any case, once there is agreement that schools should not attempt to remediate weaknesses or socialize students in particular directions, but instead should deal with them as independent learners and attempt to respond to their needs and differences, accommodating begins to make sense. Adults *are* responsible for their own choices and actions, even those that seem ill-advised. Furthermore, as adult status (however defined) becomes more and more clear, it is up to students to define and pursue their own goals and up to schools to help them in this process. Students who attain adult status should take the initiative in deciding what they want to study, where they want to study, and perhaps to some degree, how they want to study.

Thus, at the college level, it makes sense to allow students to choose a traditional versus a self-paced course in a subject area of interest, to choose courses on the basis of their interests and aptitudes, and to choose instructors on the basis of what is known about their competence and methods. Students who prefer courses with much choice of assignments and independent work can choose these courses, and those who prefer instructors who want clear and explicit requirements and tightly organized approaches to teaching and grading can get them. Better student achievement and attitudes probably will result. Similarly, there probably are many advantages to allowing students to allocate optional course work however they choose. Students interested in a relatively narrow subject-matter area probably will get more out of intensive work in this area than they would out of a mixture of required courses, whereas students who have not yet defined their interests very precisely are probably better off continuing to sample different areas while trying to find themselves. For students considered adults, then, differential learning experiences that accommodate areas of strength and preference probably are a good idea. For younger students, however, determining the implications of individual and group differences for educational experiences is a very complex problem. Usually, neither pitching to strengths nor trying to shore up weaknesses will succeed by itself, because these oversimplified approaches cause more problems than they solve. Rational program planning will require detailed analyses of why the differences exist, whether schools should take them into account, and if so, how. In turn, answering these questions will require clarity about goals, especially the issue of whether differential treatment of different students is intended to lead all students to the same goal but with different methods versus intended to encourage different students to pursue different goals. Until and unless we come to much more agreement than we have now about the nature of the ideal person and about the functions of schools, these larger issues will have to be settled through the application of value systems rather than scientific psychological information.

REFERENCES

Arlin, M. The interaction of locus of control, classroom structure, and pupil satisfaction. *Psychology in the Schools,* 1975, *12,* 279–286.

Bandura, A. *Principles of behavior modification.* New York: Holt, 1969.

Baratz, S., & Baratz, J. Early childhood intervention: The social science base of institutional racism. *Harvard Educational Review,* 1970, *40,* 29–50.

Berliner, D., & Cahen, L. Trait-treatment interaction and learning. In F. Kerlinger (Ed.), *Review of Research in Education.* Itasca, Ill.: Peacock, 1973.

Bracht, G. H. Experimental factors related to aptitude-treatment interactions. *Review of Education Research,* 1970, *40,* 627–645.

Brophy, J. E. & Evertson, C. *Learning from teaching: A developmental perspective.* Boston: Allyn & Bacon, 1976.

Brophy, J. E., & Good, T. L. *Teacher-student relationships: Causes and consequences.* New York: Holt, 1974.

Copple, C., & Suci, G. J. The comparative ease of processing standard English and black nonstandard English by lower-class black children. *Child Development,* 1974, *45,* 1048–1053.

Cronbach, L. J. Beyond the two disciplines of scientific psychology. *American Psychologist,* 1975, *30,* 116–127.

Cronbach, L. J. The two disciplines of scientific psychology. *American Psychologist,* 1957, *12,* 671–684.

Cronbach, L. J., & Snow, R. *Aptitudes and instructional methods: A handbook for research on interactions.* New York: Irvington, 1977.

Deci, E. L. *Intrinsic motivation.* New York: Plenum, 1975.

Domino, G. Interactive effects of achievement orientation and teaching style on academic achievement. *Journal of Educational Psychology,* 1971, *62,* 427–431.

Dowaliby, F., & Schumer, H. Teacher-centered versus student-centered mode of college classroom instruction as related to manifest anxiety. *Journal of Educational Psychology,* 1973, *64,* 125–132.

Eden, D. Intrinsic and extrinsic rewards and motives. Replication and extension with kibbutz workers. *Journal of Applied Social Psychology,* 1975, *5,* 348–361.

Good, T. L., & Brophy, J. E. *Educational psychology: A realistic approach.* New York: Holt, 1977.

Good, T. L., & Power, C. Designing successful classroom environments for different types of students. *Journal of Curriculum Studies,* 1976, *8,* 1–16.

Hall, V., Turner, R., & Russell, W. Ability of children from four subcultures and two grade levels to imitate and comprehend crucial aspects of standard English. *Journal of Educational Psychology,* 1973, *64,* 147–158.

Hartup, W. W. Peer interaction and social organization. In P. Mussen (Ed.), *Carmichael's manual of child psychology* (Vol. 2). New York: Wiley, 1970.

Hess, R. D. Class and ethnic influences upon socialization. In P. Mussen (Ed.), *Carmichael's manual of child psychology* (Vol. 2). New York: Wiley, 1970.

Hunt, D. Person-environment interaction: A challenge found wanting before it was tried. *Review of Educational Research,* 1975, *45,* 209–230.

Johnson, D. W., & Johnson, R. T. Instructional goal structure: Cooperative, competitive, or individualistic. *Review of Educational Research,* 1974, *44,* 213–240.

Kagan, S., & Madsen, M. C. Experimental analysis of cooperation and competition of Anglo-American and Mexican children. *Developmental Psychology,* 1972, *6,* 49–59.

Kleinfield, J. Effective teachers of Indian and Eskimo students. *School Review,* 1975, *83,* 301–344.

Labov, W. Academic ignorance and black intelligence. *Atlantic,* 1972, *229*(6), 59–67.

Miller, A., & Thomas, R. Cooperation and competition among Blackfoot Indian and urban Canadian children. *Child Development,* 1972, *43,* 1104–1110.

Nedler, S. A development process approach to curriculum design. In R. Parker (Ed.), *The preschool in action: Exploring early childhood programs.* Boston: Allyn & Bacon, 1972.

Salomon, G. Heuristic models for the generation of aptitude-treatment interaction hypotheses. *Review of Educational Research,* 1972, *42,* 327–343.

Schultz, C., & Dangel, T. The effects of recitation on the retention of two personality types. *American Educational Research Journal,* 1972, *9,* 421–430.

St. John, N. Thirty-six teachers: Their characteristics, and outcomes for black and white pupils. *American Educational Research Journal,* 1971, *8,* 635–648.

Sutter, E. *Individual differences and social conditions as they affect learning by computer-assisted instruction.* Unpublished doctoral dissertation, University of Texas, 1967.

Van de Riet, H. Effects of praise and reproof on paired-associate learning in educationally retarded children. *Journal of Educational Psychology,* 1964, *55,* 139–143.

7

Social Outcomes
of the Schooling Process
and Their Taxonomy

Daniel Bar-Tal
School of Education, Tel Aviv University

Within recent years, research in the social psychology of education has been oriented mainly toward two goals. The first, a practical goal, was to enhance the academic achievement of pupils through attention to social variables in education. The second, an epistemological goal, focused on understanding the social structure of the school and its social processes. Whereas the first goal directly concerns educators (and, perhaps, students) the latter goal has principally been the concern of social psychologists who perceive the school as a setting in which it is possible to study social behavior. In general, researchers, whose major concern has been academic performance in the classroom, have investigated the influence on achievement of social psychological variables, such as patterns of interaction, styles of leadership, and relationships between teacher and pupil. Those researchers who have visited schools in order to study the social processes per se have assumed that social behavior in schools does not really differ from social behavior in other settings. Moreover, an investigation of social behavior in the setting of the school itself allows for study in a "real world," rather than in the artificial setting of a laboratory.

It seems that one direction of research that has been relatively neglected in social-psychological educational research is the investigation of social outcomes of the schooling process. If the school is to be viewed as a socialization agency, where children spend thousands of hours interacting with their peers and teachers, then it seems reasonable to propose that social outcomes be considered as important dependent variables in the study of the schooling process. In such research, social psychologists of education can provide the conceptual frameworks and operational techniques for the illumination of the effects of the schooling process on children's social outcomes.

This chapter serves two major focuses. The first is to discuss general conceptual and empirical issues regarding social outcomes of the schooling process. The second

The author would like to thank Robert Glaser, David Lancy, Gaea Leinhardt, Lauren Resnick, and Leonard Saxe for their helpful comments on earlier drafts of this chapter.

is to propose a framework that will enable social psychologists to define, organize, and analyze various types of educationally related social outcomes.

SOCIAL OUTCOMES

Social outcomes are defined here as those social reactions of pupils that are learned or modified as a result of pupils' presence in a school. *Social reactions,* according to Allport (1968), consist of those thoughts, feelings, and behaviors influenced by the actual, imagined, or implied presence of others. Thus, according to this definition, social outcomes include attitudes, beliefs, and behaviors. Such a definition extends the scope of social outcomes beyond the traditionally discussed outcomes of affective education (cf. Kahn & Weiss, 1973), which are limited solely to attitudes.

Children acquire social reactions merely by attending school for many hours a day and by participating in the variety of school activities. In schools, pupils are introduced to new information about different subjects that may affect their social perception or attitudes concerning objects, nature, or people. In schools, children meet new people, peers and teachers, who may influence their social reactions. Finally, schools as social organizations with their particular structures, norms, and patterns of interactions may have a profound effect on pupils' beliefs, attitudes, and behaviors. Thus, it is postulated that, even if the school de-emphasizes social education, even if the school does not have any organized social activity, even if the teachers suppress informal social interactions with pupils, and even if the school explicitly ignores social objectives of education and openly states that its only objective is to teach the three Rs, the pupils in such schools nevertheless would acquire social reactions. In this vein, Silberman (1970) has pointed out that

> what educators must realize . . . is that how they teach and how they act may be more important than what they teach. The way we do things, that is to say, shapes values more directly and more effectively than the way we talk about them. Certainly, administrative procedures like automatic promotion, homogeneous grouping, racial segregation, or selective admission to higher education affect "citizenship education" more profoundly than does the social studies curriculum. And children are taught a host of lessons about values, ethics, morality, character, and conduct every day of the week, less by the content of the curriculum than by the way schools are organized, the ways teachers and parents behave, the way they talk to children and to each other, the kinds of behavior they approve or reward and the kinds they disapprove or punish. These lessons are far more powerful than the verbalizations that accompany them and that they frequently controvert. (p. 9)

It should be noted that in recent years there is a growing trend in schools to plan social objectives for the schooling process. Educators determine the desirable social outcomes, and they design special programs, curricula, and social organizations of schools so that these outcomes can be achieved by the pupils (e.g., Khan & Weiss, 1973; Kohlberg & Turiel, 1971; Levine, 1973; Schmuck & Schmuck, 1974). If pupils acquire the designed social outcomes, these outcomes are termed *directed.* In addition to directed social outcomes, schools always have nondirected social outcomes because schools are unable to design programs for each social reaction, and also, directed social outcomes are usually accompanied by latent effects of unexpected social outcomes.

Theoretical Rationale for Studying
of Social Outcomes

In view of the fact that, until recently, it was widely believed that personality dispositions, such as habits, basic attitudes or beliefs, traits, and values, are stable (e.g., Allport, 1937; Stagner, 1961), recent theorizing about the instability of social reactions makes the study of social outcomes of the schooling process particularly important and meaningful. According to the former approach, individuals were believed to behave consistently in different situations over long periods of time, and behavioral changes, as a result of environmental effects, were expected to be minor. In contrast, Mischel (1968) has reviewed extensive evidence that individuals' social reactions are, on the contrary, greatly affected by the conditions of the situation and can be modified by numerous environmental changes. He proposes a cognitive social-learning model that "shifts the unit of study from global traits inferred from behavior signs to the individual's cognitive activities and behavior patterns, studied in relation to the specific conditions that evoke, maintain, and modify them and which they, in turn, change" (Mischel, 1973, p. 265). According to this thesis, behavior is viewed as highly environment specific, and "a person will behave consistently across situations only to the extent that similar behavior leads, or is expected to lead, to similar consequences across those conditions" (Mischel, 1971, p. 74). This position recognizes the possibility that the school, as an environment where children spend much of their time, may have a profound effect on students' social reactions. Mischel (1968) specifically pointed to such a possibility in suggesting that, when an environment responds to an individual's behavior consistently for a long time, the individual acquires relatively stable patterns of reactions.

Although the schooling process may have an important impact on children's social reactions, it is further recognized that, in their later years of life, other environments may continue to shape the individuals' social reactions. Nevertheless it can be assumed that the schooling process leaves its marks for many years to come and that any understanding of human social reactions requires an investigation of the impact that the schooling process has had on individuals.

One of the best known research projects in social psychology that has demonstrated this contention was carried out by Newcomb (1943, 1963). In the earlier study, Newcomb found that college may have a profound influence on its students' political attitudes. Students in their third and fourth years of study were found to be significantly less conservative than students in their first year of college. Newcomb attributed this change to the influence of teachers' participation in college activities and to students' personal involvement in the college as a social institution. Approximately 20 years later, Newcomb recontacted his subjects and found that they still retained their nonconservative political attitudes acquired during their years of college.

Although there are only a few investigations of social outcomes of the schooling process, a number of educators and social scientists have pointed out the importance of the school as an institution where students acquire social reactions. Thus, for example, Musgrave (1972) noted that the importance of the school as a socializing agency has grown over the last century because the family has had less influence on the social development of the child and because the structure of knowledge has become complex and has been applied more fully in the economy. Morrison and McIntyre (1971) observed that "although academic and occupational objectives are overriding in the treatment of most conventional school subjects, most curricula are, with varying degrees of explicitness, intended to influence pupils' social skills and values. Both the subject content and the methods by which it is taught may contribute to the achievement of such goals" (p. 113). Havighurst (1953) recognized in his early writings the fact that the "school becomes a place where they [children] also learn the task of social development" (p. 25). According to Havighurst, the child learns in school: (a) getting along with peers, (b) sex roles, (c) attitudes toward self, (d) a concept about the world, (e) morality and values, (f) independence, and (g) attitudes toward other people and institutions. In general, Havighurst pointed out that children learn societal values and skills in school that are required in order to fulfill specific roles in the society. Parsons (1959), who urged that the classroom be viewed as an agency of socialization where children are trained to adjust to social requirements, pointed out that children in schools learn "moral" skills in addition to cognitive skills. In this vein, Dreeben (1968) wrote a book called *On What is Learned in School* in which he argued that children in schools learn social norms through informal experiences, exposure to varied subject matter, didactic efforts of teachers, and their participation in social activities. Dreeben suggested that children primarily learn four norms in school, that is, the norms of independence, achievement, univeralism, and specificity.

Writing about the social outcomes of the schooling process, Himmelweit and Swift (1969) noted that "little consideration is given to the contribution that the school makes by its values, its learning opportunities, and teacher-child relationships—school is not seen as an active socializing agent exerting an effect independent of that of the home" (p. 155). Himmelweit and Swift have conducted one of the few studies that explicitly attempted to assess the effect of schooling on students' social reactions. The research, however, was limited to the investigation of school influence upon job aspirations. Their results showed "that school rather than home affected the individual's subsequent occupational history, job level, and aspirations. Moreover, his evaluation of his own career achievements was determined far more by reference to the achievement of his classmates than to those of his family" (pp. 157–158).

Similarly, Minuchin, Biber, Shapiro, and Zimiles (1969) conducted an extensive investigation of the psychological impact of schooling. Although these researchers chose their set of social measures in an unsystematic way, their study was designed to compare the influence of different school environments. Their results showed that "the schools affected the lives and functioning of the children in ways that were pervasive and perhaps profound" (p. 390). Minuchin et al. found that children in different schools varied more in terms of social outcomes than in terms of academic performance. The school environment was found to have an impact on the children's self-perceptions, their attitudes, and the learning and performance of their roles. The authors noted, however, that "the potency of the school's orientation in affecting the children was a function of two conditions: the orientation of the home and its interaction with school influence; and the extent to which the school operated as a total integrated environment" (p. 391).

Jencks and his colleagues (Jencks, Smith, Acland, Bane, Cahen, Gintis, Heyns, & Michelson, 1972), in their influential study that attempted to assess the effects of the schooling process, recognized the importance of schooling for the development of noncognitive traits that might be crucial in the students' future success in life. They wrote:

Noncognitive attributes may play a larger role than cognitive skills in determining economic success or failure. The evidence of our senses tells us that noncognitive traits also contribute far more than cognitive skills to the quality of human life and the extent of human happiness. We therefore believe that the noncognitive effects of schooling are likely to be more important than the cognitive effects. (p. 134)

The authors also point out, however: "We would like to be able to give the factors influencing each of these traits as much attention as we gave cognitive skills, but we do not know enough to do this. We do not even have generally agreed upon names for these traits, much less a system for measuring them" (p. 131). The latter view reflects the state of investigation of the social outcomes of the schooling process.

Problems

Despite the evidence that the schooling process shapes social reactions, comparatively little research has been done in elucidating them. As Himmelweit and Swift (1969) noted, "Few measures have been developed for understanding how, why, and with what effect the school seeks to influence behavior and outlook. The tendency appears to be toward collection of measures of the child's liking for and adjustment to school, his examination records, leaving age, and ratings of his behavior by peers and teachers" (p. 155).

The fact that the study of social outcomes of the schooling process has been a neglected area in the social psychology of education can be explained in many ways. One explanation is that it has been very difficult to assess the social outcomes of the schooling process that are uniquely a product of the school. The child spends much time with family and peers, and no one can deny that these agents of socialization also have profound influences on the social development of the child. Thus, social scientists have had difficulty in distinguishing between those social outcomes that are a result of the schooling experience and those that are acquired in other settings.

A second reason for this neglect is the problem of defining school and classroom processes and structures as independent variables. Schools are complex environments, replete with various materials, interactions, and structures. As a result, researchers have difficulty in identifying the specific variables and deciding what variables might have an impact on social reactions.

An additional reason for the past disregard of social outcomes of the schooling process is the fact that students are rarely evaluated in a formal manner on the basis of social outcomes. Although a few curricula or programs exist that teach a child affective behavior, and some schools have defined affective objectives for schooling, schools do not explicitly place a high value on any specific social reactions, at least not when compared to the high value placed on academic achievement. Similarly, there is a lack of adequate instruments for measuring social reactions. For each particular social reaction, there are different instruments, and many of them do not satisfy the required criteria of validity and reliability. The existence of many different instruments is partially the result of social psychologists' disagreement on the definition of certain social reactions. Thus, for example, independent behavior is defined in several different ways (Hartup, 1963) and, as a result, has been measured with different instruments.

Finally, there is disagreement among educators and social psychologists about the scope of the definition of social outcomes. Some scientists include emotional reactions, cognitive responses, or personality characteristics, whereas others limit the definition of social outcomes to affective reactions. There have been attempts to define the scope of social outcomes of the schooling process by classifying them into differential categories (e.g., Hoepfner, Henenway, DeMuth, Tenopyr, Granville, Petrosko, Krakower, Silberstein, & Nadeau, 1972; Walker, 1973). These attempts of classification were based, however, more on intuitive knowledge than on theoretical, social-psychological bases. That is, types of social outcomes are not distinguished theoretically, or methodologically, and as a result, the scope of each category is relatively unclear and undifferentiated.

In summary, social scientists and educators have recognized the importance of studying social outcomes of schooling. For a series of reasons, however, the study of social outcomes has been relatively neglected. In the next section, a framework is suggested to overcome some of the previously stated difficulties of the investigation of social outcomes. Specifically, in the following pages, a definition of the scope of social outcomes is presented, and social outcomes are classified on the basis of systematic social-psychological criteria. Nevertheless, it is recognized that many problems of investigating social outcomes remain unresolved and should be the subjects of future concern.

TAXONOMY

A taxonomy of social outcomes of the schooling process, based on social-psychological theory, can help to organize the existing research in a meaningful way and stimulate further research by providing a proper framework for understanding the scope of social outcomes of the schooling process.

Theoretical Overview

The suggested taxonomy consists of discriminable and measurable categories for classifying social outcomes of the schooling process. Specifically, the taxonomy includes two major, though not mutually exclusive, categories. Each major category is further divided into three subcategories. The first major category classifies social outcomes by type of social reaction and consists of three subcategories: (1) beliefs, (2) attitudes, and (3) social behaviors. Each of these categories can be viewed as a reaction that the pupils learn in school. The second major category classifies the outcomes on the basis of the object toward which the reaction is directed. This dimension consists of three subcategories: (1) reactions toward self, (2) reactions toward others, and (3) reactions toward nonhuman objects.

The basic difference among social outcomes lies in the first major category (i.e., type of reaction). Distinguishing beliefs, attitudes, and behaviors reflects Allport's (1968) definition of social reactions. Such distinctions have been recognized by a number of other social psychologists (e.g., Bem, 1970; Fishbein, 1967; Fishbein & Ajzen, 1975). Beliefs consist of the cognitive knowledge that individuals have about their world or hypotheses that individuals possess concerning "the nature of the object and its relations to other objects" (Fishbein, 1967, p. 259). Attitudes are defined as evaluations on a negative–positive dimension of abstract or concrete objects or propositions. This definition of attitudes corresponds to that of many psychologists who regard evaluation or affect as the single defining dimension of attitudes (e.g., Katz & Stotland, 1959; Rosenberg, 1956; Thurstone, 1928). Finally, social behaviors are observable patterns of reactions that are carried out as a result of the influence of others.

The main reason for retaining these distinctions and studying all three types of reactions is based on the evidence that beliefs, attitudes, and behaviors are not necessarily related (e.g., Fishbein, 1967; Kiesler, Collins, & Miller, 1969). An example of a lack of relation among the three subcategories would be a child who believes that a teacher is lazy and unfair, but warm and smart. The attitude of the child toward this teacher is neutral (the child neither likes nor dislikes the teacher), and behaviorally, the child smiles at the teacher, approaches the teacher, and initiates informal interactions. In another situation, it is possible that the child believes that he or she is independent while behaving very dependently and having negative attitudes toward dependency. Thus, it is possible to assume that an individual may have beliefs and attitudes that are inconsistent with behavior.

In addition, the existence of one type of outcome does not necessarily indicate the existence of another type of outcome. Individuals may have beliefs about certain objects without forming attitudes about them, or individuals may have attitudes about other people without ever interacting with them. Thus, for example, a child may have beliefs about various objects, plants, or animals without ever evaluating them; also, a child may dislike members of different racial, ethnic, or religious groups without ever having seen one of them.

It should be noted, however, that an individual's beliefs, attitudes, and behaviors may be interrelated (see Kiesler, Collins, & Miller, 1969). Thus, for example, a child may believe that her or his teacher is unfair, lazy, and cold; the child may dislike this teacher; and the child may behave toward this teacher with much arrogance and hatred. It is also possible that the sets of beliefs individuals form may influence their attitudes (Fishbein, 1967) and behaviors (Bem, 1970). It has been also suggested, on the basis of theories of cognitive consistency, that individuals' attitudes may cause a change in their beliefs (Zajonc, 1968). Finally, much has been written about the relation between attitudes and behaviors. In spite of inconsistent findings, it is possible to state that, under certain circumstances, attitudes may change behaviors (Kiesler, Collins, & Miller, 1969); and recently it has been suggested that behavior change may induce attitude change (Bem, 1970; Festinger, 1957).

Classifying social outcomes on the basis of the object of the reaction (the second major category) is based on the assumption that individuals differ in their reactions toward self, others, and nonhuman objects. Whereas the reactions toward nonhuman objects are in most of the cases universal, general, and undifferentiated, the reactions toward people are complex, taking into account specific human characteristics. As Heider (1958) stated, people

> are usually perceived as action centers and as such can do something to us. They can benefit or harm us intentionally, and we can benefit or harm them. Persons have abilities, wishes and sentiments, they can act purposefully, and can perceive or watch us. They are systems having an awareness of their surroundings and their conduct refers to this environment, an environment that sometimes includes ourselves. (p. 21)

In addition, individuals often react differently toward self and others. The reactions toward self are always ego-involved and subjective and are often primarily directed at maintaining positive self-image. One example of a difference between reaction toward self and reaction toward an other is provided by Jones & Nisbett (1971). They collected evidence suggesting that an individual's causal beliefs concerning self-behavior and the behavior of other people differ in their direction. That is, while individuals tend to believe that their own behavior is caused by situational factors, they also tend to believe that the same behavior performed by others is a result of stable personal characteristics of the performers.

Discussion of the Categories

Beliefs

Beliefs are based on perceptions and facts-oriented information. One of the explicit goals of school education is to provide information. In school, children acquire factual information about many different, previously unfamiliar subjects. On the basis of acquired information, children form beliefs about new subjects such as war, patriotism, democracy, and so on. This new information may also modify children's previously formed beliefs. For example, children may change their beliefs about their parents, religion, or ethnic group as a result of the newly acquired information. In addition, their formal and informal interactions with teachers and peers may also affect their beliefs about their school, their neighborhood, and themselves.

Beliefs have usually been measured by self-report questionnaires or interviews. It is possible to present open-ended questions or closed-ended questions that consist of alternatives from which children can choose. A study by deCharms (1972) is an example of how instruction can affect students' beliefs concerning self-determination, personal responsibility, self-confidence, and internal control (being an "origin"). In his study, some of the students received special training to change the previously mentioned beliefs, while others did not. The training lasted between 1 and 2 years. At the end of this period, the results indicated that the students who participated in the training felt less like "pawns" and more like "origins" than students who did not participate in the training.

Attitudes

Attitudes are affective evaluations. They involve an object toward which the child has positive, neutral, or negative affections. Thus, in contrast to beliefs, which consist of knowledge of the object, attitudes consist of evaluations of the object in positive or negative terms. Many attitudes are learned in school. The teacher actively evaluates much of the information presented during the teaching process, and children may acquire these attitudes from the teachers. School experiences may affect the formation of the child's attitudes toward the school, teachers, learning, a particular subject matter, or other children. The school experience may also change some of the attitudes held before coming to school. Thus, for instance, enrollment in a desegregated school may affect white children's attitudes toward black children.

Attitudes are mainly assessed by scales composed of items that rely on respondents' self-reports of feelings or evaluations regarding the particular attitude object (Scott, 1968). An example of how the schooling process affects students' social reactions is a study done by Minuchin, Biber, Shapiro, and Zimiles (1969). Among several social reactions, the researchers compared the attitudes toward school of students from traditional schools with students from modern schools (the schools were matched on the basis of their socioeconomic and cultural levels). The results indicated that "the greatest negativism and ambivalence appeared among the traditional school children, and the greatest enthusiasm and positive identification among modern school children" (p. 263).

Social Behaviors

The school experience may shape the child's social behaviors. In school, children acquire new patterns of behavior and change some old ones. For example, schooling may affect such behaviors as aggression, self-initiation, independence, or cooperation.

Social behaviors are most directly assessed by observational techniques (Weick, 1968). Thus, for example, Thompson (1944) compared two groups of nursery school children for a number of social behaviors. The two groups were otherwise matched; in one, the teacher was instructed to minimize her involvement and to de-emphasize personal involvement relations; in the second, the teacher was instructed to actively guide the children's activities and to develop warm relations with each child. Observation indicated that, while at the beginning of the year, the two groups did not differ in their social behavior, at the end of the year, the groups differed significantly on a number of measures. Children in the second group were more ascendant, more constructive, and showed greater social participation in group activities and more leadership than children in the first group.

Reactions toward Self

Reactions toward self consist of those beliefs, attitudes, or behaviors concerned with or directed toward the self. The experience of being in school influences the children's reaction toward themselves. The reaction toward self consists, for example, of children's perceptions, feelings, and evaluations of themselves as individuals and of self-directed behaviors such as self-gratification. The school, as a primary setting for academic and social experience, influences the children's self-development. Thus, for example, psychologists have consistently documented significant relationships among such variables as academic achievement, school satisfaction, and self-concept of ability or self-esteem (e.g., Purkey, 1970).

In this vein, a study by Schmuck (1963) investigated, among other things, the effect of classroom social structure on pupils' attitudes toward self. The researcher compared centrally structured classroom groups, characterized by a narrow focus of interpersonal acceptance and rejection, with diffusely structured classroom groups, characterized by a wide range of interpersonal choices. The results of this study indicated that the positive attitude toward self is positively related to the degree of diffuseness in the classroom group.

Reactions toward Others

Reactions toward others consist of those beliefs, attitudes, or behaviors concerned with or directed toward other individuals, groups, or both. School experience influences the type of reactions that the person has toward other individuals. The child may form beliefs and attitudes about peers, teachers, or other adults. In addition, the child acquires some patterns of social-behavioral reactions toward other individuals or groups. An example of schooling effects on social reactions toward others is a study by Singer (1966), who investigated the effect of desegregation on pupils' interracial attitudes. The results of this study showed that pupils in the desegregated schools had more positive intergroup attitudes than pupils in the segregated schools.

Reactions toward Nonhuman Objects

Reactions toward nonhuman objects consist of those beliefs, attitudes, or behaviors concerned with or directed toward nature (e.g., animals, birds, plants) and toward concrete or abstract objects or propositions. The school experience shapes the children's reactions toward different objects—a living creature, a touchable object, a symbol, a slogan, or an idea. Thus, for instance, the schooling process may affect the children's attitudes toward democracy or nationalism, their beliefs about government actions or certain kinds of birds, and their patterns of political behavior or behavior toward domestic animals. A study by Langton (1967) can serve as an example for school effect on children's reactions toward nonhuman objects. This study compared Jamaican political attitudes and behaviors of working-class pupils in heterogeneous-class schools with those of working-class pupils in homogeneous-class schools. The results showed that working-class pupils in a heterogeneous class-room have more "democratic" attitudes, give greater support to civil liberties, and have more positive orientations toward voting than pupils in a homogeneous class-room. They are also more economically conservative and less supportive of the political system than working-class pupils in a homogeneous classroom.

Use

The proposed taxonomy can be seen as a framework for conceptually organizing studies of social outcomes of the schooling process, especially in light of the fact that the taxonomy enables the classification of any possible social outcomes into systematically differentiated categories. For example, according to the taxonomy, the social outcomes of independence can be measured in several ways. Thus, a child's belief concerning independence can be measured by asking if he or she likes to be independent, and a child's behavior of independence can be assessed by observing her or his behavior. In addition, one can measure a child's belief concern-ing others by asking him or her to indicate whether his or her peers are independ-ent. One can also measure his or her attitudes toward others by asking him or her if he or she likes the independence of other individuals. These examples show that the proposed taxonomy of social outcomes may facilitate research by indicating the specificity of the measured child's reaction through the distinction among the child's beliefs, attitudes, and behaviors. As long as researchers measure social reac-tions (i.e., beliefs, attitudes, and behaviors) separately, the taxonomy has a mean-ingful function. On the one hand, the taxonomy characterizes the uniqueness of each social outcome; on the other hand, it enables the study of the relationship among different social outcomes. The latter possibility suggests an investigation of the interrelation among children's beliefs, attitudes, and behaviors that are learned in school. In addition, it is possible to investigate the effect of one type of outcome on another. The focus of such research could be, for example, on the investigation of how children's beliefs formed in a school affect their previous attitudes, or how the attitudes modified or formed as a result of school experience influence their behavior. All the features of the proposed taxonomy discussed here suggest that it can serve as a framework for conceptualizing research in the social outcomes of the schooling process.

The usefulness of the taxonomy can be demonstrated if two conditions are fulfilled. First, it must be shown that the social reactions, as classified by the taxonomy, may be affected by the schooling process. This condition is demonstrable from the review of a number of studies that showed that variation in schooling processes leads to differing social outcomes. Second, it must be shown that a large number of social reactions can be classified according to the categories of the proposed taxonomy.

To examine the classification utility of the proposed taxonómy, a variety of children's social reactions were classified according to the categories of the taxonomy. These social reactions were isolated from a review of several dozen studies in the area of education and child social development. All of the reviewed studies focused on sociopsychological variables, and although only few of the studies investigated social outcomes per se, it was assumed that these variables could be utilized in research on social outcomes of the schooling process. The reviewed studies do not represent any systematic sample of socio-development studies. They were chosen merely as demonstrative examples of how to use the proposed taxonomy.

The variables were classified according to how they operated in each study (see Table 7-1); that is, it was necessary to find out how each researcher used the variable in order to classify it, because the same variable can operate as a belief, an attitude, or a social behavior.

Discussing several studies at greater length provides examples of how the researchers made the social variables operational. Thus, an experiment by Ross (1966) can serve as an example of a study that measured social behavior toward self. The outcome variable in this study was dependence. To measure this variable, nursery school children's behavior was observed in terms of whether they came to the school by themselves and whether they dressed themselves without help. A study by Kagan and Madsen (1971) is an example of an experiment that measured social behavior toward others. This study investigated competitive and cooperative patterns of behavior. Cooperative or competitive behavior was assessed by organizing a game in which two children were required to reach a goal. The game could be played competitively, in which case a child could try to receive the reward herself or himself, or cooperatively, in which case the two children could help each other and share the reward. The experimenters observed the playing of the game and thus were able to determine the nature of the behavior.

An example of a study that investigated attitudes and beliefs toward others is one by Yee and Runkel (1969). The researchers used a 100-item inventory, About My Teacher, developed by Beck (1964) to investigate pupils' attitudes toward teachers. The questionnaire consisted of attitudinal and belief items such as "Is your teacher fun to be with?" "Does your teacher succeed in keeping the pupils under control?" and "Does your teacher make you feel like learning a lot on your own?" Soares and Soares (1969) measured the self-beliefs of children by asking the children to rate themselves on 20 pairs of bipolar traits. A study by Hudgins, Smith, and Johnson (1962) investigated attitudes and beliefs toward others. Children were given four sociometric tests and asked to indicate three or four pupils who generally were the best students, three or four pupils with whom they would like to work on arithmetic problems, and three or four pupils who were most liked. In addition, the children were asked the same questions with regard to pupils who have the least ability and are the least liked. Finally, a study by Insel and Wilson (1971) measured attitudes toward other people and objects. The authors devised a conservation scale

TABLE 1 Classification of Social Variables according to the Categories of the Taxonomy

Object of reaction	Beliefs		Attitudes		Behaviors	
	Study	Variable	Study	Variable	Study	Variable
Self	Yarrow, Scott, & Waxler (1973) Trowbridge (1972) Soares & Soares (1969) Shantz & Woydanoff (1973)	Altruism Self-concept Self-perception Aggression	Schmuck (1963) Feshbach & Feshbach (1969)	Attitude toward self Empathy	Bonney & Powell (1953) Ross (1968)	Bodily self-contact Dependence
	Yee & Runkel (1969) Rothenberg (1970) Koslin, Koslin, Pargament, & Waxman (1972) Adelson, Green, & O'Neill (1969) Ehman (1969) Hudgins, Smith, & Johnson (1962) Letter (1959)	Attitudes toward teacher Social sensitivity Racial attitudes Political attitudes Political attitudes Perception of Classmates Aggression	Yee & Runkel (1969) Schmuck (1963) Hartup (1964) Hudgins, Smith, & Johnson (1972) Lesser (1959) Insel & Wilson (1971) Koslin, Koslin, Pargament, & Waxman (1972)	Attitudes toward teacher Involvement in class Friendship Perception of classmates Popularity Conservatism Racial attitudes	Kagan & Madsen (1971) Hartup (1958) Heathers (1955) McCandless, Bilous, & (1961) Walters, Pearce, & Dahms (1961) Bryan (1971) Grusec (1971) Masters (1972) Presbie & Coiteux (1971) Staub (1971)	Cooperation Dependence Dependence Popularity and dependence Aggression Altruism Altruism Altruism Altruism
Others	Ross (1966) Boehm (1957) Durkin (1959) Hoffman (1971) Luria & Rebelsky (1969) Yarrow, Scott, & Waxler (1973)	Dependence Independence Moral development Moral development Moral development Altruism				
Nonhuman objects	Epstein & Komorita (1971) Barnett & Zucker (1973) Ehman (1969) Weinheimer (1972)	Locus of control Friendliness Political attitudes Conformity	Schmuck (1963) Insel & Wilson (1971) Spenser & Horowitz (1973)	Attitudes toward school Conservatism Racial attitudes	Jegard & Walters (1960) Fagot & Patterson (1969)	Aggression Sex role

for children that consisted of 50 items to which the children were asked to indicate if they favor or believe in each particular object or concept, some examples of which are computers, Chinese food, bikinis, and so on.

Several conclusions can be drawn from the classification of the social variables according to the proposed taxonomy. First, the taxonomy appears to be a useful tool for classifying a variety of social reactions. Second, the categories of the taxonomy indicate the precise nature of the social variables: Is it belief, attitude, or behavior? This function is important because the same variable can be measured in several different ways, and often researchers measure a variable indirectly, discussing it as if it were measured directly. Thus, for example, whereas Bryan (1971) measured altruism by observing a child's behavior toward others, Yarrow, Scott, and Waxler (1973) measured the same variable by asking a child questions about his or her beliefs concerning other people in different situations. Third, the taxonomy facilitates investigation of the relationship among the subcategories of variables. That is, it is possible to investigate the relationship between different reactions. For example, it is possible to compare a child's beliefs concerning the teachers with her or his attitudes toward the teacher. Thus, it appears that the proposed taxonomy is useful in classifying social reactions. Such classification defines the scope of social outcomes of the schooling process and clarifies the meaning of the specific social reactions.

CONCLUSION

In this chapter, the attention of social psychologists of education is summoned to the study of social outcomes of the schooling process. The premise is that the classroom is a major source of socialization experiences for children. Children not only acquire academic skills in school, but they also learn social reactions that may be important for their future success in adult life. Those social reactions that are learned in the school are called social outcomes of the schooling process. The taxonomy suggested here, by making possible the classification of these social outcomes and by defining their scope, should facilitate investigation.

It is hoped that social psychologists of education will direct their efforts to investigating the beliefs, attitudes, and social behaviors that children learn in schools. Such research should function as a basis for establishing social objectives in education. Once it is determined what kind of social outcomes are learned in schools, then it should be possible to determine what kind of outcomes are desirable. Eventually, it might be useful to structure an environment in which the child will learn those social outcomes that are adaptive and desired by the society. The latter goal is a complicated one because of ethical, didactic, and organizational problems, but it seems that it is more desirable to plan at least some social outcomes, rather than leaving to chance the social development of children in schools. The route to these goals is long and complex, but even the longest march starts with the first step.

REFERENCES

Adelson, J., Green, B., & O'Neil, R. Growth of the idea of law in adolescence. *Developmental Psychology*, 1969, 1, 327–332.

Allport, G. W. *Personality: A psychological interpretation.* New York: Holt, 1937.

Allport, G. W. The historical background of modern social psychology. In G. Lindzey & E. Aronson (Eds.), *The handbook of social psychology*. Reading, Mass.: Addison-Wesley, 1968.

Barnett, D. W. & Zucker, K. B. An exploration into children's interpersonal behavior as related to their perception of social interactions. *Psychology in the Schools*, 1973, 10, 61-66.

Beck, W. H. *Pupils perceptions of teacher merit: A factor analysis of five hypothesized dimensions*. Unpublished doctoral dissertation, Stanford University, 1964.

Bem, D. J. *Beliefs, attitudes and human affairs*. Monterey, Calif.: Brooks/Cole, 1970.

Boehm, L. The development of independence: A comparative study. *Child Development*, 1957, 28, 85-92.

Bonney, M. E., & Powell, J. Differences in social behavior between sociometrically high and sociometrically low children. *Journal of Educational Research*, 1953, 46, 481-495.

Brophy, J. E. & Good, T. L. *Teacher-student relationships: Causes and consequences*. New York: Holt, 1974.

Bryan, J. H. Model affect and children's imitative altruism. *Child Development*, 1971, 42, 2061-2065.

deCharms, R. Personal causation training in the schools. *Journal of Applied Social Psychology*, 1972, 2, 95-113.

Dreeben, R. *On what is learned in school*. Reading, Mass.: Addison-Wesley, 1968.

Durkin, D. Children's acceptance of reciprocity as a justice principle. *Child Development*, 1959, 30, 189-196.

Ehman, L. H. An analysis of the relationship of selected educational variables with the political socialization of high school students. *American Educational Research Journal*, 1969, 6, 559-590.

Epstein, R., & Komorita, S. S. Self-esteem, success, failure, and locus of control of Negro children. *Developmental Psychology*, 1971, 4, 2-8.

Fagot, B. L., & Patterson, G. R. An in vivo analysis of reinforcing contingencies for sex-role behaviors in the preschool child. *Developmental Psychology*, 1969, 1, 563-568.

Feshbach, N. D., & Feshbach, S. The relationship between empathy and aggression on two age groups. *Developmental Psychology*, 1969, 1, 102-107.

Festinger, L. *A theory of cognitive dissonance*. New York: Harper, 1957.

Fishbein, M. A consideration of beliefs and their role in attitude measurement. In M. Fishbein (Ed.), *Readings in attitude–theory and measurement*. New York: Wiley, 1967.

Fishbein, M., & Ajzen, I. *Belief, attitude, intention and behavior: An introduction to theory and research*. Reading, Mass.: Addison-Wesley, 1975.

Grusec, J. E. Power and the internalization of self-denial. *Child Development*, 1971, 42, 93-105.

Hartup, W. W. Nurturance and nurturance-withdrawal in relation to the dependency behavior of preschool children. *Child Development*, 1958, 29, 191-201.

Hartup, W. W. Dependence and independence. *The 62nd Yearbook of the National Society for the Study of Education* (Pt. 1), 1963, 62, 333-363.

Hartup, W. W. Friendship status and the effectiveness of peers as reinforcing agents. *Journal of Experimental Child Psychology*, 1964, 1, 154-162.

Havighurst, R. *Human development and education*. New York: Longman's, 1953.

Heathers, G. Emotional dependence and independence in nursery school play. *Journal of Genetic Psychology*, 1955, 87, 37-58.

Heider, F. *The psychology of interpersonal relations*. New York: Wiley, 1958.

Himmelweit, H. T., & Swift, B. A model for the understanding of school as a socializing agent. In P. H. Mussen, J. Langer, & M. Covington (Eds.), *Trends and issues in developmental psychology*. New York: Holt, 1969.

Hoepfner, R., Henenway, J., DeMuth, J., Tenopyr, M. L., Granville, A. C., Petrosko, J. M., Krakower, J., Silberstein, R., & Nadeau, M. A. *CSE-RBS test evaluation: Tests of higher-order cognitive, affective, and interpersonal skills*. Los Angeles: Center for the Study of Evaluation, 1972.

Hoffman, M. L. Identification and conscience development. *Child Development*, 1971, 42, 1071-1082.

Hudgins, B. B., Smith, L. M., & Johnson, J. J. The child's perception of his classmates. *Journal of Genetic Psychology*, 1962, 101, 401-405.

Insel, P., & Wilson, G. D. Measuring social attitudes in children. *British Journal of Social and Clinical Psychology*, 1971, 10, 84-86.

Jegard, S., & Walters, R. H. A study of some determinants of aggression in young children. *Child Development*, 1960, **31**, 739-747.

Jencks, C., Smith, M., Acland, H., Bane, M. J., Cohen, D., Gintis, H., Heyns, B., & Michelson, S. *Inequality: A reassessment of the effect of family and schooling in America.* New York: Basic, 1972.

Jones, E. E., & Nisbett, R. E. *The actor and the observer: Divergent perceptions of the causes of behavior.* Morristown, N.J.: Silver Burdett, 1971.

Kagan, S., & Madsen, M. C. Cooperation and competition of Mexican, Mexican-American, and Anglo-American children of two ages under four instructional sets. *Developmental Psychology*, 1971, **5**, 32-39.

Kahn, S. B., & Weiss, J. The teaching of affective responses. In R. M. W. Travers (Ed.), *Second handbook of research on teaching.* Chicago: Rand McNally, 1973.

Katz, D., & Stotland, E. A. A preliminary statement to a theory of attitude structure and change. In S. Koch (Ed.), *Psychology: A study of a science* (Vol. 3). New York: McGraw-Hill, 1969.

Kiesler, C. A., Collins, B. E., & Miller, N. *Attitude change: A critical analysis of theoretical approaches.* New York: Wiley, 1969.

Kohlberg, L., & Turiel, E. Moral development and moral education. In G. S. Lesser (Ed.), *Psychology and educational practice.* Glenview, Ill.: Scott, Foresman, 1971.

Koslin, S., Koslin, B., Pargament, R., & Waxman, H. Classroom racial balance and students' interracial attitudes. *Sociology of Education*, 1972, **45**, 386-407.

Langton, K. P. Peer group and school and the political socialization process. *American Political Science Review*, 1967, **61**, 751-758.

Lesser, G. S. The relationships between various forms of aggression and popularity among lower-class children. *Journal of Educational Psychology*, 1959, **50**, 20-25.

Levine, E. Affective education: Lessons in ego development. *Psychology in the Schools*, 1973, **10**, 147-150.

Luria, Z., & Rebelsky, F. Children's conceptions of events before and after confession of transgression. *Child Development*, 1969, **40**, 1055-1061.

Masters, J. C. Effects of social comparisons upon the imitation of neutral altruistic behaviors by young children. *Child Development*, 1972, **43**, 131-142.

McCandless, B. R., Bilous, C. B., & Bennett, H. L. Peer popularity and dependence on adults in preschool-age socialization. *Child Development*, 1961, **32**, 511-518.

Minuchin, P., Biber, B., Shapiro, E., & Zimiles, H. *The psychological impact of schooling experience.* New York: Basic, 1969.

Mischel, W. *Personality and assessment.* New York: Wiley, 1968.

Mischel, W. *Introduction to personality.* New York: Holt, 1971.

Mischel, W. Toward a cognitive social learning reconceptualization of personality. *Psychological Review*, 1973, **80**, 252-283.

Morrison, A., & McIntyre, D. *Schools and socialization.* London: Penguin, 1971.

Musgrave, P. W. *The sociology of education.* London: Methuen, 1972.

Newcomb, T. M. *Personality and social change.* New York: Holt, 1943.

Newcomb, T. M. Persistence and regression of change attitudes: Long-range studies. *Journal of Social Issues*, 1963, **19**(4), 3-14.

Parsons, T. The school class as a social system: Some of its functions in American society. *Harvard Educational Review*, 1959, **29**, 297-318.

Presbie, R. J., & Coiteux, P. F. Learning to be generous or stingy: Imitation of sharing behavior as a function of model generosity and vicarious reinforcement. *Child Development*, 1971, **42**, 1033-1038.

Purkey, W. W. *Self-concept and school achievement.* Englewood Cliffs, N.J.: Prentice-Hall, 1970.

Rosenberg, M. Cognitive structure and attitudinal effect. *Journal of Abnormal and Social Psychology*, 1956, **53**, 367-372.

Ross, D. Relationship between dependency, intentional learning, and incidental learning in preschool children. *Journal of Personality and Social Psychology*, 1966, **4**, 374-381.

Rothenberg, B. B. Children's social sensitivity and the relationship to interpersonal competence, intrapersonal comfort, and intellectual level. *Developmental Psychology*, 1970, **2**, 335-350.

Schmuck, R. A. Some relationships of peer liking patterns in the classroom to pupil attitudes and achievement. *School Review*, 1963, **71**, 337-359.

Schmuck, R. A., & Schmuck, P. A. *A humanistic psychology of education: Making the school everybody's house.* Palo Alto, California.: Mayfield, 1974.

Scott, W. A. Attitude measurement. In G. Lindzey & E. Aronson (Eds.), *The handbook of social psychology* (Vol. 2). Reading, Mass.: Addison-Wesley, 1968.

Shantz, D. W., & Woydanoff, D. A. Situational effects on retaliatory aggression at the three age levels. *Child Development,* 1973, **44**, 149-153.

Silberman, C. H. *Crisis in the classroom.* New York: Random House, 1970.

Singer, D. *Interracial attitudes of Negro and white fifth grade children in segregated and unsegregated schools.* Unpublished doctoral dissertation, Columbia University, Teachers College, 1966.

Soares, A. T., & Soares, L. M. Self-perceptions of culturally disadvantaged children. *American Educational Research Journal,* 1969, **6**, 31-45.

Spencer, M. B., & Horowitz, F. D. Effects of systematic social and token reinforcement on the modification of racial and color concept attitudes in black and in white preschool children. *Developmental Psychology,* 1973, **8**, 46-154.

Stagner, R. *Psychology of personality.* New York: McGraw-Hill, 1961.

Staub, E. The use of role playing and induction in children's learning of helping and sharing behavior. *Child Development,* 1971, **42**, 805-816.

Thompson, G. S. The social and emotional development of preschool children under two types of educational program. *Psychological Monographs,* 1944, **58**, (5, Whole No. 258).

Thurstone, L. L. Attitudes can be measured. *American Journal of Sociology,* 1928, **33**, 529-554.

Trowbridge, N. Self-concept and socio-economic status in elementary school children. *American Educational Research Journal,* 1972, **9**, 525-537.

Walker, D. K. *Socio-emotional measures for preschool and kindergarten children.* San Francisco: Jossey-Bass, 1973.

Walters, J., Pearce, D., & Dahms, L. Affectional and aggressive behavior of preschool children. *Child Development,* 1957, **28**, 15-26.

Weick, K. E. Systematic observational methods. In G. Lindzey & E. Aronson (Eds.), *The handbook of social psychology,* Vol. 2. Reading, Mass.: Addison-Wesley, 1968.

Weinheimer, S. Egocentrism and social influence in children. *Child Development,* 1972, **43**, 567-578.

Yarrow, M. R., Scott, P. M., & Waxler, C. Z. Learning concern for others. *Developmental Psychology,* 1973, **8**, 240-260.

Yee, A. H., & Runkel, P. J. Simplicial structures of middle-class and lower-class pupils' attitudes toward teachers. *Developmental Psychology,* 1959, **1**, 646-652.

Zajonc, R. B. Cognitive theories in social psychology. In G. Lindzey & E. Aronson (Eds.), *The handbook of social psychology.* Reading, Mass.: Addison-Wesley, 1968.

8

The Psychosocial Context
of Distress at School

John C. Glidewell
University of Chicago

Children at school are often under tension, occasionally in distress. They are undergoing a process of imme'diate socialization into the social systems of the school and a process of anticipatory socialization into the social systems of the community. Both generate tensions. Socialization can be conceived as the process by which individuals become aware of the alternative modes of behavior available to them, become aware of the consequences of adopting each mode, and adopt as effective and proper those behaviors most often approved. The goal of socialization is to induce people to do *well* and to do *good*, as competence and morality are defined by the society. The nature of the process is influenced by the cultural values, the ethnic concerns, the social norms, the sex roles, and the psychosocial context of the process. The following sections contain accounts of the data relating to these social processes at school, to the inevitable tensions they generate, to the distress they occasion, and to their connections with the institutional approaches to managing the tensions.

Following the lead of John Clausen (1966), one may conceptualize schooling as a socialization process. Socialization is a conformity-inducing process as well as a competence-training process. As Dreeben (1968, pp. 63–86) has shown well, schooling is, in fact, a special socialization process that induces special kinds of conformity. It demands that one independently adapt oneself readily to many new situations; that one approach other people positively; that one apply oneself with great regularity and intensity to an achievement that is a form of self-modification; that one accept being treated as a member of a class (pupil) or an age-grade category and being treated on the basis of a few characteristics, not on the basis of one's whole person. Generally speaking, the process works well. Pupils do learn to cope with the world around them; they do develop themselves; and each generation learns a little more than the last, perhaps at a little less psychological cost.

The demands of schooling quite regularly restrict the expression of the urges felt by individuals, and thereby, produce intrapersonal tensions. They also quite regularly restrict the allocation of roles, resources, and rewards among the people involved, making them more and less appropriate to individual needs and more and less equitable. The demands of schooling thereby produce interpersonal tensions. Tensions produce contractions in individual perception and interpersonal interaction—contractions in speed, variety, and intensity. Under such tensions, people see fewer alternative approaches to problems, take fewer risks, make fewer experiments, become involved 'with fewer people, get upset more easily. The tensions are felt in the individuals, but they feel those particular tensions because they are members of that particular system. Some form of tension management is a necessary, but not sufficient, condition for getting work done.

There is a long and honorable tradition in all sorts of societies that individuals who get especially upset by socialization processes are temporarily relieved from the regular social system (neighborhood, work group, classroom) and assigned to dyads—one-to-one relationships with someone in a helping role. In such dyads, it is often possible to manage the tensions more readily while the individuals receive some form of support or assistance in seeking some realistic resolution of their conflicts. Intimate dyads facilitate learning how to modify their own behavior or learning how to initiate some modification in the larger social system. Sometimes the one-to-one interactions are called tutoring, sometimes training, sometimes consultation, sometimes gossiping, sometimes confession, sometimes therapy, and sometimes lecturing by a Dutch uncle. I have made a detailed analysis of such helping subsystems previously (Glidewell, 1972). I propose that they constitute a special case of systematic tension management. The general case is the creation of a special temporary social system—small or large—to deal with problems that are so tension producing that the tensions cannot be managed in the regular social system.

A temporary social system has several advantages. Its particular restrictive norms are less aggravating because they are temporary. Individuals will conform temporarily to restrictions they would not conform to permanently. Members can make mistakes with less threat of long-term consequences. Because mistakes are less threatening, experimentation is more attractive, and more new approaches to problems are tried. Under such conditions, tensions are less constrictive; interaction is more innovative. The temporary system provides a needed tension management—although not necessarily the needed conflict resolution. With respect to resolution, the temporary system is only enabling, not determining.

There are other forms of tension management: special roles to link one system with another, subdivision of large groups into smaller groups, games and gamesmanship, abstract goal setting, isolation, and pacing (i.e., well-timed cycles of increases and relaxations of social demands). All these forms of tension management are used by the social systems of a school in coping with individuals who become upset in responding to the socialization processes in the school.

The following sections contain a review of work on distress and tension management at school: the psychosocial antecedents, the immediate context of the classroom, the psychosocial resources, the manifestations of distress at school, and the preventive and therapeutic approaches to distress at school. All are conceptualized as parts of the necessary tensions occasioned by the socialization process, and all are conceptualized as involving those particular modes of tension management suitable to the social institutions in which they evolved.

PSYCHOSOCIAL ANTECEDENTS

One may recurrently try to piece together some of the links in the usual chain of antecedent events that lead both to individual distress and to systemic tension management at school. The phenomena can be traced, in part, to the temperaments of the children; in part, to the culturally based patterns of values on children, on expressiveness, and on health; in part, to the family-based psychosocial resources of the children; in part, to the norms and goals of the children's social strata; and in part, to the interplay of these forces in shaping the sex roles of the children.

Mechanic has pointed out, in a series of provocative papers (1962, 1964, 1965; Mechanic & Volkhart, 1961) that data about distress represent two kinds of phenomena: (1) one's condition and (2) one's reaction to one's condition. The behavior both of individuals and of their associates is influenced by both kinds of phenomena. As Padilla and Ruiz (1973) and Sue and Wagner (1973) have demonstrated, the cultural backgrounds of the individuals influence their reactions to their condition—to a small but significant extent. Following are some specifications.

Ethnic Factors

Zbarowski (1952) reported that, in a New York City hospital, Jewish and Italian adult patients related that their mothers showed great concern about possible illness or injury and great alarm at small symptoms of disorders, like coughs. Such great concerns were not so often characteristic of the parents of "old Americans" and Irish patients. Both Jews and Italians made greater use of physicians in helping roles, but they used them quite differently. The Jews were interested in understanding why they felt the pain and tended to use the helper as a teacher. The Italians, however, were interested in getting sympathy and relief from their pain and tended to use the helper as a healer. Both the variations in the use of the temporary helping dyad and the variations in the way of using it are, I propose, variations in techniques for tension management—techniques developed by the social systems within these cultures to manage the tensions generated by the distress, so that the work necessary to the reduction of the distress could take place. As shown in one of Mechanic's studies (1964), however, cultural factors, while they have significant influences, account for only a small part of the variations in the management of the tensions produced by pain and distress.

Sex Roles

The socialization of males and females is different in all cultures. As shown by the analyses of Maccoby and Jacklin (1974), the social expectations for one's sex are powerful forces in school as elsewhere—and specifically in responses to distress in school (e.g., Minuchin, 1964). Mechanic (1964) found that age-sex roles influenced the fear of getting hurt and the attention given to pain more than maternal attitudes or maternal illness behavior did. Schmuck and Van Egmond (1965) found that, for girls, the utilization of intelligence was reduced by loss of social acceptance in the classroom, whereas, for boys, it was more reduced by loss of social power. Generally, boys have poorer relations with teachers than girls do (e.g., Lippitt & Gold, 1959), and boys are more often seen by teachers as having mental health problems (Gildea, Glidewell, & Kantor, 1961). Girls are more apt to respond to classroom social pressure by conformity and more apt to approach teachers with pleas for help (Lippitt & Gold, 1959). Generally, male college students rated 3-year-old girls more favorably than boys, but female college students rated 3-year-old boys more favorably (Gurwitz & Dodge, 1975). Teachers are often female, tend to like boys, but perceive boys as "having problems." Boys have more trouble getting socialized, and they more often employ an aggressive gamesmanship. Girls have less trouble getting socialized, and they more often employ confidence games by establishing a reputation of conformity before risking a breach of norms (Hollender's idiosyncracy credit, 1958). Perhaps, if one can pretend for a time that it is just a game, one can cope with both the restrictions and the sustained effort needed in school with less disruption from tension. Conclusions concerning sex-role difference must be suspended as current social changes develop and as the results of much active, new research are available.

Social Class and Sex

Along another dimension, Koos (1954) found that the lower classes were less likely than the (relatively) upper classes to view themselves as ill when they had particular symptoms and less likely to seek medical help. Saunders (1954) found, in the U.S. Southwest, that *deprived* Spanish-speaking families were more likely to rely on folk medicine and family care than were Anglos. The tensions were managed by a helping dyad—but in the folk society. These findings would lead one to expect that lower-class mothers would report fewer behavior symptoms to an interviewer and would less often seek middle-class professional help in dealing with symptoms. The former expectation was supported by the St. Louis County data (Glidewell, Domke, & Kantor, 1959). For those children perceived by their teacher as in distress at school (subclinically disturbed and clinically disturbed) but not for others, the lower-class mothers reported fewer symptoms. The data are summarized in Table 8-1.

The latter expectation was also supported by Turner's (1960) analysis of the data from St. Louis County. She found that the lower classes were less often in contact with mental health resources, but that the making of contact, by the mother and child, was *more* closely related to the (independently assessed) severity of the child's problems than it was related to social class. It appeared that it was primarily the distress that provoked the tension management, but the social-class values set limits upon the extent to which the particular helping dyad was employed.

Meaningful data are available to show social-class differences in the responses to stress as represented by certain behavior symptoms. For symptoms reported by mothers, in white families, comparative prevalence for the middle and lower classes in St. Louis County are shown in Table 8-2.

TABLE 8-1 Mean Number of Symptoms Reported by Mothers

Teachers Ratings	Social Class				
	Upper	Upper middle	Lower middle	Lower	Total
Well adjusted	.5	1.7	2.0	1.6	1.7
No known problems	1.8	1.8	1.8	2.0	2.0
Subclinically disturbed	3.0	2.7	2.9	2.5	2.7
Clinically disturbed	4.4	4.8	2.7	2.5	3.0
Total	2.4	2.0	2.1	2.5	2.1
Number	49	157	223	398	827

TABLE 8-2 Prevalence of Behavior Symptoms in White Third-grade Children (Reported by Their Mothers)

	Rate per 100			Rate per 100	
Symptom	Middle class (N = 380)	Lower class (N = 398)	Symptom	Middle class (N = 380)	Lower class (N = 398)
Nervousness	31	34	Speech trouble	08	10
Eating trouble	28	30	Thumb-sucking	11	06
Daydreaming	22	18	Trouble sleeping	10	07
Temper tantrums	18	19	Stomach trouble	08	08
Unusual fears	17	20	Withdrawal with		
Withdrawal with			adults	02	01
children*	08	06	Acting out with		
Acting out with			adults	07	05
children*	10	07	Destructiveness	05	08
Wetting self	13	16	Resistance to		
Overactivity	14	15	school	04	05
Lying	12	15	Sex troubles	01	02
Frequent crying	12	13	Stealing	02	02
			(General Anti-		
			socialness)*	(05)	(08)

*Differences significant (p < .05).

Problems of interpersonals skills were somewhat more prevalent in the middle classes. Antisocial behavior was slightly more prevalent in these lower-class white children. Not apparent in Table 8-2 is a significant interaction of sex and adjustment. Among the *well-adjusted boys,* the middle-class children showed a higher prevalence of withdrawal in relationships with other children (8% versus 0%); but among the *maladjusted girls,* the lower classes showed a higher prevalence (32% versus 9%). (A more complete analysis of the findings is presented in Glidewell's 1968 paper.) A tendency to withdraw from social interaction in order to manage tensions was so uncommon among lower-class boys (3%) that in this sample *all* lower-class boys (versus only 40% of middle-class boys) who were withdrawn were seen by teachers as disturbed. Among lower-class girls, the prevalence of withdrawal was typical of that of most children (8%), but the symptom still alerted the teacher. Two-thirds of the lower-class girls (versus only one-fourth of middle-class girls) showing the symptom were seen by the teacher as disturbed.

One study of the *incidence* of behavior symptoms provided an analysis of social-class differences in the rates of appearance of new symptoms among white children. The social-class differences in incidence were quite small (Glidewell, 1968). It is of interest to note that, whereas lower-class boys showed a significantly lower *prevalence* of withdrawal than middle-class boys, they showed only a slightly (and not significantly) lower *incidence* of withdrawal. The conclusion is that episodes of withdrawal appeared almost as often among lower-class boys as among middle-class boys, but they did not last as long. The data suggest that the socialization forces acting on lower-class white boys move them away from passivity and toward assertiveness. For middle-class boys, on the other hand, the pressures act in both directions—in conflict. Again, the striking implication is that the social classes make differential uses of withdrawal (mulling things over) and aggressive involvement (fighting things out) to manage tensions—apparently both intrapersonal and interpersonal.

Community Contracultures

There is a more critical problem about which the data are intriguing but less precise. The cultural gap between the blacks of the rural and urban slums and the educational institution has been most difficult to close. (See the collections of articles edited by Roberts in 1967 and by Epps, 1974.) The work of Rainwater (1970) is a good example of the data available. It seems certain that the slum develops community and family organizations, roles, values, concerns, and tension-management methods markedly different from those of most schools. One would expect that the response of a slum child to distress at school would be markedly different from that of a middle-class child—white or black. The data available do not satisfactorily settle the issue, but they are provocative.

Swallow (1967) studied the nursery school behavior of a sample of 53 children of black mothers on ADC. Her data showed significant differences among the children in the process of adapting to the socialization processes of the middle-class nursery school. Some girls (more often those with warmer mothers) shifted their behavior in conformity to the teacher's requests; some girls (more often those with less warm mothers) responded only to pressure from their peers. The boys were less responsive to any social influence—mother, teacher, or peers. Swallow interpreted her data as indicating that the younger, more assertive mothers, either by modeling or by direct tuition, induced their girls to put on whatever proper performance the situation demanded for attainment of desired rewards—a confidence game in nursery school or elsewhere. The older, more stoic mothers induced their girls to accept—and to survive within—their disadvantaged position, even perhaps consciously to avoid any proper performance for rewards.

Slaughter (1977) followed 56 black children and 40 of their mothers from a summer Head Start program in 1965 through the fourth grade in 1971. She found that school experiences were discontinuous with home experiences (and presumably community experiences), that teacher evaluations interacted with parental influences to affect both cognitive and personal-social outcomes, and indeed that, after a delay, the school affected the home. Epstein and McPartland (1977), in a broad study of 4,079 *white* students in grades 6, 7, 9, and 12 in one Maryland school district, found no home-school interaction, however. Main effects of the social-power allocation at home on personal-social attributes were clear, as were main effects of power allocation at school; but interaction was not apparent.

Smith and Geoffrey (1968) made careful, coordinated observations each day for a full semester in a "split seventh-eighth grade" classroom in an urban slum school. Their observations showed a parade of dramatic events, mostly violent, which were sensational to the middle-class eye but were more nearly commonplace to the slum children. More critical than the dramatic events was the pervasive sense of defenselessness of the children—defenselessness against almost all demands from the world around them. To cope with this sort of distress, each child sought alliances, close identifications with an ingroup, full involvement in the here and now, and a pawn-like resignation toward the future. "Things happen to you and you accept them and live with them and try to pick off the better parts as well as you can" (p. 225), and get as much out of them as you can.

The most highly socialized people in a contraculture can develop an effective and integrated social system with its own roles, values, norms, language, and group-insulation methods. The perception of inverse causality, the experiencing of time in discrete units, the focus of attention on social structure to the exclusion or even perversion of social functions, and a pervasive self-consciousness—all these have been suggested as variables by which such contracultures can be distinguished in the urban slum (Davis, 1948; Deutsch, 1963; Miller, 1965; Riessman, 1962). The connections between these distinguishing variables and the expressive, quickly passing, pawnlike response to distress seems credible, but it is yet to be empirically established.

A number of social theorists (e.g., Erickson, 1962) have proposed that continuing deviance is a necessary condition to the establishment and modification of norms. Such a function seems especially useful to the socialization process because it makes public and explicit just what are the consequences of doing what one is not supposed to do. It is tempting to speculate that, as the distance between the middle and the lower classes becomes greater, as is the case in some suburbs, antisocial behavior among middle-class children becomes more prevalent. Because of the distance, there is no public and explicit demonstration of the consequences of deviance by a deviant group. Following this premise, then, the necessary demonstration is therefore provided by middle-class antisocial behavior.

It is also important to point out the widely observed fact that, once deviant roles, groups, or contracultures become established and recognized, the alienation seems irreversible. It is exceedingly difficult to move back into the dominant conventional role, group, or culture.

There is some danger that a contraculture, when perceived by the members of the dominant culture, is subject to distortion by assimilation and contrast. An upper-lower-class group, being upwardly mobile and involved in anticipatory socialization and thus being more similar to the dominant group, may *by assimilation* be perceived as more like the dominant culture than it really is. Conversely, an established contraculture, being distinctly different from the dominant culture, may *by contrast* be perceived as more different than it really is—and be perceived as "the hard-core poor." Orive and Gerard (1975) found that the extent of the father's cross-racial organizational involvement was positively associated with the number of sociometric choices received by minority (black and Mexican American) children in elementary schools in Riverside, California. At least there, assimilation was operating.

However it is appropriately conceived, whatever its connection with the appearance and course of distress in school, the children of the contracultures of the slums—rural and urban—develop special modes of individual and systemic tension management that deserve special attention. The self-consciousness may be disruptive of interpersonal skills even within the contraculture. The exclusive focus on structure and the ignorance of function could mean an ignorance of the essential functions that must be performed by individuals in structural positions within the contraculture. The conception of the world as players and pawns could mean a disruption of a sense of potency and responsibility, and a particularly threatening internal antisocial behavior. Clear and valid explication is still to be developed.

THE IN-SCHOOL CONTEXT OF DISTRESS AT SCHOOL

Social Structure of Classrooms

The social structure of classrooms develops quickly—within a few weeks at most—and remains very much the same throughout a school year (see, for example,

Bonney, 1942, 1943; Lippitt Gold, 1959, Moreno, 1934; Wellman, 1926). Almost all pupils are quite aware of the structure of the classroom social system and perceive their position in it with considerable accuracy (Gold, 1958; Goslin, 1962; Lippitt, Polansky, & Rosen, 1952; Potashin, 1946). The components of the class-room social system are mutually attracted pairs and subgroups, plus a few con-tinuing isolates (Criswell, 1939; Jennings, 1937; Moreno, 1934). The stable sub-groups tend to be composed of children—usually of the same social class and sex—who have similar values and personality traits and are often in contact with one another because of proximity in the classroom or neighborhood (Austin & Thompson, 1948; Kuhlen & Lee, 1943; Seagoe, 1933). A centralized hierarchy, as distinguished from a diffuse structure, seems to provide greater stability and to produce more accurate self-perceptions of status, but it provides a less emotionally supportive social climate (Schmuck, 1962, 1963). It is in such a social context that the schoolchild must learn the alternative modes of behavior available and the consequences of adopting each mode.

Isolation in the classroom has been a matter of considerable interest and the subject of considerable research. The findings have been consistent: Isolation is associated with anxiety, low self-esteem, poor interpersonal skills, and emotional handicaps (Bower, 1960; Gronlund, 1959; Horowitz, 1962; Mensh & Glidewell, 1958; Smith, 1958). In the classroom, isolation is not a very effective tension-management device. Instead of reducing tension and enabling conflict resolution, it increases the conflict and distorts perception.

Less interest has been shown in the development of small contracultures of pairs and subgroups who value, approve, and award status for behavior opposite of that approved by most pupils and the teacher. Especially the experiment of Kerstetter and Sargent (1940), but also the work of Kerr (1945) and Shoobs (1947), has shown the nature of such contracultures within the classroom and the resistance to their change.

Of still less interest has been the *invisible child.* Painter (1962) reported that, in the practice of child psychiatry, some quite healthy children were referred to him as "emotionally ill." Their only symptom was that they seemed to be unaware of the social expectations of them—the expectations of other children. Hudgins and Loftis (1966) have commented on the invisible child who was not rejected by other children and not an isolate in the usual sense, simply was not noticed by other children or by adults. Further, such a child did not seem to need to be noticed. Stringer and Glidewell (1965) have made similar comments. Trained observers in the classroom had great difficulty because a few children simply went unnoticed during the observation period. Gronlund (1959) and also Northway (1944) ob-served that there are some healthy, self-sufficient, or socially uninterested children who seemed to be unaware of the classroom social structure or their position in it. The nature of the personality and social adaptation of such invisible children is not clear from the data, but it is clear that they *cannot* be categorized as isolates, and they *cannot* be assumed to be in distress.

Teacher Social Power and Its Use

A large number of investigations have indicated systematic effects of (a) the degree of dispersion and the manner of employment of the social power and (b) the allocation of emotional acceptance by the teacher. Intervention of any sort at any point in the classroom social system has been demonstrated to produce effects in most of the related parts and, sometimes, throughout the classroom social system. The manner of intervention of a teacher into the behavior of any individual pupil influences, not only the response of the individual pupil, but also (a) the behavior of many watching pupils, (b) the perception by the classroom group of the fairness of the teacher, and (c) the perception by the classroom group of the target pupil's power and competence—in sum, the whole social organization and work pattern of the classroom. The dynamics of these teacher-classroom relationships were particularly well analyzed and demonstrated in the work of Thelen (1950, 1951, 1967) in the late 1940s and early 1950s, of Flanders (1951), and subsequently, of Rehage (1951), of Levitt (1955), of Leeds (1956), of Perkins (1957), of Birth and Prillwitz (1959), of Tausch (1958a, 1958b, 1960, 1962), of Cogan (1958), of Gnagey (1960), of Kounin, Gump, and Ryan (1961), of Bossert (1975), and of Brophy and Good, 1974.

Of particular significance are two studies of values. Bronfenbrenner, Devereau, Suci, and Rodgers (1965) found that children's reports of their teachers' behavior toward them showed a closer relationship to their own value reports than did their reports of their parents' behavior. Schmuck and Van Egmond (1965) also found that parental attitudes toward school and achievement were less important in affecting academic work than the children's relationships with their teachers. Epstein and McPartland (1977) found, however, that participation in family decisions combined with degree of family regulation had positive effects on self-reliance, self-esteem, and prosocial behavior and that those family effects were greater than school effects, significant as the latter were. Family and school thus compete for influence on students, but the teacher remains a powerful social agent.

The particular effects of the teachers' dispersion of their power and emotional acceptance have included: (a) increased pupil-to-pupil interaction, (b) reduced interpersonal conflicts and anxieties, (c) increased mutual public esteem and increased self-esteem, (d) wider dispersion and flexibility of peer social power, (e) greater tolerance for divergent opinions in the initial phases of problem solving, (f) greater convergence of opinion in the later phases of problem solving, (g) increased self-initiated work, and (h) increased independence of opinion. Such dispersion alone has not, however, produced any regular improvement in academic achievement. The details are covered in a prior review (Glidewell, Kantor, Smith, & Stringer, 1966) and are being further explained by the current research of Marshall (1978).

Preventive intervention into classroom socialization might well attempt to slow up the formation of the first social structure. One might be able to maintain at least temporarily a more diffuse structure than usual and, more permanently, induce a greater flexibility of structure. The research findings available suggest that such modifications could be accomplished by varying (a) the learning activities of the classrooms so that a greater variety of physical and social skills were required, (b) the physical proximity of the children in the classroom, (c) the size of the work groups assigned to learning tasks, and (d) the distribution of teacher power and emotional acceptance, including delegation of teacher power to pupils with special competencies not usually recognized.

Deliberately maintaining a more flexible, and thereby more diffuse, social structure in the classroom will also make it more difficult for children—and teacher—to be sure of their positions in the classroom social structure, make the criteria for the relevance of social behavior less clear, and induce a higher level—not a lower level—of tension in the system. Accordingly, in order for such modifications to prevent distress, they must be accompanied by some forms of tension management. The psychosocial bases for, and the nature of, some forms of tension management are analyzed in the following sections.

PSYCHOSOCIAL RESOURCES

On entry into school, the child has developed some particular set of personal psychosocial resources. It seems credible that the individual differences among children in the development of such resources are the products of the interplay among the individual differences in factors in the physical, biological, and social environment of the children. Whatever their preschool antecedents, the school and the child must work with these resources.

Temperament

Recently a number of scientists have become interested again in the interaction between nature and nurture in the development of psychiatric disorders in childhood. The longitudinal studies of Chess (1969) and Birch, Thomas, and Chess in New York (1966) represent an excellent example of the reawakened interest. Since 1956 they have followed a sample of 136 children. Data have been collected by interviews with parents and teachers, by direct observation of the children at home and at school, and by standardized tests. Psychiatric evaluation and periodic clinical follow-up examinations have been completed on each case of behavior disturbance. In most of the children, the consistency of the expressions of temperament at different ages was striking. Significant changes occurred in a few children. More important, both the constancies and the changes could be explained, in the concepts of the investigators, by the interaction between the temperaments of the children and the demands of their environment.

Analyses over the first 5 years of life indicated that the temperamental constancies and changes could be differentiated by five variables: (1) regularity of biological functions, (2) adaptability in new situations, (3) positiveness of approach, (4) mood, and (5) intensity of reactions. The most prevalent combination of these factors involved regularity of life-style, positive approach to new stimuli, easy adaptation to change, a preponderance of positive mood, and reactions of mild-to-moderate intensity. Such children are easy to socialize and they show few problems in school. Generally, they are well liked by almost everybody—parents, pediatricians, psychiatrists, and pedagogues.

The diametrically opposite combination is the least prevalent. As indicated in the foregoing section, life at school is particularly difficult for children who respond to new stimuli negatively or by withdrawal, who are slow in adapting to changes in their environment, who show frequent negative moods, and who react with great intensity. The temperament of the child is not in itself a problem. The social systems of the school can sometimes provide a consistent set of demands, tolerance for slow adaptation to change, and tension management by personal support during intense negative moods; and the difficult child adapts to the school. Teachers who understand that their role is one of influence—but not an all-determining one—on the child, often find such children interesting, predictable, dependable, independent in their opinions, and zestful in their responses to the learning demands at school.

Socialization at school is still, however, primarily a conformity-inducing process; and the intense, negative, slow-to-adapt child presents more behavior problems than other children. The New York studies have identified, in 42 of the 136 children, mild-to-severe behavior problems of some form, of both long and short duration, during the 5 years of follow-up. The environmental demands that produced stress to the point of symptom formation were not the same for all children. The intense, negative, slow-to-adapt children showed a higher incidence of behavior problems—typically in response to impatient, inconsistent, and punitive demands from adults. The moderate, positive, adaptable children showed a lower incidence of behavior problems. When they did present problems, it was in response to conflicting demands between the home and some external agent—often a school (Chess, Thomas, & Birch, 1959).

Intellect

A number of investigators have found relationships between intelligence and "acceptance" in the socialization process. The correlations range between .00 and .45, and they average about .20. Examples of such studies are those of Bonney (1942, 1943), Deitrich (1964), Grossman and Wrighter (1948), Kuhlen and Lee (1943), Laughlin (1954), Potashin (1946), Shoobs (1947), and Young and Cooper (1944). Other work has demonstrated that the utilization of intelligence increase with both social acceptance and social power in the classroom (Schmuck, 1962, 1963; Schmuck & Van Egmond, 1965; Van Egmond, 1960). On the other hand, intellectual resources were not related to the psychosocial resources as estimated by social workers (based on interviews with mothers): self-esteem, interpersonal skills, competence, responsibility, productivity, and enjoyment. These data were interpreted as meaning that resources influenced how children used their intellect but that resources were not determined, and perhaps not limited, by childrens' intellectual endowment (Stringer & Glidewell, 1967).

Work on achievement and mental health has shown that most children do not achieve in school at a steady rate; they achieve in cycles.. When the *rate of gain* as measured by achievement tests, for individual children, is plotted against the norm (mean rate for national sample), most plots show a rate higher than norm one year, followed by a rate lower than norm the next year. In schools placing much pressure on children to achieve, the high phase of the cycle may last 2 years; the low phase, 1 year. In schools placing little pressure on children to achieve, the frequency of the cycle is reduced. The findings indicate that intellectual resources can be mobilized by socialization processes, but that some occasional relaxation will occur. The data provide an excellent example of pacing as a tension-management method.

Of special interest, however, is the pattern of deviant low achievement that was identified by the research. One pattern emerged in which the alternation was rapidly reduced (not by limited intelligence) in the early school years. In the subsequent years, the pattern showed more deviant low achievement, was more often out of phase, and showed few recovery cycles, until the child's achievement rate was stabilized far below expectancy. The data implied that the tensions were not managed. A deviation-amplifying cycle had been generated. The initial kick was not clearly specified in the data, but low self-esteem was the likely starter, more likely than low intelligence (Stringer, McMahan, & Glidewell, 1962).

Interpersonal Skills

The development of interpersonal skills is a fundamental aspect of the socialization process. In order for children to become aware of the alternative modes of behavior available to them and the consequences of adopting each mode, they must make some early experiments either in initiating interaction or in waiting and watching. They must judge the nature of others' responses to their initiatives or lack of initiatives and modify their future initiatives and responses accordingly—whether they tend to conform or to deviate. A kind of self-reinforcing circular process builds up. Dominative behavior stimulates dominative behavior (Anderson, 1939). Emergent leaders must meet group norms if they are to influence the new group (Merei, 1949). Behavior that is both aggressive and noncooperative tends to provoke rejection by peers (Schmidt, 1958), but boys who exhibit active-assertive behavior that is also cooperative in the eyes of others are more often accepted—and are most responsive to peer approval (Patterson & Anderson, 1964). Hostile behavior, negative affect, and peer rejection appear to be in a close mutual connection, each reinforcing the other (Lippitt & Gold, 1959), except in schools of predominantly lower-class children, where belligerence and aggressiveness characterize a well-accepted leader among both boys and girls—a leader who is not necessarily liked but is clearly respected and influential (Pope, 1953; Lippitt, Polansky, & Rosen, 1952). The process of learning these alternatives and their consequences is a part of the process of developing the interpersonal skills necessary to any choice about acceptance, conformity, dependence, independence, influence, and cooperation.

Self-esteem

One of the concepts most commonly invoked to specify a psychosocial resource is the concept of self-esteem. A considerable body of evidence has accumulated to show that physical condition, social-class background, and intelligence have significant but *limited* influences upon the self-conception with which a pupil enters an elementary school classroom. Moreno's classroom sociometric studies of the 1930s (1934) showed such influences in New York; Bonney (1942, 1943) found similar phenomena in Texas. Neugarten (1946) and Stendler (1949) in the U.S. Midwest and Potashin (1946) in Canada also confirmed these findings. Force (1954) observed that children with obvious physical handicaps suffered in self-esteem and gained only limited acceptance by peers. Moss and Kagan (1961) reported a relationship between *increases* in self-evaluation and *increases* in IQ scores between ages 6 and 10. The question becomes: How is self-esteem further influenced by the classroom socialization process?

The connection between self-esteem and position in the social organization of the classroom is reasonably well established. Unfortunately the connection is enmeshed in a complex of interrelations with other social and personal characteristics (see, for example, Glidewell et al., 1966). The studies of Bonney (1942, 1943) showed that some of the characteristics associated with extensive social acceptance and social power in the classroom were self-confidence, self-respect, and self-awareness—all of which may be considered components of self-esteem. Kifer (1973) found over an 8-year period a steadily increasing distance between the self-evaluations of students who remained in the upper 20% of their class in achievement and those who remained in the lower 20%. Baron (1951) found that girls high in peer status in their classrooms felt a clear sense of efficacy in coping with their environmental demands, whereas low-status girls often felt inadequate to meet what they perceived as excessive environmental demands. Coopersmith (1959) found high self-esteem to be associated with more extensive acceptance by peers in the classroom. He also found that pupils with low self-esteem tended to show more anxiety. The connection with anxiety and other manifestations of distress has been confirmed by Douglas (1959), Feldhusen and Thurston (1964), Horowitz (1962), McCandless, Castameda, and Palermo (1956), and Trent (1957). Rosenberg (1965) has shown similar connections in adolescent society. Slaughter (1977) found similar connections in a longitudinal study of black Head Start pupils. These studies have been put together here in a way never originally intended by the investigators. They have been designated as studies of self-esteem in spite of the facts that each involved a somewhat different conception of what was being studied and that each employed different approaches to measuring what are here called aspects of self-esteem. In spite of these differences, the studies do show one clear convergence: There is a connection between self-evaluation, competence, status, and the capacity to cope with the stresses of the process of socialization in the classroom.

Patterns

In the St. Louis County research program, Stringer and Glidewell (1967) studied the psychosocial resources of a sample of 247 white elementary school children, predominantly middle class, of both sexes. The development of the resources was assessed by an interview with the mothers. They found that the five resources studied were themselves closely related to an estimate of the mental health of the child, that each was less closely related to the number of symptoms the child presented to his or her mother, and that each was least closely related to his or her achievement rate at school. The findings are summarized in Table 8-3.

Each of the resource scales was positively and significantly related to casework judgments of (a) the quality of the parents' marriage, and (b) family support of the child. These findings are more interesting when it is noted that these psychosocial resources were unrelated to intelligence ($r = .00$ for boys, $r - .23$ for girls and not significantly different from 0). The data suggest that these resources may well be

TABLE 8-3 Correlations between Psychosocial Resources, Mental Health, Behavior Symptoms, and Achievement ($N = 247$)

	Variables							
	1	2	3	4	5	6	7	8
1. Mental health		84	82	77	73	70	−68	31
2. Self-esteem			82	78	71	65	−63	28
3. Enjoyments				81	75	60	−62	33
4. Competence-productivity					64	63	−48	29
5. Interpersonal skills						68	−51	29
6. Coping efficiency							−45	21
7. Number of symptoms								−17
8. Achievement								

different manifestations of the same thing. That "thing" may be "mental health" or it may be success in coping with the problems of socialization—tension management. To some extent, it is the absence of behavior symptoms; but it is clearly less the absence of illness than it is the presence of health. If any one component is central to these resources, it appears to be that conceptually elusive quality, "self-esteem."

The most promising aspect of these findings is that they suggest that such resources make it possible for a child to withstand the stresses of socialization at school with less difficulty. At the risk of straining an analogy, highly developed psychosocial resources may provide something like immunity to the inevitable exposure to the stresses of socialization in the way that antibodies provide immunity to the inevitable exposure to communicable diseases. Behind mental health, self-esteem, and enjoyments is the factor of "competence-productivity," that is, the record of working effectively. Although this is not simply doing well on achievement tests, it is a record of achievement at school. Thus, such achievement may well "immunize" a child to behavior disorders (Bloom, 1976, pp. 139-160). Preliminary findings from Dolan's (1977) research confirm this "immunization effect."

Another promising aspect of these findings is that the development of such resources proceeds at school as well as at home. The development is linked in some way with the process of finding or being assigned a position in the social structure of classrooms. The chain of influences is probably a mutually causative, spiral development, such as that specified in general theory by Maruyama (1963), so that neither resources nor position is clearly the antecedent. The implication is, however, that some form of intervention into the process of classroom social organization could be an important approach to facilitating the development of resources and the prevention of behavior problems. Experiments with planned subgrouping with the classroom have not been encouraging. As soon as the enforced subgrouping is relaxed, the classroom tends to return to its prior organization (Kerr, 1945; Kerstetter & Sargent, 1940; Shoobs, 1947). Modification of teachers' uses of their social power shows much more promise. Beginning perhaps with Rehage's (1951) experiment, a number of studies have indicated that variations in the way teachers distribute their power and acceptance among children influence the social organization of the classroom (if not the academic achievement of the individual children) (Cogan, 1958; Flanders, 1951; Medley & Mitzel, 1959; Minuchin, 1964). These implications for preventive intervention require close attention to the psychosocial context of distress at school.

MANIFESTATIONS OF DISTRESS AT SCHOOL

In spite of considerable effort to validate assessments of mental health and illness at school, the specification of conceptually distinct emotional problems of school children has been unsatisfactory. Studies in Philadelphia and Los Angeles by Paynter and Blanchard (1928), in Chicago by Ackerson (1931), in Leicester by Cummings (1944), in Minneapolis by Griffiths (1952), in Berkeley by Macfarlane and her associates (Macfarlane, Allen, & Honzik, 1954), in Buffalo by Lapouse and Monk (1958), in California by Bower (1960) and in the county of Buckinghamshire by Sheperd, Oppenheim, and Mitchell (1966) and Mitchell and Sheperd (1966)—all these studies entailed analyses of the appearance and course of symptoms of emotional problems, but none of them produced clearly delineated problem entities.

Most of these studies involved a sample of school children, most of whom presented no serious problems. Perhaps the prevalence is too low to permit analyses that will do what is generally desired, specifically (a) clearly distinguish one kind of problem from another, (b) assess the degree of severity of the problem, (c) identify the significant points in the course of the development of the problem, and (d) yield some possible inferences about the nature of the factors that brought on the problem.

Analyses of the manifestations of distress in more seriously disturbed children has shown more progress. For example, Lorr and Jenkins (1953), extending the work of Hewitt and Jenkins (1946) and Jenkins and Glickman (1946) analyzed data from clinical case records and found five replicable factors: (1) socialized delinquency, (2) internal conflict, (3) unsocialized aggressiveness, (4) schizoid pattern, and (5) brain injury.

Peterson (1961), like Ackerson (1931), was able empirically to distinguish "conduct problems" (antisocial behavior) from "personality problems" (low self-esteem, withdrawal, dysphoric mood). Ruter (1965) reviewed a number of research findings and confirmed the distinction of antisocial behavior from other disorders. He also suggested that developmental disorders could be empirically distinguished from other antisocial and neurotic disorders of children. Another review by the Group for the Advancement of Psychiatry (1966) yielded a quite detailed classification, but its empirical substantiation remains to be accomplished. The factor analyses (of various reports from clinicians and parents) of Lorr and Jenkins (1953), Coan and Cattell (1959), and Peterson (1961) are difficult to summarize, but each includes a differentiation of antisocial behavior, of achievement problems, of hyperactivity, of developmental problems, of some form of intrapersonal emotional tension or neurotic problems, of very rare childhood psychosis, and of damage to the central nervous system. When similar data on general, nonclinical samples of children are analyzed, no such clear-cut factors emerge, except for the several manifestations of antisocial behavior (Glidewell, 1968).

When teachers are asked to report the behavior of children in school, they do give rather clear indications of what they consider to constitute manifestations of distress at school. For example, in some of the St. Louis County studies, factor analyses of behavior problems (reported by some 60 teachers on six samples each of 200 elementary school children) showed that teachers perceived four manifestations of psychosocial distress: intrapersonal distress, defects of interpersonal skills, antisocial behavior, and slow achievement (Glidewell, 1968). There was also a possible additional factor—hyperactivity—but it was not so clearly a separate entity. These findings converge with those of the investigators who were stimulated by Wickman's (1928) comparisons of teachers and clinicians in their views of the significance of the behavior problems of children. For example Stouffer (1952) and Beilin (1959) questioned Wickman's methods and findings and produced evidence that teachers and clinicians in the 1940s and 1950s tended to agree rather well with each other about the significance of specified behavior problems. Their data also indicate that the teachers were concerned about particular problems of the same sort: intrapersonal distress, interpersonal skills, antisocial behavior, and achievement.

To say that teachers and clinicians agree about the "significance" of these problems is not to say that either of them see the problems as mental illnesses. Agreement between teachers and clinicians about whether particular children are mentally ill has been somewhat irregular in the United States. Ullman (1952) in Maryland; Glidewell, Mensh, and Gildea (1957) in Missouri; and Bower (1960) in California found rather substantial agreement (about 70–80%) between teachers and mental health specialists, but each worked with samples selected in rather different ways. Goldfarb (1963) in Maryland found significantly less agreement (about 60%). The indications are that, to teachers, distress at school is clearly not the same thing as mental illness. The problems to which they are sensitive appear to be more accurately considered to be evidences of ineffective socialization: intrapersonal distress, interpersonal ineptness, antisocial behavior, lagging achievement. Connected with such problems or even underlying them may be some neurological defect, some psychiatric pathology such as an incipient schizophrenia, but teachers rarely undertake such judgments. Children with childhood schizophrenia very, very rarely appear in school. Children who are later to become schizophrenic in adulthood do appear in school, but effective *predictive* identification remains to be demonstrated.

An extensive survey of studies of prevalence of behavior problems has been made by Glidewell and Swallow (1968). The most prevalent problems were problems of intrapersonal distress. They included temper tantrums, daydreaming, unusual fears, and frequent crying. They appeared in about 20% of school children. The unusual fears and crying appeared more often in girls than boys. The next-most prevalent problem was the deficit of interpersonal skill, appearing in about 15% of school children, and showing no sex differences. Antisocial behavior appeared in only 5% of the children and appeared more often in boys than girls.

Although distress at school may be a manifestation of some pathological intrapsychic processes having their roots far outside the school, such distress is also, and perhaps alternately, a manifestation of problems of socialization in school. No matter how much value a society may set on originality, the socialization process is clearly a conformity-producing process. Conformity, however, is a very complex phenomenon. Learning by children of the modes of behavior available to them, and of the consequences of adopting each mode, can and does produce a wide variety of "cost-benefit analyses" by children and, accordingly, a wide variety of patterns of conforming and deviating in various degrees along many dimensions. If children are to approach the stresses involved in testing their urges against the social costs and benefits, they must use the resources and inclinations available to them to manage the tensions involved while they choose their modes of response to socialization. To be expressive or to be stoic, to talk or to act, to seek help or to help themselves, to approach family and friends or to approach teachers and doctors, to attend to people or to attend to work, to watch and wait, or to act and assert—these are the kinds of conflicts. Socialization need not reward only one side of a conflict. Children can learn to sense not only what is happening to them but also what is possible for them in their group—a judgment of prospects for accomplishing both their own goals and the goals of socialization at school.

Based upon all the foregoing work, the socialization process can be seen to be a cyclic, systemic process. One may begin an analysis at any point on the cycle. Beginning at the point of new understanding of a psychosocial process in the classroom, I propose that any new understanding increases a child's competence and productivity. The increased productivity makes the child more attractive to the other people in the classroom and makes the others more attractive to the child. Interaction thereby increases. The new interactions bring the child (sooner or later) into contact with some strange ideas and practices, and that contact increases anxiety, noise, and confusion. Tensions increase. The child wards off the tension, reduces her or his interaction rate, and seeks to regain composure and foresight. The cycle thus corrects itself.

When the tensions are well managed, work and thought continue during the cycle, and it ends with another new understanding of psychosocial processes. With that new understanding, the cycle begins again, attraction increases, interaction increases, and so forth. Tension can thus be seen to act as a governor for the speed of the cycle. When tensions are managed effectively, the cycle accelerates until tensions again become unmanageable. The cycle then decelerates until the tensions are manageable.

Groups, classrooms, and, in turn, schools develop systemic ways of maintaining the demands of socialization, maintaining the tensions involved, and, concurrently, managing the tensions with relief, support, and reduction of risks, so that they do not negate the learning opportunity. The manifestations of stress are often more accurately conceived as failures of tension management—individual or systemic—than as personal defects.

The foregoing findings show certain influences of culture, class, and family on the approaches to tension management during socialization, approaches that provide resources and limitations for preventive intervention at school. Some children will be expressive; some, stoic. Some children will seek help; some, steadfastly refuse it. Some will seek help from professionals like teachers and doctors; some, from family and friends. Some children will speak freely of their motives and emotions; some, consider their motives and emotions private matters. Some children will work on their problems with words; some, only with activity. Some will watch their problems and wait; some, attack their problems and fight. Some children will expect friendly responses to their initiatives; some, hostile responses. Some children will perceive most of their world as friendly and benign; some, as hostile and malign and seek safety in a small supportive contraculture, "us against the world." Any program of preventive intervention that depends upon an induction of conformity to any one of these approaches to tension management during socialization is necessarily limited.

The following sections contain accounts of attempts to develop preventive school mental health programs—attempts at systemic tension management to hold the line so that the people involved can work and also develop conflict resolutions.

PREVENTIVE SCHOOL MENTAL HEALTH
INTERVENTIONS

The research findings in the preceding sections have relatively clear implications for the design of programs of experimental preventive intervention into the development of distress at school. The implications are that programs based on open discussion of motives and feelings, on the recognition of the need for professional help, on verbal problem solving, and on abstractions about personal distress will run into cultural barriers. In addition, programs of training and consultation about socialization at school that are based on prime responsibility to the individual; that appeal to motives and feelings; and that focus on children, active involvement, introspection, and self-awareness will run into institutional barriers. Programs of intervention into the adult social system in the school that are based upon involvement, confrontation, and conflict resolution will run into barriers of group norms and professional privilege. Several experimental preventive programs that used clinical services are summarized, and as far as the data are available, their contact with the community is analyzed in the sections that follow.

The child-guidance clinic was developed as an innovation within the health institution. The growth of the movement and its doctrine has been traced in a collection of papers edited by Tulchin (1964). It was preventive only in the sense that treatment of children might prevent illness in adults or treatment of the family might prevent illness in other children in the family. The functional process was therapeutic. It was operated by a team of both medical and nonmedical specialists, but the codes of practice of medicine were carefully followed (Stevenson & Smith, 1934). In the eyes of the community, medical practice was the best legitimized professional practice. Psychologists and social workers—explicitly or implicitly— established the legitimacy of their professional practice when they associated themselves with "the doctor" and followed the doctor's codes and customs in taking care of "the patient." To an ill patient in distress, the customs were appropriate, because the practice of medicine, during the 1930s, had an excellent reputation for relieving distress and curing illnesses (Ackerman, 1945).

Role Confusions

There were, however, complications. The social role of "the patient" was not so clear when a child had a phobia as it was when a child had measles. In its preventive, orthopsychiatric orientation, the clinic proposed to treat the whole family even when the whole family did not consider itself to be ill. Further, in the past when a child became ill with the measles, it was clear that the parents did not cause the illness. When the child had a school phobia, however, the child-guidance clinic staff led one to believe that the child's distress just might have been caused by the way the parents had raised the child.

Still further, when a child had measles, he or she was taken out of school, kept more or less in bed, and relieved of his or her usual family and school responsibilities. When a child was painfully timid, however, he or she was often expected to continue in school, stay out of bed, and discharge the usual responsibilities. If the child had the measles, he or she was expected to try to get well as soon as possible, and the best way to get well was to do exactly what the doctor and parents told him or her to. The parents were agents of the doctor's professional expertise. In the child guidance clinic, by contrast, the child was told that the outcome of treatment depended largely upon his or her own efforts; the child could not depend on the doctor to know just what the child should do. To complicate matters further, the parents were by no means the doctor's agents; they were patients, too (Allen, 1934). The traditional role of the patient, complementary and reciprocal to the role of the doctor, so functional for treating acute communicable diseases, was vague, overlapping, inequitable, and confused in this treatment of a family for a chronic, noncommunicable distress, which might not be a disease at all, and there were high tensions.

At the point at which the school referred a child to the clinic, still further complications arose. Now the teacher, as well as the parents, was involved. It was not at all explicit whether the teacher, too, was a patient, but it was often implied that the teacher's behavior toward the child might have induced or aggravated the problems. It was often explicitly stated that the teacher *could* become a therapeutic agent—an agent of the doctor's—if only she or he could develop the proper relationship with the child and develop the proper therapeutic skills as well.

Many social scientists (e.g., Gouldner, 1960) have proposed that the viability of any social system may depend upon the development and modification of consensual norms of complementarity and reciprocity. Given such a confusion about the complementarity and reciprocity in the school-family-clinic relationship, one might expect considerable tension to be evident in their interchanges, and one might even expect some question about the viability of the relationship. I have made a more complete analysis of tension management in helping subsystems in a previous paper (Glidewell, 1972).

Tensions and Their Sources

Manifestations.

There have been a number of accounts of the tensions involved when clinical services have been extended into the schools (Board of Education, 1955; Cutts, 1955; Newton & Brown, 1967; Seeley, Sim, & Loosley, 1956; Tri-state Conference on School Psychology, 1962). The following excerpt from a report by Stringer (1962), from the St. Louis County experiences, is typical.

> A ghastly discrepancy soon appeared between what had been planned and what actually occurred, ghastly at least to those of us who worked in the schools. . . . We were foreign bodies in the system of every school we worked in. . . . They found indirect (but quite effective) means to control us. One was to encapsulate us and hold us safely inactive. . . . Another was to give us only irremediable cases to work with. . . . In two . . . districts we were clearly regarded rather as trouble-makers than as trouble-shooters; in the third, more favorably disposed district, we had roughly sixty referrals that seemed to be immovable. (p. 7)

Focus of Responsibility

In St. Louis County, one source of tension was the institutional differences in the focus of responsibility (Glidewell & Stringer, 1967). Within the community health institution, the classical clinical orientation placed the prime value on the health of the patient. Whether the patient had become ill or injured legitimately or illegitimately was irrelevant. On the other hand, in the community educational institution, the classical pedagogical orientation placed the prime value on socialization—the accommodation of the individual's motives and resources to the demands of competent citizenship in the society into which the child was being inducted. It was quite important whether the accommodation was made legitimately or illegitimately. Within the clinic, in one-to-one interaction, the clinician could, for long periods of time, give undivided attention to one patient. In the classroom, a teacher could rarely, and for very short periods of time, give undivided attention to one pupil. Accordingly, the clinician's recommendations to a teacher often demanded more responsibility and attention to the individual child than was appropriate in the classroom. The teacher's suggestions often demanded more responsibility and attention to the classroom and community norms than was appropriate to the clinical requirements for therapy. Similar discrepancies between focuses of responsibility have been reported by Lindemann (1957) of the Wellesley group by Neubauer and Beller (1958) and by Sarason (1966).

Intrapersonal versus Interpersonal Sources

Another institutional difference appears to be the usual assumption about the seat of the problem. The traditional clinical assumption has been that, however generated, the significant problem lies within the individual. In contrast, the traditional educational assumption has been that the significant problem lies in the approach of some socialization agent (usually a parent) to inducing behavior change in the child. To the clinician, experience has indicated that modification of the patient's environment will lead only to new manifestations of the problem. To the teacher, experience has indicated that modification of a pupil's environment often leads to the end of the problem. Both clinician and teacher have had their views reinforced by their experience, but each was dealing with a different kind of problem and a different population of children. Sanford (1966), although working at the college level, made a discerning analysis of the conflict. He found that the educational process must, in the interest of learning, induce tensions in students. Education must include the support of ideas in profound conflict with cherished and long-standing beliefs of the pupil, beliefs about the nature of the world and the nature of the self. The conflict is unsettling, tension generating.

Educators can, however, by modifying their organizations, roles, or policies, improve the institutional management of the tensions of students. Counselors in the school, Sanford found, were appropriately used for individual support of students who were vulnerable but functioning, and clinicians were more appropriately used when the student must be temporarily removed from school and relieved of his or her student role.

Behavior-change Induction

A third frustration seemed to have arisen from differing assumptions about effective approaches to behavior change. Glidewell and Stringer (1967) found that the teacher regularly employs—and is regularly rewarded for—appeals to the intellect. Most children respond readily. The clinician is seldom rewarded for appeals to the intellect; most clinical patients do not respond. The clinician regularly employs—and is regularly rewarded for—appeals to motives and emotions. Her or his patients may not respond so readily, but they respond to nonintellectual appeals much more readily than to intellectual appeals. Frequently, that is why they are in the clinic and not in the classroom.

In summary, among the fundamental differences between the health institution and the educational institution, there were three that generated understandable tensions: (1) the differences in focus of responsibility: recovery of individual health versus accommodation of individual and society, (2) the differences in the perception of the locus of the problem: inside the person or in the social system, and (3) the differences in the assumptions about the most effective way of inducing behavior change: appeal to motives and emotions versus appeals to intellect. Thus, the social psychology of the educational institution was in conflict with the social psychology of the health institution.

Psychosocial Forces against Referral

A number of studies (e.g., in Glidewell & Swallow, 1968) of histories of children referred by elementary schools for clinical services have shown that the behavior that prompted the referral had been apparent in the very early grades. About 60% could have been referred, on the data in their records, from 1 to 8 years before they were referred. One-third of them could have been identified as early as grade 1; two-thirds, by grade 3. The children in distress were much more likely to fail a grade than their functioning classmates. Where the distress was accompanied by academic failure, very few children were able to cope with their distress without special help (Stringer, 1963). When a sample of 12 third-grade, 12 fourth-grade, and 12 fifth-grade teachers was given opportunity for unlimited referral, they actually referred less than one-half of those children whom they believed needed clinical help (Glidewell & Swallow, 1968). In discussions, such teachers have identified two strong forces delaying referral. From the teacher's point of view, and indeed in fact, to be referred to a mental health professional is a blow to the self-respect of a child and the child's family, and referral stigmatizes a child in the school and the neighborhood. In addition, such symptoms as those usually prompting referral often disappear within a year. In fact, in St. Louis County, 80% of them disappeared within a year (Glidewell, Gildea, & Kauffman, 1973). Still further, once having referred a child, the teacher seldom had received clinical comments or recommendations that were considered useful. From the point of view of the teacher, it was unwise to risk the prospect of so little gain against the prospect of so much loss. It was sensible and realistic to delay referral. In one sense, the teacher was adopting the folk-reliant attitude of the lower classes and of some closely knit ethnic groups. It seems a surprising attitude for a middle-class professional teacher.

From the point of view of the clinician, the referral ought to have been made earlier, but clinicians, too, felt the strain of the problems of reporting and recommending action to teachers. In the report of the analysis of the work of the Bureau of Child Guidance of the New York City schools (Board of Education, 1955), the clinicians, too, expressed a belief that the traditional clinical team approach "yields information of a kind that . . . does not lend itself readily to the formulation of a plan whereby the school may work more effectively with the child" (p. 13). Similar concerns about the linkage between the clinic and the school or, indeed, between the school psychologist and the teacher within the school, were recorded at the Thayer Conference in 1952 (Cutts, 1955) and at the Tri-state Conference on School Psychology (1962), and they have been made the subject of a cogent historical analysis by Lighthall (1963).

Summary: Clinical Services for School

Most of the observations just cited indicate that teachers regularly seek relief from the very real stresses generated by the behavior of markedly deviant children in their classrooms. Even though the number of children is exceedingly small, the problems they induce are acute and, in a classroom, pervasive. These stresses are psychosocial forces toward referral, but the referrals are seldom represented as prompted by the teacher's needs. The interest in special classrooms, classrooms attached to clinics, and other ways of segregating children in distress is partly occasioned by the need of the teacher and the classroom for relief from these stresses. Currently, the clinical and educational wisdom of such segregation is a matter of controversy. Perhaps new data from current research will help in planning to meet these real needs for simple relief.

The development of orthopsychiatric teamwork clinical services for children has created new kinds of clinical roles, confusingly different—to the public—from the traditional doctor-patient-parent roles appropriate to acute, infectious diseases of childhood. Such services for schools introduce additional complications as a result of differences in focus of responsibility, assumptions about the locus of the problem, and approaches to behavior-change induction. Teachers are inclined to hope for maturation or classroom intervention to reduce problems, are concerned about the stigma associated with referral, and are often doubtful about the practical outcome of clinical treatment, but they do need and seek relief from the stresses generated in a classroom by repeated deviant behavior.

PARENT EDUCATION

Conceiving distress at school to be based fundamentally in the nature of the parent-child relationship, many people involved in preventive mental health have invested their efforts in parent education programs. The basic assumption is that most problems are, at least in part, amenable to resolution by information and applied intelligence. It is an assumption that has had a long and honorable history. In the light of such a history, it seemed altogether sensible for a professional practitioner to undertake to provide concerned parents with straightforward information about the nature of child development and the nature of the processes of parent-child interaction in everyday life.

Generally, however, such educational activities were the subject of much controversy, particularly during the 1950s in the United States. The controversies were well represented in the proceedings of the National Assembly on Mental Health Education held at Cornell University, Ithaca, New York, in September 1958. The conclusions of the assembly were depressing. There were no convincing data available to support the idea that mental health education for parents had any impact at all on the prevention of distress in either parents or children.

A number of parent education programs have been observed and analyzed in a variety of ways. Brim (1959) published an especially comprehensive survey of the developments in parent education up to 1958. The working paper on educational practices in the proceedings of the National Assembly on Mental Health Education (Pennsylvania Mental Health, Inc., 1960) presented a competent review and analysis. None of these efforts revealed any clear support for the presumed effects of parent education.

As mentioned before, many community leaders were well acquainted with the tensions that accompanied the confusions about the roles of doctors and patients in dealing with social-emotional problems. The planners of parent education programs usually designed the approach to encourage the practitioner to provide relevant—and, if possible, interesting—general information but to avoid giving any specific advice about the problems of particular children. At the same time, the practitioner was often confronted in public by individuals who made urgent requests for advice about the problems of particular children. To refuse to give such needed and requested advice seemed to be too stubborn, but to offer it in such a setting seemed to be too hazardous. Tensions mounted.

In addition, troubles arose because some of the clear and straightforward information given by the professional practitioners was disturbing. The information itself seemed to produce tensions in people. Some form of tension management was needed to go along with these informational confrontations.

Some program planners decided upon what I submit was a tension-management device: They decided not to use professional practitioners at all. The popularity of group-discussion techniques reinforced this trend during the 1950s, and a number of programs were developed and offered as discussions among laypeople led by laypeople, and planned by laypeople. These efforts were supported by the experiments of Lewin and his students on the induction of behavior and attitude change by discussion and decision (Lewin, 1947). Mental health associations in many parts of the United States—including St. Louis, Missouri; Austin, Texas; and Westchester County, New York—developed such discussion programs. Other uses of laymen roles in tension management are now vigorously under development (e.g., Cowan, Trost, Lorion, Dorr, Izzo, & Isaacson, 1975).

The St. Louis Program

History

In St. Louis, a layperson–led, group-discussion, parent education program was initiated in the fall of 1949 by two St. Louis organizations: The Mental Hygiene Society and the Council for Parent Education. The two organizations later merged into the Mental Health Association of St. Louis. In three 2-hour workshops conducted by two professional consultants of the organizations, 20 people—5 men and 15 women—were trained as discussion leaders. The services of these volunteer discussion leaders were offered to all known parent organizations in the area, especially to school-connected organizations.

The program grew rapidly during the first 3 years, reaching a peak in 1953. Many leaders were trained. They conducted 245 discussion programs involving about 8,000 parents. Since that year, the activity has leveled off at about 150–200 discussion programs involving about 6,000 parents per year. Some organizations scheduled a series of two or three discussion programs for the same participants, aiming at cumulative impact. Detailed accounts of the origin and development of the program have been published by Brashear, Kenney, Buchmueller, and Gildea, (1954) and Gildea (1959).

Leadership Method

The typical program was opened by a 5-minute introduction by the discussion leader, explaining the purposes of the association, the film or skit and the discussion method to be used, and his or her role as discussion leader. He or she pointed out that he or she was a layperson, trained only in discussion leadership, not in mental health theory or practice.

Gildea has presented the philosophical position advocated in the training:

> For the purpose of this type of discussion, it was not considered necessary for the leaders to learn the content of the theory behind the structure of the film or skit used. Attitude and points of view were the things to be communicated, rather than facts; and it was held that there were no facts in the area of human relations that were incontrovertibly true for everyone in all social

classes and walks of life. The leaders were especially warned against being drawn into the position of experts in the field of parent-child relations. They were to maintain that they were lay people like the audience and equally interested in the issues under discussion. The atmosphere of relaxed exchange of ideas was sought. (Gildea, 1959, pp. 91–92)

Groups were limited to 20 or 30 for each discussion program. Larger groups were subdivided for discussion, each subgroup assigned its own leader.

A film or play was introduced and presented. Following the presentation, the discussion leader opened the discussion by raising questions about possible points of view concerning some aspect of parent-child relations portrayed in the film or play. Contributions by any member of the group were readily accepted by the leader and, sometimes, restated or clarified, if, in the leader's judgment, such a clarification would be supportive of further participation. Once participation was initiated, the leader followed the interests of the group. The leader sometimes summarized, organized, clarified, or restated the contributions for the orientation of the group but very rarely expressed personal opinions. No group decision or public commitment to try any new behavior was expected or requested.

Research reported by Gildea (1959) suggested that the "successful" lay discussion leader in the particular program was one who generally interacted vigorously with the group but was not upset by long pauses or periods of low activity. The leader was also slow to intervene in disagreements within the group except to clarify the issues or orient the discussion. She or he did not demand interaction or contribution by the members but did readily reinforce that interaction which did appear. The successful leader primary expressed concern was that the group be accurately oriented to the goals of the discussion, the issues under analysis, and the current contributions of the discussants. I suggest that the emphasis on goal orientation is also a form of tension management. It is as if the participants say, "We may disagree about how to accomplish them, but we all agree that we are seeking the same goals—the welfare of our children."

The Audience Attracted

Within the first 3 years, it became apparent that the groups most readily involved in the mental health discussions were those associated with elementary schools. Such groups contained significantly more mothers than fathers—even those groups meeting in the evenings. The discussion programs were most in demand by middle-class and upper-middle-class groups—groups typically concerned about their responsibilities as parents and about reaching future goals or preventing future problems.

Evaluation

Initially the success of the programs was defined simply by the continued requests for them. The failures—the discontinuation of the requests—were analyzed by Brashear and her associates (1954) and by Gildea (1959). Black groups and lower-class groups were difficult to get involved and at times openly hostile toward the method. Captive groups—those groups who agreed to the program but did not spontaneously request it—rejected the method more often than those who took the initiative in requesting the programs.

Armstrong (1958) investigated the interrelations among several factors involved in program evaluation and found two clusters of relationships. The reported satis-

TABLE 8-4 Interrelations between Variables Recorded for 193 Group-discussion Programs in Mental Health Education

	1	2	3	4	5	6	7	8
1. Program chairman's evaluation		.54	.39	.43	−.05	.05	.16	−.02
2. Discussion leader's evaluation			.50	.20	−.10	.16	−.08	−.00
3. Adequacy of physical situation				.16	−.03	.29	−.14	−.23
4. Ratings of leader effectiveness					.10	.25	−.07	−.10
5. Programs previously requested						.62	−.40	.10
6. Programs subsequently requested							−.50	.33
7. Number of people attending								−.34
8. Social class of neighborhood								

Note. Interrelations are tetrachoric correlation coefficients.

faction of the discussion leader and of the client group's program chairperson were associated with each other and with the physical setting. These three variables, along with ratings of leader effectiveness, made up the first cluster (see Table 8-4). This cluster was, however, surprisingly unrelated to the second cluster, which indicated that smaller middle-class groups repeatedly ask for mental health education programs and that the larger lower-class groups do not repeat their requests. Whether or not programs were repeatedly requested was, however, almost unrelated to the satisfaction participants reported with the programs.

The tentative interpretation was that the middle classes, being committed to working for future rewards and to a great faith in education as a way of improving life, keep trying to solve their problems by education—even in the face of variable outcomes. On the other hand, the lower classes, seeking immediate rewards and having less faith in education as a way of improving life, discontinue their efforts when faced by variable outcomes.

The discussion led by a layperson may be a method of managing the tensions induced by role confusions and by disturbing new ideas or practices. If the "doctor" role is eliminated, the role confusion is avoided. If the "expert" role is eliminated, the disturbing information may be more comfortably questioned, challenged, or analyzed for applicability without risk of being shown to be "wrong." If this is the case, the method of tension management must be more attractive to the middle classes than to the lower classes. One is constrained to compare a group discussion among laypeople to the development of folk medicine or, at least, to an attempt at local consensus development. The comparison must be to folk medicine in the process of formation in communities in which there were few consensual beliefs about child rearing. Indeed, most of the reported negative reactions to layperson-led discussions by participants in St. Louis took the form of demands for authoritative answers to questions—answers not available from the lay discussion leader. The data indicated that the middle classes reject folk medicine. As a group, however, the middle classes supported discussions led by laypeople. One must consider that the middle classes have less confidence in the expertise of the psychiatrist than they have in other medical practitioners. Child psychiatry, unlike pediatrics, may fall into the area of folk medicine for the middle classes. The middle classes thus may place more reliance on folk medicine in psychiatry than in pediatrics.

Accepting tentatively such speculations, what is the situation in the lower classes? The data still indicate that the lower classes tend to rely on folk medicine even in psychiatry. Why, then, do they find group discussions so unattractive? Group discussion led by laypeople must be considered folk medicine in formation and, accordingly, without authority. Lower-class parents want authoritative determination, even in their folk medicine. For the lower-class parent, I would maintain, the cures must be fully endorsed by the folk society.

Attitude Change

The conception of the particular attitudes to be changed by the program was eclectic in the beginning. Over time, however, a concept of "healthful" attitudes evolved. The consultants associated with the program gave great emphasis to the concept of parents' responsibility for the behavior of their children (see, for example, Glidewell, Gildea, & Kauffman, 1973). In the course of developing a research design for evaluating the effects of the program, the concept was further elaborated into four components: (1) certainty about child-rearing practices, (2) attitude toward own (parent) responsibility for influencing the outcome of the behavior problems of one's children, (3) awareness of multiple influences on the outcome of such behavior problems, and (4) feeling of potency to influence the outcome of such behavior problems (Gildea et al., 1961). The research demonstrated that the prevalence of in-school behavior problems is associated with these four attitudinal factors. The higher prevalence of behavior problems was associated with uncertainty, awareness of only single causation, denial of responsibility, and feeling of impotence to influence the outcome of the problem.

Experimental Assessment

During the period 1954-1957, a field experiment was mounted in St. Louis County. The design was carefully developed, and it included a test of the actual attitude change induced by the discussion programs in specified schools, with the parents of children in a sample of classrooms being randomly assigned to experimental and control conditions ($N = 426$). The details of the design were reported by Glidewell and his colleagues (1973).

Random assignment to experimental and control conditions required a significant deviation from the usual practice. Whereas ordinarily program requests were altogether voluntary and generated within the school organization, in the experiment, the randomly designated experimental groups were *asked* to request and attend the discussion programs. The control groups were asked not to attend. There was considerable early enthusiasm about the experiment and the discussion programs, but over the first-year series (three programs), attendance dropped sharply. In some schools—mostly upper-class and lower-class rather than middle-class—the drop in attendance was so sharp that the programs were discontinued. The attitude changes, however, were assessed regularly by interview with the mothers of the children. There were very few refusals—2% per year. A sample of the data is presented in Table 8-5.

The findings were that the programs had effects on the parents of boys only and that those effects occurred primarily during the first 12 months of the program—as might be expected by the drop in attendance. The male children of the parents in the experimental groups developed fewer new behavior symptoms at school and at home than did the male children of the parents in the control groups—as reported by mothers. The attitude changes were quite complex, however. The data have been subjected to more intensive analysis by Kantor, Gildea, and Glidewell (1969).

The findings were consistent with the findings of a similar experiment conducted subsequently in Austin, Texas. Hereford (1963) reported that parent education programs led by laypeople showed significant effects on 648 parents (mostly mothers). The effects included changed attitudes toward acceptance of child behavior, understanding of child behavior, and trust of children. The programs also, however, increased the parents' concern about their own adequacy as parents, a finding different from the increased certainty about child-rearing practices found in St. Louis. The children of parents in the experimental groups (compared to the children of parents in control groups) showed increased interpersonal attractiveness to their peers at school. Against teachers' ratings, however, the children showed no improvement.

Judged against the background of Bronfenbrenner's (1958) review of changes in child-rearing practices through time and across social classes, the data available suggest that parent education lay-led discussion does have some impact. The impact must be small increments of change in parent attitude and behavior accumulating over time, first in the middle classes and then, probably more by diffusion than by education, in the lower classes, with a constant lag between the two social classes over time.

The Milwaukee Project

The Rehabilitation Research and Training Center in Mental Retardation of the University of Wisconsin at Madison selected 40 low-income black mothers with IQ test scores (WAIS) below 75, each of whom had just delivered a child. Of the 40, 20 were assigned to a preventive program and 20 to a control group. The mothers in the program were given long-term training to improve their homemaking and child-rearing skills and to enhance their employment opportunities. The children were trained all day, 5 days a week, 12 months each year to enhance perceptual motor skills, cognitive and language development, and social-emotional skills. The effects upon the children of this complex, all-out effort have been marked. Intelligence test scores began at the same level in both groups; by 18 months, the two groups were different; at 66 months, the mean IQ in the experimental group was 122 and in the control group, 91. Learning, development, language skills, and social skills continue to be more favorable in the experimental group. The control group has begun to show the decline in IQ scores often found in black children; the experimental group has maintained its gains (Heber & Garber, 1975).

IN-SCHOOL PREVENTION

During the early 1950s, the St. Louis County Health Department began the development of a program of mental health services based on secondary preven-

TABLE 8-5 Change in Means of Attitude Scale: Certainty about Child-rearing Practices and Ideas

	Boys	Girls
Education	442	410
Control	58	579

tion—early identification and treatment of subclinical behavior problems to prevent their becoming more severe. The work began with an attempt to mount a program of group therapy with parents of children with subclinical problems, a program designed after that of Buchmueller and Gildea (Gildea, 1959). After 3 years of pilot work, it became apparent that such therapy groups were not viable in the suburban settings of St. Louis County.

From the pilot work there evolved a program of secondary prevention that has been described in detail and analyzed by Glidewell and Stringer (1967). The approach was consciously electic and experimental. As experience and data accumulated, theories were refined. The processes of research, as well as the findings influenced the practices (see especially Stringer's 1962 analysis).

A psychiatric social worker was made available to the schools on a regularly scheduled basis. The worker's prime purpose was to identify and arrest the first evidences of behavior disorders in children. A variety of screening methods was developed, but the primary investment was in improving the teacher's judgment in identifying the early manifestations of behavior problems in pupils. Particular attention was given also to the use of achievement rates as one screening device.

Consultation was provided to teachers and administrators. Consultation with teachers was case consultation, concerned with the management of particular children in the classroom. Consultation with administrators was concerned with the mental health implications of school policies such as promotions and retentions, truancy, pregnancy, classroom assignment, and the like.

A considerable investment was made in in-service training for teachers. In the early stages, such training was subject to the same tensions that had developed from school-clinic interaction. The differences between the school and the clinic in the focus of responsibility on the group and on the individual, the differences in the assumptions about the intra-individual problems and the interpersonal problems, the differences in the assumptions about induction of behavior change by appeal to the intellect and appeal to the emotions—all these institutional differences produced tensions in the in-service training activity. Over time, however, the tension management by the temporary social system of the in-service training group permitted the development of a mutually satisfying and clear role differentiation between the mental health professional and the educational professional, so that complementary and reciprocal interaction became possible. The details of this development have been published by Glidewell and Stringer (1967).

An important function was that of referral and liaison. Children having clinically severe problems were referred to appropriate community resources, and the worker undertook to provide a linking role between the clinical treatment facility and the school. This use of a system linkage by an overlapping role was a particularly difficult and particularly needed method of tension management.

In 1954 the program of prevention was widely expanded in St. Louis County, and the expansion made possible a comprehensive field experiment. It was possible to develop an effective experimental design both to test the effects of a dual program, including this secondary prevention service along with a parent education program, and to compare the dual program to the education program alone. The details of the final design were published by Glidewell et al. (1973).

Several criteria of effectiveness were employed: reports from mothers, ratings and reports from teachers, ratings by peers, psychological tests, and observations of interaction in the classroom. One of the most reliable of the criteria of effect was an index based upon the report of behavior symptoms by the mother of the child involved. The following sections contain a report of the findings of the effects of the program of prevention and the education program, as measured by the mothers' reports of symptoms.

New Symptoms

One preventive objective of the school mental health services was the reduction in the number of new symptoms presented by a child to his or her mother. Accordingly, a count was made of the number of symptoms reported on the second interview, but not on the first; and on the third interview, but not on the second. The mean number of such new symptoms for each sex in each classroom was taken as one criterion of preventive effectiveness.

Mothers were also asked to recall the duration of each symptom. As in all retrospective reporting, some inconsistencies appeared. For example, some mothers reported a symptom that they had not reported on the prior interview, but they reported that it had its onset *before* the prior interview. Others reported a symptom that had been reported on the prior interview but reported that it had its onset *after* the prior interview. In order to estimate the influences of such inconsistencies on the data analysis, two indexes were developed. One was a count of all new symptoms—reported on the second or third interview but not on the prior one—without regard to the consistency with the duration report. A second index was a count of only those new symptoms that were reported consistently with the duration report.

Critical Analyses

The effects of the school mental health programs on the mean number of new symptoms reported by mothers were tested by an analysis of a special incomplete-blocks design developed by Cochran. The means of the three program levels for the two periods and for the total time are shown in Tables 8-6 and 8-7.

The data show that the experimental programs accomplished a significant prevention of new symptoms in boys but not in girls. The findings were affected by inconsistencies in reporting new symptoms, but the preventive effects for the 30-month period are confirmed when only the consistently reported new symptoms are considered.

The inconsistencies deserve some attention. Generally, during the second interview, the mothers subject to the experimental programs had a particular tendency to report symptoms they had not reported on the first interview, but to recall their onset as prior to the first interview. Because of the well-known inaccuracies of retrospective reporting, one might assume that the first interview was more accurate than the recall on the second interview. In view of the ambiguity of these data, however, the analysis of the consistent reports only was taken as an adequate confirmation of the preventive effects on boys.

Social-class Mediation

The preventive effects showed some variation from one social class to another. Generally, the upper-middle and middle classes reported fewer new

TABLE 8-6 Preventive Effects: Mean Number
of New Symptoms

Program	Period of program availability (in months)		
	First period (12)	Second period (18)	Both periods (30)
Boys			
Dual	.78	.23*	1.06
Education	.65	.16*	.86
Control	.61	.49*	1.10
Total ($\bar{x}$)	.68	.29	1.01
Girls			
Dual	.52	.29	.82
Education	.67	.26	.92
Control	.52	.14	.60
Total ($\bar{x}$)	.57	.23	.78

Note. Means are adjusted for the effects of the initial number
of symptoms presented.

*Experimental programs showed significantly ($p < .05$)
lower mean number of new symptoms than the controls.

symptoms than the lower classes—during the first year of the experiment.
During the second year, however, the lower classes showed an equally low
number of new symptoms. This lag in the responsiveness of the lower classes
held over all programs for both boys and girls but was more pronounced for
the boys.

TABLE 8-7 Preventive Effects: Mean Number
of Consistently Reported New Symptoms

Program	Period of program availability (in months)		
	First period (12)	Second period (18)	Both periods (30)
Boys			
Dual	.37*	.04	.42*
Education	.19*	.04	.23*
Control	.50*	.11	.62*
Total	.35	.06	.42
Girls			
Dual	.27	.06	.33
Education	.30	.08	.36
Control	.17	.03	.18
Total	.25	.06	.29

Note. Means are adjusted for the effects of the initial number
of symptoms presented.

*Experimental programs showed significantly ($p < .05$)
lower mean number of new symptoms than the controls.

The interaction effects of social class and time on new symptoms were clear and significant, but the second-order interaction of social class, time, and program showed only a trend. To a small extent, the preventive effects (experimental versus control) were more pronounced during the second year in the lower classes; during the first, but not the second, year in the middle classes; and during both the first and the second year in the upper-middle classes.

In sum, the data show that the availability of the experimental programs had the effect of reducing the number of new symptoms presented by boys to their mothers. There was no such effect on girls. There was a slight tendency for the lower classes to respond later than the middle and upper-middle classes.

PRIMARY PREVENTION

Preschool Checkup

In the early 1950s, the Wellesley group undertook to mount a comprehensive preschool psychiatric checkup (Lindemann, 1957). Their findings were that the practice made possible the identification of behavior problems 1–4 years earlier than had been possible in the past without such checks. They also found that identification was tension inducing as well as informative. Some teachers and parents were not very sympathetic with the early identification, and the service ran into the typical difficulties associated with therapeutic clinical services in schools.

Stringer, in the early 1960s, undertook a somewhat different attempt to accomplish the same results. All the mothers of children entering kindergarten were requested to come to the school for an interview with a psychiatric social worker. The interview was to be accomplished as a part of the research project on child development. No offer of assistance or advice to the mother was made. An offer was made, however, for future conferences on the initiative of the mother, if she wished to discuss further any of her relationships with any of her children. About 40% of the mothers took advantage of the opportunity for the additional conferences. In the course of this program, the clinicians found very few of the typical concerns about stigma, parental inadequacy, or premature intervention into a problem the child will grow out of. The tentative interpretation is that the mothers were not asked to take the patient role, as they have been, by implication, in other such programs. Data are not yet available on the preventive effectiveness of this program (Stringer & Glidewell, 1965).

Spivak and Shure (1974), in Philadelphia, have developed a preventive program for nursery and kindergarten children. They use an adaptation of the Bereiter and Englemann language program to teach children listening, language, logic, and interpersonal skills in solving actual problems, but in game form—a tension-management device. Children receiving training offered significantly more solutions to interpersonal problems than controls and maintained their gains for 2 years. Work on this program continues.

Mental Health Consultation in Schools

Gerald Caplan (1959), at Harvard, has been the initiator of a new and well-defined practice of mental health consultation with teachers. The consultants may be from any one of the several disciplines—psychiatry, psychology, social work, nursing, or education. They are made available to the teachers in the schools at specified times. They develop their roles in the schools gradually but regularly insist that they are not in the schools to see children. They will consult with any teacher about her or his difficulties with any child who is hard to teach, but they do not take any direct action with the children. A considerable literature has developed around the technique; case histories in detail have been reported; and further literature is developing. Mannino, MacLennan, and Shore (1975) have compiled an exhaustive review of mental health consultation and of research on the process (Mannino & Shore 1972) and on the outcomes (Mannino & Shore 1975). They conclude that an integration of the findings is premature. I would point out again, however, that the consultant-consultee-client triad is a temporary system for tension management.

System Intervention in Schools

Lighthall, in Chicago, has developed a more clearly defined approach to preventive intervention at the system level. Such a program of intervention may include—in addition to the clarification of the role to school personnel—regular observation, data collection, and analyses of psychosocial phenomena at school; reporting to the members of the school social systems the outcomes of observations, data collections, or analyses; confrontations of appropriate people with stress-inducing information; development of temporary social systems or subsystems for dealing with stressful situations at school; and development of new methods of tension management and conflict resolution in the social systems at school. The approach, like Caplan's, is adult oriented, but unlike Caplan's, it is not individual oriented. The focus is upon the system. The approach is altogether speculative; experience is yet to be evaluated (e.g., Lighthall & Zientek, 1976). A similar systems approach with a focus on consultation has been mounted in the Bronx, New York (Andolfi, Stein, & Skinner, 1977).

CONCLUSION

Distress at school appears, is responded to, is managed, and is relieved—all within a potent psychosocial context. Ethnic values and beliefs; sex-role norms and demands; social-class beliefs, habits, and perceptions, all influence the use of tension management by helping dyads, by gamesmanship, by discussions of goal orientations, and by pacing, and by a variety of temporary social systems. Special contracultures also exert powerful, but less clearly explicated, influences.

Classroom social systems develop values, beliefs, roles, and demands reflecting the community but having particular characteristics of their own. Isolation reflects distress; "invisibility" does not. The variations in the dispersion of the teacher's power and acceptance have potent influence upon pupil-to-pupil interaction, interpersonal conflict, tension management, and self-esteem. The psychosocial resources of the pupil—intellect, interpersonal skills, and self-esteem—lead to a record of achievement. That record provides a kind of immunization to the inevitable exposure to the stresses of socialization at school. The management of tension at one time point leads, not only to new contacts and further demands of new tensions, but also to enhanced skills at managing new tensions.

Distress at school manifests itself more as defects of tension management than as defects of personality: intrapersonal distress, interpersonal ineptness, antisocial behavior, and lagging achievement.

Experiments in preventive intervention have shown the effects of community forces and institutional differences in tension management. The provision of traditional clinical services has led to sharp role confusions: conflict between school focus on the group and clinical focus on the individual, between school behavior-change induction by appeal to intellect and clinical appeal to motivation and emotion, between school concern with modifying interpersonal distress and clinical concern with modifying intrapersonal distress. Experiments with parent education have suggested that lay-led discussion programs do provide forms of tension management (goal orientation in temporary systems) attractive to middle-class groups. They do produce some small increments of change in parental attitudes, which become apparent in the middle classes over long periods of time. Experiments with training in cognitive and social skills for lower-class mothers have also provided prevention of distress.

The data from the St. Louis County experimental program of prevention showed that the availability of the program had the effect of reducing the number of new symptoms presented by boys to their mothers. There was no such effect for girls. There was a tendency for the lower classes to respond later than the middle or upper classes. The preventive usefulness of a variety of tension-management methods in such a program was established at a reliable level.

Current experiments with, and innovations in, preventive intervention assign the mental health specialist a nonclinical role, often as trainer-consultant; give primary attention to the school as a social system rather than to individuals; and do not expect that the system or its members take the patient role.

REFERENCES

Ackerman, N. W. What constitutes intensive psychotherapy in a child guidance clinic? *American Journal of Orthopsychiatry*, 1945, **15**, 711–720.

Ackerson, L. *Children's behavior problems*. Chicago: University of Chicago Press, 1931.

Allen, F. H. Therapeutic work with children. *American Journal of Orthopsychiatry*, 1934, **4**, 193–202.

Anderson, H. H. The measurement of domination and of socially integrative behavior in teachers' contacts with children. *Child Development*, 1939, **10**, 73–89.

Andolfi, M., Stein, D. D., & Skinner, J. A systems approach to the child, school, family and community in an urban area. *American Journal of Community Psychology*, 1977, **5**, 33–43.

Armstrong, J. *Program evaluation research*. St. Louis, Mo.: Mental Health Association of St. Louis, 1958. (Locally published report)

Austin, M. C., & Thomas, G. G. Children's friendships: A study of the bases on which children select and reject their best friends. *Journal of Educational Psychology*, 1948, **39**, 101–116.

Baron, D. Personal-social characteristics and classroom social status: A sociometric study of fifth and sixth grade girls. *Sociometry*, 1951, **14**, 32–42.

Beilin, H. Teachers and clinicians attitudes toward the behavior problems of children: A reappraisal. *Child Development*, 1959, **30**, 9–25.

Birch, H. D., Thomas, A., & Chess, S. *Implications for concepts of behavior disorders of children of renewed interest in early individual differences*. Paper presented at the meeting of the American Psychological Association, New York, 1966.

Birth, K., & Prillwitz, G. Leadership types and group behavior in school children. *Zeitschrift fur Psychologie*, 1959, **163**, 230–235.

Bloom, B. S. *Human characteristics and school learning*. New York: McGraw-Hill, 1976.

Board of Education. *Bureau of Child Guidance of the New York Public Schools: A survey*. New York, 1955.

Bonney, M. E. A study of social status on the second grade level. *Journal of Genetic Psychology*, 1942, **60**, 271–305.

Bonney, M. E. The relative stability of social, intellectual, and academic status in grades II to IV, and the inter-relationships between these various forms of growth. *Journal of Educational Psychology*, 1943, **34**, 88–102.

Bossert, S. *The organization of work and the social organization of the classroom.* Unpublished doctoral. Dissertation, University of Chicago, 1975.

Bower, E. M. *Early identification of emotionally handicapped children in school.* Springfield, Ill.: Thomas, 1960.

Brashear, E. L., Kenney, E. T., Buchmueller, A. D., & Gildea, M. C. L. A community program of mental health education using group discussion methods. *American Journal of Orthopsychiatry,* 1954, **24**, 554–568.

Brim, O. G., Jr. *Education for child rearing.* New York: Russell Sage, 1959.

Bronfenbrenner, U. Socialization and social class through time and space. In E. E. Maccoby, T. M. Newcomb, & E. L. Hartley (Eds.), *Readings in social psychology.* New York: Holt, 1958.

Bronfenbrenner, U., Devereau, E. C., Jr., Suci, G. J., & Rodgers, R. R. *Adults and peers as sources of conformity and autonomy.* Unpublished manuscript, 1965. (Available from Urie Bronfenbrenner, Cornell University, Department of Child Development and Family Relations, Ithaca, New York.

Brophy, J. E., & Good, T. L. *Teacher-student relationships: Causes and consequences.* New York: Holt, 1974.

Caplan, G. *Concepts of mental health and consultation.* Washington: U.S. Department of Health, Education, and Welfare, Childrens Bureau, 1959.

Chess, S. Genesis of behavior disorders. In J. G. Howells (Ed.), *Modern perspectives in international child psychiatry.* Edinburgh: Oliver & Boyd, 1969.

Chess, S., Thomas, A., & Birch, H. G. Characteristics of the individual child's behavioral responses to the environment. *American Journal of Orthopsychiatry,* 1959, **29**, 791.

Clausen, J. A. Family structure, socialization and personality. In L. W. Hoffman & M. L. Hoffman (Eds.), *Review of child development research* (Vol. 2). New York: Russell Sage, 1966.

Coan, R. W., & Cattell, R. B. The development of the early school personality questionnaire. *Journal of Experimental Education,* 1959, **28**, 143–152.

Cogan, M. L. The behavior of teachers and the productive behavior of their pupils: I. "Perception" analysis. *Journal of Experimental Education,* 1958, **27**, 89–105.

Coopersmith, S. A method for determining types of self-esteem. *Journal of Abnormal Social Psychology,* 1959, **59**, 87–94.

Cowan, E. L., Trost, M. A., Lorion, R. P., Dorr, D., Izzo, L. D., & Isaacson, R. V. *New ways in school mental health: Early detection and prevention of school maladaptation.* New York: Human Sciences, 1975.

Criswell, J. H. Social structure revealed in a sociometric retest. *Sociometry,* 1959, **11**, 69–75.

Cummings, J. D. The incidence of emotional problems in school children. *British Journal of Educational Psychology,* 1944, **14**, 151–161.

Cutts, N. E. (Ed.). *School psychologists at midcentury.* Washington: American Psychological Association, 1955.

Davis, A. *Social class influences on children's learning.* Cambridge: Harvard University Press, 1948.

Deitrich, F. R. Comparison of sociometric patterns of sixth grade pupils in two school systems: Ability grouping compared with heterogeneous grouping. *Journal of Educational Research,* 1964, **57**, 507–513.

Deutsch, M. The disadvantaged child and the learning process. In A. H. Passov (Ed.), *Education in depressed areas.* New York: Teachers College Press, 1963.

Dolan, L. *The affective consequences of home support, instructional quality, and achievement: A quasi-longitudinal study.* Unpublished doctoral dissertation, University of Chicago, 1977.

Douglas, V. The development of two families of defense. *Dissertation Abstracts,* 1959, **20**, 1438.

Dreeben, R. *On what is learned in school.* Reading, Mass.: Addison-Wesley, 1968.

Epps, E. (Ed.). *Cultural pluralism.* Berkeley: McCutchan, 1974.

Epstein, J. L., & McPartland, J. M. *Family and school interactions and main effects on nonacademic outcomes.* Unpublished manuscript, 1977. (Available from J. L. Epstein, Johns Hopkins University, Center for Social Organization of Schools, Baltimore, Maryland)

Erickson, K. T. Notes on the sociology of deviance. *Social Problems,* 1962, **9**, 307–314.

Feldhusen, J. F., & Thurston, J. R. Personality and adjustment of high and low anxious children. *Journal of Educational Research,* 1964, **56**, 265–267.

Flanders, N. A. Personal-social anxiety as a factor in experimental learning situations. *Journal of Educational Research,* 1951, **45**, 100–110.

Force, D. G., Jr. A comparison of physically handicapped children and normal children in the same elementary school classes with reference to social status and self-perceived status. *Dissertation Abstracts*, 1954, **14**, 104.

Gildea, M. C. L. *Community mental health.* Springfield, Ill.: Thomas, 1959.

Gildea, M. C. L., Glidewell, J. C., & Kantor, M. B. Maternal attitudes and general adjustment in school children. In J. C. Glidewell (Ed.), *Parental attitudes and child behavior.* Springfield, Ill.: Thomas, 1961.

Glidewell, J. C. Studies of mothers' reports of behavior symptoms in their children. In S. B. Sells (Ed.), *The definition and measurement of mental health.* Washington: National Center for Health Statistics, 1968.

Glidewell, J. C. A social psychology of mental health. In S. E. Golan & C. Eisdorfer (Eds.), *Handbook of community mental health.* New York: Appleton, 1972.

Glidewell, J. C., Domke, H. R., & Kantor, M. B. Behavior symptoms in children and adjustment in public school. *Human Organization*, 1959, **18**, 123-130.

Glidewell, J. C., Gildea, M. C. L., & Kauffman, M. K. The preventive and therapeutic effects of two school mental health programs. *American Journal of Community Psychology*, 1973, **1**, 295-329.

Glidewell, J. C., Kantor, M. B., Smith, L. M., & Stringer, L. A. Socialization and social structure in the classroom. In L. W. Hoffman, & Hoffman, M. L. (Eds.), *Review of child development research* (Vol. 2). New York: Russell Sage, 1966.

Glidewell, J. C., Mensh, I. N., & Gildea, M. C. L. Behavior symptoms in children and degree of sickness. *American Journal of Psychiatry*, 1957, **114**, 47-53.

Glidewell, J. C., & Stringer, L. A. The educational institution and the health institution. In E. M. Bower & W. G. Hollister (Eds.), *Behavioral science frontiers in education*, New York: Wiley, 1967.

Glidewell, J. C., & Swallow, C. S. *The prevalence of maladjustment in elementary school children.* Washington: Joint Commission on the Mental Health of Children, 1968.

Gnagey, W. J. Effect on classmates of a deviant student's power and response to a teacher-exerted control technique. *Journal of Educational Psychology*, 1960, **51**, 1-8.

Gold, M. Power in the classroom. *Sociometry*, 1958, **21** 50-60.

Goldfarb, A. Teacher ratings in psychiatric case finding. *American Journal of Public Health*, 1963, **53**, 1919-1927.

Goslin, D. A. Accuracy of self perception and social acceptance. *Sociometry*, 1962, **25**, 283-296.

Gouldner, A. W. The norm of reciprocity: A preliminary statement. *American Sociological Review*, 1960, **25**, 161-178.

Griffiths, W. *Behavior difficulties in children as judged by parents, teachers, and children themselves.* Minneapolis: University of Minnesota Press, 1952.

Gronlund, N. E. *Sociometry in the classroom.* New York: Harper, 1959.

Grossman, B., & Wrighter, J. The relationship between selection, rejection and intelligence, social status, and personality amongst sixth grade children. *Sociometry*, 1948, **11**, 346-355.

Group for the Advancement of Psychiatry. *Psychopathological disorders in childhood: Theoretical considerations and a proposed classification.* New York, 1966.

Gurwitz, S. B., & Dodge, K. A. Adults' evaluation of a child as a function of sex of adult and sex of child. *Journal of Personality and Social Psychology*, 1975, **32**, 822-828.

Heber, R., & Garber, H. The Milwaukee Project: A study of the use of family intervention to prevent cultural-familial mental retardation. In B. Z. Friedlander, G. M. Sterritt, & G. E. Kirk (Eds.), *The exceptional infant: Assessment and intervention* (Vol. 3). New York: Bruner/Mazel, 1975.

Hereford, C. F. *Changing parental attitudes through group discussion.* Austin. University of Texas Press, 1963.

Hewitt, L. E., & Jenkins, R. L. *Fundamental patterns of maladjustment: The dynamics of their origin.* Springfield: State of Illinois, 1946.

Hollender, E. P. Conformity, status, and idiosyncrasy credit. *Psychological Review*, 1958, **65**, 117-127.

Horowitz, F. D. The relationship of anxiety, self concept and sociometric status among 4th, 5th, and 6th grade children. *Journal of Abnormal Social Psychology*, 1962, **65**, 212-214.

Hudgins, B. B., & Loftis, L. The invisible child in the arithmetic class: A study of teacher-pupil interaction. *Journal of Genetic Psychology*, 1966, **108**, 143-152.

Jenkins, R. L., & Glickman, S. Common syndromes in child psychiatry. *American Journal of Orthopsychiatry*, 1946, 16, 244-252.

Jennings, H. H. Structure of leadership-development and sphere of influence. *Sociometry*, 1937, 1, 99-120.

Kantor, M. B., Gildea, M. C. L., & Glidewell, J. C. Preventive and therapeutic effects of maternal attitude change in the school setting. *American Journal of Public Health*, 1969, 59, 490-502.

Kerr, M. A. A study of social acceptability. *Elementary School Journal*, 1945, 45, 257-265.

Kerstetter, L. M., & Sargent, J. Re-assignment therapy in the classroom as a preventive measure in juvenile delinquency. *Sociometry*, 1940, 3, 293-306.

Kifer, E. *The effects of school achievement on the affective traits of the learner.* Unpublished doctoral dissertation, University of Chicago, 1973.

Koos, E. *The health of Regionville.* New York: Columbia University Press, 1954.

Kounin, J. S., Gump, P. V., & Ryan, J. J. The ripple effect in discipline. *Elementary School Journal*, 1961, 59, 158-162.

Kuhlen, R. G., & Lee, B. J. Personality characteristics and social acceptability in adolescence. *Journal of Educational Psychology*, 1943, 34, 321-340.

Lapouse, R., & Monk, M. A. En epidemiologic study of behavior characteristics in children. *American Journal of Public Health*, 1958, 48, 1134-1144.

Laughlin, F. *The peer status of sixth and seventh grade children.* New York: Columbia University, Bureau of Publications, 1954.

Leeds, C. H. Teacher attitudes and temperament as a measure of teacher-pupil rapport. *Journal of Applied Psychology*, 1956, 40, 333-337.

Levitt, E. E. Effect of a "causal" teacher training program on authoritarianism and responsibility in grade school children. *Psychological Report*, 1955, 1, 449-458.

Lewin, K. Frontiers in group dynamics. *Human Relations*, 1947, 1, 5-26.

Lighthall, F. F. School psychology: An alien guild. *Elementary School Journal*, 1963, 63, 361-364.

Lighthall, F. F., & Zientek, J. Organizational behavior: A basis for relevant interchange between psychologists and educators. In J. C. Glidewell (Ed.), *The social context of learning and development.* New York: Gardner, 1976.

Lindemann, E. *Mental health in the classroom: The Wellesley experience.* Paper presented at the annual meeting of the American Psychological Association, New York, 1957.

Lippitt, R., & Gold, M. Classroom social structure as a mental health problem. *Journal of Social Issues*, 1959, 15, 40-58.

Lippitt, R., Polansky, N., & Rosen, S. The dynamics of power: A field study of social influence in groups of children. *Human Relations*, 1952, 5, 37-64.

Lorr, M., & Jenkins, R. L. Patterns of maladjustment in children. *Journal of Clinical Psychology*, 1953, 9, 16-27.

McCandless, B. R., Castameda, A., & Palermo, D. S. Anxiety in children and social status. *Child Development*, 1956, 27, 385-392.

Maccoby, E. E., & Jacklin, C. N. *The psychology of sex differences.* Stanford: Stanford University Press, 1974.

Macfarlane, J. W., Allen L., & Honzik, M. P. *Behavior problems of normal children.* Berkeley and Los Angeles: University of California Press, 1954.

Mannino, F. V., MacLennon, B. W., Shore, M. F. *The practice of mental health consultation.* New York: Gardner, 1975.

Mannino, F. V., & Shore, M. F. Research in mental health consultation. In S. E. Golan & C. Eisdorfer (Eds.), *Handbook of community mental health.* New York: Appleton, 1972.

Mannino, F. V., & Shore, M. F. The effects of consultation: A review of empirical studies. *American Journal of Community Psychology*, 1975, 3, 1-21.

Marshall, R. E. *The effects of classroom organization and teacher-student interaction on the distribution of status in the classroom.* Unpublished doctoral dissertation, University of Chicago, 1978.

Maruyama, M. The second cybernetics: Deviation-amplifying, mutual causal processes. *American Scientist*, 1963, 51, 164-179.

Mechanic, D. The concept of illness behavior. *Journal of Chronic Disorders*, 1962, 15, 189-196.

Mechanic, D. The influence of mothers on their children's health attitudes and behavior. *Pediatrics*, 1964, 33, 444-455.

Mechanic, D. Perception of parental responses to illness. *Journal of Health and Human Behavior,* 1965, **6**, 253-261.

Mechanic, D., & Volkart, E. H. Stress, illness behavior, and the sick role. *American Sociological Review,* 1961, **26**, 51-60.

Medley, D. M., & Mitzel, H. E. Some behavioral correlates of teacher effectiveness. *Journal of Educational Psychology,* 1959, **50**, 239-246.

Mensh, I. N., & Glidewell, J. C. Children's perceptions of relationships among their family and friends. *Journal of Experimental Education,* 1958, **27**, 65-78.

Merei F. Group leadership and institutionalization. *Human Relations,* 1949, **2**, 23-39.

Miller, W. Focal concerns of lower class culture. In L. A. Ferman, J. L. Kornblum, & A. Haber (Eds.), *Poverty in America.* Ann Arbor: University of Michigan Press, 1965.

Minuchin, P. *Children's sex role concepts as a function of school and home.* Paper presented at the meeting of the American Orthopsychiatric Association, Chicago, 1964.

Mitchell, S., & Sheperd, M. A comparative study of children's behavior at home and at school. *British Journal of Educational Psychology,* 1966, **36**, 248.

Moreno, J. L. *Who shall survive?* (Pub. No. 58). Washington: Nervous & Mental Disease Publication Company, 1934.

Moss, H. A., & Kagan, J. Stability of achievement and recognition-seeking behaviors from early childhood through adulthood. *Journal of Abnormal and Social Psychology,* 1961, **62**, 504-513.

Neubauer, P. B., & Beller, E. K. Differential contribution of educator and clinician in diagnosis. In M. Krugman (Ed.), *Orthopsychiatry and the school.* New York: American Orthopsychiatric Association, 1958.

Neugarten, B. L. Social class and friendship among school children. *American Journal of Sociology,* 1946, **51**, 305-313.

Newstetter, W. I., Feldstein, M. J., & Newcomb, T. M. *Group adjustment.* Ashtabula, Ohio: Western Reserve Press, 1938.

Newton, R., & Brown, R. A preventive approach to developmental problems in children. In E. M. Bower & W. G. Hollister (Eds.), *Behavioral science frontiers in education.* New York: Wiley, 1967.

Northway, M. L. Outsiders: A study of the personality patterns of children least acceptable to their age mates. *Sociometry,* 1944, **7**, 10-25.

Orive, R., & Gerard, H. B. Social contact of minority parents and their childrens' acceptance by classmates. *Sociometry,* 1975, **38**, 518-524.

Padilla, A. M., & Ruiz, R. A. *Latino mental health: A review of literature.* Washington: U.S. Government Printing Office, 1973.

Painter, P. Personal Communication, 1962.

Patterson, G. R., & Anderson, D. Peers as social reinforcers. *Child Development,* 1964, **35**, 951-960.

Paynter, R. H., & Blanchard, P. *Educational achievement of children with personality and behavior difficulties.* New York: Commonwealth Fund (Harvard University Press), 1928.

Pennsylvania Mental Health, Inc. *Mental health education: A critique.* Philadelphia, 1960.

Perkins, H. V. A study of selected factors influencing perceptions of and changes in children's self-concepts. *Dissertation Abstracts,* 1957, **17**, 567.

Peterson, D. R. Behavior problems of middle childhood. *Journal of Consulting Psychology,* 1961, **25**, 205-209.

Pope, B. Prestige values in contrasting socioeconomic groups of children. *Psychiatry,* 1953, **16**, 381-385.

Potashin, R. A. A sociometric study of children's friendships. *Sociometry,* 1946, **9**, 48-70.

Rainwater, L. *Behind ghetto walls.* Chicago: Aldine, 1970.

Rehage, K. J. A comparison of pupil-teacher planning and teacher directed procedures in eighth grade social studies classes. *Journal of Educational Research,* 1951, **45**, 111-115.

Riessman, F. *The culturally deprived child.* New York: Harper, 1962.

Roberts, J. I. (Ed.). *School children in the urban slum.* New York: Free Press, 1967.

Rosenberg, M. *Society and the adolescent self-image.* Princeton: Princeton University Press, 1965.

Ruter, M. Classification and categorization in child psychiatry. *Journal of Clinical Psychology & Psychiatry,* 1965, **6**, 71-80.

Ruter, M., & Graham, P. Psychiatric disorder in 10 and 11 year old children. *Proceedings of the Royal Society of Medicine,* 1966, **59**, 382.

Sanford, N. A. *Self and society*. New York: Atherton, 1966.

Sarason, S. *Psychology in a community setting*. New York: Wiley, 1966.

Saunders, L. *Cultural differences in medical care*. New York: Russell Sage, 1954.

Schmidt, B. A. *The relationship between social status and classroom behavior*. Saint Louis, Mo.: Washington University, Graduate Institute of Education, 1958.

Schmuck, R. A. Sociometric status and utilization of academic abilities. *Merrill-Palmer Quarterly*, 1962, 8, 165–172.

Schmuck, R. A. Some relationships of peer liking patterns in the classrooms to pupil attitudes and achievement. *School Review*, 1963, 71, 337–359.

Schmuck, R. A., & Van Egmond, E. Sex differences in the relationship of interpersonal perceptions to academic performance. *Psychology in the Schools*, 1965, 2, 32–40.

Seagoe, M. V. Factors influencing the selection of associates. *Journal of Educational Research*, 1933, 27, 32–40.

Seeley, J., Sim, R., & Loosley, E. *Crestwood Heights*. New York, Basic, 1956.

Sheperd, M., Oppenheim, A. N., & Mitchell, S. Childhood behavior disorders and the child guidance clinic: An epidemiological study. *Journal of Child Psychology & Psychiatry*, 1966, 7, 39–52.

Shoobs, N. E. Sociometry in the classroom. *Sociometry*, 1947, 10, 154–164.

Slaughter, D. T. Relation of early parent-teacher socialization influences to achievement orientation and self-esteem in middle childhood among low-income black children. In J. C. Glidewell (Ed.), *The social context of learning and development*. New York: Gardner, 1977.

Smith, L. M. The concurrent validity of six personality and adjustment tests for children. *Psychological Monographs*, 1958, 77, (Whole No. 457).

Smith, L. M., & Geoffrey, W. *The complexities of an urban classroom*. New York: Holt, 1968.

Spivak, G., & Shure, M. B. *Social adjustment of young children: A cognitive approach to solving real life problems*. San Francisco: Jossey-Bass, 1974.

Stendler, C. B. *Children of Brasstown*. Urbana: University of Illinois, College of Education, Bureau of Research & Service, 1949.

Stevenson, G. S., & Smith, G. *Child guidance clinics*. New York: Commonwealth Fund (Harvard University Press), 1934.

Stouffer, G. A. W., Jr. Behavior problems of children as viewed by teachers and mental hygienists. *Mental Hygiene*, 1952, 36, 271–285.

Stringer, L. A. *The development of a school mental health service in a local health department*. Paper presented at the Eighth Annual Symposium on School Health, University of Kansas Medical School, Kansas City, Kans., 1962.

Stringer, L. A. The role of the school and the community in mental health programs. *Journal of School Health*, 1963, 33, 385.

Stringer, L. A., & Glidewell, J. C. *Mothers as colleagues in school mental health work*. Unpublished manuscript, 1965. (Available from L. A. Stringer, St. Louis County Health Department, Clayton, Missouri)

Stringer, L. A., & Glidewell, J. C. *Early detection of emotional problems in children* (Final Report). Clayton, Mo.: St. Louis County Health Department, 1967.

Stringer, L. A., McMahan, A., & Glidewell, J. C. *A normative study of academic progress in elementary school children*. Unpublished manuscript, 1962. (Available from L. A. Stringer, St. Louis County Health Department, Clayton, Missouri)

Sue, S., & Wagner, N. N. *Asian-Americans: Psychological perspectives*. Palo Alto, Calif.: Science & Behavior, 1973.

Swallow, C. S. *Patterns of mothering ADC children*. Unpublished master's thesis, Washington University, 1967.

Tausch, A. M. Experimental studies on the behavior of teachers toward children in difficult training situations. *Zeitschrift fur Exper. Angewandte Psychologie*, 1958, 5, 127–136.

Tausch, A. M. Special training situations in practical school instruction: Frequency, cause and type of solution by teachers: An empirical study. *Zeitschrift fur Exper. Angewandte Psychologie*, 1958, 5, 657–668. (b)

Tausch, A. M. The effect of the kind of verbal prohibitions. *Zeitschrift fur Psychologie*, 1960, 164, 215–226.

Tausch, A. M. Various non-autocratic behavior forms in their effect upon children in conflict situations. *Zeitschrift fur Exper. Angewandte Psychologie*, 1962, 9, 339–347.

Thelen, H. A. Educational dynamics: Theory and research. *Journal of Social Issues*, 1950, 6, 5–29.

Thelen, H. A., (Ed.), Experimental research toward a theory of instruction. *Journal of Educational Research,* 1951, **45**, 89–136.

Thelen, H. A. *Classroom grouping for teachability.* New York: Wiley, 1967.

Trent, R. D. The relationship of anxiety to popularity and rejection among institutionalized delinquent boys. *Child Development,* 1957, **28**, 379–384.

Tri-state Conference on School Psychology. *Proceedings.* 1962.

Tulchin, S. H. (Ed.). *Child guidance.* New York: American Orthopsychiatric Association, 1964.

Turner, V. *Effects of sex, social class, and extent of maladjustment on approaches to mental health resources.* Unpublished manuscript, 1960. (Available from V. Turner, St. Louis County Health Department, Clayton, Missouri)

Ullman, C. A. *Identification of maladjusted school children* (Public Health Monograph No. 7). Washington: U.S. Public Health Service, 1952.

Van Egmond, E. *Social interrelationship skills and effective utilization of intelligence in the classroom.* Unpublished doctoral dissertation, University of Michigan, 1960.

Wellman, B. The school child's choice of companions. *Journal of Educational Research,* 1926, **14**, 126.

Wickman, E. K. *Children's behavior and teachers' attitudes.* New York: Commonwealth Fund (Harvard University Press), 1928.

Young, L. L., & Cooper, D. H. Some factors associated with popularity. *Journal of Educational Psychology,* 1944, **35** , 513–535.

Zbarowski, M. Cultural components in responses to pain. *Journal of Social Issues,* 1952, 8, 16–20.

9

Sociocultural Origins
of Achievement Motivation

Martin L. Maehr
University of Illinois at Urbana-Champaign

Teachers and parents know that achievement is not just a function of competence, opportunity, or good fortune. Somehow, where there's a will, there's a way.
Therewith, achievement motivation has emerged as a popular explanatory concept.
Whether the focus is on "culturally disadvantaged" preschoolers, obstreperous sixth
graders, or adolescent dropouts, it is widely assumed that trying, aspiring, inner
drive—or *motivation*—makes a difference. Moreover, there is a fond belief that
social and cultural factors condition such psychological imperatives. The poor
school performance of the Chicano, black, or American Indian child is thought to
relate to membership in these social or cultural groups, and particularly to motivational problems that ensue with such membership. Such commonsense observations
are, of course, supported by a raft of social science theory, opinion, and research.
Indeed, it is well-nigh impossible to deny the pervasive effects of culture on achievement motivation. Yet, there is little general understanding of how, to what extent,
and with what inevitability social and cultural factors will influence achievement
motivation and thereby condition work styles, classroom performance, and career
patterns.

My purpose in this chapter is, first of all, to provide a panoramic view of the
work on culture and achievement motivation, and then to use that panoramic view
as a backdrop for a particular perspective on how social and cultural factors may
influence achievement motivation.

AN ANALYSIS OF CULTURE AND WILL: THE WORK
OF DAVID McCLELLAND

Perhaps no one is more closely identified with the study of culture and achievement motivation than David McClelland. As a result, discussion of the issues involved properly begins with his seminal and still-influential work.

Culture, Personality, and Achievement

Essentially, McClelland's concern with achievement is reflected in the perspective of an auto-industry executive I happened to meet on an Iran Air flight from

Teheran to Paris (via Moscow!). After an apparently successful trip, this executive was enthusiastic about the business possibilities in Iran—especially about the possibilities of producing and selling cars. Interestingly enough, in describing these possibilities, he spoke little of mineral resources or stability of government. Rather, he talked almost exclusively about the "character" of the people. He sensed a "vibrant nature," the energy, the will or whatever, to move the country forward. In pre-oil cartel 1972, "personality of the people" was given as the primary rationale for a business venture in Iran. Obsessed as everyone is today with the economics of the Middle East, this same executive may now have different reasons; but the fact remains that international decision makers in government and industry often rely, in making their decisions, on some basic generalizations about the character of people. So do most of us. Particularly, as one tries to explain achievement, one is likely to look to some driving force that resides in individuals. David McClelland's work has encouraged this predilection by providing an empirically based rationale.

In *The Achieving Society* (1961) and elsewhere, McClelland (1971; McClelland & Winter, 1969) argued persuasively that cultures and societies wax and wane as they foster the development and encourage the utilization of the achievement-motivated person. Such an assertion is not all that unusual, of course. What is significant about McClelland's work is that he initiated a thorough analysis of the achievement-motivated person and put his ideas about culture, person, and society to extensive empirical test.

McClelland, then, has first considered how culture affects achievement motivation. A significant aspect of culture (cf. Maehr, 1974b; 1975b) is the pattern of norms that guide family behavior and child-rearing practices and, in general, establish the early learning experiences that the child will have. These early learning experiences, according to McClelland, create enduring personality patterns that persist through adulthood and determine achievement motivation. By encouraging independence, challenge seeking, and delay of gratification through exhortation, modeling, or selective reinforcement, the parent not only establishes appropriate habit patterns but, most important, creates affective responses that cause the child to approach or avoid achievement situations. Certainly in the earlier work, it was generally accepted that basic patterns of achievement motivation were fairly well established by the age of 10. In later work, however, McClelland and his colleagues have made a special point of showing how such early learning experiences can be reversed in adulthood if one wishes to put forth the effort (see, e.g., McClelland & Winter, 1969). Still, the assumption is that achievement motivation resides largely in the individual. It is a trait that the person possesses and is likely to demonstrate across a wide variety of situations. It is, if you will, part of the person's character.

A major feature of McClelland and his colleague's efforts was the development of measurement technology. If one assumes that a personality trait is responsible for achievement behavior, it follows that means for assessing this trait must be developed. Following a cue provided by Freud, it was assumed that an inner motive, such as achievement motivation, would be best expressed indirectly, in fantasy. Accordingly, McClelland and his colleagues went about establishing a standard situation for obtaining samples of a person's unguarded thoughts or fantasy life as they might relate to achievement. What they settled upon was the presentation of ambiguous pictures (Thematic Apperception Test [TAT] cards) with a requirement that an individual write a short interpretative story about them. These pictures were generally suggestive of achievement situations, portraying, for example, a teen-age boy sitting in a classroom, gazing past an open book (Atkinson, 1958).

Obviously, individuals are likely to interpret such situations differently, and it was the assumption of McClelland and his colleagues that such interpretations would reveal enduring motivational inclinations. Indeed, it was found that variations in response could be related, in some general sense, to orientation toward achieving. Individuals who write themes that focus on achievement, particularly on the positive and negative feelings associated with competing against some standard of excellence, are likely to behave quite differently in achievement situations. They will, for example, exhibit moderate risk taking and readily confront challenge in competitive games and business; and overall, they seem to exhibit a peculiar concern with performing well (McClelland, 1961).

But perhaps the most dramatic accomplishment of McClelland has been to consider how personality affects culture or society. An outline of his bold hypothesis is presented in Figure 9-1. The logic is simple enough. Within each society, certain early learning experiences are, willy nilly, established for the child. This early learning may be more or less effective in fostering achievement motivation. To the degree that it is effective, it will create a pool of potential leaders who happen to be achievement motivated. Assuming that there is nothing to prevent the society from drawing its leadership from this pool, an achievement-motivated leadership should come to dominate the society's affairs. The ultimate result is that the society as a whole should act like an achievement-motivated person and, within its capacity to do so, achieve. While one might, in theory, define *societal achievement* rather broadly, McClelland has focused especially on economic achievement, a kind of achievement that may be relatively easy to measure in comparing differing societies. Now, several points should be kept clearly in mind. The child-rearing practices that are predominant within a society are a *variable*. That is, not only will societies differ from each other in how children are raised, they will, over time, exhibit striking variations in their own practices. Thus, war, population changes, and ideological shifts, such as occurred with the Reformation (cf. Weber, 1904/1930), may effect major changes in child-rearing practices. One may also guess that McClelland would now add that Great Society intervention programs could be similarly influential. It is such changes in child-rearing practices that should play a major role in later variation in societal achievement.

Amazingly enough, across a wide variety of cultures and against seemingly insurmountable odds, McClelland did, in fact, find evidence that the existence of

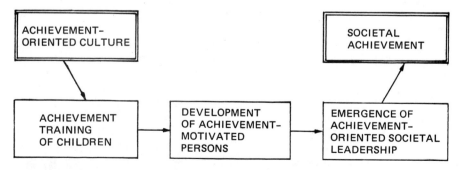

FIGURE 9-1 McClelland's hypothesis regarding culture, personality, and the achieving society.

achievement-oriented child-rearing practices at some time point was likely to eventuate—25 years later—in an "achieving society." Basically, this evidence consisted of correlations between the economic achievement of a society (adjusted for potential in terms of natural resources) and an index of the learning environment that would have been experienced by the then-adults of the society when they were children. While these correlations are not high and there are anomalies in the data, it does seem that McClelland's bold hypothesis is more than mere speculation. A society does insure its future as it rears its children. That has been said before, but McClelland may be the first to put that truism to such extensive, empirical test.

Problems with McClelland's Approach

In an important sense, McClelland's work has opened up most of the questions that must be considered in the analysis of motivation. By no means has it solved all the problems. Indeed, there are many serious criticisms of this work, and it is in several important respects a questionable guide for current research.

Measurement

A first criticism is not an unusual one as far as a complex area of study is concerned: The measurement procedures were inadequate. Although the use of achievement imagery as an index of achievement motivation may prove workable for certain purposes, serious problems exist here. Some of these relate to such technicalities as the reliability and utility of the thematic measures (see, e.g., Entwisle, 1972; Klinger, 1966, 1967; Weinstein, 1969). More basic as far as analyzing culture and achievement is concerned is the self-evident cultural bias that exists in these measures. The TAT stimuli that are characteristically employed in eliciting achievement imagery are manifestly ethnocentric in nature. They were developed in an American setting and show it. They probably are not even appropriate for subcultural groups in the United States, as research with blacks (see, e.g., Mingione, 1965, 1968) and women (see, e.g., Alper, 1974; French & Lesser, 1964; Lesser, Krawitz, & Packard, 1963) would suggest. Adaptation of the stimuli to a particular culture can and has been done, but this too is not without its problems. For example, if one wishes to create a culture-fair test of achievement motivation for Chicanos, pictures of Chicanos might well be used as the eliciting stimuli. One has, however, created an essentially new test in this instance; and the relationship of this test to the original is open to question (see, e.g., Maehr, 1974a, 1974c). Such questions of cross-cultural comparability of measures are not, of course, unique to the area of achievement motivation (see, e.g., Frijda & Jahoda, 1966; Triandis, 1972). The use of socially defined contexts, however—whether expressed in pictures or words—is likely to elicit stereotypical images that may or may not relate to anything that one might wish to label "achievement motivation."

Ethnocentric Conception of Achievement Motivation

Most disturbing is the question of whether the whole theory of achievement motivation is hopelessly ethnocentric in nature (cf. Maehr, 1974a, 1974c). For McClelland and his colleagues, achievement motivation is an internal system or process, the existence of which is verified by certain behaviors. Although the process of inferring the psychic existence or nonexistence of something is a common and time-honored practice among psychologists, it is not without its problems—especially so, when dealing with cross-cultural phenomena.

An example may clarify the point. A decade or so ago, educators focused their concern on so-called culturally disadvantaged children. The poor have been with us always; but a combination of economic, political, and social events made their plight—and ultimately the schools' plight—especially salient. Manifestly, children from certain social and cultural backgrounds were likely to have difficulty in school. They entered with what was judged to be poor preparation and barely managed to keep up through the course of schooling (see, e.g., Coleman, Campbell, Hobson, McPartland, Mood, Weinfeld, & York, 1966; Mosteller & Moynihan, 1972). It is easy to see that the inference was quickly made that there was a lack of competence involved. Not that many were willing to stress genetic differences (cf. Humphreys, 1975), but, rather, it was argued that their culture had deprived them of appropriate *learning experiences*. As a result, they were judged to be lacking in competence or intelligence and in need of remedial training before they could participate in the average classroom. In particular, it was believed that these children had limited linguistic skill because they were unable to produce the complex syntactic structures of their favored peers and could not make the necessary discriminations in hearing the spoken word. Perhaps that was the reason for their poor. showing in school and the cause of a fundamental lack in intelligence.

Certainly, there was a lack of school performance, and the language used by these children in the school setting could only be described as impoverished; but the inference that a lack of linguistic competence existed was made too soon. Various linguists, such as William Labov (1970; 1972), began to observe the linguistic behavior of these "culturally deprived" children in a variety of social settings. True, they did not exhibit linguistic competence in school, but things were altogether different in an extraschool setting such as the family living room. There, where they were comfortable and free to be themselves and where the content of their conversation was uncensored, no lack in linguistic competence was evident. Of course, this example does not say that no inferences about psychological processes can be made, nor does it say that developmental or educational deficiencies do not exist. It merely lays stress on the importance of viewing the behavior upon which such inferences are to be made in a variety of contexts before assuming a lack in, or nonexistence of, a psychological process.

A central concern in this chapter, of course, is that a very similar thing is likely to occur in the motivational area. At the base of McClelland's work is a conception of achievement motivation that is obviously Western in origin. One cannot help but suggest that it is the Protestant ethic (Weber, 1904/1930) that is achievement motivation. Although such an ethic may be found in some form in all cultures and thus have some explanatory value in making cross-cultural comparisons, it may not do full justice to the propensities and potential of these other cultures. It is all too easy to assume motivational deficiency in one or another cultural group simply because this motivation is not demonstrated in the standardized situation selected by the researcher. Thus, while some black ghetto children do not exhibit anything like high motivation to achieve at school, they may do so in another context. Granted that their lack of achievement in a school setting is an important fact to cope with, it is not sufficient reason to assume no achievement motivation. Conceivably, they can and do exhibit such motivation in another context. Thus, I personally have often been impressed with how some children who are "lazy" in school really "work" at play, exhibiting an all-consuming motivation to achieve in athletics. The point, of course, is that, in the study of culture and achievement motivation, one dare not focus on the person to the exclusion of the context. Indeed, it may be argued that by focusing so heavily on the role of personality in achievement, McClelland and his colleagues have done just that. Therewith, they have created an ethnocentric approach to motivation, an approach that simply compares other cultures to a Western prototype (see Maehr, 1974a, 1974c) without doing justice to the potential for excellence that exists within these cultures.

Intervention

Educators have yet another reason for not focusing exclusively on the role of personality in achievement. Such a focus may suggest that there is little or nothing that can be done by the teacher to foster an interest in achievement: If the child happens to possess it—of course, make the most of it—but what teacher can presume to initiate basic changes in personality? As a result, when achievement motivation is viewed narrowly and exclusively in terms of personality patterns, intervention programs inevitably involve activities the primary base of which is outside the typical classroom. The focus has to be on parenting or specialized counseling. While such intervention is possible, it is expensive (see Maehr & Lysy, in press, for a review of these issues). Moreover, the teacher is left hanging with the question: But what do *I* do? All of this suggests that a slightly different approach to the understanding of achievement motivation might be in order.

THERE IS A WILL—WHAT ARE THE WAYS?

An alternative approach to that taken by McClelland is to assume a will to achieve that is essentially *universal* and then to focus on the ways and conditions under which this will is actualized. Such an approach involves a fundamental reconsideration of the nature of achievement motivation and its causes.

The Behavioral Basis for Motivational Inferences

A basic question that one should ask when considering achievement motivation is, What is it? To answer that question, one does well to consider first the behavioral basis for motivational inferences. What is the behavior that prompts motivational inferences? Any answer to that question is bound to be debatable, but most answers would probably focus on the *direction* and *persistence* of behavior, while also looking carefully at certain instances of variations in *performance*. These three patterns comprise most of the instances in which motivational inferences are made. For the purposes of this chapter, at least, it may be asserted that these patterns are the basic data of motivation. Considering these patterns more closely, several things may be noted.

First, "variation in performance" requires fuller definition. Obviously, not all instances of variation in performance are the basis for motivational inferences. In actuality, one is likely to accept variation in performance as a fitting datum for motivational inferences only when one can rule out certain external causes (e.g., variation in task difficulty, luck, or good fortune) and certain internal ones (e.g., variation in skill level). As research on attributional processes indicates, there are specifiable conditions that lead us to judge that the variation in performance is due to the *effort* put forth by the individual (cf., e.g., Weiner, 1974). It is performance variation in these instances that is a basic datum for motivational inferences.

Second, it may be noted that persistence behavior also represents directional behavior and that both selection of behavioral alternatives and persistence could be comprised under the category of choice behavior (see, e.g., Maehr, 1967). Be this as it may, an initial behavioral emphasis suggests that one keep these behavioral categories separate until one is, in fact, sure that the same rules cover both instances.

In brief, the behavioral basis for motivational inferences is, in the first instance, three distinguishable types of behavior: directional change, persistence, and certain instances of variation in performance.

A Definition of Achievement Motivation

When the term *achievement motivation* is employed, the focus of study is, then, restricted further to certain examples of persistence, directional change and variation in performance. More specifically, three delimiting principles are operative in restricting the range of observations to achievement. First, the persistence, the directional change, the performance variation, or some combination must occur in a task for which there is a *standard of excellence;* in other words, the activity must be such that it can be evaluated in terms of success or failure. A second defining condition is that the outcome on the task is potentially *attributable to the individual's performance.* This does not necessarily mean that achievement is only an individualistic activity. The point, however, is that achievement is something to which the person makes a contribution. Something is done *by* the individual; it is not done *to* the individual. Third, some level of *challenge* and, therewith, a certain related sense of uncertainty of outcome must be involved.

Implications of the Definition

This definition of achievement motivation is derived directly from theory and research initiated by McClelland and his colleagues (cf. Atkinson & Feather, 1966; Atkinson & Raynor, 1974; McClelland, 1961; McClelland, Atkinson, Clark, & Lowell, 1953). It involves a major shift in emphasis, however—one that has broad significance so far as the cross-cultural study of achievement motivation is concerned. By definition, achievement motivation is made to be a universal phenomenon. The behavioral patterns identified as the indicants of motivation are certainly not behavioral patterns that are limited to one or another cultural group. Similarly, the delimiting principles that define these patterns as achievement related are logically assumed to be pancultural. Certainly, tasks exist in all cultures for which there are standards of excellence, levels of challenge, and the possibility of self-attribution of some sort. Whatever difference there may be, then, between cultures in the exhibition of achievement motivation, this difference relates to the tasks on which it would be demonstrated. It might be said, then, that this new definition assumes a universal will to achieve; the question is merely in which of the ways, conditions, and contexts this will is actualized.

It should be stressed that this definition not only suggests a greater openness in viewing the motivation of different cultural groups; it should also lead to an important, substantive shift in interpreting and promoting achievement behavior. The characteristic focus on the person and personality variables in achievement-motivation research gives way to a focus on situations, contexts, and immediately impinging events. If all people demonstrate achievement motivation at some place or time, the questions become: Why do some demonstrate it *here* and others *there*; What is it about "here" and "there" that makes a difference? Admittedly, work on achievement motivation has not, in the past, absolutely ruled out a role for situational factors; but by stressing the role of personality, rather than focusing on *behavioral patterns in context,* situational control over achievement motivation has been played down or even ignored. This new definition suggests an approach whereby such a wrong could be redressed. Accordingly, in the rest of this chapter, I focus on situational and contextual causes of achievement. Moreover, by placing the focus on achievement situations and contexts, practical ends are also served. Conceivably, schools and teachers can do more about achievement situations and contexts than they can about enduring personality patterns. This point should become evident as the role of situations and contexts in fostering achievement motivation is considered.

THE SITUATIONAL–CONTEXTUAL CAUSES OF ACHIEVEMENT MOTIVATION

Granted the importance of considering achievement situations and contexts, how does one conceptualize these? What variables are important? What observations should be made? While it is difficult to provide a simple, well-integrated, theoretical statement on situational-contextual causes of achievement motivation, it is nevertheless possible to identify situational-contextual dimensions that are critical (see Figure 9-2).[1]

Expectation of Others

An individual exhibits achievement motivation as a member of certain social groups. Human behavior, and most particularly achievement behavior, does not occur in a social vacuum. As a result, the expectations of others are bound to be significant in shaping when, how, and under what conditions such behavior will occur. There are at least three kinds of expectations that one can identify. These may be referred to as *normative, role-related,* and *individualized expectations.*

Normative Expectations

The existence of a social group inevitably eventuates in the development of norms for behavior. Families, clubs, schools—or even play groups—cannot exist without some sort of minimally agreed-on set of expectations regarding how members should behave or even think and believe. These expectations exist with reference to all aspects of life, but they also exist most especially in the achievement domain. Thus, within groups there are likely to be normative expectations with reference both to what can be done and to what is worth doing. In other words, the norms of a group deal, in the first instance, with the range of possible

---

[1] Identifying contemporary social factors as primary causes of behavior does not obviate a consideration of social-learning processes. After all, how do people come to accept a group as significant to them? A stress on the importance of groups in achievement behavior is simply a tacit recognition of the fact that achievement motivation not only is a function of having acquired an individualized drive but also depends on the acquisition of a certain responsiveness to, and dependency on, the needs, wishes, and hopes of others (cf. Moore, 1969).

SOCIAL EXPECTATIONS   TASK CHARACTERISTICS

FIGURE 9-2 Model of situational-contextual factors that condition achievement motivation.

or allowable behavior; but within this range, they are likely also to encourage some behavior patterns more than others. It is no secret that, within certain groups, school achievement is not only an allowable but also a highly valued possibility. Within other groups, this possibility may be allowable but hardly valued. Even within a presumably highly advanced and complex society, such as the United States, in which the desirability of school achievement is formalized in written code, there remains considerable variation in the acceptance of the code within subgroups (see, e.g., Coleman, 1961, 1974). When one wonders why a certain child seems turned off by school, it seems appropriate to consider first the various social groups in which that child participates. In this regard, it is interesting to note that programs directed to helping the underachiever—as an individual—are likely to fail unless something is done about group membership (cf. Kolb, 1965).

Normative expectations also exist with reference to *how* something can or should be done. The prevailing view in the United States is that achievement is an individualistic and totally self-serving thing; in other words, people achieve on their own and perhaps at the expense of others. Indeed, one almost takes it for granted that achievement will involve competition with others. Although this matter has only been researched in a preliminary way, it seems reasonably clear that different social groups may vary not only in the definition of what is possible and worth striving for but also in the definition of how one should achieve. Employing atlas data contained in Osgood, May, and Miron (1975), Salili and Maehr (1976), for example, found distinct variations in the meaning that achievement-related concepts had in four different countries, the United States, Iran, Japan, and Thailand. Most interesting were the interrelationships between words defining *locus of causality, styles,* and *goals* in achievement, which suggested greater commonality in achievement ends than means. Also, the results suggested that the role of self as initiator of achievement was viewed quite differently in these four different groups.

In summary, it may be suggested that social groups hold generalized expectations of achievement areas, goals, and means. Although all individuals are probably allowed to strive their hardest in some area, it is apparent that this striving is to some degree prescribed. Rate busters and curve raisers can be severely punished. Yet, there do exist, probably for all individuals, areas in which they are encouraged to put forth their fullest effort. Achievement striving is to an important degree a product of the norms of the social group of which the individual is a member.

Role Expectations

Particularized normative expectations that apply especially to individuals who happen to occupy a specific position in a group constitute role expectations. An example might be the set of expectations that could exist for an individual who happens to be the leader of a group. There is, of course, a rich literature on the effects of role expectations on behavior (see, e.g., Sarbin & Allen, 1968). The point that is important to consider here is whether occupying a particular position in a social group affects achievement motivation. There is considerable evidence to indicate that it does. Klinger and McNelley (1969), for example, have suggested that role and status changes do, in fact, eventuate in changes in achievement motivation. Indeed, they suggest that whatever is thought to be achievement motivation by those who have followed McClelland and Atkinson is, in fact, to a considerable degree a role-associated behavior. In this regard, a most interesting and illustrative study is one conducted by Zander and Forward (1968). In this study, subjects were first identified as high and low in achievement motivation according to usual procedures. Subsequently, they participated in a three-person group-performance situation in which leader and follower roles were rotated. What is most intriguing about the results is that, while in the leadership role, the low-achievement-motivated subjects exhibited the same achievement patterns as high-achievement-motivated subjects. Apparently, the high-achievement-motivation patterns *were* a part of their reportoire under the right eliciting conditions. In this case, the temporary switch in social roles was sufficient to change their style of performing so that it was similar to that of highly achievement-motivated people. Subjects who had been identified as high in achievement motivation exhibited the style of performance assumed to be typical for such people in both leader and follower roles. Although this latter finding may be taken as supportive of the proposition that personality is more critical than role, that conclusion should be approached with caution. One might wonder whether, if the highly achievement-motivated subjects had participated as followers in the same group for a longer period of time, they too might have conformed to the role expectations. One exposure to the follower role in this kind of group may not have been enough to teach them their "place." In any case, it seems reasonable to conclude that those who exhibit what appears to be a low-achievement-motivation pattern can reverse themselves dramatically given the appropriate situational-contextual conditions.

The finding that a switch in social roles within a group can change an individual's style of pursuing a task is hardly trivial. Similarly, the possibility that achievement motivation is associated with social status in a group, as suggested by Klinger and McNelley (1969), has profound implications. Briefly put, it further supports the notion that achievement motivation is by no means irrevocably set in early childhood. Rather, it is regularly subjected to modification as one joins new groups, changes positions, and attempts new tasks.

Individualized Expectations

Not all social expectations can be readily classed as normative or role related. Some seem to be associated with the individual, exclusive of role and group membership. Although these expectations may be influenced by norm and role factors, there is some value in recognizing that individualistic expectations do exist and may be equally critical in some instances. Take for example, the assumption on the part of a teacher that a child is "smart" or "dumb." Such an assumption, while it is not readily included within the two previous expectation categories, is probably a very important one for determining the behavior of the teacher and, subsequently, the achievement of the child.

Recently, considerable research has been conducted on such "particularized expectations." One line of research has focused on teachers' expectations for students. Here, the so-called Pygmalion phenomenon became for a while a cause célèbre (see, e.g., Rosenthal, 1969; Rosenthal & Jacobson, 1968; Thorndike, 1968, 1969). Out of all the effort and emotion that were embroiled in the dialogue on this phenomenon, certain understandings seem to have emerged. First, there is evidence that teachers readily slot children into certain categories, much as people who are placed in certain positions or levels in any social group are slotted. With this slotting goes a set of expectations for each person's performance and actions that will work toward insuring the realization of the expectations held (cf. Rubovits & Maehr, 1971, 1973, 1975). In other words, a self-fulfilling prophesy is operative. Of course, many things remain quite unclear about such expectations. Although expert judgments (e.g., test scores as in Rosenthal & Jacobson, 1968, or Rubovits & Maehr, 1971), ethnic stereotypes (see, e.g., Rubovits & Maehr, 1973) or certain salient behaviors, such as language usage (see, e.g., Domingo-Llacuna, 1976) appear to be important sources for the development of such expectations, there is little else we know about antecedents. Similarly, it seems that the persistence, pervasiveness, and, possibly, the *effects* of such expectancies may vary with teachers (see, e.g., Rubovits & Maehr, 1973, 1975). Some teachers simply seem to be more open than others to learning from what they see students doing. Finally, there is no clear understanding of how the teacher's expectations might create student achievement. There are, of course, a number of possibilities that can be considered. Following up on the previous discussion of norms and roles, it can be noted that the teacher is often a major influence on the norms, roles, and status hierarchy established in the classroom—especially in the early grades when, incidentally, teacher-expectancy effects seem to be the most important (Rosenthal & Jacobson, 1968). For example, teachers can and often do assign leadership roles, and as previously suggested, such role assignments may have major motivational effects. Complementing this is the possibility that teachers' behavior influences children's basic beliefs that they can (or cannot) do something if they try (see, e.g., Maehr, 1975a; Weiner & Kukla, 1970).

Of course, teachers' expectations are not the only important example of such particularized expectations. Those of parents and peers are also likely to be crucial, as Doris Entwisle and her colleagues (Entwisle & Hayduk, in press; Entwisle & Webster, 1972, 1973, 1974; Webster & Sobieszek, 1974) have pointed out in a most fascinating series of studies.

Task Characteristics

Obviously enough, an important part of the achievement situation or context is the achievement task. Whether or not a person will demonstrate motivation toward achievement is critically dependent on task characteristics. That there is important variation from task to task seems highly likely (cf. Crandall & Battle, 1970; Maehr, 1974a). What are the characteristics of tasks that are likely to make a difference in the demonstration of achievement motivation?

Sociocultural Definition

In discussing the effects of social expectations, I have already anticipated a first answer to this question. The sociocultural groups in which one participates define the appropriateness of achieving on a particular task. Certain task areas are acceptable areas in which to put forth effort and some are not. Indeed, within each sociocultural group, various task areas probably have a certain prestige ranking and, as Barkow (1975) suggests, it may be that this single fact alone best explains the demonstration of achievement striving in any given instance. Of course, much of this is at least implied in the previous review of the effects of social expectations on achievement motivation. The point here is that, in viewing task effects, one should remember that a task is a sociocultural phenomenon. Whether one can perform it at all or how it will be performed depends in large part on the meaning it has in the sociocultural context.

Interpersonal Demands

Closely related to the sociocultural definition of the task are the interpersonal demands. Different sociocultural groups have different expectations for what is desirable in interpersonal relationships. Different groups, for example, lay different degrees of stress on individualism, cooperation, and competition. Thus, it is not at all surprising that tasks organized to pit peer against peer in a competitive fashion may reduce the motivation of sociocultural groups that stress affiliative relationships and group solidarity. Again, I have anticipated this point previously, but the reminder here is that most tasks, particularly those confronted by children in school settings, have an interpersonal dimension to them.

Work versus Play

What I have not previously alluded to is a particular kind of task definition that apparently can significantly change task performance. For handy labeling, it may be referred to as a "work-versus-play" definition. While these terms have considerable surplus meaning, they do convey the essence of a certain situational distinction of importance in all cultures. Does the task primarily involve doing one's own thing or someone else's thing? Is it performed for extrinsic or intrinsic reasons?

Recently, a considerable literature has evolved that focuses on how extrinsic rewards may modify motivation to perform a task (see, e.g., Deci, 1975; Greene & Lepper, in press; Staw, 1976). A major finding has been that when extrinsic rewards are added to a task that is already interesting to the person, a certain reduction in motivation is likely to occur. More specifically, a continuing interest in performing the task, apart from the extrinsic rewards, will suffer. What was once intrinsically interesting is no longer so once it is done for extrinsic reasons. Inasmuch as learning in many cases seems to be intrinsically interesting (cf., e.g., Furth, 1970), it has been quickly pointed out that schools, through the use of gold stars, M & M's—or grades—may actually be subverting the intrinsic interests of children in learning. In a phrase, such extrinsic motivators might be turning play into work. It does seem as if an emphasis on extrinsic rewards in achievement settings can have a distinctly negative effect on motivation. Moreover, it appears that merely emphasizing external evaluation in a classroom setting may have similar negative effects across widely diverse cultural groups. In a series of studies in Iran and the United States (Kremer, 1976; Maehr & Stallings, 1972; Salili, Maehr, Sorensen, & Fyans, 1976), for example, it was found that performance of a challenging task under external-evaluation conditions reduced children's continuing motivation in subsequently performing this task on their own, apart from the evaluative setting. In contrast, a self-evaluation condition that de-emphasized external evaluation by teachers and school officials enhanced such continuing motivation (see also Maehr, 1976; 1977).

Yet, regardless of how extrinsic rewards may turn off the child in one case, they may also be the sine qua non in another. In this regard, research conducted by Sorensen (1975; 1976) may be of interest in working toward a fuller understanding of the principles involved. Briefly, Sorensen hypothesized that different kinds of reinforcement (tangible, verbal, or in the form of praise or knowledge of results) would have different motivational effects depending on the *attainment value* (Crandall & Battle, 1970) of the task. More specifically, it was predicted that tangible reinforcers would reduce motivation when the task had high attainment value; given low attainment value, one would not expect this to be the case. Results confirmed this hypothesis in the case of performance data. That is to say, performance was decreased by tangible reinforcers on the task with high attainment value. These results seem to suggest that there is no particular danger in using extrinsic rewards if the task is not already of interest. Indeed, that may be the only way an individual can be motivated to confront a task in such instances. The problem comes when one *adds* extrinsic motivators to tasks that are already of value.

Sorensen's results are very suggestive of the dual role that extrinsic motivators can play. One interpretation is that extrinsic motivators play such a dual role as they coincidentally redefine the behavior for the person. Thus, when the behavior is contracted and paid for, it is "work" and the rules of work obtain. When, however, the individual happens to perform freely, that is, apart from such contingencies, "play rules" obtain.

A first such rule seems to be that, once a task is paid for, intrinsic interest in performing it is reduced. The definition of a task as "work" means that extrinsic motivators will be critical. One does not work without pay. A second, less tautological, rule may also be suggested: Work and play are differentially controlled by level of success and the assurance of receiving a reward of some kind. If an extrinsic reward is the goal of behavior, one does not typically experiment with means, manners, and styles in achieving the goal. The surest route to success is preferred, and risk taking is eschewed. The greater the degree of success, the higher the motivation. If, however, extrinsic reasons for performing the task are minimal, then a different relationship is posited to exist between level of success and motivation. In this latter case, there is a certain freedom to experiment, take risks, and seek out challenges; instead of preferring sure success, the individual is attracted by *uncertainty* in outcome. Thus, in the play situation, one may expect motivation to be highest when uncertainty in outcome is highest, in most achievement-motivation studies, this is phrased as a subjective probability-of-success level of .50. In the work situation, the preference is for *certainty* of success; no value is attached to unpredictability and success is paramount. Thus, the higher the level of probable or actual success, the greater the motivation. Figure 9-3 presents a graphic summary of this hypothesis.

Strictly speaking, the validity of this hypothesis remains to be proven. One may deduce from studies by Maehr and Stallings (1972) that it has some degree of plausibility, however. Thus, in an external evaluation (and possibly, a "work") situation, students developed quite different kinds of attractions to tasks than they did in a self-evaluation (and possibly, a "play") situation. Briefly, whereas continuing interest in working with a "challenging" task developed when that task was originally confronted in a play situation, this did not occur in a work situation. Rather, in the work situation, a continued attractiveness toward the easy task was observed.

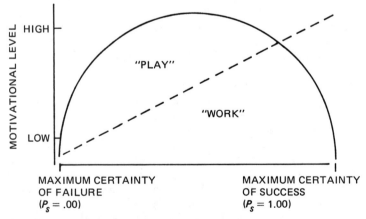

FIGURE 9-3 Hypothesized differential effects of success levels on motivation under "play" and "work" conditions.

All in all, then, the work–play definition of the situation conceivably has important effects on the motivation that will be displayed. Particularly intriguing is the hypothesis that such definitions of the situation will significantly affect the individual's willingness to confront challenge. This situational factor deserves more extensive scrutiny, not only by those interested in physical education, but by educators generally.

Intrinsic Interest

The work–play situation distinction inevitably leads to considerations of what it is about the task itself–quite apart from its sociopsychological definition–that makes it intrinsically interesting. Research on *intrinsic motivation* (see, e.g., Day & Berlyne, 1971; Deci, 1975; Hunt, 1965) has repeatedly emphasized that various structural features of the task may be critical in eliciting motivation. While we by no means have a full and complete definition of the structural features that will make a task intrinsically interesting, there are two important assertions that can be made. First, there is considerable evidence that a task that possesses an optimum level of uncertainty and unpredictability about what leads to what will be attractive. Thus, tasks that are novel, complex, ambiguous, or incongruous can be intrinsically interesting when certain socially determined factors such as competition, anxiety, and fear of failure are minimized. More generally, it seems that the human organism is basically an information-seeking mechanism, and thus tasks vary in attractiveness partly because of their information value. Social and cultural factors can subvert such intrinsic motivation, as noted previously, but they do not control it completely. A second and related point is that the information value of a task is likely to depend significantly on the level of cognitive development of a person confronting the task. Again, this factor–while it is a critical feature of achievement–should be minimally influenced by sociocultural factors. In conclusion, then, it is well to take cognizance of the fact that achievement motivation may well have an important cognitive base that exists regardless of culture or social experience.

Situation, Self, and Achievement

The third, and integrating, component in this situational-contextual analysis of achievement is the *self*. Clearly, any thorough consideration of the achieving situation must consider the self. Wary as one may be of making achievement motivation an individualistic thing, it is necessary to recognize that the achiever's thoughts about and expectations for *self* must be considered. Indeed, it may well be argued that the various theories of achievement motivation converge toward agreement as they posit the importance of self-regard in framing achievement behavior (Maehr, 1976). Of course, these theories have all been developed in Western society and have had only limited, if any, testing outside this context. Nevertheless, the evidence is such that one must consider self as a critical variable, even though one may wish to leave open the possibility of how critical any given facet of selfhood may be in a particular culture. Like *tasks*, and social *expectations, self* is simply another component to be considered in a situational-contextual analysis of achievement motivation. There are at least three facets to selfhood that are important to a situational-contextual analysis of achievement: *identity*, judged *competence*, and *self-as-initiator*.

Identity

By identity is meant, first of all, that the individuals perceive themselves to be associated with certain groups and hold selected others to be significant. Self-evidently, the effects of the social expectations discussed earlier are significantly dependent on whether or not individuals recognize these expectations as appropriate to themselves. Of course, how, why, and to what extent a person establishes and maintains such associations are questions of major and extensive concern. For this focus on a situational analysis of achievement motivation, one must confine oneself simply to recognizing that such identifications *exist*, that they can be identified, and that they are correlated in a significant way with the achievement motivation that will be demonstrated in any given instance.

Competence

A second facet of selfhood that is important in analyzing achieving behavior is an individual's judged competence to perform the task. While such judged competence may generalize across situations, with certain individuals judging themselves to be competent or incompetent across a wide variety of areas, judged competence is also demonstrably subject to variation due to immediate situational factors (see, e.g., Haas & Maehr, 1965; Ludwig & Maehr, 1967; Maehr, Mensing, & Nafzger, 1962). Moreover, it is clear that the perception of competence is a critical component in the motivation that will be demonstrated. Most theories of achievement motivation take cognizance of the role of judged competence to perform a task. Perhaps no one has explicated this in a more thorough fashion than John W. Atkinson (see, e.g., Atkinson & Feather, 1966; Atkinson & Raynor, 1974). Passing over much of the detail of his model, it may simply be noted that, following McClelland, Atkinson places stress on the fact that different kinds of *people* will react quite differently when confronted with tasks for which they hold different levels of expectancy for success or failure. The highly achievement-motivated person is presumably most motivated when the possibility of success is in the moderate range. Such a person is least motivated when success is in the low or high ranges. The inverse is true for the low-achievement-oriented person, as can be seen in Figure 9-4.

This is an intriguing hypothesis, although in many particulars it is lacking in empirical support. For example, the person who is not oriented to achievement does not typically exhibit a lowered motivation in the moderate success range, as is predicted, but rather, exhibits the same basic curve, although at a lowered level (see, e.g., Kukla, 1972, 1975; Maehr & Sjogren, 1971; Meyer, Folkes, & Weiner, 1976). What is particularly bothersome about this analysis is that a personality variable that cannot necessarily be generalized cross-culturally is made to be the critical moderator of judged competence effects on motivation. It is in this regard that attributional analyses of achievement motivation may prove helpful. Rather than stressing needs, drives, or enduring affective traits, this work has focused on the thoughts that an individual has about the achieving situation. Specifically, the focus is on the beliefs that a person may have about the causes of success and failure. Weiner (see, e.g., 1972a; 1974), for example, has reinterpreted the work of McClelland and Atkinson in these terms, arguing that the personality trait of achievement motivation can be properly viewed as a preferred way of assigning causes in achievement situations. Thus, high-achievement-motivated people are es-

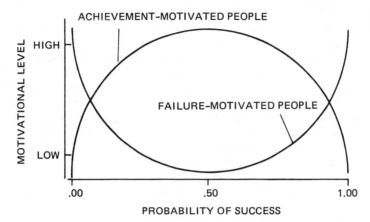

FIGURE 9-4 Hypothesized motivational patterns of achievement-motivated and failure-motivated personality types (after Atkinson).

sentially those who attribute success to self, to their own ability and effort. When such people fail, however, the failure is attributed to bad luck or not trying. Throughout, high-achievement-motivated people retain a cognitive set that they *can* do something if they *try*. In these terms, then, it is really judged competence to perform a task that will be related to the seeking out and preference for challenging tasks in the manner described by Atkinson. Simply put, people who believe in themselves will take moderate risks or confront challenge in an achieving situation.

While it may already be obvious, it will do no harm to add that an attributional analysis of achievement motivation is likely to prove more compatible with the situational, culturally relativistic approach presented in this chapter. As Weiner points out, and as is also evident in work on "learned helplessness" (Dweck, 1975, 1977; Dweck & Bush, 1976; Dweck & Reppucci, 1973), attributions, while they may have a certain durability, are not immutable. They will vary with situations, and one can teach people to assign causes differently.

Self-as-Initiator

The third facet of selfhood deals with the perceived origin of an act. Does the individual initiate it? Is it prompted by others—people, things, or events? Recent work on attributional processes, already alluded to, has relevance here also. It is deCharms (1968, 1972, 1976) who has called special attention to the initiatory role of self. In his concept of self as an *origin* or a *pawn* in an achievement situation, he has stressed that the perceived locus of an activity will moderate that activity in critical ways. Specifically, if the origin of the activity is *self*, then motivation is generally enhanced. This intriguing hypothesis has received some support in an extensive study of classroom motivation in inner-city school settings. Yet, in view of some evidence that the importance of self in achievement varies from culture to culture (see, e.g., Salili & Maehr, 1976), it must be retained as a hypothesis of interesting, but essentially untested, cross-cultural validity.

Regardless of the specific status of deCharms's hypothesis, his notions here are very suggestive of a possibility of particular relevance to the present analysis. The initiator–follower roles of self might profitably be conceptualized as the subjective side of work and play, as discussed previously. Play and work do exist cross-culturally and, hypothetically, with similar definition. In any case, by interpreting deCharms's hypothesis in work–play terms, it can be tied in with the previous analysis of these behavioral situations. Such a tie-in suggests something more specific than that the perception of self as origin or initiator will enhance motivation. It suggests that contrasting patterns of motivation will be exhibited depending on the perception of one's causal role in a situation. Specifically, when self is perceived as the initiator, highest motivation is exhibited when there is most challenge; when self is perceived as a pawn, to use deCharms's word, then a linear relationship is posited to exist between judged competence and motivation; in other words, the individual chooses to do, persists at, or demonstrates maximum motivation at tasks that provide maximum success (see Figure 9-5). It may be noted that this hypothesis, unlike that of Atkinson, assumes that all individuals will exhibit the convex motivational curve—given the right (i.e., a "play") situation. Likewise, in a work situation, all will exhibit a heightened motivation to achieve as success is more probable. Essentially, this hypothesis is implicit in White's (1959, 1960) notions of "competence motivation," as I have suggested elsewhere (1967, 1969). Certainly also, one might surmise that deCharms originally had in mind that the "origin perception" would eventuate in challenge seeking, although it is less clear, from his work, what motivational pattern should eventuate in the "pawn perception" state. In any case, the play–work ideas presented here are not without logical precedent. As such, they are deserving of direct experimental testing, which, as yet, they have not had. In terms of theory building, further consideration must be given to the hypothesis proposed above, to the effect that both high judged competence and the play situation lead to essentially the same behavior: challenge seeking. Is it possible that the situation is more likely to have the character of play for individuals who judge themselves to be competent to perform well? Or does play affect judged competence? These and similarly intriguing questions need to be answered.

In sum, the initiator facet of selfhood quite possibly plays a major role in the conditioning of motivation to achieve. Again, like all facets of perceived selfhood, it is not only a critical part of the achievement situation; it is also subject to situa-

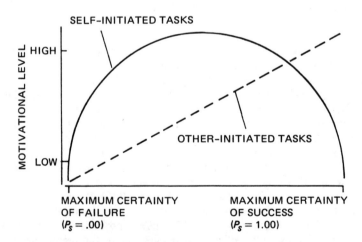

FIGURE 9-5 Hypothesized motivational patterns in self-initiated and other-initiated tasks (cf. also Figure 9-3).

tional change. Without ignoring the importance of personal history in influencing perception of self in a situation, the importance of situational-contextual variability deserves emphasis.

CONCLUSION

My consideration of sociocultural origins of achievement motivation focuses particularly on a situational-contextual analysis of achievement motivation. I have taken this tack, not only because there seems to be limited, systematic attention given to the importance of that which is situational and contextual, but also because of an assumption that such an approach may better do justice to the possibilities that exist within a given society or cultural group. Admittedly, there is point and purpose in pursuing a culture-personality hypothesis such as McClelland's. This chapter is obviously in debt to the massive efforts this approach has stimulated. Moreover, one cannot ignore the fact that a person is a part of any achieving situation and that any person has a history that has in some sense uniquely influenced that person's orientation toward achievement. The point, however, is that, in the consideration of the patterns of motivation that exist across social and cultural groups, situational-contextual variables deserve primary attention. Because the culture-personality orientation has dominated achievement theory heretofore, there is a need to modify the situation a bit. I hope this chapter has served that goal.

In stressing the situational-contextual basis of achievement motivation, I hope that a second goal has also been achieved. While it would be foolish to rule out the consideration of the *person* as a key element in achievement, particularly as one focuses on behavior *within*, rather than *across*, cultural groups, there is a necessity to emphasize concepts of the person that are responsive to situational-contextual change. It should be clear that I am inclined, in this regard to consider self-perceptions as a critical personal variable. While these perceptions will be responsive to situational-contextual factors, they are also informed by a social-learning history and structured by a cognitive capacity (cf. Salili, 1975; Salili, Maehr, & Gillmore, 1976; Weiner & Peter, 1973). Thus, they are not wholly ephemeral. Moreover, the analysis of selfhood in this chapter underscores the importance of values—which are often personalized—in creating the form that achievement will take. This again provides an entrée to the consideration of the constancies of achievement behavior in individuals.

All in all, this analysis suggests that future considerations of achievement behavior should revolve around two focuses. First and foremost, the achievement situation or context must be of major concern in considering variation in achievement motivation across social and cultural groups. Second, as one becomes interested in the individual achiever, one does well to return to an analysis of selfhood, particularly to the thoughts and perceptions the achiever holds toward self, others, and task in the situation. Incidentally, an analysis of achievement motivation that pays special attention to the situation and to the achiever's thoughts is bound to be of more help to education. Essentially, teachers and schools are in the business of creating motivation on the spot—in the classroom, on the playing field—by manipulating *situations*. They, in most cases, cannot afford to engage in reversing the individual's learning history. If one assumes that motivational change only comes through personality change, one inevitably accepts a certain fatalistic outlook as a teacher. How many personality changes can a teacher—or even the best special education program—affect in a given year? But while emphasizing the situation, I do not mean to ignore the individual achiever. Indeed, I have suggested an approach to analyzing individual differences in achievement that may actually prove to have more utility than those traditionally employed by McClelland, Atkinson, and their colleagues. Rather than focusing on inner needs expressed indirectly through fantasy, one would do well to consider conscious *thoughts* that can be readily verbalized about self and the achievement task. That is indeed the road that much of the achievement research is consciously or unconsciously following anyway (Maehr, 1976; Weiner, 1972b). Moreover, there is some hope that such a path will lead more directly to usable measurement scales of achievement motivation for education.

REFERENCES

Alper, T. G. Achievement motivation in college women: A now-you-see-it-now-you don't phenomenon. *American Psychologist,* 1974, **29**, 194–203.

Atkinson, J. W. (Ed.). *Motives in fantasy, action and society.* New York: D. Van Nostrand, 1958.

Atkinson, J. W., & Feather, N. T. (Eds.). *A theory of achievement motivation.* New York: Wiley, 1966.

Atkinson, J. W., & Raynor, J. O. (Eds.). *Motivation and achievement.* Washington. Winston, 1974.

Barkow, J. H. Prestige and culture: A biosocial interpretation. *Current Anthropology,* 1975, **16**, 559–561.

Coleman, J. S. *The adolescent society.* New York: Free Press, 1961.

Coleman, J. S. (Chair). *Youth: Transition to adulthood—Report of the panel on youth of the president's advisory committee.* Chicago: University of Chicago Press, 1974.

Coleman, J. S., Campbell, E. Q., Hobson, C. J., McPartland, J. M., Mood, M. A., Weinfeld, F. D., & York, R. L. *Equality of educational opportunity.* Washington: U.S. Government Printing Office, 1966.

Crandall, V. C., & Battle, E. S. The antecedents and adult correlates of academic and intellectual achievement effort. In J. Hill (Ed.), *Minnesota Symposium on Child Psychology.* Minneapolis: University of Minnesota Press, 1970.

Day, H. I., & Berlyne, D. E. Intrinsic motivation. In G. S. Lesser (Ed.), *Psychology and educational practice.* Glenview, Ill.: Scott, Foresman, 1971.

deCharms, R. *Personal causation.* New York: Academic, 1968.

deCharms, R. Personal causation training in the schools. *Journal of Applied Social Psychology,* 1972, **2**, 95–113.

deCharms, R. *Enhancing motivation.* New York: Irvington, 1976.

Deci, E. L. *Intrinsic motivation.* New York: Plenum, 1975.

Domingo-Llacuna, E. *The effect of pupil race, social class, speech and ability on teacher stereotypes and attribution.* Unpublished doctoral dissertation, University of Illinois at Urbana-Champaign, 1976.

Dweck, C. S. The role of expectations and attributions in the alleviation of learned helplessness. *Journal of Personality and Social Psychology,* 1975, **31**, 674–685.

Dweck, C. S. Learned helplessness and negative evaluation. *Educator,* 1977, **19**, 44–49.

Dweck, C. S., & Bush, E. S. Sex differences in learned helplessness: Differential debilitation with peer and adult evaluators. *Developmental Psychology,* 1976, **12**, 147–156.

Dweck, C. S., & Reppucci, N. D. Learned helplessness and reinforcement responsibility in children. *Journal of Personality and Social Psychology,* 1973, **25**, 109–116.

Entwisle, D. R. To dispel fantasies about fantasy-based measures of achievement motivation. *Psychological Bulletin,* 1972, **77**, 377–391.

Entwisle, D. R., & Hayduk, L. A. *The academic outlook of young children: Too great expectations.* Baltimore: John Hopkins Press, in press.

Entwisle, D. R., & Webster, M. Raising children's performance expectations. *Social Science Research,* 1972, **1**, 147–158.

Entwisle, D. R., & Webster, M. Status factors in expectation raising. *Sociology of Education,* 1973, **46**, 115–126.

Entwisle, D. R., & Webster, M. Raising children's expectations for their own performances: A classroom application. In J. Berger, T. Conner, & M. H. Fisek (Eds.), *Expectation states theory: A theoretical research program.* Cambridge, Mass.: Winthrop, 1974.

French, E. G., & Lesser, G. S. Some characteristics of the achievement motive in women. *Journal of Abnormal and Social Psychology,* 1964, 68, 119–128.

Frijda, N. & Jahoda, G. On the scope and methods of cross-cultural research. *International Journal of Psychology,* 1966, 1, 110–127.

Furth, H. *Piaget for teachers.* Englewood Cliffs, N.J.: Prentice-Hall, 1970.

Greene, D., & Lepper, M. R. (Eds.). *The hidden costs of reward.* Hillsdale, N.J.: Erlbaum, in press.

Haas, H. I., & Maehr, M. L. Two experiments on the concept of self and the reaction of others. *Journal of Personality and Social Psychology,* 1965, 1, 100–105.

Humphreys, L. G. Race and sex differences and their implications for educational and occupational equality. In M. L. Maehr & W. M. Stallings (Eds.), *Culture, child, and school.* Monterey, Calif.: Brooks/Cole, 1975.

Hunt, J. McV. Intrinsic motivation and its role in psychological development. In D. Levine (Ed.), *Nebraska Symposium on Motivation.* Lincoln: University of Nebraska Press, 1965.

Klinger, E. Fantasy need achievement as a motivational construct. *Psychological Bulletin,* 1966, 66, 291–308.

Klinger, E. Modeling effects on achievement imagery. *Journal of Personality and Social Psychology,* 1967, 7, 49–62.

Klinger, E., & McNelley, F. W. Fantasy need achievement and performance: A role analysis. *Psychological Review,* 1969, 76, 574–591.

Kolb, D. A. Achievement-motivation training for underachieving high school boys. *Journal of Personality and Social Psychology,* 1965, 2, 783–792.

Kremer, B. *Pupil reactions and evaluation conditions as a function of developmental level and evaluative context.* Unpublished doctoral dissertation, University of Illinois at Urbana-Champaign, 1976.

Kukla, A. Foundations of an attributional theory of performance. *Psychological Review,* 1972, 79, 454–470.

Kukla, A. Preferences among impossibly difficult and trivially easy tasks: A revision of Atkinson's theory of choice. *Journal of Personality and Social Psychology,* 1975, 32, 338–345.

Labov, W. The logic of nonstandard English. In F. Williams (Ed.), *Language and poverty.* Chicago: Rand McNally, 1970.

Labov, W. Academic ignorance and black intelligence. *Atlantic,* 1972, 229(6), 59–67.

Lesser, G. S., Krawitz, R. N., & Packard, R. Experimental arousal of achievement motivation in adolescent girls. *Journal of Abnormal and Social Psychology,* 1963, 66, 59–66.

Ludwig, D. J., & Maehr, M. L. Changes in self concept and stated behavioral preferences. *Child Development,* 1967, 38, 453–467.

Maehr, M. L. *Competence revisited.* Paper presented at the meeting of the American Educational Research Association, New York, February 1967.

Maehr, M. L. Self concept, challenge, and achievement. *Lutheran Education,* 1969, 105, 50–57.

Maehr, M. L. Culture and achievement motivation. *American Psychologist,* 1974, 29, 887–896. (a)

Maehr, M. L. *Sociocultural origins of achievement.* Monterey, Calif.: Brooks/Cole, 1974. (b)

Maehr, M. L. Toward a framework for the cross-cultural study of achievement motivation: McClelland considered and redirected. In M. G. Wade & R. M. Martens (Eds.), Psychology of motor behavior and sport. *Proceedings of the annual conference of the North American Society for the Psychology of Sport and Physical Activity.* Urbana, Ill.: Human Kinetics, 1974. (c)

Maehr, M. L. *Expectations in the classroom: Status effects.* Discussant's comments in a symposium at the meeting of the American Psychological Association, Chicago, September 1975. (a)

Maehr, M. L. Sociocultural influences on behavior and development. In M. L. Maehr & W. M. Stallings (Eds.), *Culture, child, and school.* Monterey, Calif.: Brooks/Cole, 1975. (b)

Maehr, M. L. Continuing motivation: An analysis of a seldom considered educational outcome. *Review of Educational Research,* 1976, 46, 443–462.

Maehr, M. L. Turning the fun of school into the drudgery of work: The negative effects of certain grading practices on motivation. *Educator,* 1977, 19, 10–14.

Maehr, M. L., & Lysy, A. Motivating students of diverse sociocultural backgrounds to achieve. *International Journal of Intercultural Relations*, in press.

Maehr, M. L., Mensing, J., & Nafzger, S. Concept of self and the reaction of others. *Sociometry*, 1962, **25**, 353-357.

Maehr, M. L., & Sjogren, D. Atkinson's theory of achievement motivation: First step toward a theory of academic motivation? *Review of Educational Research*, 1971, **41**, 143-161.

Maehr, M. L., & Stallings, W. M. Freedom from external evaluation. *Child Development*, 1972, **43**, 177-185.

McClelland, D. C. *The achieving society*. New York: Free Press, 1961.

McClelland, D. C. *Motivational trends in society*. Morristown, N.J.: Silver Burdett, 1971.

McClelland, D. C., Atkinson, J. W., Clark, R. A., & Lowell, E. L. *The achievement motive*. New York: Appleton, 1953.

McClelland, D. C., & Winter, D. G. *Motivating economic achievement*. New York: Free Press, 1969.

Meyer, W., Folkes, V., & Weiner, B. The perceived informational value and affective consequences of choice behavior and intermediate difficulty task selection. *Journal of Research in Personality*, 1976, **10**, 410-423.

Mingione, A. D. Need for achievement in Negro and white children. *Journal of Consulting Psychology*, 1965, **29**, 108-111.

Mingione, A. D. Need for achievement in Negro, white, and Puerto Rican children. *Journal of Consulting and Clinical Psychology*, 1968, **32**, 94-95.

Moore, W. E. Social structure and behavior. In G. Lindzey & E. Aronson (Eds.), *The handbook of social psychology* (2nd ed., Vol. 4). Reading, Mass.: Addison-Wesley, 1969.

Mosteller, F., & Moynihan, D. (Eds.). *On equality of educational opportunity*. New York: Random House, Vintage, 1972.

Osgood, C. E., May, W., & Miron, M. *Cross-cultural universals of affective meaning*. Urbana: University of Illinois Press, 1975.

Rosenthal, R. Empirical vs. decreed validation of clocks and tests. *American Educational Research Journal*, 1969, **5**, 708-711.

Rosenthal, R., & Jacobson, L. *Pygmalion in the classroom: Teacher expectation and pupils' intellectual development*. New York: Holt, 1968.

Rubovits, P. C., & Maehr, M. L. Pygmalion analyzed: Toward an explanation of the Rosenthal-Jacobson findings. *Journal of Personality and Social Psychology*, 1971, **19**, 197-203.

Rubovits, P. C., & Maehr, M. L. Pymalion black and white. *Journal of Personality and Social Psychology*, 1973, **25**, 210-218.

Rubovits, P. C., & Maehr, M. L. Teacher expectations: A special problem for black children with white teachers? In M. L. Maehr & W. M. Stallings (Eds.), *Culture, child and school*. Monterey, Calif.: Brooks/Cole, 1975.

Salili, F. *The development of achievement and moral judgment in Iranian children*. Unpublished doctoral dissertation, University of Illinois at Urbana-Champaign, 1975.

Salili, F., & Maehr, M. L. *A cross-cultural analysis of achievement-related concepts*. Unpublished research report, Center for Instructional Research and Curriculum Evaluation, University of Illinois at Urbana-Champaign, 1976.

Salili, F., Maehr, M. L., & Gillmore, G. Achievement and morality: A cross-cultural analysis of causal attribution and evaluation. *Journal of Personality and Social Psychology*, 1976, **33**, 327-337.

Salili, F., Maehr, M. L., Sorenson, R. L., & Fyans, L. J. A further consideration of the effects of evaluation on motivation. *American Educational Research Journal*, 1976, **13**, 85-102.

Sarbin, T. R., & Allen, V. L. Role theory. In G. Lindzey & E. Aronson (Eds.), *The handbook of social psychology* (2nd Ed., Vol. 1). Reading, Mass.: Addison-Wesley, 1968.

Sorensen, R. L. *Attainment value and type of reinforcement: A hypothesized interaction effect*. Unpublished doctoral dissertation, University of Illinois at Urbana-Champaign, 1975.

Sorenson, R. L. Attainment value and type of reinforcement: A hypothesized interaction effect. *Journal of Personality and Social Psychology*, 1976, **34**, 1155-1160.

Staw, B. M. *Intrinsic and extrinsic motivation* (University Programs Modular Studies). Morristown, N.J.: Silver Burdett, 1976.

Thorndike, R. L. Review of Pygmalion in the classroom. *American Educational Research Journal*, 1968, **5**, 708-711.

Thorndike, R. L. But do you know how to tell time? *American Educational Research Journal*, 1969, **6**, 692.

Triandis, H. C. *The analysis of subjective culture.* New York: Wiley, 1972.

Weber, M. *[The protestant ethic and the spirit of capitalism]* (T. Parsons, Trans.). New York: Scribner, 1930. (Originally published, 1904.)

Webster, M., & Sobieszek, B. I. *Sources of self-evaluation.* New York: Wiley, 1974.

Weiner, B. Attribution theory, achievement motivation and the educational process. *Review of Educational Research,* 1972, **42**, 203–215. (a)

Weiner, B. *Theories of motivation.* Chicago: Rand McNally, 1972. (b)

Weiner, B. Achievement motivation as conceptualized by an attribution theorist. In B. Weiner (Ed.), *Attribution theory and achievement motivation.* Morristown, N.J.: Silver Burdett, 1974.

Weiner, B., & Kukla, A. An attributional analysis of achievement motivation. *Journal of Personality and Social Psychology,* 1970, **15**, 1–20.

Weiner, B., & Peter, N. A cognitive-developmental analysis of achievement and moral judgments. *Developmental Psychology,* 1973, **9**, 290–309.

Weinstein, M. S. Achievement motivation and risk preference. *Journal of Personality and Social Psychology,* 1969, **13**, 153–172.

White, R. W. Motivation reconsidered: The concept of competence. *Psychological Review,* 1959, **66**, 297–333.

White, R. W. Competence and the psychosexual stages of development. In M. R. Jones (Ed.), *Nebraska Symposium on Motivation.* Lincoln: University of Nebraska Press, 1960.

Zander, A., & Forward, J. Position in group, achievement motivation, and group aspirations. *Journal of Personality and Social Psychology,* 1968, **8**, 282–288.

V

THE CLASSROOM GROUP

10

Applications
of Social Psychology
to Classroom Life

Richard A. Schmuck
Center for Educational Policy and Management and Department
of Educational Psychology, University of Oregon

Many school practitioners and educational psychologists put insufficient emphasis on the social-psychological aspects of classroom life. The concepts of such seminal thinkers as George H. Mead, Charles Cooley, and Kurt Lewin are unfamiliar to them, and John Dewey is mostly remembered for an association with progressivism rather than for his social-psychological insights into the nature of schooling. Indeed, the popular and conventional view of the educational process among educators seems to be that teaching and learning occur in two-person units involving the teacher and each individual student. The group dynamics within the classroom are often de-emphasized.

Educational psychologists also have used a dyadic view as a guiding principle in their research on teaching and learning, but they generally have not been successful in presenting consistent empirical relationships to support it. Although research from the behaviorist's perspective has had some payoff for understanding teaching and learning, educational researchers have not shown consistent relationships between teachers' personality characteristics or behavioral styles on the one hand and individual students' achievement or attitudes on the other. As Glick (1968) has indicated in his review of the empirical literature on this topic, the lack of consistent empirical associations between individual-teacher and individual-student variables is not surprising from the perspective of social psychology. A simple, dyadic view of teaching and learning is shortsighted and grossly oversimplified when one recognizes the power of other social dynamics that regularly occur in the classroom.

An anecdote about my 9-year-old son illustrates the multifarious dynamics present in today's classrooms. During the summer of 1976 when Allen was 8, he attended a special reading class for 1 hour, 5 days a week, to improve his reading skills. The class was designed from the perspectives of reinforcement theory and behavior modification; the curriculum was systematic and sequential; supportive reinforcements were to be issued at appropriate times by the teacher; and teacher-student interaction was emphasized whereas student-student relationships were underplayed. Our son made progress. We were pleased; he was pleased; and the teacher was pleased. I have no idea how pleased Allen's peers were, but at the final conference the teacher noted a behavior pattern typical of Allen that was unusual in her experience. She said, "He reinforces other kids. Often after a youngster has successfully read a difficult passage, Allen will reach over to pat him on the back and say, 'You did a good job!' I've just not seen that happen much before in my classes." I was good for Allen, for the teacher, and for the other students.

Although classroom teachers do frequently interact with individual students, virtually all of teachers' behaviors within the classroom occur in the social context of the student peer group. The formal interventions and informal behaviors of teachers are continually mediated by the informal group processes of the student peer group; even a succinct directive aimed at one student by a teacher does *not* occur simply in the narrow dyadic context of teacher-student interaction. A teacher's directives occur within the context of the classroom group, and any student's responses to those directives are influenced by the feelings, attitudes, and relationships shared within the student peer group. In this fashion, students continually influence one another to attend to particular teacher behaviors and not to others.

THE CLASSROOM AS SOCIAL CONTEXT

Cognitive, affective, and behavioral events in the classroom are fundamentally social phenomena. This social-psychological orientation to the classroom has been touched on in the thorough review of theory and research by Getzels (1969); in the comprehensive book of readings by Miles and Charters (1970); in the analyses of classroom interaction by Jackson (1968) and Schmuck and Schmuck (1975); and in several general texts by Backman and Secord (1968), Guskin and Guskin (1970), Johnson (1970), and Bany and Johnson (1975).

All these authors view the social context of the classroom as being constituted of both formal and informal processes. The formal processes are ways various classroom participants work toward carrying out official or publically specified goals. In the classroom, for example, a formal aspect of group processes is the manner in which any youngster is expected to perform the role of academic student as it is defined by teacher, school district, and adult community at large. Informal group processes, on the other hand, involve the unique ways in which each classroom participant relates to others as persons. In most classes, an important aspect of informal processes is the way in which the students' friendships for one another are distributed. Friendships and other aspects of informal life in classrooms often have an important bearing on the ways formal processes, in particular teaching and learning, are carried out.

Sociological research carried out two generations ago within industrial organizations by Roethlisberger and Dickson (1939) pointed to the importance of informal relationships for accomplishing the goals of production in small work groups. Employees in industry were viewed by these researchers as being motivated not primarily for wages but also for self-esteem. What the employees hoped for, in the main, was credit for work done well, interesting and stimulating tasks, appreciation, approval, and congenial relations with fellow workers. Industrial administrators were encouraged to understand the informal person-to-person relationships on the job because the social and affective lives of the employees were viewed as importantly related to the production goals of the company.

Several systematic studies of military behavior during World War II tended to substantiate these early results from industry. Shils and Janowitz (1948) showed that the breakdown of the German army was not due primarily to flaws in its formal organization but, instead, arose out of dissolution of friendships among small units of soldiers. They concluded that the informal, supportive relationships of closeness among the soldiers were necessary for full realization of the formal goals of winning the war. A similar result showed up in Goodacre's study (1953) of American rifle squads. He found that the men in the high-performing squads reported their group as having a significantly greater number of men buddying around together on the post after duty hours, as having fewer disagreements among the men in the squad, and as having an attractive group from the points of view of other soldiers on the post.

These classical studies of group behavior along with a host of others, including the important works of Wilfred Bion and Jacob Moreno, have shown that informal relationships among people are inevitable in any formal organization and that, if the formal organization fails to take such informal relationships into consideration, discord, strife, and conflict can appear at the formal level of group functioning. The classroom with its multifarious peer-group dynamics presents a clear example of this point. If informal group processes, in the form of peer relations and norms, are not supportive, unproductive interpersonal tensions can occur, and the students' learning of the formal curriculum can be negatively affected.

In the classroom, the student peer group presents some of the most salient and meaningful rewards and punishments there can be, in any given day, for individual students. Starting in the third and fourth grades for most youngsters, peer-group members exert strong influence on one another's values, attitudes about school, developing aspirations, and school behavior. The impact of the classroom peer group is especially significant for upper elementary students, who typically spend 4–8 hours together every day. Although junior and senior high students, in contrast, have a wider number of peer settings for interaction both within and outside the school, a secondary student who has difficulty relating to classmates also tends to experience tensions with peers in other settings and vice versa. In any case, no matter how well a student of any age may fit into informal groups outside the school, every youngster spends a large part of each weekday in classroom situations, and many students who are pinpointed by teachers for psychological help tend to be isolated or rejected by peers.

My research has shown that classroom groups with supportive friendship patterns enhance academic learning, whereas more interpersonally tense classroom environments in which peer-group rejections are strong and frequent get in the way of learning (Schmuck, 1963; Schmuck, 1966; Schmuck, 1971). These studies showed that the classroom peer group characterized by a wide dispersion of friendships had more cohesiveness than groups with concentrations of liked and disliked members. My data on elementary classes tended to replicate Muldoon's (1955) finding that the concentration of liked and disliked members in high school classrooms was negatively associated with cohesiveness. He found that the more clearly a class recognized and designated its popular and unpopular members, the less the class functioned as a unit, worked cooperatively under stress, and manifested overt friendliness. Muldoon's finding, as well as those in my own inquiries, indicate that the profusion of emotional support for students in the diffusely structured group increases the attractiveness of the class for the students.

My research went beyond an analysis of the group dynamics of the classroom peer group to include measurement of such psychological variables as students' self-esteem, their attitudes toward school, and their academic performance. The data indicated that the students' academic performances were highly correlated with their feelings about themselves—especially their self-appraisals as effective peers and as effective students—and that these self-appraisals were influenced, at least in part, by the students' friendships and influence relationships with their classmates. In other words, the pattern of peer-group friendship and influence relationships within the class had an impact upon the students' self-concepts and attitudes toward school, which, in turn, affected the students' academic performance—or so at least could go one plausible explanation of my correlational data.

This explanation of my research findings has been essentially corroborated in a more recent study by Lewis and St. John (1974) that dealt with the achievement of black students in classrooms that had a majority of whites. In an effort to study the dynamics of racially integrated classes, Lewis and St. John set out to test the conception derived from the 1954 Supreme Court decision that integrated school experiences would facilitate the achievement of black students. They collected extensive data from 154 black sixth graders in 22 majority-white classrooms. Their results showed that a rise in the achievement of blacks depended on two factors. (1) norms stressing achievement in the classrooms and (2) acceptance of black students into the classroom peer group. This second factor was shown to be especially important. The mere presence of academically achieving white students was insufficient to raise achievement levels of black students. The performance of blacks was strongly influenced by their being accepted as friends by white students.

Informal group interactions in the classroom do make a difference in the accomplishment of the formal goals of the school. Students who receive unfavorable and negative feedback from their peers are put in a threatening environment for many hours each day; their anxiety and insecurity reduce their self-esteem; and their lack of adequate self-worth, in turn, decreases their efforts to succeed in academic work. A lack of peer acceptance undermines students' self-confidence and debilitates their motivation to persist in the face of tough academic obstacles.

LEARNING GROUPS

Many strong demands exist today for improving human relationships in schools and for both legitimizing pluralism and making it operational in the educational establishment. These demands have precipitated a large number of educational experiments and instructional innovations that can be grouped under the banner of alternative schools. Many public school districts are experimenting with or fully implementing some kind of alternative school at this very moment. Although one contemporary faction of alternative educators wishes to get students back to the basics and to restore teacher authority, most experiments in alternative education continue to emphasize individual differences, student freedom and responsibility, and relaxed and supportive interpersonal relationships. The *learning group*—in contrast to the classroom group—is a useful social-psychological concept for thinking about teaching and learning in this contemporary context.

By the *learning group*, I refer to a collection of school participants, including teachers and students, working together, at least in part, on learning tasks. Note that any given classroom does not necessarily constitute a learning group, nor do all learning groups exist only within the classroom setting. The variety of learning groups in our contemporary schools can be limitless. There are ungraded classrooms in which students are tentatively grouped according to their level of skill or degree of interest; instructional groups, based primarily on learner goals, that may last from 2 days to 2 years; long-term extracurricular groups such as career-guidance and student-government groups; and learning groups formed for specific short-term purposes, such as special seminars or theater groups.

An example of a classroom that does not have learning groups in the strict sense of the concept is a language laboratory with individualized programs. The students are not required to work together to implement their learning tasks, and interpersonal interactions are intentionally underplayed. Moreover, although the learning goals for all students may be the same, the students do not function interdependently in attempting to reach those goals; in fact, each student acts more or less autonomously from all others. Another example is the physical arrangements employed at a local Oregon private school, which has classrooms in which student desks are positioned around the walls of the room. Students are obliged to face the walls, and large partitions are used to separate students from one another. The classroom is physically designed to keep interaction among the students at a minimum.

Although the language laboratory and the private school classroom with cubicles do not facilitate the development of learning groups, formal and informal social processes are nonetheless at work to some degree. As we pointed out in our text on humanistic psychology (Schmuck & Schmuck, 1974), even the most individuated classroom settings are influenced by some aspects of interpersonal life. The mere physical presence of other students does have some effect on a student's performance even as she or he engages the simplist of learning tasks. In addition, when the informal peer relations increase in power and salience—as they do with teen-agers— the student's self-appraisals become more and more vulnerable to the influence of the peer group. Even in the language laboratory or in the classroom with cubicles, each student's self-concept can be altered depending on whether the quality of informal relationships is threatening and debilitating, or supportive and enhancing, to the development of self-esteem. In any classroom, despite a teacher's or an aide's attempts to discourage interaction between students, the students still do carry out some informal interchanges with one another that can have impact on their self-esteem as students, and on their attitudes toward school.

Indeed, physical proximity and extended time together are fundamental ingredients for the formation of any group. At the same time, proximity and time together are not in themselves sufficient for the formation of a learning group. Some students meet together for a whole academic year in the same room, ostensibly working toward similar goals, while still not learning the first names of some of their peers. Such an anonymous class, along with some language laboratories and some clusters of students engaged in individually prescribed instruction, would be located at the lower end of a dimension of "groupness." On the other hand, a collection of students can work together for only a short period of time, as in rehearsing a play, in raising funds for the school, or even in a small group seminar, and while doing so, display the features of collaboration and interdependence that would place them on the higher end of a dimension of groupness. Particular classrooms and even entire schools can be categorized according to their location on a dimension of groupness. Obviously, some are much more like learning groups than others. Although a class's ideal place on this dimension depends on one's philosophy and values, the concepts and skills of applied social psychology take on more relevance and importance for those classes on the higher end of the dimension that exhibit the features of an interdependent learning group.

A Social Psychology of Effective Learning Groups

I take the value position that most, if not all, students should have some academic experiences in effectively functioning learning groups. Interaction and interdependence are facts of life in the late 1970s, and students should learn to cope effectively with these conditions. Moreover, although student alienation is prominent in schools, it does not follow, even in our largest urban schools, that learning groups must be impersonal or inhumane. Collective life can introduce a multitude of new issues and conflicts to individuals who have lived primarily in small, low-tension primary groups, but these conflicts can be solved creatively and constructively only if the participants have had some experience and practice in learning how to work effectively together to cope with group problems.

Our understanding of the dimension of groupness in classrooms can be enhanced, and our ability to take action to establish effective learning groups can be strengthened, by keeping three clusters of social-process variables in mind: (1) interaction and interdependence among the members, (2) movement toward some shared goals, and (3) interaction through a social structure. The degree to which these social-psychological characteristics are present reflects the nature of the classroom as a social unit; their quality is associated with the potential psychological effectiveness of the classroom learning group. Classrooms that do not have some of the social-psychological characteristics discussed here will be likely to be individuated and lonely, whereas those that exhibit them are more likely to be psychologically supportive and facilitative of group and individual learning.

The first characteristic, *interaction and interdependence,* refers to teachers and students communicating face to face and possessing some reciprocal influence in relation to one another. This sociological property, discussed in detail by Cartwright and Zander (1969), excludes mere human aggregates in physical proximity, such as students in a lecture hall or students at a school assembly, or collections of school participants with some characteristic in common such as redheads or all the members of a particular grade or school. It represents the most fundamental defining attributes of a group.

For example, if a dozen students from different high schools are lying by chance in the sun on the same Florida beach, they do not, as such, constitute a group; but if someone in the water cries for help and the 12 students respond by trying to save the swimmer from drowning in some kind of concerted manner, they have become a group in that they now interact interdependently in relation to a function.

Parsons (1951) suggested five modes of social interaction and interdependence that are useful in trying to gain clarity about the effective dynamics of learning groups.

1. *Affective–Nonaffective.* A class with effective learning groups has an atmosphere of affective support and openness. It is a social environment in which expressions of feelings are welcomed and reinforced and in which there are more expressions of favorable, than of unfavorable, feelings. In contrast, classes that

do not manifest the characteristics of effective learning groups feature more students who keep their happy feelings or feelings of displeasure to themselves.

2. *Self-Collective.* Effective learning groups alternate between a focus on self and a focus on the collective. Some learning tasks are carried out by individuals; others are done by group members striving to produce a product through their conjoint efforts.

3. *Universalism–Particularism.* In some rare classrooms, the teacher treats all students alike; but usually, in classes with effective learning groups, individual variations are expected and rewarded. Indeed, no pretense is made that all students should be treated alike; rather, individual strengths and learning needs are publically specified and discussed.

4. *Achievement-Ascription.* In many classrooms, a student's standing is achieved through personal effort, but in some, the status one enters with can influence the status eventually arrived at in the group. Both individual and group achievement are expected and rewarded in classes with effective learning groups.

5. *Specificity–Diffuseness.* In some classes, discussions are focused entirely on the curriculum, while classrooms with effective learning groups display a broad array of personal and impersonal topics that are viewed as legitimate and appropriate.

As classrooms exhibit flexibility and variability along these five Parsonian dimensions of interaction and interdependence, they are more likely to become supportive environments for the development of effective learning groups.

With regard to the second social-psychological characteristic, *shared goals,* the members of effective learning groups move toward at least a few preferred, understandable, and consensual end states. The pursuit of subject-matter learning is, of course, an example of a common, formal group goal in most classrooms. Other goals that may be less obvious but are important for effective learning groups have to do with maintaining cohesiveness and identity as a miniculture. Along with academic and social-emotional goals, classrooms that are constituted of effective learning groups also possess goals that are focused on individual achievement as well as goals that emphasize the group, as such, producing some output. As we have described elsewhere (Schmuck & Schmuck, 1975), learning groups can become increasingly effective as they are able to fulfill several of these goal categories at the same time. Thus, learning groups increase in effectiveness as they sometimes have all members pursuing subject-matter projects together; other times have individuals or subgroups doing their own things; still other times have group discussions about how the total body is working; and finally include time for small friendship clusters to get together informally.

Classrooms can also be categorized according to the nature of their social structures. Structured interaction is regular, repetitive, and to some extent expected and predicted by the participants. The traditional classrooms may define the teacher always as educational leader, whereas effective learning groups call for other social structures through which students take the teacher role in relation to one another and through which the formal teacher can act as a student occasionally. Some learning groups may decide to have officers, or a steering committee, or several of the members occupying special interfacing and linkage roles with external groups and library resources. Perhaps most of the recent innovativeness in our schools, especially with alternative schools, has arisen from creative thinking about possibilities of different sorts of social structures for learning groups.

Psychodynamics in Effective Learning Groups

To round out this social-psychological orientation to classroom life, I must add a few important psychological variables to the social processes of interaction, interdependence, shared goals, and social structures. Within the context of the array of social processes in the learning group, students experience thoughts and feelings about themselves. At the same time, they bring their own previously developed motivational structures to the classroom. As they proceed through school, the interplay of the social processes in classrooms and the students' developing motivational structures are mutually influential.

The motivational structures of students, while quite varied one from the other, are all undergirded by a master motive, that being a continuous striving for self-esteem and self-respect. Any student's personal striving for self-esteem can be viewed as transpiring in at least three psychodynamic domains: (1) the striving for *competence*, also labeled as achievement, efficacy, mastery, and curiosity; (2) the striving for *power* or influence in relation to others; and (3) the striving for *affiliation* with and affection from others. The basic psychological questions for students in learning groups are: What can I accomplish by dint of personal effort? How can I exert my will by taking appropriate initiative? and Who will go with me when I offer myself as a friend? Typical feelings that are associated with frustrations of these three motivational structures within learning groups are feelings of inferiority, worthlessness, being put down, loneliness, betrayal, lack of interest, and dullness. *Incompetence, powerlessness,* and *rejection* are the most serious psychological problems in the school.

LEVERAGE POINTS FOR INTERPERSONAL IMPROVEMENT

To develop effective learning groups, one must be conscious of the interplay between the social processes and the psychodynamics discussed above. On the one hand, there are the social processes of interaction, interdependence, shared goals, and social structure; on the other, there are the motivational structures of competence, power, and affiliation. These latter psychodynamics, representing the substance of student self-esteem, constitute key leverage points for improving the quality of life in learning groups. By using the strivings for competence, power, and affiliation as points of departure, one can begin to build rudimentary designs for the social processes of effective learning groups.

The Striving for Competence

Students, for the most part, strive to act competently. Indeed, as White (1959) has so eloquently stated, the search for competence is a basic human drive. Ways in which students behave to prove to themselves that they are competent are influenced decidedly by their self-expectations for personal success. Students with low confidence in their own abilities will behave differently than students who have high self-confidence. Classroom situations are used often as testing grounds for a student's self-expectations. A student who believes that an excellent job has been done on an assignment and who receives a similar evaluation from the teacher will feel bolstered by the school experience. If a low evaluation had been received, the dissonance would have motivated the student to reassess capabilities and to expect a somewhat lower level of personal performance on subsequent occasions. Effective learning groups provide ways in which students can realistically assess their competence and positively strengthen their self-esteem.

Research has shown that classroom performance can be altered by changes in students' self-images. Benjamin (1950) asked 48 senior high students to rank themselves at their own intelligence level. Next, he administered an intelligence test, after which he presented false information to each student about his or her performance. To half of the students, Benjamin presented scores that were one level above what the students expected; to the other half, he presented scores below actual student predications. Finally, Benjamin administered another form of the same intelligence test. A majority of scores for the second test changed in the direction of the falsely reported ranks; students who thought they did better than they had expected performed better on the second test, whereas students who believed they did poorer than they had expected actually did do poorer on the second test.

In other research, Sears (1940) showed that a student's level of aspiration is influenced by past success or failure experiences. She tested upper elementary students on their arithmetic and reading performances, making estimates of the time each student took to complete a page of work. Students who experienced failure on these tests set their levels of aspiration at unrealistically high or unrealistically low levels. These unrealistic students had a high fear of failure, lacked self-confidence, and viewed themselves as "losers." Either they set up each situation so that they would most certainly succeed and be able to dismiss their success by saying, "Anyone can do that!" or they set goals that they could not possibly achieve, once again proving that they were incompetent. Those students who set realistic goals had experienced successes in the past. They chose moderate levels of aspiration that were challenging but that also offered high probabilities of success.

DeCharms (1968, 1972), in more recent work, theorized that students differ according to the extent that they act as "pawns" and as "origins." Pawns possess very little self-confidence, feeling that others are in control and that they themselves do not often make deliberate choices about the direction of their lives. Students who are origins, on the other hand, direct their own lives, having confidence that they can make choices on their own and that they can plan and pursue their own interests. DeCharms work is important because it demonstrates the impact of teacher behavior upon the self-concepts of students.

DeCharms tested two important hypotheses from this theory about student pawns and origins. First, he posited that student pawns and origins are created out of the expectations that other key people hold for them. Second, he posited that a relationship exists between originlike student behavior and successful academic achievement. He conducted a 3-year intervention and evaluation program in an urban district to test these hypotheses, collecting data from fifth graders and following these same students during their sixth and seventh grades.

At the same time that deCharms was collecting data from the fifth graders, he was training sixth- and seventh-grade teachers on how to help students develop more originlike behavior. The teachers were trained to use exercises for bolstering their self-concept and procedures for stimulating achievement striving, and they were taught concepts related to the pawn–origin dimension. DeCharm's evaluation data showed that the experimental teachers changed their classroom behaviors and that their students gained in academic achievement and in originlike behaviors compared to control groups. DeCharms showed that students' expectations about their own behavior can be crucial to what happens in the students' striving for academic achievement and that a teacher can have significant influence on the self-expectations that students develop.

The works of White, Benjamin, Sears, and deCharms overlap significantly with recent research on attribution theory (Bem, 1972; Nisbett & Valins, 1971; Weiner, 1974). According to attribution theory, students' perceptions of the causes of their behavior influence how they behave on future occasions. Students presumably judge their motivation to achieve, in other words, partly from the circumstances under which they behave. If they perform activities for external rewards, they infer a lack of personal interest, whereas if they perform without external inducement, like deCharms's origins, they judge themselves to be intrinsically interested in the activities. In Deci's (1975) view, rewards reduce intrinsic motivation to strive for competence by creating the impression that one's behavior is externally prompted and by weakening feelings of competence and self-determination.

Another social-psychological process that is related to the strengthening or weakening of students' feelings of competence involves teachers communicating their expectations for student performance to the students. In a summary of a host of empirical findings on how teachers communicate expectations for student achievement, Rosenthal (1973), the originator of the "Pygmalion effect," discussed four social-psychological mechanisms.

The first labeled *climate,* states that high expectations for another's behavior give rise to a climate of warmth, attention, and emotional support. The second variable is *feedback*; teachers give more encouragement and praise to students for whom they have high expectations. Third, Rosenthal points to the sort of *input* that teachers present to students for whom they have high expectations; they rephrase questions, give helpful hints to answers, and give more constructive information to students they believe know an answer than to students they believe have "low ability." Finally, the fourth mechanism in Rosenthal's summary involves the teachers' *encouragement* for the output of student responses. Rosenthal points out that teachers wait longer for answers from "high-ability" students than from their "low-ability" peers.

Although competent teaching helps students move a step beyond where they are presently, it is obvious from the research (Brophy & Good, 1970, 1972; Rosenthal, 1973; Rosenthal & Jacobson, 1968; Rubovitz & Maehr, 1971) that many teachers provide it only for those students for whom they hold high expectations. For most teachers, their bias in favor of high-ability youngsters is unconscious. If teachers are to be instrumental in helping each student perform optimally, however, a point of leverage for student improvement must be the teacher's own expectations for a student's achievement. Teachers need to become aware of their natural tendency to focus more on the students who are doing well and need to pursue a consistent course of appropriate and equitable support and encouragement for all students. Through introspection, teachers may be able to understand how they are unwittingly behaving in discriminatory ways toward students.

The Striving for Power

While, for some social psychologists, competence and power are conceptualized as overlapping in so far as both refer to an individual's need to predict and control the environment, I prefer to keep them separated, especially in discussions about the classroom and learning groups. For me, the striving for competence has to do primarily with mastery over academic subject matter within the school. It may also refer to striving to master physical tasks, as in sports, or to growing intellectually so that new possibilities in the school's curriculum are available. In contrast, the striving for power always takes place in relation to other human beings, such as one's peers, older students, or the teacher.

The issues of social power—who has interpersonal influence and how it is used— are highly important for an understanding of interpersonal relations in classrooms. Effective learning groups feature students who feel powerful and influential and who are happy, effective, and curious. Class members with some degree of influence feel secure and useful. In contrast, students who feel powerless possess poor images of themselves; they feel negative about school and do not perform at levels conso- nant with their abilities. Powerlessness induces anxiety; the classroom becomes a threatening and insecure place. An effective learning group has a social climate in which all students see themselves as having some influence.

An analysis of the bases of social influence is helpful for an understanding of interpersonal processes in learning groups. French and Raven (1959) created a set of helpful categories for understanding the bases of influence. The set includes *expert power* (the extent of knowledge that a person is viewed as possessing), *referent power* (the extent of identification or closeness that others perceive in relation to a person), *legitimate power* (stemming from internalized values that others have in relation to the accepted right of a person to be influential), *reward power* (the extent to which a person is viewed as having ability to give rewards), and *coercive power* (the extent to which a person is viewed as being able to punish others). According to research by Hornstein, Callahan, Fisch, and Benedict (1968), teachers want to work with a principal who employs expert or referent power, but not with one who imposes legitimate or coercive power. Our observations of class- rooms indicate that much the same is true for students in relation to their teacher.

Teachers enter their classes with particular bases of social power ascribed to them. Students typically view teachers as having legitimate authority and coercive power, and as holding the possibilities for giving out rewards. The actual power of teachers appears to be enhanced if they distribute group functions to the students, encourage independence, stimulate open communication, and attempt to become attractive to the students. Holding on tightly to authority and only occasionally allowing students to influence the class often leads to high dependency as well as resistance and interpersonal tension and friction. In short, the wise teacher attempts to establish influence relationships with students based on referent and expert power to go along with the legitimate, reward, and coercive bases of power.

Even though students do not hold legitimate authority, they do have significant power in their classrooms. They can get their peers to do things by rewarding them with smiles, gifts, or other inducements; they can also be influential by coercing peers through threats of physical punishment or exclusion. Some students are influ- ential because they are charismatic; that is, others find them attractive and can identify with them. Still others are able to get their peers to follow them because they are viewed as experts.

Several studies have systematically and empirically explored the characteristics of students with high power in classrooms (Gold, 1958; Polansky, Lippitt, & Redl, 1950). This research generally has indicated that the influential students possess attributes that are valued by members of the peer group. Students who held positions of high power were good at doing things (expert power) and possessed a cluster of highly valued personal characteristics (referent power) such as strength, good looks, friendliness and helpfulness in interpersonal relations. Moreover, the actions of powerful students are observed more closely by their peers than the actions of others in the classroom. Thus, they could measurably enhance or inhibit the effective dynamics of their classes by their actions.

The teacher who can help influential students feel involved in the classroom will have an easier time influencing the entire group than a teacher who is in conflict with the high-power students. Research on the "ripple effect" by Kounin, Gump, and Ryan (1961) indicated that the ripples of disturbance in the learning group were greatest when students with high power were the targets of the teacher's disciplinary actions. The entire class showed tension and behavioral disturbances when the high-power students showed defiance toward the teacher's requests. Conversely, detrimental and disturbing ripple effects were barely discernible when low-power students were the targets of a teacher's discipline.

The bases of teacher power are especially undermined when overt conflict occurs with high-power students. Because the power of students is frequently based on their being identification figures who are attractive (referent power) and because teacher power is based primarily on legitimacy, high power students have more influence over the peer group than the teacher does. When teachers face overt conflict situations, they cannot achieve influence and increase student learning simply by resorting to their legitimate authority or by using punishment. Coercion may gain short-term, overt compliance, but punitive actions reduce the students' sustained interest and lessen the likelihood of reaching educational goals. Direct, open encounters between students and teacher—encounters recognizing the right of students to have some power over their own learning-group procedures—can be used as a means for developing plans and procedures acceptable to both. Although shared influence is difficult to establish in a learning group, a teacher can begin by distributing part of the legitimate power to students and by arranging for students to participate actively in classroom leadership positions. Teachers who can learn some of the skills of shared decision making that are presented in Johnson and F. P. Johnson (1975) and Schmuck and Schmuck (1975) will generally achieve some degree of referent power and in fact have fewer instances of overt power struggles.

The Striving for Affiliation

Despite the obvious importance of friendship patterns in learning groups, some teachers still maintain that they are employed to teach content and that they should not have to be concerned with their students's social relationships, especially insofar as their popularity within the peer group is concerned. Such a view significantly oversimplifies the social-psychological realities of the classroom. Teaching and learning involve an interpersonal process; and once that process is under way, it is complicated and affected by the many relations among the students, and between the students and teacher. Learning groups have a hidden world of attraction and hostility among peers that influences the academic performances of the individual students. Students who feel some support from friendly peers use their intellectual potential more completely than do their fellow students who are rejected by the peer group (see Schmuck, 1963, for details).

From the thorough reviews on affiliation by Berscheid and Walster (1969) and Rubin (1973), and from my own reviews of classroom research (Schmuck, 1969), it can be surmised that liked students, more than unpopular students, will be physically attractive, well-coordinated at motor skills, outgoing and socially effective, intellectually competent, and mentally healthy. Some differences between social classes have also been noted; for example, lower-class boys in predominately lower-class schools have traditionally gained acceptance by being more defiant and physically aggressive than their peers and middle-class counterparts. The research also shows that students are often rejected for one or more reasons, such as (a) being limited in their physical ability, (b) having difficulties in relating socially to others, (c) having intellectual limitations, and (d) having mental health difficulties. In many classrooms, the social behaviors of lower-class students lead to their being rejected when their overt aggression or passive dependency run counter to middle-class values.

These findings can be understood in terms of a theory developed by Lippitt, Polansky, Redl, and Rosen (1952) and explained by Gold (1958). The theory states that all students possess properties that are defined as personal characteristics. Physical attributes, personality characteristics, and intelligence are examples of personal properties. These properties are converted into resources when they are valued for their usefulness by the group. Because different students and learning groups value different things, a property of a student that is a valuable resource in one social context may not be a useful resource in another. Similarly, as the same learning group faces various situations or developmental stages, different properties of group members may be valued or reevaluated. This theory links the concept of resource with the concept of liking by assuming that a resource has the function of inducing those who value it to be attracted by one who possesses it. Gold states that this is essentially an economic theory. "On the one hand, we have someone who possesses something the other wants or wishes to avoid; on the other hand, we have someone who wants or wishes to avoid it (p. 51-52), and the outcome is attraction. Gold goes on to state: "It is not enough for someone to be capable of being warm and friendly; he must be able to bestow this warmth and friendliness on another if it is to be considered a resource in the relationship" (p. 52).

Friendship formation in learning groups develops in systematic ways. Physical appearances and proximity trigger the friendship. Students who strike each other as attractive as well as those who initially sit close to each other commence interaction. Then, provided there are not significant threats to the students' common needs for status and security, communication between the students will continue. The discovery of common attitudes, values, and interests deepens the relationship and encourages informal meetings outside the classroom. The favorable reactions from each other enhance each student's self-worth and they react favorably. The presence of complementarity and interlocking personality needs buttress the relationship and help to maintain it.

My best guess about the development of interpersonal attraction in learning groups involves a series of *filtering factors*, with proximity, physical attraction, and social-status similarities operating early, granting status and security to the other by favorable approval operating next, discovering consensus on values and interests coming somewhat later, and need complementarity still later, always through the enhancement of self-esteem by getting and giving favorable reactions to others. A mismatch at any point in this developmental sequence could cause the friendship to be dissolved.

Sex differences also exist in learning groups' liking patterns. Boys appear to be more psychologically affected by having low influence in the group than girls are. Girls, in contrast, are more affected by having low liking status (Van Egmond, 1960). These findings are consistent with theoretical and empirical work of Horner (1972), who has posited that the achievement motive is secondary to the affiliation motive for girls. In attempting to isolate variables affecting the academic performance of boys and girls, Schmuck and Van Egmond (1965) found that girls were significantly influenced by their position in the peer group, their satisfaction with the teacher, and their level of perceived parental support. Boys, on the other hand, were influenced primarily by their relationships in the peer group and with the teacher and not significantly by the interactions they were having with their parents.

At the group level, liking patterns have been described in terms of peer-group sociometric structures. Elsewhere (Schmuck, 1963; Schmuck, 1966), I have described two types of sociometric structures: (1) centrally structured groups, characterized by a narrow focus of interpersonal acceptance and rejection, and (2) diffusely structured groups, characterized by a wide range of positive and negative choices with little or no focus of interpersonal acceptance and rejection on just a few members. In centrally structured groups, a large number of students agreed in selecting a small cluster of their classmates as highly accepted or rejected. Diffusely structured groups, on the other hand, were not typified by small clusters of highly accepted and highly rejected students; in other words, there were no distinct subgroups whose members received most of the sociometric choices.

The research on these several varieties of informal friendship structures indicated that students were more accurate in estimating their liking status in centrally structured groups than in diffusely structured groups. The theoretical bases for this finding originated with gestalt perceptual theory on the one hand (Kohler, 1947), and group dynamics theory on the other (Cartwright & Zander, 1969). The assumption from gestalt theory was that at least one significant determinant of perceptual veridicality must lie in the structure of the distal stimulus, that is, for example, its "good form," clarity, symmetry, or distinctiveness. Centrally structured peer groups, compared to diffusely structured ones, represented clearer and more distinct social stimuli for individual students. From group dynamics, studies on communication nets and group structure (Leavitt, 1951) indicated that task leadership was recognized more quickly and easily in centrally structured groups. Social-emotional status could also be expected to be more easily recognized in groups with centrally structured liking patterns.

The theories of cognitive validation (Pepitone, 1964), cognitive balance (Newcomb, 1961), and self-esteem (Jones, 1973) are useful for understanding the effects of different sociometric group structures. Validation theory argues that students will strive to evaluate themselves in the eyes of their peers by trying to find out their position in the liking structure. If the sociometric structure is so ordered that only a few students are clearly the most liked, then it should be relatively easy for them to determine their places in the peer group.

The perceptions of students in centrally structured classes are in close agreement with the actual structure. With a psychological thrust for cognitive balance at work, a sense of rejection by others leads to negative opinions about one's self-worth, which, in turn, lead to a perception of the learning group as offering a threatening cluster of interactions. Moreover, according to the self-esteem theorists, rejection by others would usually lead to frustrations in enhancing self-worth and to dislike for those who are negative. Even though the need for cognitive validation is strong for students in diffusely structured groups, the status patterning is unclear. Students receive about the same number of favorable and supportive choices as their peers; more students view themselves as highly liked or at least as secure. In diffusely structured classrooms, the students' cognized positions of high status encourage high self-esteem, which facilitates their performance on academic learning. The peer group is not a threat, and students feel a sense of security and status.

Another aspect of my empirical work (Schmuck, 1966) indicated that a student's perceived sociometric position within the class had implications for the accomplishment of that student's academic work. Those students who were accurate when estimating their position in the liking structure and who were negatively placed in that structure were lower utilizers of academic abilities and had less favorable attitudes toward self and school than students who were accurate and positively placed. Moreover, students who thought of themselves as being liked, as they did quite frequently in diffusely structured groups, were using their abilities more highly and had more favorable attitudes toward self and school, even though objectively they often had low liking status within the classroom peer group. Finally, the research indicated that students who had very few friends outside the classroom were more influenced by their liking status in the group than were students who had more nonclass friends.

Teachers' reactions toward their students also are fraught with affect. Teachers tend to like students who are attractive to peers, who exhibit friendly feelings toward other people, and who adjust to the school's demands. On the other hand, teachers tend to dislike students who create disturbances and who keep other students from attending to schoolwork.

Girls typically have more compatible relationships with their teachers than boys (see Maccoby & Jacklin, 1974, for a thorough review of sex differences in the classroom). Boys, more often than girls, are disliked by teachers. Teachers have been found to give most negative feedback to boys with low status in the peer-liking structure. Lippitt and Gold (1959) showed that teachers often paid closer attention to the social behavior than to the academic performance of low-peer-status boys and that the low-status boys received more overt rebuke and criticism than other students. At the same time, teachers appeared to grant low-peer-status girls support and affection. These findings were accompanied by others showing that low-status boys were aggressive and disruptive, whereas low-status girls tended to be more dependent, passive, and affectionate.

Flanders and Havumaki (1960) showed how teachers' behaviors can influence friendship patterns in learning groups. They asked teachers to respond positively and consistently to selected students and not to others. For a week, teachers interacted with and praised only students seated in odd-numbered seats. In comparison groups, all students were encouraged to speak, and the teachers' praise was directed to the whole class. Students in the odd-numbered seats, in the former situation, later received more sociometric choices from their peers than did students in the evennumbered seats. In the comparison classrooms, the difference between the sociometric choices of students in the odd-and-even numbered seats was insignificant. The peer choices were spread around more evenly, indicating greater general acceptance. Retish (1973) similarly showed that planned and systematic teacher reinforcement of rejected students can result in significant net gains of the sociometric statuses of the targeted students.

Further research indicated that teachers of more diffusely structured classrooms, compared to other teachers, attended to and talked with a larger variety of students per hour (Schmuck, 1966). Teachers with centrally structured peer groups tended to call on fewer students and seemed especially to neglect the slower, less involved students. Teachers working with the most supportive peer groups tended to reward students with specific statements for helpful behaviors and to control behavioral disturbances with general, group-oriented statements. Teachers with less supportive liking patterns in their classrooms tended to reward individuals less often and to reprimand them publically more often for breaking classroom rules.

Satisfaction with one's teacher is an important facilitative condition for a student's academic performance. Students are attracted to teachers who provide them with a boost of status in the peer group and who grant them security. Teachers who reward frequently and who do not rebuke or demean students in the eyes of their peers are attractive. Students who are satisfied with their teachers usually feel good about school, learning, and themselves. The continual rejection of an overtly aggressive student by both classroom peers and the teacher feeds the negative cycle of low self-esteem, unfriendly overtures to others, and poor performance in academic work.

THE CULTURE OF CLASSROOMS

As I have already implied, the student's search for personal competence, power, and affiliation occurs within the context of a surrounding classroom culture. By classroom culture, I mean the quality of emotional and intellectual interplay between individuals and subgroups; it can be informally assessed by observing physical movements and bodily gestures of students and the teacher. One might ask: How do students move toward the teacher? Do they stand close or far away? Are they physically at ease or tight and tense? How often is affection indicated by smiles, winks, or pats on the back? Do the students move quietly and unobtrusively with measured steps or do they walk freely and easily in ways that indicate the classroom is truly their own? Are students reticient to approach clusters of teachers? Are teachers similarly slow to approach clusters of students? How do the students relate to one another? Are they quiet, distant, and formal, or do they talk easily and laugh spontaneously? Along with analyses of group processes having to do with the motives of competence, power, and affiliation, the culture of a classroom can be formally analyzed by investigating its norms and goal structures.

Norms

Norms are shared expectations or attitudes about procedures and behaviors that are appropriate for the classroom. Students and teachers are typically motivated to adhere to the norms. Norms are strong stabilizers of behavior because the members of the class monitor one another's behaviors. The strength of group norms in a classroom arises out of two kinds of forces: (1) forces within the student to reduce conflict felt when personal actions are different from those held by others and (2) forces induced by others who wish to influence the student's behavior.

A definition of norms must emphasize sharing; thus, norms are group phenomena, constituting the culture; they are not psychological processes that can be separated from the group. Norms are individuals' expectations or attitudes that are shared in a group. When a norm is present, most group participants know that their expectations or attitudes are also held by others, and the others expect them to have the expectation or attitude and to behave accordingly. Norms influence perception (how students view the physical and social world of the learning group), cognition (how students think about the learning group), evaluation (how they feel about aspects of the classroom), and behavior (how the students overtly act in the classroom). In the real world of classrooms, it is difficult to separate perceptual, cognitive, evaluative, and behavioral processes.

Students feel insecure when their personal response is in opposition to a group norm. Hoffman (1957) experimented with the relationship between anxiety and disagreements with group norms. He had students state opinions about a series of social attitudes, and then, 6 weeks later, they were asked again for attitudes on the same items—this time after hearing the experimenter present false group norms. Hoffman measured anxiety, using galvanic skin responses. He found that subjects' anxieties were lowest when their opinions were in agreement with the norms both times. As the subjects changed their opinions, from the first to the second time, toward the bogus norms, there was a moderate degree of skin response; but for those subjects whose opinions both times were quite different from the group norms, there was the highest amount of galvanic skin response.

Many students fear being rejected by their peers and tend to go along with peers' perceptions of group norms in order not to be rejected. Students make the norms of the peer group their own attitudes as they become more and more involved in and rewarded by the group. High-influence students in the peer group usually exhibit most allegiance to group norms and have attitudes very similar to the norms. Peer groups also have goals toward which they are moving, and highly involved students become committed to these. Students who are actively working toward peer-group goals may willfully allow themselves to be infringed upon personally and even put themselves out in order to help the group.

One particularly dramatic illustration of the power of the norms of the peer group in relation to school achievement was presented by Hargreaves (1967) in his study of "streaming" in an all-male, English secondary school for boys. Hargreaves studied the psychological impact of the norms of several different peer-group cultures. The results show how deeply the norms of a peer group can affect the behavior of individual students.

Hargreaves's analysis focused on interpersonal processes in the peer groups of the fourth and last year because the boys in these groups represented the "final products" of the schooling process; they had spent the longest time being indoctrinated into the values of the school. The study dealt with four streams of four distinct peer groups. It showed that each stream had its unique set of norms that persisted even when the composition of the streams changed as boys were shifted among them.

The highest stream, labeled A, held norms that were consonant with the school's formal goals; boys valued academic achievement, looked down upon fooling around in class, discouraged fighting, thought that teachers should be obeyed, and thought that cheating should be strictly against the student code. In contrast, boys in Stream B were opposed to working hard on academics, disliked students who obeyed teachers readily, tried to avoid schoolwork whenever possible, and encouraged fooling around.

Stream C was composed of three subgroups. Like Stream B, most of the members strongly devalued academic work; but, whereas in B, fun was valued more than work, and "messing around" was encouraged for its own sake, the high-status clique of C apparently was interested in behaving contrary to school values and defying the school administration. The C group was negatively oriented toward the establishment of the school, while the B group was more fun loving. One subgroup in C, however, continued to hold norms very different from the rest of the C group. For example, the "deviant" C subgroup valued work, obeyed teacher demands, dressed well, and attended school regularly.

Stream D held even stronger norms in opposition to the school; in fact, one criterion for status seemed to be doing poor academic work. Truancy was encouraged; physical violence was used against low-status boys who went along with the teachers; and delinquent acts of all sorts were frequent and valued by the high-status clique in the D stream.

Members of these four streams entered into very little interaction with one another except when students were switched from one stream to another and when there was some mixing while participating on the school's rugby team. Most participants in the school both students and staff held stereotypic conceptions of members in the different groups. For example, the As were viewed as snobby whereas the Ds were seen as delinquent. Hargreaves also showed that the students' identifications with their own group were very strong. For example, at times the boys in the lower streams behaviorally manifested the importance of the norms by decreasing their performance on tests purposefully so that they would not be rejected by the members of their stream.

Goal Structures

Goals are norms that give direction to student behavior. A key idea about a goal is that it is an ideal or target, a "place" toward which one is striving. The motivating factor of a goal is not so much the fact that it is attractive but the fact that being there is more attractive than being where one is now. It is the discrepancy between where one is and where one would like to be that motivates one to action. This is as true for a classroom group as it is for an individual student.

Johnson and R. T. Johnson (1975) offer an analysis of goals in relation to learning groups. They state that "students are motivated to achieve learning goals within goal structures" (p. 29). Goal structures are constituted to different sorts of interpersonal interdependencies, and learning groups typically manifest three kinds of student interdependence. The first is cooperative interdependence, in which students work together to accomplish shared goals. The second is competitive interdependence, wherein only one or a few students may be successful. The third is individualistic interdependence, wherein students work alone to accomplish goals that are unrelated to the goals of others.

In the cooperative goal structures, the goals of individual students are linked together so that one student cannot meet his or her goal unless others reach theirs. When a student acts so as to reach a preferred goal state, the chances that others will reach their goals are increased. Sometimes, of course, striving after one's own goal could be detrimental to a cooperative effort. In competitive goal structures, the goals of individual students are linked together so that one student can meet her or his goal only if others do *not* reach theirs. When a student acts so as to reach a personal goal, the chances that others will reach their goals are decreased. The goals of individual students are independent in the individualistic goal structures. Whether or not a student accomplishes a set goal has no bearing whatsoever upon whether others reach theirs.

Teachers should give conscious attention to the goal structure that is set into motion for a given learning activity. Although the cooperative structure might be chosen more often than the other two, no single goal structure is superior in all ways. The appropriate goal structure should be chosen to accomplish the learning objectives of a particular content area. Cooperative goal structures typically are appropriate both for academic learning and for engaging members of a learning group in working on improving the interpersonal processes of the group. Johnson and R. T. Johnson view the cooperative structures as the most important because of the multiple gains for students.

TYPES OF INNOVATIVE LEARNING GROUPS

Traditionally American schools have stressed both the academic and intellectual development of students and competitive goal structures in the classroom. Today, however, in our crowded and complex world, to stress the intellectual through a competitive mode may be narrow, out of date, and unwise. Schools need to teach students more about who they are and how they might use what they have. A storehouse of knowledge is not very useful to contemporary students who cannot apply what they have learned.

Indeed, there has been a growing outcry in America that many of our traditional schools are emotionally destructive. The criticisms have to do primarily with the quality of interpersonal relationships among school participants. Fewer and fewer criticisms seem to be aimed just at curricula, facilities, or instructional strategies; criticisms about joylessness, fear, mutual lack of respect among teachers and students, the absence of spontaneity, growing alienation, and personal disinterest have become dominant. The crisis of our schools lies in interpersonal conditions; the changes demanded are in the area of human relationships; applications are needed from social psychology.

Through the use of theory and research from social psychology, Schmuck and Schmuck (1974) have proposed an innovative school organization constituted primarily of three different learning groups. This organizational format aims to provide a supportive context for both academic learning and self-development. Each student and faculty member would spend some time in a group focused on guidance or personal growth, some time in groups oriented toward academic and intellectual development, and some time in other groups that aim to help students apply and use their knowledge. These three types of learning groups are, respectively, the *guidance group* (with special attention to emotional dynamics), the *instructional group* (with emphasis on intellectual development), and the *application group* (with attention to realistic problem solving).

Although some aspects of these learning groups are now found in most schools, few schools give equal attention to each. Most public schools are structured around instructional groups. I agree with Coleman (1972), however, who pointed out that contemporary students tend to receive too much information and too little chance to apply it. I also think that students should have greater opportunity to work through their personal and emotional concerns. Public schools need to structure more educational experiences on guidance and application and fewer on formal instruction.

Many alternative schools stress personal-growth experiences, thus offering learning experiences within guidance groups. I also agree, however, with Kozol's criticism (1972) that many free schools have failed to provide adequate opportunities to learn basic skills needed for survival. Vocational schools traditionally have focused on the practical uses of information but have emphasized skills required for specific jobs. Most young people will have a number of jobs and many other tasks and problems before their careers are completed. Attempts to help students to cope only with specific job skills are inadequate.

Along with my own efforts at designing organizational structures that might serve well the multiple needs of contemporary youth, a number of others are offering fresh and creative designs. For example, Postman and Weingartner (1973) recommend some procedures with which parents and students can try to influence the social dynamics in the school. Rotzel (1971) shows how a small group of parents went about designing a humanistic school. Mahan and Moeller (1971) show how administrators and teachers can go about changing their own organization to respond to the changing demands and needs of their students. Each of these efforts, in one way or another, refers to guidance, instruction, and application as fundamental to the curriculum of the modern, comprehensive school.

The Guidance Group

Experience in guidance groups would help students develop a basic core of self-esteem and develop ways to strive for self-knowledge. The central philosophical goals are self-oriented: to know, to accept, and to continue to improve oneself. The group interaction would be designed to build awareness of individuals, to gain self-confidence by learning how one's behaviors affect other people, and to increase understanding and acceptance of others.

The kinds of activities used to reach these goals would include teaching how to distinguish among personal thoughts, personal feelings, and perceptions of others; teaching how to gather valid information about one's strengths and weaknesses in relation to others; and encouraging group members to discuss the interpersonal impact of each person's behavior. Useful resources for such classes are the books by Castillo (1974), Gazda (1973), Harmin, Kirschenbaum, and Simon (1973), Johnson and F. P. Johnson (1975), and Lyon (1971).

The overall task of the guidance group would be to provide emotionally meaningful experiences to facilitate the personal growth and psychic integration of the members. So-called discipline problems can be greatly relieved when guidance groups are offered. Moreover, instructional groups can be greatly strengthened if the members periodically discuss their emotional stresses, interpersonal attractions, and individual irritations. The interpersonal processes of living are just as important—given this emphasis—as the development of academic cognitions.

Recently, I observed an elementary teacher and his class carrying out some guidance activities. On the particular day I observed, the teacher was leading the class in a strength-building exercise he called "finding our resources." The goal of this practice was to build the self-esteem of individual students, and perhaps to develop classroom cohesiveness, by the sharing of favorable characteristics of everyone in the class.

The teacher started by leading a discussion on the variety of personal traits of people—valuable traits—and on the importance of knowing who is good at what things. Students were then given a large sheet of newsprint paper and were asked to put their names at the top and to list in large letters what they considered to be their individual strengths. Every student was encouraged to have at least three important items on the list.

These sheets were then hung up around the room, and the students were asked to add strengths to other students' lists, strengths that they had perceived in the past. Each student was encouraged to add something, to the other sheets. A few days later, the teacher mimeographed sheets about all the students' resources and spent 5 hours discussing ways of using the strengths in the class. The teacher reported high satisfaction with the impact of the activity.

The Instructional Group

Instructional groups are aimed at helping students develop cognitive skills. They deal with traditional subject matter such as reading, writing, arithmetic, science, and a category of integrated subject matter with a problem-oriented approach. Such learning groups could be organized in many ways with many curriculum aids, materials, and instructional procedures. The most prominent norm for instructional groups should be support for a continual process of inquiry; thus curiosity, spontaneity, logic, experimentation, and creativity all would be valued. Expectations would support clarifying the issues of study, seeking information from many sources, compiling the information systematically, and helping one another to learn about the salient points of the subject matter.

There are a number of possible innovative ways to mobilize peer-group interaction to support instruction and the development of cognitive skills. Recently, in an urban middle school, I observed a teacher giving her students an opportunity to teach their own lesson plans to one another. The goals seemed to be to establish increased feelings of ownership for the curriculum on the part of the students and to help the students develop some leadership skills by formally leading the class.

The teacher commenced the practice by dividing the class into subgroups of six students each. Each of these groups was told that it would work together for 1 hour daily to study designated topics. The concepts to be learned were listed. Each group was told that every student would be expected to be the leader of a group for 1 week of the term. The teacher described the responsibilities of the leader and asked each group to select its first leader.

These initial leaders were asked to draw up lesson plans for 1 week. A lesson-plan format was presented by the teacher. The teacher met with the instructional leaders during lunch one day and went over their plans. Some leadership skills were discussed, and each leader was able to meet individually with the teacher if there was a need for additional help. The leaders were given total responsibility for teaching and evaluating for their 1 week. Their week was completed after they had supplied the teacher with written reports on the progress of their group.

A popular innovation for instruction that is being tried in many urban schools today is cross-age tutoring. In this instructional procedure, an older student is paired with a younger student to tutor the younger student in some academic area.

The actual tutoring behaviors of the older students can vary considerably; in some instances, for example, a younger student might be taken to the library and read to, whereas in other instances a younger student might be assigned some specific lessons in reading or arithmetic.

Many of the teachers that I have talked with about cross-age tutoring find that the older student gains more from the tutoring relationship; older students, for example, who have trouble with reading may well be assigned to a beginning reader; or as another example, an older student who has problems in math may benefit from teaching a younger student simple mathematical skills. One teacher I observed used cross-age tutoring with a group of junior high–age boys who had severe reading disabilities; their reading skills as well as their understanding of personal problems were greatly enhanced through tutoring younger students in reading.

A host of recent studies and research reports can be helpful in offering creative ideas for the improvement of instructional groups. Among them are: Flanders (1970), Good and Brophy (1973), Kounin (1970), Nyberg (1971), Rosenthal and Jacobson (1968), Schmuck and Schmuck (1975), Sommer (1967), and White and Lippitt (1960). An entire issue of a journal entitled, *The History and Social Science Teacher* (1976), focused on alternative classroom environments and includes many very useful strategies for ameliorating instructional groups.

The Application Group

Application groups are action oriented groups; they are neither as introspective as guidance groups nor as devoted to academic disciplines as instructional groups. Students and faculty apply their knowledge, insights, and skills to find out what will work and what will not work in solving real problems. The problems chosen for concentration can come from inside specific classrooms, from the school organization, or from the community outside the school.

Application groups are more fluid and flexible than guidance or instructional groups; several ad hoc groups might exist simultaneously for a short time, disbanding as soon as their purposes are accomplished. Those that are developed to deal with community problems may also tackle various issues and organize in different ways. They provide ways and opportunities for students to find ways of linking personal values and academic information to their own behavior as responsible and intelligent citizens. Application groups also can provide behavioral experience that will help students to see the practical relevance of what they learn in the guidance and instructional groups.

The role of the teacher in the application group differs somewhat from the role of the teacher in the other two groups. In the guidance group, teachers strive to facilitate closeness and openness by being honest and informal themselves and often by describing their own feelings as an equal member of the group. In instructional groups, teachers take on more formal leadership functions; there is cognitive material to be mastered, and the teachers often are more resourceful than the students in initiating a sequence of learning steps and choosing learning materials. In instructional groups, teachers should assume an active influence relationship with students. The application group calls for a blend of these two teacher roles.

Application groups deal with personal values, academic information, and behavioral tryouts. The teacher should attempt to be facilitative and personal when values are being described and shared. On the other hand, the information to be provided about problem solving and the academic content of specific problem-solving activities call for teachers to be more directive and structured. Planning for, executing, and giving feedback about new behaviors all call for a blending of the directive and the facilitative. In taking action, all individuals, whether students or teacher, should be urged to make decisions for themselves.

For the past several years, I have been collaborating with others (Arends, Schmuck, Milleman, & Wiseman, in press) in the development of a curriculum in organizational psychology for senior high students. This.curriculum module, an example of the sort of material that might be used in application groups, aims to help students understand how their needs for competence, power, and affiliation come into play as they participate in learning groups. Moreover, it attempts to help students explore how the school organization influences both the dynamics of learning groups and the satisfaction of their individual motives. Finally, by linking cognitive learning with action taking, this curriculum strives to help students plan on ways they can help their own school as well as other organizations become better places in which to satisfy basic psychological needs.

CONCLUSION

Classroom learning constitutes a transactional social process involving the exchange of a school curriculum between teachers and students and among the students. Thus, teaching and learning transactions are particular kinds of multiple interpersonal relationships. How students experience the curriculum is influenced, not only by their relationships with the teacher, but also through their contacts with peers. From these relationships, students strive to obtain feelings of competence, power, and affiliation. Students' daily behaviors in the school are shaped significantly by the norms and goal structures of their learning groups. The teacher typically has been singled out as the most influential classroom participant because he or she is formally designated to present the curriculum and to improve interpersonal relationships. In contrast, my focus here is on learning groups as entities with an influence of their own. A larger number of learning objectives and interpersonal motives can be reached in schools where learning groups are divided into guidance, instructional, and application groups.

REFERENCES

Arends, R. I., Schmuck, R. A., Milleman, M., & Wiseman, J. *Learning about school life through organizational psychology*. Washington. American Psychological Association, in press.

Backman, C. W., & Secord, P. F. *A social psychological view of education*. New York: Harcourt, 1968.

Bany, M. A., & Johnson, L. V. *Educational social psychology*. New York: Macmillan, 1975.

Bem, D. J. Self-perception theory. In L. Berkowitz (Ed.), *Advances in experimental social psychology* (Vol. 6). New York: Academic, 1972.

Benjamin, J. Change in relation to influences upon self-conceptualization. *Journal of Abnormal and Social Psychology*, 1950, **45**, 573–580.

Berscheid, E., & Walster, E. *Interpersonal attraction*. Reading, Mass: Addison-Wesley, 1969.

Brophy, J. E. & Good, T. L. Teachers' communication of differential expectations for children's classroom performance: Some behavioral data. *Journal of Educational Psychology*, 1970, **61**, 365–374.

Brophy, J. E., & Good, T. L. Teacher expectations: Beyond the Pygmalion controversy. *Phi Delta Kappan*, 1972, **54**, 276–278.

Cartwright, D., & Zander, A. *Group dynamics: Research and theory*. New York: Harper, 1969.

Castillo, G. *Left-handed teaching: Lessons in affective education.* New York: Praeger, 1974.
Coleman, J. S. The children have outgrown the schools. *Psychology Today*, February 1972, 5(9), 72.
DeCharms, R. *Personal causation.* New York: Academic, 1968.
DeCharms, R. Personal causation training in the schools. *Journal of Applied Social Psychology*, 1972, **2**, 295–313.
Deci, E. L. *Intrinsic motivation.* New York: Plenum, 1975.
Flanders, N. A. *Analyzing teaching behavior.* Reading, Mass: Addison-Wesley, 1970.
Flanders, N. A., & Havumaki, S. The effect of teacher-pupil contacts involving praise on the sociometric choices of students. *Journal of Educational Psychology*, 1960, **51**, 65–68.
French, J., & Raven, B. The bases of social power. In D. Cartwright (Ed.), *Studies of social power.* Ann Arbor: Institute for Social Research, 1959.
Gazda, G. *Human relations development: A manual for educators.* Boston: Allyn & Bacon, 1973.
Getzels, J. W. A social psychology of education. In G. Lindzey & E. Aronson (Eds.), *The handbook of social psychology* (2nd ed., Vol. 5). Reading, Mass.: Addison-Wesley, 1969.
Glick, O. The educational process in the classroom. *School Review*, 1968, **76**, 339–351.
Gold, M. Power in the classroom. *Sociometry*, 1958, **21**, 50–60.
Good, T. L., & Brophy, J. E. *Looking at classrooms.* New York: Harper, 1973.
Goodacre, D. M. Group characteristics of good and poor performing combat units. *Sociometry*, 1953, **16**, 168–178.
Guskin, A. E., & Guskin, S. L. *A social psychology of education.* Reading, Mass.: Addison-Wesley, 1970.
Hargreaves, D. H. *Social relations in a secondary school.* Atlantic Highlands, N.J.: Humanities, 1967.
Harmin, M., Kirschenbaum, H., & Simon, S. *Clarifying values through subject matter: Applications for the classroom.* Minneapolis: Winston Press, 1973.
History and Social Science Teacher, 1976, **12** (2). (Whole issue)
Hoffman, M. L. Conformity as a defense mechanism and a form of resistance to genuine group influence. *Journal of Personality*, 1957, **25**, 412–424.
Horner, M. Toward an understanding of achievement related conflicts in women. *Journal of Social Issues*, 1972, **28**, 157–175.
Hornstein, H., Callahan, D., Fisch, E., & Benedict, B. Influence and satisfaction in organizations: A replication. *Sociology of Education*, 1968, **41**, 380–389.
Jackson, P. W. *Life in classrooms.* New York: Holt, 1968.
Johnson, D. W. *The social psychology of education.* New York: Holt, 1970.
Johnson, D. W., & Johnson, F. P. *Joining together: Group theory and group skills.* Englewood Cliffs, N. J.: Prentice-Hall, 1975.
Johnson, D. W., & Johnson, R. T. *Learning together and alone: Cooperation, competition, and individualization.* Englewood Cliffs, N. J.: Prentice-Hall, 1975.
Jones, S. Self and interpersonal evaluations: Esteem theories versus consistency theories. *Psychological Bulletin*, 1973, **79**, 185–199.
Kohler, W. *Gestalt psychology.* New York: Liveright, 1947.
Kounin, J. S. *Discipline and group management in classrooms.* New York: Holt, 1970.
Kounin, J. S., Gump, P. E., & Ryan, J. J. Explorations in classroom management. *Journal of Teacher Education*, 1961, **12**, 235–246.
Kozol, J. *Free schools.* Boston: Houghton Mifflin, 1972.
Leavitt, H. J. Some effects of certain communication patterns on group performance. *Journal of Abnormal and Social Psychology*, 1951, **46**, 38–50.
Lewis, R., & St. John, N. Contributions of cross-racial friendship to minority group achievement in desegregated classrooms. *Sociometry*, 1974, **37**, 79–91.
Lippitt, R., & Gold, M. Classroom social structure as a mental health problem. *Journal of Social Issues*, 1959, **15**, 40–58.
Lippitt, R., Polansky, N., Redl, F., & Rosen, S. The dynamics of power. *Human Relations*, 1952, **5**, 37–64.
Lyon, H. C. *Learning to feel–Feeling to learn.* Columbus, Ohio: Merrill, 1971.
Maccoby, E. E., & Jacklin, C. N. *The psychology of sex differences.* Stanford: Stanford University Press, 1974.
Mahan, D., & Moeller, G. H. *The faculty team: School organization for results.* Chicago: Science Research, 1971.

Miles, M., & Charters, W. W., Jr. (Eds.). *Learning in social settings: New readings in the social psychology of education.* Boston: Allyn & Bacon, 1970.

Muldoon, J. F. The concentration of liked and disliked members in groups and the relationship of the concentration to group cohesiveness. *Sociometry,* 1955, 18, 73-81.

Newcomb, T. M. *The acquaintance process.* New York: Holt, 1961.

Nisbett, R. E., & Valins, S. *Perceiving the causes of one's own behavior.* Morristown, N. J.: Silver Burdett, 1971.

Nyberg, D. *Tough and tender learning.* Palo Alto, Calif. Mayfield, 1971.

Parsons, T. *The social system.* New York: Free Press, 1951.

Pepitone, A. *Attraction and hostility.* New York: Atherton, 1964.

Polansky, N., Lippitt, R., & Redl, F. An investigation of behavioral contagion in groups. *Human Relations,* 150, 3, 319-348.

Postman, N., & Weingartner, C. *The school book.* New York: Dell, 1973.

Retish, P. M. Changing the status of poorly esteemed students through teacher reinforcement. *Journal of Applied Behavioral Science,* 1973, 9, 44-50.

Roethlisberger, F. J., & Dickson, W. J. *Management and the worker.* Cambridge. Harvard University Press, 1939.

Rosenthal, R. The Pygmalion effect lives. *Psychology Today,* 1973, 7(4), 56-63.

Rosenthal, R., & Jacobson, L. *Pygmalion in the classroom: Teacher expectation and pupils' intellectual development.* New York: Holt, 1968.

Rotzel, G. *The school in Rose Valley.* Baltimore: Johns Hopkins Press, 1971.

Rubin, Z. *Liking and loving: An invitation to social psychology.* New York: Holt, 1973.

Rubovitz, P. C., & Maehr, M. L. Pygmalion analyzed: Toward an explanation of the Rosenthal-Jacobson finds. *Journal of Personality and Social Psychology,* 1971, 19, 197-204.

Schmuck, R. A. Some relationships of peer liking patterns in the classroom to pupil attitudes and achievement. *School Review,* 1963, 71, 337-359.

Schmuck, R. A. Some aspects of classroom social climate. *Psychology in the Schools,* 1966, 3, 59-65.

Schmuck, R. A. Group processes. In P. L. Ebel (Ed.), *Encyclopedia of educational research.* London: Collier MacMillan, 1969.

Schmuck, R. A. Influence of the peer group. In G. Lesser (Ed.), *Psychology and educational practice.* Glenview, Ill.: Scott, Foresman, 1971.

Schmuck, R. A., & Schmuck, P. A. *A humanistic psychology of education: Making the school everybody's house.* Palo Alto, Calif.: Mayfield, 1974.

Schmuck, R. A., & Schmuck, P. A. *Group processes in the classroom* (2nd ed.). Dubuque, Iowa: Brown, 1975.

Schmuck, R. A., & Van Egmond, E. Sex differences in the relationship of interpersonal perceptions to academic performance. *Psychology in the Schools,* 1965, 2, 32-40.

Sears, P. Levels of aspiration of academically successful and unsuccessful children. *Journal of Abnormal and Social Psychology,* 1940, 35, 498-536.

Shils, E., & Janowitz, M. Cohesion and disintegration in the Wehrmacht in World War II. *Public Opinion Quarterly,* 1948, 12, 280-315.

Sommer, R. Classroom ecology. *Journal of Applied Behavioral Science,* 1967, 3, 489-503.

Van Egmond, E. *Social interrelationship skills and effective utilization of intelligence in the classroom.* Unpublished doctoral dissertation, University of Michigan, 1960.

Weiner, B. *Achievement motivation and attribution theory.* Morristown, N.J.: Silver Burdett, 1974.

White, R. K., & Lippitt, R. *Autocracy and democracy: An experimental inquiry.* New York: Harper, 1960.

White, R. W. Motivation reconsidered: The concept of competence. *Psychological Review,* 1959, 66, 297-333.

11

The Effects of
a Cooperative Classroom Structure
on Student Behavior and Attitudes

Elliot Aronson, Diane L. Bridgeman, and Robert Geffner
University of California at Santa Cruz

Children learn a great many things in elementary school classrooms. Some of the learnings are explicit, for example, reading, writing, arithmetic, social studies. Other learnings are implicit, for example, how to relate to other people or an understanding of oneself. It would be advantageous if, in addition to acquiring specific skills and information, children could use the classroom to experience and learn productive ways of relating to others and to develop, as well, a reasonable and positive view of themselves as people. In this essay, we consider how these implicit learnings take place. We consider the influence of social-interaction groups that utilize cooperative learning, and we consider the effect these groups have on students' self-esteem, academic performance, interpersonal relations, and role-taking ability.

Over the past 30 years, cooperative groups have been the focus of many empirical inquiries. Deutsch's (1949) definition of cooperation has been used as a guide for structuring many of these investigations. He defined a *cooperative social situation* as one in which each individual can reach a goal only if all the individuals achieve their goals. When this is attained, the individuals are then said to be promotively interdependent. In a more recent theoretical treatment of cooperation, Deutsch (1969) outlined his view of the initiation of cooperative behaviors. He suggested that cooperative interactions will enable the participants to experience a highlighting of mutual interests, coordinated efforts, equal power distribution, trust, helpful attitudes, and honest and open communication. In a similar vein, Johnson and Johnson (1975) suggested that cooperative interaction is the coordination of behavior among individuals to achieve mutual goals.

Recently, several investigators have begun an exploration of the interrelationships among aspects of cooperative learning groups and their underlying mechanisms. For example, some investigators (e.g., Slavin, DeVries, & Hulten, 1975) have shown that cooperative reward structures increase norms to enhance the attainment of the group's goal. Slavin (1977a) has examined the distinction between team

Much of the research reported in this paper was supported by grants from the National Science Foundation and the National Institutes of Health, awarded to Elliot Aronson.

effects and peer-tutoring effects in classroom situations and has suggested a complex model of team learning that involves time and task variables. On the other hand, Bridgeman (1977) focused on social variables of cooperation and found an enhancement of role-taking abilities in students who participated in 8 weeks of cooperative independent learning. Further research (summarized by Johnson & Johnson, 1975) offers impressive evidence for the superiority of cooperative, over competitive, goal-structured environments for many of the variables considered here (e.g., performance, self-esteem, liking, prejudice reduction, and role taking).

Many of the social behaviors suggested by Deutsch and by Johnson and Johnson as necessary for attaining successful cooperative behavior are also met in a cooperative, interdependent learning process recently developed by Aronson and his colleagues (Aronson, Blaney, Sikes, Stephan, & Snapp, 1975). It should be noted that Aronson and his colleagues utilized a model of cooperation that differs somewhat from the Deutsch and the Johnson and Johnson models; in the Aronson model, individuals cooperate to master a task, but their performance occurs and is evaluated on an individual basis.

For the remainder of this chapter, we focus on a few specific variables that are important to the educational process and to a student's personal growth. We discuss some of the theoretical perspectives as well as some of the recent research investigating the effects of cooperation upon students' social behaviors and attitudes.

SELF-ESTEEM

A person's self-concept generally consists of all the attitudes, abilities, and assumptions that individual holds concerning himself or herself that act as a guide for behavior (Coopersmith & Feldman, 1974; LaBenne & Greene, 1969). One aspect of self-concept that is important in educational research is self-esteem. It is usually considered to be the evaluative component of self-concept. Coopersmith (1967) defines *self-esteem* as the amount of worthiness an individual perceives in herself or himself. Where does one find evidence about one's own worthiness? Cooley (1902) believed that an individual's self-esteem reflected the real or imagined appraisals of others (i.e., the "looking glass self"). This emphasis on social-comparison processes has been an important aspect of many of the theories of the development of self-esteem (e.g., Mead, 1934). Snygg and Combs (1949) presented a more phenomenological view; they emphasized that how one acts is a result of the perceptions of oneself and the situation at a particular time.

Thus, one major conception of self-esteem has been the amount of self-worth one comes to perceive in oneself as a result of interpersonal interactions with relevant others, such as family members, teachers, and friends. Over 40 years ago, Mead (1934) suggested a "multidimensional self" that consisted of home attitudes, school attitudes, and social attitudes. More recent investigators have also presented such a view of self-esteem (Crandall, 1973; Gergen, 1971), and research involving factor analyses or other conceptual breakdowns seems to indicate that self-esteem is probably multidimensional (e.g., Bailey, 1970; Stanwyck & Felker, 1971). As far as the source of self-esteem is concerned, two factors seem vital: One factor, "outer" or "external" self-esteem, involves the reflected appraisals of relevant others, whereas the second factor, "inner" or "personal" self-esteem, involves personal experiences, accomplishments, and abilities (Coopersmith & Feldman, 1974; Franks & Marolla, 1976).

Thus, it has been suggested that there is an external self-esteem acquired from interacting with other people and a personal self-esteem concerning one's confidence in one's abilities acquired from more active interaction with physical objects. These dimensions, however, are not mutually exclusive; they may overlap as well as interact with each other.

In education, these two dimensions of self-esteem develop from children's interpretations of the feedback from teachers and classmates as well as from their own learning experiences. In a traditional classroom that emphasizes competition among students, high performance is produced partly by instilling students with a fear of failure. This competitiveness in schools produces a situation in which there are "winners" and "losers," which often leads to low self-esteem for the losers once they begin to internalize the failures (Coopersmith & Feldman, 1974). This virtually guarantees continual low performance for the losers, creating a vicious circle.

Effects of Cooperation on Self-Esteem

One method that can be used to accomplish positive outcomes for students is to change from a competitive to a cooperative environment in the classroom. The production of "losers" is virtually eliminated in this environment. With a cooperative environment, it is likely that the students will experience greater success as well as an increase in support from their classmates. As these phenomena occur, they will almost certainly produce an increase in self-esteem (Covington & Beery, 1976; Johnson, 1970). This, too, occurs as a function of the positive feedback received from group members and of the skills and abilities gained by the members when they help teach their classmates (peer teaching).

In this chapter, we focus primarily on research with a specific technique that we ourselves have been most directly involved with. This technique was developed as an attempt to incorporate the beneficial features of cooperation and peer teaching into the highly structured atmosphere of the more traditional classroom (Aronson et al., 1975). Dubbed the "jigsaw technique," it is a method of learning that, by its very nature, requires the students to work together and teach each other so that the students must depend on each other to accomplish their goals. It is a situation in which beating the other person has no payoff; rather, the students are reinforced for helping one another. Moreover, the jigsaw structure requires the students to utilize one another as resources rather than to depend on the teacher as the major provider of information—a state of affairs that is the hallmark of the traditional classroom. The students also reinforce one another—instead of allowing the teacher to be the sole provider of the rewards in the classroom. Inasmuch as all students participate, it was predicted that even students with low self-esteem would begin having successful experiences and would, as a consequence, begin to realize that they, too, have special abilities and talents. Thus, in this highly structured process, the cycle of negative, self-fulfilling prophecies would theoretically begin to break down. Further, it was expected that the other students who had considered the "failure" students as having little ability and worth would come to realize that their perceptions might have been in error.

Let us look at the jigsaw process in some detail. The jigsaw paradigm is a synthesis of small-group dynamics and social-interaction principles. In this model, students are placed in small groups of five or six in which each student is given one segment of the day's lesson and is responsible for teaching it to the other group members. The process resembles the assembling of a jigsaw puzzle. Because the other members have no other access to this information, interdependence is established. In a typical classroom, there are five groups of six students. That means that there are five students (one from each group) who have the same segment of information. In order to assist the students in transmitting their information to the members of their *jigsaw group,* those students (one from each group) meet as a *counterpart group.* The counterpart group precedes the jigsaw group and serves as a vehicle for assisting students to master the material for presentation to their jigsaw group by helping them to put their segment of the material into their own words, to exchange ideas of presentation, and to anticipate the kinds of questions the members of the original group might ask. Thus, the situation, by its very nature, not only induces children to imitate and model skills of group dynamics and social interaction, such as listening carefully and asking good questions, but also requires them to integrate these skills cognitively in their interactions with their group members.

It is the element of structured interdependence that makes this a unique and powerful learning process. By temporarily assuming the role of teacher, each student becomes a valuable resource for the others. Learning from each other gradually diminishes the need to try to outlearn each other, because one student's learning enhances the learning of the other students instead of inhibiting it. In the cooperative paradigm, the classroom teacher learns to be a facilitating resource person who, instead of lecturing to students, shares in the learning and teaching process with the students. Rather than being passively dependent on the teacher as the sole human resource, each student is required to be an active participant and to be responsible for what he or she learns.

Keeping this presentation simple results in an overly glossy picture of how the jigsaw process functions in the classroom. Not all of our endeavors have run smoothly; not all students easily adapt to a cooperative classroom. Some students are poor readers; some students prefer to work alone; and for some students, English is their second language. Such situations present serious problems, but with the aid of a little ingenuity on the part of the teacher, they are not insolvable. In most cases, the teacher has been able to find a way to turn some of these difficulties into strengths. To take one example, poor readers and bilingual students can be encouraged to use their classmates as helpful models. The counterpart section of the jigsaw format allows such students to view the way a more experienced or more articulate student formulates thoughts and ideas so that active modeling, feedback, and then rehearsal of the material to be presented can take place.

One other problem needs to be made explicit. As one might expect, children who have spent several years in a competitive classroom situation do not switch immediately to a cooperative strategy as soon as the jigsaw technique is implemented. The first 2 or 3 weeks frequently involve a slow and painful transition marked by occasional regression to competitive behavioral strategies such as putdowns, name calling, and other derogating acts. Invariably the students learn, however, that these strategies do not pay off, and gradually cooperative behavior comes to predominate.

This interdependent learning process illustrates that encouraging a cooperative environment is not antithetical to providing a guiding structure in which expectations are flexible yet clear. Many proponents of this innovation support stressing the basics in education. One advantage of the process is that it is not dependent on a specific curriculum. The jigsaw paradigm has been used with the same curriculum as more traditional classrooms, and it has also been used with more humanistic curricula. But does it work? Does it encourage the kinds of social exchanges discussed at the beginning of this chapter?

It is relatively easy to assess the extent to which students attain this integration of shared knowledge: by observing the student groups, by having discussions and asking pertinent questions about the material afterward, by giving essay questions that cover everyone's part in the curriculum, or more traditionally, by giving standard quizzes and tests at the end of each week of cooperative group learning. By the same token, one can also measure the effects of cooperation on self-esteem, interpersonal relations, academic performance, and role taking.

Jigsaw Research and Self-esteem

The first systematic experiment to investigate the effects of the jigsaw technique on students' self-esteem was conducted by Blaney, Stephan, Rosenfield, Aronson, and Sikes (1977). The schools in Austin, Texas, had recently been desegregated, producing a great deal of tension that was apparently being exacerbated by the competitive atmosphere existing in most classrooms. The jigsaw technique was introduced in 10 fifth-grade classrooms in seven elementary schools. From among those same schools, 3 classes were also utilized as controls for this study. The experimental classes met in jigsaw groups for about 45 minutes a day, 3 days a week, for 6 weeks. Each jigsaw group consisted of approximately three Anglos, one black, and one Mexican American student. The curriculum was basically the same for the experimental and control classes. Measures were administered before the introduction of the jigsaw technique and again 6 weeks later.

The self-esteem of the students was measured by summing the responses to four attitude questions: "How much do you like being yourself?" "When you are in the classroom, how important do you feel?" "When you are in the classroom, how smart do you feel?" and "When you are in class, how often do you feel you can learn whatever you try to learn?" In general, the results indicated that the experimental subjects significantly increased in self-esteem while the control subjects decreased.

Another recent experiment was conducted to investigate self-esteem in more depth and to control for possible Hawthorne effects that may have been present in the Blaney et al. research. To control for Hawthorne effects, interdependent learning groups were compared to other novel cooperative groups as well as to traditional methods of learning. In his PhD dissertation, Geffner (1978) used an attitude questionnaire and a modified version of A Pictorial Self-Concept Scale for Children (Bolea, Felker, & Barnes, 1971). This modified scale consists of cartoonlike pictures of stick figures in various types of situations and includes the five dimensions of self-esteem deemed important by the students themselves: scholastic abilities, athletic abilities, physical appearance, social interactions, and family interactions. The research was carried out over an 8-week period in 10 fifth-grade classes from four elementary schools in Santa Cruz County, California.

The results of the attitude questionnaire essentially replicated those of Blaney et al. In general, students in both the jigsaw groups and the other cooperative groups improved in self-esteem, with the former groups improving the most. With the pictorial measure of self-esteem, Geffner also found that interdependent learning either maintained or improved the students' self-esteem, whereas the more traditional methods of teaching generally produced a drop in self-esteem. Specifically, the cooperative conditions, in comparison to the more traditional ones, improved the students' self-images regarding their social interactions and their scholastic abilities and even generalized to improve their confidence in athletic abilities and family interactions. Positive feedback, support, and successful experiences of many of the students in the cooperative classes probably led to the generalized improvement in self-esteem and the feelings of competence. Summarizing the two field experiments, it appears that students learning in independent classes for a few days per week do show gains in self-esteem. But what about the effects of cooperation on academic performance? How do students feel about cooperating with their classmates? Does cooperation affect the students' attitudes toward their school? These questions are the subject of our next section.

ACADEMIC PERFORMANCE AND CLASSROOM ATTITUDES

Effects of Cooperation on Academic Performance

Although it is clear that cooperative techniques can produce improved self-esteem, their affects on academic performance are still equivocal. Some studies show that where students teach each other (peer tutoring), both "tutors" and "pupils" improve in their academic abilities; the tutors also show improved self-esteem and more confidence in their skills (Cloward, 1967; Lippitt & Lohman, 1965). (An extensive review of the literature on peer tutoring can be found in Devin-Sheehan, Feldman, & Allen, 1976.) Other research has shown that competition can at least have a beneficial effect on performance in adults. Interestingly enough, this was the major finding of one of the earliest experiments ever done in social psychology (Triplett, 1898).

Some innovative procedures, while making students happy, have produced decreases in performance. Indeed, recent reports (Chalupsky & Coles, 1977) indicate that most general innovative classroom procedures are not associated with maintained or improved academic achievement. In addition, there are well-founded reports that some students are graduating from high school without being able to read and write. It is little wonder, then, that a "back to basics" phase in education may well overshadow newly emerging research that examines not only specific types of innovations but also the social variables involved in classroom learning. What is clear from the conflicting evidence is that not all innovations are helpful and that some can be detrimental. Whether results are beneficial depends upon the precise nature of the innovation as well as on the skill and attitude of the teacher. For example, a laissez-faire, unstructured innovation may provide students with feelings of freedom and creativity but is probably not conducive to learning. Effective classroom learning requires a creative teacher who allows students to take responsibility for their learning while providing a stimulating structure within which to do so.

Recent research indicates that, in complex situations like problem solving and academic activities, cooperation does produce better performance than competition (DeVries, Edwards, & Wells, 1974; Wheeler, 1977; Wodarski, Hamblin, Buckholdt, & Ferritor, 1973). There is substantial evidence that students with high self-esteem generally have high achievement levels (e.g., Brookover, Paterson, & Thomas, 1964). In summaries of the research in this field, Covington and Beery (1976) and

Purkey (1970) also suggest that high self-esteem leads to better academic perform-ance and, conversely, that high performance leads to high self-esteem. It appears that the positive experiences, higher expectations, and anticipated successes are all involved in self-fulfilling prophecies (e.g., Rosenthal & Jacobson, 1968; Weiner, 1974) that lead to improved self-esteem and subsequently to higher achievement levels in school.

Lucker, Rosenfield, Sikes, and Aronson (1977) designed an experiment to deter-mine the effects of the jigsaw technique of interdependent learning on academic performance for fifth- and sixth-grade students. Inasmuch as self-esteem improved with the use of the jigsaw, it was hypothesized that achievement levels would also improve. Therefore, six classrooms were taught with the jigsaw method for 2 weeks while five classrooms were taught in a traditional manner and were the controls for this experiment. Achievement tests were administered to all students before and after the jigsaw was instituted in the experimental classrooms.

The analyses of the data indicated that the students in the jigsaw classes showed significantly more improvement in achievement than the students in the control classes. It appears that these results were mainly due to the increased performance of the ethnic-minority students in the jigsaw classes, especially in comparison to the minority students' performance in the traditional classrooms. Thus, Anglos per-formed about the same in jigsaw and traditional classes, but minority students performed much better with the interdependent teaching method. Lucker et al. also found that the above results were not related to the particular ability level of the students. In other words, high-ability Anglos and minorities benefited as much from the jigsaw technique as low-ability Anglos and minorities. Therefore, being in the jigsaw groups did not cause high-ability students to decrease in their achievement performance. The data for improved minority performance have been replicated by Slavin (1977b) and Garibaldi (1977) using other types of cooperative groups in the classroom.

Jigsaw Research and Classroom Attitudes

In the experiment by Blaney et al. (1977), attitudes of students toward school were assessed by the following questions: "How much do you like school this year?" "When you are in the classroom, how happy do you feel?" and "When you are in the classroom, how bored do you feel?" Significant results were ob-tained for this measure. It was found that Anglo students in jigsaw classes in-creased in their liking for school while control Anglos decreased in their liking for school. The black students in the jigsaw classes decreased somewhat in their liking for school, but the control blacks decreased substantially. The Mexican American students in control classes improved substantially, however, in liking for school, while the experimental Mexican Americans increased only slightly. The researchers speculated that these latter results may have been due to lan-guage barriers faced by the Mexican American students in the jigsaw groups when they were "forced" to participate in the peer teaching. These results of improved attitudes toward school are consistent with previous research by Dunn and Gold-man (1966) and by Wheeler and Ryan (1973).

Blaney et al. also found that jigsaw students decreased in "wanting to beat a classmate at schoolwork" while the control students increased in this type of com-petitiveness. The students in the jigsaw classes also increased in feeling that "they could learn from their classmates" while the responses of the students in the control classes decreased for this question.

INTERPERSONAL RELATIONS

Effects of Cooperation on Interpersonal Relations

An important aspect of the classroom situation is the manner in which students relate to each other. Cooperative reward-structure situations seem to enhance interpersonal relations (Blanchard, Adelman, & Cook, 1974; Deutsch, 1949; Johnson & Johnson, 1972). Recent research indicates that cooperation leads to more acceptance, more concern, and more trust among the group members; in other words, the members come to value each other more than they do in competitive situations (Garibaldi, 1977; Johnson & Johnson, 1974; Slavin, 1977b). Research at the elementary school level (Phillips & D'Amico, 1956), at the junior high school level (Gottheil, 1955), and at the college level (Deutsch, 1949) has indicated that cooperation leads to increased liking and better relations among classmates. Research on the jigsaw technique has also confirmed these results. For example, Blaney et al. (1977) reported that the students in the jigsaw groups did come to like their group members significantly more than the other students, and they even increased their liking for their other classmates, too. These findings are important because increased liking for a student is a first step to the student being accepted and given support by her or his classmates.

Thus, the research has shown that cooperation in the classroom (especially interdependence) leads to improved self-esteem, improved attitudes toward school, increased academic performance for minority students, and more liking for classmates. It is appropriate now to discuss some of the possible reasons for these beneficial outcomes.

Attribution theory has a good deal of relevance to this situation. Basically, the proponents of attribution theory state that people will go beyond the available information in order to try to explain the causes of someone's behavior, even their own (Heider, 1958; Jones & Davis, 1965). In general, when viewing one's own behavior, one will make dispositional attributions to explain one's successes (e.g., success was due to my ability) and situational attributions to try to explain one's failures (e.g., failure was due to poor lighting). Thus, self-attributions generally protect self-esteem. In the classroom, then, a student who performs well would probably attribute this to his or her personal ability, knowledge, and intelligence, and this would enhance the student's inner self-esteem. Indeed, Covington and Beery (1976) report that success-oriented students generally make dispositional attributions when they perform well, and they usually attribute failure to a lack of effort. Other researchers have suggested that attributions of success and failure in achievement-oriented situations like school are made along two dimensions: a dispositional-situational dimension described above, and a stability dimension (Weiner, 1974; Weiner, Frieze, Kukla, Reed, Rest, & Rosenbaum, 1971). In other words, ability is considered relatively stable while such things as luck and task difficulty are more variable over time. Thus, consistent performance will lead to attributions of ability, and this will enhance self-esteem.

What happens when a child experiences failure? Covington and Beery (1976) state that the lack of successful experiences and the scarcity of rewards in many classrooms can lead some students to learn to expect failure. These students give up and stop trying to succeed; low self-esteem and low achievement are maintained through negative self-fulfilling prophecies. In these cases, it appears that the students make situational attributions (e.g., luck) for the few successes they might have and dispositional attributions for their failures (e.g., poor ability and low self-worth). These same kinds of attributions are often made by classmates and even by some teachers with regard to those students who are failing in school (Weiner, 1974). Thus, the interactions among students can also lead to these self-defeating, self-fulfilling prophecies.

The emphasis in cooperative, interdependent interactions, however, is on all participants working together to accomplish a mutual goal. The students support each other in achieving success, and this is likely to increase the positive feedback given to the group members. Thus, cooperative interactions promote positive self-fulfilling prophecies, and students who might be considered "losers" in many traditional classrooms (e.g., slow-achieving Anglos and minority students) seem to change their attributions about their performance from negative ones to more ego-enhancing ones. This would account for the improved self-esteem and better achievement found in several recent studies (e.g., Blaney et al., 1977; Garibaldi, 1977; Geffner, 1978; Lucker et al., 1977; Slavin, 1977b).

In order to focus more directly on some of these assumed mechanisms underlying the impact of jigsaw learning on student attitudes and classroom performance, two laboratory experiments were designed and conducted. In these experiments, students were removed from the hustle and bustle of the classroom and tested under more controlled, laboratory conditions. In one such study, Stephen, Kennedy, and Aronson (1977) set up a situation in which sixth-grade students succeeded or failed at a motor task (throwing bean bags at a target) that was performed cooperatively, competitively, or independently. Recall that in previous research it was found that individuals make dispositional attributions to explain their own success and situational attributions to explain their failures. Stephan et al. demonstrated that the world is a little more complicated than that. They found that whether or not ego-enhancing attributions were made depended on the kind of interaction and whether or not the partner was a friend. For example, in the competition condition with a friend, the usual ego-enhancing attribution process was reversed so that winners were less likely than losers to attribute their performance on the task to skill. It looks as though people are reluctant to lord it over a friend whom they beat—at least temporarily.

A similar experiment was designed to look more closely at the kind of attributions made by college students in interdependent, cooperative, and competitive interactions with other students (Stephan, Presser, Kennedy, & Aronson, in press). Each subject was paired with a confederate of the experimenters in the training and testing of artistic judgments. The subjects' results were manipulated to indicate task success or failure. Again, ego-enhancing attributions were generally made by the student to explain her or his success or failure. In the cooperative and interdependent conditions, similar attributions were made for the partner's success or failure (i.e., dispositional attribution for success and situational attribution for failure). In the competition condition, however, the process was reversed so that partner failure was attributed dispositionally and success situationally. In short, cooperation leads individuals to treat their partners in the same ego-enhancing manner in which they treat themselves. Competition creates a harsh difference.

Thus, firm evidence exists for the conjecture that an interdependent, cooperative environment can change the self-defeating attributions and negative self-fulfilling prophecies made by the students who are considered failures by others and themselves. This line of research lends credence to the model developed earlier: Poor performance in a competitive or hostile environment can trigger mechanisms (negative dispositional attributions by others and by the person himself or herself) that, together with feelings of ineffectiveness (from the poor performance itself), can combine to perpetuate poor performance. The research discussed above demonstrates that this trend can be reversed either by enhancing the performance of the individual or by changing the attributions that tend to be made as a function of a cooperative (as opposed to a competitive) environment.

Effects of Cooperation on Interethnic Relations

The competitive environment of the typical traditional classroom may serve to retard some of the expected beneficial effects of desegregated schools. In 1954, when the Supreme Court decided that schools must be desegregated, it was expected that desegregation would have beneficial effects on the self-esteem and performance of ethnic children and on the reduction of interethnic prejudice. Recent, thorough reviews of research on the effects of desegregation (St. John, 1975; Miller, 1977) show few if any benefits, however. Indeed, if anything, there is some evidence for a reduction in self-esteem among ethnic children following desegregation.

It is our hunch that a highly competitive situation works a special hardship on ethnic children. Many of these children come from ghetto schools where the atmosphere and facilities are below average. They are suddenly forced to compete with middle-class Anglo children who are better prepared and more accustomed to the competitive process. The situation is one that makes poor performance likely—which, as we have seen, can have a deleterious effect on self-esteem as well as on feelings of friendship across ethnic lines.

Allport (1954) and Cook (1969) have suggested that certain criteria must be met in order to reduce ethnic prejudice. These conditions include: equal status contact between ethnic-group members; cooperative interactions, preferably with successful outcomes (e.g., interdependence); social norms that encourage interethnic interaction (i.e., the teacher or authority figure must support the cooperative interethnic interaction); situations that promote friendly relations; and situations that enhance the generalization of improved attitudes to other ethnic-group members and other situations. Cook (1969) found substantial improvement in interethnic attitudes in a quasi-naturalistic work environment involving extremely prejudiced Anglos. His experimental situation met many of the above criteria for repeated interethnic contact in a cooperatively oriented environment. Katz (1955) also reported that cooperative interactions between Anglo and black teen-agers in recreational groups led to a reduction of ethnic prejudice. Harding, Proshansky, Kutner, and Chein (1969) reviewed many studies that met the above criteria in various settings, and these studies also indicated that interethnic relations improved.

What happens when a cooperative structure is substituted for a competitive one in the classroom? In recently desegregated schools in Colorado, Weigel, Wiser, and Cook (1975) instituted some cooperative techniques for 4 months and assessed the effects on cross-ethnic relations and attitudes. They did find more cross-ethnic helping behavior in their experimental classes compared to the traditional control classes, and they also found some positive attitudinal changes among the ethnic groups (Anglo, black, and Mexican American). Other research in classroom situations also indicates that cross-ethnic helping and cross-ethnic liking improved with the introduction of a cooperative structure (Blanchard et al., 1974; DeVries & Edwards, 1974; DeVries & Slavin, 1976).

Research in social psychology has also shown that interdependence seems to reduce intergroup hostilities and tensions (e.g., Sherif, Harvey, Hood, White, & Sherif, 1961). Theoretically, then, the jigsaw method of learning should also reduce interethnic prejudice in the classroom. To test this assumption, Geffner (1978) investigated the interethnic and intraethnic perceptions of Mexican American and Anglo students. The results of his research indicate that the interdependent and cooperative methods of learning yielded some important beneficial outcomes. For example, in the cooperative classes, there was significant improvement for the Anglos' perceptions of how Mexican American students view themselves and their classmates; however, in traditional classes there was no improvement in the Anglos' perceptions of Mexican Americans, and there was a decline in the Mexican Americans' opinions of other Mexican Americans. The jigsaw and other cooperative group conditions also showed improvement in their students' perceptions of Anglos' academic abilities and self-worth, while the traditional condition showed a substantial decrease. In summary, Geffner found that being in interdependent classrooms tended to raise Mexican American students' perceptions of the academic abilities of Anglos and tended to maintain the remaining interethnic and intraethnic perceptions as well as self-perceptions in this category. Being in traditional classrooms, however, tended to lower the self-perceptions of all students as well as to lower the Mexican American students' perceptions of the academic abilities of Anglos and other Mexican Americans.

Summarizing all the research on the jigsaw technique (e.g., Blaney et al., 1977; Geffner, 1978; Lucker et al., 1977), it appears that this interdependent learning method enhances the students' self-esteem, improves their academic performance, increases liking for their classmates, and improves some of their interethnic and intraethnic perceptions. These changes are important for students because they seem to promote ego-enhancing attributions for the students themselves, as well as for their peers. The resulting positive self-fulfilling prophecies should theoretically improve academic achievement and self-satisfaction in the long run too, but these still need to be investigated. In addition, it appears that the groundwork for reducing prejudice in the classroom has been established, assuming that the cooperative interaction among students is sustained. It also appears that the jigsaw technique of interdependent learning is most effective in classes that were previously taught in a traditional manner, especially in situations in which there is interethnic interaction (e.g., in newly desegregated schools).

ROLE TAKING

Why does cooperative interaction enhance interpersonal behavior in the classroom? One of the crucial mechanisms underlying the beneficial effects of cooperative behavior on liking, positive attributions, self-esteem, and performance is the ability to take the role of another person. According to Piaget's (1932) theory, children learn and develop by interacting with their environment. Through the active process of resolving social and cognitive conflicts, children construct their ways of viewing the world. If children engage in a cooperative, rather than a competitive, process, the nature of their interaction should increase their abilities to take one another's perspective. More specifically, Piaget suggested that egocentrism and role taking are negatively correlated in children's development; that is, social interactions that enhance role taking would diminish egocentrism because the dove-tailing of responses involved in effective social interaction demands that each participant modify her or his intended behavior in anticipation of the other's reaction to this behavior. Inasmuch as Piaget also suggested that egocentrism can be overcome by dissonant information in verbal exchanges with peers and that social interaction allows a child to recognize the difference between his or her own preoccupations and the concerns of others, it seems likely that the cooperative process would provide a framework for enhancing social development in a structural sense.

Thus, in order to cooperate with other individuals, one must have the ability to take the perspective of oneself and of others in shared situations. Without this perspective-taking ability and without the ability to feel concern for others, one is limited in one's ability to carry out positive social behaviors. Johnson (1975) stressed the importance of the relationship between cooperation and role taking when he urged that individuals interested in developing effective perspective-taking abilities in children should emphasize cooperative goal structures in schools. Aron-son's cooperative, interdependent paradigm meets such a requirement.

Jigsaw Research and Role Taking

The hypothesis stated above was recently tested by Bridgeman (1977) in her PhD dissertation. Specifically, she assessed the relationship between cooperative learning and role-taking abilities with 120 fifth-grade students from three Santa Cruz County elementary schools. A revised version of Chandler's (1973) role-taking cartoon series was used to assess the students' perspective-taking abilities. Each of the cartoons depicts a central character caught up in a chain of psychological cause and effect such that the character's subsequent behavior was shaped by and fully comprehensible only in terms of the events preceding it. In one of the sequences, for example, a boy who had been saddened by seeing his father off at the airport began to cry when he later received a gift of a toy airplane similar to the one that had carried his father away. Midway into each sequence, a second character is introduced in the role of a late-arriving bystander who witnessed the resultant behaviors of the principal character but was not privy to the antecedent events that brought them about. It is possible to place the subject in a privileged position relative to the story character whose role the subject is later asked to assume, and to specify the degree to which the subject is able to set aside facts known only to her or him and adopt a perspective measurably different from her or his own. These role-taking tasks were administered to all students before and after 8 weeks of classroom learning. The cooperative, interdependent classes constituted the experimental condition, and the more traditional, teacher-centered classes constituted the control condition.

The results indicated that students in the cooperative classrooms were better able to put themselves in the bystander's place, while students in the control classroom made significantly more egocentric statements on behalf of the role of the bystander. For example, when the mailman delivered a toy airplane to the little boy, students in traditional classrooms tended to assume that the mailman knew the boy would cry; that is, they believed that the mailman knew that the boy's father had recently left town on an airplane—simply because they (the subjects) were privy to this information. On the other hand, students who had participated in a jigsaw group were much more successful at taking the mailman's role—realizing that the mailman could not possibly have predicted that the boy would cry upon receiving a toy airplane.

The results from this study (Bridgeman, 1977) are consistent with both Piaget's assumptions and the assumptions underlying the cooperative process. Both role taking of rational thought (considering the logical perspective of another) and role taking of affective thought (considering the emotional perspective of another) showed a significant increase after the cooperative experience. There was no change in the role-taking abilities of the students in the control classrooms who were taught in more traditional ways. Thus, in addition to clarifying the social-developmental importance of cooperative learning, the results of this experiment demonstrate that the cooperative paradigm's role-taking effects transfer from a classroom setting to a nonclassroom setting. Specifically, the results demonstrate that the effects of the curriculum-incorporated role-taking experiences from the cooperative interactions carried over into the noncurriculum tasks on Chandler's role-taking stories.

Further, these data confirm our notion that empathic role taking may be a key ability that mediates other interpersonal behaviors. It seems logical to assume that, if cooperative learning (which requires role taking) enhances role taking, and if the process of role taking is essential to the development of a sense of self (Mead, 1934), then cooperation should enhance self-esteem as well. In accordance with Mead, Piaget theorizes that the ability to take a role is necessary to the development of a consciousness of self, for an egocentric mind cannot be conscious of its own processes. It also follows that role taking should enhance liking for others. In short, once one has the ability to see the world from another's perspective, it follows that one will see that person in a more positive, more differentiated, less stereotypic way. This process seems to work according to a feedback principle. That is, it also seems reasonable that people who feel secure about themselves could better understand the perspective of others. If one is able, therefore, to take the role of another while enhancing one's self-esteem, it would seem then that one might become more tolerant and less prejudiced toward others.

There are still many unexplored aspects of cooperative learning that need to be addressed, such as: long-term effects, sex differences, cognitive development, prejudice reduction, motivation, power distribution, and stereotyping, to name a few. Our results thus far seem promising. It is clear to us that cooperation does affect attitudes and social behaviors in the classroom and therefore should be given serious consideration by educators and social policy-makers.

REFERENCES

Allport, G. W. *The nature of prejudice.* Reading, Mass.: Addison-Wesley, 1954.

Aronson, E., Blaney, N. T., Sikes, J., Stephan, C., & Snapp, M. Busing and racial tension: The jigsaw route to learning and liking. *Psychology Today,* February, 1975, pp. 43–59.

Bailey, S. Independence and factor structure of self-concept metadimensions. *Journal of Counseling Psychology,* 1970, 17, 425–430.

Blanchard, F. A., Adelman, L., & Cook, S. W. The effect of group success and failure upon interpersonal attraction in cooperating interracial groups. *Journal of Personality and Social Psychology,* 1974, **31**, 1020–1030.

Blaney, N. T., Stephan, C., Rosenfield, D., Aronson, E., & Sikes, J. Interdependence in the classroom: A field study. *Journal of Educational Psychology,* 1977, **69**, 139–146.

Bolea, A. S., Felker, D. W., & Barnes, M. D. A pictorial self-concept scale for children in K-4. *Journal of Educational Measurement,* 1971, **8**, 223–224.

Bridgeman, D. L. *The influence of cooperative, interdependent learning on role taking and moral reasoning: A theoretical and empirical field study with fifth grade students.* Unpublished doctoral dissertation, University of California at Santa Cruz, 1977.

Brookover, W. B., Paterson, A., & Thomas, S. Self-concept of ability and school achievement. *Sociology of Education,* 1964, **37**, 271–278.

Chalupsky, A. B., & Coles, G. J. *The unfulfilled promise of educational innovation.* Paper presented at the meeting of the American Educational Research Association, New York City, 1977.

Chandler, M. J. Egocentrism and antisocial behavior: The assessment and training of social perspective-taking skills. *Developmental Psychology,* 1973, **9**, 326–332.

Cloward, R. Studies in tutoring. *Journal of Experimental Education,* 1967, **36**, 14–25.

Cook, S. W. Motives in a conceptual analysis of attitude-related behavior. In W. J. Arnold & D. Levine (Eds.), *Nebraska Symposium on Motivation* (Vol. 17). Lincoln: University of Nebraska Press, 1969.

Cooley, C. H. *Human nature and the social order.* New York: Scribner's, 1902.

Coopersmith, S. *The antecedents of self-esteem.* San Francisco: W. H. Freeman, 1967.

Coopersmith, S., & Feldman, R. Fostering a positive self-concept and high self-esteem in the classroom. In R. H. Coop & K. White (Eds.), *Psychological concepts in the classroom,* New York: Harper, 1974.

Covington, M. V., & Beery, R. G. *Self-worth and school learning.* New York: Holt, 1976.

Crandall, R. The measurement of self-esteem and related constructs. In J. P. Robinson & P. R. Shaver (Eds.), *Measures of social psychological attitudes* (rev. ed.). Ann Arbor: Institute for Social Research, 1973.

Deutsch, M. An experimental study of the effects of cooperation and competition upon group process. *Human Relations,* 1949, **2**, 199–231.

Deutsch, M. Socially relevant science. *American Psychologist.* 1969, **24**, 1076–1092.

Devin-Sheehan, L., Feldman, R., and Allen, V. Research on children tutoring children: A critical review. *Review of Educational Research,* 1976, **46**, 355–385.

DeVries, D. L., & Edwards, K. J. Student teams and learning games: Their effects on cross-race and cross-sex interaction. *Journal of Educational Psychology,* 1974, **66**, 741–749.

DeVries, D. L., Edwards, K. J., & Wells, E. H. *Teams-games tournament in the social studies classroom: Effects on academic achievement, student attitudes, cognitive beliefs, and classroom climate.* (Tech. Rep. No. 173). Johns Hopkins University, Center for Social Organization of Schools, 1974.

DeVries, D. L., & Slavin, R. E. *Teams-games tournament: A final report on the research* (Tech. Rep. No. 217). Johns Hopkins University, Center for Social Organization of Schools, 1976.

Dunn, R. E., and Goldman, M. Competition and noncompetition in relationship to satisfaction and feelings toward own group and nongroup members. *Journal of Social Psychology,* 1966, **68**, 229–311.

Franks, D. D., & Marolla, J. Efficacious action and social approval as interacting dimensions of self-esteem: A tentative formulation through construct validation. *Sociometry,* 1976, **39**, 324–341.

Garibaldi, A. M. *Cooperation, competition, individualization and black students' problem solving and attitudes.* Paper presented at the annual convention of the American Psychological Association, San Francisco, 1977.

Geffner, R. A. *The effects of interdependent learning on self-esteem, inter-ethnic relations, and intra-ethnic attitudes of elementary school children: A field experiment.* Unpublished doctoral dissertation, University of California at Santa Cruz, 1978.

Gergen, K. J. *The concept of self.* New York: Holt, 1971.

Gottheil, E. Changes in social perceptions contingent upon competing or cooperating. *Sociometry,* 1955, **18**, 132–137.

Harding, J., Proshansky, H. M., Kutner, B., & Chein, I. Prejudice and ethnic relations. In G. Lindzey & E. Aronson (Eds.), *Handbook of social psychology* (Vol. 5). Reading, Mass.: Addison-Wesley, 1969.

Heider, F. *The psychology of interpersonal relations.* New York: Wiley, 1958.

Johnson, D. W. *The social psychology of education.* New York: Holt, 1970.

Johnson, D. W. Cooperativeness and social perspective taking. *Journal of Personality and Social Psychology,* 1975, **31**, 241-244.

Johnson, D. W., & Johnson, R. T. Instructional goal structure: Cooperative, competitive, or individualistic. *Review of Educational Research,* 1974, **44**, 213-240.

Johnson, D. W., & Johnson, R. T. *Learning together and alone: Cooperation, competition, and individualization.* Englewood Cliffs, N.J.: Prentice-Hall, 1975.

Johnson, D. W., & Johnson, S. The effects of attitude similarity, expectation of goal facilitation, and actual goal facilitation on interpersonal attraction. *Journal of Experimental Social Psychology,* 1972, **8**, 197-206.

Johnson, D. W., & Lewicki, R. J. The initiation of superordinate goals. *Journal of Applied Behavioral Science,* 1969, **5**, 9-24.

Jones, E. E., & Davis, K. E. From acts to dispositions. In L. Berkowitz (Ed.), *Advances in experimental social psychology* (Vol. 2). New York: Academic, 1965.

Katz, I. *Conflict and harmony in an adolescent interracial group.* New York: New York University Press, 1955.

La Benne, W. D., & Greene, B. I. *Educational implications of self-concept theory.* Santa Monica, Calif.: Goodyear, 1969.

Lippitt, P., & Lohman, J. Cross-age relationships: An educational resource. *Children,* 1965, **12**, 113-117.

Lucker, G. W., Rosenfield, D., Sikes, J., & Aronson, E. Performance in the interdependent classroom: A field study. *American Educational Research Journal,* 1977, **13**, 115-123.

Mead, G. H. *Mind, self and society.* Chicago: University of Chicago Press, 1934.

Miller, N. *Principles relevant to successful school desegregation.* Unpublished manuscript, University of California at Riverside, 1977.

Phillips, B. N., & D'Amico, L. A. Effects of cooperation and competition on the cohesiveness of small face-to-face groups. *Journal of Educational Psychology,* 1956, **47**, 65-70.

Piaget, J. *Judgment and reasoning in the child.* New York: Harcourt, 1932.

Purkey, W. W. *Self-concept and school achievement.* Englewood Cliffs, N.J.: Prentice-Hall, 1970.

Rosenthal, R., & Jacobson, L. *Pygmalion in the classroom: Teacher expectation and pupils' intellectual development.* New York: Holt, 1968.

Sherif, M., Harvey, O. J., White, B. J., Hood, W., & Sheriff, C. *Intergroup conflict and cooperation: The robbers cave experiment.* Norman: University of Oklahoma Institute of Intergroup Relations, 1961.

Slavin, R. E. *Decomposing a student team technique: Team reward a team task.* Paper presented at the annual meeting of the American Psychological Association, San Francisco, 1977. (a)

Slavin, R. E. *Student team learning techniques: Narrowing the achievement gap between the races* (Tech. Rep. No. 228). Johns Hopkins University, Center for Social Organization of Schools, 1977. (b)

Slavin, R. E., DeVries, D. L., & Hulten, B. H. *Individual vs. team competition: The interpersonal consequences of academic performance* (Tech. Rep. No. 188). Johns Hopkins University, Center for Social Organization of Schools, 1975.

Snygg, D., & Combs, A. W. *Individual behavior.* New York: Harper, 1949.

Stanwyck, D. J., & Felker, D. W. Measuring the self-concept: A factor analytic study. Cited in P. A. Zirkel. Self-concept and the "disadvantage" of ethnic group membership. *Review of Education Research,* 1971, **41**, 211-225.

Stephen, C., Kennedy, J. C., & Aronson, E. The effects of friendship and outcome on task attribution. *Sociometry,* 1977, **40**, 107-111.

Stephan, C., Presser, N. R., Kennedy, J. C., & Aronson, E. Attributions to success and failure in cooperative, competitive and interdependent interactions. *European Journal of Social Psychology,* in press.

St. John, N. *School desegregation: Outcomes for children.* New York: Wiley, 1975.

Triplett, N. The dynamogenic factors in pace-making and competition. *American Journal of Psychology,* 1898, **9**, 507-533.

Weigel, R. H., Wiser, P. L., & Cook, S. W. The impact of cooperative learning experiences on cross-ethnic relations and attitudes. *Journal of Social Issues,* 1975, **31**(1), 219-244.

Weiner, B. *Achievement motivation and attribution theory.* Morristown, N.J.: Silver Burdett, 1974.

Weiner, B., Frieze, I., Kukla, A., Reed, L., Rest, S., & Rosenbaum, R. M. *Perceiving the causes of success and failure.* Morristown, N.J.: Silver Burdett, 1971.

Wheeler, R. *Predisposition toward cooperation and competition: Cooperative and competitive classroom effects.* Paper presented at the annual meeting of the American Psychological Association, San Francisco, 1977.

Wheeler, R. C., & Ryan, F. L. Effects of cooperative and competitive classroom environments on the attitudes and achievement of elementary school students engaged in social studies inquiry activities. *Journal of Educational Psychology,* 1973, 65, 402–407.

Wodarski, J. S., Hamblin, R. L., Buckholdt, D., & Ferritor, D. E. Individual consequences versus different shared consequences contingent on the performance of low-achieving group members. *Journal of Applied Social Psychology,* 1973, 3, 276–290.

VI

THE SCHOOL AS AN ORGANIZATION

12

Alternative Organizations for Schools and Classrooms

Dean Tjosvold
Pennsylvania State University

Students, teachers, and administrators continually organize themselves by making decisions and then influence each other until these decisions are implemented. Because of their high degree of interdependence, educators and students must coordinate their activities if they are to reach their goals.

Decision making and resulting influence both follow a pattern. In most schools, as in most organizations, a few people in the top positions are expected to coordinate the activities of the members by making decisions and by overseeing their implementation. In most classrooms, the teacher is expected to determine the major learning activities and to induce the students to become involved in them. Principals are expected to make decisions about the overall management of the school; teachers and students are expected to carry out these decisions. In recent years, however, educators and students have demonstrated their dissatisfaction with this traditional, centrally controlled way of organizing schools and classrooms.

In this chapter, I identify major characteristics of centrally controlled organizations and review research that suggests the effects these characteristics have on the organizational life of schools and on the learning of students and educators. I also propose a model of collaborative organization for schools as a feasible alternative to the centrally controlled organization.

Educational research has the advantage of pertaining directly to schools. Comparatively little educational research, however, has studied the organization of schools (Bidwell, 1965; Corwin, 1962; Schlectly, 1976). Because this educational research has not used important organizational concepts and has relied on correlational findings and questionnaire data, its uses are limited. Social-psychological research suggests useful concepts and insights into the organization of schools. In this chapter, while not ignoring methodological strengths and shortcomings of the research, I emphasize the reasonable implications of research for educational practice.

My position here is that schools and classrooms are too dependent on centrally controlled organizations. In many educational settings, collaborative organizations are more useful for facilitating educational goals, although in some situations, a

The author thanks Joseph J. Rubin for his helpful comments during the preparation of this chapter.

centrally controlled organization is appropriate and effective. Many schools and classrooms depend on an unspecified organization. As a result, participants have different expectations about their roles, obligations, and rights. They feel that their rights have been violated or they remain unaware of the expectations that others have for them. To avoid these common dilemmas, educators and students should use both organizational structures appropriately and be aware of when each structure is being used. Moreover, they should develop the attitudes and skills needed to make each organizational structure work.

DISENCHANTMENT
WITH CENTRALLY CONTROLLED SCHOOLS

Dramatic changes have occurred in the daily life of schools. The switch and paddle, once symbols of authority, are gone. The courts and educators have argued that coercive, corporal punishment is too debilitating to be used regularly (Bidwell, 1965). Many educators are experimenting with alternative ways of making school decisions and influencing students (Walberg & Thomas, 1972). Free schools and open classrooms are visible attempts to find more effective ways of organizing. The changing values of educators and students are sources of this dissatisfaction with centrally controlled organizations.

Educators' Aspirations

Many educators seek a more active role in making school decisions. Through associations and unions, teachers have tried to influence classroom size and other aspects of their work. Like other professionals (Bennis, 1969), they believe that their vocation should be personally rewarding and that they should possess the freedom and power to make their work more enhancing. They believe that they are capable of participating in the governance of the school rather than of being unilaterally controlled by administrators. Fortunately, some administrators welcome faculty involvement.

Some educators want students to take a more active and responsible role in shaping their school lives. Those committed to affective education think students should learn to accept responsibility, communicate openly, manage conflicts, and live and work with others in a productive and enjoyable manner. It is vital, then, that the school and classroom offer appropriate models of organization. The school thereby becomes a laboratory in which students, teachers, and administrators join in experiments in organizing.

Many humanistically oriented educators believe that relationships in school are too often sour, mechanical, and devoid of excitement and positive feelings (Herndon, 1968; Silberman, 1971). They envision that students will acquire the values and attitudes that foster humanizing capabilities and interactions (Johnson & Johnson, 1975). They want kindness, compassion, empathy, and responsiveness, rather than the impersonality, force, and cruelty of dehumanized relationships. In their view, the traditional organization is a major source of dehumanization in schools.

Violence in Schools

A significant minority of students have challenged the authority of schools to regulate their lives. They have argued that this control is demeaning and inconsistent with their attempts to become self-directing, educated people. They have attempted to increase their control over their school lives; they have protested and initiated lawsuits (Chesler & Lohman, 1971).

The breakdown of effective organization in many schools, owing in part to the increased number of alienated young people, underscores the urgency of developing alternative organizations. In too many schools, educators and students are psychologically and physically brutalized by each other. Despite the presence of over 700 assistants charged with maintaining order in Philadelphia schools, teachers have been assaulted by parents and students (Mallowe, 1976). In 1975, serious injuries of nearly 300 teachers in this school system resulted in follow-up reports. Furthermore, it is likely that only a fraction of the actual assaults were reported. Frustrated teachers have been observed tolerating, perhaps even relishing, the physical beating of "tough" students by official "enforcers." Students, according to Marlowe, have also been subject to shakedowns, beatings, and even murder at the hands of other students. National statistics collected by the recent U.S. Senate Subcommittee to investigate Juvenile Delinquency (1975) indicate that, between 1970 and 1973, assaults on students increased by 85%; assaults on teachers increased by 77%; and homicides by 19%. The presence of such disorder in schools demonstrates the need to devise new and effective organizational structures for schools.

The growing number of alienated young people seems to contribute to the present organizational problems. Bronfenbrenner (1974) argued that the ravages of poverty, the rat race, and divorce have led to the deterioration of the American family as a socialization agent. Children in many families lack meaningful relationships; they remain alienated from the adult world, from their peers, and from themselves. They are angry, disaffected, and, at times, antisocial and criminal. The accelerating abuse of alcohol and drugs by adolescents, the growing rate of juvenile delinquency, and the increasing incidence of suicides among adolescents appear to be symptoms of the deterioration of the family and the consequent alienation of the young (Bronfenbrenner, 1974). Alienated youth, it can be conjectured, are unlikely to be committed to their own development; they often reject the legitimacy of the school to make decisions for them; they do not value the resources (e.g., grades and social approval) that educators have traditionally used to induce reluctant students to learn. These young people are very much in need of socializing experiences; yet they avoid activities designed for their learning and fail to build meaningful relationships with educators. Organizations to involve alienated students in learning and socialization experiences are needed.

THE CONCEPT OF ORGANIZATIONAL EFFECTIVENESS

Although it is obvious that chaotic, violent schools are ineffectively organized, researchers disagree over the definition and criteria by which organizational effectiveness should be measured. Given that the primary objective of schools is to facilitate learning, student learning has often been considered the criterion of a school's effectiveness (e.g., Boocock, 1972; Coleman, Campbell, Hobson, McPartland, Mood, Weinfield, & York, 1966; Jencks, 1972). Although equating and measuring an organization's effectiveness by the attainment of its primary objective appears to be only common sense, there are in fact several serious shortcomings of this concept. For a school, or any organization, to be effective, it must not only reach its primary objective in the short run, but it must also strengthen its ability to do so in the future. In addition, measuring an organization's effectiveness by the extent to which its primary objective has been reached can be misleading. Many other factors can account for its success or failure in reaching the primary objective. It is widely recognized that students often learn because of nonschool influences. Finally, limiting the definition of organizational effectiveness to the attainment of the primary objective does not encourage observing, understanding, or improving the organizational dynamics of schools (Schlechty, 1976).

Argyris (1964, 1970) has proposed an alternative concept of organizational effectiveness. In his judgment, an organization not only must achieve its primary goal but must achieve two maintenance objectives: (1) internal strength and (2) adaption to the external environment. To reach its primary and auxiliary objectives, an organization must develop the capabilities to generate valid information, resolve and manage conflicts, solve problems, and make and implement decisions. Members should become internally committed to the decisions of the organization so that these decisions are implemented. All of their resources should be utilized to solve problems in such a way that these problems do not recur. Because members often have opposing opinions and interests, conflicts must be resolved to maintain the decision-making and problem-solving capabilities at an effective level. Indeed, problems should be solved and decisions should be made in such a way that these capabilities of the organization are enhanced (Argyris, 1970).

Argyris emphasized communication of information, decision making, influencing, and resolving conflicts, all as processes related to a school's capacity to reach primary and auxiliary maintenance objectives. A major implication of this concept of organizational effectiveness is that researchers and practitioners should develop ways of measuring and strengthening the capabilities of communication, conflict resolution, and problem solving (Miles & Schmuck, 1971).

CENTRALLY CONTROLLED ORGANIZATIONS

There are three major characteristics of the dominant mode of organization, and a review of the educational and social-psychological research suggests the consequences these characteristics have on school life and learning.

1. *Control Orientation.* It is assumed that members of the organization need continuous direction and supervision if they are to coordinate their activities. People in the managerial positions are expected to exercise unilateral control over those lower in the hierarchy (Argyris, 1970).
2. *Centralization of Decisions-making Authority and Power.* People in the managerial positions are responsible for the well-being of the organization and are expected to control members by making and implementing the major decisions. They are given control over valued resources; that is, they are given power, by which they can reward and punish members so that their decisions are implemented (Katz & Kahn, 1966).
3. *Rational-task Orientation.* Members are expected to accomplish their assigned duties. Neither feelings, personal relationships, nor individual characteristics are expected to interfere with their role performance (Weber, 1947).

These three characteristics are highly related. The control orientation implies that decision-making authority and power, the instruments with which control is exercised, should be centralized; members must comply with directives. The organization typically structures the members' environment so that compliance gains tangible benefits (Weber, 1947). As is argued below, the control orientation and centralization of decision making and power often results in negative feelings. As the organization may be ill equipped to cope with the open expression of hostility, the rational-task orientation may be functional for the organization, at least in the short run.

Control Orientation

Waller (1932) portrayed schools as preoccupied with the control of students. More recent observers have also concluded that educators are intent on maintaining order and discipline (e.g., Willower & Jones, 1967). Indeed, the control of students is often equated with teaching competence (Gordon, 1957), and popular symbols of schools (e.g., the paddle, rules, teacher's furrowed brow) also suggest this preoccupation. Educational research has focused on educators' beliefs about the control of students and their directive behavior toward students.

Teacher Directiveness

Many observation studies have tried to document the impact that directive and controlling teachers have on classroom social processes and learning. Anderson and his associates (e.g., Anderson, 1939; Anderson & Brewer, 1945) divided teacher behavior into dominative (controlling) and integrative (collaborative) categories. Drawing upon this distinction, Flanders (1959) classified teacher communication acts as either direct or indirect influence attempts. Direct influence attempts (e.g., lectures, commands) are believed to restrict freedom of action; indirect influence attempts (e.g., accepts feelings, asks questions) increase freedom of action. Withall's (1949) Climate Index categorizes teachers' verbal behavior into statements that support the teacher (teacher-centered) and those that support the learners (student-centered).

Research suggests that teachers who are directive (dominant and teacher-centered) have students who are dependent, fail to achieve, and dislike school compared to students whose teachers are indirective (see reviews by Dunkin & Biddle, 1974; Rosenshine & Furst, 1973). Several problems with the research limit the confidence that this generalization warrants (see Dunkin & Biddle, 1974).

Control Idealogy

Research on educators' control beliefs (Willower, 1975) provides additional evidence that a control orientation may have destructive effects on the organizational life of schools. Control-minded, custodial teachers have been found to perceive students as irresponsible and lacking self-discipline. To compensate for these deficiencies, the teachers believe that schools must emphasize their authority by making and enforcing decisions. Humanistic teachers, on the other hand, perceive students as capable of self-direction and as committed to learning. They believe that schools should be more communally arranged with power and decision-making responsibility widely shared among administrators, teachers, and students. Willower has also noted that educators' control ideology is related to their personality dispositions. Humanistic teachers are more open-minded, creative, self-actualizing, and professionally oriented; they have a greater sense of control over their personal lives than do custodial teachers.

Research on control beliefs suggests that the control orientation of schools is so dominant that its acceptance may be a major outcome of professional socialization. Teachers have been found to be more custodial in centrally controlled schools than in schools where teachers influence school decisions (Jones, 1969). Teachers appear to become more custodial with experience, perhaps because they find adopting custodial attitudes a prerequisite for acceptance by other educators (Hoy, 1968, 1969). Beginning teachers may feel obligated to act in a controlling way and develop attitudes to justify their actions (Tjosvold & Kastelic, 1976), or they may discover that students are unprepared and unwilling to make and implement classroom decisions (Rhea, 1968; Tjosvold & Santamaria, 1977).

Educators' control beliefs may also affect their relationship with and actions toward students. Custodial teachers have been found to teach in a directive way (Rexford, Willower, & Lynch, 1972); as research just reviewed suggests, this may impede student achievement and induce a negative classroom climate. Consistent with this reasoning, faculty custodial beliefs have been found to be positively related to student absenteeism, dislike of school, and alienation (Pritchett & Willower, 1975; Rafalides & Hoy, 1971). Research on the control ideology of educators explores important aspects of the organizational life of schools and suggests that norms and values that sanction the unilateral control of students may induce teachers to adopt custodial attitudes and to act in a directive way. These controlling attitudes and actions may in turn induce students to dislike school and to withdraw from full involvement.

Controlling Influence Patterns

The control orientation of school implies that members typically attempt to influence others by trying to control them. Social-psychological research suggests that these attempts can induce resistance to compliance and may weaken the relationship between the influencer and the target of the influence so that future influence attempts are less successful and future exchanges, less rewarding. Reactance theory (Brehm, 1966) and personal causation theory (de Charms, 1968) suggest that people want to be the cause or the origin of their own behavior and that they resent attempts by others to control them. Consistent with these ideas, research on influence strategies indicates that people resist controlling influence attempts. Individuals, for example, have been found to defy threats, and to counterthreaten if possible, perhaps because they experience the threats as restricting their free choice (Deutsch, 1973; Heilman & Garner, 1975). Individuals have refused to comply with an influence attempt, though resistance was costly, when they believed the influencer intended to control them (Tjosvold, 1978).

Kipnis (1972, 1974, 1976) has explored the effects of controlling influence attempts on the *influencer*. Individuals who used their superior power to influence a subordinate were found to devalue the subordinate's performance and to maintain social distance, possibly as a result of their perceived control of the subordinate. Individuals who use less controlling influence methods may have more positive perceptions of the target and develop more open relationships. In summary, research has found that controlling influence attempts induce (a) resistance, (b) negative attitudes toward the influencer and toward the influenced, and (c) the perception of a competitive relationship. Controlling influence patterns may contribute significantly to organizational ineffectiveness.

Centralization of Decision making and Power

Individuals given the responsibility for coordinating the actions of other members of the organization need to be able to make decisions that are obeyed and also need the power to reward compliance and to punish noncompliance. Because little educational research has explored the possible effects of this centralization, a review of relevant social-psychological research is appropriate.

The studies of Lewin and his colleagues (Lewin, Lippitt, & White, 1939; White & Lippitt, 1960) on leadership styles were early experimental attempts to ascertain the impact of centralization of decision making and power on groups of children. "Autocratic" leaders were instructed to assert their authority by determining the group's activities and to use their power by praising and criticizing the group members. "Democratic" leaders were to attempt to help group members decide their activities for themselves; these leaders were to avoid praising and criticizing the members. "Laissez-faire" leaders were to do little to help the group members make decisions or influence each other.

Autocratically led groups were characterized by interpersonal conflict, scapegoating, and productivity. Democratically led group members were more group minded and less productive, though they did work longer without supervision. Members in the laissez-faire groups were unproductive and appeared to be frustrated. Methodological problems limit the usefulness of these results, for it is possible that the leadership styles may have been confounded with the expression of affect. McCandless (1961), who was one of the leaders in the experiment, has argued that leaders, because of their ideological commitment, may have been warm in the democratic, cold in the autocratic, and detached in the laissez-faire conditions.

The centralization of decision making and power can also be examined by analyzing its major components. This section treats research relevant to the issues of (a) methods of increasing control capabilities, (b) unequal relationships, and (c) effects of dependency on learning.

Strengthening Control Capabilities

Educators under pressure to control students and other subordinates may, to gain confidence, attempt to enhance their decision-making authority and relative power; but the methods of enhancing authority and increasing power have negative effects on the social processes and on the learning of the members of the organization.

Enhancing Decision-making Authority. In a centrally controlled organization, a status authority hierarchy is established based on a sequence of subordinate positions (Sampson, 1963; Johnson & Allen, 1972). Administrators have more status than teachers, for example, because of their position in the school authority hierarchy. Higher status is a basis for influence because the norms and roles of the organization typically indicate that members ought to obey legitimate orders (Michener & Burt, 1974).

Role theory (e.g., Sarbin & Allen, 1968) suggests how high-status people may strengthen their ability to control people in lower positions. Teachers, for example, may clarify to students that obedience to orders is an important role expectation. Students should understand that the role of the teacher includes directing and controlling and that people in their role are expected to obey. The teacher can strengthen the impact of these role expectations by enlisting other students, teachers, administrators, and parents to inform the students that they, too, expect the students to comply with the teacher's decision. This consensual role expectation indicates to the students how they can obtain the approval of others. In addition, the teacher can convince the students that their obedience is justified because he or she has the competence to make effective decisions (Michener & Burt, 1974).

Increasing Power. Power can be defined as the capacity to affect another's rewards and costs (Thibaut & Kelley, 1959) or, in field theory terms, as the control of valued resources (Kipnis, 1976). A teacher has power with respect to a student when the student perceives that the teacher controls the distribution of resources that the student values. Social power, then, depends on a need–resource correspondence (Strong & Matross, 1973). The power of the teacher is determined by the extent to which the student values her or his resources. This value depends in turn, upon the incentive the student has for the goal which is affected by the teacher's resources and upon the availability of alternative sources of the teacher's resources.

Power is one basis for influencing other people. Positively valued resources (e.g., high grades, esteem) can be promised or given conditionally upon the basis of desired performance. Negatively valued resources (e.g., detention, disapproval) can be threatened or administered as a consequence of undesired behavior. The person subjected to power is then likely to do as requested in order to be rewarded or to avoid punishment.

Teachers have more power over students than students have over teachers; likewise, administrators have more power over teachers than they have over administrators. The superior power of administrators and teachers derives directly from their position in the organization rather than from their personal characteristics, though these too can contribute. While students have lesser power, they are seldom powerless, for they have resources (e.g., acceptance) that can facilitate and frustrate the goals of educators.

Although few empirical studies have considered the ways of increasing relative power, several theorists have suggested methods for developing such power (e.g., Strong & Matross, 1973; Michener & Suchner, 1972). For example, in the teacher-student relationship, teachers can make their resources known and valued. Teachers can publicize their resources and in order to persuade students of their need for these resources, the teachers can withdraw them for a short time. Persuading students that they have few alternative sources can also increase the relative power of the teacher. Similar methods can be used by administrators who want to increase their power over teachers.

Educators who want to increase their relative power can also try to decrease their dependence. They might, for example: (a) belittle others' resources, (b) maintain that they are not needed, (c) demonstrate alternative sources, and (d) convince these people that they can forgo their resources when they become costly.

Strengthening the decision-making authority and power of educators implies their own enhancement—they are the ones who have the competence to make important decisions and control the valuable resources—and the belittlement both of other educators and also of the students, who possess few valuable resources, are inexperienced, and are too narrow minded for decision making. In centrally controlled schools, teachers may conclude that they are not competent to make important school decisions and that they control few valuable resources.

Unequal Relationships

The unequal relationships that are characteristic of a centrally controlled organization may "corrupt" relationships among educators and students. Applied psychologists have argued that unequal power and status undermine relationships. Many psychotherapists, for example, believe that they can be more successful when they develop a relationship immune from the client and therapist roles; these unequal power and status roles may make mutually open, growth-producing liaisons difficult (Laing, 1967; Rogers, 1951).

Research on unequal status relationships suggests that low-status people are likely to perceive higher status people as capable because they are believed to have the competence needed to hold high-status positions (French, 1963). The perceived competence of the high-status person may engender identification by the low-status person (Kohlberg, 1969). This identification can take the form of (a) attraction and perceived similarity (Mulder, 1960), (b) the magical belief that one is the high-status person (Lippitt, Polansky, & Rosen, 1952; Polansky, Lippett, & Redl, 1950), (c) frequent and supportive communication with the high-status person (Kelley, 1951; Thibaut, 1950), and (d) imitation of the behavior of the high-status person (Bandura, 1969).

High-status people, on the other hand, may believe that the low-status person is incompetent and, therefore, may have little incentive to identify with her or him. They may be unwilling to convey their own confusions and feelings of incompetence but be very willing to criticize the shortcomings of the low-status people (Kelley, 1951). High-status people also appear to want low-status people to agree with their positions on issues relevant to their high status (Jones, 1964). They may be self-protective when they fear that maintaining their superior position is threatened and respond by perceiving low-status people as incompetent and withholding approval as a way of minimizing their threat (Kelley, 1951; Zander, Cohen, & Stotland, 1957).

Research on unequal power relationships suggests that people with low power are apt to feel uncertainty about their future goal facilitation and frustration because these both depend heavily on the unpredictable behavior of the high-power person (Cohen, 1959). These feelings of uncertainty and anxiety provoke several reactions: (a) increased vigilance and attempts to understand and predict the high-power person's behavior (Johnson & Ewens, 1971; Tjosvold & Okun, 1976), (b) distorted perceptions of the positive intent of the high-power person toward the low-power person (Pepitone, 1950; Thibaut & Riecken, 1955), (c) attraction mixed with fear toward the high-power person (Hurwitz, Zander, & Hymovitch, 1968), (d) stifling of criticism of the high-power person (Cohen, 1958), (e) unwillingness to clarify one's position to the high-power individual (Alkire, Collum, Kaswin, & Love, 1968), and (f) ingratiation, conformity, flattery, and effacing self-presentation to induce the high-power person to like and to reward the low-power person (Jones, 1964, Tjosvold, in press). In conflict situations, low-power people may expect exploitation because, lacking retalitory capabilities, they believe that they are vulnerable (Solomon, 1960; Tedeschi, Lindskold, Horai, & Gahagan, 1969).

High-power people may feel less threatened and less uncertain, though they appear to be concerned with maintaining superior power. They may be defensive and self-protective, especially if they fear that they may be removed from their position (Cohen, 1958). They may underestimate the low-power person's positive intent because they believe the low-power person helps only because of their superior power (Thibaut & Riecken, 1955). They may devalue the low-power person as dependent and controlled by external forces, such as high-power people (Kipnis, 1972). High-power people have been found to be inattentive to the communications of the low-power person and unresponsive to cooperative gestures. They attempt to protect their superior power by rejecting demands for change (Deutsch, 1973; Tedeschi, Lindskold, Horai, & Gahagan, 1973; Tjosvold, 1974; 1977a, 1977b, 1977c; Tjosvold & Okun, 1976).

Effects of Dependency

Social-psychological research suggests that the sense of competence and self-control of both educators and students may be undermined by their placement in a low-status and low-power position in school. Self-esteem, which is related to academic performance as well as to psychological well-being, indicates the extent to which a person believes that she or he is competent, worthwhile, and successful (Coopersmith, 1967, Johnson, 1970). The findings of social-psychological research suggest that low-status and low-power positions may reduce self-esteem.

The symbolic interactionist approach to self-esteem emphasizes that people evaluate themselves as they perceive they are evaluated (Mead, 1934). Several studies suggest that (a) low-status and low-power positions are believed to require modest competencies and that negative characteristics are attributed to the holders of these positions and (b) negative evaluations are communicated to them (Berger, Cohen, & Zelditch, 1972; French, 1963; Zander & Cohen, 1955). The negative feedback and snubbing are likely to lower self-esteem. On the other hand, positive feedback and deferential behavior are likely to increase the self-esteem of high-power and high-status people. Prolonged membership in either a high-power and high-status position or a low-power and low-status position has been found to affect self-esteem (Heiss & Owens, 1972; Maykovich, 1972; Yancy, Rigsby, & McCarthy, 1972).

Organizational members with low power and low status are also likely to lose self-esteem because they have few opportunities for psychological success and many for failure. According to Argyris (1970), psychological success experiences are the bases for concluding that one is a capable person because one has behaved competently. The opportunities for psychological success increase (and for failure, decrease) as (a) people are able to define their own goals, (b) the goals are relevant to their central needs, (c) the activities involve their important abilities, and (d) the goals represent a challenging level of aspiration. People in dependent positions generally have more opportunities for psychological failure than for success (Argyris, 1970). Those in low-status and low-power positions then, are apt to experience psychological failure that lowers self-esteem.

To occupy a dependent position may also induce alienation in the form of powerlessness. Seeman (1959) defined *powerlessness* as the expectancy that one cannot by one's actions obtain desired outcomes or achieve goals. Because the goal attainment or frustration of low-status and low-power people depends in large part on the wishes of high-power people, it is probable that they develop (and realistically so) general expectancies that their own lives are beyond self-control (Rotter,

1966; DeCharms, 1976). Low-status and low-power minority groups have been found to possess feelings of powerlessness (Baltzell, 1964; Clark, 1965).

The sense of powerlessness is apt to significaltly affect behavior. People who believe that they are powerless have been found to be less resistant to influence attempts, to place less value on skill than on luck, to lack commitment to social-change movements, to fail to seek and to obtain useful information about their situation, and to influence other people ineffectively (Lefcourt, 1966; Rotter, 1966; Seeman, 1971). Coleman et al. (1966) argued that feeling powerless contributes greatly to the academic failure of students. Students and educators whose outcomes are controlled by others and whose decisions are made by others may not develop the skills of being independent, self-directing people.

The Effects of Centralization on Schools

The centralization of decision-making authority and power may seriously impair organizational processes and the learning and growth of students. Communication with people of unequal status and power may be impoverished and distorted. People in dependent positions may be unwilling to express their ideas and feelings directly and may even mislead and deceive their superiors. These interruptions in the flow of valid information and creative ideas can deteriorate organizational capabilities for problem solving, decision making, and conflict resolution (Argyris, 1970; Bennis, 1969). Without valid information, problems are not easily recognized and examined; nor are the requirements and consequences of decisions accurately estimated; nor are the incidence and underlying causes of conflicts identified. Moreover, fewer ideas are discussed to help solve problems, improve decision making, and manage and resolve conflicts. As a result, the effectiveness of the school and the classroom is reduced.

These organizational processes also directly affect the learning of students and other organizational members. To the extent that centralization inhibits open conflict resolution and problem solving, students do not learn the skills and values associated with effective problem solving and conflict resolution; instead, they learn to suppress their dissatisfaction, demands for change, and ideas for change. Whereas learning compliance to authority is probably useful, for it is sometimes required in the adult world of work and citizenship, learning to obey as the primary or only legitimate response to authority is unlikely to be a valuable skill. Strong reliance on authority may also promote antidemocratic intolerance for minority groups and for freedom of expression (Adorno, Frenkel-Brunswik, Levinson, & Sanford, 1950). The emphasis on the decision making and on the power of educators to control is unlikely to help students learn the skills and values (e.g., the legitimacy of dissent) necessary for democratic citizenship. In addition, a centrally controlled school provides few opportunities for students to articulate their moral ideas, to understand the moral reasoning of classmates, or to act consistently with their moral ideas (Kohlberg, 1975; Tjosvold & Johnson, 1977). Schools, then, may fail to stimulate student moral development and, ultimately, fail to facilitate student commitment to democracy, equality, and freedom (Kohlberg & Turiel, 1971).

Contrary to some popular beliefs, the exercise of control over students is unlikely to teach discipline or self-control. As suggested by Rogers (1951) and de Charms (1968, 1976), in order for students to exercise self-control, they need to be aware of their own needs and values; they must be able to determine alternatives, set goals, and be willing to take the necessary risks to reach these goals. Rather than have their decisions made for them, students need opportunities and training to develop these capabilities.

Students may also learn how to act in a dependent position. Many appear to resign themselves to their dependency and lack of control over major aspects of their school lives. Rhea (1968) suggested that students often accept their dependency by attributing to educators the competence to make wise decisions. Students also know that accepting their dependent position spares them the difficult task of making decisions and, indeed, of developing decision-making capabilities. Though students accept dependency, they may still attempt to increase the outcomes they receive from educators by trying to compile a record of good grades that they believe will be useful (Rhea, 1968). Bidwell (1965) has argued that students often seek to manipulate teachers' approval of them into special favors, especially high grades. Students have been found to believe that bluff and charm are more useful than knowledge in getting good grades (Rhea, 1968).

A second, complementary response is for students to develop their own subcultures (Willower, 1965). These can help students deny that the praise, grades, and knowledge of educators are important; in turn, success in athletics, clothes, popularity among peers, and so forth are overvalued (Coleman, 1961). These subcultures may obstruct the goals of schooling (Boocock, 1972; Bidwell, 1965; Coleman, 1961). Students may also respond to their dependent position by psychologically withdrawing from schools (Rafalides & Hoy, 1971). A minority of students have attempted to increase their influence over their school lives by presenting demands and protesting restrictions (Chesler & Lohman, 1971).

Students may respond to their dependent position with active confrontation, the development of subcultures, acceptance, withdrawal, or some combination of these; they may respond by alternating among these possibilities. Indeed, they may expend considerable energy in trying to resolve conflicts over how they should react to their dependent position. Research is needed to clarify the conditions that affect the response to dependent positions in centrally controlled schools and the consequences of these responses on school life and learning.

Rational-task Orientation

In a centrally controlled organization, members are expected to relate to each other according to established rules rather than to individual styles or personalities. Affective relationships among educators and students inevitably develop and influence school life. These relationships can interfere with decision making and implementing in centrally controlled schools. Teachers may become so dependent on the students for emotional support that they do not exercise their authority legitimately. Gordon (1957) argued that teachers exchange higher grades and other preferential treatment for emotional support. The authority of teachers and the value of grades to promote and symbolize academic excellence are thus diminished.

Personal, emotional relationships also develop among teachers and among students. Waller (1932) argued that teachers and students form two cohesive "fighting" groups. Teachers represent the wider culture and demand academic achievement; students seek more immediate rewards, such as satisfying relationships with their peers. These opposing interests and values may result in what Waller characterized as a "cold war."

Relationships among teachers are likely to affect their effectiveness and their relationships with students and community members (McPherson, 1972; Schmuck, 1971). Noting that little research has been done on teacher groups, Bidwell (1965) speculated that they develop cohesive, cooperative relationships because of the similarity of position and backgrounds. Case studies (e.g., McPherson, 1972) suggest, however, that teachers often develop competitive, minimally supportive groups. The inattention of researchers to the impact of teacher collegial groups on schools is paralleled by the inattention of educational practitioners to the development of groups that promote effective schooling.

Argyris (1964, 1970) has outlined the consequences on the effectiveness of an organization of being made up of members who value cognitive rationality and task accomplishment while denying the rationality and even the existence of their feelings and, relatedly, their interpersonal concerns. According to Argyris, people in such rational-task environments are under pressure to hide their feelings and to suppress concerns about their relationships. Because interpersonal difficulties are seldom openly considered and resolved, members tend to be confused and develop feelings of interpersonal failure. They tend to disown their feelings and become intolerant of the feelings of associates. Problem-solving and decision-making discussions tend to focus on ideas and issues that evoke little emotionality and bar the unleashing of suppressed feelings. Members then become less open to experimental ideas and risk taking. In this climate, emphasis is on appeasing those who have power. Conformity, dependence, and ineffective information and idea generation undermine problem-solving and decision-making capabilities.

Research by Gordon (1957) and Coleman (1961) suggests that the values and life-styles of student groups may conflict with adult expectations. The pressures these groups place on gaining extracurricular success appear to divert students away from academic goals. Educators should seek to develop affective relationships that promote the objectives of schools; attempts to do this are discussed below.

The research reviewed does not support the present dominant use of centrally controlled organizations for schools. They may contribute to organizational ineffectiveness of schools and impede the learning and growth of students. I now turn to collaborative organization as a feasible alternative to the centrally controlled way of organizing.

COLLABORATIVE ORGANIZATIONS

In this section, the major characteristics of collaborative organizations are identified and research that suggests their consequences on school life is reviewed. This model of collaborative organization is similar to alternative organizations proposed by several researchers (e.g., Bennis, 1969; Johnson, 1970; Katz & Kahn, 1966; McGregor, 1960). The major characteristics of collaborative organizations can be summarized as:

1. *Collaborative Orientation.* Members of organizations are expected to recognize that they must use their resources and work together to accomplish the goals of the organization. Members are expected to respect individual abilities and self-determination. A collaborative orientation also implies shared decision making.
2. *Shared Decision-making Authority and Power.* All members are responsible for the well-being of the organization. They or their representatives determine poli-

cies and allocate resources. Members realize that all the people in the organization have valuable resources (power) that can contribute to the effectiveness of the organization.
3. *Emotional-Interpersonal and Rational-task Orientation.* Members are expected to attain the goals of the organization and to complete their tasks. In addition, they must realize that the development and strengthening of interpersonal relationships can help the organization attain these goals.

Examples of Collaborative Organizations

What would a collaborative classroom or school look like in concrete terms? The following examples suggest the variety of ways in which this type of organizational structure can be implemented. Merriam and Guerney (1973) trained elementary teachers in communication and group decision-making skills to help them conduct effective classroom decision-making discussions. The teachers scheduled at least two 30–45-minute sessions a week in which the students were encouraged to discuss planning and implementing issues in class organization during lunch and recess, in room excuses, and in interpersonal problems. One classroom attempted to find a fair and effective way of excusing students to use the bathroom; another class sought to resolve the conflict resulting from the attempt of a student to kiss unresponsive classmates. In these legislative meetings, all students were encouraged to express their own viewpoints and to make decisions by consensus or by majority vote. The teachers considered the class discussions productive and valuable. Several other positive effects on students and classroom life also seemed to occur. For example, students appeared to be ready to form groups to discuss and resolve problems.

Under the direction of Kohlberg and his associates, a "just community" school was recently opened (Kohlberg, 1975). As suggested by Kohlberg's theory, group discussions and controversies facilitate moral development. In the first weeks, 60 students and six teachers decided governing processes. After rules were established, a student discipline committee began to oversee their enforcement. The issues this legislature discusses are limited to matters of justice because Kohlberg maintains that staff, courses, and schedules involve lengthy discussions that bore students. Although only impressionistic data are available, educators and students at their school appear to have developed a sense of community, high morale, and the ability to resolve their conflicts openly and fairly. Students seem to act responsibly and to be committed to following rules and to pursuing important goals. Although they come from a variety of backgrounds, they appear to cooperate with each other and avoid cliques. In addition to the effect on moral development, this collaborative organization appears to improve organizational processes of schools and facilitate other educational objectives.

Collaborative Orientation

Research based on observation of teachers' controlling behavior in the classroom (Dunkin & Biddle, 1974) and on measurement of the control ideology of educators (Willower, 1975) suggests collaboration as an effective alternative to a control orientation. Collaborative teachers attempt to influence students indirectly so that freedom of action and perceived alternatives are increased. Collaborative teachers have been found to have students who take initiative and achieve. Educators who do not have strong beliefs that students need to be controlled argue that they should share in the decision making and power in schools. Educators with these collaborative beliefs have students who are involved in school.

Social-psychological research suggests that collaborative influence can induce acceptance of the influence attempt and strengthen the relationship between the influencer and the influenced. People have been found to comply when the influencer indicated a desire to collaborate with them, rather than to control them (Tjosvold, 1978). These targets of the collaborative influence also felt accepted by the influencer and believed their relationship was cooperative. A collaborative orientation is also demonstrated in the way decisions are made and power is distributed.

Shared Decision-making Authority and Power

A number of social psychologists have argued that giving groups within organizations the autonomy to make some important decisions and to regulate their internal affairs can make organizations more effective (e.g., Bennis, 1969; Schein, 1969). From this perspective, decision making should be shared among members of the organization who have relevant information and must implement the decisions and those in administrative positions. Sharing decision-making authority in schools implies that educators and students, along with the principal, would make decisions that affect the whole school, whereas the students and teacher would make many decisions that are related to classroom life.

Considerable research supports the procedure of sharing decision-making authority among groups within an organization (see reviews by Bucklow, 1966; Campbell, Dunnette, Lawler, & Weick, 1970; Lowin, 1968). Under most conditions, groups have been found to solve problems and to make decisions more effectively than individuals (Watson & Johnson, 1972). Because group members together have more useful information and more varied perspectives, they recognize and consider more alternatives than do individuals. In addition, groups that make their own decisions are likely to be committed to their implementation. Members are likely to understand the decision and its rationale and to be aware of how they are to act in order to implement the decision. They are also likely to believe that, because other group members are committed to the decision, they must contribute to implementing the decision if they are to gain the esteem of others.

Members of an organization who participate in decision making are also apt to feel personally enhanced. They may gain greater esteem from others; their participation in an effective decision-making and implementing group can help them feel they are contributing to the welfare of the organization (French, 1963). They are also likely to experience psychological success; involvement in the challenging tasks of making decisions and solving problems can help them develop their social and intellectual capabilities (Argyris, 1970). The experience of making decisions may contribute to their feelings that they can shape their own lives (Rotter, 1966; deCharms, 1976). The cooperative interaction of group decision making should strengthen the group as a source of support for its members (Deutsch, 1949; Johnson & Johnson, 1974).

Given the advantages of group decision making described above and the increase in members feelings of accomplishment and competence, organizations that encourage their members to participate in decision making should be more effective. In a test of this idea, Coch and French (1948) found that small groups of employees who evaluated and redesigned their jobs, when compared to employees who did not participate in these changes, were found to be both more productive and—as suggested by the indexes of lower absenteeism and turnover—more fulfilled in their work. Similar research also suggests that student and teacher participation in making decisions can help schools reach their primary goal of promoting student learning as well as their maintenance goal of strengthening themselves internally.

Decision-making groups must also control some of the resources of the organization in order to help them implement decisions (Katz & Kahn, 1966). Power also involves the valued personal resources of individual members. Members working and making decisions together may often recognize that their personal resources are valuable to the group. They are also likely to help other members develop and use their resources to help in the accomplishment of goals (Deutsch, 1949; Johnson & Johnson, 1974).

Both the distribution of the control of organizational power among groups and the recognition of individual resources of group members imply that relationships in collaborative organizations may not be so unequal in power. Research reviewed earlier suggests that, as relationships approach equality of power, they are likely to be characterized by effective communication, decision making, problem solving, and conflict resolution. In addition, the relationships in collaborative organizations may be largely cooperative. As the group members work toward common goals, they are more likely to believe that members are using their resources cooperatively to achieve success (Johnson & Johnson, 1974). Under these conditions, the uncertainty, suspicion, and defensiveness of many unequal relationships may be moderated. People in highly cooperative, even though unequally powerful, relationships may communicate openly, develop trust, and resolve conflicts effectively (Deutsch, 1973).

Emotional-Interpersonal Orientation

A collaborative organization encourages members to examine interpersonal concerns and openly to express their feelings. Strengthening interpersonal relationships is necessary to make the groups within the collaborative organization effective. Moreover, as research already reviewed suggests, relationships are likely to be largely cooperative and their feelings positive. Discussing interpersonal issues and expressing feelings is likely to be seen as nonthreatening and productive when done within this supportive context.

In collaborative organizations, groups are explicitly established and given responsibility to accomplish tasks that contribute to the organization. For example, teachers may be charged as a group with helping each other develop and use more effective classroom practices. Schmuck (1971) found that teachers who fashioned a cohesive, cooperative peer group and were consulted about their classroom behavior were able to improve the social processes in their classrooms. As noted by Coleman (1972) and Johnson and Johnson (1974), the power of the relationships among students is now greatly underutilized in schools. Placing students in groups and structuring cooperative relationships can increase group support and encouragement for learning and affective development (Johnson & Johnson, 1974). The explicit structuring of cooperative groups is a largely untapped source of organizational effectiveness for schools.

ATTITUDES AND SKILLS

To make either the centrally controlled or the collaborative organization work effectively, the members must have appropriate attitudes and use appropriate skills. A number of attitudes and skills are useful for both types of organizations. All members of a school, for example, should value learning and, in particular, the education of the young. Without such commitment, the activities of schools can become ritualistic. Educators and students should perceive that all members, though they have different responsibilities, are working to accomplish the goal of the school. Members must also realize that they need to contribute energy and resources to the organization in return for the benefits it provides. Yet centrally controlled and collaborative organizations appear to be based on some opposing attitudes and to require different skills.

The appropriate attitudes and skills for centrally controlled organizations appear to be:

1. Recognition that each member is responsible for completing assigned tasks and for following directions of those with authority
2. Compliance skills of following directions and giving valid information to the decision makers
3. Belief that people with greater authority have the knowledge to make effective decisions
4. Recognition that feelings and personalities should not interfere with task accomplishment and obligations

The appropriate attitudes and skills for collaborative organizations appear to be:

1. Recognition that all members are responsible for the well-being of the organization and for those functions over which their groups have been given specific authority
2. Interpersonal and group skills of developing trust, resolving conflicts, making decisions, and solving problems
3. Belief that members with expertise and the capacity to implement should make decisions
4. Recognition that personal involvement with other members is legitimate and helpful for accomplishing goals

Because of their experience, students can be expected to have the skills and attitudes associated with centrally controlled organizations; they may lack those appropriate for collaborative schools (Argyris, 1974; Watson & Johnson, 1972). For example, many students may resist accepting greater decision-making responsibilities partly because they do not believe they can make effective decisions (Rhea, 1968). A recent study (Tjosvold & Santamaria, in press) reveals that educators can modify these attitudes. Students who cooperated with each other and whose teacher credibly supported their competence to make decisions were found to have more favorable attitudes toward making classroom decisions. Students may also be reluctant to take more decision-making responsibility because they fear they lack the ability (Rhea, 1968). Several skill-development programs are available to help students and educators develop group skills (e.g., Johnson & Johnson, 1975) and self-directing skills (deCharms, 1976). In addition, students and educators can learn the appropriate attitudes and skills for collaborative schools through experience.

WHEN TO USE COLLABORATION
AND WHEN TO USE CENTRAL CONTROL

The method of organization affects the quality of life in schools and the extent to which schools attain their objective of helping students become competent young adults. The research reviewed in this chapter suggests that centrally controlled schools and classrooms have been too extensively depended on to coordinate the activities of educators and students. Collaboratively organized schools and classrooms generally facilitate school effectiveness and student learning, but centrally controlled schools and classrooms can actually obstruct the attainment of educational objectives.

Although collaboration is a viable alternative, a centrally controlled organization can be more useful under certain conditions. I do not suggest that all school or classroom decisions be made collaboratively. Ideally, both organizations would be used. The policies decided through collaboration would be limited; other decisions would be made unilaterally by teachers or administrators. Educators and students should understand whether decisions are going to be made collaboratively or unilaterally. They should also know their rights and obligations in each organization.

The following guidelines can be used to decide whether to use a collaborative or a centrally controlled organization.

1. *Internal Commitment to the Decision.* Decisions to which members of the organization must be internally committed should be made by collaborative procedures. Eduators who do not want to be obligated to close supervision, but who want their students to be more internally committed to classroom rules and assignments, may find collaboration useful. Principals, for example, who want their teachers to try to make faculty reorganization effective may want the teachers to participate in the reorganization process. Decisions (e.g., student locker assignment) in which it is unimportant whether people are internally committed can be made in a centrally controlled manner.
2. *Significance of the Decision.* For divisive issues, collaborative decision making is generally preferred. If decisions on such issues are made unilaterally, opponents are apt to feel resentful and estranged from the decision makers and uncommitted to implementing the decision, and they may even try to sabotage the decision by withdrawing their support from its implementation. In collaborative decision making, people are more likely to feel that their views have been examined, to believe that others are committed, and to be more aware of the advantages of the decision.
3. *Participants' Skills and Attitudes.* If students and educators do not have appropriate attitudes and skills, collaborative decision making can be inefficient and can exacerbate internal divisions. Without experience, however, it is hardly surprising that the people do not have these attitudes and skills. Educators and students should be given opportunities to develop skills and attitudes through experience as well as through training programs.
4. *Energy.* Collaborative decision making usually takes more energy and time than does centrally controlled decision making. Communicating the decisions and

gaining commitment to them often takes less energy, however, than in centrally controlled schools. In emergencies like fire drills or other situations in which there is little time to make decisions, centrally controlled organizations are preferred.

CONCLUSION

Characteristics of centrally controlled and collaborative organizations have been identified; their consequences on the organizational processes of school and on the learning of students have been outlined; and the appropriate attitudes and skills of the participants and the conditions under which each organization may be effective have been proposed. The research reviewed challenges the reliance of most schools and classrooms on the centrally controlled ways of organizing. Many educators want students to learn effective and alternative ways of coordinating their activities. Changing values of students, especially the increasing number of alienated children, appear to limit further the usefulness of centrally controlled organizations.

Social-psychological research has been extensively relied on to clarify organizational issues of schools. The usefulness of educational research is limited because of the tendency to rely on correlational methods and questionnaire data. In addition to methodological problems, these empirical methods are tied closely to present educational practice. At best, these research methods can isolate the most effective practice among those presently employed. There are valuable practices, however, that are now very much underutilized. Because schools tend to be homogeneously organized (Corwin, 1962), nonexperimental studies are unlikely to identify useful alternative organizations.

Perhaps more important than its methodological shortcomings, educational research has largely ignored important concepts of social psychology and organizational behavior. Similarly, educational practitioners appear to ignore these concepts and have tended to simplify the issues of organization to one of "discipline." Educational researchers and practitioners should use a range of organizational concepts to analyze classrooms and schools and as bases for effective intervention. Independent variables such as decision-making patterns and the distribution of power, and dependent variables such as capabilities for communication, conflict resolution, and problem solving should be used to guide research and practice.

The emphasis in this chapter has been on the implications of research for educational practice rather than on critically reviewing the available research. Given the shortcomings of this research, however, future research is needed to challenge and modify the propositions advanced here. Research is needed to investigate the relevance of the insights and findings from social-psychological research. Researchers may find that some special conditions of schools modify the usefulness of collaborative organizational procedures. For example, the short time perspective of elementary school children may restrict the benefits of giving them decision-making authority. Researchers can also develop methods of implementing collaborative organizations.

I hope that the ideas presented here will encourage experimenting with the organization of schools, both by researchers and by practitioners. A control orientation, centralization of decision making and power, and a rational-task orientation are *not* the only feasible and effective ways of organizing schools. Collaboration between researchers and practitioners may be able to devise and implement organizational procedures that can coordinate and enhance the energies of students, teachers, and administrators by helping them make decisions, solve problems, and resolve conflicts.

REFERENCES

Adorno, T. W., Frenkel-Brunswik, E., Levinson, D. J., & Sanford, R. N. *The authoritarian personality.* New York: Harper, 1950.

Alkire, A. A., Collum, M. E., Kaswin, J., & Love, L. R. Information exchange and accuracy of verbal communication under social power conditions. *Journal of Personality and Social Psychology,* 1968, 9, 301–308.

Anderson, H. H. Domination and integration in the social behavior of kindergarten children in an experimental play situation. *Genetic Psychology Monographs,* 1939, 21, 357–385.

Anderson, H. H., & Brewer, H. M. Studies of teachers' classroom personalities. I. Dominative and socially integrative behavior of kindergarten teachers. *Applied Psychological Monographs,* 1945.

Argyris, C. *Integrating the individual and the organization.* New York: Wiley, 1964.

Argyris, C. *Intervention theory and method.* Reading, Mass.: Addison-Wesley, 1970.

Argyris, C. Alternative schools: A behavioral analysis. *Teachers College Record,* 1974, 75, 429–452.

Baltzell, E. D. *The Protestant establishment: Aristocracy and caste in America* New York: Random House, 1964.

Bandura, A. Social learning theory of identificatory processes. In D. A. Goslin (Ed.), *Handbook of socialization theory and research.* Chicago: Rand McNally 1969.

Bennis, W. G. *Organization development: Its nature, origins, and prospects.* Reading, Mass.: Addison-Wesley, 1969.

Berger, J., Cohen, B. P., & Zelditch, M., Jr. Status characteristics and social interaction. *American Sociological Review,* 1972, 37, 241–255.

Bidwell, C. E. The school as a formal organization. In J. G. March (Ed.), *Handbook of organizations.* Chicago: Rand McNally, 1965.

Boocock, S. S. *An introduction to the sociology of learning.* Boston: Houghton Mifflin, 1972.

Brehm, J. W. *A theory of psychological reactance.* New York: Academic, 1966.

Bronfenbrenner, U. The origins of alienation. *Scientific American,* 1974, 231, 53–58.

Bucklow, M. A. A new role for the work group. *Administrative Science Quarterly,* 1966, 11, 59–78.

Campbell, J. P., Dunnette, M. D., Lawler, E. E., & Weick, K. E. *Managerial behavior, performance, and effectiveness.* New York: McGraw-Hill, 1970.

Chesler, M. A., & Lohman, J. E. Changing schools through student advocacy. In R. A. Schmuck & M. B. Miles (Eds.), *Organization development in schools.* Palo Alto, Calif.: Mayfield, 1971.

Clark, K. B. *Dark ghetto: Dilemmas of social power.* New York: Harper, 1965.

Coch, L., & French, J. R. P., Jr. Overcoming resistance to change. *Human Relations,* 1948, 1, 512–532.

Cohen, A. R. Upward communication in experimentally created hierarchies. *Human Relations,* 1968, 11, 41–53.

Cohen, A. R. Situational structure, self-esteem, and threat-oriented reactions to power. In D. Cartwright (Ed.), *Studies in social power.* Ann Arbor: Institute for Social Research, 1959.

Coleman, J. S. The children have outgrown the schools. *Psychology Today,* 1972, 5, 72–75.

Coleman, J. S., Campbell, E. Q., Hobson, C. J., McPartland, J. M., Mood, M. A., Weinfeld, F. D., & York, R. L. *Equality of education opportunity.* Washington. U.S. Government Printing Office, 1966.

Coopersmith, S. *The antecedents of self-esteem.* San Francisco: W. H. Freeman, 1967.

Corwin, R. G. Education and the sociology of complex organizations. In D. Hansern & J. Gerstl (Eds.), *On education: Sociological perspectives.* New York: Wiley, 1962.

de Charms, R. *Personal causation.* New York: Academic, 1968.

de Charms, R. *Enhancing motivation in the classroom.* New York: Irvington, 1976.

Deutsch, M. An experimental study of the effects of cooperation and competition upon group process. *Human Relations,* 1949, 2, 199–231.

Deutsch, M. *The resolution of conflict.* New Haven: Yale University Press, 1973.

Dunkin, M., & Biddle, B. *The study of teaching.* New York: Holt, 1974.

Flanders, N. A. Teacher-pupil contacts and mental hygiene. *Journal of Social Issues,* 1959, 15, 30–39.

French, J. R. P., Jr. The social environment and mental health. *Journal of Social Issues,* 1963, 19, 39–56.

Gordon, C. W. *The social system of the high school.* New York: Free Press, 1957.

Heilman, M. E., & Garner, K. A. Counteracting the boomerang: The effects of choice on compliance to threats and promises. *Journal of Personality and Social Psychology,* 1975, 31, 911–917.

Heiss, J., & Owens, S. Self-evaluation of blacks and whites. *American Journal of Sociology,* 1972, 78, 360–370.

Herndon, J. *The way it spozed to be.* New York: Bantam, 1968.

Hoy, W. K. The influence of experience on the beginning teacher. *School Review,* 1968, 76, 312–323.

Hoy, W. K. Pupil control ideology and organization socialization: A further examination of the influence of experience on the beginning teacher. *School Review,* 1969, 77, 257–265.

Hurwitz, J., Zander, A., & Hymovitch, B. Some effects of power in the relations among group members. In D. Cartwright & A. Zander (Eds.), *Group dynamics,* New York: Harper, 1968.

Jencks, C. *Inequality: A reassessment of the effect of family and schooling in America.* New York: Basic, 1972.

Johnson, D. W. *The social psychology of education.* New York: Holt, 1970.

Johnson, D. W., & Allen, S. Deviation from organizational norms concerning the relationship between status and power: Equity vs self-interest theory. *Sociological Quarterly,* 1972, 13, 174–182.

Johnson, D. W., & Johnson, R. T. Instructional goal structure: Cooperative, competitive or individualistic. *Review of Educational Research,* 1974, 44, 213–240.

Johnson, D. W., & Johnson, F. P. *Joining together: Group theory and group skills.* Englewood Cliffs, N.J.: Prentice-Hall, 1975.

Johnson, M. P., & Ewens, W. Power relations and affective style as determinants of confidence in impression formation in a game situation. *Journal of Experimental Social Psychology,* 1971, 7, 98–110.

Jones, E. E. *Ingratiation.* New York: Appleton, 1964.

Jones, T. E. *The relations between bureaucracy and the pupil control ideology of secondary schools and teachers.* Unpublished doctoral dissertation, Oklahoma State University, 1969.

Katz, D. & Kahn, R. L. *The social psychology of organizations.* New York: Wiley, 1966.

Kelley, H. H. Communication in experimentally created hierarchies. *Human Relations,* 1951, 4, 39–56.

Kipnis, D. Does power corrupt? *Journal of Personality and Social Psychology,* 1972, 24, 33–41.

Kipnis, D. The powerholder. In J. T. Tedeschi (Ed.), *Perspectives on social power.* Chicago: Aldine, 1974.

Kipnis, D. *The powerholders.* Chicago: University of Chicago Press, 1976.

Kohlberg, L. Stage and sequence: The cognitive-developmental approach to socialization. In D. A. Goslin (Ed.), *Handbook of socialization theory and research.* Chicago: Rand McNally, 1969.

Kohlberg, L. The cognitive-developmental approach to moral education. *Phi Delta Kappan,* June 1975, pp. 670–677.

Kohlberg, L., & Turiel, E. Moral development and moral education. In G. S. Lesser (Ed.), *Psychology and educational practice.* Glenview, Ill.: Scott, Foresman, 1971.

Laing, R. D. *The politics of experience.* New York: Ballantine, 1967.

Lefcourt, H. M. Internal versus external control: A review. *Psychological Bulletin,* 1966, 65, 206–220.

Lewin, K., Lippitt, R., & White, R. K. Patterns of aggressive behavior in experimentally created social climates. *Journal of Social Psychology,* 1939, 10, 271–299.

Lippitt, R., Polansky, N., Redl, F., & Rosen, S. The dynamics of power. *Human Relations,* 1952, 5, 37–64.

Lowin, A. Participants decision making: A model, literature critique, and prescriptions for research. *Organization Behavior and Human Performance,* 1968, 3, 68–106.

Mallowe, M. Fear and loathing in the classroom. *Philadelphia Magazine,* April 1976, pp. 118–123.

Maykovich, M. K. Reciprocity in racial stereotypes: White, black, and yellow. *American Journal of Sociology*, 1972, 77, 876–897.

McCandless, B. R. *Children and adolescents: Behavior and development*. New York: Holt, 1961.

McGregor, D. *The human side of enterprise*. New York: McGraw-Hill, 1960.

McPherson, G. H. *Small town teacher*. Cambridge: Harvard University Press, 1972.

Mead, G. H. *Mind, self, and society*. Chicago: University of Chicago Press, 1934.

Merriam, M., & Guerney, B. G., Jr. Creating a democratic elementary school classroom: A pilot training program, involving teachers, administrators, and parents. *Contemporary Education*, 1973, 45, 34–41.

Michener, H. A., & Burt, M. R. Legitimacy as a base of social influence. In J. T. Tedeschi (Ed.), *Perspectives in social power*. Chicago: Aldine, 1974.

Michener, H. A., & Suchner, R. W. The tactical use of social power. In J. T. Tedeschi (Ed.), *The social influence process*. Chicago: Aldine, 1972.

Miles, M. B., & Schmuck, R. A. Improving schools through organization development: An overview. In R. A. Schmuck & M. B. Miles (Eds.), *Organization development in schools*, Palo Alto, Calif.: Mayfield, 1971.

Mulder, M. The power variable in communication experiments. *Human Relations*, 1960, 13, 241–256.

Packwood, J. S., & Willower, D. J. Pluralistic ignorance and pupil control ideology. *Journal of Educational Administration*, 1972, 10, 78–87.

Pepitone, A. Motivational effects in social perception. *Human Relations*, 1950, 3, 57–76.

Polansky, N., Lippitt, R., & Redl, F. The use of near-sociometric data on group treatment processes. *Sociometry*, 1950, 13, 39–62.

Pritchett, W., & Willower, D. J. Teacher public control behavior and student attitudes toward high school. *Alberta Journal of Educational Research*, 1975, 12, 110–115.

Rafalides, M., & Hoy, W. K. Student sense of alienation and pupil control orientation of high schools. *High School Journal*, 1971, 55, 102.

Rexford, G. E., Willower, D. J., & Lynch, P. D. Teachers' pupil control ideology and classroom verbal behavior. *Journal of Experimental Education*, 1972, 40, 78–82.

Rhea, B. Institutional paternalism in high school. *Urban Review*, 1968, 2, 13–15.

Rogers, C. R. *Client-centered therapy: Its current practice, implications, and theory*. Boston: Houghton Mifflin, 1951.

Rotter, J. B. Generalized expectancies for internal revenue versus external control of reinforcement. *Psychological Monographs*, 1966, 86 (1, Whole No. 609).

Rosenshine, B., & Furst, N. F. The use of direct observation of study teaching. In R. M. W. Travers (Ed.), *Second handbook of research on teaching*. Chicago: Rand McNally, 1973.

Sampson, E. E. Status congruence and cognitive consistency. *Sociometry*, 1963, 26, 146–162.

Sarbin, T. R., & Allen, V. L. Role theory. In G. Lindzey & E. Aronson (Eds.), *The handbook of social psychology*. (Vol. 1). Reading, Mass.: Addison-Wesley, 1968.

Schein, E. H. *Process consultation: Its role in organizational development*. Reading, Mass.: Addison-Wesley, 1969.

Schlechty, P. C. *Teaching and social behavior: Toward an organizational theory of instruction*. Boston: Allyn & Bacon, 1976.

Schmuck, R. A. Improving classroom group processes. In R. A. Schmuck & M. B. Miles (Eds.), *Organization development in schools*. Palo Alto, Calif.: Mayfield, 1971.

Seeman, M. On the meaning of alienation. *American Sociological Review*, 1959, 24, 783–791.

Selman, M. The urban alienations: Some dubious theses from Marx to Marcuse. *Journal of Personality and Social Psychology*, 1971, 19, 135–143.

Silberman, C. E. *Crisis in the classroom*. New York: Random House, Vintage, 1971.

Solomon, L. The influence of some types of power relationship and game strategies upon the development of interpersonal trust. *Journal of Abnormal and Social Psychology*, 1960, 61, 223–230.

Strong, S., & Matross, R. Change processes in counseling and psychotherapy. *Journal of Counseling Psychology*, 1973, 20, 25–37.

Tedeschi, J. T., Lindskold, S., Horai, J., & Gahagan, J. P. Social power and the credibility of promises. *Journal of Personality and Social Psychology*, 1969, 13, 253–261.

Thibaut, J. An experimental study of the cohesiveness of underprivileged groups. *Human Relations*, 1950, 3, 251–278.

Thibaut, J., & Kelley, H. H. *The social psychology of groups.* New York: Wiley, 1959.

Thibaut, J. W., & Riecken, H. W. Some determinants and consequences of the perception of social causality. *Human Relations,* 1955, **24**, 113–133.

Tjosvold, D. Threat as a low-power person's strategy in bargaining: Social face and tangible outcomes. *International Journal of Group Tensions,* 1974, 4 494–510.

Tjosvold, D. Commitment to justice in conflict between unequal status persons. *Journal of Applied Social Psychology,* 1977, 6, 149–162. (a)

Tjosvold, D. The constituent's affirmation and the opposing negotiator's self-presentation in conflict between unequal status groups. *Organization Behavior and Human Performance,* 1977. **18**. 146–157. (b)

Tjosvold, D. Low-power person's strategies in bargaining: Negotiability of demand, maintaining face, and race. *International Journal of Group Tensions,* 1977, 7, 20–41. (c)

Tjosvold, D. *Control strategies and social face.* Paper presented at the American Educational Research Association, Toronto, 1978.

Tjosvold, D. The affirmation of the high power person and his position: ingratiation in conflict. *Journal of Applied Social Psychology,* in press.

Tjosvold, D., & Johnson, D. W. The effects of controversy on cognitive perspective-taking. *Journal of Educational Psychology,* 1977, 69, 679–774.

Tjosvold, D. & Kastelic, T. The effects of student motivation and the principal's values on teacher directiveness. *Journal of Educational Psychology,* 1976, 68, 768–774.

Tjosvold, D., & Okun, M. *The "corrupting" influence of power: Cognitive perspective-taking and cooperation.* Paper presented at the meeting of the American Psychological Association, Washington, 1976.

Tjosvold, D., & Santamaria. P. Effects of cooperation and teacher support on student attitudes toward decision-making in the elementary science classroom, *Journal of Research in Science Teaching,* in press.

U.S. Senate Subcommittee to Investigate Juvenile Delinquency. *Our nation's schools—A report card: "A" in school violence and vandalism.* Washington. U.S. Government Printing Office. 1975.

Walberg, H. J., & Thomas, S. C. Open education: An operational definition and validation in Great Britain and United States. *American Educational Research Journal,* 1972, 9, 197–208.

Waller, W. *The sociology of teaching.* New York: Wiley, 1932.

Watson, G., & Johnson, D. W. *Social psychology: Issues and insights.* Philadelphia: Lippincott, 1972.

Weber, M. *The theory of social and economic organization.* New York: Oxford University Press, 1947.

White, R. K., & Lippitt, R. *Autocracy and democracy: An experimental inquiry.* New York: Harper, 1960.

Willower, D. J. Hypotheses on the school as a social system. *Educational Administration Quarterly,* 1965, **1**, 40–51.

Willower, D. J. Some comments on inquiries on school and pupil control. *Teachers College Record,* 1975, 77, 219–230.

Willower, D. J., & Jones, R. G. Control in an educational organization. In J. D. Raths (Ed.), *Studying teaching.* Englewood Cliffs, N.J.: Prentice-Hall, 1967.

Withall, J. The development of a technique for the measurement of socioemotional climate in the classrooms. *Journal of Experimental Education,* 1949, 17, 347–361.

Yancey, W. L., Rigsby, L., & McCarthy, J. D. Social position and self-evaluation: The relative importance of race. *American Journal of Sociology,* 1972, 78, 338–357.

Zander, A., & Cohen, A. R. Attributed social power and group acceptance: A classroom experimental demonstration. *Journal of Abnormal and Social Psychology,* 1955, 51, 490–492.

Zander, A., Cohen, A. R., & Stotland, L. *Role relations in the mental health professions.* Ann Arbor: University of Michigan, 1957.

13

Conflict Management in
the School and Classroom

David W. Johnson
University of Minnesota

A student walks down the hall proclaiming, in a loud voice and using unusually foul language, that someone has stolen her notebook. A teacher demands that the student stop swearing, but the student continues. The teacher then grabs the student by the arm to march her to the principal's office, but the student strikes the teacher several times, breaks away, and runs down the hallway.

A group of teachers meets to make decisions about the curriculum materials they would like to recommend for use next year. A heated debate develops between two factions committed to different approaches to teaching their subject. Both factions refuse to compromise and the argument continues and continues.

The school is an organization (Johnson, 1970), and like any organization its operation cannot be understood without noting the significance of conflict (Johnson, 1973; Robbins, 1974). Conflicts among school personnel, between students and school personnel, and among students are inevitable. Such conflicts are a moment of truth, a test of the health of the relationships within the school, and a crisis that weakens or strengthens school relationships. Conflicts are critical events that may bring increased learning, creative insight, high-quality problem solving, and closer relationships; or they may bring lasting resentment, smoldering hostility, psychological scars, closed minds, and a refusal to perform role responsibilities. Conflicts can push people away from each other or pull them into closer and more cooperative relationships. Conflicts may contain the seeds of destruction or the seeds of a more unified and cooperative organization. Conflicts may bring aggression or mutual understanding. Conflicts have the potential for producing both highly constructive and highly destructive consequences.

Most people can easily recognize when they or others are in a conflict; yet the concept of conflict has not been an easy one for social scientists to define. In trying to define conflict, some social scientists have mentioned frustration; others have focused on decisions among attractive or unattractive alternatives; and some have concentrated on the feelings of the people involved (such as rage, anger, distrust, and rejection). Probably the most influential definition is that of Deutsch (1969): A *conflict* exists whenever incompatible activities occur. An activity that is incompatible with another activity is one that prevents, blocks, interferes with, or injures the second activity or in some way makes the second activity less likely or less effective. The two types of conflict that are the focus of this chapter are controversy and conflicts of interest. *Controversy* exists when one person's ideas, information, conclusions, theories, or opinions are incompatible with those of another person, and the two seek to reach an agreement. The conflict resides in the two people's attempt to resolve their disagreement. When two students, for example, must come to an agreement on the answer to a math problem, and they disagree as to what the answer should be, a controversy exists. A *conflict of interest* exists when the incompatible activities desired by the people involved are based on:

1. Differences in needs, values, and goals (such as those between educators in favor of ethnic integration and those opposed)
2. Scarcities of certain resources, such as power, money, time, space, and position (students, for example, may resist the exercise of authority by school personnel as the students attempt to increase their own power in the school)
3. Competition or rivalry for rewards and privileges (such as two students competing to see who can obtain the highest score on a test)

Controversies and conflicts of interest will inevitably and regularly occur in any school. How these conflicts are managed is of great importance for the effectiveness and efficiency of the school as an organization.

Many people in our society fear conflict. They believe that conflicts are bad and should be avoided. They think that a good school or classroom is one in which there are no conflicts. Many discussions of conflict talk about it causing divorces, psychological distress, violence, social disorder, breakdown of authority, and the termination of relationships. Deutsch (1969) notes that a superficial reading of many psychological theories that emphasize tension reduction, dissonance reduction, good balance, and good form would seem to imply that psychological utopia would be a conflict-free existence. Many married couples go to great lengths to avoid open discussion of conflicts (Bach & Wyden, 1968). Members of most organizations in our society do not encourage open expressions of conflict; the avoidance of conflict is characteristic of many hospitals, mental health organizations, government agencies, churches, businesses, industrial organizations, and other kinds of organizations (Argyris, 1970; Beckhard, 1969; Blake & Mouton, 1969; Deutsch, 1973; Johnson, 1973; Robbins, 1974; Walton, 1969).

DeCecco and Richards (1974) conducted a study of over 8,500 junior and senior high school students in the New York, Philadelphia, and San Francisco areas. They found that both the school personnel and the students avoided the expression of anger and the open negotiation of conflicts. They also found that, in 61% of the conflicts reported by students, the students perceived the outcomes as negative (only in 9% did they report constructive outcomes), and in 91% of the conflicts, students reported that their tension level was not lowered by the way in which the conflicts were managed. The continuation of high tension levels in students creates the possibility of further conflicts and general resistance to the educational program of the school. Walton (1969) observes that, when conflicts are not discussed openly, they will be expressed indirectly at organizational costs, and that the indirect expression of conflicts persists longer than do directly confronted conflicts.

Although many people fear and avoid the open expression of conflict, it should be remembered that it is not the presence of conflict that causes psychological distress, violence, termination of relationships, and social disorder. It is the destructive and ineffective management of conflict that causes all these disastrous and unfortunate things. Conflicts are a natural and desirable part of any relationship and, when managed constructively, they are extremely valuable.

Conflicts are managed constructively when (a) all people involved are satisfied with the outcomes; (b) the ability of the people involved to work together cooperatively has been improved; and (c) their ability to resolve future conflicts constructively has been improved. In order for conflicts to be managed constructively, (a) the overall social context has to be cooperative; (b) the school norms and values have to support constructive conflict management; and (c) the school personnel and students have to have the skills, attitudes, and strategies needed to manage conflicts constructively.

Conflicts are absolutely necessary if schools are to maintain their viability and effectiveness. Too few school personnel accept conflict, and almost none attempt to stimulate it. Many, if not most, schools and classrooms need more conflict, not less. More schools and classrooms are dying from complacency and apathy than are dying from an overabundance of conflict. More classrooms suffer from boredom and routine than from conflict. It does matter though, what kinds of conflicts occur in schools and classrooms and how these conflicts are managed. It is to the two kinds of conflicts that I now turn.

CONTROVERSY

> *Since the general or prevailing opinion on any subject is rarely or never the whole truth, it is only by the collision of adverse opinion that the remainder of the truth has any chance of being supplied.*
>
> (John Stuart Mill)

In a social studies class, a teacher is presenting a lesson on the United States Congress. The students are discussing in small groups the reasons why citizens want to be representatives in Congress. One student says the major reason is a desire to help your neighbors and your country. Another student says being a member of Congress is just a way to get rich and quotes Roger Mudd (CBS News, December 24, 1976) that a representative in Congress receives more than $400,000 per year in salary and benefits. Voices rise as the argument continues. What does the teacher do? Would the teacher encourage the argument, helping students find evidence to support and argue their positions? Or would the teacher try to calm things down and change the topic of discussion?

In any learning situation, such conflicts among ideas or opinions are inevitable. They will occur no matter what the teacher does. Learning situations are filled with conflicts among students, between the teacher and the student, and between what a student currently understands and new information being learned. Current evidence indicates that, in most classrooms, such conflicts are avoided and suppressed (DeCecco & Richards, 1974) and that teachers and students lack the skills and procedures needed for effective conflict management (Blake & Mouton, 1970; Deutsch, 1973; Johnson, 1970). By avoiding and suppressing certain kinds of conflicts, teachers lose valuable opportunities to increase student motivation, creative insight, cognitive development, and learning. Conflicts have the potential for producing either highly constructive or highly destructive outcomes, depending on how they are managed.

Controversy is the most important kind of conflict for increasing the quality of students' learning experiences. It resides in the two people's attempt to resolve their disagreement. A closely related kind of conflict is *conceptual conflict,* which exists when two incompatible ideas exist simultaneously within a student's mind and must be reconciled (Berlyne, 1957, 1966). A common source of conceptual conflict is receiving new information that does not fit with what one already knows (Hunt, 1964).

The process by which controversy sparks learning is outlined in Figure 13-1. It begins, as does all learning, with a student categorizing and organizing current personal information and experiences so that a conclusion is derived. When the student realizes that other students or the teacher have a different conclusion and that they challenge and contest her or his conclusion, a state of internal conceptual conflict, uncertainty, or disequilibrium is aroused. The uncertainty motivates an active search (called "epistemic curiosity" by Berlyne, 1971) for more information, new experiences, and a more adequate cognitive perspective and reasoning process in the hope of resolving the uncertainty. The student derives more adequate cognitive perspective and reasoning process by more accurately understanding opponents' cognitive perspective and reasoning process and then adapting his or her own cognitive perspective and reasoning process accordingly. Out of the argumentation and debate, a joint agreement is reached as to the correct conclusion. In reaching the joint conclusion, the student employs the new cognitive perspective

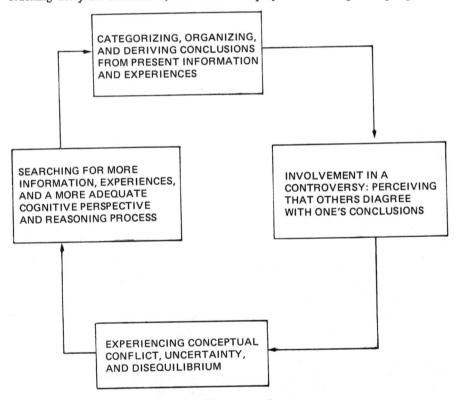

FIGURE 13-1 The process of controversy.

and reasoning process, which results in a higher quality and more creative conclusion than the one originally held. This process can be repeated. Thus, controversies might lead to positive outcomes. The appearance of the positive outcomes is, however, contingent upon the conditions under which the controversy occurs.

Outcomes

As discussed previously, the process of controversy may lead to the following outcomes: epistemic curiosity, accuracy of cognitive perspective taking, transition to the upper stage of cognitive reasoning, good ability to solve problems and make decisions, and creativity.

Conceptual Conflict and Epistemic Curiosity

Controversy among students or between the students and the teacher creates conceptual conflict, which leads to epistemic curiosity in students. Disagreement with another person can be a source of conceptual conflict that provokes attempts to explore the other person's ideas (Berlyne, 1966). Conceptual conflict has high arousal potential; it can motivate attempts to resolve it by seeking new information or by trying to reorganize the knowledge one already has (Berlyne, 1960, 1963, 1965; Burdick & Burnes, 1958, Gerard & Greenbaum, 1962; Kiesler & Pallak, 1976; Tjosvold & Johnson, 1977, in press). The greater the disagreement among students or between the teacher and the students, the more frequently the disagreement occurs, the greater the number of people disagreeing with a student's position, the more competitive the context of the controversy, and the more affronted the student feels, the greater the conceptual conflict and uncertainty the student will experience (Asch, 1952; Burdick & Burnes, 1958; Festinger, 1964; Gerard & Greenbaum, 1962; Tjosvold & Johnson, 1977, in press; Tjosvold, Johnson, & Faber, 1968; Worchel & McCormick, 1963). Thus, there is evidence that controversy can create conceptual conflict and epistemic curiosity.

Accuracy of Cognitive Perspective Taking

In resolving controversies, students need to be able both to comprehend the information being presented by their opposition and to understand the cognitive perspective their opposition is using to organize and interpret the information. A *cognitive perspective* consists of the cognitive organization being used to give meaning to a person's knowledge and the structure of a person's reasoning. Tjosvold and Johnson (1977, in press) conducted a pair of experiments in which they found that the presence of controversy promotes greater understanding of another person's cognitive perspective than does the absence of controversy. Subjects engaging in a controversy were better able subsequently to predict what line of reasoning their opponent would use in solving a future problem than were subjects who interacted without any controversy. The more competitive the context and the more affronted the students feel, the more accurate they are in predicting the line of reasoning used in solving a future problem by their opponent. These findings are especially important as accurate perspective taking is central to cognitive development, moral reasoning, self-esteem, social intelligence, cooperation, communication effectiveness, problem solving, and conflict resolution (Asch, 1952; Falk & Johnson, 1977; Flavell, 1968; Johnson, 1971d, 1975a, 1975b; Kohlberg, 1969; Mead, 1934; Piaget, 1948, 1950; Rogers, 1951).

Transition from One Stage of Cognitive Reasoning to Another

Cognitive development theorists (Flavell, 1963; Kohlberg, 1969; Piaget, 1948, 1950) have posited that it is repeated interpersonal controversies, arguments, and disagreements (in which the person is forced again and again to take cognizance of the perspective of others) that promote cognitive and moral development, the ability to think logically, and the reduction of egocentric reasoning. Such interpersonal conflicts are posited to create disequilibrium within a person's cognitive structures, which motivates a search for a more adequate and mature process of reasoning. There are several studies that have found that, when pairing a conserver with a nonconserver and giving the pair conservation problems to solve, the conserver's answer prevails in the great majority of conservation trials (Botvin & Murray, 1975; Miller & Brownell, 1975; Murray, 1972; Silverman & Geiringer, 1973; Silverman & Stone, 1972; Smedlund, 1961c). The solution of the problems is not based on general social dominance but, rather, on the greater certainty and superior logic of the conservers (Miller & Brownell, 1975). Murray (1972) use a three-person discussion group in which one nonconserver and two conservers reached a group decision as to the answer to a series of conservation problems. When tested later individually, all subjects made significant gains in conservation judgments and explanations on the same problems, as well as on parallel forms of the problems and on new conservation problems; nonconservers made the greater gains. Murray and Botvin (1974) demonstrated that, when internal disequilibrium was created by having nonconserving subjects argue publicly for correct solutions of conservation problems, the subjects increased in ability to solve correctly conservation problems compared to a control group who did not publicly espouse a conservation position. These gains, furthermore, were not extinguished when the subjects then publicly argued an incorrect nonconserving solution to conservation problems. Jensen and Larm (1970) conducted a similar study in which they found that argumentation among subjects increased their ability to include intentions as well as consequences in making judgments in response to stories compared to a control group and subjects who were reinforced for including intentions as well as consequences in their judgments. Taken together, these studies indicate that controversy among students, and the conceptual conflict it generates, are an important factor in cognitive growth.

Besides the research on Piaget's theory of cognitive development, there are several studies, based primarily on Kohlberg's (1969) theory of moral development, investigating the experiences that lead to a transition to higher stages of moral reasoning. The basic format of these studies is to place subjects in a situation requiring the making of a decision as to how a moral dilemma should be resolved with other people who use higher stages of moral reasoning than the subject. Such controversies result in advances in level of moral reasoning (Blatt, 1969; Blatt & Kohlberg, 1973; LeFurgy & Woloshin, 1969; Maitland & Goldman, 1974; Rest, Turiel, & Kohlberg, 1969; Turiel, 1966).

Although these studies support the assumption that controversy leads to conceptual conflict, which, in turn, promotes the transition to higher stages of cognitive and moral reasoning, simply presenting students with a differing opinion does not mean that a conflict will ensue. If the conflicts presented are not related to the students' existing stage of cognitive and moral reasoning as well as to their emerging stage, the conflicts are unlikely to be experienced (Inhelder, Bovet, Sinclair, &

Smock, 1966; Inhelder & Sinclair, 1969; Langer, 1969). In addition, many of the above studies do not clearly indicate whether their results are due to controversy, to direct conformity to social pressure, or to the imitation of models.

The cognitive development theorists, as well as Berlyne, assume that the accuracy of cognitive perspective taking resulting from conceptual conflict and the resulting information-seeking behavior will promote the transition to a higher stage of conceptual reasoning and to reorganization within a person's cognitive structures. Tjosvold and Johnson (in press) conducted a pair of experiments that do not support such an assumption. They found that a competitive context (compared to a cooperative one) and feelings of being affronted by the opponent (compared to the absence of such feelings) increased conceptual conflict and information-seeking behavior, increased accuracy of cognitive perspective taking, but also resulted in feelings of dissonance and closed-mindedness. The dissonance experienced tended to be resolved by derogating the opponent's perspective and the opponent as a source of influence.

Taken together, however, the above studies do provide evidence that controversies among students can promote transitions to higher stages of cognitive and moral reasoning. Such findings are important, as there is little doubt that higher levels of cognitive and moral reasoning cannot be directly taught (Inhelder & Sinclair, 1969; Sigel & Hooper, 1968; Sinclair, 1969; Smedslund, 1961a, 1961b; Turiel, 1973; Wallach & Sprott, 1964; Wallach, Wall, & Anderson, 1967; Wohlwill & Lowe, 1962).

Quality of Problem solving and Decision making

The interpersonal controversies that lead to conceptual conflict and feelings of uncertainty in turn lead to a search for additional information and experiences, to greater accuracy of cognitive perspective taking, and to the transition to a more mature cognitive and moral reasoning process, seem to promote high-quality problem solving and decision making. Certainly, the purpose of controversy within a cooperative group is to arrive at the highest quality solution or decision that is possible. There are many social scientists who have noted the value of controversy for high-quality problem solving, decision making, and learning (Dewey, 1933; Ewbank & Auer, 1946; Harnack & Fest, 1964; Howell & Smith, 1956; Johnson, 1970, 1973; Johnson & Johnson, F. P., 1975; Kelley & Thibaut, 1969; Petelle, 1964; Simmel, 1957). There are, moreover, studies that confirm such opinions (Boulding, 1964; Glidewell, 1953; Hall & Williams, 1966, 1970; Hoffman & Maier, 1961; Hoffman, Harburg, & Maier, 1962; Maier & Hoffman, 1964; Maier & Solem, 1952). Thus, there is evidence that controversies among members of a group will result in high-quality problem solving and decision making.

Creativity

Creativity is bringing something new into existence by a process consisting of an overlapping sequence such as (a) recognizing and experiencing a challenging problem, (b) gathering the necessary knowledge and resources for a long-term and intense effort to solve the problem, (c) experiencing an incubation period wherein one temporarily withdraws from the issue after experiencing feelings of failure, tension, and discomfort owing to the failure to solve the problem, (d) seeing the problem from different perspectives and reformulating it in a way that lets new orientations to a solution emerge in a moment of insight or inspiration (often accompanied by intense feelings of illumination and excitement), and (e) elaborating, detailing, and testing the solution against reality.

Controversies, disagreements, arguments, debates, presenting opposing viewpoints and diverse information and ideas, all are important aspects of gaining creative insight. There is evidence that such interpersonal interaction increases the number of ideas, quality of ideas, feelings of stimulation and enjoyment, and originality of expression in creative problem solving (Bahn, 1964; Bolen & Torrance, 1976; Dunnette, Campbell, & Jaastad, 1963; Falk & Johnson, 1977; Peters & Torrance, 1972; Torrance, 1970, 1971, 1973; Triandis, Bass, Ewen, & Mikesele, 1963). There is also evidence that controversies result in more creative problem solutions, with more member satisfaction, compared to group efforts that do not include controversies (Glidewell, 1953; Hall & Williams, 1966, 1970; Hoffman, Harburg, & Maier, 1962; Maier & Hoffman, 1964; Rogers, 1970). These studies demonstrated that controversies both can encourage group members to dig into a problem, raise issues, and settle them in ways that show the benefits of using a wide range of ideas and can result in a high degree of emotional involvement in and commitment to solving the problems the group is working on.

Summary of the Controversy Process

There is evidence, therefore, that controversy can arouse conceptual conflict, subjective feelings of uncertainty, and epistemic curiosity; increase accuracy of cognitive perspective taking; promote transitions from one stage of cognitive and moral reasoning to another; increase the quality of problem solving; and increase creativity. These findings support the hypothesized process by which controversy promotes learning. That is, the situation begins with students categorizing and organizing their present information and experiences so that a conclusion is derived. When they realize that other students (or the teacher) have a different conclusion, either conceptual conflict, uncertainty, or disequilibrium is aroused. The conceptual conflict leads to epistemic curiosity, which, in turn, motivates a search for more information, new experiences, and a more adequate cognitive perspective and reasoning process. The more adequate cognitive perspective and reasoning process is derived from a more accurate understanding of the perspective and reasoning process of the students' opponents and an adaptation of their own perspective and reasoning process accordingly. Next, a joint agreement is reached as to the correct conclusion, employing the more adequate cognitive perspective and reasoning process, and a higher quality and more creative solution to the problem is generated.

Conditions of Controversy

Although controversy can operate in a beneficial way, it will not do so under all conditions. As with all conflict, the potential for either constructive or destructive outcomes is present in a controversy. Whether positive or negative consequences result depends on the conditions under which the controversy occurs and the way in which it is managed. These conditions and procedures include:

1. The context within which controversy occurs
2. The differences in personality, sex, attitudes, background, social class, cognitive-reasoning strategies, cognitive perspectives, information, and skills among the students involved

3. The amount of relevant information distributed among students
4. The perspective-taking skills of the students.

The Context of Controversy

Deutsch (1973) emphasizes that the context within which conflicts occur has important effects on whether the conflict turns out to be constructive or destructive. There are two possible contexts for controversy: cooperation and competition. A *cooperative context* is one in which people perceive that they obtain their goal if and only if the other people with whom they are linked can obtain their goals; if one person achieves his or her goal, all people with whom he or she is linked achieve their goal (Deutsch, 1962). In a *competitive context,* people perceive that they can obtain their goal if and only if the other people with whom they are linked fail to obtain their goal; if one person achieves her or his goal, all other people with whom she or he is linked fail to achieve their goal (Deutsch, 1962). There are literally hundreds of studies documenting the relative effects of cooperation and competition (Johnson & Johnson, R. T., 1974, 1975). There are several ways in which a cooperative context facilitates constructive controversy whereas a competitive context promotes destructive controversy:

1. In order for controversy to be constructive, information must be accurately communicated. Within a cooperative context, communication tends to be open and honest, whereas, in a competitive context, communication tends to be non-existent or misleading (Johnson, 1974; Johnson & Johnson, R. T., 1975). Cooperative contexts, compared to competitive ones, promote more accurate communication of information, more verbalization of ideas and information, greater efforts in seeking others' information and ideas, more attentiveness to others' statements, utilization of others' information in more optimal ways, more acceptance of and willingness to be influenced by others' ideas and information, fewer difficulties in communicating with and understanding others, more confidence in one's own ideas and in the value that others attach to one's ideas, and greater feelings of agreement between oneself and others (Crawford & Haaland, 1972; Johnson, 1974; Johnson & Johnson, R. T., 1975; Laughlin & McGlynn, 1967). Blake and Mouton (1961) provide evidence, furthermore, that competition biases a person's perceptions and comprehension of the viewpoints and positions of other individuals. Tjosvold and Johnson (in press), however, found that a competitive context promoted a more accurate understanding of the opponent's cognitive perspective but a closed-minded refusal to utilize it.
2. Constructive controversies require supportive climates in which people feel safe enough to challenge each other's ideas. Deutsch (1958, 1960, 1962) and other researchers (Johnson, 1974) have found that trust is built through cooperative interaction and destroyed through competitive interaction. Cooperativeness is related to beliefs that peers and authority figures are supportive and accepting of one as a person and of one's achievement efforts (Johnson & Ahlgren, 1976; Johnson, Johnson, Johnson, & Anderson, 1976).
3. Cooperative learning experiences, compared with individualized ones, promote a belief that controversy is constructive (Johnson, Johnson, & Scott, 1978).
4. Constructive controversy requires dealing with feelings as well as with ideas and information. There is evidence that cooperativeness is related to an ability to understand what other people are feeling and why they are feeling that way,

whereas competitiveness is not (Johnson, 1975a, 1975b; Johnson, Johnson, Johnson, & Anderson, 1976).

5. How controversies are defined has great impact on how constructively they are managed. Within a cooperative context, conflicts tend to be defined as problems to be jointly solved, whereas within a competitive context, conflicts tend to be defined as win–lose situations (Deutsch, 1973; Rubin & Brown, 1975).

Heterogeneity of People Involved in Controversy

Heterogeneity leads to potential controversy. The differences in personality, sex, attitudes, background, social class, cognitive-reasoning strategies, cognitive perspectives, information, and skills that are found among students lead potentially to diverse organization and processing of present information and experiences. Deriving different conclusions from one's present information and experiences begins the cycle of controversy. There is evidence that more controversy occurs in heterogeneous groups than in homogeneous ones (Fiedler, Meuwese, & Oonk, 1961; Torrance, 1961).

Because heterogeneity among students creates the potential for controversy does not mean that such controversies will be constructively managed. There is contradictory evidence concerning the effectiveness of homogeneous and heterogeneous groups in problem solving. Several studies have found heterogeneous groups to be superior to homogeneous groups in quality of group solution, creativity of group solution, and member satisfaction with the solution (Amaria, Biran, & Leith, 1969; Ghiselli & Lodahl, 1958; Goldman, 1965; Hoffman, 1959; Hoffman & Maier, 1961; Hoffman, Harburg, & Maier, 1962; Pelz, 1956; Triandis, Hall, & Ewen, 1965; Ziller, 1955; Ziller & Exline, 1958). Other studies have found either that homogeneous groups arrive at better solutions than do heterogeneous groups or that there is no difference between heterogeneous and homogeneous groups in quality of group solutions (Altman & McGinnies, 1970; Falk & Johnson, 1977; Fiedler, Meuwese, & Oonk, 1961; Haythorn, Couch, Haefner, Langham, & Carter, 1956; Schultz, 1955, 1958; Shaw, 1960). The failure of heterogeneous groups always to outperform homogeneous groups raises the possibilities that, when relevant expertise is lacking in the group, heterogeneity may not affect quality of problem solving; or when group members do not have the skills to exchange information effectively, heterogeneity may not be utilized productively. These possibilities are discussed next.

Relevant Information Available

If controversy is to lead to learning, the group members must possess information relevant to the solution of the problem on which they are working. The more information is available, the easier it should be to solve their problem. There are a number of studies that indicate that groups that have more information about a problem usually perform better than do groups with less information (Goldman, 1965; Laughlin & Branch, 1972; Laughlin, Branch, & Johnson, 1969; Laughlin & Johnson, 1966; Laughlin, Kerr, Davis, Haiff, & Marciniak, 1975; Tuckman, 1967). Having relevant information available, however, does not mean that it will be utilized. When the task is such that the correct answer is immediately recognizable when it is proposed, it tends to be immediately accepted (Laughlin & Bitz, 1975), but when the task is such that the correct answer is not immediately recognizable, it may require one group member to propose the answer and another member to support it before the group adopts it (Laughlin, Kerr, Davis, Halff, & Marciniak, 1975). Laughlin and his associates (1975), furthermore, found that, when no member of a group knew the correct answer to a problem, the group would still figure it out about 20% of the time, indicating that the quality of the group discussion can affect the successful solution of problems even when member expertise is low.

Perspective-taking Skills

In order for controversies to be managed constructively, they need to take place within a cooperative context; students need to be sufficiently heterogeneous to disagree with one another; and the information relevant for jointly solving learning problems must be available. For heterogeneity to contribute to learning, and for information to be exchanged and utilized, students need a minimal level of communication skills. Perhaps the most important set of skills for exchanging information and opinions is *perspective taking*: the ability to understand how a problem or situation appears cognitively and affectively to another person. The opposite of perspective taking is *egocentrism*, embeddedness in one's own perspective to the extent that one is unaware of other perspectives and of the limitations in one's perspective. The level of students' perspective-taking abilities will tend to affect the

1. *Amount of Information Disclosed.* More information, both personal and impersonal, is disclosed when one is interacting with a person engaging in perspective-taking behaviors (Colson, 1968; Noonan-Wagner, 1975; Sermat & Smyth, 1973; Taylor, Altman, & Sorrentino, 1969).
2. *Phrasing of Messages so that Others Can Comprehend Their Meaning.* People high in perspective-taking ability are better able to phrase messages so that others can understand than are people low in perspective-taking ability (Feffer & Suchotliff, 1966; Flavell, 1968; Hogan & Henley, 1970).
3. *Comprehension and Retention of Others' Messages.* Johnson (1967, 1968, 1971a) found that engaging in perspective-taking behaviors in conflicts results in increased understanding and retention of the opponent's messages and perspective. Flavell (1968), in a series of studies with children, found that perspective-taking ability facilitates the comprehension of messages from another person. Feffer and Suchotliff (1966) and Hogan and Henley (1970) found similar results with adults.
4. *Quality of Problem Solving.* During controversies, perspective-taking behaviors, compared to egocentrically emphasizing one's own information and perspective, results in more creative and higher quality solutions (Falk & Johnson, in press) and in greater gains in accuracy of problem solving (Johnson, 1977).
5. *Perceptions of Learning Experience.* Perspective-taking behaviors promote more positive perceptions of the information-exchange process, of fellow problem solvers, and of the problem-solving experience (Falk & Johnson, 1977; Johnson, 1971c, 1977; Noonan-Wagner, 1975).

The presence of diverse information and opinions does not ensure that constructive controversy will take place. When information and insights relevant to solving a problem are distributed among group members, there is no guarantee that the information and insights will be exchanged in a way that ensures their utilization. The level of students' perspective-taking and other communication skills will influence the extent to which controversy occurs, to which information and insights are effectively exchanged, and to which the controversy is managed in a constructive, rather than a destructive, way.

Summary of Conditions Affecting Outcomes of Controversy

Whether or not controversy among students leads to increased motivation, cognitive development, and learning will depend upon the conditons under which it occurs. To be constructive, controversy needs to occur within a cooperative context; sufficient differences among students must exist to ensure diverse conclusions being derived from information and experiences; information relevant to the solution of the learning task must be distributed among students; and students must have a certain level of competency in exchanging information accurately, especially the ability to view problems and situations from other people's perspectives.

Conclusions about Controversy

Disagreements among students' ideas, conclusions, theories, and opinions are an important source of learning in all instructional situations. When occurring within facilitative conditions, there is evidence that such conflicts will create conceptual conflict, feelings of uncertainty, and epistemic curiosity; will increase students' accuracy of cognitive perspective taking; will promote students' transitions from one stage of cognitive and moral reasoning to another; will increase the quality of students' problem solving; and will increase students' creativeness. There is also evidence indicating that the conditions affecting the constructiveness of controversy are the goal structure within which the controversy occurs, the heterogeneity among students, the amount of relevant information students' possess, and the perspective-taking skills of students. Although a great deal more evidence is needed to validate firmly the potential outcomes of controversy in instructional situations and the conditions that facilitate constructive outcomes, there is enough evidence to suggest that creating controversy is an important teaching strategy for increasing learning and intellectual development.

The available evidence also points toward some specific suggestions for teachers who wish to capitalize fully on the intellectual disagreements that arise within instructional situations. Available research suggests that teachers who wish to promote constructive controversy should structure learning activities cooperatively, ensure that each cooperative group is heterogeneous, promote controversies within each cooperative group, teach perspective-taking skills to students, and emphasize rational argument.

CONFLICTS OF INTEREST

John teaches American history. Sam is a student taking American history. Sam hates history and wants to get by with as little effort as possible while he concentrates his energies on chemistry and automobile mechanics, both of which he loves. He is content to get a D in American history. John believes that every student should achieve up to his or her potential, and he recognizes that Sam is an intelligent student. He thinks, therefore, that Sam should spend considerable time studying American history so he can get an A in the course. John tells Sam to study harder. Sam tells John to mind his own business. John and Sam are locked in a conflict of interest. Sam's interests of wanting to do minimal work for a minimally passing grade in American history are in conflict with John's interests of wanting Sam to do maximal work for the maximal grade of A.

Students do have different interests than teachers. High school students, for example, may want to focus their energies on resolving their conflicts around dependence and independence on adults and on creating secure relationships with their peers, whereas teachers may want students to be academically motivated and committed to becoming experts in the subject areas taught. Teachers do have different interests from administrators. Administrators may concentrate on coordinating the school's activities with those of other schools in the same district, whereas teachers focus on their own instructional interests. English teachers may have different concerns and perspectives from science teachers. In any school, different people will have different values and goals, will seek scarce resources such as money and power, and will compete with each other for status and rewards. The management of such conflicts of interest is an important aspect of maintaining the cooperation among the school staff and between the students and the school staff that is necessary for schools to operate effectively.

Conflicts of interest exist when the actions of one person attempting to maximize her or his advantages or benefits prevent, block, interfere with, or injure the actions of another person trying to maximize advantages or benefits or in some way make that second person's actions less effective. The term *interest* is used with the meaning of benefit, profit, advantage, concern, right, or claim. Conflicts among people's interests can be based on:

1. Differences in needs, values, and goals
2. Scarcities of certain resources such as power, influence, money, time, space, popularity, and position
3. Competition or rivalry

There is no way to eradicate conflicts of interest in the classroom or school. There are times when school personnel will be in conflict over how money, space, students, and recess time are to be allocated. There will never be enough resources to meet everyone's needs, and therefore, there will be conflicts over how the resources are to be divided and who will receive how much. There are times when school personnel and students will be in conflict over the imposition of rules, regulations, assignments, and responsibilities, over the amount of independence allowed students, over the amount of effort committed to academic learning, and over the personal relevance to students' immediate concerns of what is being taught. The differences in needs, values, and goals and the differences in power will always create conflicts of interest between students and school personnel. There are times when students will compete with each other for grades and the recognition and affection of the teacher or peers and will see the meeting of their needs as being in opposition to the meeting of the needs of others. One student, for example, may crack jokes to gain attention while another student is making a speech on love and friendship. Conflicts of interest will regularly occur among school personnel, between students and school personnel, and among students no matter what the educational practices and philosophy of a school are. It is a face of life: People's interests often conflict with each others, and the teacher must be skilled in negotiating settlements to such conflicts and in teaching students the procedures for doing so.

Constructive Outcomes

Conflicts of interest are not to be avoided; they are to be encouraged and managed constructively. They do have important outcomes that are essential for socialization and the functioning of an effective instructional program. Here are a few of the more important benefits to be derived from the constructive management of conflicts of interest:

1. The key developmental conflicts are expressed, managed, and worked through in interpersonal relationships. In order to resolve their developmental conflicts constructively, students need to be skilled in the negotiating of resolutions of conflicts of interest.
2. Negotiating skills are essential for the maintenance of healthy and growth-producing relationships with peers, family, and associates. In their daily lives, as future adults, for a successful career, and for the maintenance of close and personal relationships, students will have to be able to negotiate settlements to conflicts of interest. One of the important socialization goals of the school, therefore, is to promote student skills in conflict management.
3. Students gain greater self-understanding as a result of conflicts with others. Having to talk about their needs, values, and goals helps clarify them. Finding out what one can and cannot compromise about helps clarify one's values and self-image.
4. Participation in, and successful resolution of, conflicts of interest is essential for developing the competencies needed for healthy social development. Negotiating resolutions of conflicts of interest is essential for building and maintaining trust in the affection, support, and cooperation of other people; for developing the ability to see situations from the perspectives of others with opposing or different interests; for clarifying one's goals and directions; for increasing one's awareness of one's interdependence with others; for clarifying and cohering one's identity as a person; and for building and maintaining one's self-esteem.
5. Instruction cannot be fully successful if there are underlying resentments, dissatisfactions, tensions, and hostilities among students or between students and the teacher. Conflicts of interest provide an avenue for bringing relationship problems out into the open, for arriving at solutions, for resolving tensions and resentments, and for stabilizing and integrating relationships.
6. There are sometimes basic changes that need to be made within a school or a classroom for outmoded and inappropriate procedures to be changed to more effectively meet the instructional and socialization needs of students and the community. Often discipline problems, rebellion against authority, and widespread anger are signs that some adaptive change needs to take place within the school or classroom. Conflicts of interest, when they are negotiated with skill, can lead to both organizational and personal change, adaptation, and growth. The basic sources of dissatisfaction are ended by allowing rival claims of students and teachers to be immediately and directly resolved. The underlying sources of anger, resentment, and rebellion against authority can be alleviated through changes promoted by negotiating resolutions of conflicts of interest. Skillful negotiations of conflicts of interest also help maintain the basic cooperation among students and school personnel and within the school staff that is absolutely essential for the effective functioning of the school personnel. Likewise,

basic cooperation among the school staff, absolutely essential for the effective functioning of the school, is also promoted by skillful negotiating of settlements to conflicts of interest.

7. The reasons students are obstructing the instructional activities of the teacher is often a puzzle. The teacher does not understand the motivations for the students' actions and, therefore, does not know where to start in finding more constructive ways of meeting the students' needs. Through negotiating conflicts of interest, the teacher and the students can become more aware of what the antagonistic interests are and how strong they are. Such an awareness can lead to a readjustment of teacher and student behavior better to meet the needs of both.

8. Athletics, chess, bridge, poker, and many games and activities are highly structured conflicts of interest. Conflicts of interest can be fun when they become part of a process of testing and assessing oneself and experiencing the pleasure of the full and active use of one's capabilities. Friendly rivalries can be enjoyable and add some spice to everyday activities. If for no other reasons, conflicts of interest should be promoted in the classroom to capitalize on the fun, enjoyment, excitement, and motivation they generate. The appropriate use of interpersonal and intergroup competition are examples.

To Avoid or to Resolve—That Is the Question

When conflicts of interest arise, the teacher is usually faced with the decision of whether to try to control and avoid the conflict or to face it directly and try to resolve it. In order to make such a decision the teacher will need to understand what events trigger the expression of the conflict and what barriers exist to beginning negotiations (Walton, 1969). To avoid the conflict, the triggering events must be removed and the barriers to negotiation must be built up. To resolve the conflict, the teacher must increase the frequency of the triggering events and decrease the barriers to negotiations.

An event triggers the expression of the conflict by setting off a hostile interaction or a confrontation. A triggering event may be as simple as two students being physically near each other or as complex as two students being in competition while a certain mutual friend observes. Put-downs, negative remarks, sarcasm, and criticism on sensitive points are frequently triggering events. Feeling deprived, neglected, and ignored is a common triggering event. Through understanding the triggering events, one can head off a conflict interchange or one can precipitate the expression of the conflict.

Within many conflicts of interest, there are barriers to expressing the conflict and seeking its resolution. These barriers may be internal, such as attitudes, values, fears, anxieties, and habitual patterns of avoiding conflicts; or they may be external, such as time constraints, group norms disapproving the open expression of conflict, pressures to maintain a congenial public image, and faulty perceptions of one's own vulnerability and the other's strength. Physical separation is an often-used barrier to the expression of conflicts of interest. By placing students in different classes, by avoiding being in the teachers' lounge with certain other teachers, or by removing a student from school, conflicts of interest can be suppressed.

To understand a conflict, one must determine what kinds of barriers are customarily operating and what triggers the expression of the conflict. Because an important aspect of conflict management is choosing the right time and place for negotiations, an understanding of the barriers and triggering events allows one either temporarily to suppress the expression of the conflict until the time and place is more appropriate or to precipitate the expression of the conflict when the time and place is appropriate. Some triggering events, furthermore, may trigger a malevolent expression of the conflict, whereas other triggering events may lead to a constructive confrontation. Being teased, for example, may begin a physical fight between two students, whereas competing on a spelling drill may result only in name calling. By understanding what events trigger a conflict, one can ensure that events that would spark a verbal confrontation are present rather than events that would trigger more destructive expressions of a conflict of interest.

Not every conflict of interest is negotiable. The opponent or the people involved may be too anxious, defensive, or psychologically unstable to negotiate effectively. Their motivation to change may be very low. It is a mistake to assume that one can *always* openly negotiate the resolution of a conflict, for there are times when conflicts are better avoided. Usually, however, conflicts of interest can be settled constructively. The vast majority of conflicts of interest in schools could be negotiated if the participants would attempt to do so.

Promoting Negotiations

Once it has been decided to resolve a conflict of interest, there are many procedures available. Legal actions, third-party roles (such as therapists, counselors, arbitrators, mediators, and student advocates), violence, and negotiations are all examples. Usually, the preferred procedure will be negotiations, for it is by far the most effective for constructively resolving conflicts in schools.

Negotiating is a process by which people who want to come to an agreement to resolve a conflict, but who disagree about the nature of the agreement, try to work out a settlement. Negotiations are aimed at achieving an agreement that specifies what each party gives and receives in a transaction between them. The discussion of negotiations in this chapter focuses on the situation in which two or more members of the same organization (the school) have a conflict of interest. There are two basic goals for negotiating a conflict of interest within an organization: (1) reaching an agreement and (2) not damaging (but, if possible, improving) the basic cooperation among the people involved. Within an organization, members have to be concerned about both the primary and the secondary gains achieved for themselves through negotiations. The *primary gain* is determined by the nature of the agreement; the more favorable the agreement is to the member's short-term goals, the greater the primary gain for that person. The *secondary gain* is determined by the effectiveness of the organization; the more effective the school, the more the member's long-term goals will be met, and therefore, the greater the long-term gain for that person. Consequently, in negotiating a resolution to a conflict of interest, a person has to be concerned, not only with what is most personally desirable, but also with what is most desirable for improving the effectiveness of the school or classroom.

Negotiations have several important characteristics (Johnson & Johnson, F. P., 1975): (a) There are at least two persons, groups, organizations, or nations involved; (b) there are both cooperative interests (both parties wish to reach an agreement) and competitive interests (both parties wish to reach an agreement as favorable to themselves as possible) present; (c) both parties are dependent on the other for reaching an agreement; (d) each party is in the dilemma of wanting to propose an agreement that is highly favorable to itself but not wanting to risk making the other party so mad that it refuses to negotiate; (e) each party is dependent on the other to provide information about what a reasonable agreement is from the other's perspective; (f) there are contractual norms that spell out acceptable behavior during negotiations; and (g) the negotiations have a beginning, a middle, and an end.

Junior high and high school students from all parts of the United States reported that they preferred direct negotiations to resolve student-student and teacher-student conflicts of interest (DeCecco & Richards, 1974). They preferred a committee as the best means of managing conflicts between students and administrators. Despite their preferences, the students perceived little choice among alternatives for resolving conflicts. Of all students questioned, 81% saw no alternative to the method actually used for resolving conflict. They reported that negotiations were tried in only about 17% of the conflicts, while decisions were imposed by school authorities in 55%. Thus, negotiating is not a commonly used method in most secondary schools in the United States. Inasmuch as it is the most effective method, school personnel and students are not availing themselves of the procedures needed for constructive conflict management.

Confronting the Opposition.

The first step in negotiating a constructive settlement of a conflict is to confront the opposition (Argyris, 1970; Beckard, 1969; Bach & Wyden, 1969; Johnson & Johnson, F. P., 1975; Walton, 1969). A *confrontation* is the direct expression of one's view of the conflict and one's feelings about it while inviting the opposition to do the same. Confrontations involve clarifying and exploring the conflict issues, the nature and strength of the underlying needs of the participants in the conflict, and their current feelings. They are deliberate attempts to begin, with opposition, a direct and problem-solving discussion about the conflicts.

There has been a series of studies comparing confrontations with other strategies for dealing with conflicts of interest. Burke (1969) found that problem-solving confrontations were strongly associated with constructive resolution of conflicts, whereas forcing the other person to accept one's position was strongly associated with ineffective conflict management. Lawrence and Lorsch (1967) examined, in six organizations, the use of confrontation, of forcing the other person to accept one's position, and of smoothing over conflict. They found that high organizational performance was associated with the use of confrontation in dealing with conflicts. Burke (1970) asked 74 managers to describe the way they and their immediate superiors dealt with conflicts. Although both effective and ineffective managers reported the use of confrontation, ineffective managers reported much higher use of forcing the other person to accept one's position.

Perhaps the most difficult aspect of confrontation is the open expression of current feelings; yet it is usually necessary. Often, if emotions are not directly expressed verbally, they will be expressed in deeds or misdeeds later. Feelings such as anger and resentment are especially difficult for many people to express constructively during confrontations. Unexpressed anger can be turned inward and become apathy, depression, and guilt, or it can be displaced onto other people and situations. DeCecco and Richards (1974) found that, when students or school personnel did not express the anger they felt, the anger did not vanish but was expressed nonverbally in the sudden eruption of physical violence and assaults on both people and property. When one person expressed anger and the other did not, anger seemed to build to even higher levels. The failure to express anger verbally was found to result in violence, intimidation, coercion, and the displacement of anger onto issues, personal differences, and actions that could not be negotiated. When anger was skillfully expressed by both participants in the conflict, it had such positive functions as communicating what issues needed to be resolved and where commitments were. The verbal expression of anger also seemed to generate motivation to resolve conflicts and to abide by the agreements made. An important factor in the skillful expression of anger was focusing the anger on issues and conditions that could be changed with reasonable amounts of effort and time. DeCecco and Richards concluded that the expression of anger must be focused on issues. Anger focused on people often took the form of verbal threats and was more often a prelude to violence than to negotiations. Feshbach (1970) also found that the verbal expression of anger can be a substitute for physical aggression. Levi-Strauss (1969) states that structured ways of expressing anger and other "raw" feelings, such as verbalizing them in negotiations, transforms them into more "cooked," civilized feelings. Johnson (1971b) found that the expression of anger in ways that communicate rejection of the opponent as a person decreases the likelihood that the opponent will change her or his attitudes about the conflict being negotiated. The person expressing the anger, furthermore, tended to underestimate the alienating effect of anger on the opponent.

An important aspect of confrontations, therefore, is the direct, verbal expression of anger focused on the issues, not on the persons, involved in the conflict. The emotional statement of issues is the means of structuring the anger by directing it toward issues that can be negotiated. All participants in the conflict need to be able to express their anger in words and to focus such expressions on the issues being negotiated.

Besides anger, negotiators will also want to express warmth. Johnson (1971b, 1971c) found that the expression of warmth (compared to coldness and rejecting anger) results in more agreements being reached in negotiations, in one's being better liked by one's opponents, and in the opponents developing positive attitudes toward the negotiations and feeling accepted.

Jointly Defining the Conflict.

It takes two or more people to create a conflict of interest, and it takes two or more people to resolve one. In order to reach an agreement on how the conflict is to be resolved, the conflict must be defined in a way that both sides can accept. Here are some helpful guidelines in defining the conflict constructively.

Focus on behavior, not on psychological states and personality characteristics. There is a tendency in defining conflicts to attribute the causes of the conflict to inner psychological states of the opponent (Blake & Mouton, 1962; Chesler & Franklin, 1968; Sherif & Sherif, 1965). Defining a conflict as the sick and perverted actions of a vicious troublemaker is less constructive than defining a conflict as a specific set of actions by an opponent. People want to appear strong and capable to others, and if they believe one is trying to label them as sick, weak, incompetent, or ineffective, they will refuse to compromise or negotiate flexibly (Brown, 1968; Tjosvold, 1974; Tjosvold, Johnson, & Fabrey, 1978). Make sure the conflict is over issues, not personalities.

A conflict defined as a problem to be solved is much easier to resolve constructively than a conflict defined as a win–lose situation (Blake & Mouton, 1962; Deutsch & Lewicki, 1970). The total benefits for all sides in negotiations are higher when problem-solving strategies are used rather than win–lose strategies (Lewis & Pruitt, 1971). Defining a conflict as a win–lose situation leads to adopting win–lose strategies such as making an opening proposal highly favorable to oneself, refusing to modify it, trying to persuade the opponent that one's position is reasonable, using threats and promises to coerce and entice the opponent to accept one's proposals, and ignoring all of the opponent's arguments concerning the validity of his or her position (Chertkoff & Esser, 1976; Johnson, 1974; Rubin & Brown, 1975; Walton & McKersie, 1965). Although win–lose strategies often pay off in the short run, the damage they cause to future cooperation significantly reduces their secondary gains. Win–lose strategies commonly impose the position of the negotiator with the most power in the school upon the other participants. They undermine trust, inhibit dialogue and communication, and generally diminish the likelihood that the conflict will be resolved constructively. In a win–lose negotiation, every action of all participants is viewed as an attempt to dominate. Negotiators tend to deny the legitimacy of their opponents' interests and to consider their own needs. They try to force the opponent to give in while trying to augment their own power and undermine the power of their opponents. The losers have little motivation to carry out the actions agreed on, resent the winner, and often try to sabotage the agreement. The winner finds it hard to enforce the agreement. Severe damage to interpersonal relationships results. Generally, the winner and the losers will be hostile toward each other in the future. Because of the damage to the long-term cooperation among students and school personnel, win–lose strategies should be avoided.

Despite the high probability of secondary losses, win–lose strategies of negotiation are often used in schools. Both Flanders (1964) and Gump (1964) have observed that teachers try to dominate students by coercing them into doing what the teachers want. Such negotiation strategies tend to provoke student resistance to the teachers' influence attempts (Flanders, 1964). Rafalides and Hoy (1971), in a study of 45 high schools involving 3,000 teachers and administrators, concluded that, when a school emphasizes authoritarian control and expects students to accept teacher decisions without questions, students become alienated from the school. DeCecco and Richards (1974) note that 55% of the conflicts they studied were resolved by school personnel coercively imposing decisions on students. They concluded that coercion and threats of punishment by school personnel frequently escalated conflict and prevented negotiations.

The smaller and more precise the conflict, the easier it will be to resolve (Deutsch, Canavan, & Rubin, 1971). It is easier, for example, to resolve a conflict over a small rule infraction than a conflict over disrespect toward adult authority. The more general and ambiguous the definition of the conflict, the harder it is to resolve constructively.

Communicating Cooperative Intentions

Numerous studies indicate that the unambiguous expression of cooperative intentions in negotiations of conflicts of interest results in (a) agreements being reached in shorter periods of time; (b) a reduction of the opponents' defensiveness and egocentrism, allowing them to consider other perspectives; (c) increased attitude change; (d) reduction of the felt importance to have the "right" ideas about the issues being negotiated; (e) greater comprehension and retention by each opponent of the other's position and arguments; and (f) increased perceptions by each opponent that the other accurately understands the opponent's position, is an understanding and accepting person, and is one in whom she or he would like to confide (Johnson, 1971d, 1974; Johnson, McCarty, & Allen, 1976).

Negotiation and Perspective Taking

In order to negotiate successfully, one needs to become sufficiently detached from one's original position to be able to see the situation from new perspectives. Negotiation requires both a realistic assessment of common and opposed interests and a sacrifice of some of the opposed interests in order to build on the common ones. The basis of rational problem solving is a clear understanding of all sides of an issue and an accurate assessment of their validity and relative merits. In order to achieve this, one must be able to understand the perspectives of opponents. The balancing of gains and losses best occurs when both negotiators can view the conflict from all varying perspectives. The attitude modification and changes in position necessary for an agreement to be reached in negotiations are greatly dependent on perspective taking. Part of negotiating is both seeing the conflict from the opponent's perspective and inducing the opponent to view the conflict from one's own perspective.

In their study of conflict in schools, DeCecco and Richards (1974) found that the inability to take other people's perspectives seriously impeded negotiations as a means of conflict resolution. The failure of teachers and administrators correctly to perceive the interests of students resulted in destructive conflict management. Without perspective taking, the common interests of school personnel and students were not recognized and sought after by either school personnel or students. The younger the students, furthermore, the more difficulty they had in taking other people's perspectives, indicating that perspective-taking abilities are related to cognitive development.

When one argues one's opponent's position, one publicly espouses a set of attitudes with which one disagrees. By temporarily arguing an opponent's position, one increases one's understanding of the other person's perspective and position, thus achieving a reorientation that allows one to arrive at broader and more productive alternative agreements. There are a series of studies that demonstrate greater modification of attitudes after publicly espousing a set of attitudes with which one disagrees than after passive exposure to the same persuasive materials (e.g., Culbertson, 1957; Greenwald & Albert, 1968; Janis & Gilmore, 1965; Janis & King, 1954; King & Janis, 1956; Zimbardo, 1965). Johnson (1966, 1967, 1971a) and Muney and Deutsch (1968) found that, in direct negotiations of conflicts of interest, people who temporarily argued their opponent's position (compared to people who negotiated without doing so) changed their attitudes significantly more on the issue being negotiated. These studies did not find significant differences in the ease of reaching agreement. Johnson (1966, 1967), however, found that the vast majority of pairs of subjects that temporarily argued each other's position and reached an agreement had at least one person who was highly accurate in representing the opponent's position, feelings, and perspective.

A central aspect of indicating to one's opponent that one is attempting to see the conflict from the opponent's perspective is accurately to paraphrase the opponent's position and feelings. Johnson (1971c) found that the accurate restatement of the opponent's position and feelings induces the opponent to modify personal attitudes about the issue being negotiated. He also found that more agreements resulted from the accurate restatement of the opponent's position and feelings than from the inaccurate restatement of the opponent's position and feelings. The more competitive the negotiator, however, the less likely it is that she or he will be influenced by listening to her or his opponent accurately restating his or her position, feelings, and perspective (Johnson & Dustin, 1970).

The temporary arguing of the opponent's position has been found to increase a negotiator's understanding and retention of the content and perspective of the opponent's position, to clarify misunderstandings and misperceptions of the opponent's position, and to increase the positiveness of attitudes toward the opponent and the negotiations (Johnson, 1966, 1967, 1968, 1971a, 1971c). Johnson (1971c) found that hearing one's opponent accurately paraphrase one's position, feelings, and perspective resulted in more favorable perceptions of the opponent and the negotiations.

A central aspect of successful negotiations, therefore, is the overt taking of the perspective of one's opponents and influencing them to do the same.

STUDENT REBELLION AGAINST AUTHORITY

Any kind of controversy or conflict of interest may turn into violent rebellion. There is some evidence that violence against people and property has been rapidly increasing in American schools. The U.S. Senate Subcommittee to Investigate Juvenile Delinquency (1975) conducted a nationwide survey of 750 school districts. They found that, between 1970 and 1973, burglaries of school buildings increased by 12%; robberies increased by 37%; assaults on students increased by 85%; assaults on teachers increased by 77%; rapes and attempted rapes increased by 40%; and homicides increased by 19%. According to the National Educational Association (reported in the February 3, 1976 issue of the *Wall Street Journal*) students committed 100 murders, 12,000 armed robberies, 9,000 rapes, and 270,000 school burglaries and caused $600 million in school property damage during the 1974–1975 school year. Such incidences of violence against people and property represent a breakdown of authority in the school.

The most difficult conflict for many school personnel to manage is student rebellion against the authority hierarchy of the school. Examples of such student rebellion can be found in most schools. Incidences such as unidentified students appearing in a classroom and refusing either to leave or to give their names, students ignoring teacher directives to stop standing in the hall and go to class, students in bathrooms smarting off to teachers who are telling them to go to class, and students appearing in the library without passes and refusing to leave when told to do so are all examples. School personnel often experience both fear and anger when students flaunt violations of school regulations.

There are many possible reasons why students, especially in junior and senior high schools, rebel against the authority vested in school personnel. Stinchcombe (1964) concludes from an extensive study that student rebellion is based on either (a) failure to achieve up to the school's criteria for success by middle-class males who want to be academically successful but are unable to be so or (b) disinterest in the school's criteria for success by males who see themselves destined for the manual-labor market and females who are planning on early marriages (they see little value in grades and instead strive for adult privileges that are more important and more satisfying for them). DeCecco and Richards (1974) conclude, on the basis of their study, that student rebellion is often based on the failure to express anger about an issue directly to school personnel within the context of negotiations. The failure to express anger directly around an issue causes students to express anger indirectly through violence toward each other, school personnel, and property. Rhea (1968) concludes that students are more present oriented, less motivated toward future success, and less likely to believe in the school's benevolent paternalism. Chesler and Franklin (1968) believe that many incidences of student rebellion are based on student concern about the lack of personal communication with school personnel and resentment about the dehumanizing way students are treated.

The research of DeCecco and Richards (1974) indicates that 19% of the conflicts reported by students involved the use of violence. School personnel used violence in about 11% of the conflicts, while students used force with other students in about 5% of the conflicts. Students used force against school personnel in about 3% of the conflicts reported. Students reported more violence in urban (22%) than in suburban (16%) junior and senior high schools. Students reported more peer violence in junior (9%) than in senior (5%) high schools. They reported more adult use of force, however, in senior (9%) than in junior (4%) high schools. Students believed that they were victims of adult violence four or five times as often as they believed that they were the perpetrators. School personnel, however, believed that they were more often the victims than were the students.

It may be possible to prevent much of the rebellion against authority now occurring in schools. Eash and Sparkis (1973) conducted a study of two inner-city junior high schools in a major metropolitan area. Their study focused on the students who were sent to the principal's office or the guidance office more than once a month. Being sent to these offices usually meant that the student was involved in some form of violence against people or property and that the teacher felt unable to control the student. In one junior high school, less than 7% of the students were involved in more than one incident a month, and in the other junior high school, less than 15% were involved in more than one incident a month. By concentrating the social services of the schools on these students and by giving special attention to their program of studies for the following year, their disruptive behavior was reduced to practically zero within 1 year.

CONCLUDING NOTE

Schools will never eradicate conflict, but through encouraging controversies and the skillful negotiation of conflicts of interest, the destructiveness currently resulting from conflicts within many schools can be greatly reduced. Through training students and school personnel in constructive argumentation and negotiating, conflicts can be a source of growth, excitement, learning, and creativity.

REFERENCES

Altman, I., & McGinnies, E. Interpersonal perception and communication in discussion groups of varied attitudinal composition. *Journal of Abnormal and Social Psychology,* 1960, **60,** 390-395.

Amaria R., Biran, L., & Leith, G. Individual versus cooperative learning. *Educational Research,* 1969, 11, 95-103.

Argyris, C. *Intervention theory and method.* Reading, Mass.: Addison-Wesley, 1970.

Asch, S. *Social Psychology.* Englewood Cliffs, N.J.: Prentice-Hall, 1952.

Bach, G., & Wyden, P. *The intimate enemy.* New York: Morrow, 1969.

Bahn, C. *The interaction of creativity and social facilitation in creative problem solving.* Unpublished doctornal dissertation, Columbia University, 1964.

Beckhard, R. *Organizational development.* Reading, Mass.: Addison-Wesley, 1969.

Berlyne, D. E. Uncertainty and conflict: A point of contact between information-theory and behavior-theory concepts. *Psychological Review,* 1957, 64, 329-339.

Berlyne, D. E. *Conflict, arousal, and curiosity.* New York: McGraw-Hill, 1960.

Berlyne, D. E. Exploratory and epistemic behavior. In S. Koch (Ed.), *Psychology: A study of science* (Vol. 2). New York: McGraw-Hill, 1963.

Berlyne, D. E. Curiosity and education. In J. Krumboltz (Ed.), *Learning and the educational process.* Chicago: Rand McNally, 1965.

Berlyne, D. E. Notes on intrinsic motivation and intrinsic reward in relation to instruction. In J. Bruner (Ed.), *Learning about learning* (Cooperative Research Monograph No. 15). Washington: U.S. Department of Health, Education, and Welfare, Office of Education, 1966.

Berlyne D. E. *Aesthetics and psychobiology.* New York: Appleton, 1971.

Blake, R., & Mouton, J. Comprehension of own and outgroup positions under intergroup competition. *Journal of Conflict Resolution,* 1961, 5, 304-310.

Blake, R., & Mouton, J. The intergroup dynamics of win-lose conflict and problem-solving collaboration in union-management relations. In M. Sherif (Ed.), *Intergroup relations and leadership.* New York: Wiley, 1962.

Blake, R., & Mouton, J. *Building a dynamic corporation through torid organizational development.* Reading, Mass.: Addison-Wesley, 1969.

Blake, R., & Mouton, J. The fifth achievement. *Journal of Applied Behavior Science,* 1970, 6, 413-426.

Blatt, M. The effects of classroom discussion upon children's level of moral judgement. Unpublished doctoral dissertation, University of Chicago, 1969.

Blatt, M., & Kohlberg, L. The effects of classroom moral discussion upon children's level of moral judgement. In L. Kohlberg (Ed.), *Collected papers on moral development and moral education.* Cambridge: Harvard University, Moral Education and Research Foundation, 1973.

Bolen, L., & Torrance, E. *An experimental study of the influence of locus of control, dyadic interaction, and sex, on creative thinking.* Paper presented at the American Educational Research Association, San Francisco, April, 1976.

Botvin, G., & Murray, F. The efficacy of peer modeling and social conflict in the acquisition of conservation. *Child Development,* 1975, 45, 796-799.

Boulding, E. Further reflections on conflict management. In R. Kahn & E. Boulding (Eds.), *Power and conflict in organizations.* New York: Basic, 1964.

Brown, B. The effects of the need to maintain face on interpersonal bargaining. *Journal of Experimental Social Psychology,* 1968, 4, 107-122.

Burdick, H., & Burnes, A. A test of "strain toward symmetry" theories. *Journal of Abnormal and Social Psychology,* 1958, 57, 367-369.

Burke, R. Methods of resolving interpersonal conflict. *Personnel Administration,* July 1969, pp. 48-55.

Burke, R. Methods of resolving superior-subordinate conflict: The constructive use of subordinate differences and disagreements. *Organizational Behavior and Human Performance,* 1970, 5, 393-411.

Chertkoff, J., & Esser, J. A review of experiments in explicit bargaining. *Journal of Experimental Social Psychology,* 1976, 12, 464-487.

Chesler, M., & Franklin, J. *Interracial and intergenerational conflict in secondary schools.* Paper presented at The American Sociological Association meeting, Boston, August 1968.

Colson, W. *Self-disclosure as a function of social approval.* Unpublished master's thesis, Howard University, 1968.

Crawford, J., & Haaland, G. Predecisional information seeking and subsequent conformity in the social influence process. *Journal of Personality and Social Psychology,* 1972, 23, 112-119.

Crockenberg, S., & Nicolayev, J. *Stage transition in moral reasoning as related to conflict experienced in naturalistic settings.* Paper presented at the Meeting Society for Research in Child Development, New Orleans, March 1977.

Culbertson, F. Modification of an emotionally held attitude through role playing. *Journal of Abnormal and Social Psychology*, 1957, **54**, 230–233.

DeCecco, J., & Richards A. *Growing pains: Uses of school conflict*. New York: Aberdeen, 1974.

Deutsch, M. Trust and suspicion. *Journal of Conflict Resolution*, 1958, **2**, 265–179.

Deutsch, M. The effect of motivational orientation upon trust and suspicion. *Human Relations*, 1960, **13**, 123–139.

Deutsch, M. Cooperation and trust: Some theoretical notes. In M. Jones (Ed.), *Nebraska Symposium on Motivation*. Lincoln: University of Nebraska Press, 1962.

Deutsch, M. Conflicts: Productive and destructive. *Journal of Social Issues*, 1969, **25**, 7–43.

Deutsch, M. *The resolution of conflict*. New Haven: Yale University Press, 1973.

Deutsch, M., Canavan, D., & Rubin, J. The effects of size of conflict and set of experimenter upon interpersonal bargaining. *Journal of Experimental Social Psychology*, 1971, **7**, 258–267.

Deutsch, M., & Lewicki, R. "Locking in" effects during a game of chicken. *Journal of Conflict Resolution*, 1970, **14**, 367–378.

Dewey, J. *How we think*. Lexington, Mass. Heath, 1933.

Dunnette, M. D., Campbell, J., & Jaastad, K. The effect of group participation on brainstorming effectiveness of two industrial samples. *Journal of Applied Psychology*, 1963, **47**, 30–37.

Eash, M., & Sparkis, V. *Analysis of behavioral incidents reported in discipline cases in two junior high schools* (Mimeographed Rep.). Chicago: University of Illinois at Chicago Circle, Office of Evaluation Research, 1973.

Ewbank, H., & Auer, J. *Discussion and debate*. New York: Appleton, 1946.

Falk, D., & Johnson, D. W. The effects of perspective-taking and egocentrism on problem-solving in heterogeneous and homogeneous groups. *Journal of Social Psychology*, 1977, **102**, 63–72.

Feffer, M., & Suchotliff, L. Decentering implications of social interaction. *Journal of Personality and Social Psychology*, 1966, **4**, 415–422.

Feshbach, S. Aggression. In P. Mussen (Ed.), *Carmichael's manual of child psychology* (Vol. 2). New York: Wiley, 1970.

Festinger, L., & Maccoby, N. On resistance to persuasive communications. *Journal of Abnormal and Social Psychology*, 1964, **68**, 359–366.

Fiedler, F., Meuwese, W., & Oonk, S. An exploratory study of group creativity in laboratory tasks. *Acta psychologica*, 1961, **18**, 100–119.

Flanders, N. A. Some relationships among teacher influence, pupil attitudes, and achievement. In B. Biddle & W. Ellena (Eds.), *Contemporary research on teacher effectiveness*. New York: Holt, 1964.

Flavell, J. *The development psychology of Jean Piaget*. New York: D. Van Nostrand, 1963.

Flavell, J. *The development of role taking and communication skills in children*. New York: Wiley, 1968.

Gerard, H. & Greenbaum, C. Attitudes toward an agent of uncertainty reduction. *Journal of Personality*, 1962, **30**, 485–495.

Ghiselli, E., & Lodahl, T. Patterns of managerial traits and group effectiveness. *Journal of Abnormal and Social Psychology*, 1958, **57**, 61–66.

Glidewell, J. C. *Group emotionality and production*. Unpublished doctoral dissertation, University of Chicago, 1953.

Goldman, M. A comparison of individual and group performance of varying combinations of initial ability, *Journal of Personality and Social Psychology*, 1965, **1**, 210–216.

Greenwald, A., & Albert, R. Acceptance and recall of improvised arguments. *Journal of Personality and Social Psychology*, 1968, **8**, 31–35.

Gump, P. V. Environmental guidance of the classroom behavioral system. In B. Biddle & W. Ellena (Eds.), *Contemporary research on teacher effectiveness*. New York: Holt, 1964.

Hall, J., & Williams, M. A comparison of decision making performances in established and ad hoc groups. *Journal of Personality and Social Psychology*, 1966, **3**, 214–222.

Hall, J., & Williams, M. Group dynamics training and improved decision making. *Journal of Applied Behavioral Science*, 1970, **6**, 39–68.

Harnack, V., & Fest, T. *Group discussion: Theory and technique*. New York: Appleton, 1964.

Haythorn, W., Couch, D., Haefner, D., Langham, P., & Carter, L. The behavior of authoritarian and equalitarian personalities in groups. *Human Relations*, 1956, **9**, 57–74.

Hoffman, L. Homogeneity of member personality and its effect on group problem-solving. *Journal of Abnormal and Social Psychology*, 1959, 58, 27–32.

Hoffman, L., Harburg, E., & Maier, N. Differences and disagreements as factors in creative problem solving. *Journal of Abnormal and Social Psychology*, 1962, 64, 206–214.

Hoffman, L., & Maier, N. Sex differences, sex composition, and group problem-solving. *Journal of Abnormal and Social Psychology*, 1961, 63, 453–456.

Hogan, R., & Henley, N. *A test of the empathy-effective communication hypothesis* (Research Rep. 84). Baltimore: Johns Hopkins University, Center for Social Organization of Schools, 1970.

Howell, W., & Smith, D. *Discussion.* New York: Macmillan, 1956.

Hunt, J. Introduction: Revisiting Montessori. In M. Montessori (Ed.), *The Montessori method.* New York: Shocken, 1964.

Inhelder, B., Bovet, M., Sinclair, H., Smock, C. On cognitive development. *American Psychologist*, 1966, 21, 160–164.

Inhelder, B., & Sinclair, H. Learning cognitive structures. In P. Mussen, J. Langer, & M. Covington (Eds.), *Trends and issues in developmental psychology.* New York: Holt, 1969.

Janis, I., & Gilmore, J. The influence of incentive conditions on the success of role-playing in modifying attitudes. *Journal of Personality and Social Psychology*, 1965, 1, 17–27.

Janis, I., & King, B. The influence of role playing on opinion change. *Journal of Abnormal and Social Psychology*, 1954, 49, 211–218.

Jensen, L., & Larm, C. Effects of two training procedures on intentionality in moral judgments among children. *Developmental Psychology*, 1970, 2, 310.

Johnson, D. W. *The use of role reversal in intergroup competition.* Unpublished doctoral dissertation, Columbia University, 1966.

Johnson, D. W. The use of role reversal in intergroup competition. *Journal of Personality and Social Psychology*, 1967, 7, 135–141.

Johnson, D. W. *The effects on cooperation of commitment to one's position and engaging in or listening to role reversal.* Unpublished manuscript, 1968. (Available from L. D. W. Johnson, Department of Educational Psychology, University of Minnesota, Minneapolis, Minn.)

Johnson, D. W. *The social psychology of education.* New York: Holt, 1970.

Johnson, D. W. The effectiveness of role reversal: The actor or the listener. *Psychological Reports*, 1971, 28, 275–282. (a)

Johnson, D. W. The effects of the order of expressing warmth and anger upon the actor and the listener. *Journal of Counseling Psychology*, 1971, 18, 571–478. (b)

Johnson, D. W. The effects of warmth of interaction, accuracy of understanding, and the proposal of compromises on the listener's behavior. *Journal of Counseling Psychology*, 1971, 18, 207–216. (c)

Johnson, D. W. Role reversal: A summary and review of the research. *International Journal of Group Tensions*, 1971, 1, 318–334. (d)

Johnson, D. W. *Contemporary social psychology.* Philadelphia: Lippincott, 1973.

Johnson, D. W. Communication and the inducement of cooperative behavior in conflicts. *Speech Monographs*, 1974, 41, 64–78.

Johnson, D. W. Affective perspective-taking and cooperative predisposition. *Developmental Psychology*, 1975, 11, 869–870. (a)

Johnson, D. W. Cooperativeness and social perspective taking. *Journal of Personality and Social Psychology*, 1975, 31, 241–244. (b)

Johnson, D. W. *The distribution and exchange of information in problem solving dyads.* Manuscript submitted for publication, 1977.

Johnson, D. W., & Ahlgren, A. Relationship between student attitudes about cooperation and competition and attitudes toward schooling. *Journal of Educational Psychology*, 1976, 68, 92–102.

Johnson, D. W., & Dustin, R. The initiation of cooperation through role reversal. *Journal of Social Psychology*, 1970, 82, 193–203.

Johnson, D. W., & Johnson, F. P. *Joining together: group theory and group skills.* Englewood Cliffs, N.J.: Prentice-Hall, 1975.

Johnson, D. W., & Johnson, R. T. Instructional goal structure: Cooperative, competitive, or individualistic. *Review of Educational Research*, 1974, 44, 213–240.

Johnson, D. W., & Johnson, R. T. *Learning together and alone: Cooperation, competition, and individualization.* Englewood Cliffs, N.J.: Prentice-Hall, 1975.

Johnson, D. W., Johnson, R. T., Johnson, J., & Anderson, D. The effects of cooperative vs. individualized instruction on student prosocial behavior, attitudes toward learning, and achievement. *Journal of Educational Psychology*, 1976, **68**, 446–452.

Johnson, D. W., Johnson, R. T. & Scott, L. The effects of cooperative and individualized instruction on student attitudes and achievement. *Journal of Social Psychology*, 1978, **104**, 207–216.

Johnson, D. W., McCarty, K., & Allen, T. Congruent and contradictory verbal and nonverbal communications of cooperativeness and competitiveness in negotiations. *Communication Research*, 1976, **3**, 275–292.

Keasey, C. Experimentally induced changes in moral opinions and reasoning. *Journal of Personality and Social Psychology*, 1973, **26**, 30–38.

Kelley, H., & Thibaut, J. Group problem solving. In G. Lindzey & E. Aronson (Eds.), *Handbook of Social Psychology* (Vol. 4). Reading, Mass.: Addison-Wesley, 1969.

Kiesler, C., & Pallak, M. Arousal properties of dissonance manipulations. *Psychological Bulletin*, 1976, **83**, 1014–1025.

King, B., & Janis, I. Comparison of the effectiveness of improvised versus nonimprovised role-playing in producing opinion changes. *Human Relations*, 1956, **9**, 177–186.

Kohlberg, L. Stage and sequence: The cognitive-developmental approach to socialization. In D. A. Goslin (Ed.), *Handbook of socialization theory and research*. Chicago: Rand McNally, 1969.

Krause, R., & Deutsch, M. Communication in interpersonal bargaining. *Journal of Personality and Social Psychology*, 1966, **4**, 572–577.

Kuhn, D., Langer, J., Kohlberg, L., & Haan, N. The development of formal operations in logical and moral judgment. *Genetic Psychological Monographs*, in press.

Langer, J. Disequilibrium as a source of development. In P. Mussen, J. Langer, & M. Covington (Eds.), *Trends and issues in developmental psychology*. New York: Holt, 1969.

Laughlin, P., & Bitz, D. Individual versus dyadic performance on a disjunctive task as a function of initial ability level. *Journal of Personality and Social Psychology*, 1975, **31**, 487–496.

Laughlin, P., & Branch, L. Individual versus tetradic performance on a complementary task as a function of initial ability level. *Organization Behavior and Human Performance*, 1972, **8**, 201–216.

Laughlin, P., Branch, L., & Johnson, H. Individual versus triadic performance on a unidimensional complentary task as a function of initial ability level. *Journal of Personality and Social Psychology*, 1969, **12**, 144–150.

Laughlin, P., & Johnson, H. Group and individual performance on a complementary task as a function of initial ability level. *Journal of Experimental Social Psychology*, 1966, **2**, 407–414.

Laughlin, P., Kerr, N., Davis, J., Haiff, H., & Marciniak, K. Group size, member ability, and social decision schemes on an intellective task. *Journal of Personality and Social Psychology*, 1975, **31**, 522–535.

Laughlin, P., & McGlynn, R. Cooperative versus competitive concept attainment as a function of sex and stimulus display. *Journal of Personality and Social Psychology*, 1967, **7**, 398–402.

Lawrence, P., & Lorsch, J. *Organization and environment: Managing differentiation and integration.* Cambridge: Harvard University, Graduate School of Business Administration, Division of Research, 1967.

LeFurgy, W., & Woloshin, G. Immediate and long-term effects of experimentally induced social influence in the modification of adolescents' moral judgments. *Journal of Personality and Social Psychology*, 1969, **12**, 104–110.

Levi-Strauss, C. *Raw and the cooked: Introduction to a science of mythology.* New York: Harper, 1969.

Lewis, S., & Pruitt, D. Organization, aspiration level, and communication freedom in integrative bargaining. *Proceedings of the American Psychological Association*, 1971, **6**, 221–222.

Maier, N., & Hoffman, L. Financial incentives and group decision in motivating change. *Journal of Social Psychology*, 1964, **64**, 369–378.

Maier, N., & Solem, A. The contributions of a discussion leader to the quality of group thinking: The effective use of minority opinions. *Human Relations*, 1952, **5**, 277–288.

Maitland, D., & Goldman, J. Moral judgment as a function of peer group interaction. *Journal of Personality and Social Psychology*, 1974, **30**, 699–704.

Mead, G. *Mind, self, and society*. Chicago: University of Chicago Press, 1934.

Miller, S., & Brownell, C. Peers, persuasion, and Piaget: Dyadic interaction between conservers and nonconservers. *Child Development*, 1975, **46**, 992–997.

Muney, B., & Deutsch, M. The effects of role reversal during the discussion of opposing viewpoints. *Journal of Conflict Resolution*, 1968, **12**, 345–356.

Murray, F. Acquisition of conservation through social interaction. *Developmental Psychology*, 1972, **6**, 1–6.

Murray, F., & Botvin, G. *The acquisition of conservation through cognitive dissonance*. Paper presented at the American Educational Research Association, Chicago, March 1974.

Noonan-Wagner, M. *Intimacy of self-disclosure and response processes as factors affecting the development of interpersonal relationships*. Unpublished doctoral dissertation, University of Minnesota, 1975.

Pelz, D. Some social factors related to performance in a research organization. *Administrative Science Quarterly*, 1956, **1**, 310–325.

Petelle, J. The role of conflict in discussion. *Speaker and gavel*, 1964, **2**, 24–28.

Peters, R., & Torrance, E. Dyadic interaction of preschool children and performance on a construction task. *Psychological Reports*, 1972, **30**, 747–750.

Piaget, J. *The moral judgment of the child*. New York: Free Press, 1948.

Piaget, J. *The psychology of intelligence*. New York: Harcourt, 1950.

Rafalides, M., & Hoy, W. K. Student sense of alienation and pupil control orientation of high schools. *High School Journal*, 1971, **55**, 102.

Rest, J., Turiel, E., & Kohlberg, L. Relations between level of moral judgment and preference and comprehension of the moral judgment of others. *Journal of Personality*, 1969, **37**, 225–252.

Rhea, B. Institutional paternalism in high schools. *Urban Review*, 1968, **2**, 13–15, 34.

Robbins, S. *Managing organizational conflict*. Englewood Cliffs, N.J.: Prentice-Hall, 1974.

Rogers, C. R. *Client-centered therapy: Its current practice, implications, and theory*. Boston: Houghton Mifflin, 1951.

Rogers, C. R. Towards a theory of creativity. In P. Vernon (Ed.), *Readings in creativity*. London: Penguin, 1970.

Ross, E. *The principles of sociology*. New York: Appleton, 1920.

Rubin, J., & Brown, B. *The social psychology of bargaining and negotiation*. New York: Academic, 1975.

Schultz, W. What makes groups productive. *Human Relations*, 1955, **8**, 429–465.

Schultz, W. *FIRO: A three-dimensional theory of interpersonal behavior*. New York: Holt, 1958.

Sermat, V., & Smyth, M. Content analysis of verbal communication in the development of a relationship: Conditions influencing self-disclosure. *Journal of Personality and Social Psychology*, 1973, **26**, 332–346.

Shaw, M. A note concerning homogeneity of membership and group problem-solving. *Journal of Abnormal and Social Psychology*, 1960, **60**, 448–450.

Sigel, I., & Hooper, F. (Eds.). *Logical thinking in children: Research based on Piaget's theory*. New York: Holt, 1968.

Silverman, I., & Geiringer, E. Dyadic interaction and conservation induction: A test of Piaget's equilibration model. *Child Development*. 1973, **44**, 815–820.

Silverman, I., & Stone J. Modifying cognitive functioning through participation in a problem-solving group. *Journal of Educational Psychology*, 1972, **63**, 603–608.

Simmel, G. Conflict association. In L. Coser & B. Rosenberg (Eds.), *Sociological theory: A book of readings*. New York: Macmillan, 1957.

Sinclair, H. Developmental psycho-linguistics. In D. Elkind & J. Flavell (Eds.), *Studies in cognitive development: Essays in honor of Jean Piaget*. New York: Oxford University Press, 1969.

Smedslund, J. The acquisition of conservation of substance and weight in children: II. External reinforcement of conservation of weight and the operations of addition and subtraction. *Scandinavian Journal of Psychology*, 1961, **2**, 71–84. (a)

Smedslund, J. The acquisition of conservation of substance and weight in children: III. Extinction of conservation of weight acquired "normally" and by means of empirical controls on a balance. *Scandinavian Journal of Psychology*, 1961, **2**, 85–87. (b)

Smedslund, J. The acquisition of conservation of substance and weight in children. V. Practice in conflict situations without external reinforcement. *Scandinavian Journal of Psychology,* 1961, 2, 156–160. (c)

Stinchcombe, A. *Rebellion in a high school.* New York: Quadrangle/The New York Times Book Co., 1964.

Taylor, D., Altman, I., & Sorrentino, R. Interpersonal exchange as a function of rewards and costs and situational factors: Expectancy confirmation-disconfirmation. *Journal of Experimental Social Psychology,* 1969, 5, 324–339.

Tjosvold, D. Threat as a low-power person's strategy in bargaining: Social face and tangible outcomes. *International Journal of Group Tensions,* 1974, 4, 494–510.

Tjosvold, D. Low-power person's strategies in bargaining: Negotiability of demand, maintaining face, and race. *International Journal of Group Tensions,* 1977, 7, 20–41.

Tjosvold, D., & Johnson, D. W. The effects of controversy on cognitive perspective-taking. *Journal of Educational Psychology,* 1977, 69, 679–685.

Tjosvold, D., & Johnson, D. W. *Controversy, cooperation and competition, and accuracy of cognitive perspective-taking. Contemporary Educational Psychology,* in press.

Tjosvold, D., Johnson, D. W., & Fabrey, L. *The effects of controversy and defensiveness on cognitive perspective-taking.* Manuscript submitted for publication, 1978.

Torrance, E. Can grouping control social stress in creative activity? *Elementary School Journal,* 1961, 62, 139–145.

Torrance, E. Influence of dyadic interaction on creative functioning. *Psychological Reports,* 1970, 26, 391–394.

Torrance, E. Stimulation, enjoyment, and originality in dyadic creativity. *Journal of Educational Psychology,* 1971, 62, 45–48.

Torrance, E. *Dyadic interaction in creative thinking and problem solving.* Paper presented at the meetings of the American Educational Research Association, New Orleans, February 1973.

Triandis, H. C., Bass, A., Ewen, R., & Mikesele, E. Teaching creativity as a function of the creativity of the members. *Journal of Applied Psychology,* 1963, 47, 104–110.

Triandis, H. C., Hall, E., & Ewen, R. Member heterogeneity and dyadic creativity. *Human Relations,* 1965, 18, 33–55.

Tuckman, B. Group composition and group performance of structured and unstructured tasks. *Journal of Experimental Social Psychology,* 1967, 3, 25–40.

Turiel, E. An experimental test of the sequentiality of developmental stages in the child's moral judgment. *Journal of Personality and Social Psychology,* 1966, 3, 611–618.

Turiel, E. Stage transition in moral development. In R. M. W. Travers (Ed.), *Second handbook of research on teaching.* Chicago: Rand McNally, 1973.

U.S. Senate Subcommittee to Investigate Juvenile Delinquency. *Our nation's schools—A report card: "A" in school violence and vandalism.* Washington: U.S. Government Printing Office, 1975.

Wallach, L., & Sprott, R. Inducing number conservation in children. *Child Development,* 1964, 35, 1057–1071.

Wallach, L., Wall, A., & Anderson, L. Number conservation: The roles of reversibility, addition-subtraction, and misleading perceptual cues. *Child Development,* 1967, 38, 425–442.

Walton, R. *Interpersonal peacemaking.* Reading, Mass.: Addison-Wesley, 1969.

Walton, R., & McKersie, R. *A behavioral theory of labor negotiations.* New York: McGraw-Hill, 1965.

Wohlwill, J., & Lowe, R. Experimental analysis of the development of the conservation of number. *Child Development,* 1962, 33, 153–167.

Worchel, P., & McCormick, B. Self-concept and dissonance reduction. *Journal of Personality,* 1963, 31, 589–599.

Ziller, R. Scales of judgment: A determinant of the accuracy of group decisions. *Human Relations,* 1955, 8, 153–167.

Ziller, R., & Exline, R. Some consequences of age heterogeneity in decision-making groups. *Sociometry,* 1958, 21, 198–211.

Zimbardo, P. The effect of effort and improvisation on self-persuasion produced by role-playing. *Journal of Experimental Social Psychology,* 1965, 1, 103–120.

VII

THE SCHOOL AND THE COMMUNITY

School Desegregation
and Intergroup Relations

Janet Ward Schofield
University of Pittsburgh

School desegregation has been one of the most controversial issues on the American political scene during the last quarter century. No other domestic policy issue in recent years has aroused such strong feeling and widespread political activity among vast numbers of Americans. Proponents of desegregation have doggedly pursued litigation against segregated school districts year after year in spite of huge costs and interminable delays. Opponents have sought a constitutional amendment against "forced busing," which would have the practical consequence of severely limiting desegregation. Opposition to desegregation has been the cornerstone of national as well as local political careers and the moving force behind the founding of over 3,000 private academies.

The historic *Brown v. Board of Education* case of 1954, which overturned the earlier separate-but-equal doctrine, had relatively little concrete impact on the country's heavily segregated schools for more than a decade, although public reaction to the ruling was immediate and intense, especially in the South (Read, 1975). Substantial desegregation efforts began largely as a result of federal court orders in the late 1960s after the passage of the Civil Rights Act of 1964 and several Supreme Court decisions that emphasized the importance of rapid desegregation. So, for example, in 1964, a full 10 years after the Brown decision, about 98% of the black children in the South were still in all-black schools. By 1974, however, about 45% of southern black children were in schools that were more than one-half white (Holsendolph, 1976). Such changes were much more dramatic in the South than in the rest of the country, although a trend toward slowly decreasing segregation has been evident in most other regions of the country, with the important exception of some large urban areas (Farley, 1975; Pettigrew, 1969a). Although 67% of all black children were still in predominantly minority schools in the 1974–1975 school year, the impact of the school desegregation efforts of the preceding decade was widely

The author wishes to express her thanks to Tom Pettigrew and Stuart Cook for their helpful comments on an earlier draft of this chapter. Some of the work necessary for the preparation of this chapter was supported by the author's contract 400-76-0011 with the National Institute of Education. Other expenses related to its preparation were covered by grant 5-S05-RR07084 from the Biomedical Research Support Program of the National Institute of Health.

329

felt (Holsendolph, 1976). For example, the proportion of white Americans who reported that the grade school nearest their home was all white dropped from 59% in 1964 to 36% in 1970. Similarly, the proportion of blacks reporting that the nearest elementary school was all black fell from 40% to 13% during that same period (Campbell, 1971).

The *Brown v. Board of Education* decision was based on the constitutional principle of equal protection (Read, 1975; Wisdom, 1975). Nonetheless, the work of social scientists on the effects of racial segregation figured quite noticeably in the proceedings. Over 40 social scientists and educators testified in the case, and 32 signed a lengthy statement, "The Effects and Consequences of Desegregation: A Social Science Statement," which supported the plaintiff's position (Wisdom, 1975). Also, the pioneering work of social scientists like Gunner Myrdal and Kenneth Clark was cited by the Court in the now-famous footnote 11.

At the time of the 1954 decision and for the following 10–15 years, there was a widely shared optimism among social scientists about the probable beneficial effects of desegregation. Social scientists' widely shared faith in contact as a means of fostering improved understanding and interracial harmony is reflected in the 1968 report of the National Advisory Commission on Civil Disorders. The commission urged that school desegregation be adopted as "the priority education strategy" saying, "In this last summer's disorders we have the consequences of racial isolation at all levels, and of attitudes toward race, on both sides, produced by three centuries of myth, ignorance, and bias. It is indispensable that opportunities for interaction between the races be expanded" (p. 12).

At least partly because changes in intergroup attitudes and behavior are seen as having such potentially important social consequences, considerable research has explored the impact that desegregated schooling has on such attitudes and behavior. The results of this work are far from conclusive, however. In fact, in recent years, unusually sharp controversies have arisen in the academic community about the probable effects of desegregation on intergroup relations. For example, Armor (1972) and Pettigrew, Useem, Normand, and Smith (1973) differ dramatically in their interpretation of the data on how desegregation influences racial attitudes. Similarly, the views of Coleman, Kelly, and Moore (1975) on the relation between school desegregation and white flight have been sharply challenged by the work of other researchers (Farley, 1975; Pettigrew & Green, 1976a, 1976b; Rossell, 1975–1976).

In light of the great public concern about desegregation and the considerable controversy among social scientists about the implications of their findings, it seems important to ask both what social-psychological theory and research have to say about desegregation and intergroup relations and how such research can be made more fruitful. I approach these tasks first by demonstrating the striking inconclusiveness of the literature to date regarding the impact of desegregation on intergroup relations. Then, I review the social-psychological theory relating to desegregation with an emphasis on showing how the lack of attention to theory has contributed to the inconclusiveness of the empirical literature. Next, I discuss conceptual and methodological problems that have also contributed seriously to making the desegregation literature difficult to interpret. Finally, on a more positive note, I highlight recent trends that desegregation research has taken and new paths it could follow that might help to make it more rewarding theoretically as well as more useful to the policy maker and practitioner.

Because of space limitations, this review deals exclusively with the impact of desegregation on interracial attitudes and behavior, although there has also been considerable work on the impact of desegregation on children's academic achievement, self-esteem, and self-concepts. Readers interested in the latter topics are referred to St. John's (1975) recent book, which contains an extensive bibliography.

OVERVIEW OF THE RESEARCH FINDINGS ON DESEGREGATION AND INTERGROUP RELATIONS

Desegregation and Intergroup Attitudes

St. John (1975) recently reviewed the literature from 1937 through 1973 on the impact of school desegregation on interracial attitudes. Like other recent reviewers of this research (Amir, 1976; Carithers, 1970; Cohen, 1975; Stephan, 1978), St. John concludes that its most striking feature is the inconsistency of the findings. Many studies suggest that desegregation tends to lead to more positive interracial attitudes (Gardner, Wright, & Dee, 1970; Jansen & Gallagher, 1966; Mann, 1959; Singer, 1966; U.S. Commission on Civil Rights, 1967). Others suggest precisely the opposite (Barber, 1968; Dentler & Elkins, 1967; Taylor, 1967). Still others suggest that desegregation has a positive effect on the attitudes of whites and a negative effect on the attitudes of blacks (McWhirt, 1967) or vice versa (Crooks, 1970; Kurokawa, 1971; Webster, 1961). Finally, some like Lombardi (1962) or Trubowitz (1969) suggest no effect at all.

A brief presentation of a few representative studies should illustrate the wide variety of methodologies and conclusions that characterize the literature. Singer's (1966) study of fifth-grade students in three suburban schools is fairly typical of well-designed studies that seek to assess the effect of desegregation on students' interracial attitudes. Singer compared the attitudes of black and white students in segregated schools to those of fifth graders in a school that was approximately 65% white and 35% black. Attitudes were assessed with the Bogardus Social Distance Scale as well as with a questionnaire and a gamelike test. Singer concluded that students in the desegregated school generally showed more positive intergroup attitudes than those in the segregated schools. Desegregated black and white students showed more favorable attitudes toward the other group on the social-distance questionnaire than did their segregated counterparts of similar IQ and socioeconomic background. This was true in spite of the fact that desegregated whites saw blacks as more aggressive and as less likely to do well academically than did segregated whites. In another frequently cited study, Webster (1961) obtained responses to social-distance questions from 60 whites and 44 blacks just a few months before they were transferred from segregated elementary schools to a newly desegregated junior high school. Retesting of the same students after 6 months of desegregated schooling showed that, whereas white students had become less accepting of blacks, the black students were more accepting of whites.

McPartland's (1968) secondary analysis of data from a survey conducted by the U.S. Office of Education is a good example of the large-scale survey research on desegregation and interracial attitudes. Analyzing data on a sample of high school students living in the Northeast, McPartland found that previous interracial contact was associated with positive interracial attitudes. In a survey of white students attending suburban schools near Boston that enrolled black students through a voluntary busing program, Useem (1976) also found a clear positive relationship between prior interracial experience and the students' attitudes toward the busing program. In addition, she found a weak positive relation between interracial contact in extracurricular activities and white students' attitudes. Classroom contact with black students was not associated with positive attitudes, however.

St. John (1975) categorized the studies she reviewed in numerous ways to see if, once the studies were properly grouped, some patterns could be found in their seemingly inconsistent and contradictory results. This effort, however, showed few clear-cut results. For example, there was little relation between the design of a study (cross-sectional versus longitudinal) and its findings. Also, there was little relation between the kind of desegregation (neighborhood, voluntary, mandatory) and its effect on interracial attitudes. The research published since 1973 is just as inconclusive as that reviewed by St. John.

I present no comprehensive review of the research on desegregation and intergroup attitudes here because, cumulatively, the literature yields so few firm conclusions. Rather, after a brief examination of the literature on desegregation's effect on intergroup behavior, I focus attention on exploring why the research findings in these areas are so inconclusive and on suggesting directions future work might more profitably take.

Desegregation and Intergroup Behavior

St. John's (1975) review lists 19 studies that deal with the relationship between desegregated schools and intergroup behavior. Many of these studies are routinely cited in similar discussions of the literature (Carithers, 1970; Cohen, 1975; Pettigrew, 1969b). Rather remarkably, only one of these studies involved actual observation of intergroup behavior in a desegregated school.[1] A large majority use variants on traditional sociometric techniques (Moreno, 1934) that involve asking people to report with whom they would chose to interact in various situations rather than observation of actual choice behavior. Similarly, sociometric or other nonobservational methods predominate in the work bearing on interracial interaction produced since 1973 (e.g., Gerard & Miller, 1975; Green & Gerard, 1974; Schofield, 1975). Because sociometric studies are such a large part of the research on the effect of desegregation on intergroup relations, I first present a few representative examples. Then, separately and in more detail, I discuss studies that have involved actual systematic observation of behavior.

As St. John's (1975) analysis suggests, the findings on the relation between desegregation and interracial behavior are as contradictory and confusing as those on desegregation and intergroup attitudes. Several studies using sociometric techniques to assess the relation between desegregation and interracial behavior have concluded that the children in desegregated schools became less accepting of members of other groups over time. For example, Shaw (1973) asked all students in the fourth, fifth, and sixth grades of a recently desegregated school to name the three students they would most like in their classroom and the three students they would least like in their classroom. This sociometric test was administered in February and June during the first year of desegregation. It was readministered in February of the following year. Analysis of this data suggested that "association with members of

---

[1] This count does not include the classic Yarrow, Campbell, and Yarrow (1958) study that was conducted in a desegregated camp.

the other race, at least in the school studied, leads to less acceptance of members of the race" (p. 151). Gerard and Miller's (1975) massive longitudinal study of the schools in Riverside, California, comes to much the same conclusion. In this study, questionnaires that asked each child to indicate his or her first, second, and third choices for friends, schoolwork partners, and members of a ball team were administered to several thousand white, black, and Mexican American children. Gerard and Miller focus their analysis on the number of times children belonging to the various groups were chosen by their peers on the sociometric tests. For example, they report that the average Anglo boy received 2.56 choices in the year before desegregation and 2.93 in the following year, compared to black boys, who received 2.18 choices before desegregation and 1.80 during the first year of desegregation. Although the primary focus of their analysis concerns overall friendship, work, and play status without special regard for who chooses whom, Gerard and Miller also do some analyses and draw some conclusions about the amount of interracial contact and longitudinal trends in this contact. They write, "The unprecedented amount of data we have examined points unmistakably to the conclusion that, with the exception of playground interaction, little or no real integration occurred during the relatively long-term contact situation represented by Riverside's desegregation program. If anything we found some evidence that ethnic cleavage becomes more pronounced over time" (p. 237).

Other studies using sociometric or other techniques designed to judge behavioral tendencies come to somewhat different conclusions, however. For example, Yarrow, Campbell, and Yarrow (1958) found that both black and white children who had attended an interracial summer camp were less likely to choose white cabin mates at the end of the 2-week experience, suggesting that desegregated experience can decrease whites' tendencies to in-group choice. Also, Schofield (1975) found that, after 1 year of mandatory desegregation, black elementary students were more likely to place themselves with an integrated group in a picture game than were their still-segregated counterparts.

Studies based on observation of actual interracial behavior in desegregated schools are extremely few and far between. As a matter of fact, examination of the studies from 1937 to 1973 catalogued by St. John (1975) and a search of *Psychological Abstracts, Sociology Abstracts,* and the *ERIC* indexes from 1974 to 1976 revealed only three studies that employed true systematic observational techniques to assess changes in students' interracial behavior. These studies, like the attitude studies and those employing sociometric techniques, show very mixed results. Aronson and Noble (1966) observed student seating patterns in a summer school program for black and white students in West Hartford, Connecticut. They found no changes in these patterns over time. Consistent with the results of many sociometric studies, however, they found more interracial seating in the elementary grades than in high school. Silverman and Shaw (1973) studied interracial interaction in three Florida schools during the first semester of court-ordered desegregation. Observers who recorded the total number of students interacting and the number who were interacting in racially mixed groups were stationed in the school during the 3rd, 8th, and 13th weeks of the semester. Silverman and Shaw found a weak trend for an increase in interracial interaction from the 3rd week to the 8th week and a subsequent decrease by the 13th week. The apparent trends were not statistically significant, however. Schofield and Sagar (1977b) charted interracial interaction during the first year of desegregated schooling for seventh and eighth graders voluntarily attending a new magnet school. They recorded seating patterns in the school cafeteria weekly from the fourth month of school through the end of the school year. In the seventh grade, where classes were racially balanced, the seating patterns showed a significant increase in racial mixing over time; but in the eighth grade, which was tracked into a heavily white, accelerated academic group and a heavily black regular group, the opposite pattern was found.

The only finding that emerges consistently from sociometric and observational studies in desegregated schools is that students interact more with others of their own group than would be expected if race were not an important grouping criterion (Criswell, 1939; Gerard & Miller, 1975; Green & Gerard, 1976; Jansen & Gallagher, 1966; Moreno, 1934; Shaw, 1973; Schofield & Sagar, 1977a, 1977b). The extent of the racial clustering in desegregated schools varies markedly, but it appears to occur almost everywhere. In some schools, the resegregation seems almost total. For example, Cusick and Ayling (1973) report that they were unable to have an informal discussion with a racially mixed group over lunch at a high school because the informal pattern of segregated black and white tables was so strong that students were unwilling to break it. Silverman and Shaw (1973) found that interracial interactions ranged from a low of .67% of all interactions observed to a high of 10.3% in three schools that were from 30% to 50% black. Schofield and Sagar (1977a, 1977b) found somewhat more mixing than the studies just cited, but they report levels of interracial interaction that are still quite low. For example, at the end of 1 year of desegregation under very favorable circumstances, black and white students sat next to each other at lunch about one-fifth as often as they would have if race did not enter into seating choices.

THEORY IN DESEGREGATION RESEARCH

Cohen (1975) and St. John (1975) both argue convincingly that the lack of theoretical perspective in desegregation research is a major contributing factor to the inconclusiveness of the literature taken as a whole. Typically, researchers have studied a particular example of desegregation and looked for changes in students' attitudes or behaviors that could be attributed to their desegregated experience. Because they bring no theoretical framework that would suggest what characteristics of the desegregated setting might relate to those changes, researchers pay little attention to what the desegregated setting is actually like. Because desegregated schools differ so dramatically on so many variables, contradictory outcomes are found. Without a theoretical perspective, one has little idea of what patterns to look for in the data, and confusion abounds.

Contact Theory

Among social psychologists, the most widely shared theoretical perspective on desegregation and intergroup relations has been that suggested by Allport's (1954) contact theory. Allport's basic thesis is relatively straightforward. He argues that intergroup contact may reinforce previously held stereotypes and increase intergroup hostility unless the contact situation is structured in a way that provides equal status for minority- and majority-group members and provides strong institutional support for positive relations. Allport also stresses the necessity of cooperative interaction aimed toward the achievement of shared goals. According to Allport, unless these conditions are met, improvement in intergroup relations is unlikely.

Building on Allport's work, Pettigrew has argued that it is a mistake to use one word, *desegregation,* to apply to all kinds of interracial schooling. He has drawn a distinction between what he calls *merely desegregated schools* and *genuinely integrated schools.* Pettigrew (1973) writes: "Desegregation is achieved by simply ending segregation and bringing blacks and whites together; it implies nothing about the quality of interracial interaction" (pp. 92-93). Integration, on the other hand, is achieved only when Allport's conditions for fostering positive intergroup contact have been met. Pettigrew (1973) argues, for example, that Allport's equal-status criterion requires that the integrated school provide equal access to sources of social status as well as to physical facilities and materials. Hence he contends that an integrated school's staff must be interracial at all levels and that positions that give students formal or informal status, such as student council member or cheerleader, must not be monopolized by either group. Pettigrew also sees strict ability grouping based on test scores as incompatible with the equal-status criterion when it leads to heavily resegregated classrooms with differential status. In addition, he stresses the vital importance of the attitudes of school authorities, such as the principal, arguing that positive attitudes about desegregation are crucial to creating the supportive atmosphere Allport hypothesized was necessary for improved intergroup relations.

Although contact theory is routinely invoked in reports on desegregation research, it has, in actuality, had a remarkably small impact on the design and reporting of that research. For example, contact theory appears to have had extremely little impact on the kind of information given in published reports about the effects of desegregation. Researchers often tip their hats to contact theory in the introductory passages of a research report and then fail entirely to give information on topics the theory suggests should be vital to predicting the likely outcomes of the interracial experience. Webster's (1961) study is fairly typical in this regard. He mentions contact theory in the first paragraph of his study. In discussing his results, he states that the criteria specified by contact theory as conducive to positive change were met. The extent to which these criteria were actually met in the study is, however, unclear. For example, the only information Webster (1961) gives about authorities' stand on desegregation is that the change in district boundaries that resulted in the desegregation was ordered by the school board because of overcrowding and socioeconomic-status differentials between schools. There is no specific information on the attitudes of others, such as principals or teachers, who could reasonably be argued to be authorities more important than the school board in the eyes of the desegregated junior high school students. In addition, no information is given on the racial composition of the school's staff. Webster's study provides a specific example of research that takes a contact-theory perspective without supplying data that the perspective would suggest is important, but many others do precisely the same thing.

The number of studies that omit basic descriptive data on the desegregated situation, as well as the sort of data that contact theory suggests, is extraordinary. Studies frequently neglect to indicate whether the school studied was experiencing mandatory, voluntary, or neighborhood desegregation, and even whether classrooms within the school were desegregated. Many studies fail to mention the racial mix of the students (Crooks, 1970; Kurokawa, 1971), and the majority neglect to give such information about the school's staff. Cohen (1975) found that only 3 of the 24 studies she reviewed had detailed information on the attitudes of teachers and administrators.

Unfortunately, although contact theory is often used to explain the results of studies that find that interracial contact has led to increased friction or to no change, it has rarely been used to structure studies of desegregation's effects. The very few studies that have taken contact theory really seriously have had generally promising results: That is, interracial attitudes or behavior appeared to be related to the conditions of desegregation much as Allport (1954) has suggested. For example, Lachat (1972) studied racial attitudes in an all-white, an integrated, and a desegregated high school. Although there was a considerable amount of voluntary segregation in informal social activities in the integrated school as well as in the desegregated one, the white students were almost twice as likely to hold positive attitudes toward blacks in the former school as in the latter (71% versus 37%). Also, Schofield and Sager (1977b) found different trends in the amount of interracial interaction in different grades of the same school that were characterized by different classroom-assignment policies. In the grade with a low-status, heavily black track and a high-status, heavily white track, racial aggregation increased over time; but in the nontracked grade, it decreased.

Clearly the most ambitious efforts to apply and develop contact theory are those of Stuart Cook and his associates. Cook (1969) reviewed the literature on intergroup relations and concluded that five aspects of the interracial contact situation are especially crucial in determining whether attitudinal change will occur as a result of intergroup contact. Three of these aspects were very similar to Allport's (1954) original contact theory and Pettigrew's (1969a) later discussion of it:

1. Equal status within the setting for members of both groups
2. Mutual interdependence
3. A social climate that has norms favorable to interracial association

The two new items added by Cook (1969) were:

1. The attributes of the disliked group member in the contact situation contradict prevailing stereotyped belief.
2. The association reveals personal information about the disliked group member so that others interacting with that member are encouraged to perceive him or her as an individual.

After isolating the above factors as crucial to attitude change, Cook carefully went about constructing a contact situation that fulfilled these criteria. The actual procedures are described in detail elsewhere (Cook, 1969). In brief, Cook selected highly prejudiced white college students and then exposed each to a black confederate daily for about 4 weeks in an experimental situation that the students believed to be a part-time job. Approximately 2 months after this exposure, subjects were retested for attitude change. Of Cook's subjects, 35% showed a favorable attitude change of 1 or more standard deviations. (The standard deviation used was based on analysis of the test scores of other college students living in the same town as the experimental subjects.) Only 1 of the 23 subjects showed a clear negative change, as did 2 of the control subjects. A later replication of this study found essentially the same results as the initial study (Cook, 1971). Cook's work is an extraordinarily clear demonstration that planned experiences that incorporate the conditions suggested by contact theory can bring about substantial attitude change. Interestingly, a recent study of intergroup relations in a prison housing unit that closely replicated the conditions created in Cook's work also found significant decreases in racial prejudice over time (Foley, 1976). Because studies that test contact theory's predictions about positive change are so few and far between, however, it is difficult to assess how adequately this theory has isolated the variables that effect the outcomes of interracial contact.

A Theory of Status Characteristics and Expectation States

Although contact theory was, for many years, the most wisely accepted theoretical perspective on intergroup relations, in the last decade a few other theoretical positions have inspired noteworthy work that explores the factors conducive to change in interracial attitudes and interaction patterns.

Berger, Cohen, and Zelditch (1966, 1972) have developed a theory of status characteristics and expectation states that Cohen and her colleagues have applied to studying interracial interaction. In brief, their theory argues that the status order in society engenders expectations about competence that become widely held by members of both the higher ranked and the lower ranked groups. When members of these groups come in contact, these mutually held expectations about competence may lead to dominance and actually superior performance by the higher ranked group. The theory further holds that to influence behavior expectations need not be conscious.

Cohen (1972) argues that, in American society, race is one of the status characteristics that lead to the self-fulfilling prophecy predicted by the theory. This argument gains strong support from Cohen's demonstration that white junior high school students working in biracial groups dominate interaction even though the experimental situation was carefully constructed to eliminate all factors, aside from the students' expectations, that might promote dominance by either race. I. Katz (1964) and his colleagues had previously found similar dominance by white college students in biracial work groups.

Cohen and Roper (1972) reasoned that if expectation states help to account for white domination of interaction in biracial states, then changes in expectations should lead to changes in such patterns. Hence, they used a specially designed training experience to influence black children's expectations about their own competence. Black children were taught how to build a radio and also instructed how to teach the skill to others. Then these children viewed a film of themselves constructing the radios. A group of white children viewed the film as well. Next, some of the black children taught white children how to build the radios while others taught the skill to a black administrator. Then all children participated in small biracial groups. The groups in which black children had taught whites how to make the radio showed a pattern of equal-status interaction. The other groups showed the familiar pattern of white dominance, however. Cohen and Roper (1972) concluded that unequal interaction patterns will persist unless the expectations of both groups are treated.

As is apparent, Cohen's theory has somewhat different practical implications than contact theory. Whereas contact theory holds that positive relations will evolve if a cooperative equal-status environment is created, expectation theory suggests that, even in such an environment, biased expectations of both whites and blacks may lead to continued white dominance unless active steps are taken to reverse the perhaps-unconscious expectations. Hence, instead of equal status, this theory calls for an at-least-temporary reversal of superior and subordinate roles. In one experiment, Cohen, Lockheed, and Lohman (1976) found that both expectation training and a control condition that involved a noncompetitive curriculum and an interracial staff resulted in equal-status behavior after a period of 1 week. After this initial period, all students participated in a 6-week program that was structured to require cooperation. At the end of the 6-week period, the black males in the expectation-training group showed some tendency to dominate the white males. Just the reverse was true in the control group, in which white females tended to dominate black females. The findings from this study generally support expectation theory. They also suggest that cooperative interaction in a setting that gives equal status to both groups can, at least in the short run, affect intergroup behavior without specifically planned expectation training.

Other Theoretical Orientations

Contact theory and the theory of status characteristics and expectation states on which Cohen's work is based are obviously theoretical positions that are directly oriented toward illuminating intergroup relations. Other theoretical perspectives not directed specifically to this end also present a fertile source of ideas for exploring the factors that account for the course of intergroup relations in desegregated schools. In recent years, investigators have begun to apply insights gained from other theories to studying factors that affect intergroup attitudes and behavior.

A number of investigators have shown that reinforcement techniques can be successfully used to change interracial attitudes and behavior in young children (Edwards & Williams, 1970; Hauserman, Walen, & Behling, 1973; McMurty & Williams, 1972). For example, Hauserman et al. (1973) used simple reinforcement techniques to promote interracial seating in first-grade students. During the baseline period, observations of the seating pattern in the school cafeteria and of play patterns immediately following lunch were made. Then a program was instituted in which all children were verbally encouraged to sit with a new friend during lunch. In addition, children who sat next to a new friend were given tokens redeemable for desirable objects. After approximately 2 weeks, the reinforcement was discontinued. Although there was marked intersubject variability, "posttreatment" measures taken the following week suggested an increase in interracial seating as well as in interracial interaction during the free-play period compared to the base-line period.

Taking a very different perspective, Pettigrew (1967) has explored the implications of social-comparison processes for the interracial school. He argues that "many of the consequences of interracial classrooms . . . are a direct function of the opportunities such classrooms provide for cross-racial self-evaluation. It follows from such a hypothesis that the more opportunities for cross-racial self-evaluation a school provides, the greater the consequences" (p. 287). Pettigrew's contention that interracial classrooms lead to cross-racial comparisons, whereas segregated ones do not, is supported by Rosenberg and Simmon's (1971) study of black students in Baltimore.

Several other researchers have fruitfully begun to explore the ways in which ideas derived from social-psychological research on person perception can illuminate processes that lead to the formation and maintenance of stereotypes (Ashmore & DelBoca, 1976). For example, Duncan (1977) started with the basic premise, which is supported by much social-psychological research, that an individual's perception of others may be heavily influenced by personal needs, wishes, or expectations. He then demonstrated experimentally that white students are more likely to label an ambiguous shove as violent when the perpetrator is black than when he is white. In addition, working within the framework of attribution theory, Duncan investigated students' perceptions of the causes of the violent act. He found that when the harm-doer was black the students were more likely to interpret the aggressive behavior as due to stable personal dispositions than when the harm-doer was white. In the latter situation, students more frequently invoked situational explanations for the negative behavior. Such findings clearly illuminate psychological processes that may underlie the maintenance of negative stereotypes in situations in which the in-group and out-group members actually behave quite similarly.

CONCEPTUAL AND METHODOLOGICAL PROBLEMS IN DESEGREGATION RESEARCH

Although the atheoretical nature of much past research on desegregation clearly contributes significantly to the inconclusiveness of the literature, basic conceptual and methodological problems also plague the field and contribute markedly to the general confusion. I next discuss some of these problems before proceeding in the last section to suggest ways in which some of these problems can be ameliorated.

What Is Desegregation?

Frequently, in laboratory research, investigators working on a topic at very different institutions will employ the same or extremely similar methods of operationalizing a concept. For example, as Cartwright (1973) points out, a large majority of the research on the risky shift used the same instrument to study that phenomenon. Although the exclusive use of a single specific operationalization of a concept leaves unanswered very serious questions about the generality of the phenomenon under study, as both Cartwright (1973) and Campbell and Fiske (1959) have noted, it is, of course, conducive to consistency of results.

One of the major reasons for the apparent inconsistency of the results of research on desegregation is that researchers have studied vastly different situations, all of which have been subsumed under one term: *desegregation.* Most researchers are not in a position to create instances of desegregation that embody precisely the characteristics they see as crucial to the concept or to control for or eliminate unwanted aspects of the situation they are studying. Typically, they hear about instances of interracial mixing in the schools that are occurring somewhere in their general locale and then try to gain access to the appropriate schools for study. Hence, there is often little motivation to go through the conscious step of deciding how one can best operationalize the concept of desegregation, for the practical problems involved in finding and gaining access to a site or sites that embody these characteristics are often overwhelming.

The social situations that our society labels as "desegregated schools" vary to an extraordinary extent. The problem is, as Cohen (1975) points out, that "desegregation is a political-legal concept, used in widely differing ways by different courts. And when researchers attempt to locate settings in which to study desegregation, they too differ as to what constitutes desegregation" (p. 274). Schools that are considered desegregated in one study might well be considered segregated in another. For example, Singer (1966) classifies a school that is 80% black as segregated, whereas Porter (1971) calls a classroom that is 70% black desegregated. Useem (1976) analyzes racial attitudes in a "token desegregated school" that is over 95% white. Kurokawa (1971) compares a "white" school to a "mixed school." Although he does not give the precise proportion of whites, blacks, and Japanese-Americans at these two schools, he obtained one-third of his minority-group sample from the "white" school, which clearly means that it was not entirely white.

Obviously, the most basic criterion used by researchers and the courts in deciding whether a school is desegregated is the racial mix of the student body. Other factors clearly come into play, however. For example, a suburban school that receives bused inner-city blacks like the one Useem (1976) studied is called "desegregated" even though it was less than 5% black, but a school that is less than 5% black would undoubtedly be classified as segregated if it were located in an area with a substantial black population whose children attended a heavily black school. Hence, the demographic characteristics of the community surrounding the school appear to influence what black/white ratio is considered segregated or desegregated. Warshauer and Dentler (1967) have suggested that a school should be considered desegregated only if the percentage of students of each group in the student body is between 50% and 200% of that group's representation in the entire community. In addition, the race of the group that predominates in the school appears to influence the mathematical proportion of students required to achieve a situation that is called "desegregation." For example, a school that is 90% white and 10% black would be classified as desegregated under some circumstances, whereas a school that was 90% black and 10% white would never be so classified.

Research has quite clearly shown the ratio of black to white in a desegregated situation is related to intergroup attitudes (Dentler & Elkins, 1967; McPartland, 1968; St. John & Lewis, 1975; U.S. Commission on Civil Rights, 1967). For example, St. John and Lewis (1975) used a sociometric technique in which children reported their degree of liking for their classmates to assess peer popularity in desegregated classrooms. These researchers found that being part of the majority group in their classroom increased interracial popularity for both black and white children. So, blacks were most popular with whites in majority-black classrooms, whereas whites were most popular with blacks in majority-white classrooms. There is also some evidence that interracial friendship patterns are influenced by whether black students attend a desegregated neighborhood school or a more distant desegregated school (St. John & Lewis, 1975; Willie, 1973). Hence, it seems likely that the wide variation in the particular racial mix of the schools studied and in the schools' community settings contributes substantially to making it difficult to draw any overall conclusions about the impact of desegregation on interracial attitudes and behavior.

Differential Implementation of Similar Desegregation Programs

Recent work in the field of evaluation research suggests other factors that also contribute importantly to making the desegregation literature inconclusive and difficult to interpret. Evaluative researchers stress the importance of recognizing that programs vary tremendously in the degree to which and in the way in which they are implemented (Cook & Campbell, 1976; Guttentag & Struening, 1975). Thus, even if one program looks superficially like another, one cannot safely assume that they actually take similar shape. Even if the instances of desegregation studied were similar in the ratios of blacks to whites in the schools and the surrounding communities, there would probably still be such substantial differences between the situations that they might be expected to produce widely varying results. For example, some schools clearly distribute black and white students throughout their classes in proportions roughly similar to their proportion in the school (Schofield, 1976). Others resegregate black and white students within the school building (National Institute of Education, 1977). Hence, one desegregated school with 30% black students might have these students distributed equally in all classes, whereas another school might informally resegregate its classes so that students would have little or no classroom contact with students of the other group. It is reasonable to speculate that two such schools could have entirely different effects on the intergroup attitudes of their students, with the resegregated school reinforcing prejudiced attitudes and tendencies toward in-group choice. Indeed, a study by Koslin, Amarel, and Ames (1969) found less racial polarization in classrooms that closely reflected the racial balance of the school they were in than in classrooms in which the racial composition differed from that of the school. Interestingly, in spite of the fact that almost a decade has passed since Cook (1969) drew attention to the importance of the contact situation's acquaintance potential, extremely few published research reports give even crude information on this topic. Cohen (1975), who reviewed the literature on school desegregation and intergroup relations, notes that only one-fifth of the studies done between 1968 and 1974 reported on whether there was actual interracial contact in the classrooms of the schools studied.

The fact that instances of desegregation that appear similar on the surface may differ markedly in critical aspects of implementation such as the extent of actual interracial contact has important implications for the interpretation of large-scale studies that analyze outcome variables in a number of segregated and desegregated schools and conclude that desegregation has no impact. Indeed, it could be that desegregation has an impact that is masked because of the tremendous variance caused by other uncontrolled variables. Alternatively, the positive impact of desegregation in some schools' classrooms might be counterbalanced by the negative impact in others. Sometimes investigators recognize these kinds of problems. For example, in a chapter titled "Effects of Desegregation on Achievement-Relevant Motivation," Biener and Gerard (1975) write

> Our statistical design allowed us to examine differences between samples of minority children at different points . . . —zero years in the receiving schools, versus one year, versus three years—controlling for variations in response due to age and sex within each group. Considering the large amount of uncontrolled variability in the children's actual school experience, it is surprising that we found any differences at all. (p. 146)

More often, however, the problem is completely ignored.

Variations in the Context of Desegregation Efforts

In addition to suggesting that the conclusion, no effect, drawn by some studies may be incorrect, the work of evaluative researchers also suggests why findings of some effect vary so greatly in their conclusions about the nature of that effect. Guttentag (1973) writes

> Programs really are the inverse of the carefully designed and manipulated single variables of the experimental paradigm. And whereas the measurement of outcomes tacitly assumes that the social setting of the program—the when, where, and how a program is administered, and so forth—accounts for less of the variance than treatment effects, this is likely not to be the case at all. (p. 61)

Thus even instances of desegregation that appear roughly equivalent in black/white ratios and implementation strategies may have very different effects depending on the context in which they occur. The huge variations in the context of instances of desegregation that have been studied can be illustrated by brief discussion of the studies cited by St. John's (1975) review. Some of the early studies reviewed by St. John were carried out when laws requiring racial segregation were still in effect and strictly enforced in parts of this country (Criswell, 1939; Kupferer, 1954; Lundberg & Dickson, 1952). Others were conducted during the surge of militant-integrationist civil rights activity in the 1960s (Dentler & Elkins, 1967; McPartland, 1968). Still other studies were done in the 1970s after Presidents Nixon and Ford, as well as some prominent black leaders, had seriously reopened the issue of whether integration was a desirable goal (Eddy, 1975; Schofield & Sagar, 1977b). Also, the region of the country in which these studies were conducted varies from southern states like North Carolina and Kentucky to northern states like New York and Massachusetts to western states such as Oklahoma and California. Cohen (1975) points out that, at present, we do not know what specific changes in our social history constitute factors likely to effect the desegregation process and its impact on students. However, the importance of social-context factors like region or historical era of desegregation is suggested by St. John's (1975) conclusion that studies performed in the South, which also tend to be early studies, are more likely than those performed in the North to find that desegregation negatively influences interracial attitudes. The work of Coles (1968) also suggests that social context can play a vital role in affecting children's reactions to desegregated schooling.

Variation in the Participants in the Desegregation Program

School desegregation varies widely, not only in the how, when, and where of its implementation, but also in the who—the characteristics of the students involved. For example, studies of school desegregation and interracial attitudes and behavior have been conducted in settings ranging from nursery schools (Porter, 1971) through high schools (Useem, 1976). In addition, both the absolute and the relative social class of the black and white students involved vary widely. Reviews of the literature suggest that factors such as age, sex, and social class are related to students' reactions to desegregation (Carithers, 1970; Cohen, 1975; St. John, 1975). Often these factors appear to have interactive effects. For example, although black girls seem to find desegregation more difficult than black boys do, the reverse may be true for whites (Patchen, Davidson, Hofmann, & Brown, 1977; Singer, 1966; Yarrow, Campbell, & Yarrow, 1958). Not surprisingly, behavior in desegregated schools appears to be related to personal factors such as students' aggressiveness and initial racial attitudes (Patchen et al., 1977). One might expect that such factors would also influence the rate and direction of change in interracial attitudes and behavior. Hence, it seems unwise to search for "the effect" of desegregation. One would expect different outcomes depending on the particular situation. In addition, even within a particular setting, a host of variables such as age, sex, and minority- or majority-group membership might be expected to influence how a student reacts to the desegregated experience.

Focus on a Narrow Range of Outcomes rather than on Process

Typically, researchers studying desegregated schools have tried to assess the effects of desegregation without simultaneously exploring the social processes that might account for these effects (National Institute of Education, 1974; St. John, 1975). The lack of attention given in the desegregation research literature to classroom social process is striking. This point is well illustrated by the fact that, in his discussion of the dynamics of the interracial classroom, Pettigrew (1967) cites just three major studies or groups of studies. Two of these, *Equality of Educational Opportunity* (a survey by Coleman, Campbell, Hobson, McPartland, Mood, Weinfeld, & York, 1966) and *Racial Isolation in the Public Schools* (U.S. Commission on Civil Rights, 1967), were, as Pettigrew (1967) notes, broad-gauged surveys that, though they can describe and statistically relate variables, "can only hint at the basic . . . processes at work" (p. 285). The third group of studies, reported in I. Katz (1964), is much more useful in understanding the dynamics in interracial interaction because biracial groups were observed in a variety of experimental situations. Katz's work suggests that the academic performance of black Americans in biracial situations may be influenced by four factors: (1) lowered probability of success, (2) social threat, (3) failure threat, and (4) a social-facilitation effect.[2] The people participating in Katz's experiments were primarily college age or older, however, so it is unclear how well his findings about interracial social processes would apply to a schoolroom situation with students of a very different age. As a matter of fact, later work by Katz and his colleagues (Katz, I., Henchy, & Allen, 1968) suggests that the social-facilitation effect observed in the earlier experiments did not operate for black children in a ghetto elementary school.

The focus on desegregation's effects has undoubtedly stemmed at least partially from the fact that researchers and funding agencies have often hoped to use the results of the research in political ways to support or, less frequently, to undermine the national policy of school desegregation. Obviously, for political purposes, it is

[2] As blacks come less and less to idealize whites and to denigrate blacks, this added incentive value of white approval compared to black approval should disappear. Hence, although the social-facilitation effect may have helped increase black achievement in desegregated settings in the past, ultimately one would expect that it would cease to operate.

much more useful to be able to say that desegregation improves or harms inter-group relations than it is to delineate the processes that may lead to these results.

The heavy emphasis on effects to the exclusion of process is an especially severe problem because desegregation research tends to be nonexperimental and does not lend itself well, from a statistical point of view, to unambiguous causal statements. Given this state of affairs, the causal statements that are made would be much more convincing if one could demonstrate processes that occur in the desegregated set-ting and plausible links between the processes and the outcomes that are found (Suchman, 1967).

I would argue that potential political use of studies on desegregation has led, not only to a focus on effects rather than process, but also to a study of a narrow range of effects that tend to be relatively easily interpreted as "good" or "bad" while ignoring others that might be equally important (Sagar, 1977). For example, a great many studies of desegregation and intergroup attitudes have used measurement techniques like doll choice and social-distance questionnaires to assess change in generalized affect toward the outgroup. Relatively few studies, however, have inves-tigated changes in factors like the ability to differentiate between out-group mem-bers. Laboratory research has suggested that such ability is related to prejudice, at least in white children (Katz, P., 1976). Given that notable disparities exist between the average social, economic, and educational status of blacks and whites, the ability on the part of whites to differentiate between blacks rather than to assume that all blacks share what are most probably perceived as negative characteristics is of considerable importance.

Problems in Measuring Interracial Attitudes

Researchers who want to investigate the impact of desegregation on interracial attitudes face a very difficult task. First, they must face the numerous thorny issues routinely encountered in attempts to measure attitudes (cf. Scott, 1968). Second, they are likely to have to deal with the complex technical issues often involved in the measurement of change (cf. Linn & Slinde, 1977). As each of these topics has a large literature of its own. I do not review all of these problems here. Rather, I turn to a brief consideration of the special problems faced by researchers trying to measure attitudes in an area as controversial and emotionally involving as race relations.

Rosenberg (1969) has argued convincingly that participants in the research pro-cess are often quite concerned with presenting themselves in a way that will earn the researcher's approval. Although this "evaluation apprehension" is most proba-bly operative in a wide variety of research situations, it seems especially likely to influence subjects' responses when the research is dealing with a controversial topic like race relations (Gaertner, 1976). Subjects concerned about making a good im-pression may be particularly careful to present their racial attitudes in a way they believe will win favor because these attitudes are so closely linked to cultural norms and values. For example, it seems unlikely that subjects would feel that the re-searcher's judgment of them would be much influenced by the subjects' expressed preferences for vanilla over chocolate ice cream or vice versa. In this case the expressed attitudes have little to do with important social norms or values, and disagreement with the researcher seems unlikely to have major consequences for the researcher's evaluation of the subjects. In race relations, however, where feelings often run strong and people frequently characterize those who disagree with them as stupid or immoral, precisely the opposite is true.

Gaertner (1976) points out that, when responding to questions about their racial attitudes, individuals are presenting themselves not only to the researcher but also to themselves. Following a train of thought of similar to D. Katz's (1960) discussion of the value-expressive function that attitudes can serve, Gaertner argues that many whites desire to see themselves as unprejudiced even though their basic feelings about blacks may be negative or ambivalent. Hence, they may well make unprejudiced statements in order to convince themselves as well as others that they are not prejudiced. This line of reasoning gains some empirical support from the finding that, among liberals, those whose affective responses to blacks are the least positive sometimes act in the most positive manner toward blacks (Weitz, 1972), if they are anxious about denying their negative or ambivalent feelings.

Another set of problems that may sometimes impede the fruitful study of interracial attitudes in a desegregated school centers around the ethical and practical dilemmas of assessing actively hostile feelings or negative sterotypes. In a great many, if not all, desegregated schools, there is at least the potential for outbursts of negative feeling or behavior between blacks and whites. Hence, administrators and teachers in such schools are often, with good reason, leery of letting a researcher employ a balanced attitude-assessment instrument that may contain negative as well as positive statements; for there is always the possibility that the presentation of such negative statements will help legitimize stereotyped antiblack or antiwhite points of view or serve as a trigger to set off undesirable conflict.

Given the difficulties that plague relatively straightforward attempts to measure racial attitudes, measures that are unlikely to arouse the subjects' awareness that their racial attitudes are being studied seem desirable. In recent years, a number of relatively nonreactive measures of attitudes have been developed (cf. Crosby, Bromley, & Saxe, 1977; Gaertner, 1976). Examples of such measures include judgment of voice tone (Weitz, 1972) and Gaertner and Bickman's (1971) wrong-number technique. Such measures, however, have very rarely if ever been used in the study of the effects of school desegregation on interracial attitudes.

Problems in Measuring Interracial Behavior

As mentioned previously, a great many of the studies designed to investigate the relation between desegregation and interracial behavior use sociometric techniques to assess interracial behavior. Unfortunately, there are several potentially serious problems with the use of such techniques. Almost all the data suggesting that choices on sociometric tests reflect actual behavior choices have been gathered in white classrooms (Biehler, 1954; Bonney & Powell, 1953; Byrd, 1951). Also, sociometric measures may well be as open to distortion by evaluation apprehension as attitude measures. It seems reasonable to expect that the responses of students in desegregated schools to sociometric tasks might be seriously influenced by their perceptions of what school authorities believe is the proper relationship between blacks and whites. Hence, sociometric measures may well be less reliable indicators of actual behavior in desegregated schools than in segregated ones. In fact, it might even be argued that such measures could better serve as crude indicators of perceived racial norms than of actual interracial behavior (Pettigrew, 1977).

Even if sociometric choices were shown to be strongly associated with actual behavioral patterns in desegregated classrooms, there is still some question of how appropriate these techniques are for assessing the impact of desegregation on intergroup behavior. Typically, sociometric measures require the child to give the names of a very small number of other children who are the most preferred companions for various activities. So although such measures allow assessment of the child's closest friends or most preferred partners, they are generally very insensitive to changes in patterns of social interaction that do not involve the development of especially strong relationships. Cohen (1975) has written:

> The mechanism of desegregation is not intended to create universal love and brotherhood. The goal of the desegregation process is a reasonable degree of social integration and a lack of overt conflict whereby blacks and whites, given an objective important to both, can trust each other and listen to each other sufficiently well to complete the task at hand, whether it be a vocational task, an educational task, or a political task. (p. 273)

To the extent that one accepts Cohen's argument, sociometric techniques seem to measure an outcome that, though desirable, is not of the highest priority. Obviously this is not a criticism of the sociometric technique per se. Rather, it is a suggestion that sociometric techniques tap a specific kind of behavior that from the point of view of social policy is less crucial than many other kinds of intergroup behavior.

In addition, it should be noted that the most frequently used sociometric techniques tend to assess behaviors that are relatively unlikely to change over short periods of time. For example, it seems reasonable to expect that a child who initially avoids playing with members of an outgroup would become willing to play cooperatively with out-group members if a conducive situation should arise long before the child would ever select an out-group member as a playmate when allowed to single out a few special students. In light of this fact, it is especially unfortunate that studies of school desegregation typically span just the first year of the desegregation process. In addition, the majority of the desegregation studies have been conducted in schools where desegregation stems from the transfer of children from one school to another rather than from residential desegregation. There is evidence suggesting that new children in a school, regardless of their race, do not immediately become fully integrated into the peer network (St. John & Lewis, 1975; Willie, 1973). It seems unrealistic, therefore, to expect that sociometric techniques would indicate marked changes in interracial behavior in the space of a year or less, even if the school came close to meeting Allport's (1954) criteria. Unfortunately, because studies of intergroup behavior in desegregated schools very rarely use other measures of behavior that may be more rapidly influenced by interracial contact, generalizations about the effect of desegregation are based almost exclusively on the study of this one particular kind of behavior that is relatively resistant to change.

The clear effect of ethical and practical constraints against openly investigating really negative intergroup relations (mentioned briefly in the previous section) can be seen in an examination of the sociometric measures used to explore intergroup relations in desegregated schools. Although there are notable exceptions (Shaw, 1973), recent studies using sociometric peer-nomination techniques almost invariably ask children to name those they want to interact with most but avoid asking for the names of those with whom they are least likely to want to interact (Gerard &

Miller, 1975; Schofield, 1978). The same tendency to avoid strong negative categories is also clear in sociometric rating studies in which children are asked to rate others on a continuum. For example, Schofield's (1978) five rating categories go from "I'd like to work with this person very much" to "I'd rather not work with this person." There is no strong negative statement such as "I'd dislike working with this person very much" to parallel the rather strong positive statement. Not infrequently, attempts to avoid negative statements while keeping a continuum with 5 or more points lead to psychometric problems. For example, St. John and Lewis (1975) instructed students to designate "best friends" by a 1, "good friends" by a 2, "kids who are not your friends but OK" by a 3, and "kids you don't know very well" by a 4. The researcher then assigned a 5 to children who were not rated on a given paper on the assumption that these were the respondents' "least liked or most ignored classmates" (p. 350). As can be seen, the first three ratings on the scale seem to refer to the degree of positive affect. The fourth rating, however, refers to degree of acquaintance, which may be quite different; for it seems quite possible that a student might want to be friends with another student whom he or she does not happen to know well. Hence, the 5-point linear scale seems to shift the entity it measures in midstream. St. John and Lewis's (1975) scale is far from unique in this respect. This tendency to avoid the measurement of negative behavior and to focus on more positive behaviors may have serious consequences. The work of Patchen et al. (1977) suggests that the best predictors of positive interracial behavior are not the same factors that best predict negative behavior, so work that focuses exclusively on factors influencing positive behavior may be of little help to theorists or practitioners who are trying to understand the origins of negative behaviors and mechanisms for reducing such behaviors.

Given the serious problems associated with using sociometric techniques to measure desegregation's impact on intergroup behavior, direct measurement of the behavior itself seems much preferable. Of course, it is possible that, like sociometric measures, behavior may be influenced by evaluation apprehension, but in recent years investigators have found ways to record behavior that appear to be quite nonreactive. For example, Silverman and Shaw (1973) had graduate assistants with counters concealed in their pockets loiter where they could see students leaving school at the end of the day. In the Schofield and Sager (1977b) study, observers were stationed on a ramp that overlooked the cafeteria; they only entered the cafeteria itself when there was doubt about the race or sex of a student. Inasmuch as the seating positions of all 300–400 students in the cafeteria were mapped in the course of 15 minutes during each lunch period, students were hardly likely to feel that they, as individuals, were being judged by the observers.

Another advantage of behavioral measures is, of course, that they can easily be used to measure things, like seating patterns, that may show either positive or negative change well before the more intense relationships that most sociometric techniques are designed to tap. In addition, they can be used, when desired, to tap the same sort of choice behavior that sociometric techniques are designed to measure. For example, Schofield (1976) reports the use of a game, run by teachers as part of ordinary classroom activity, that was developed specifically to allow direct observation of student friendship choices.

Given the numerous advantages of behavioral measures, the question arises as to why sociometric techniques have been so much more widely used. It would seem that practical considerations most probably account for the widely shown preference for sociometric techniques. Sociometric questionnaires can be administered relatively quickly and easily to large numbers of students. In addition, they pose relatively little threat to teachers or administrators in the school being studied, although they may pose more of a threat to students than relatively unobtrusive behavioral measures. On the other hand, behavioral observations in the classroom generally require the presence of the researcher while the teacher is actually teaching. Also, although there are numerous widely known and used observational systems that focus on teacher-student interaction, there are relatively few that focus on student-student interaction (Simon & Boyer, 1967). The task of developing reliable systems for coding classroom behavior is formidable. Thus, researchers primarily interested in desegregation and interracial interaction are compelled to use sociometric techniques or relatively simple coding systems unless they want to work on a quite different and extremely time-consuming task—the development of measures of peer interracial interaction. In spite of the practical difficulties associated with the use of behavioral measures, the advantages of using them seem great enough to suggest that researchers interested in gauging interracial interaction should make a serious effort to see whether they can be used, either in place of traditional sociometric techniques or in addition to them.

Design Problems in Desegregation Research

Even if desegregation research had dealt adequately with the problems discussed above, it would still have to face the very severe practical and methodological problems that are posed when one attempts to assess the impact of an ongoing and highly controversial social policy. As Crain (1976) points out, there are strong pressures on researchers involved with studies on desegregation to complete their work rapidly. Often school boards give permission for studies in their districts in the hope that the study will supply useful information for their decision making. Similarly, funding agencies or the governing bodies of which the funding agencies are a part often sponsor desegregation research in order to generate data to guide policy decisions. These decisions are frequently pressing, so the idea of waiting for research results for any large number of years is highly unattractive (cf. Weiss, 1977). These pressures for rapid results are of course compounded by the academic reward structure, which also strongly encourages rapid publication. Hence, for a variety of reasons, including the fact that cross-sectional studies are generally less expensive than longitudinal studies, the large majority of the research dealing with desegregation and intergroup relations is cross-sectional rather than longitudinal. Rather ironically, cross-sectional data, which is attractive to policy-makers because of its relatively low cost and quick payoff, does not allow one to make the causal inferences with which policy-makers are frequently concerned. For example, it seems about as reasonable to interpret the positive relation McPartland (1968) found in survey data between intergroup contact and racial attitudes as suggesting that positive attitudes lead to contact as it does to interpret it as suggesting that contact leads to positive attitudes. Unfortunately, because the data are cross-sectional, they give little indication of the relative importance of these two causal sequences in accounting for the relationship found between contact and positive attitudes.

Although longitudinal studies have a distinct advantage over cross-sectional studies, they too frequently have serious problems. First, one must have the financial resources and long-term cooperation from a school that longitudinal studies require. The pressures and difficulties of doing long-term longitudinal work are so great that very few desegregation studies span more than 1 year. Although occasional studies do span 2-5 or more years (e.g., Gerard & Miller, 1975; Schofield & Sagar, 1977a), they almost inevitably tend to encounter potentially serious problems. For example, in the 3 years between 1966 and 1969 Gerard and Miller (1975) lost approximately one-third of their original sample. The tendency of longitudinal studies to cover short periods at the beginning of students' desegregated schooling severely limits the extent to which it is appropriate to generalize from their findings.

In addition to covering short periods of time, many longitudinal studies of desegregation employ no control group. Rather, they simply measure a group of students before and after desegregation. Writing about this kind of design, Campbell and Stanley (1963) say: "While this design . . . is judged as . . . worth doing where nothing better can be done . . . it is introduced . . . as a 'bad example' " (p. 7) of a research strategy. Campbell and Stanley go on to point out the serious threats to internal validity in designs such as this. Because there is no control group, the researcher has little idea of whether the effect found, if any, stems from factors like historical change or maturation of the subjects rather than from the treatment being investigated.

The importance of having control groups in longitudinal studies of school desegregation and intergroup relations is heighted by the fact that research suggests there are indeed both age trends and clear historical trends in interracial attitudes and behavior. For example, Criswell's (1939) early work on age trends suggests that black and white children interact fairly readily until third grade, when students increasingly begin to interact with others of their own race. Other research supports Criswell's early finding of increasing hostility and racial cleavage with age (Aronson & Nobel, 1966; Deutschberger, 1946; Dwyer, 1958; Trager & Yarrow, 1952). Hence, changes in interracial attitudes owing to age may confound changes resulting from desegregation unless a control group is available to which the desegregated group can be compared. Similarly, survey research suggests that there have been definite shifts in the racial attitudes of both whites and blacks during the last 15 years (Campbell, 1971; Schuman & Hatchett, 1974). Thus, there is a very real possibility that, in research without a control group, changes resulting from desegregation will be confounded with changes owing to larger societal trends. The desirability of having control groups in longitudinal studies of desegregation is illustrated by a study performed by Williams and Venditti (1969). These researchers found that, over the course of a year, black students in both segregated and desegregated schools became more negative in their attitudes toward certain aspects of their schools and the students in these schools. If measures had been taken only in the desegregated schools, the changes in attitudes might well have been incorrectly attributed to the desegregation experience.

Desegregation researchers recognize the importance of control groups but often are unable to locate or gain access to such groups in spite of serious thought and effort. Finding appropriate control groups is much more difficult than it might appear, as many of the desegregation programs that are most easily accessible to researchers are voluntary programs. Inasmuch as volunteers in these programs are self-selected for their interest in attending a desegregated school, a control group of students who have not volunteered for such a program is clearly of questionable value. Students interested in the desegregation program who were not admitted would make a good control group only if a random selection process were used in deciding which of the applicants would be admitted to the program. There apparently has been only one study of a desegregation program in which students were randomly assigned to desegregated and control groups (Pettigrew, 1977).

Studies attempting to judge the impact of desegregation on interracial behavior, whether they use observational measures or sociometric techniques, face a special control-group problem. As St. John (1975) points out: "Interracial behavior cannot be compared in segregated and integrated settings or before and after desegregation; it can be examined only if the races are in contact" (p. 65). One can compare responses of segregated and desegregated students to attitude measures like social-distance questions, but one can hardly make meaningful comparisons between the in-school interracial behavior of segregated and desegregated students because segregated students have no out-group members with which they can interact. In essence, this means that studies of behavior are hard pressed to find reasonable control groups. There are a number of partial solutions to this problem, although none are completely satisfactory. First, if longitudinal studies with no control group find trends that are clearly counter to the trends one might expect due to maturation, one can at least make a reasonably strong argument that desegregation is responsible for that effect. This argument would be greatly strengthened if hypotheses about the effects of desegregation based on our theoretical understanding of the process had been formulated in advance. For example, Schofield and Sager (1977b) hypothesized a trend toward increasing racial mixing in the seventh grade of a school and a trend toward decreasing mixing in the eighth. Given the available data on developmental trends, one would predict no change or decreased mixing in both grades. Schofield and Sagar's hypotheses, which were based on differences in the school's policies regarding tracking of students in the two grades, were confirmed.

There is another way to handle the control-group problem in studies of intergroup behavior, a way that is methodologically more satisfying than the one just discussed. One could present students actually enrolled in segregated and desegregated schools with an interracial situation outside of their schools in which their behavior could be observed. Assuming that segregated students who constitute a reasonable control group could be found (this is the same problem found in attitude studies), the behavior of the segregated and desegregated students could be compared. For example, students from the segregated and desegregated schools could be observed during a summer camp experience. Using this strategy, one could assess quite well whether interracial schooling influences students' behaviors in quite different interracial situations. Unfortunately, this strategy would not test whether behavior changes owing to desegregation are occurring in the desegregated school itself. There is evidence that an individual's interracial behavior varies considerably from setting to setting depending on the requirements and norms of the various situations (Minard, 1952), so positive or negative changes in intergroup relations within the desegregated school might well be missed.

Finally, there are problems even with a design that has longitudinal data on reasonably well-matched students at one desegregated and one segregated school. The principal problem is that the impact of the schools as institutions may be confounded with the impact of desegregated classrooms, which is only one aspect of those schools. Obviously schools that are similar in most objective respects on which "experimental" and "control" schools are usually matched can differ significantly in other respects that may have implications for the students' development.

For example, a number of studies have suggested that the principal of a desegregated school has a very major impact on how intergroup relations develop in the school (St. John, 1975). Hence, the conclusions drawn from research comparing racial attitudes in one desegregated and one segregated school might be affected greatly by the principal who happened to be at the desegregated school. To avoid such problems, one could study a whole array of segregated and desegregated schools, but this strategy requires vast amounts of time, money, and effort. In addition, the "error variance" due to differences between the various desegregated schools might well mask whatever effect or effects desegregation might have.

In addition to facing several control-group problems, desegregation studies are often plagued by self-selection problems, both at the institutional and the individual level, that limit their external validity. As Pettigrew (1969a) points out, schools that agree to make themselves available to researchers interested in desegregation are clearly not a random sample of all desegregated schools. For example, such well-regarded school systems as those in New Haven, White Plains, and Berkeley have allowed significant studies of desegregation, whereas many less well-regarded systems, including Cleveland, Chicago, and Los Angeles, refused to permit their students to participate in a major federal survey of desegregated schools even though participation by school districts in this study was ordered by Congress in the Civil Rights Act of 1964 (Pettigrew, 1969a). Similarly, it is reasonable to hypothesize that children whose parents refuse to let them participate in research on desegregation may well not be a random sample of the children in such schools.

THE FUTURE OF RESEARCH ON SCHOOL DESEGREGATION

There are some encouraging new trends in thinking and research about desegregation that I now discuss, along with some suggestions about future directions.

The Development and Refinement of Contact Theory

There seem to be two very closely related contact-theory-inspired lines of work that are now much needed. First, much remains to be done in conceptually working out the way in which the rather general concepts employed by contact theory apply to and operate in the school situation. Second, more work and study are needed on the effects of the contact-theory variables taken one at a time.

The need for systematic conceptual work on the development and refinement of contact theory can be illustrated by discusion of the very varied ways in which the concept of equal status within the contact situation has been conceptualized. Some social scientists have considered the equal-status criterion met when members of both groups have equal access to the same institution. For example, as mentioned previously, Webster (1961) considered the equal-status condition as met when blacks and whites were assigned to attend the same school. Pettigrew (1975), however, emphasizes the importance of equal access to all sources of both formal and informal status. Webster (1961) discusses equal access to the school but says nothing about the racial composition of the school's staff or about internal arrangements such as tracking that clearly affect students' status. Hence, Pettigrew's position th t contact theory requires equal formal status for both the staff and the clients of an institution goes well beyond the requirements for equal status as they are operationalized in many contact studies like Webster's.

St. John (1975), Cohen (1975) and Armor (1972) have gone a step further and emphasized the difficulty of actually achieving equal status within the contact situation when students bring with them very different backgrounds. Discussing contact theory's requirements for equal status, St. John (1975) writes: "Black and white children may be unequally prepared to be successful students or may be accorded unequal status in the peer group because of differential family background" (p. 98). After studying interaction between black and white students, Cohen (1975) writes

> The inference may be drawn that even though blacks and whites might be brought together in a desegregated school in an "equal status" manner, it is still quite possible for the racial difference to act as a strong status differential triggering expectations for whites to do better.... If this occurs in the school situation, then the racial sterotypes which contribute to these expectations are only reinforced and confirmed by the interracial interaction. (p. 294)

As can be seen, in these statements the emphasis is on the way that the characteristics the group members bring with them influence the development of informal status and consequent intergroup relations.

There is little theoretical or empirical work to suggest which of the varied sources of equal or unequal status—the law, administrative policy, formal organizational structure, or informal structure resulting from status-related personal characteristics—is most crucial for the development of intergroup relations. The same lack of clarity about the precise referents of contact theory's general propositions that has been illustrated with this discussion of "equal status" is generally evident in the literature for the other criteria Allport (1954) specified. Work that refines and clarifies contact theory's suggestions should be of great practical, as well as theoretical, utility. It would suggest to school districts involved in desegregation where their resources might most profitably be invested as well as lead to new insights about the nature of intergroup relations.

The second line of work I would suggest, the study of the way in which variables isolated by contact theory operate when taken one at a time, is a natural outgrowth of the conceptual elaboration and refinement suggested above. Studies such as those reviewed earlier (Cook, 1969; Lachet, 1972; Schofield & Sagar, 1977b) suggest that when all or most of the conditions specified by contact theory are met attitude or behavioral change tends to occur. As Cook (1969) and Weissback (1976) have pointed out, however, this sort of work does not allow one to determine which of the variables specified by contact theory, or which combination of these variables is instrumental in bringing about the changes that do occur.

The beginning of a trend toward investigating the operation of the contact-theory variables singly is evident both in recent theorizing about equal status and in the studies on the effect of cooperative dependence on relations between black and white students. For example, Amir (1976) has questioned whether equal status is indeed a sine qua non for improved intergroup relations or whether it is merely one possible way of achieving this goal.

Also, a number of investigators have begun to ask whether cooperative dependence can, by itself, improve intergroup relations (Aronson, Blaney, Sikes, Stephan, & Snapp, 1975; DeVries & Edwards, 1974; Katz, I., & Benjamin, 1960; Katz, I., Goldston, & Benjamin, 1958; Weigel, Wiser, & Cook, 1975; and Witte, 1972).

Aronson et al. (1975) set up cooperative work groups in fifth- and sixth-grade classrooms in newly integrated schools. Tasks were structured so that cooperation was essential for individual success. For example, each child on a team was given one paragraph from a biographical sketch of a well-known individual. Then, after students had had time to learn their paragraphs and to teach their paragraphs to the others, each child was tested on the figure's complete biography. Aronson et al. found that such cooperative interaction increased peer liking significantly in the desegregated groups. No parallel increase was found in control classes with more traditional competitive structures.

In a similar experiment, Weigel et al. (1975) examined the effect of cooperative dependence on cross-ethnic respect and liking in junior and senior high school students. These students participated in English classes that either did or did not stress cooperation. In the experimental "cooperative" classrooms, teachers had group representatives give reports and gave rewards to students based on their group's performance. In contrast, these same teachers stressed individual assignments and rewards in the control "traditional" classrooms. At the end of about one semester of school, measures of students' respect and liking for their classmates as well as of their sociometric choices were obtained. White students in the cooperative classrooms showed greater respect and liking for their Mexican American classmates than did their peers in the control classrooms, as contact theory would predict. Neither white students' respect and liking for blacks nor their sociometric choice of blacks appeared to be influenced by the cooperative experience, however. Similarly, blacks and Mexican Americans in the cooperative classrooms were no more likely to show respect and liking for out-group members or to choose them on the sociometric test than were those in the traditional classrooms. Finally, a survey on interracial attitudes administered to students in their homes 3 months after the end of the classroom experience found no differences between the cooperative and the traditional groups. The study also concluded, however, that intergroup relations were "more harmonious [in the cooperative program] as reflected by a smaller proportion of cross-ethnic conflict and a higher proportion of cross-ethnic helping" (p. 239). These findings are consonant with my earlier contention that important changes in intergroup behavior may occur well before any changes in friendship patterns are evident on sociometric tests.

Studies of the effects of cooperative dependence generally show improved intergroup attitudes or increased interaction, although some show little or no change. It is very important, however, to note that, unlike many other studies of mere contact, they do not find negative results. This suggests that cooperative dependence is, as contact theory suggests, conducive to the development of positive intergroup relations. Nonetheless, the mixed results also suggest the need for further exploration of why and how cooperative dependence operates to influence intergroup attitudes. Study of the operation of the other variables specified by contact theory has hardly been begun but is much needed.

In addition to illustrating a promising trend in the refinement of contact theory, the cooperative-dependence studies just cited also represent a promising trend in conceptualization and design. These studies ask specific well-thought-out questions that can be answered experimentally in ongoing schools. Hence, they tend to have the advantages of experiments that lead to greater certainty in inference while at the same time they are actually conducted in the kinds of ongoing situations to which the results of the experiment are meant to generalize.

Utilization of New and Diverse Theoretical Perspectives

In general, researchers have been quite slow to apply the theoretical ideas developed in social psychology to the study of desegregated schools. As discussed previously, the last decade has seen the application of ideas taken from such diverse perspectives as reinforcement theory and attribution theory to illuminating processes that affect race relations (Duncan, 1977; Williams, 1972). Most of this work has been done in laboratories, however, and with rare exceptions, it has not been used to a significant extent by researchers working in desegregated schools.

To illustrate the potential value of applying theory and research from other areas of social psychology to the study of intergroup relations in desegregated settings. I shall present a brief discussion of theory and research on interpersonal attraction to show their relation to studies of desegregation. Although I use the area of interpersonal attraction for illustrative purposes, many other areas of theory and research have equal potential for suggesting important avenues of investigation. Attraction theory and research emphasize the importance of propinquity in the development of positive interpersonal relations. Numerous studies have shown how personal relations are clearly influenced by both the physical and the functional distance between individuals' apartments (Caplow & Forman, 1950; Festinger, Schachter, & Back, 1950). Other studies have shown that propinquity has a strong effect on interpersonal relations in the classroom. For example, Byrne and Buehler (1955) have shown that students who are assigned adjacent seats tend to become acquainted with each other. Also, Byrne (1971) demonstrated that the number of friendships a student forms in school can be increased if the teacher changes the assigned seating pattern during the course of a semester. The findings of interpersonal-attraction research suggest that school policies, like tracking or seating-assignment policies, that influence the proximity of white and black students within a desegregated school may have a crucial impact on the effect of desegregation on intergroup relations. Such hypotheses could clearly be investigated.

One explanation for the frequently found relation between propinquity and interpersonal attraction is the possibility that propinquity makes it likely that individuals will have the opportunity to discover shared attitudes. Similarity of attitudes is frequently held to be crucial to the development of interpersonal attraction, and the evidence supporting this contention is strong (Newcomb, 1961; Schachter, 1951). Applying this perspective to intergroup relations, Rokeach, Smith, and Evans (1960) have argued that whites' rejection of blacks stems from their belief that blacks tend to hold different values and beliefs. There is considerable research that suggests that these assumed differences are indeed a factor contributing to whites' disinclination to interact with blacks (Rokeach & Mezei, 1966; Rokeach, Smith, & Evans, 1960; Smith, Williams, & Willis, 1967). The strength of these effects seems to depend greatly on the kind of behavior in question (Triandis & Davis, 1965). Recent research suggests that belief similarity can indeed be a strong factor in whites' attraction to black individuals (Moss & Andrasik, 1973), but it also yields an interesting qualification to the generalization that similarity yields attraction. Moss and Andrasik (1973) found that whites who are highly prejudiced are less attracted to blacks who share their negative attitudes toward interracial interaction than to blacks who favor such interaction. Hence, some individuals react negatively to belief similarity when such similarity may be interpreted as a negative reaction to themselves or to a group to which they belong. Although the laboratory research on belief similarity and interracial acceptance has been justly criticized for its artificiality and for other failings (Dienstbier, 1972), it raises some provocative questions. For example, it stimulates thought about the possible negative consequences of interaction between whites and blacks who may hold very divergent beliefs because of differences in cultural, social-class, and educational backgrounds.

In this very cursory discussion of the interrelation between theory on interpersonal attraction and intergroup relations, I have attempted to show how desegregation research can profit from the application of theoretical perspectives that have not been developed with the specific purpose of illuminating intergroup relations in desegregated situations. Similarly, findings from research on relations between blacks and whites can help to refine and develop theory on interpersonal attraction. If such a mutually useful relationship between social-psychological theory and research on desegregation can be fully developed, then desegregated schools may indeed become the valuable "natural laboratory" for social science research that Williams, Fisher, and Janis (1956) long ago envisioned. Equally if not more important from a practical standpoint, research on desegregation may begin to clarify the numerous processes that account for the very different outcomes of desegregation in various circumstances.

Dealing with the Fact that Desegregation Is not a Traditional Independent Variable

The diversity of the phenomena traditionally labeled as "desegregation" has been amply documented earlier in this chapter. Inasmuch as such diversity is likely to remain a fact because of vastly different social and demographic conditions under which biracial schooling is instituted, social psychologists need to develop some ways for thinking more precisely about the phenomena. Pettigrew (1969b) has made a beginning in this direction by distinguishing between desegregation and integration, but much more thought needs to be given to determining what factors are sufficiently crucial to warrant using separate terms to distinguish between the various kinds of interracial schooling that occur. For example, because it appears that the black/white ratio in racially mixed schools and classrooms influences the way in which peer social relations develop (St. John & Lewis, 1975), it might be wise to classify schools or classrooms by the racial mix of students. One might classify schools and classrooms according to their degree of racial balance, where balance is defined by the percentage of the student body that is black or white. Biracial classrooms or schools that fall between 35% and 65% black or white could be called "balanced," whereas those with more than 65% of either group might be termed "imbalanced." This usage of the word *balance* is obviously quite different from the one in which *balance* describes the fit between the black/white ratio in a school district or community and the black/white ratio in a school. Rather, it focuses on the experience the student is likely to have within the school's walls and suggests that having a clear numerical minority group in the school, be it white or black, may well result in the development of quite different intergroup relations than a situation in which the two groups have relatively equal numbers.[3]

I have suggested that the numerical mix of blacks and whites in an interracial school may be sufficiently important to merit using different words to describe schools with different black/white ratios. Other researchers might find other distinctions more crucial. In order to avoid a confusing proliferation of terms, what is needed is a conceptual analysis supported, of course, by empirical explorations, that suggests the particular variables that are so crucial that they must be considered when one is describing an interracial school. Such an analysis is beyond the scope of this chapter, but it should be of the highest priority.

I suggest that, until more thought and research have gone into determining which aspects of the interracial school are most crucial in affecting the processes that occur and what impact they have on intergroup relations, researchers studying desegregated schools should almost without exception gather the following information on those schools:

1. The proportion of students, faculty, and administrators who belong to each racial or ethnic group
2. The extent to which the school resegregates students through tracking or other methods
3. The size of the school and the racial composition of the school before desegregation
4. The characteristic mode or modes of instruction
5. Any major changes in curriculum or teaching style made in anticipation of, or reaction to, desegregation
6. The type of desegregation (mandatory, voluntary, neighborhood)
7. The attitudes of the community and the school staff toward desegregation
8. The socioeconomic status of the various groups of students as well as their age and grade level

If full information cannot be obtained on these items, an attempt to at least estimate them should be made. For example, it is impractical to expect the researcher primarily interested in interracial interaction within a school to conduct a sample survey to gather information on the community's attitude toward desegregation. Such an effort could be a major study in itself. The researcher might, however, be able to review newspaper accounts of community actions that are indicative of local sentiment. If space constraints in journals prohibit reporting fully on these factors, supplemental descriptive material might be routinely prepared and made available to interested scholars.

The above list of items was constructed admittedly somewhat arbitrarily. One might well be able to make strong arguments that omitted items should be included or that items appearing on the list should be dropped. The rather arbitrary way in

---

[3] Clearly, *balance*, as it is used here, need not be conceptualized as a dichotomous variable. In fact, for many purposes, it might better be conceptualized as continuous. The 65/35% criterion for balance is suggested to emphasize that, beyond this point, it may be virtually impossible for the smaller group to prevail when issues that come up tend to polarize students by race. Even if the smaller group gains more power per person than the larger through factors such as good relations with the teachers or the ability to physically intimidate other students, they may find it hard to significantly influence the situation if they are too outnumbered.

which some items were included and others excluded is a reflection of the fact that we have relatively little guidance from either theory or empirical evidence about the factors that influence the way desegregation affects students. Until such guidance is available, the inclusion of the above may make it easier to cumulate studies and to begin to find patterns.

The recommendation that the information listed above should be included in research reports may appear unnecessary to those unfamiliar with the desegregation literature who might, therefore, make the erroneous assumption that such basic data would be a part of any study. But the incredible lack of attention to important characteristics of desegregated schools being studied can be vividly illustrated by an incident that occurred just this year at the national convention of a research-oriented professional association. At that meeting, a researcher who presented a paper on the effects of desegregation on intergroup relations was unable to answer a question from the audience about whether the desegregated school had any black faculty. His reply was, "Well, I guess so, but I'm really not too familiar with the staff at the school."

Need for Increased Attention
to Quasi-experimental Methods

Desegregation rarely, if ever, occurs in a way that meets the conditions necessary for experimental work. Random assignment to treatments, appropriate control groups, and reasonable control over nontreatment factors are all extremely difficult to attain. Occasionally, situations do occur that come relatively close to providing the random assignment and equivalent control group required by the logic of experimental design (Gerard & Miller, 1975; Schofield, 1975). Even in these situations, one generally encounters error variance on account of uncontrolled factors that may be great enough to mask even a sizable impact of desegregation (Cook & Campbell, 1976; Green & Gerard 1974). Hence, researchers interested in assessing the impact of desegregation on students need to consider more carefully quasi-experimental designs that might be appropriate. In addition, further attention needs to be devoted to the development and utilization of statistical techniques such as path analysis, cross-lagged correlation, and treatment-effect correlations designed to facilitate causal inference from nonexperimental data. For a clear discussion of the various quasi-experimental designs and correlational techniques available, readers are referred to Cook and Campbell's (1976) recent work.

CONCLUSION

The utter inconclusiveness of the research on the effect of desegregation on intergroup relations is clearly disappointing to those who had hoped to find a simple, straightforward answer to the question, What effect does desegregation have on intergroup attitudes and behavior? These results are doubly disappointing to those whose interest stems from a desire to gain clear support for their position in the heated national debate about desegregation.

Yet the tremendously varied conclusions drawn from different studies do teach, if painfully and later than desirable, a most important lesson. They suggest that the fact that black and white students attend schools together has a much less crucial impact on intergroup relations than the particular circumstances in which this contact occurs. Allport (1954) made this point nearly a quarter of a century ago; yet social scientists, like policy-makers and the general public, have been slow to respond to its full implications.

The inconclusiveness of the research suggests that people need to stop thinking about desegregation as a well-defined program with a predictable effects that are "good" or "bad" depending on one's value system. Rather, they need to recognize that racial mixing is just one aspect of the schooling children receive in desegregated schools, and that other aspects of that schooling may be far more crucial in determining how children's attitudes and behavior develop. This shift from seeing desegregation as a variable that in and of itself will have clear positive or negative consequences is entirely proper given that the policy of desegregation stems from constitutional considerations rather than from any positive or negative psychological effects that might be attributed to desegregation.

Given the demonstrated fruitlessness of searching for "the effect" of desegregation and the fact that desegregation is a legal imperative not dependent on proof of positive or negative effects for its implementation, the clear need is now to ask a new question, What types of factors influence how interracial schooling will affect children? Exploration of this question is an exciting prospect for two reasons. First, it should lead to a richer development and a fuller application of theory relevant to understanding the social and cognitive processes that account for students' reactions to desegregated schooling. Second, theory and research on these processes should be of considerable utility to policy-makers and practitioners who are faced with the challenge of structuring desegregated schools so that the impact they have on students is desirable from both a personal and a societal perspective.

REFERENCES

Allport, G. W. *The nature of prejudice.* Reading, Mass.: Addison-Wesley, 1954.

Amir, Y. The role of intergroup contact in change of prejudice and ethnic relations. In P. Katz (Ed.), *Towards the elimination of racism.* New York: Pergamon, 1976.

Armor, D. J. The evidence on busing. *Public Interest,* Summer 1972, pp. 90–124.

Aronson, E., Blaney, N. T., Sikes, J., Stephan, C., & Snapp, M. Busing and racial tension: The jigsaw route to learning and liking. *Psychology Today,* February 1975, pp. 43–120.

Aronson, S., & Noble, J. *Urban-suburban school mixing: A feasibility study.* Unpublished manuscript, 1966. (Available from S. Aronson, West Hartford Board of Education, West Hartford, Conn.)

Ashmore, R., & DelBoca, F. Psychological approaches to understanding intergroup conflict. In P. Katz (Ed.), *Towards the elimination of racism.* New York: Pergamon, 1976.

Barber, R. W. *The effects of open enrollment on anti-negro and anti-white prejudices among junior high students in Rochester, New York.* Unpublished doctoral dissertation, University of Rochester, 1968.

Berger, J., Cohen, E., & Zelditch, M. Status characteristics and expectation states. In J. Berger, M. Zelditch, & B. Anderson (Eds.), *Sociological theories in progress.* Boston: Houghton Mifflin, 1966.

Berger, J., Cohen, E., & Zelditch, M. Status conceptions and social interaction. *American Sociological Review,* 1972, 37, 241–255.

Biehler, R. F. Companion choice behavior in the kindergarten. *Child Development,* 1954, 25, 45–50.

Biener, L., & Gerard, H. Effects of desegregation on achievement-relevant motivation. In H. Gerard & N. Miller (Eds.), *School desegregation.* New York: Plenum, 1975.

Bonney, M. E., & Powell, J. Differences in social behavior between sociometrically high and sociometrically low children. *Journal of Educational Research,* 1953, 46, 481–495.

Byrd, E. A study of validity and constancy of choices in a sociometric test. *Sociometry,* 1951, 14, 175–181.

Byrne, D. *The attraction paradigm*. New York: Academic, 1971.

Byrne, D., & Buehler, J. A. A note on the influence of propinquity upon acquaintanceships. *Journal of Abnormal Social Psychology*, 1955, 51, 147–148.

Campbell, A. *White attitudes toward black people*. Ann Arbor. Institute for Social Research, 1971.

Campbell, D. T., & Fiske, D. W. Convergent and discriminant validation by the multitrait-multimethod matrix. *Psychological Bulletin*, 1959,,56, 81–105.

Campbell, D. T., & Stanley, J. *Experimental and quasi-experimental designs for research*. Chicago: Rand McNally, 1963.

Caplow, T., & Forman, R. Neighborhood interaction in a homogeneous community. *American Sociological Review*, 1950, 15, 357–366.

Carithers, M. W. School desegregation and racial cleavage, 1954–1970: A review of the literature. *Journal of Social Issues*, 1970, 26,(4) 25–47.

Cartwright, D. Determinants of scientific progress: The case of research on the risky shift. *American Psychologist*, 1973, 28, 222–231.

Cohen, E. Interracial interaction disability. *Human Relations*, 1972, 25, 9–24.

Cohen, E. The effects of desegregation on race relations. *Law and Contemporary Problems*, 1975, 39, 271–299.

Cohen, E., Lockheed, M., & Lohman, M. The center for interracial cooperation: A field experiment. *Sociology of Education*, 1976, 49, 47–58.

Cohen, E., & Roper, S. Modification of interracial interaction disability: An application of status characteristics theory. *American Sociological Review*, 1972, 37, 643–657.

Coleman, J. S., Campbell, E. Q., Hobson, C. J., McPartland, J. M., Mood, A. M., Weinfeld, F. D., & York, R. L. *Equality of educational opportunity*. Washington: U.S. Government Printing Office, 1966.

Coleman, J. S., Kelly, S.,D., & Moore, J. A. *Recent trends in school desegregation*. Paper presented at the meeting of the American Educational Research Association, Washington, April 1975.

Coles, R. Northern children under desegregation. *Psychiatry*, 1968, 31, 1–15.

Cook, S. W. Motives in a conceptual analysis of attitude-related behavior. In W. J. Arnold & D. Levine (Eds.), *Nebraska Symposium on Motivation* (Vol. 17). Lincoln: University of Nebraska Press, 1969.

Cook, S. W. *The effect of unintended interracial contact upon racial interaction and attitude change*. (Project No. 5-1320), Final Report, U.S. Office of Education, 1971.

Cook, T. D., & Campbell, D. T. The design and conduct of quasi-experiments and true experiments in field settings. In M. D. Dunnette (Ed.), *Handbook of industrial and organizational psychology*. Chicago: Rand McNally, 1976.

Crain, R. Why academic research fails to be useful. *School Review*, 1976, 84, 337–351.

Criswell, J. H. A sociometric study of racial cleavage in the classroom. *Archives of Psychology*, 1939, 33 (Whole No. 235).

Crooks, R. C. The effects of an interracial preschool program upon racial preference, knowledge of racial differences and racial identification. *Journal of Social Issues*, 1970, 26(4), 137–144.

Crosby, F., Bromley, S., & Saxe, L. Recent unobtrusive studies of racial discrimination and prejudice: A literature review. Unpublished manuscript, 1977. (Available from Dept. of Psychology, Yale University, New Haven, Conn.)

Cusick, P. A., & Ayling, R. *Racial interaction in an urban secondary school*. Paper presented at the meeting of the American Educational Research Association, New Orleans, February 1973.

Dentler, R. A., & Elkins, C. Intergroup attitudes, academic performance, and racial composition. In R. A. Dentler, B. Mackler, & M. E. Warshauer (Eds.), *The urban R's*. New York: Praeger, 1967.

Deutschberger, P. Interaction patterns in changing neighborhoods: New York and Pittsburgh. *Sociometry*, 1946, 9, 303–315.

DeVries, D. L., & Edwards, K. J. Student teams and learning games: Their effects on cross-race and cross-sex interaction. *Journal of Educational Psychology*, 1974, 66, 741–749.

Dienstbier, R. A. A modified belief theory of prejudice emphasizing the mutual causality of racial prejudice and anticipated belief differences. *Psychological Review*, 1972, 79, 146–160.

Duncan, B. Differential social perceptions and attributions of intergroup violence: Testing the lower limits of stereotyping of blacks. *Journal of Personality and Social Psychology,* 1977, **34**, 590–598.

Dwyer, R. J. A report on patterns of interaction in desegregated schools. *Journal of Educational Sociology,* 1958, **31**, 253–356.

Eddy, E. Educational innovation and desegregation: A case study of symbolic realignment. *Human Organization,* 1975, **34**, 163–172.

Edwards, C. D., & Williams, J. E. Generalization between evaluative words associated with racial figures in preschool children. *Journal of Experimental Research in Personality,* 1970, **4**, 144–155.

Farley, R. Residential segregation and its implications for school integration. *Law and Contemporary Problems,* 1975, **39**, 104–193.

Festinger, L., Schacter, D., & Back, K. *Social pressures in informal groups: A study of a housing community.* New York, Harper, 1950.

Foley, L. Personality and situational influences on changes in prejudices: A replication of Cook's railroad game in a field setting. *Journal of Personality and Social Psychology,* 1976, **34**, 846–856.

Gaertner, S. Nonreactive measures in racial attitude research: A focus on liberals. In P. Katz (Ed.), *Towards the elimination of racism.* New York: Pergamon, 1976.

Gaertner, S., & Bickman, L. Effects of race on elicitation of helping behavior: The wrong number technique. *Journal of Personality and Social Psychology,* 1971, **20**, 218–222.

Gardner, B. B., Wright, B. D., & Dee, R. *The effects of busing black ghetto children into white suburban schools,* 1970. (ERIC Document Reproduction Service No. ED 048 389)

Gerard, H., & Miller, N. *School desegregation.* New York: Plenum, 1975.

Green, J., & Gerard, H. School desegregation and ethnic attitudes. In H. Fromkin & J. Sherwood (Eds.), *Integrating the organization: A social psychological analysis.* New York: Free Press, 1974.

Guttentag, M. Subjectivity and its use in evaluation research. *Evaluation,* 1973, **1**, 60–65.

Guttentag, M., & Struening, E. The handbook: Its purpose and organization. In M. Guttentag & E. Struening (Eds.), *Handbook of evaluation research* (Vol. 2). Beverly Hills, Calif.: Sage, 1975.

Hauserman, N., Walen, S. R., & Behling, M. Reinforced racial integration in the first grade: A study in generalization. *Journal of Applied Behavior Analysis,* 1973, 6 193–200. (Summary)

Holsendolph, E. Figures show integration lag. *New York Times,* June 20, 1976, p. 24.

Jansen, V. G., & Gallagher, J. J. The social choices of students in racially integrated classes for the culturally disadvantaged talented. *Exceptional Children,* 1966, **33**, 222–226.

Katz, D. The functional approach to the study of attitudes. *Public Opinion Quarterly,* 1960, **24**, 163–204.

Katz, I. Review of evidence relating to effects of desegregation on the performance of Negroes. *American Psychologist,* 1964, **19**, 381–399.

Katz, I., & Benjaman. L. Effects of white authoritarianism on biracial work groups. *Journal of Abnormal and Social Psychology,* 1960, **61**, 448–465.

Katz, I., Goldston, J., & Benjaman, L., Behavior and productivity in biracial work groups. *Human Relations,* 1958, **11**, 123–141.

Katz, I., Henchy, T., & Allen, H. Effects of race of tester approval–disapproval and need on Negro children's learning. *Journal of Personality and Social Psychology,* 1968, 8, 38–42.

Katz, P. Attitude change in children: Can the twig be straightened? In P. Katz (Ed.), *Towards the elimination of racism.* New York: Pergamon, 1976.

Koslin, S., Amarel, M., & Ames, N. A distance measure of racial attitudes in primary grade children: An exploratory study. *Psychology in the Schools,* 1969, **6**, 382–385.

Kupferer, H. J. An evaluation of the integration potential of a physical education program. *Journal of Educational Sociology,* 1954, **28**, 89–96.

Kurokawa, M. Mutual perceptions of racial images: White, black, and Japanese-Americans. *Journal of Social Issues,* 1971, **27**(4), 213–235.

Lachat, M. *A description and comparison of the attitudes of white high school seniors towards black Americans in three suburban high schools: An all white, a desegregated and an integrated school.* Unpublished doctoral dissertation, Columbia University, Teachers College, 1972.

Linn, R., & Slinde, J. The determination of the significance of change between pre and post testing periods. *Review of Educational Research,* 1977, **47**, 121–150.

Lombardi, D. N. *Factors affecting changes in attitudes toward Negroes among high school students.* Unpublished doctoral dissertation, Fordham University, 1962.

Lundberg, G. A., & Dickson, L. Selective association among ethnic groups in a high school population. *American Sociological Review,* 1952, **17**, 23–35.

Mann, J. H. The effects of inter-racial contact on sociometric choices and perceptions. *Journal of Social Psychology,* 1959, **50**, 143–152.

McMurty, C. A., & Williams, J. E. The evaluation dimension of the affective meaning system of the preschool child. *Developmental Psychology,* 1972, **6**, 238–246.

McPartland, J. M. *The segregated student in desegregated schools: Sources of influence on Negro secondary students* (Report No. 21). Baltimore: John Hopkins University, Center for the Study of Social Organization of Schools, 1968.

McWhirt, R. A. *The effects of desegregation on prejudice, academic aspiration and the self-concept of tenth grade students.* Unpublished doctoral dissertation, University of South Carolina, 1967.

Minard, R. Race relationships in the Pocahontas coal field. *Journal of Social Issues,* 1952, **8**(1), 29–44.

Moreno, J. L. *Who shall survive? A new approach to the problems of human interrelations.* Washington: Mental Disease Publishing Col, 1934.

Moss, M. K., & Andrasik, F. Belief similarity and interracial attraction. *Journal of Personality,* 1973, **41**, 192–205.

National Advisory Commission on Civil Disorders. Washington: U.S. Government Printing Office, 1968.

National Institute of Education. *Field studies in urban desegregated schools* (RFP-NIE-R-75-0023). Washington: 1974.

National Institute of Education. *Resegregation: A second generation school desegregation issue.* Unpublished manuscript. Desegregation Studies Unit, Washington, 1977.

Newcomb, T. M. *The acquaintance process.* New York: Holt, 1961.

Patchen, M., Davidson, J., Hofman, G., & Brown, W. Determinants of students' interracial behavior and opinion change. *Sociology of Education,* 1977, **50**, 55–75.

Pettigrew, T. Social evaluation theory: Convergences and applications. In D. Levine (Ed.), *Nebraska Symposium on Motivation* (Vol. 15). Lincoln: University of Nebraska Press, 1967.

Pettigrew, T. The Negro and education: Problems and proposals. In I. Katz & P. Gurin (Eds.), *Race and the social sciences.* New York: Basic, 1969(a).

Pettigrew, T. Racially separate or together. *Journal of Social Issues,* 1969, **25**(1), 43–68. (b)

Pettigrew, T. The case for the racial integration of the schools. In O. Duff (Ed.), *Report on the future of school desegregation in the United States.* Pittsburgh: University of Pittsburgh, Consultative Resource Center on School Desegregation and Conflict, 1973.

Pettigrew, T. *Racial discrimination in the United States.* New York, Harper, 1975.

Pettigrew, T. Personal communication, January 5, 1977.

Pettigrew, T., & Green, R. A reply to professor Coleman. *Harvard Educational Review,* 1976, **46**, 225–233. (a)

Pettigrew, T., & Green, R. School desegregation in large cities: A critique of the Coleman "white flight" thesis. *Harvard Educational Review,* 1976, **46**,(1), 1–53. (b)

Pettigrew, T., Useem, E., Normand, C., & Smith, M. Busing: A review of the evidence. *Public Interest,* Winter 1973, pp. 88–118.

Porter, J. D. *Black child-white child.* Cambridge: Harvard University Press, 1971.

Read, F. Judicial evolution of the law of school integration since *Brown v. Board of Education. Law and Contemporary Problems,* 1975, **39**, 7–49.

Rokeach, M., & Mezei, L. Race and shared belief as factors in social choice. *Science,* 1966, **151**, 167–172.

Rokeach, M., Smith, P. W., & Evans, R. I. Two kinds of prejudice or one? In M. Rokeach, (Ed.), *The open and closed mind.* New York: Basic, 1960.

Rosenberg, M. J. The conditions and consequences of evaluation apprehension. In R. Rosenthal & R. L. Rosnow (Eds.), *Artifact in behavior research.* New York: Academic, 1969.

Rosenberg, M., & Simmons, R. *Black and white self-esteem: The urban school child.* Washington: American Sociological Association, 1971.

Rossell, C. School desegregation and white flight. *Political Science Quarterly,* 1975–1976, **90,** 675–695.

Sagar, H. A. *Interracial contact in the public schools: Theory, research and application.* Unpublished manuscript, 1977. (Available from Department of Psychology, University of Pittsburgh, Penn. 15260)

Schacter, S. Deviation, rejection and communication. *Journal of Abnormal and Social Psychology,* 1951, **46,** 120–207.

Schofield, J. W. *To be or not to be (black).* Paper presented at the meeting of the American Psychological Association, Chicago, September 1975.

Schofield, J. W. *Ethnographic study of a "nearly integrated" middle school.* Unpublished manuscript, 1976. (Available from Department of Psychology, University of Pittsburgh, Pittsburgh, Penn. 15260)

Schofield, J. W. *Social process and peer relations in a "nearly integrated" middle school.* (Contract No. 400-76-0011, 1977). Final project report, 1977.

Schofield, J. W. *Peer nomination v. ranking on sociometric tests.* Unpublished manuscript, 1978. (Available from Department of Psychology, University of Pittsburgh, Pittsburgh, Penn. 15260)

Schofield, J. W., & Sagar, H. A. *Interracial behavior in a "magnet" school.* Paper presented at the American Psychological Association, San Francisco, August 1977. (a)

Schofield, J. W., & Sagar, H. A. Peer interaction patterns in an integrated middle school. *Sociometry,* 1977, **40,** 130–138. (b)

Schuman, H., & Hatchett, S. *Black racial attitudes: Trends and complexities.* Ann Arbor: Institute for Social Research, 1974.

Scott, W. A. Attitude measurement. In G. Lindzey & E. Aronson (Eds.), *The handbook of social psychology* (Vol. 2) Reading, Mass.: Addison-Wesley, 1968.

Shaw, M. E. Changes in sociometric choices following forced integration of an elementary school. *Journal of Social Issues,* 1973, **29**(4), 143–157.

Silverman, I., & Shaw, M. E. Effects of sudden mass desegregation on interracial interaction and attitudes in one southern city. *Journal of Social Issues,* 1973, **29**(4), 133–142.

Simon, A., & Boyer, E. G. (Eds.), *Mirrors for behavior: An ethology of classroom observation instruments* (15 vols.). Philadelphia: Research for Better Schools, 1967.

Singer, D. *Interracial attitudes of Negro and white fifth grade children in segregated and unsegregated schools.* Unpublished doctoral dissertation, Columbia University, Teachers College, 1966.

Slavin, R. E. How student learning teams can *integrate* the desegregated classroom. *Integrated Education,* 1977, **15**(6), 56–58.

Smith, C., Williams, L., & Willis, R. Race, sex, and belief as determinants of friendship acceptance. *Journal of Personality and Social Psychology,* 1967, **5,** 127–134.

Stephan, W. G. School desegregation: An evaluation of predictions made in *Brown v. Board of Education. Psychological Bulletin,* 1978, **85,** 217–238.

St. John, N. *School desegregation: Outcomes for children.* New York: Wiley, 1975.

St. John, N., & Lewis, R. Race and the social structure of the elementary classroom. *Sociology of Education,* 1975, **48,** 346–368.

Suchman, E. A. *Evaluative research: Principles and practice in public service and social action programs.* New York: Russell Sage, 1967.

Taylor, C. P. *Some change in self-concept in the first year of desegregated schooling.* Unpublished doctoral dissertation, University of Delaware, 1967.

Trager, H. G., & Yarrow, M. R. *They learn what they live.* New York: Harper, 1952.

Triandis, H. C., & Davis, E. E. Race and belief as determinants of behavior intentions. *Journal of Personality and Social Psychology,* 1965, **2,** 715–725.

Trubowitz, J. *Changing the racial attitudes of children.* New York: Praeger, 1969.

U.S. Commission on Civil Rights. *Racial Isolation in the public schools.* Washington: U.S. Government Printing Office, 1967.

Useem, E. L. Correlates of white students' attitudes towards a voluntary busing program. *Education and Urban Society.* 1976, 8(4). 441–476.

Warshauer, M. E., & Dentler, R. A. A new definition of school segregation. In R. A. Dentler, B. Mackler, & M. E. Warshauer (Eds.), *The urban R's.* New York: Praeger, 1967.

Webster, S. W. The influence of interracial contact on social acceptance in a newly integrated school. *Journal of Educational Psychology,* 1961, **52,** 292–296.

Weigel, R. H., Wiser, P. L., & Cook, S. W. The impact of cooperative learning experiences on cross-ethnic relations and attitudes. *Journal of Social Issues,* 1975, 31(1), 219–244.

Weiss, C. Using social research in public policy making. Lexington, Mass.: Lexington Books, 1977.

Weissback, T. A. Laboratory controlled studies of change of racial attitudes. In P. Katz (Ed.), *Towards the elimination of racism.* New York: Pergamon, 1976.

Weitz, S. Attitude, voice and behavior: A repressed affect model of interracial interaction. *Journal of Personality and Social Psychology,* 1972, 24, 14–21.

Williams, J. E. *Racial attitudes in preschool children: Modification via operant conditioning, and revised measurement procedure.* Paper presented at the meeting of the American Psychological Association, Honolulu, September 1972.

Williams, R. M., Fisher, B. R., & Janis, I. L. Educational desegregation as a context for basic social research. *American Sociological Review,* 1956, 21, 577–583.

Williams, R., & Vendetti, F. Effect of academic integration on southern Negro students' expressed satisfaction with school. *Journal of Social Psychology,* 1969, 20, 203–209.

Willie, C. *Race mixing in the public schools.* New York: Praeger, 1973.

Wisdom, J. Random remarks on the role of social sciences in the judicial decision-making process in school desegregation cases. *Law and Contemporary Problems,* 1975, 39, 135–149.

Witte, P. *The effects of group reward structure on interracial acceptance peer tutoring and academic performance.* Unpublished doctoral dissertation, Washington University, 1972.

Yarrow, M. E., Campbell, J. D., & Yarrow, L. J. Acquisition of new norms: A study of racial desegregation. *Journal of Social Issues,* 1958, 14(1), 8–28.

Author Index

Pressey, S. L., 14, 16, 22
Prillwitz, G., 173, 197
Pritchett, W., 280, 296
Proshansky, H. M., 28, 51, 266, 270
Pruitt, D., 316, 317, 324
Purkey, W. W., 157, 163, 263, 271

Rafalides, M., 280, 286, 296, 317, 325
Rainwater, L., 201
Rausch, H. L., 55, 81
Raven, B., 241, 254
Raynor, J. O., 211, 220, 224
Read, F., 329, 330, 361
Read, W. H., 46, 51
Rebelsky, F., 163
Redl, F., 241, 243, 254, 255, 283, 295, 296
Reed, L., 264, 272
Rehage, K. J., 173, 178, 201
Reitz, J. G., 83n., 109
Reppucci, N. D., 221, 224
Resnick, J. H., 28, 51
Rest, J., 304, 325
Rest, S., 264, 272
Retish, P. M., 245, 255
Rexford, G. E., 280, 296
Rhea, B., 280, 286, 291, 296, 320, 325
Rice, A. K., 28, 52
Richards, A., 300, 301, 315–318, 320, 322
Richards, E. A., 14
Riecken, H. W., 283, 287
Riegel, K. F., 58, 80
Riessman, F., 171, 201
Rigsby, L., 284, 297
Robbins, S., 299, 300, 325
Roberts, J. I., 170, 201
Robinson, J. P., 94, 110
Rodgers, R. R., 173, 198
Rodin, J., 58, 80
Roethlisberger, F. J., 13, 22, 232, 255
Rogers, C. R., 10, 19–20, 22, 283, 285, 296, 303, 306, 325
Rohwer, W. D., 17, 21
Rokeach, M., 354, 361
Roper, S., 337, 359
Rosen, S., 172, 176, 200, 243, 254, 283, 295
Rosenbaum, R. M., 264, 272
Rosenberg, M., 28, 51, 163, 177, 201, 338, 344, 361
Rosenfield, D., 261, 263, 270, 271
Rosenshine, B., 279, 296
Rosenthal, R., 11, 17–18, 22, 28, 51, 58, 72, 80, 83, 110, 215, 216, 226, 240, 252, 255, 263, 271

Rosnow, R. L., 28, 52
Ross, D., 159, 163
Ross, E. A., 12, 13, 22
Rossell, C., 330, 361
Rothenberg, B. B., 163
Rotter, J. B., 284–285, 289, 296
Rotzel, G., 250, 255
Rubin, J., 308, 317, 325
Rubin, Z., 243, 255
Rubovits, P. C., 215, 226, 240, 255
Ruiz, R. A., 167, 201
Runkel, P. J., 59–60, 67, 70, 77–78, 80, 159, 164
Russell, W., 142, 147
Ruter, M., 179, 201
Ryan, F. L., 263, 272
Ryan, J. J., 173, 200, 242, 254

Sagar, H. A., 333, 334, 336, 342, 344, 349, 350, 352, 361, 362
St. John, N., 144, 148, 234, 266, 271, 331–334, 340, 342, 343, 346, 347, 350, 352, 355, 362
Salili, F., 214, 217, 221, 223, 226
Salomon, G., 137, 148
Sampson, E. E., 281, 296
Sanford, N., 28, 51, 83n., 86, 110, 184, 202
Sanford, R. N., 10, 21, 285, 294
Santamaria, P., 280, 291, 297
Sarason, S., 184, 202
Sarbin, T. R., 214, 226, 281, 296
Sargent, J., 172, 178, 200
Saunders, L., 168, 202
Saxe, L., 345, 359
Schacter, S., 354, 362
Schatzman, L., 87, 92, 96n., 98–100, 105, 110
Schein, E. H., 289, 296
Schlechty, P. C., 275, 278, 296
Schmidt, B. A., 176, 202
Schmuck, P. A., 150, 164, 232, 235, 237, 242, 249, 252, 255
Schmuck, R. A., 51, 67, 70, 80, 150, 157, 163–164, 167, 172, 173, 175, 202, 232, 223, 235, 237, 242–246, 249, 252, 253, 255, 278, 287, 290, 296
Schofield, J. W., 332–334, 336, 341, 342, 347, 349, 350, 352, 357, 362
Schön, D. A., 294
Schultz, C., 138, 148
Schultz, W., 308, 325
Schuman, H., 349, 362

Wellman, B., 172, 203
Wells, E. H., 262, 270
Wells, M. G., 86, 109
Wheeler, R., 262, 272
Wheeler, R. C., 263, 272
White, B. J., 15, 22, 267, 271
White, R. K., 10, 13, 15, 21, 252, 255, 281, 295, 297
White, R. W., 222, 227, 238, 240, 255
Wickman, E. K., 7, 22
Wickman, E. V., 179, 203
Wiley, D. E., 102, 110
Willems, E. P., 55, 81
Williams, J. E., 338, 354, 360–362
Williams, L., 354, 362
Williams, M., 305, 306, 322
Williams, R., 349, 362
Williams, R. M., 355, 362
Willie, C., 340, 346, 363
Willis, R., 354, 362
Willower, D. J., 128, 130, 132, 279, 280, 286, 296, 297
Wilson, G. D., 159, 161, 162
Winter, D. G., 206, 226
Wisdom, J., 330, 363
Wiseman, J., 253
Wiser, P. L., 266, 271, 352, 362
Withall, J., 279, 297
Witte, P., 352, 363
Wodarski, J. S., 262, 272
Wohlwill, J., 305, 326
Wolcott, H. F., 120, 132
Woloshin, G., 304, 324

Wood, H., 117, 124, 132
Woodruff, A. D., 15, 22
Woydanoff, D. A., 164
Wright, H. S., 117, 131
Wright, B. D., 331
Wright, J. M., 94, 110
Wrighter, J., 175, 199
Wyant, S. H., 70, 77–78, 80
Wyden, P., 300, 315, 321

Yancey, W. L., 284, 297
Yarrow, L. J., 332n., 333, 343, 363
Yarrow, M. E., 332n., 333, 343, 362, 363
Yarrow, M. R., 161, 164, 349, 362
Yee, A. H., 159, 164
York, R. L., 91, 92, 109, 209, 224, 277, 294, 343, 359
Young, L. L., 175, 203

Zajonc, R. B., 155, 164
Zander, A., 214, 227, 236, 244, 253, 283, 284, 295, 297
Zbarowski, M., 167, 203
Zelditch, M., Jr., 284, 294, 337, 358
Zientek, J., 196, 200
Ziller, R., 308, 326
Zimbardo, P., 318, 326
Zimiles, H., 152, 156–157, 163
Zucker, K. B., 162

Subject Index

Achievement
and intelligence, 175
motivation, 138–139, 205–227, 238
behavioral basis for interference in, 210–211
culture and, 205–209, 216
definition of, 211–212
ethnocentric approach to, 208–210
expectations in, 212–216
intrinsic interest in, 219
McClelland's study of, 205–210
measurement of, 206–208
personality and, 205–207
self in, 219–223
situational-contextual causes of, 212–223
task characteristics, 216–219
work vs. play, 217–219
Action:
no-line, 30–31, 33–34, 49
off-line, 32, 33, 39, 45
on-line, 30–31, 32n., 33–35, 49
sideline, 32–33, 39, 43, 46, 48
Action research, 28
Analysis of covariance (ANCOVA), 103
Analysis of variance (ANOVA), 103
Annual Review of Psychology, 15n.
Aptitude-by-treatment interaction, 135–137
Attitudes, evaluation of, 156–157
Aversion therapy, 90

Behaviorism, 29
vs. humanism, 19–20
Behavior reinforcement, 84, 89–90
Beliefs, evaluation of, 156

Blacks:
contraculture in schools, 170–171
in cooperative classrooms, 263, 266–267
culture in study programs, 142
in desegregated schools (*see* School desegregation)
dialect, 142
parent education program for, 191
teachers with, 142, 144
Brown v. Board of Education, 329, 330

Center for the Study of Evaluation, 94
Child-rearing practice and achievement, 206–208
Children (*see* Students)
Civil Rights Act, 329, 351
Classrooms, 111–132, 276
application group, 252–253
breaching (behavior), 124–125
careers of pupils, 125–130
cognitive maps in, 119–120, 125
conflict in (*see* Conflict management; Conflict of interest; Controversy)
cooperative structure, 257–272
goal structures in, 248–249
group interactions, 233–234
guidance groups, 250–251
instructional groups, 251–252
integrated (*see* School desegregation)
language laboratory, 235
learning groups, 234–238, 249–253
model of, 122–125
norms in, 246–248
participant observation in, 117–119
passing (behavior), 124–125
phenomenology of, 111–112, 115, 130–131

DATE DUE

MR 3'81			
MR 2 3'81			
AP 6'81			
AP 2 1'81			
GAYLORD			PRINTED IN U.S.A.